Parametric Modeling

with Autodesk Inventor R4

Randy H. Shih
Oregon Institute of Technology

SDC
PUBLICATIONS
Mission, Kansas

Schroff Development Corporation

P.O. Box 1334
Mission KS 66222
(913) 262-2664
www.SDCACAD.com

Shih, Randy H.
Parametric modeling with Autodesk Inventor R4/
Randy H. Shih

ISBN 1-58503-072-4

Printed and bound in the United States of America.

Preface

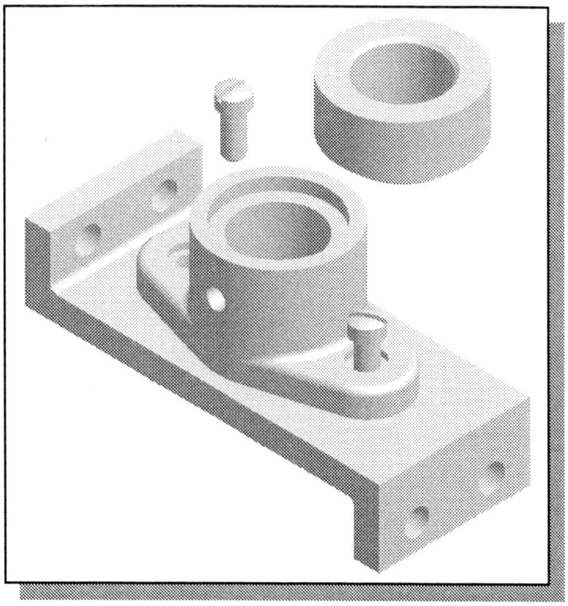

The primary goal of ***Parametric Modeling with Autodesk Inventor R4*** is to introduce the aspects of **Solid Modeling** and **Parametric Modeling**. This text is intended to be used as a training guide for students and professionals. This text covers *Autodesk Inventor R4* and the lessons proceed in a pedagogical fashion to guide you from constructing basic shapes to building intelligent solid models and creating multi-view drawings. This text takes a hands-on, exercise-intensive approach to all the important *Parametric Modeling* techniques and concepts. This textbook contains a series of ten tutorial style lessons designed to introduce beginning CAD users to **Autodesk Inventor**. This text is also helpful to Autodesk Inventor users upgrading from a previous release of the software. The solid modeling techniques and concepts discussed in this text are also applicable to other parametric feature-based CAD packages. The basic premise of this book is that the more designs you create using *Autodesk Inventor*, the better you learn the software. With this in mind, each lesson introduces a new set of commands and concepts, building on previous lessons. This book does not attempt to cover all of the *Autodesk Inventor*'s features, only to provide an introduction to the software. It is intended to help you establish a good basis for exploring and growing in the exciting field of **Computer Aided Engineering**.

Acknowledgments

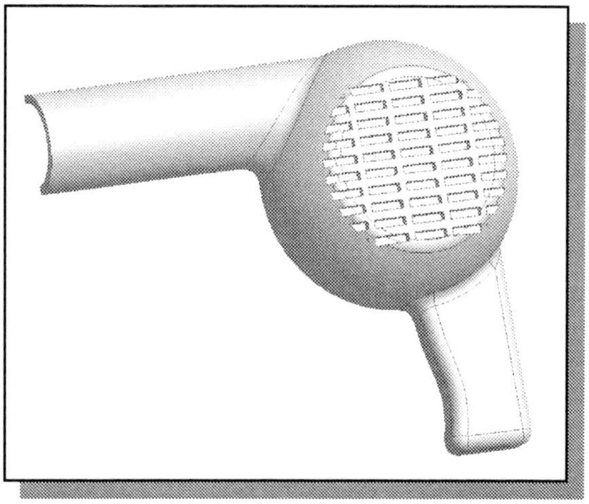

This book would not have been possible without a great deal of support. First, special thanks to two great teachers, Prof. George R. Schade of University of Nebraska-Lincoln and Mr. Denwu Lee, who taught me the fundamentals, the intrigue, and the sheer fun of Computer Aided Engineering.

The effort and support of the editorial and production staff of Schroff Development Corporation is gratefully acknowledged. I would especially like to thank Stephen Schroff and Mary Schmidt for their support and helpful suggestions during this project.

I am grateful that the Mechanical and Manufacturing Engineering Technology Department of Oregon Institute of Technology has provided me with an excellent environment in which to pursue my interests in teaching and research.

Finally, truly unbounded thanks are due to my wife Hsiu-Ling and my daughter Casandra for their understanding and encouragement throughout this project.

Randy H. Shih
Klamath Falls, Oregon

Table of Contents

Lesson 2

Constructive Solid Geometry Concepts

Lesson 3

Model History Tree

Lesson 4
Parametric Constraints Fundamentals

Lesson 5
The BORN Technique and Work Features

Lesson 6
Part Drawings and Associative Functionality

Lesson 7
Symmetrical Features in Designs

Lesson 10
Assembly Modeling - Putting It All Together

Notes:

Introduction

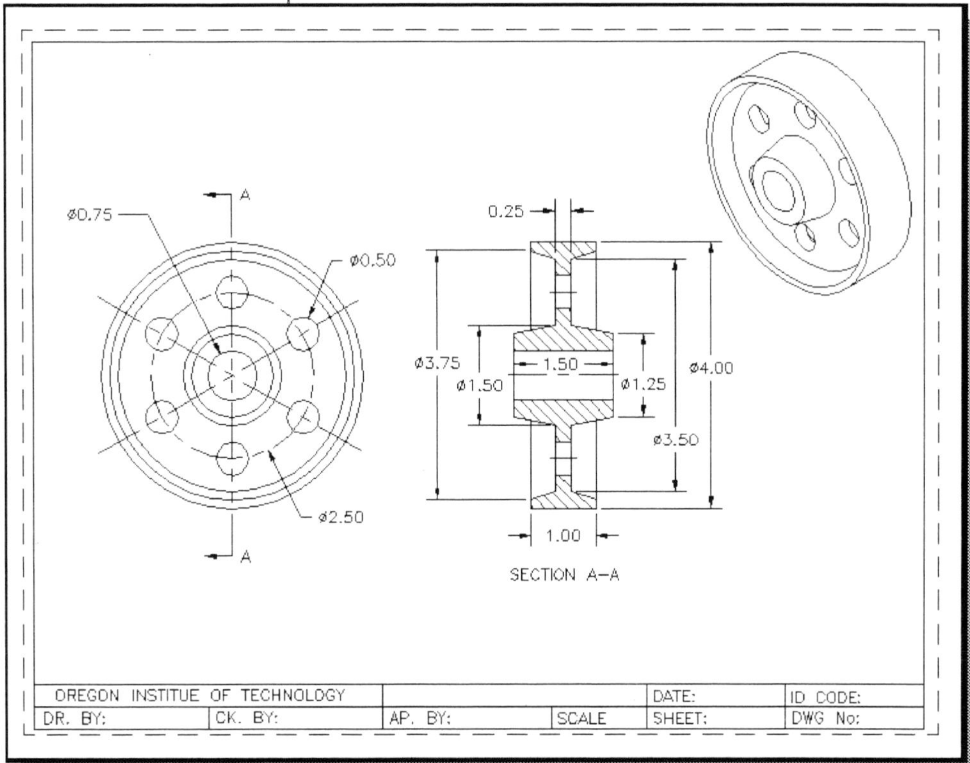

Learning Objectives

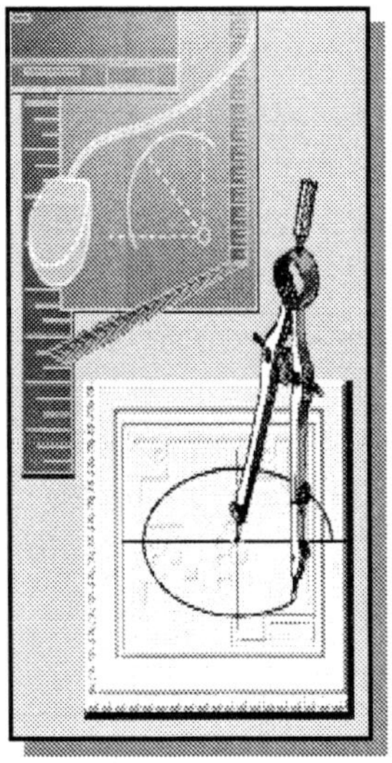

- ♦ Development of Computer Geometric Modeling
- ♦ Feature-Based Parametric Modeling
- ♦ Getting Started with Autodesk Inventor
- ♦ Startup Options and Units Setup
- ♦ Autodesk Inventor Screen Layout
- ♦ Mouse Buttons
- ♦ Autodesk Inventor On-Line Help

Introduction

The rapid changes in the field of **Computer Aided Engineering** (CAE) have brought exciting advances in the engineering community. Recent advances have made the long-sought goal of **concurrent engineering** closer to a reality. CAE has become the core of concurrent engineering and is aimed at reducing design time, producing prototypes faster, and achieving higher product quality. ***Autodesk Inventor*** is an integrated package of mechanical computer aided engineering software tools developed by *Autodesk, Inc.* ***Autodesk Inventor*** is a tool that facilitates a concurrent engineering approach to the design and stress-analysis of mechanical engineering products. The computer models can also be used by manufacturing equipment such as machining centers, lathes, mills, or rapid prototyping machines to manufacture the product. In this text, we will be dealing only with the solid modeling modules used for part design and part drawings.

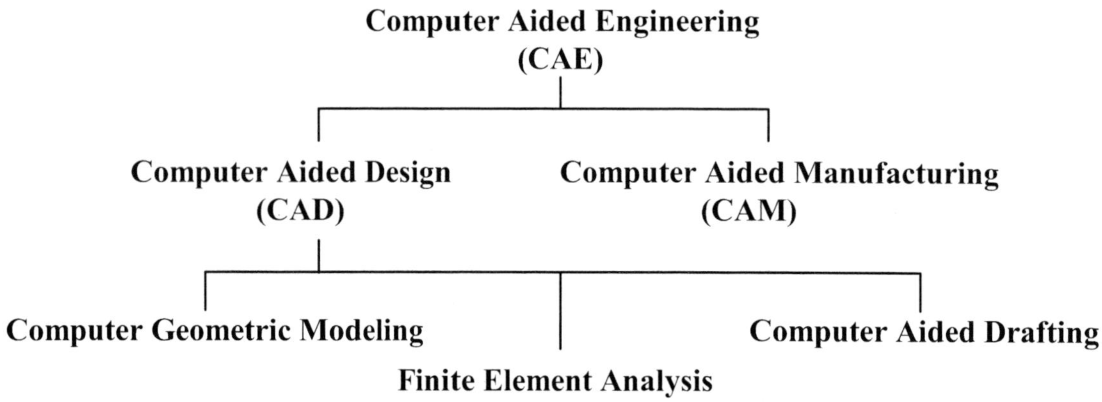

Development of Computer Geometric Modeling

Computer geometric modeling is a relatively new technology and its rapid expansion in the last fifty years is truly amazing. Computer-modeling technology advanced along with the development of computer hardware. The first generation CAD programs, developed in the 1950s, were mostly non-interactive; CAD users were required to create program-codes to generate the desired two-dimensional (2D) geometric shapes. Initially, the development of CAD technology occurred mostly in academic research facilities. The Massachusetts Institute of Technology, Carnegie-Mellon University and Cambridge University were the lead pioneers at that time. The interest in CAD technology spread quickly and several major industry companies, such as General Motors, Lockheed, McDonnell, IBM, and Ford Motor Co., participated in the development of interactive CAD programs in the 1960s. Usage of CAD systems was primarily in the automotive industry, aerospace industry, and government agencies that developed their own programs for their specific needs. The 1960s also were marked as the beginning of the development of finite element analysis methods for computer stress analysis and computer aided manufacturing for generating machine toolpaths.

The 1970s are generally viewed as the years of the most significant progress in the development of computer hardware, namely the invention and development of **microprocessors**. With the improvement in computing power, new types of 3D CAD programs that were user-friendly and interactive became reality. CAD technology quickly expanded from very simple **computer aided drafting** to very complex **computer aided design**. The use of 2D and 3D wireframe modelers was accepted as the leading edge technology that could increase productivity in industries. The developments of surface modeling and solid modeling technology were taking shape by the late 1970s; but the high cost of computer hardware and programming slowed the development of such technology. During this period of time, the available CAD systems all required expensive room-sized mainframe computers that were extremely high in cost.

In the 1980s, improvements in computer hardware brought the power of mainframes to the desktop at less cost and with more accessibility to the general public. By the mid-1980s, CAD technology had become the main focus of a variety of manufacturing industries and was very competitive with traditional design/drafting methods. It was during this period of time that 3D solid modeling technology had major advancements, which boosted the usage of CAE technology in industry.

The introduction of the *feature-based parametric solid modeling* approach, at the end of the 1980s, elevated the CAD/CAM/CAE technology to a new level. In the 1990s, CAD programs evolved into powerful design/manufacturing/management tools. CAD technology has come a long way, and during these years of development, modeling schemes progressed from two-dimensional (2D) wireframe to three-dimensional (3D) wireframe, to surface modeling, to solid modeling and, finally, to feature-based parametric solid modeling.

The first generation CAD packages were simply 2D **Computer Aided Drafting** programs, basically the electronic equivalents of the drafting board. For typical models, the use of this type of program would require that several to many views of the objects be created individually as they would be on the drafting board. The 3D designs remained in the designer's mind, not in the computer database. The mental translations of 3D objects to 2D views are required throughout the use of the packages. Although such systems have some advantages over traditional board drafting, they are still tedious and labor intensive. The need for the development of 3D modelers came quite naturally, given the limitations of the 2D drafting packages.

The development of three-dimensional modeling schemes started with three-dimensional (3D) wireframes. Wireframe models are models consisting of points and edges, which are straight lines connecting between appropriate points. The edges of wireframe models are used, similar to lines in 2D drawings, to represent transitions of surfaces and features. The use of lines and points are also a very economical way to represent 3D designs.

The development of the 3D wireframe modeler was a major leap in the area of computer geometric modeling. The computer database in the 3D wireframe modeler contains the locations of all the points in space coordinates and it is typically sufficient to create just one model rather than multiple views of the same model. This single 3D model can then be viewed from any direction as needed. Most 3D wireframe modelers allow the user to create projected lines/edges of 3D wireframe models. In comparison to other types of 3D modelers, the 3D wireframe modelers require very little computing power and generally can be used to achieve reasonably good representations of 3D models. However, because surface definition is not part of a wireframe model, all wireframe images have the inherent problem of ambiguity. Two examples of such ambiguity are illustrated.

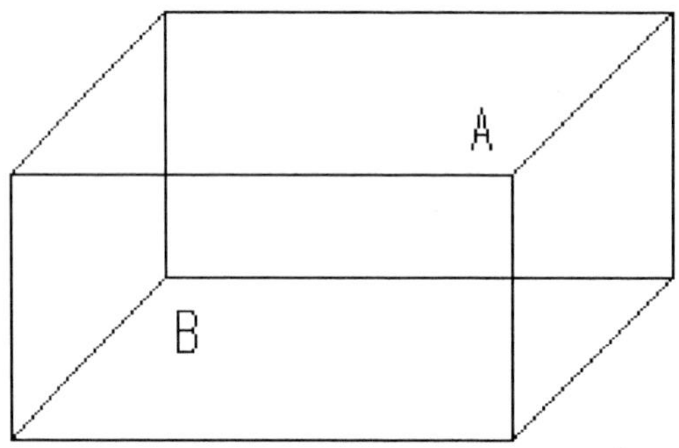

Wireframe Ambiguity: Which corner is in front, A or B?

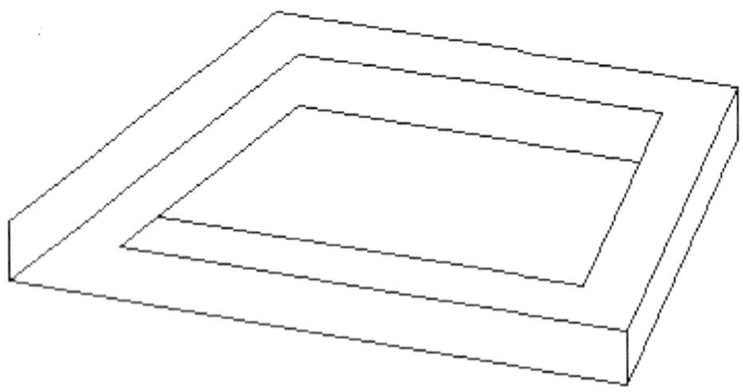

A non-realizable object: Wireframe models contain no surface definitions.

Surface modeling is the logical development in computer geometry modeling to follow the 3D wireframe modeling scheme by organizing and grouping edges that define polygonal surfaces. Surface modeling describes the part's surfaces but not its interiors. Designers are still required to interactively examine surface models to insure that the various surfaces on a model are contiguous throughout. Many of the concepts used in 3D wireframe and surface modelers are incorporated in the solid modeling scheme, but it is solid modeling that offers the most advantages as a design tool.

In the solid modeling presentation scheme, the solid definitions include nodes, edges, and surfaces, and it is a complete and unambiguous mathematical representation of a precisely enclosed and filled volume. Unlike the surface modeling method, solid modelers start with a solid or use topology rules to guarantee that all of the surfaces are stitched together properly. Two predominant methods for representing solid models are **constructive solid geometry** (CSG) representation and **boundary representation** (B-rep).

The CSG representation method can be defined as the combination of 3D solid primitives. What constitutes a "primitive" varies somewhat with the software but typically includes a rectangular prism, a cylinder, a cone, a wedge, and a sphere. Most solid modelers also allow the user to define additional primitives, which are shapes typically formed by the basic shapes. The underlying concept of the CSG representation method is very straightforward; we simply **add** or **subtract** one primitive from another. The CSG approach is also known as the machinist's approach as it can be used to simulate the manufacturing procedures for creating the 3D object.

In the B-rep representation method, objects are represented in terms of their spatial boundaries. This method defines the points, edges, and surfaces of a volume, and/or issues commands that sweep or rotate a defined face into a third dimension to form a solid. The object is then made up of the unions of these surfaces that completely and precisely enclose a volume.

By the 1980s, a new paradigm called *concurrent engineering* had emerged. With concurrent engineering, designers, design engineers, analysts, manufacturing engineers, and management engineers all work together closely right from the initial stages of the design. In this way, all aspects of the design can be evaluated and any potential problems can be identified right from the start and throughout the design process. Using the principles of concurrent engineering, a new type of computer modeling technique appeared. The technique is known as the *feature-based parametric modeling technique*. The key advantage of the *feature-based parametric modeling technique* is its capability to produce very flexible designs. Changes can be made easily and design alternatives can be evaluated with minimum effort. Various software packages offer different approaches to feature-based parametric modeling, yet the end result is a flexible design defined by its design variables and parametric features.

Feature-Based Parametric Modeling

One of the key-elements in the *Autodesk Inventor* solid modeling software is its use of the **feature-based parametric modeling technique**. The feature-based parametric modeling approach has elevated solid modeling technology to the level of a very powerful design tool. Parametric modeling automates the design and revision procedures by the use of parametric features. Parametric features control the model geometry by the use of design variables. The word ***parametric*** means that the geometric definitions of the design, such as dimensions, can be varied at any time during the design process. Features are predefined parts or construction tools in which users define the key parameters. A part is described as a sequence of engineering features, which can be modified/changed at any time. The concept of parametric features makes modeling more closely match the actual design-manufacturing process than the mathematics of a solid modeling program. In parametric modeling, models and drawings are updated automatically when the design is refined.

Parametric modeling offers many benefits:

- **We begin with simple, conceptual models with minimal detail; this approach conforms to the design philosophy of "shape before size."**
- **Geometric constraints, dimensional constraints, and relational parametric equations can be used to capture design intent.**
- **The ability to update an entire system, including parts, assemblies and drawings after changing one parameter of complex designs.**
- **We can quickly explore and evaluate different design variations and alternatives to determine the best design.**
- **Existing design data can be reused to create new designs.**
- **Quick design turn-around.**

One of the key-features of *Autodesk Inventor* is the use of an assembly-centric paradigm, which enables users to concentrate on the design without depending on the associated parameters or constraints. Users can specify how parts fit together and the *Autodesk Inventor assembly-based fit function* automatically determines the parts' sizes and positions. This unique approach is known as the **Direct Adaptive Assembly approach**, which defines part relationships directly with no order dependency.

The *Adaptive Assembly approach* is a unique design methodology that can only be found in *Autodesk Inventor.* The goal of this methodology is to improve the design process and allows you, the designers, to **Design the Way You Think**.

Getting Started with *Autodesk Inventor*

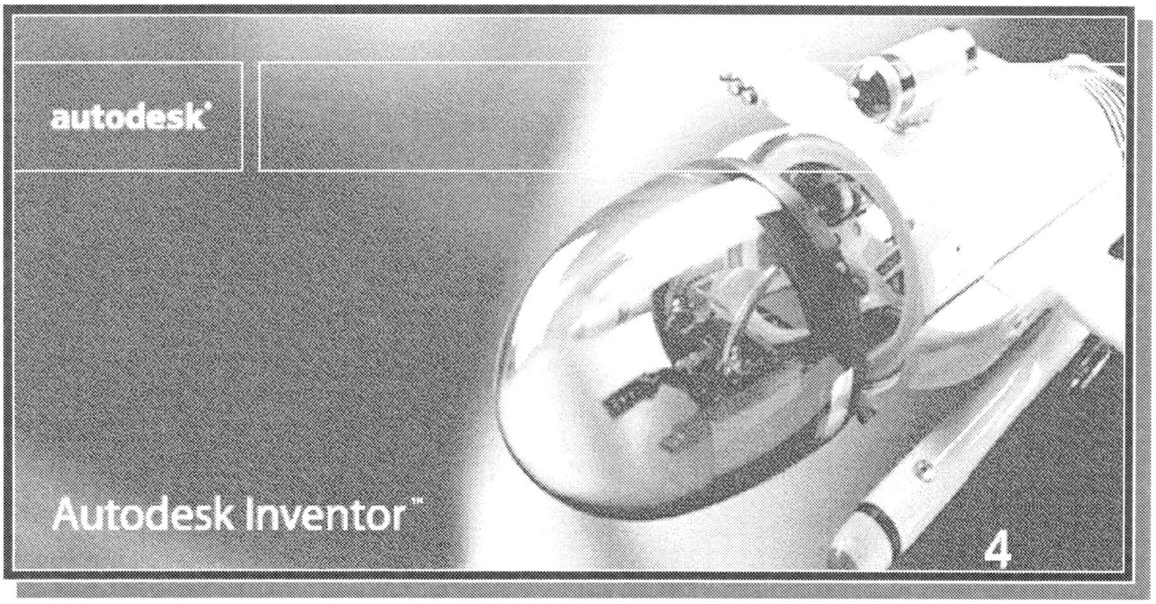

- *Autodesk Inventor* is composed of several application software modules (these modules are called *applications*), all sharing a common database. In this text, the main concentration is placed on the solid modeling modules used for part design. The general procedures required in creating solid models, engineering drawings, and assemblies are illustrated.

Starting *Autodesk Inventor*

How to start ***Autodesk Inventor*** depends on the type of workstation and the particular software configuration you are using. With most *Windows* systems, you may select ***Autodesk Inventor*** on the *Start* menu or select the ***Autodesk Inventor* icon** on the desktop. Consult your instructor or technical support personnel if you have difficulty starting the software.

The program takes a while to load, so be patient. Eventually the ***Autodesk Inventor*** *Startup* dialog box will appear on the screen.

The tutorials in this text are based on the assumption that you are using ***Autodesk Inventor****'s* default settings. If your system has been customized for other uses, some of the settings may not work with the step-by-step instructions in the tutorials. Contact your instructor and/or technical support personnel to restore the default software configuration.

The Startup dialog box and Units Setup

Once the program is loaded into the memory, the *Startup* dialog box appears at the center of the screen.

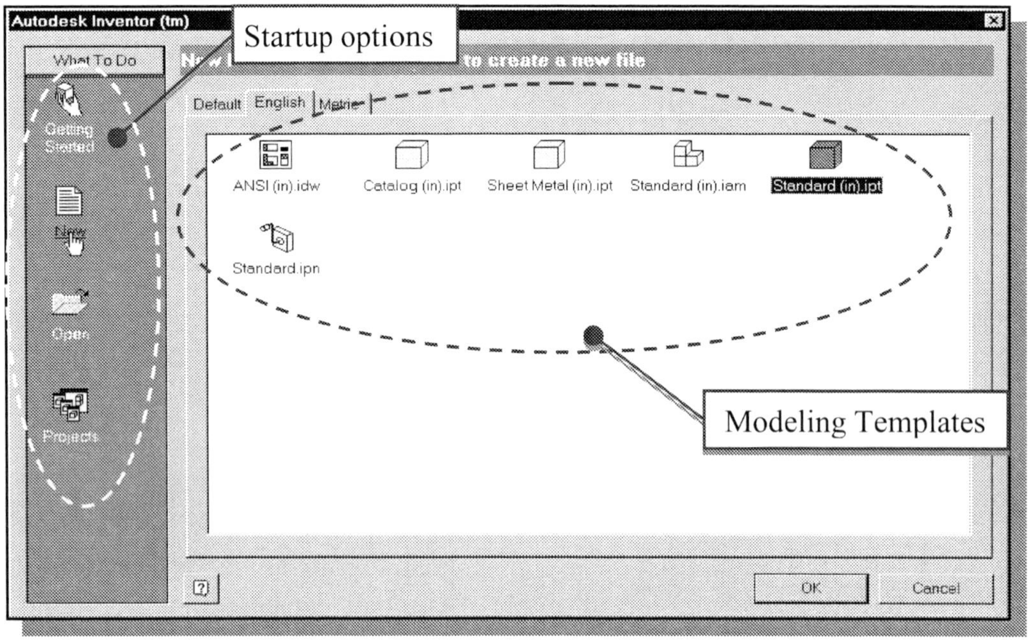

The following three startup options are available: *New, Open*, and *Getting Started*. The *New* option allows us to start a new modeling task. The *Open* option allows us to open an existing model file. The *Getting Started* option provides some quick helps that illustrate the features and general procedures of using *Autodesk Inventor*.

➢ Select the ***New*** icon with a single click of the left-mouse-button in the *What to Do* dialog box.

➢ Select the **English** tab as shown below. When starting a new CAD file, the first thing we should do is to choose the units we would like to use. We will use the English (feet and inches) setting for this example.

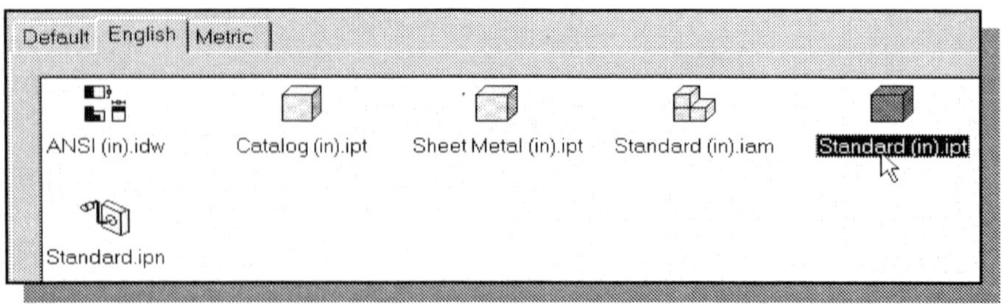

➢ In the *New - Choose Template* area, select the **Standard(in).ipt** icon as shown. The six icons allow us to specify the type of modeling to be used. The **idw** file type stands for *Inventor* drawing file, the **iam** file type stands for *Inventor* assembly file, and the **ipt** file type stands for *Inventor* part file. The **ipn** file type stands for assembly presentation. Pick **OK** in the *Startup* dialog box to accept the selected settings.

Autodesk Inventor Screen Layout

The default *Autodesk Inventor* drawing screen contains the *pull-down* menus, the *Standard* toolbar, the *Features* toolbar, the *Command* toolbar, the *Sketch* toolbar, the *Drawing Area*, the *Browser Area*, and the *Status Bar*. A line of quick text appears next to the icon as you move the *mouse cursor* over different icons. You may resize the *Autodesk Inventor* drawing window by click and drag at the edges of the window, or relocate the window by click and drag at the window title area.

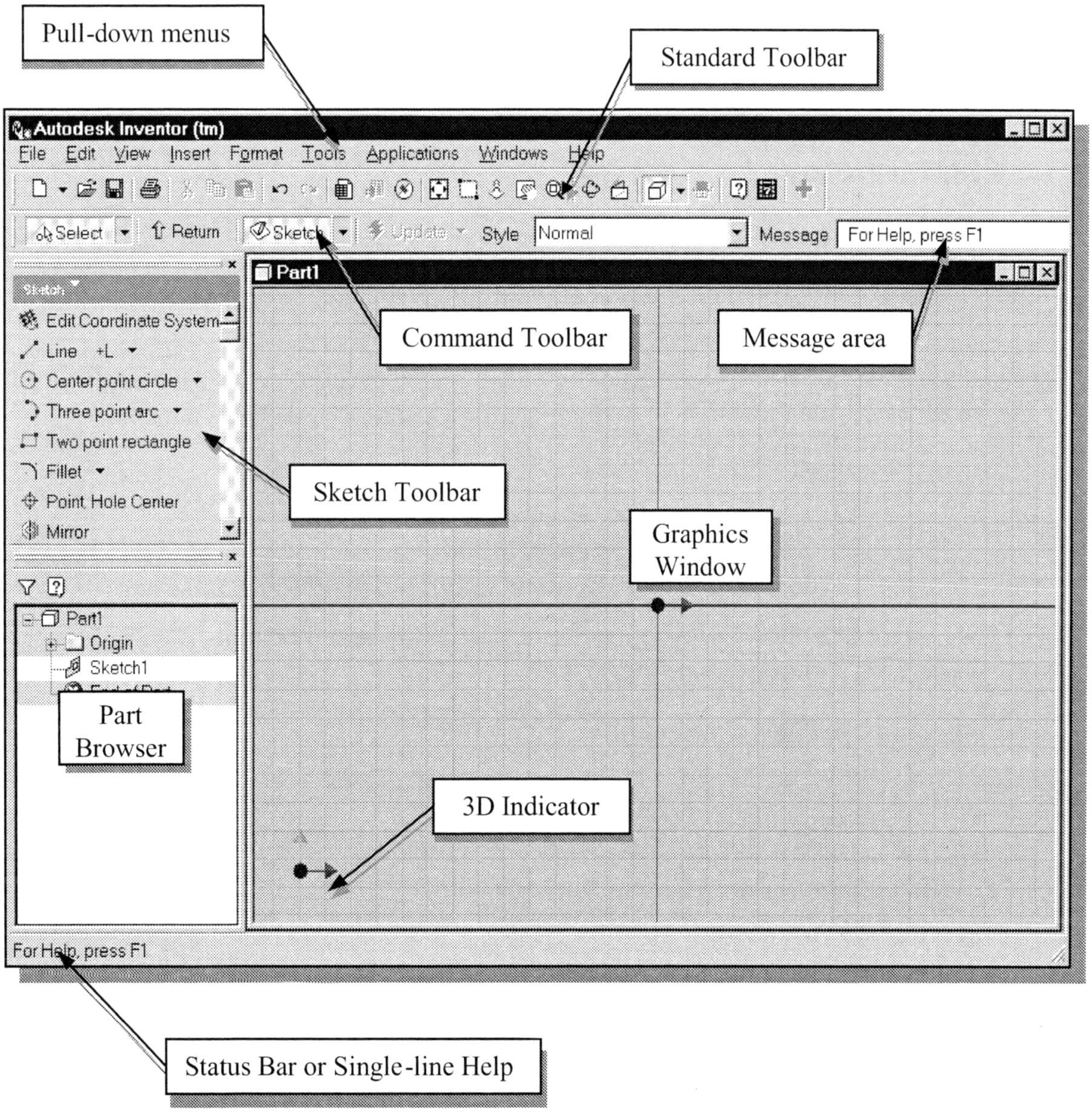

- **Pull-down Menus**

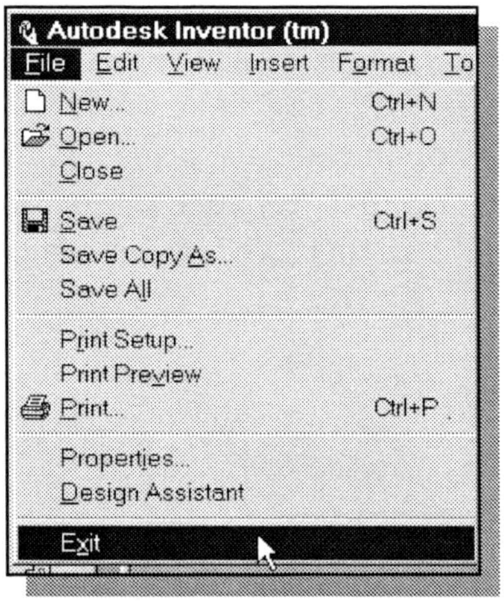

The *pull-down* menus at the top of the main window contain operations that you can use for all modes of the system.

- **Standard Toolbar**

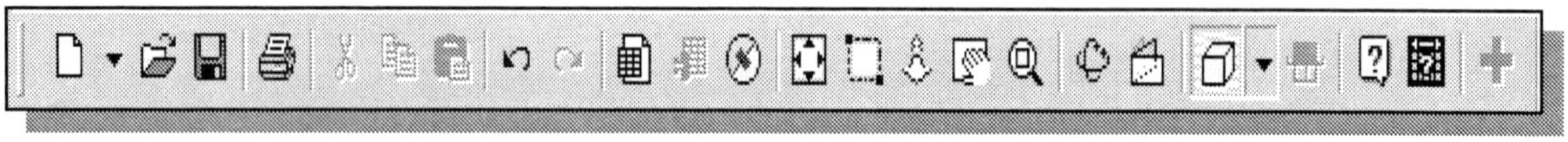

The *Standard* toolbar at the top of the screen window allows us quick access to frequently used commands. For example, the view-related commands, commands such as *Zoom*, *Pan*, and *Rotate*, are tools to help manipulate the viewing of graphical objects.

- **Feature Toolbar**

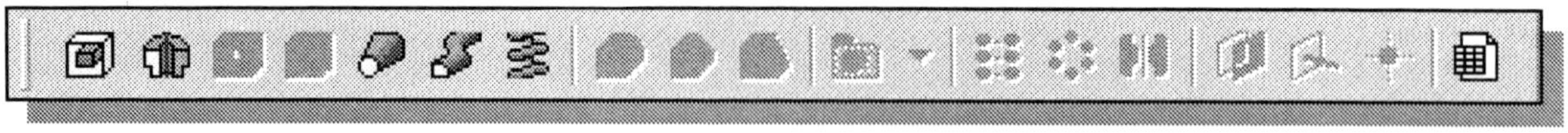

The *Feature* toolbar allows us quick access to frequently used features-related commands, such as *Extrude*, *Revolve*, and *Patterns*.

- **Command Toolbar**

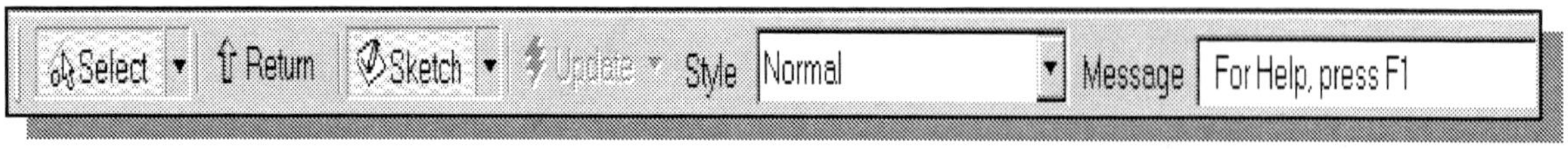

The *Command* toolbar provides status information for an operation and it is also the area for basic operation selection. *Command* is a special toolbar that is always visible when the *Autodesk Inventor* window is open and active.

- **Sketch Toolbar**

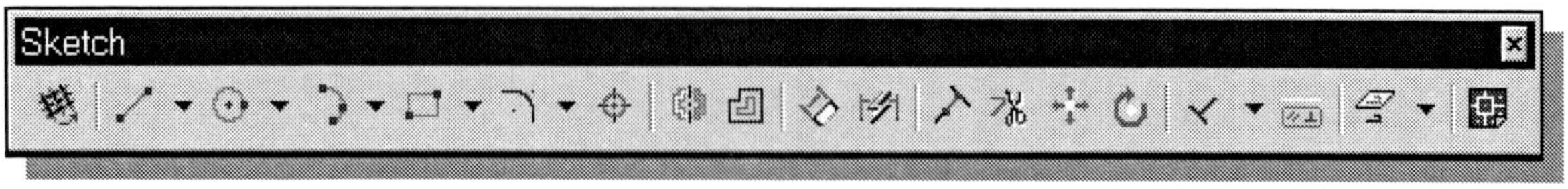

The *Sketch* toolbar provides tools for creating the basic geometry that can be used to create features and parts.

- **Graphics Window**

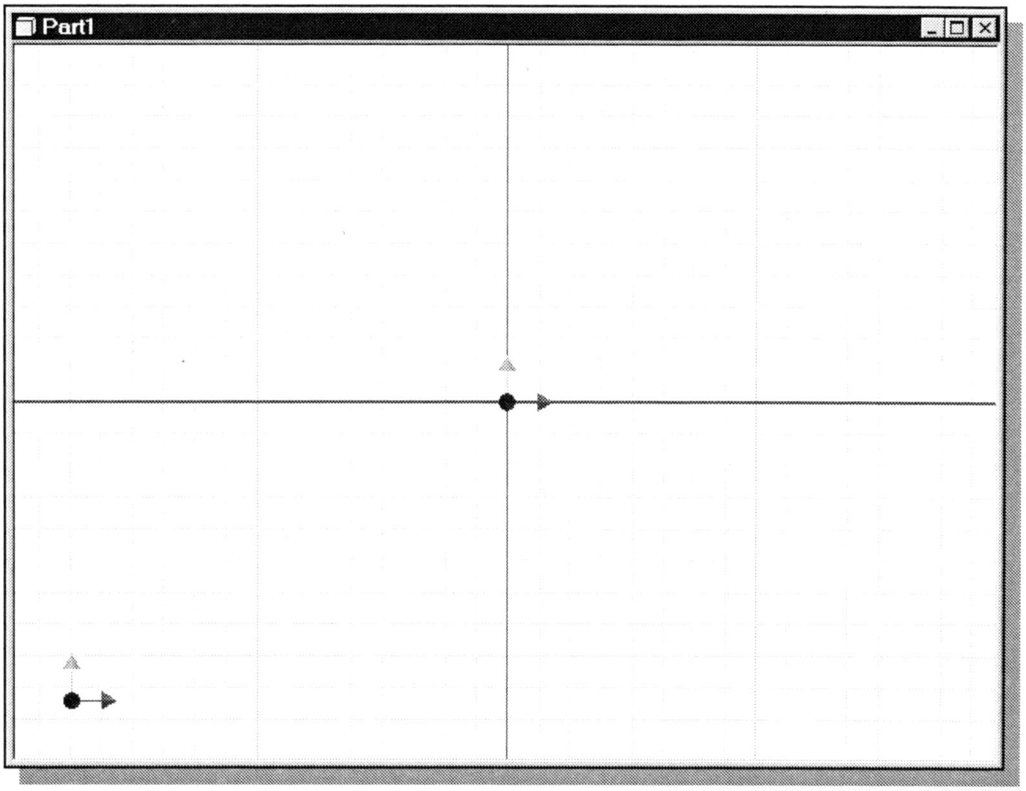

The *graphics window* is the area where models and drawings are displayed.

- **Graphics Cursor or Crosshairs**

The *graphics cursor*, or *crosshairs*, shows the location of the pointing device in the graphics window. During geometric construction, the coordinate of the cursor is displayed in the *Status Bar* area, located at the bottom of the screen. The cursor's appearance depends on the selected command or option.

- **Status Bar**

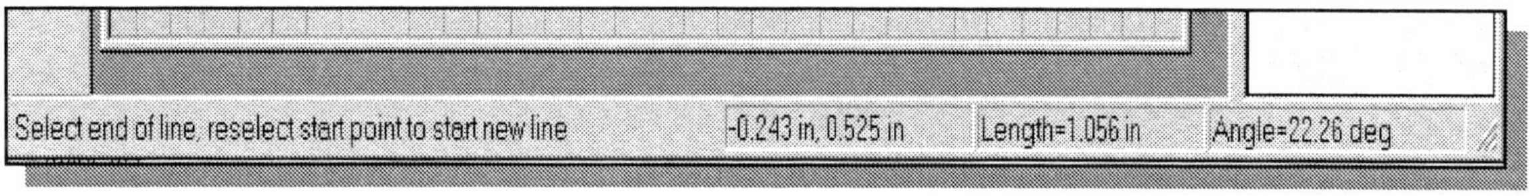

The *Status Bar* area shows a single-line help when the cursor is on top of an icon. This area also displays information pertinent to the active operation. For example, in the above figure, the coordinates and length information of a line are displayed while the *Line* command is activated.

- **Browser**

The *browser window* shows and hides selected features, filters contents, manages access to feature and editing, and provides alternate access to functions in the context menu.

Mouse Buttons

Autodesk Inventor utilizes the mouse buttons extensively. In learning *Autodesk Inventor's* interactive environment, it is important to understand the basic functions of the mouse buttons. It is highly recommended that you use a mouse or a tablet with *Autodesk Inventor* since the package uses the buttons for various functions.

- **Left mouse button**

The **left-mouse-button** is used for most operations, such as selecting menus and icons, or picking graphic entities. One click of the button is used to select icons, menus, and form entries, and to pick graphic items.

- **Right mouse button**

The **right-mouse-button** is used to bring up additionally available options. The software also utilizes the **right-mouse-button** as the same as the **ENTER** key, and is often used to accept the default setting to a prompt or to end a process.

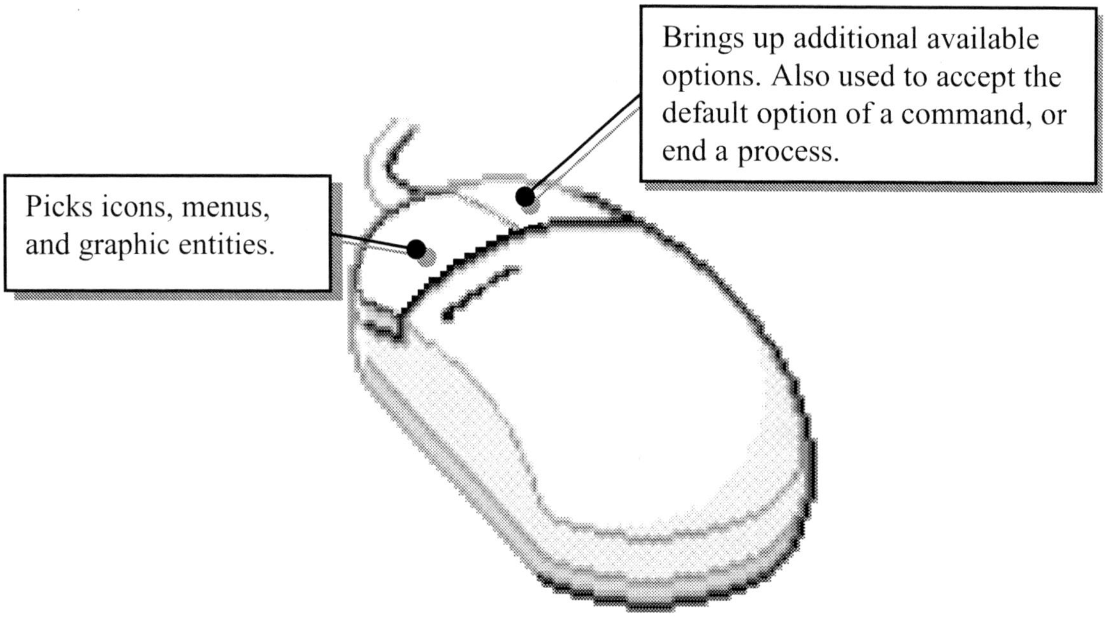

[Esc] - Canceling commands

The [**Esc**] key is used to cancel a command in *Autodesk Inventor*. The [**Esc**] key is located near the top-left corner of the keyboard. Sometimes, it may be necessary to press the [**Esc**] key twice to cancel a command; it depends on where we are in the command sequence. For some commands, the [**Esc**] key is used to exit the command.

On-Line Help

❖ Several types of on-line help are available at any time during an *Autodesk Inventor* session. *Autodesk Inventor* provides many on-line help functions, such as:

- The *Help* menu: Click on the ***Help*** option in the pull-down menu to access the *Autodesk Inventor* ***Help*** **menu system**.
- On-line manuals and tutorials: Three icons are available in the *Standard* toolbar to access the on-line manuals and tutorials: ***Help Topics*** and ***Visual Syllabus***.
- Help quick key: Press the [**F1**] key to access the ***On-line Help*** **system**.

Leaving Autodesk Inventor

➢ To leave *Autodesk Inventor*, use the left-mouse-button and click on **File** at the top of the *Autodesk Inventor* screen window, then choose **Exit** from the pull-down menu.

Creating a CAD files folder

It is a good practice to create a separate folder to store your CAD files. You should not save your CAD files in the same folder where the *Autodesk Inventor* application is located. It is much easier to organize and backup your project files if they are in a separate folder. Making folders within this folder for different types of projects will help you organize your CAD files even further. When creating CAD files in *Autodesk Inventor*, it is strongly recommended that you *save* your CAD files on the hard drive.

To create a new folder:

1. In *My Computer*, or start the **Windows Explorer** under the *Start* menu, open the folder in which you want to create a new folder.
2. On the **File** menu, point to **New**, and then click **Folder**. The new folder appears with a temporary name.
3. Type a name for the new folder, and then press **ENTER**.

NOTES:

Lesson 1
Parametric Modeling Fundamentals

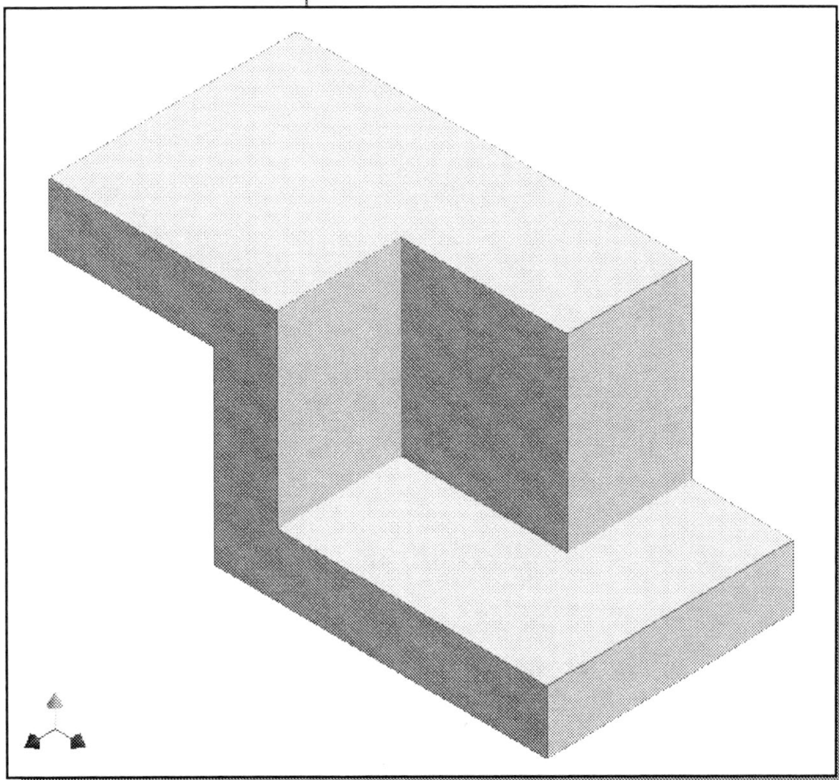

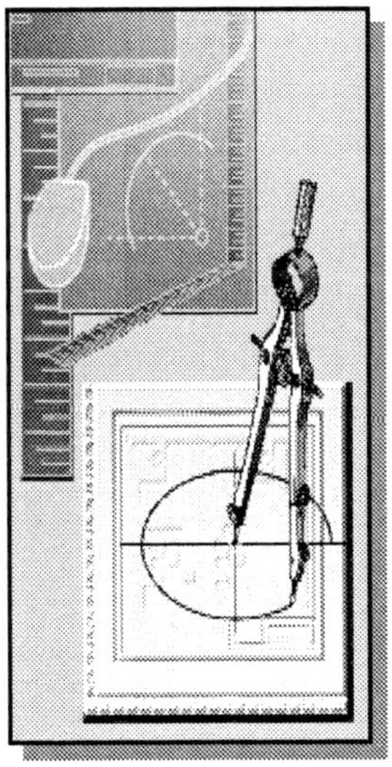

Learning Objectives

When you have completed this lesson, you will be able to:

- ♦ Create Simple Extruded Solid Models.
- ♦ Understand the Basic Parametric Modeling Process.
- ♦ Create 2-D Sketches.
- ♦ Understand the "Shape before size" approach.
- ♦ Use the Dynamic Viewing commands.
- ♦ Create and Modify Parametric Dimensions.

Introduction

The **feature-based parametric modeling** technique enables the designer to incorporate the original **design intent** into the construction of the model. The word ***parametric*** means the geometric definitions of the design, such as dimensions, can be varied at any time in the design process. Parametric modeling is accomplished by identifying and creating the key features of the design with the aid of computer software. The design variables, described in the sketches and described as parametric relations, can then be used to quickly modify/update the design.

In *Autodesk Inventor*, the parametric part modeling process involves the following steps:

1. **Create a rough two-dimensional sketch of the basic shape of the base feature of the design.**

2. **Apply/modify constraints and dimensions to the two-dimensional sketch.**

3. **Extrude, revolve, or sweep the parametric two-dimensional sketch to create the base solid feature of the design.**

4. **Add additional parametric features by identifying feature relations and complete the design.**

5. **Perform analyses on the computer model and refine the design as needed.**

6. **Create the desired drawing views to document the design.**

The approach of creating two-dimensional sketches of the three-dimensional features is an effective way to construct solid models. Many designs are in fact the same shape in one direction. Computer input and output devices we use today are largely two-dimensional in nature, which makes this modeling technique quite practical. This method also conforms to the design process that helps the designer with conceptual design along with the capability to capture the ***design intent***. Most engineers and designers can relate to the experience of making rough sketches on restaurant napkins to convey conceptual design ideas. *Autodesk Inventor* provides many powerful modeling and design-tools, and there are many different approaches to accomplishing modeling tasks. The basic principle of **feature-based modeling** is to build models by adding simple features one at a time. In this chapter, the general parametric part modeling procedure is illustrated; a very simple solid model with extruded features is used to introduce the *Autodesk Inventor* user interface. The display viewing functions and the basic two-dimensional sketching tools are also demonstrated.

The *Z-Block* design

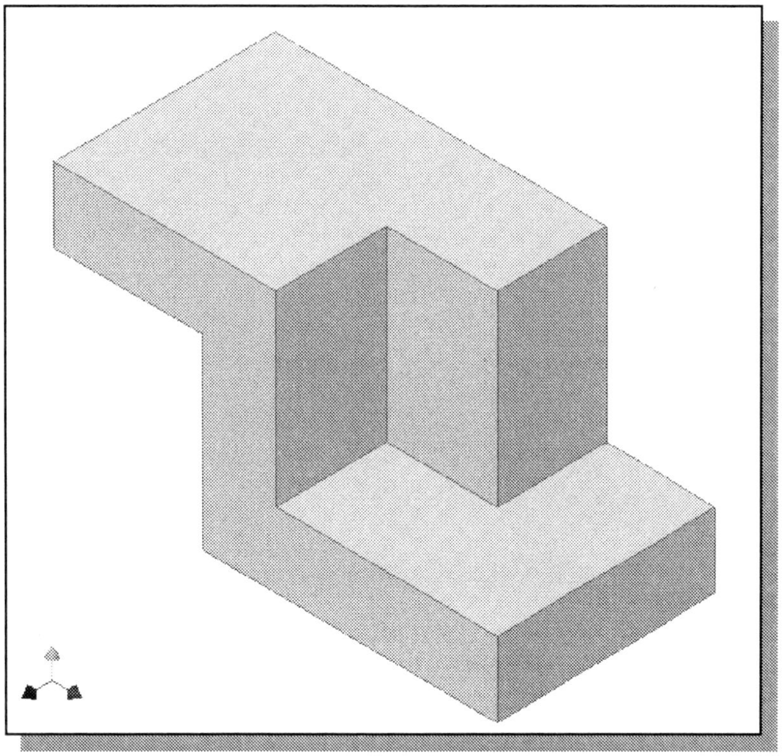

Starting Autodesk Inventor

1. Select the ***Autodesk Inventor*** option on the *Start* menu or select the ***Autodesk Inventor*** icon on the desktop to start *Autodesk Inventor*. The *Autodesk Inventor* main window will appear on the screen.

2. Once the program is loaded into the memory, the *Startup* dialog box appears at the center of the screen.

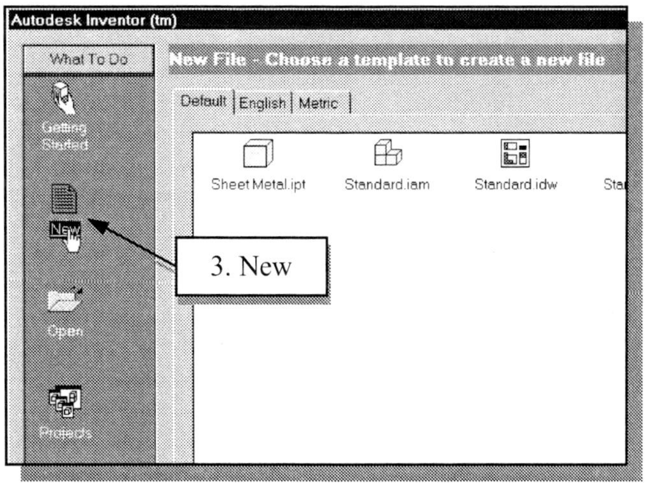

3. Select the ***New*** icon with a single click of the left-mouse-button in the *What to Do* dialog box.

4. Select the **English** tab as shown below. When starting a new CAD file, the first thing we should do is to choose the units we would like to use. We will use the English setting (inches) for this example.

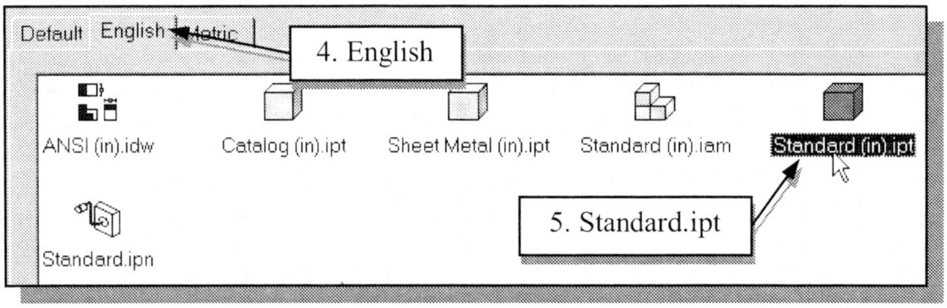

5. In the *New - Choose Template* area, select the ***Standard(in).ipt*** icon as shown.

6. Pick **OK** in the *Startup* dialog box to accept the selected settings.

Autodesk Inventor Screen Layout

The default *Autodesk Inventor* drawing screen contains the *pull-down* menus, the *Standard* toolbar, the *Command* toolbar, the *Sketch* toolbar, the *graphics* window, the *Browser* area, and the *Status Bar*.

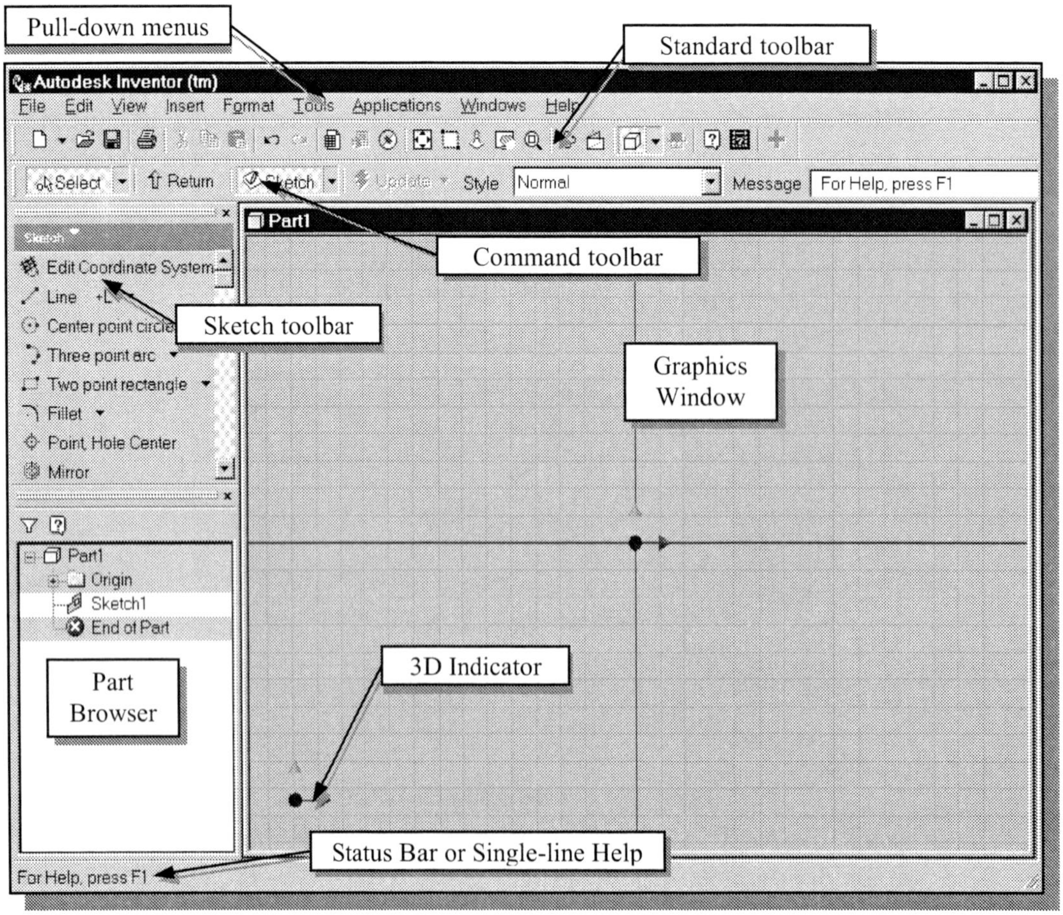

Creating Rough Sketches

Quite often during the early design stage, the shape of a design may not have any precise dimensions. Most conventional CAD systems require the users to input the precise lengths and locations of all geometric entities defining the design, which are not available during the early design stage. With *parametric modeling*, we can use the computer to elaborate and formulate the design idea further during the initial design stage. With *Autodesk Inventor*, we can use the computer as an electronic sketchpad to help us concentrate on the formulation of forms and shapes for the design. This approach is the main advantage of *parametric modeling* over conventional solid-modeling techniques.

As the name implies, ***rough sketches*** are not precise at all. When sketching, we simply sketch the geometry so that it closely resembles the desired shape. Precise scale or lengths are not needed. *Autodesk Inventor* provides us with many tools to assist us in finalizing sketches. For example, geometric entities such as horizontal and vertical lines are set automatically. However, if the rough sketches are poor, it will require much more work to generate the desired parametric sketches. Here are some general guidelines for creating sketches in *Autodesk Inventor*:

- **Create a sketch that is proportional to the desired shape.** Concentrate on the shapes and forms of the design.

- **Keep the sketches simple.** Leave out small geometry features such as fillets, rounds and chamfers. They can easily be placed using the *Fillet* and *Chamfer* commands after the parametric sketches have been established.

- **Exaggerate the geometric features of the desired shape.** For example, if the desired angle is 85 degrees, create an angle that is 50 or 60 degrees. Otherwise, *Autodesk Inventor* might assume the intended angle to be a 90-degree angle.

- **Draw the geometry so that it does not overlap.** The geometry should eventually form a closed region. *Self-intersecting* geometry shapes are not allowed.

- **The sketched geometric entities should form a closed region.** To create a solid feature such as an extruded solid, a closed region is required so that the extruded solid forms a 3D volume.

➢ **Note:** The concepts and principles involved in *parametric modeling* are very different, and sometimes they are totally opposite, to those of conventional computer aided drafting. In order to understand and fully utilize *Autodesk Inventor's* functionality, it will be helpful to take a *Zen* approach to learning the topics presented in this text: **Temporarily forget your knowledge and experiences of using conventional Computer Aided Drafting systems.**

Step 1: Creating a rough sketch

➢ The *Sketch* toolbar provides tools for creating the basic geometry that can be used to create features and parts.

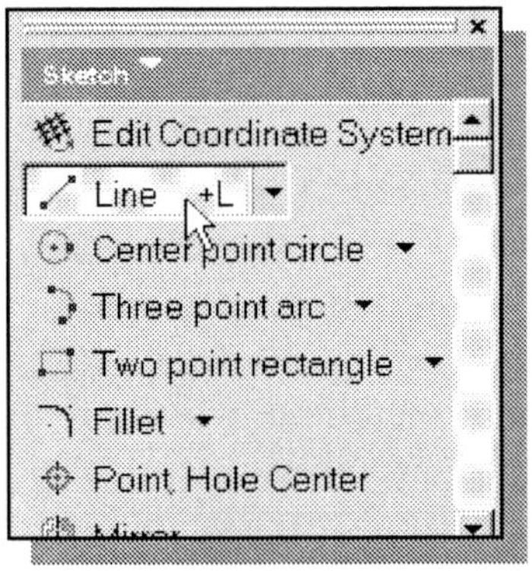

1. Move the graphics cursor to the ***Line*** icon in the *Sketch* toolbar. A *Help-tip box* appears next to the cursor and a brief description of the command is displayed at the bottom of the drawing screen: *"Creates Straight line segments and tangent arcs."*

2. Select the icon by clicking once with the **left-mouse-button**; this will activate the *Line* command. In the command prompt area, near the bottom of the *Autodesk Inventor* drawing screen, the message *"Specify start point, drag off endpoint for tangent arcs"* is displayed. *Autodesk Inventor* expects us to identify the starting location of a straight line.

Graphics Cursors

Notice the cursor changes from an arrow to a crosshair when graphical input is expected.

1. Left-click a starting point of the shape, roughly near the lower center of the graphics window as shown below.

2. As you move the graphics cursor, you will see a digital readout in the *Status Bar* area at the bottom of the window. The readout gives you the cursor location, the line length, and the angle of the line measured from horizontal. Move the cursor around and you will notice different symbols appear at different locations.

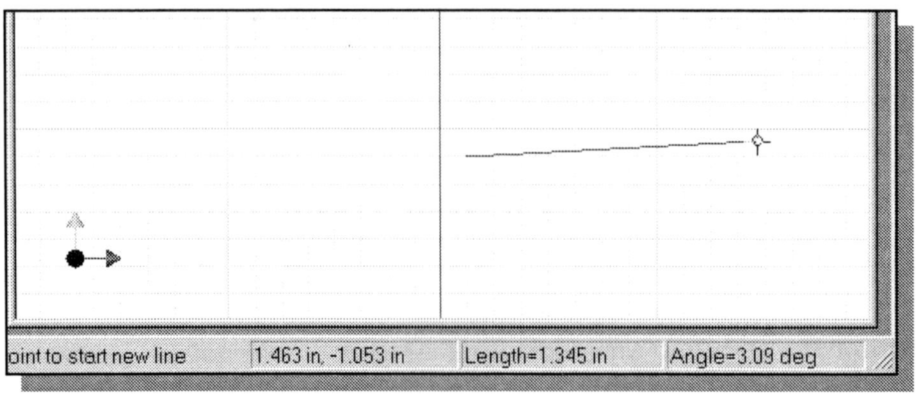

3. Move the graphics cursor toward the right side of the graphics window and create a horizontal line as shown below (**Point 2**). Notice the geometric constraint symbol displayed.

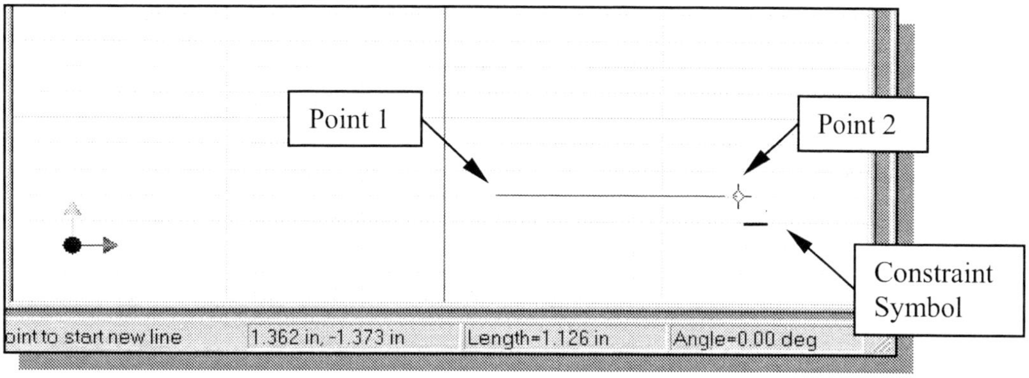

Geometric Constraint Symbols

Autodesk Inventor displays different visual clues, or symbols, to show you alignments, perpendicularities, tangencies, etc. These constraints are used to capture the *design intent* by creating constraints where they are recognized. *Autodesk Inventor* displays the governing geometric rules as models are built. To prevent constraints from forming, hold down the [**Ctrl**] key while creating an individual sketch curve. For example, while sketching line segments with the ***Line*** command, endpoints are joined with a *coincident constraint*, but when the [**Ctrl**] key is pressed and held, the inferred constraint will not be created.

	**Vertical**	indicates a line is vertical
	**Horizontal**	indicates a line is horizontal
	Dashed line	indicates the alignment to the center point or endpoint of an entity
	**Parallel**	indicates a line is parallel to other entities
	**Perpendicular**	indicates a line is perpendicular to other entities
	**Coincident**	indicates the cursor is at the endpoint of an entity
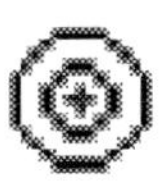	**Concentric**	indicates the cursor is at the center of an entity
	**Tangent**	indicates the cursor is at tangency points to curves

4. Complete the sketch as shown below, creating a closed region ending at Point 1. Do not be concerned with the actual size of the sketch. Note that all line segments are sketched horizontally or vertically.

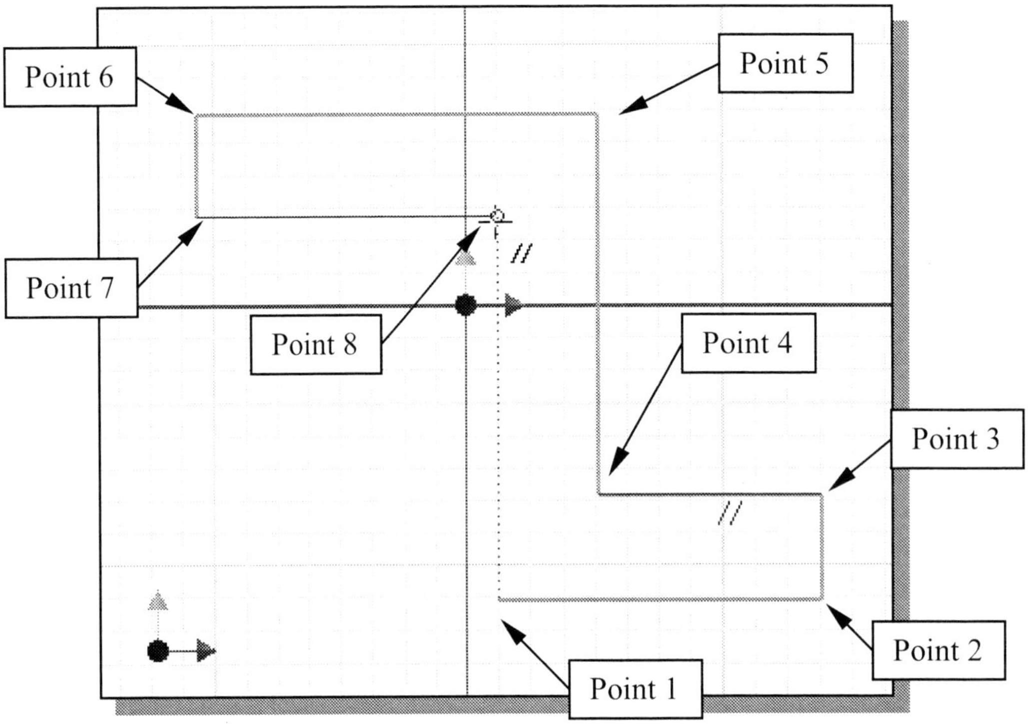

5. Inside the graphics window, click once with the **right-mouse-button** to display the option menu. Select **Done[Esc]** in the popup menu, or hit the [Esc] key once, to end the *Sketching Line* command.

Step 2: Apply/modify constraints and dimensions

As the sketch is made, *Autodesk Inventor* automatically applies some of the geometric constraints (such as horizontal, parallel, and perpendicular) to the sketched geometry. We can continue to modify the geometry, apply additional constraints, and/or define the size of the existing geometry. In this example, we will illustrate adding dimensions to describe the sketched entities.

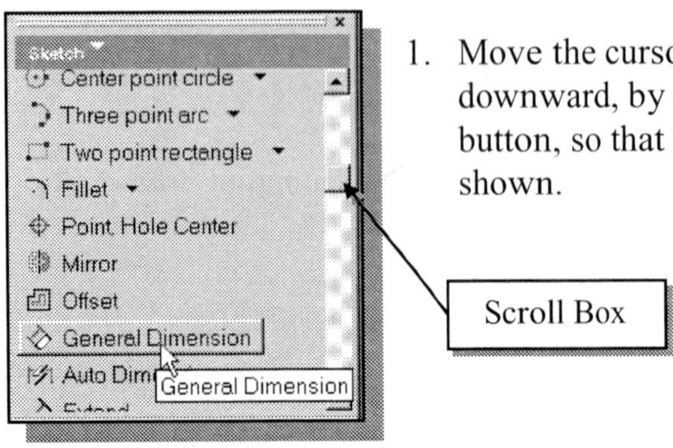

1. Move the cursor to the *Sketch* toolbar area and scroll downward, by dragging the *scroll box* with the left-mouse-button, so that the *General Dimension* icon is visible as shown.

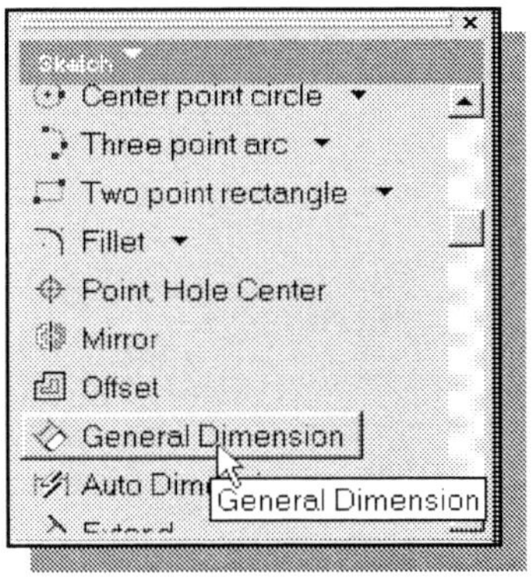

2. Move the cursor on top of the *General Dimension* icon. The *General Dimension* command allows us to quickly create and modify dimensions. Left-click once on the icon to activate the *General Dimension* command.

3. The message "*Select Geometry to Dimension*" is displayed in the *Status Bar* area, at the bottom of the *Inventor* window. Select the bottom-horizontal line by left-clicking once on the line.

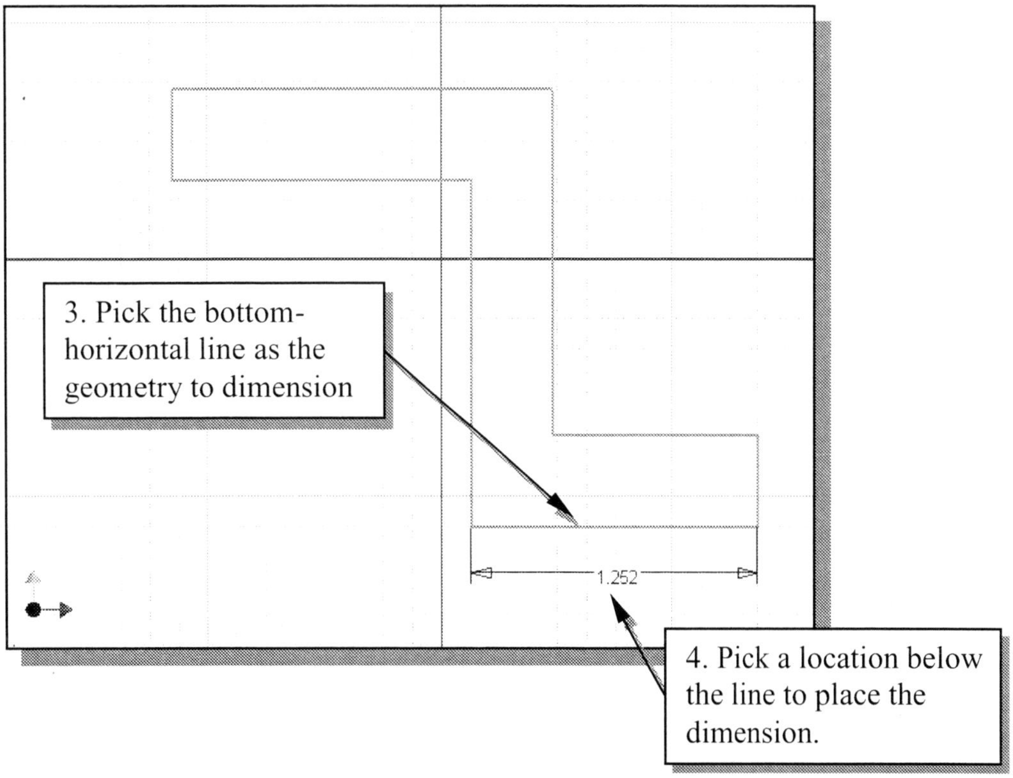

4. Move the graphics cursor below the selected line and left-click to place the dimension. (Note that the value displayed on your screen might be different than what is shown in the above figure.)

5. The message "*Select Geometry to Dimension*" is displayed in the *Status Bar* area, at the bottom of the *Inventor* window. Select the left-vertical line.

6. Pick a location toward the left of the sketch to place the dimension.

❖ The *General Dimension* command will create a length dimension if a single line is selected.

7. The message "*Select Geometry to Dimension*" is displayed in the *Status Bar* area, at the bottom of the *Inventor* window. Select the left-vertical line as shown below.

8. Select the far-right-vertical line as shown below.

9. Pick a location toward the bottom of the sketch to place the dimension, as shown below.

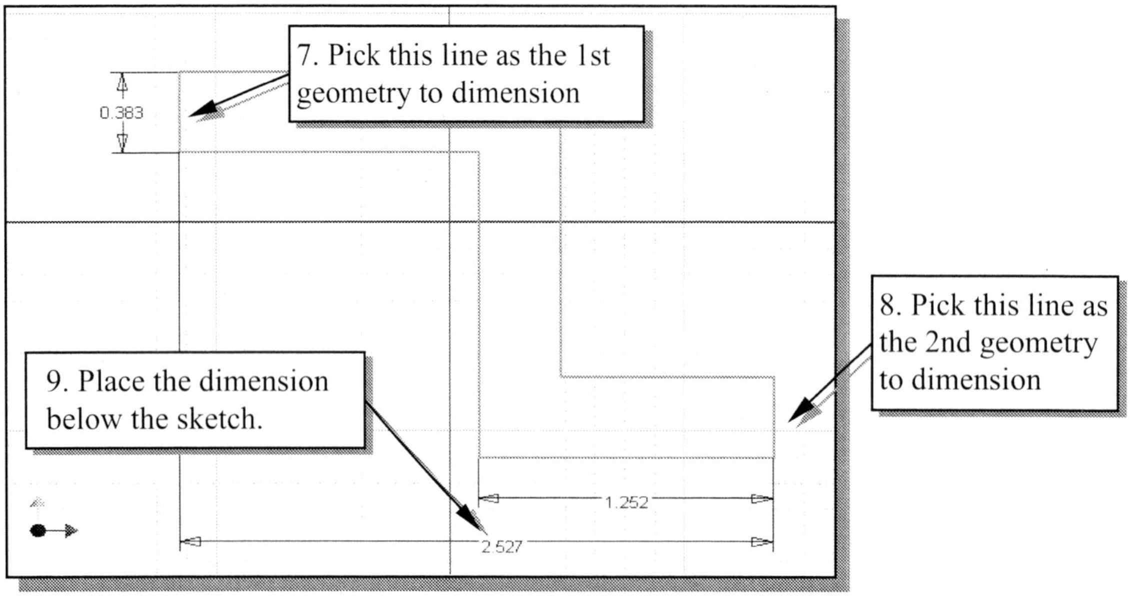

❖ When two parallel lines are selected, the *General Dimension* command will create a dimension measuring the distance in between.

10. On you own, repeat the above steps and create additional dimensions so that the sketch appears as shown below.

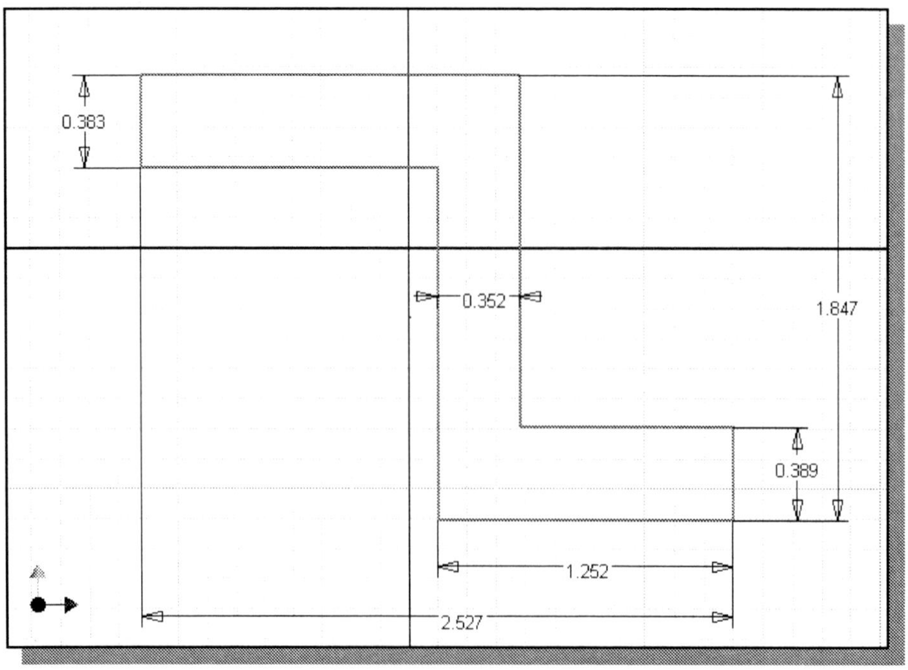

Modifying the dimensions of the sketch

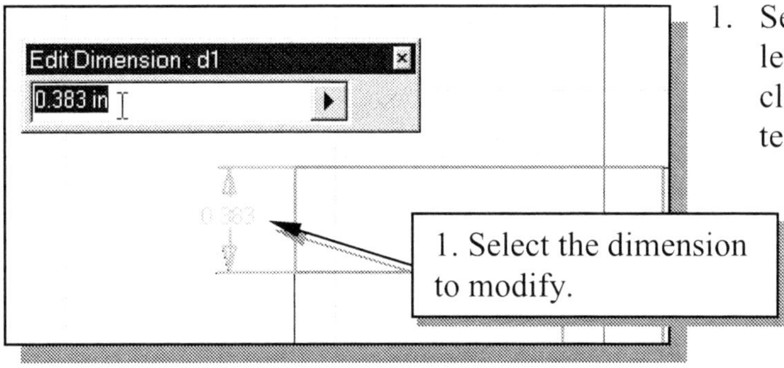

1. Select the dimension that is to the left side of the sketch by left-clicking once on the dimension text.

2. In the *Edit Dimension* window, the current length of the line is displayed. Enter **0.375** to set the length of the line to 0.375 inches.

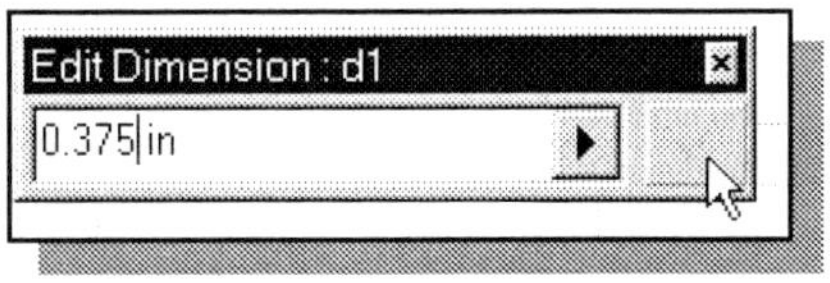

3. Click on the ***Accept*** icon to accept the entered value.

➢ *Autodesk Inventor* will now update the profile with the new dimension value.

4. On you own, repeat the above steps and adjust the dimensions so that the sketch appears as shown below.

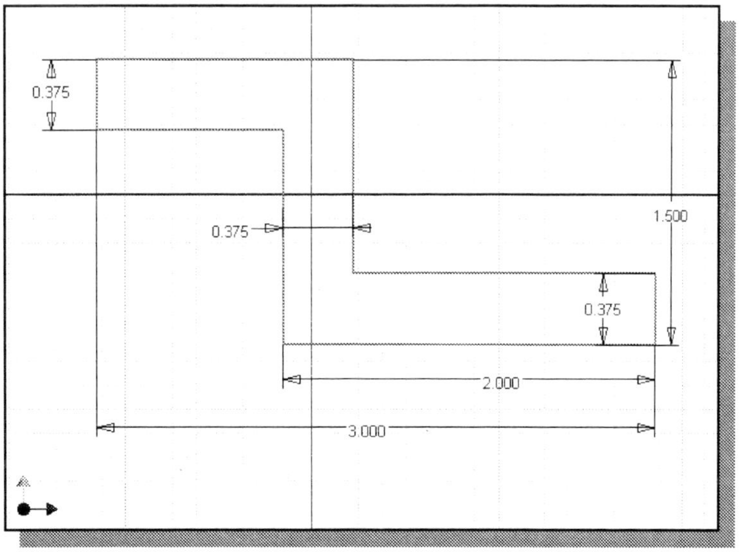

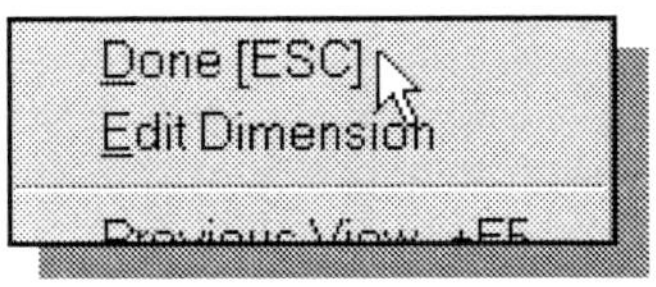

5. Inside the graphics window, click once with the **right-mouse-button** to display the option menu. Select **Done** in the popup menu to end the *General Dimension* command.

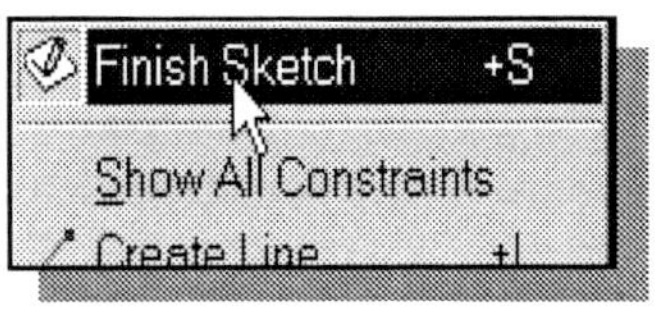

6. Inside the graphics window, click once with the **right-mouse-button** to display the option menu. Select **Finish Sketch** in the popup menu to end the *Sketch* option.

Step 3: Completing the Base Solid Feature

Now that the 2D sketch is completed, we will proceed to the next step: create a 3D part from the 2D profile. Extruding a 2D profile is one of the common methods that can be used to create 3D parts. We can extrude planar faces along a path. We can also specify a height value and a tapered angle. In *Autodesk Inventor*, each face has a positive side and a negative side, the current face we're working on is set as the default positive side. This positive side identifies the positive extrusion direction and it is referred to as the face's ***normal***.

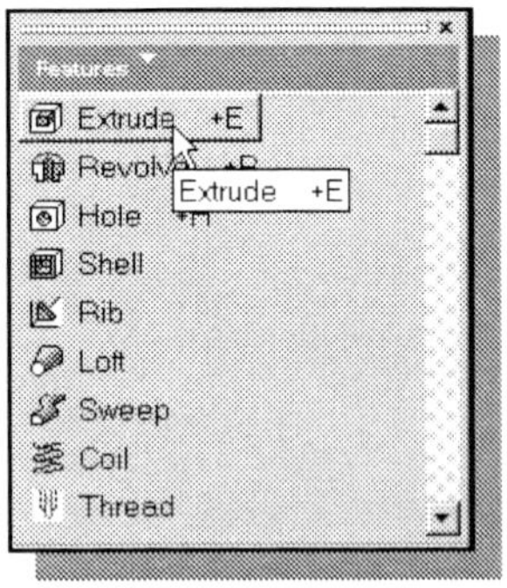

1. In the *Feature* toolbar (the toolbar that is located to the left side of the graphics window), select the ***Extrude*** command by releasing the left-mouse-button on the icon.

2. In the *Extrude* popup window, enter **1.5** as the extrusion distance. Notice that the sketch region is automatically selected as the extrusion profile.

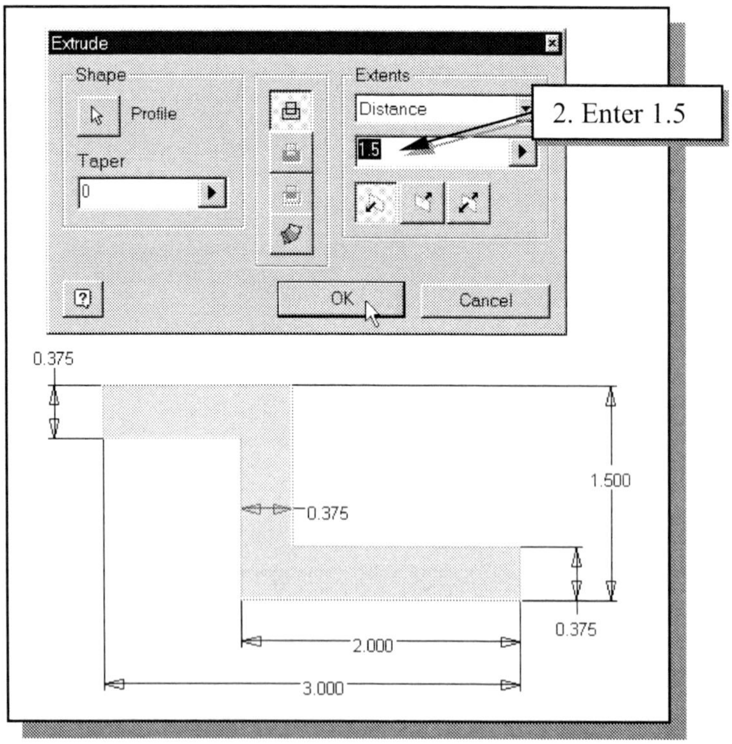

3. Click on the **OK** button to proceed with creating the 3D part.

- Note that all dimensions disappeared from the screen. All parametric definitions are stored in the ***Autodesk Inventor* database** and any of the parametric definitions can be displayed and edited at anytime.

Isometric View

❖ *Autodesk Inventor* provides many ways to display views of the three-dimensional design. Several options are available that allow us to quickly view the design to track the overall effect of any changes being made to the model. We will first orient the model to display in the *isometric view*, by using the pull-down menu.

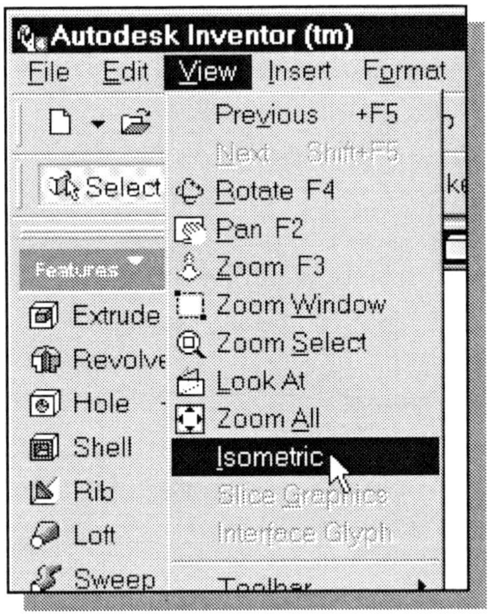

1. Select ***Isometric View*** in the **View** pull-down menu to change the display to the isometric view.

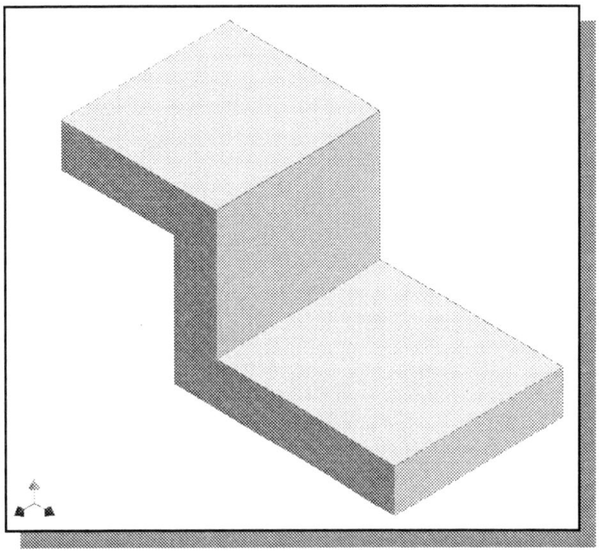

❖ Notice the other view-related commands that are available under the **View** pull-down menu. Most of these commands are also accessible through the *Standard* toolbar and/or *function keys*.

Dynamic Viewing Functions - *Zoom* and *Pan*

Autodesk Inventor provides a special user interface called *Dynamic Viewing* that enables convenient viewing of the entities in the graphics window.

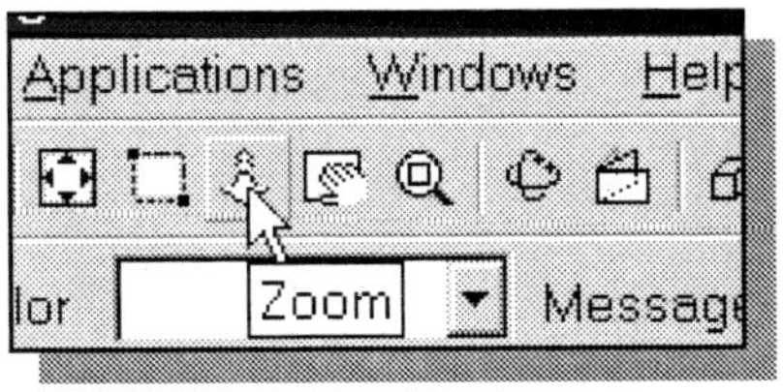

1. Click on the ***Zoom*** icon, located in the *Standard* toolbar as shown.
2. Move the cursor near the center of the graphics window.
3. Inside the graphics window, **press and hold down the left-mouse-button**, then move downward to enlarge the current display scale factor.
4. Press the [**Esc**] key once to exit the *Zoom* command.

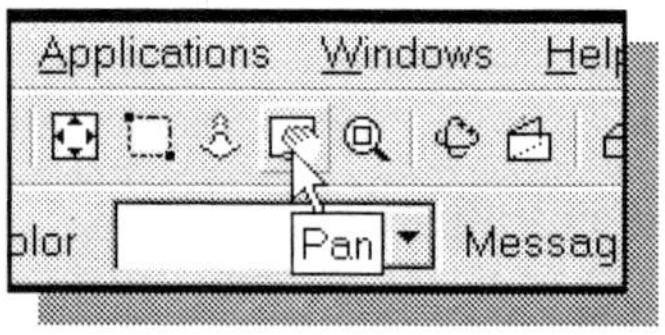

5. Click on the ***Pan*** icon, located next to the *Zoom* command in the *Standard* toolbar. The icon is the picture of a hand.

➢ The *Pan* command enables us to move the view to a different position. This function acts as if you are using a video camera.

6. On your own, use the *Zoom* and *Pan* options to reposition the sketch near the center of the screen.

Dynamic Rotation of the 3D block - *3D Rotate*

The *3D Rotate* command allows us to:

- Rotate a part or assembly in the graphics window. Rotation can be around the center mark, free in all directions, or around the X/Y-axes in the *3D-Rotate* display.
- Reposition the part or assembly in the graphics window.
- Display isometric or standard orthographic views of a part or assembly.
- The *3D Rotate* tool is accessible while other tools are active. *Autodesk Inventor* remembers the last used mode when you exit the *Rotate* command.

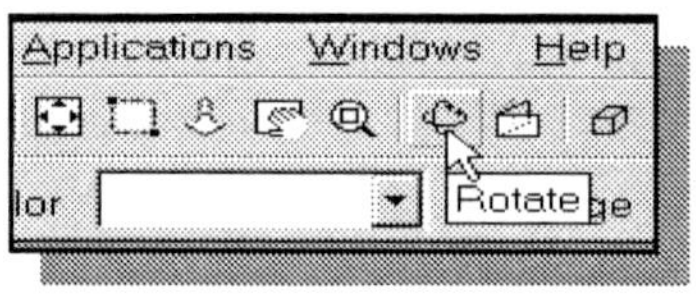

1. Click on the ***Rotate*** icon in the *Standard* toolbar.

The *3D Rotate* display is a circular rim with four handles and a center mark. *3D Rotate* enables us to manipulate the view of 3D objects by clicking and dragging with the left-mouse-button:

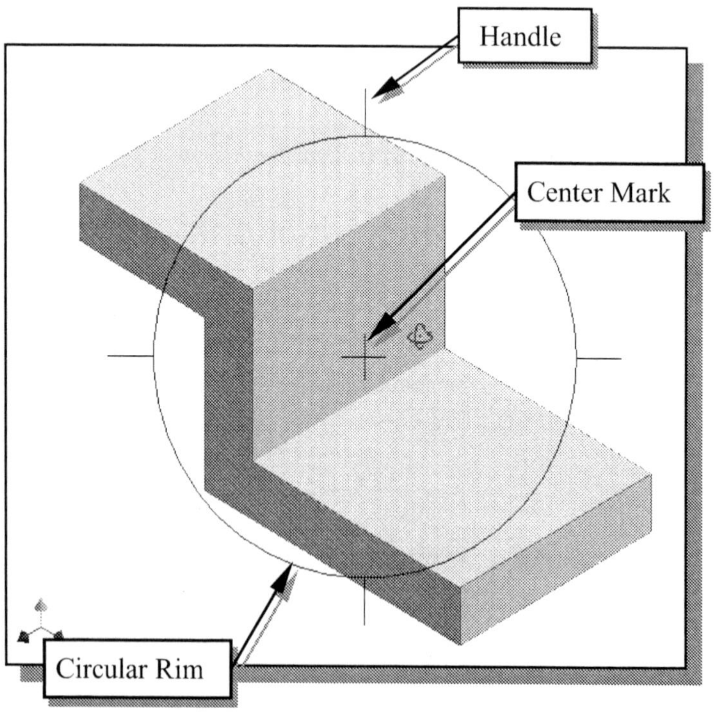

- Drag with the left-mouse-button near the center for free rotation.
- Drag on handles to rotate around the horizontal or vertical axes.
- Drag on the rim to rotate about an axis that is perpendicular to the displayed view.
- Single left-mouse-click to align the center mark of the view.

2. Inside the *circular rim*, press down the left-mouse-button and drag in an arbitrary direction, the *3D Rotate* command allows us to freely rotate the solid model.

3. Move the cursor near the circular rim and notice the cursor symbol changes to a single circle. Drag with the left-mouse-button to rotate about an axis that is perpendicular to the displayed view.

4. Single left-mouse-click near the top-handle to align the selected location to the center mark in the graphics window.

5. Press the [**Space bar**] to activate the *Common Views* option.

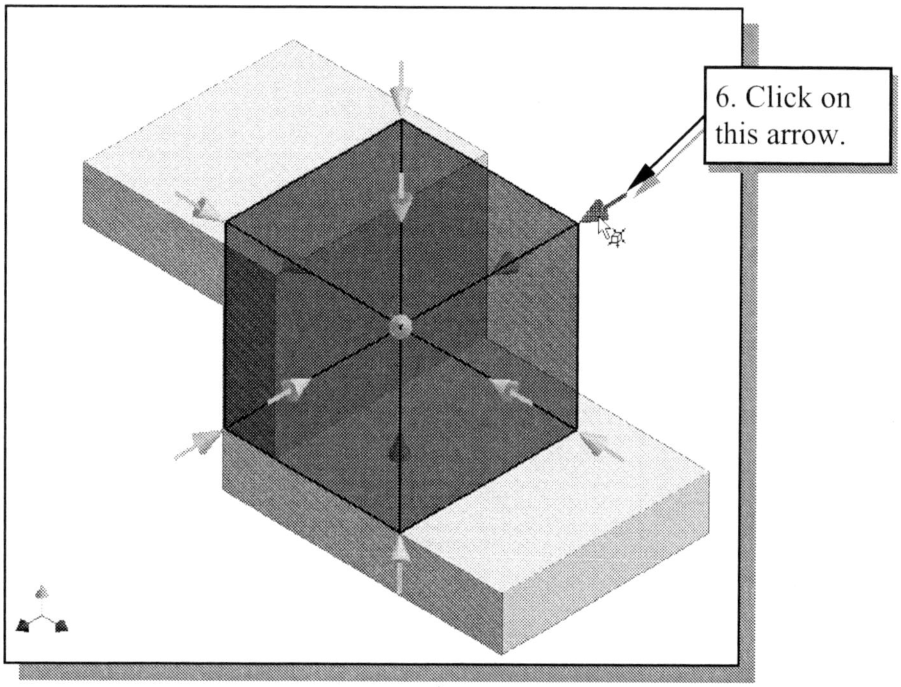

6. The displayed arrows represent the viewing directions of the pre-defined common views. Change the viewing direction by left-clicking once on the top-right arrow as shown in the above figure. Hit the [Esc] key once to exit the *3D Rotate* command.

7. On your own, use the different options described in the above steps and familiar yourself with the *3D Rotate* command. Reset the display to the *Isometric* view as shown in the above figure before continuing to the next section.

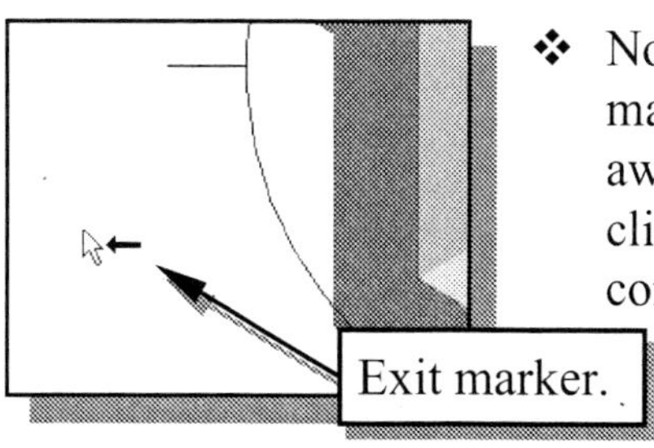

❖ Note that while in the *3D Rotate* mode, a horizontal marker will be displayed next to the cursor if the cursor is away from the circular rim. This is the **exit marker.** Left-clicking once will allow you to exit the *3D Rotate* command.

Dynamic Viewing - Quick Keys

We can also use the function keys on the keyboard and the mouse to access the *Dynamic Viewing* functions.

❖ Panning – F2 and the mouse

Hold the **F2** function key down, and drag with the left-mouse-button to pan the display. This allows you to reposition the display while maintaining the same scale factor of the display.

Pan

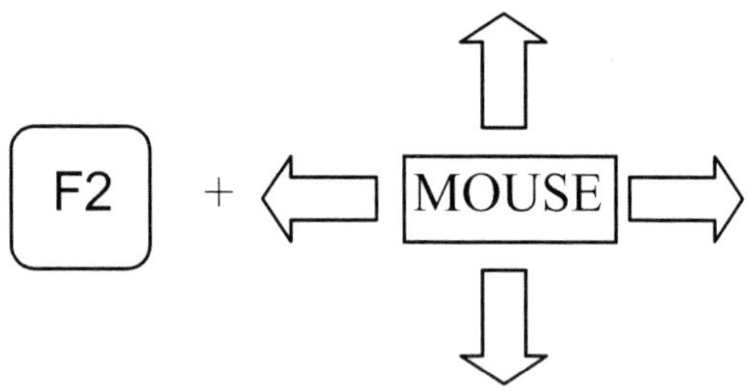

❖ Zooming – F3 and the mouse

Hold the **F3** function key down, and drag with the left-mouse-button vertically on the screen to adjust the scale of the display. Moving upward will reduce the scale of the display, making the entities display smaller on the screen. Moving downward will magnify the scale of the display.

Zoom

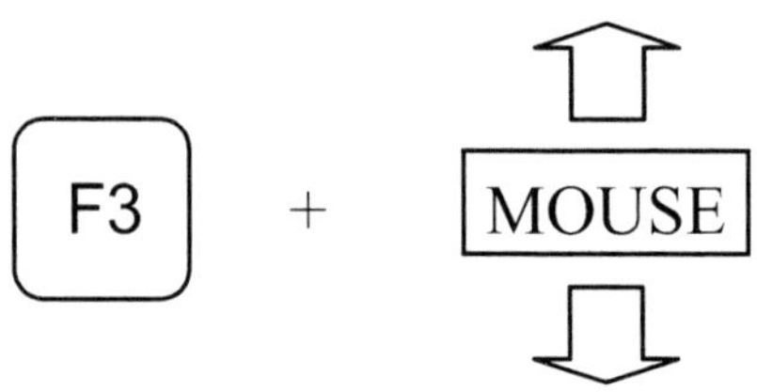

❖ 3D Dynamic Rotation – F4 and the mouse

Hold the **F4** function key down and move the mouse to rotate the display. The *3D Rotate* rim with four handles and the center mark appears on the screen. Note that the *Common View* option is not available when using the **F4** quick key.

Dynamic Rotation

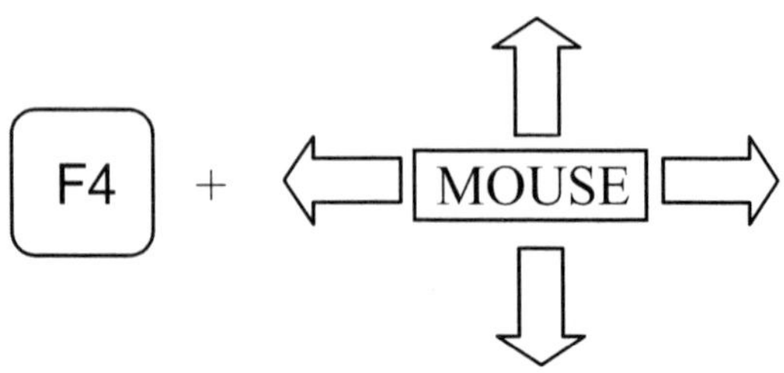

Display Modes: Wireframe, Shaded, Hidden Edge

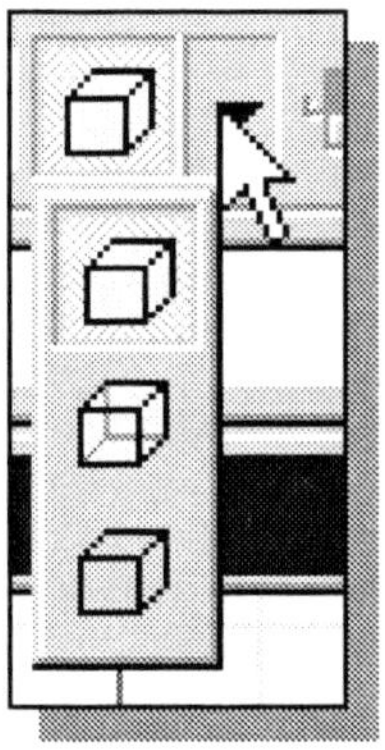

- The display in the graphics window has three display-modes: wireframe, shaded, and shaded with hidden edge display. To change the display mode in the active window, click on triangle icon next to the display mode button on the *Standard* toolbar, as shown in the figure.

❖ **Shaded Solid:**

The third icon in the display mode button group generates a shaded image of the 3D object.

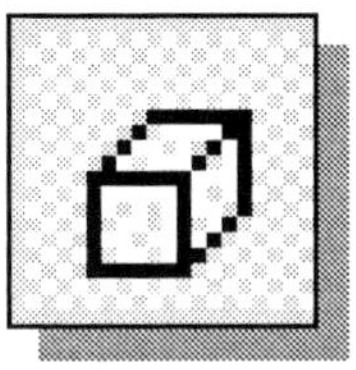

Shaded Solid

❖ **Hidden-Edge Display:**

The second icon in the display mode button group can be used to generate an image of the 3D object with all the back lines shown.

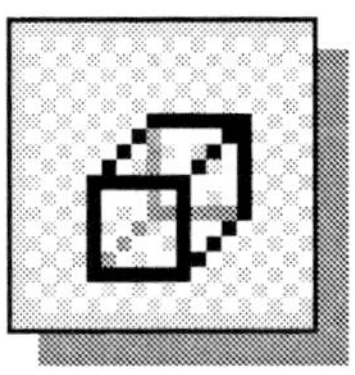

Hidden-Edge Display

❖ **Wireframe Image:**

The first icon in the display mode button group allows the display of the 3D objects using the basic wireframe representation scheme.

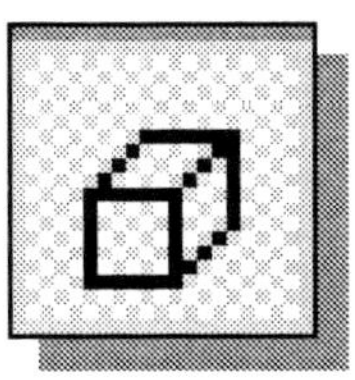

Wireframe

➢ On your own, use the different options described in the above sections to familiarize yourself with the 3D viewing/display commands. Reset the display to the standard isometric view before continuing to the next section.

Sketch plane – It is an XY CRT, but an XYZ World

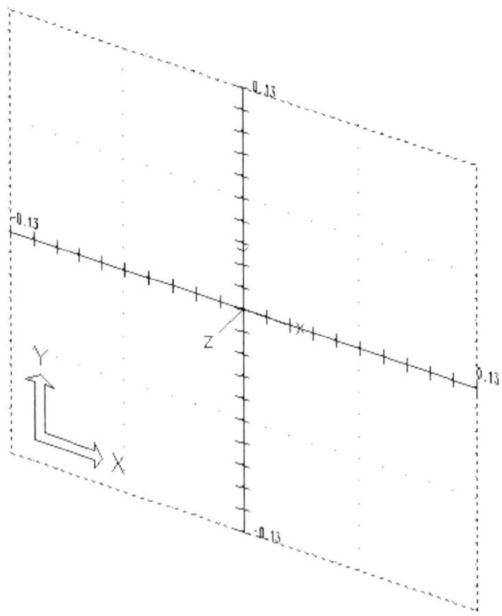

Design modeling software is becoming more powerful and user friendly, yet the system still does only what the user tells it to do. When using a geometric modeler, we therefore need to have a good understanding of what its inherent limitations are. We should also have a good understanding of what we want to do and what to expect, as the results are based on what is available.

In most 3D geometric modelers, 3D objects are located and defined in what is usually called **world space** or **global space**. Although a number of different coordinate systems can be used to create and manipulate objects in a 3D modeling system, the objects are typically defined and stored using the world space. The world space is usually a **3D Cartesian coordinate system** that the user cannot change or manipulate.

In most engineering designs, models can be very complex, and it would be tedious and confusing if only the world coordinate system were available. Practical 3D modeling systems allow the user to define **Local Coordinate Systems (LCS)** or **User Coordinate Systems (UCS)** relative to the world coordinate system. Once a local coordinate system is defined, we can then create geometry in terms of this more convenient system.

Although objects are created and stored in 3D space coordinates, most of the geometry entities can be referenced using 2D Cartesian coordinate systems. Typical input devices such as a mouse or digitizers are two-dimensional by nature; the movement of the input device is interpreted by the system in a planar sense. The same limitation is true of common output devices, such as CRT displays and plotters. The modeling software performs a series of three-dimensional to two-dimensional transformations to correctly project 3D objects onto a 2D picture plane.

The *Autodesk Inventor* ***sketch plane*** is a special construction tool that enables the planar nature of the 2D input devices to be directly mapped into the 3D coordinate system. The *sketch plane* is a local coordinate system that can be aligned to the world coordinate system, an existing face of a part, or a reference plane. By default, the *sketch plane* is aligned to the world coordinate system.

Think of a sketch plane as the surface on which we can sketch the 2D profiles of the parts. It is similar to a piece of paper, a white board, or a chalkboard that can be attached to any planar surface. The first profile we create is usually drawn on the default sketch plane, which is in the current coordinate system. Subsequent profiles can then be drawn on sketch planes that are defined on **planar faces of a part**, **work planes attached to part geometry**, or **sketch planes attached to a coordinate system** (such as the World XY, XZ, and YZ sketch planes). The model we have created so far used the default settings where the sketch plane is aligned to the XY plane of the world coordinate system.

1. In the *Standard* toolbar select the ***Sketch*** command by left-clicking once on the icon.

2. In the *Status Bar* area, the message: "*Select face, workplane, sketch or sketch geometry.*" is displayed. *Autodesk Inventor* expects us to identify a planar surface where the 2D sketch of the next feature is to be created. Move the graphics cursor on the 3D part and notice that *Autodesk Inventor* will automatically highlight feasible planes and surfaces as the cursor is on top of the different surfaces. Pick the top face of the horizontal portion of the 3D object.

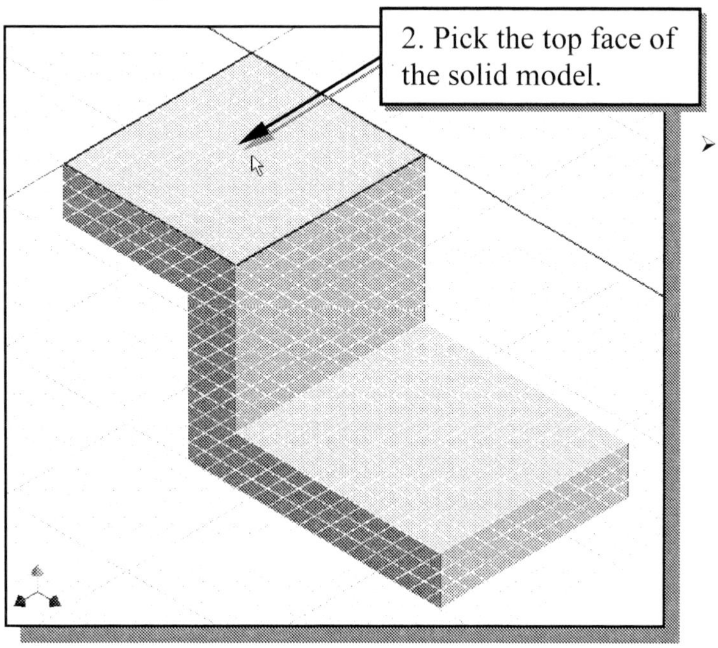

- Note that the sketch plane is aligned to the selected face. *Autodesk Inventor* automatically establishes a User-Coordinate-System (UCS), and records its location with respect to the part on which it was created.

Step 4: Adding additional features

- Next, we will create and profile a rectangle, which will be used to create another extrusion feature that will be added to the existing solid object.

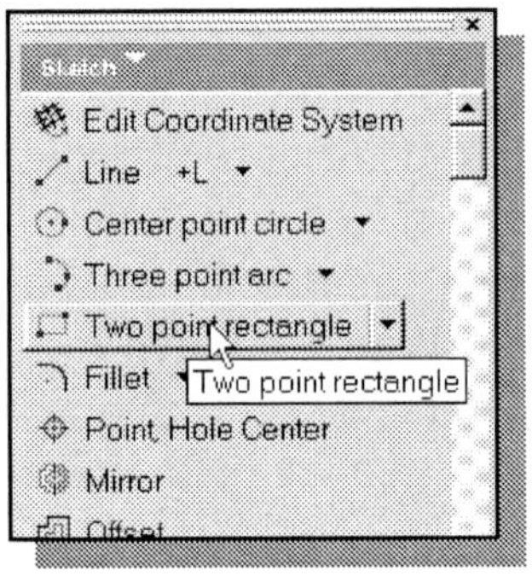

1. Select the ***Two point rectangle*** command by clicking once with the **left-mouse-button** on the icon in the *Sketch* toolbar.

2. Create a rectangle by picking the top right corner of the solid model as shown below.

3. Move the cursor downward and select a location as shown below.

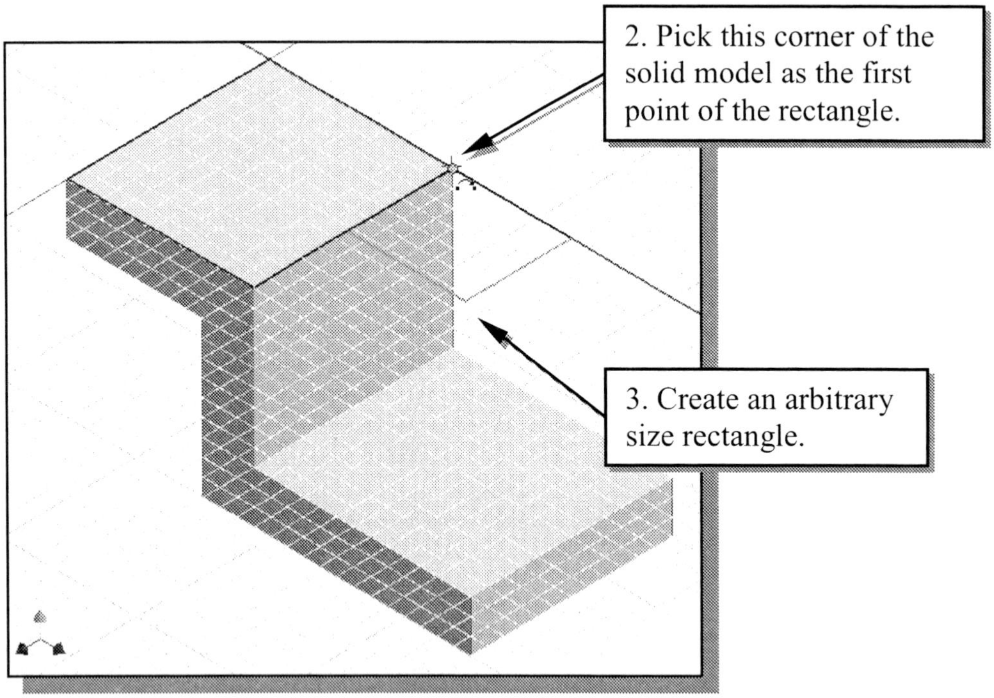

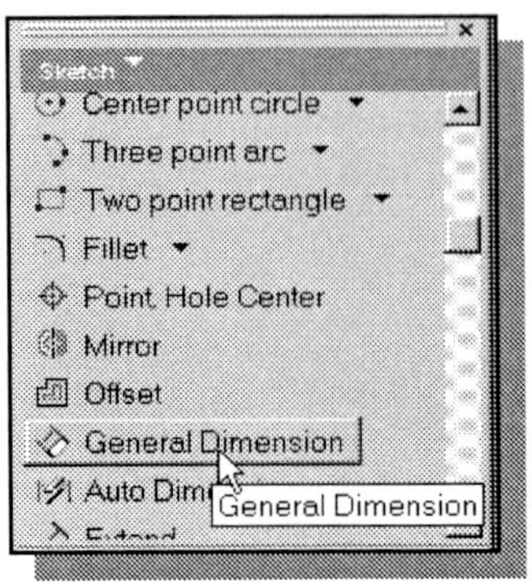

4. Select the ***General Dimension*** command in the *Sketch* toolbar. The *General Dimension* command allows us to quickly create and modify dimensions. Left-click once on the icon to activate the *General Dimension* command.

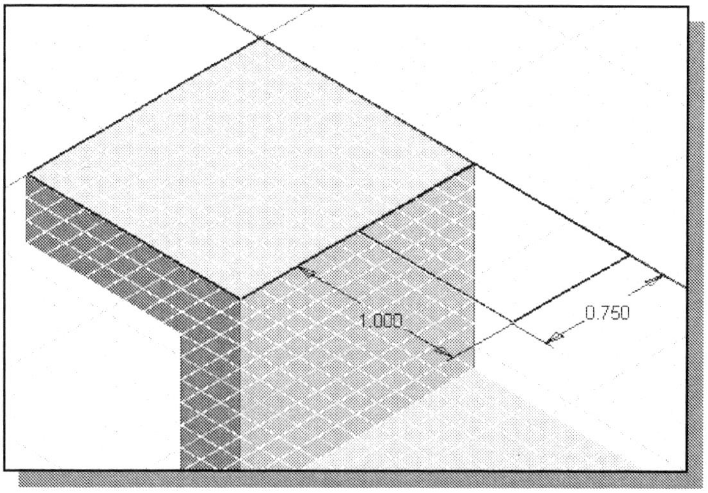

5. The message "*Select Geometry to Dimension*" is displayed in the *Status Bar* area, at the bottom of the *Inventor* window. Create the two dimensions as shown in the figure below.

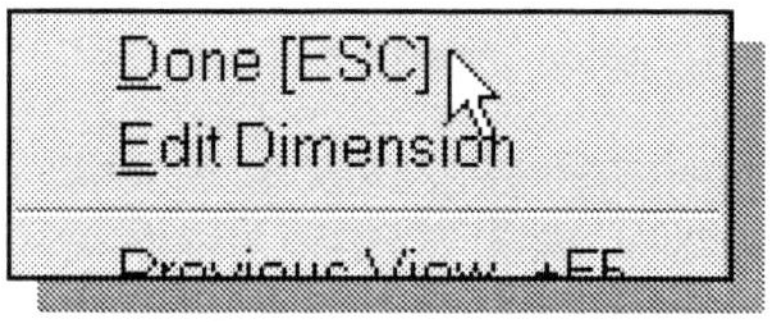

6. Inside the graphics window, click once with the **right-mouse-button** to display the option menu. Select **Done** in the popup menu to end the *General Dimension* command.

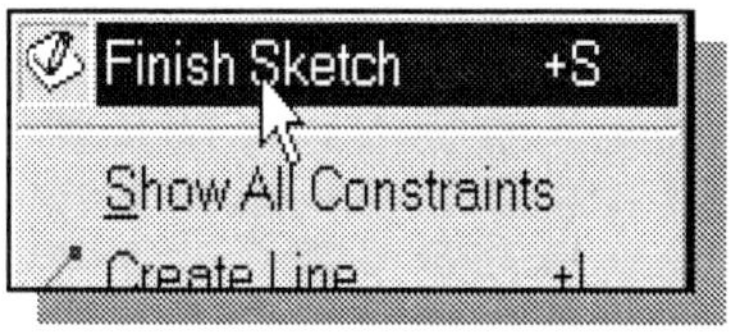

7. Inside the graphics window, click once with the **right-mouse-button** to display the option menu. Select **Finish Sketch** in the popup menu to end the *Sketch* option.

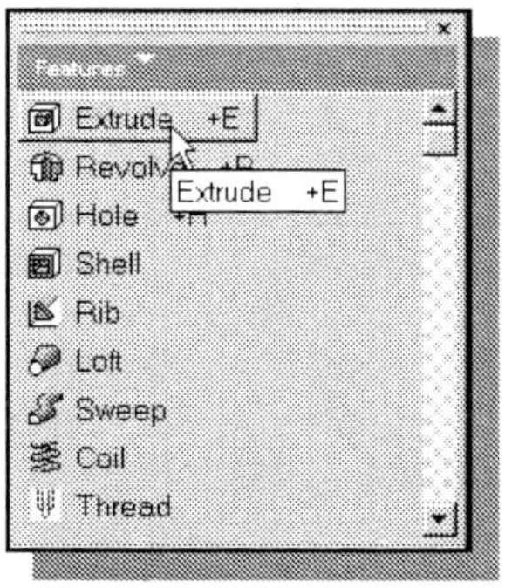

8. In the *Feature* toolbar (the toolbar that is located to the left side of the graphics window), select the ***Extrude*** command by releasing the left-mouse-button on the icon.

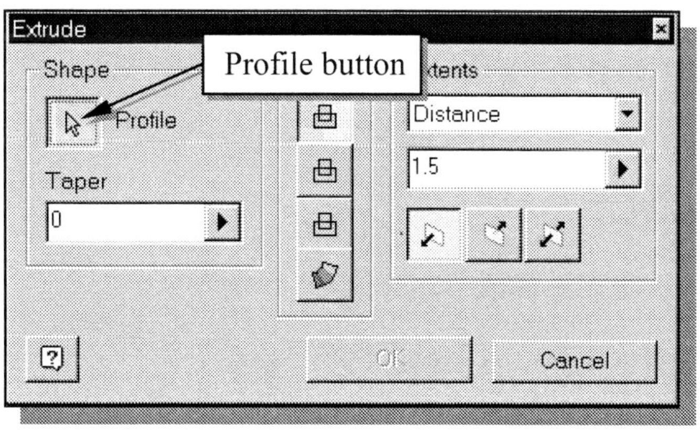

9. In the *Extrude* popup window, the **Profile** button is pressed down; *Autodesk Inventor* expects us to identify the profile to be extruded.

10. Move the cursor inside the rectangle we just created and left-click once to select the region as the profile to be extruded.

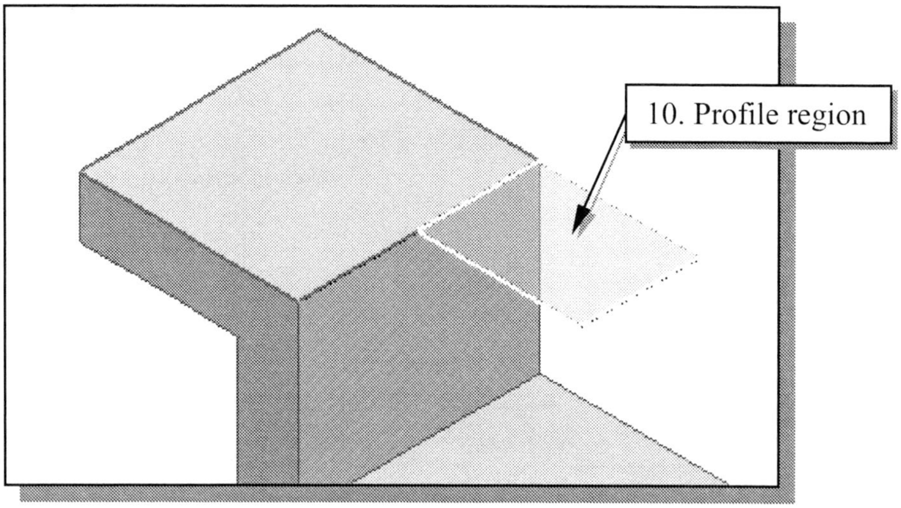

11. In the *Extrude* popup window, select **To Next** as the extent method as shown. Notice that the arrow direction is automatically set to point toward the center of the solid model.

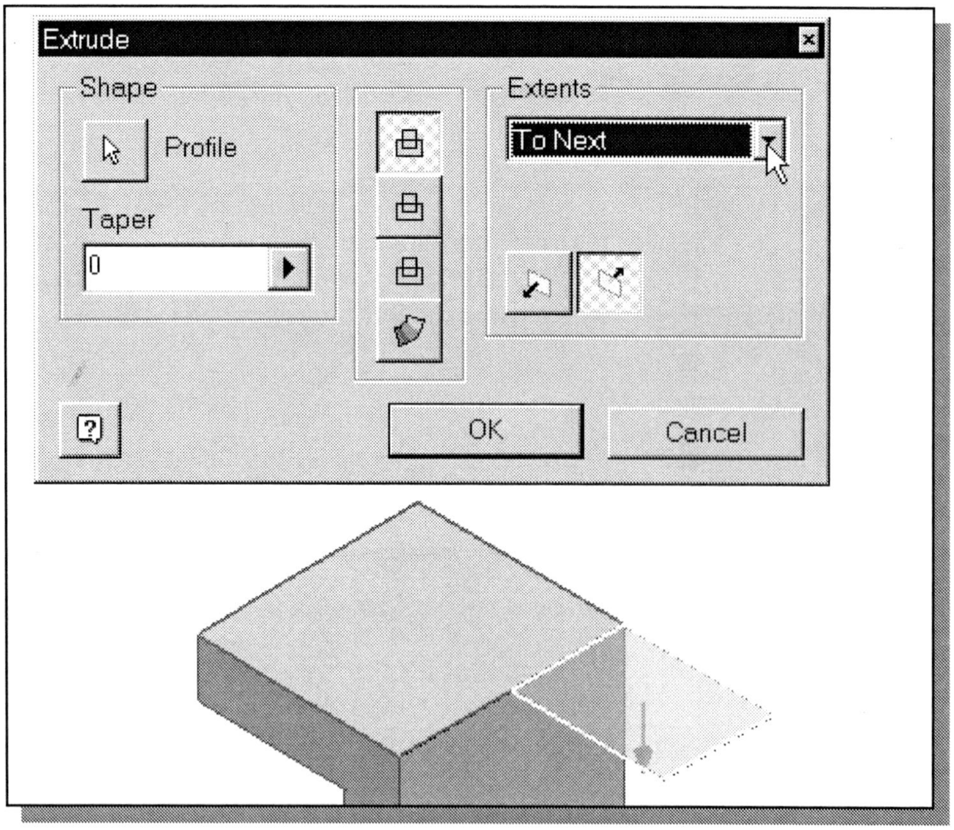

12. Click on the **OK** button to proceed with creating the 3D part.

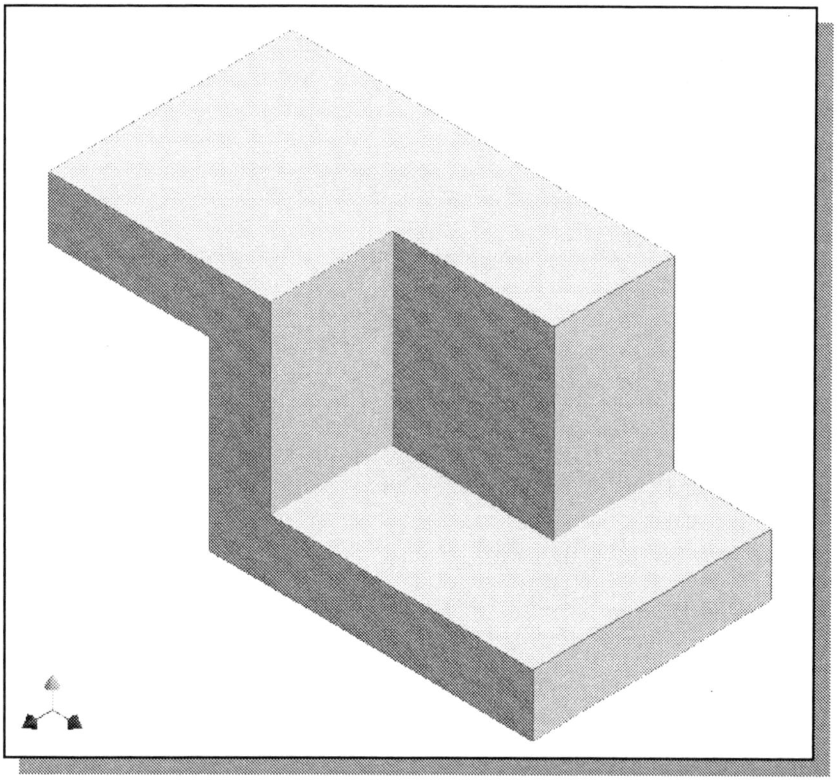

Save the Part

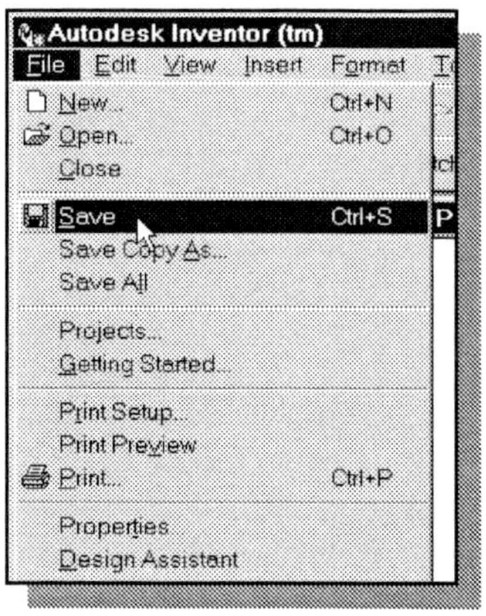

1. Select **Save** in the *Standard* toolbar, or you can also use the "**Ctrl-S**" combination (press down the "Ctrl" key and hit the "S" key once) to save the part.

2. In the popup window, enter ***Locator*** as the name of the file.

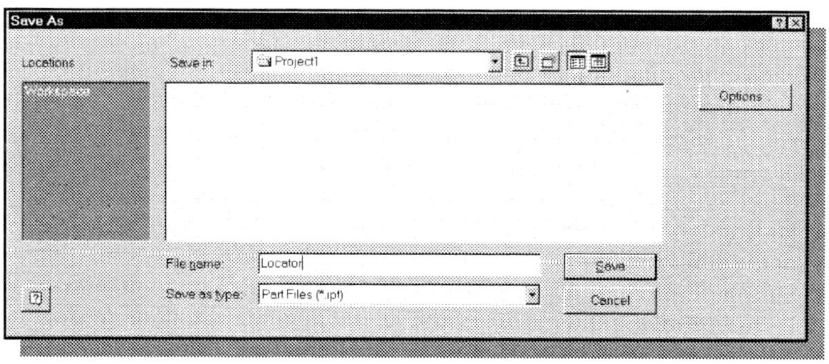

3. Click on the **SAVE** button to save the file.

❖ It is a good habit to save your model periodically, just in case something might go wrong while you are working on it. In general, you should save your work onto the disk at an interval of every 15 to 20 minutes. You should also save before you make any major modifications to the model.

Questions:

1. What is the first thing we should set up in *Autodesk Inventor* when creating a new model?

2. Describe the general *parametric modeling* procedure.

3. What is the main difference between a rough sketch and a *profile*?

4. List two of the geometric constraint symbols used by *Autodesk Inventor*.

5. What was the first feature we created in this lesson?

6. Describe the steps required to define the orientation of the sketching plane?

7. Identify the following commands:

(a)

(b)

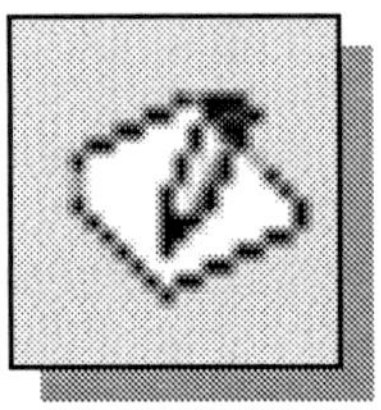

(c)

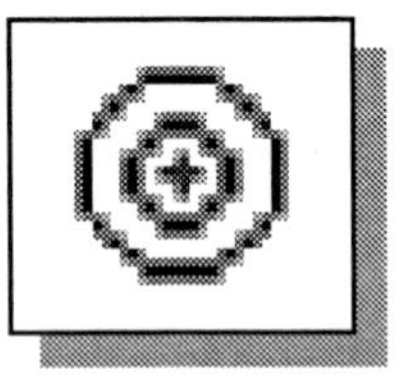

(d)

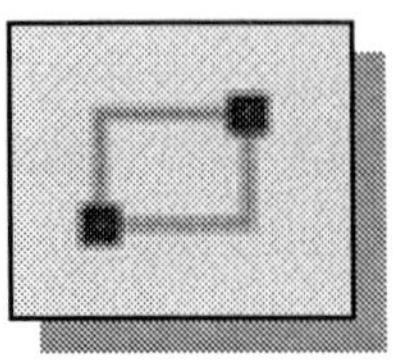

Exercises:

1. Plate Thickness: 0.25

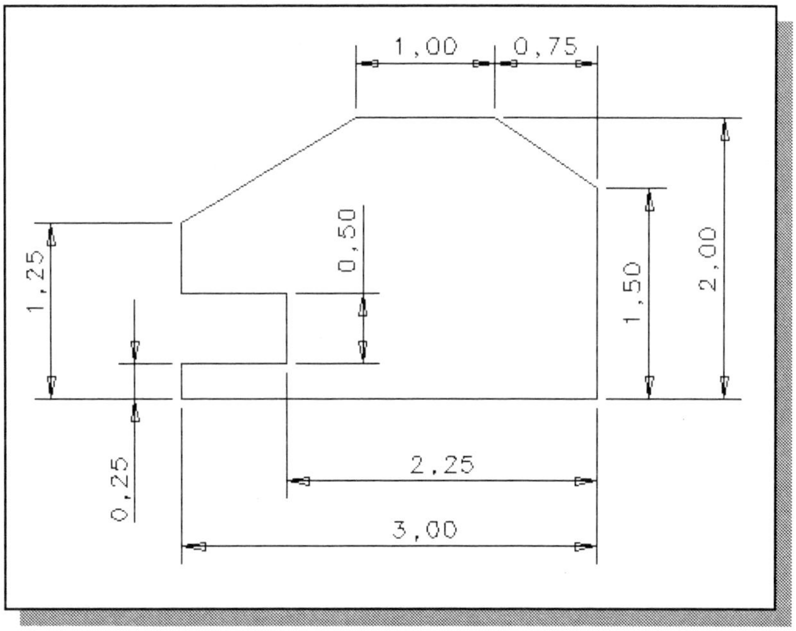

2. Plate Thickness: 0.5

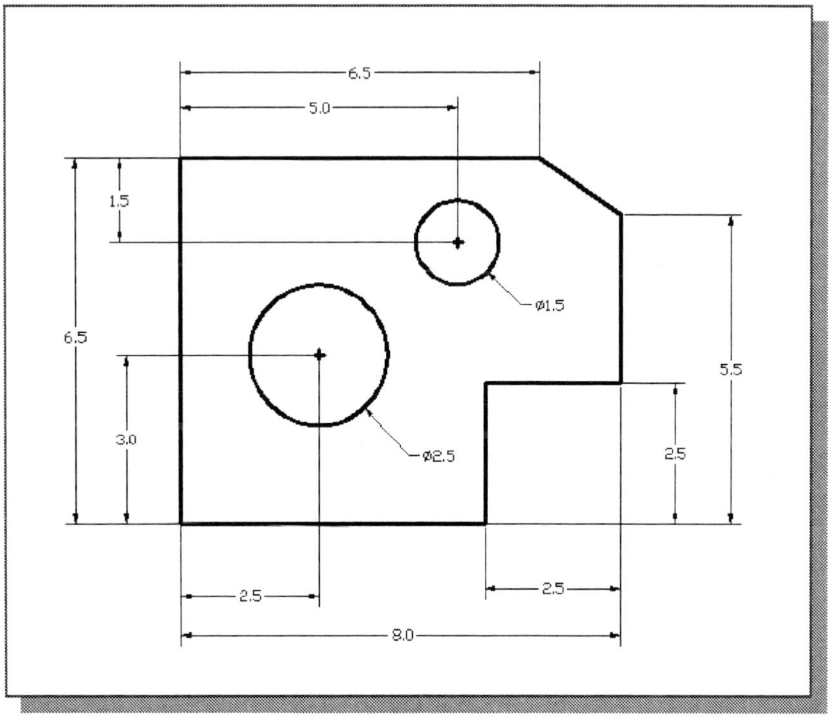

NOTES:

Lesson 2
Constructive Solid Geometry Concepts

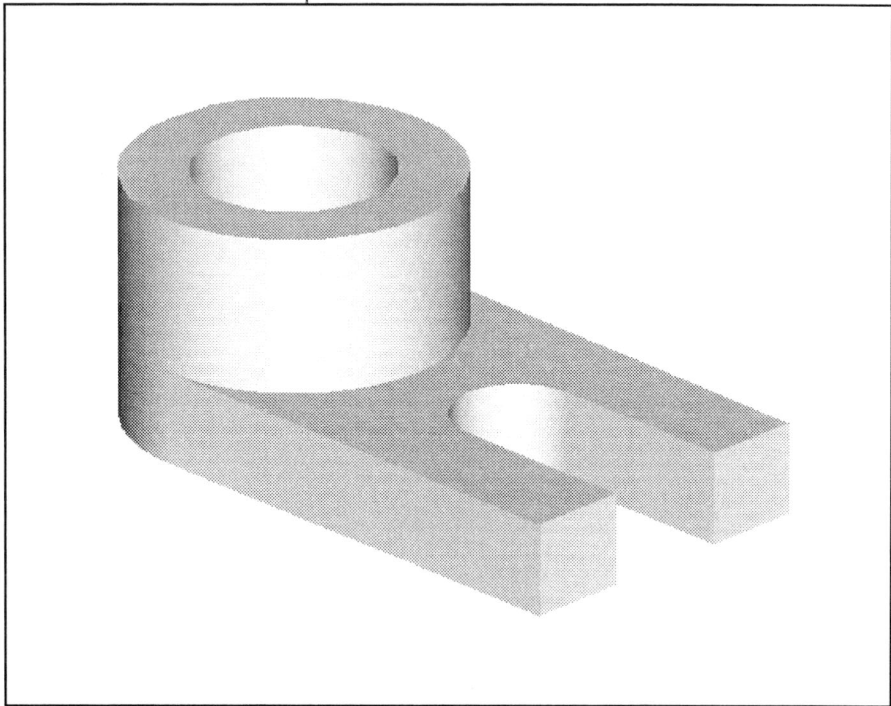

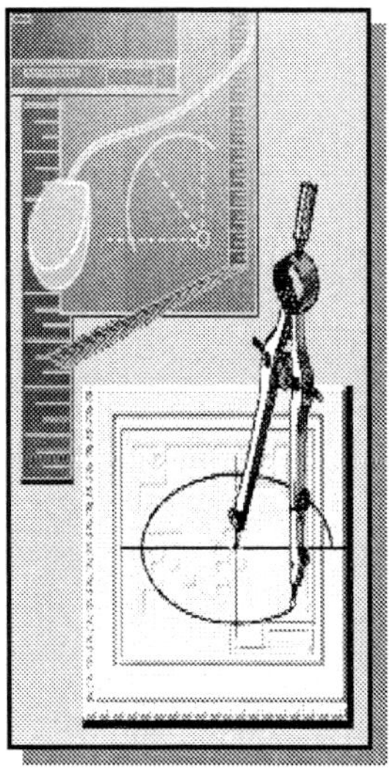

Learning Objectives

When you have completed this lesson, you will be able to:

- ♦ Understand the Constructive Solid Geometry Concepts.
- ♦ Create a Binary Tree.
- ♦ Understand the basic Boolean Operations.
- ♦ GRID and SNAP intervals Setup.
- ♦ Understand the importance of Order of Features.
- ♦ Create Placed Features.
- ♦ Use the different Extrusion options.

Introduction

In the 1980s, one of the main advancements in **Solid Modeling** was the development of the **Constructive Solid Geometry** (CSG) method. CSG describes the solid model as combinations of basic three-dimensional shapes (**Primitive Solids**). The basic primitive solid set typically includes: Rectangular-prism (Block), Cylinder, Cone, Sphere, and Torus (Tube). Two solid objects can be combined into one object in various ways using operations known as **Boolean operations**. There are three basic Boolean operations: **JOIN (Union)**, **CUT (Difference)**, and **INTERSECT**. The *JOIN* operation combines the two volumes included in the different solids into a single solid. The *CUT* operation subtracts the volume of one solid object from the other solid object. The *INTERSECT* operation keeps only the volume common to both solid objects. The CSG method is also known as the **Machinist's Approach**, as the method is parallel to machine shop practices.

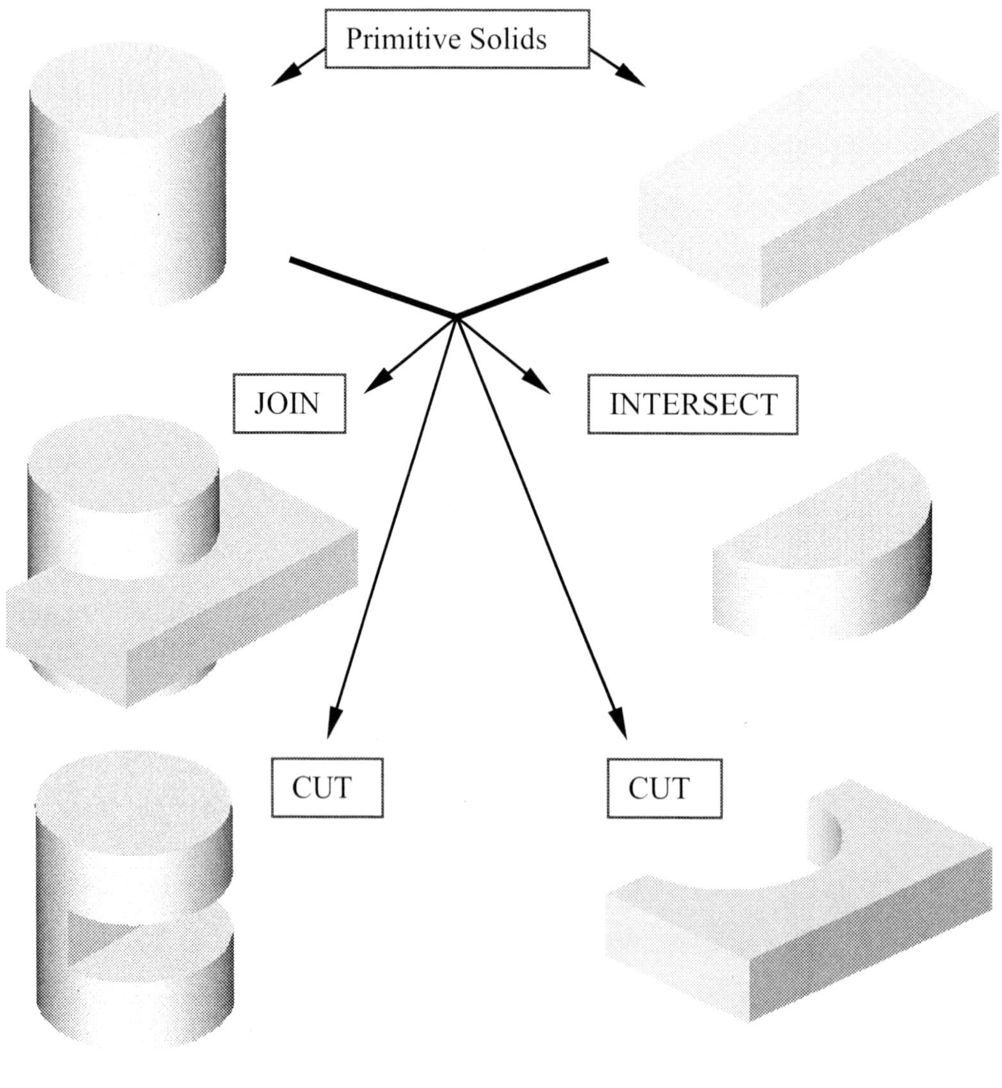

Binary Tree

The CSG is also referred to as the method used to store a solid model in the database. The resulting solid can be easily represented as what is called a **binary tree**. In a binary tree, the terminal branches (leaves) are the various primitives that are linked together to make the final solid object (the root). The binary tree is an effective way to keep track of the *history* of the resulting solid. By keeping track of the history, the solid model can be re-built by relinking through the binary tree. This provides a convenient way to modify the model. We can make modifications at the appropriate links in the binary tree and relink the rest of the history tree without building a new model.

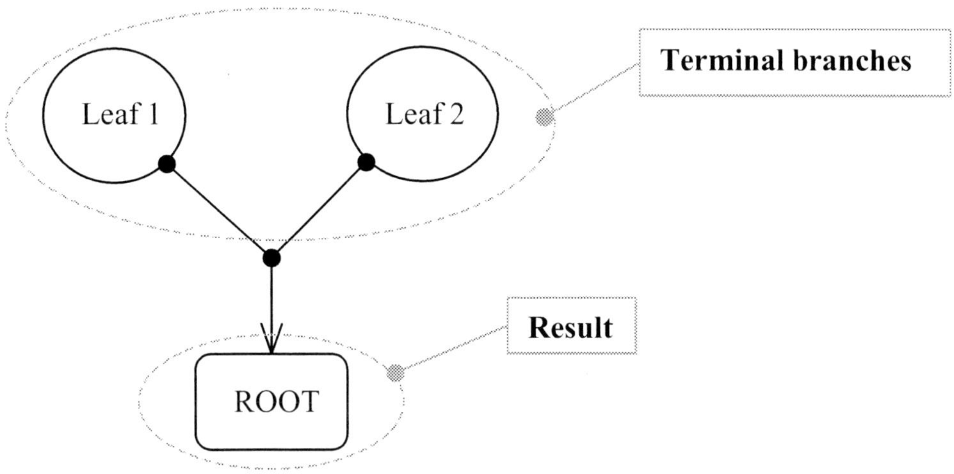

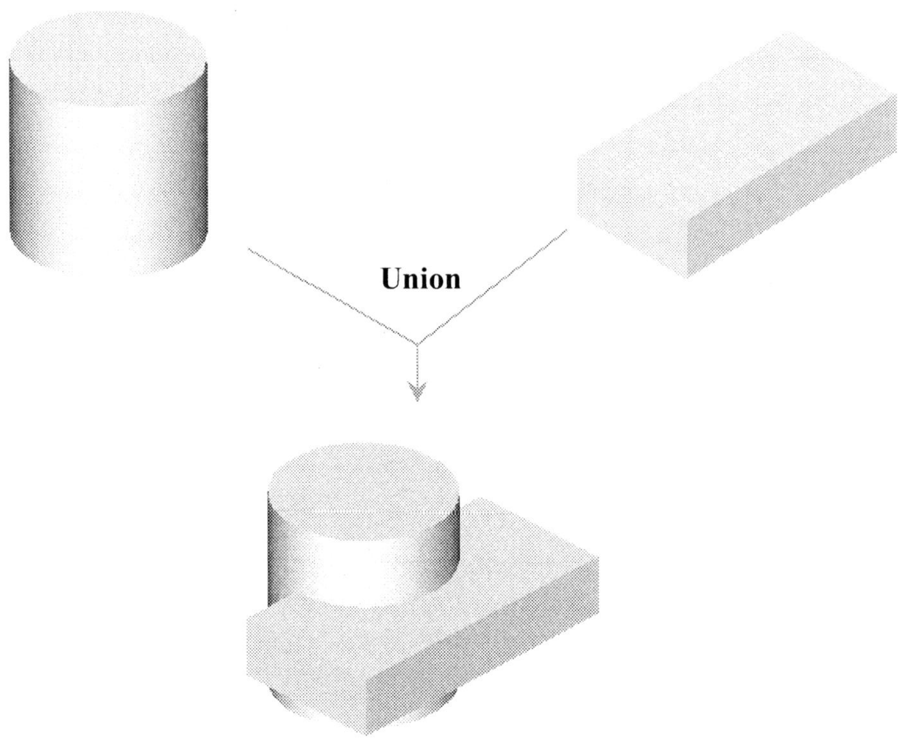

The *Locator* Design

The CSG concept is one of the important building blocks for feature-based modeling. In *Autodesk Inventor*, the CSG concept can be used as a planning tool to determine the number of features that are needed to construct the model. It is also a good practice to create features that are parallel to the manufacturing process required for the design. With parametric modeling, we are no longer limited to using only the predefined basic solid shapes. In fact, any solid features we create in *Autodesk Inventor* are used as primitive solids; parametric modeling allow us to maintain full control of the design variables that are used to describe the features. In this lesson, a more in-depth look at the parametric modeling procedure is presented. The equivalent CSG operation for each feature is also illustrated.

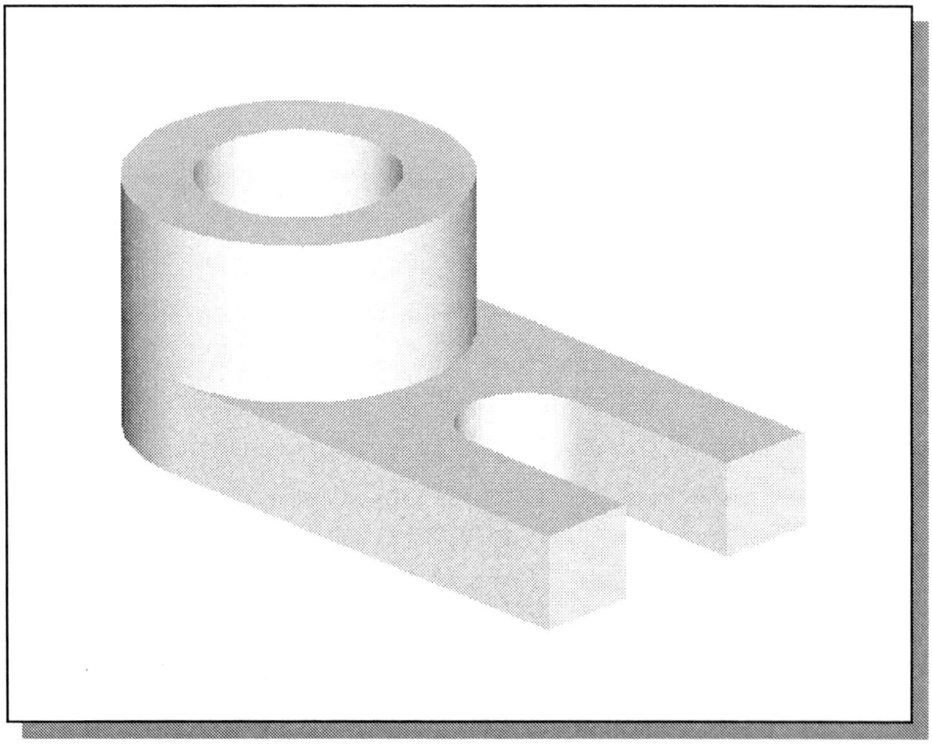

- Before going through the tutorial, on your own, make a sketch of a CSG binary tree of the ***Locator*** design using only two basic types of primitive solids: cylinder and rectangular prism. In your sketch, how many *Boolean operations* will be required to create the model? What is your choice of the first primitive solid to use, and why? Take a few minutes to consider these questions and do the preliminary planning by sketching on a piece of paper. Compare the sketch you make to the CSG binary tree steps shown on page 2-7. Note that there are many different possibilities in combining the basic primitive solids to form the solid model. Even for the simplest design, it is possible to take several different approaches to creating the same solid model.

Starting Autodesk Inventor

1. Select the ***Autodesk Inventor*** option on the *Start* menu or select the ***Autodesk Inventor*** icon on the desktop to start *Autodesk Inventor*. The *Autodesk Inventor* main window will appear on the screen.

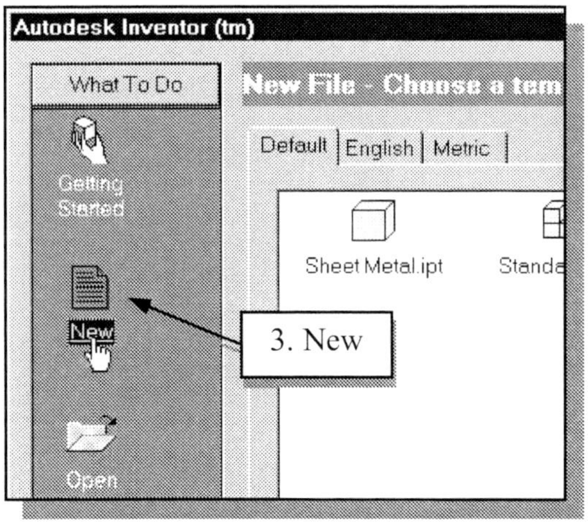

2. Once the program is loaded into the memory, the *Startup* dialog box appears at the center of the screen.

3. Select the ***New*** icon with a single click of the left-mouse-button in the *What to Do* dialog box.

❖ Every object we construct in a CAD system is measured in units. We should determine the value of the units within the CAD system before creating the first geometric entities. For example, in one model, a unit might equal one millimeter of the real-world object; in another model, a unit might equal an inch. In *Autodesk Inventor*, the ***Choose Template*** option is used to control how *Autodesk Inventor* interprets the coordinate and angle entries. In most CAD systems, setting the model units does not always set units for dimensions. We generally set model units and dimension units to the same type and precision.

4. Select the **Metric** tab as shown below. We will use the millimeter (mm) setting for this example.

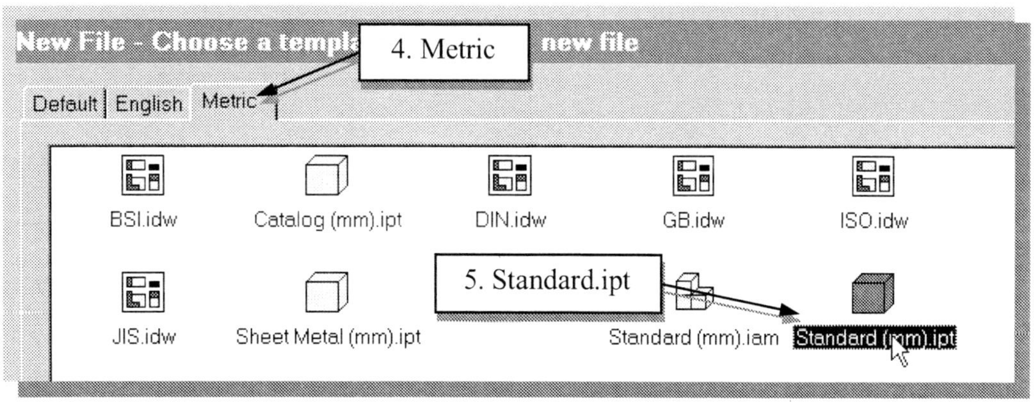

5. In the *New - Choose Template* area, select the **Standard(mm).ipt** icon as shown.

6. Pick **OK** in the *Startup* dialog box to accept the selected settings.

GRID and *SNAP* Intervals Setup

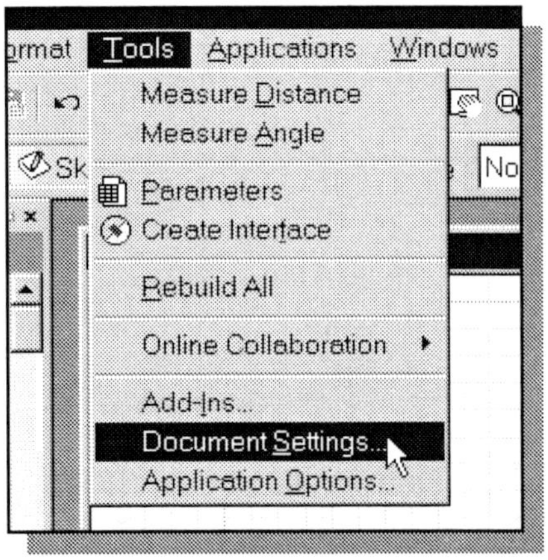

1. In the pull-down menu, select

   Tools → Document Settings

2. In the *Document Settings* dialog box, click on the **Sketch** tab as shown in the below figure.

3. In the *Drafting Settings* dialog box, set the X and Y *SNAP Spacing* to **5 mm**.

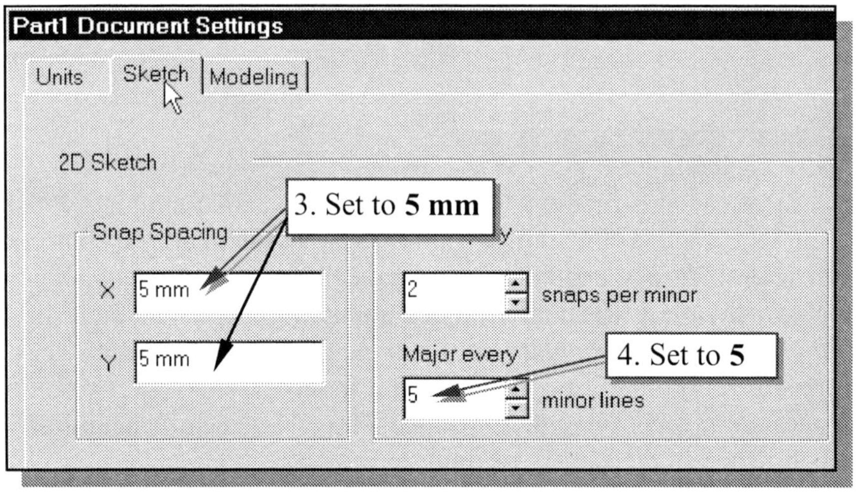

4. Change *Grid Display* to display one *major line* every **5** *minor lines*.

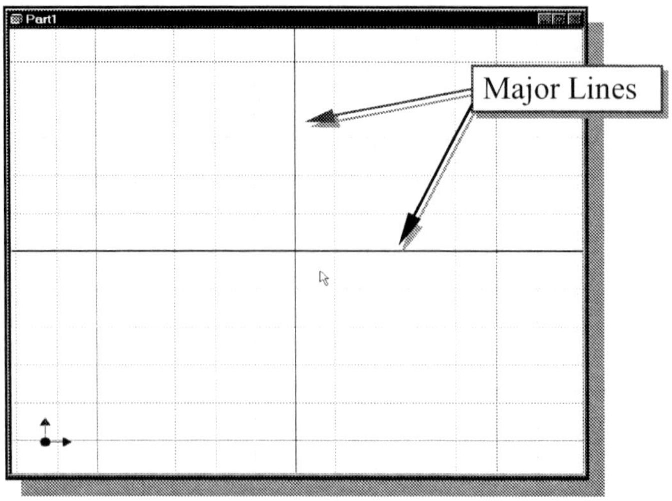

5. Pick **OK** to exit the *Sketch Settings* dialog box.

❖ Note that although the *SNAP* option is also available in *Autodesk Inventor*, its usage in parametric modeling is not recommended.

Modeling Strategy - CSG Binary Tree

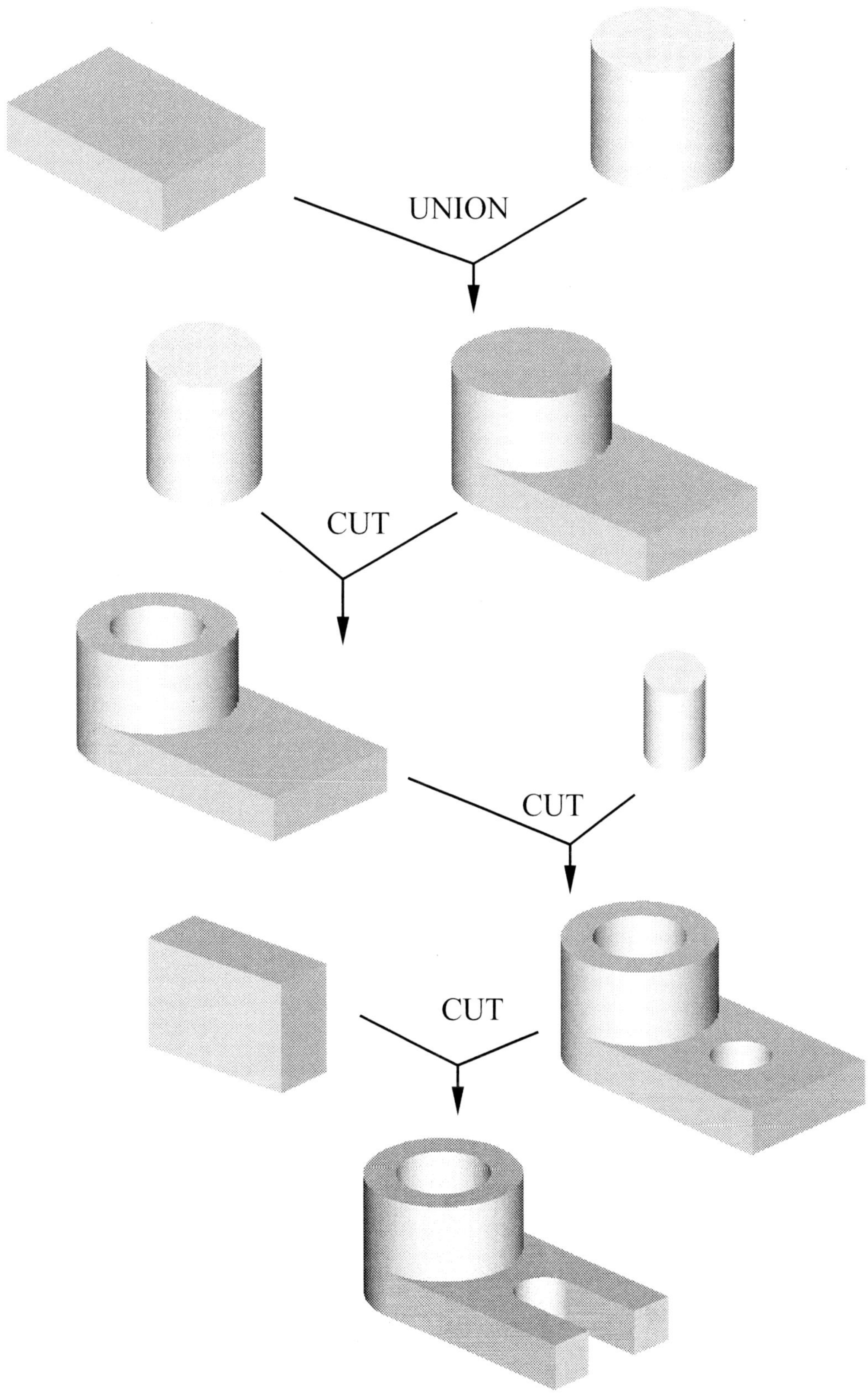

Base Feature

In *parametric modeling*, the first solid feature is called the **base feature,** which usually is the primary shape of the model. Depending upon the design intent, additional features are added to the base feature.

Some of the considerations involved in selecting the base feature are:

- **Design intent** - Determine the functionality of the design; identify the feature that is central to the design.

- **Order of features** – Choose the feature that is the logical base in terms of the order of features in the design.

- **Ease of making modifications** - Select a base feature that is more stable and is less likely to be changed.

We will create a rectangular block as the base feature of the ***Locator*** design.

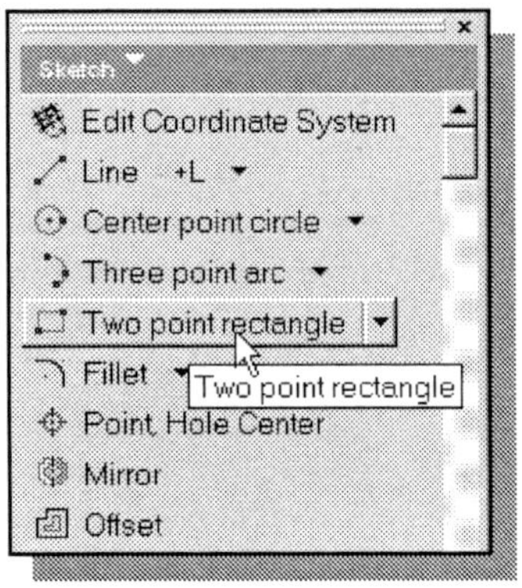

1. Select the *Two point rectangle* command by clicking once with the **left-mouse-button** on the icon in the *Sketch* toolbar.

2. Create a rectangle of arbitrary size by selecting two locations on the screen as shown below.

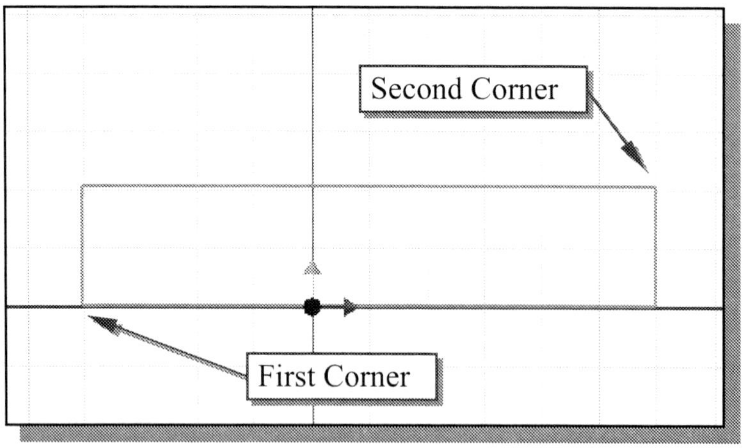

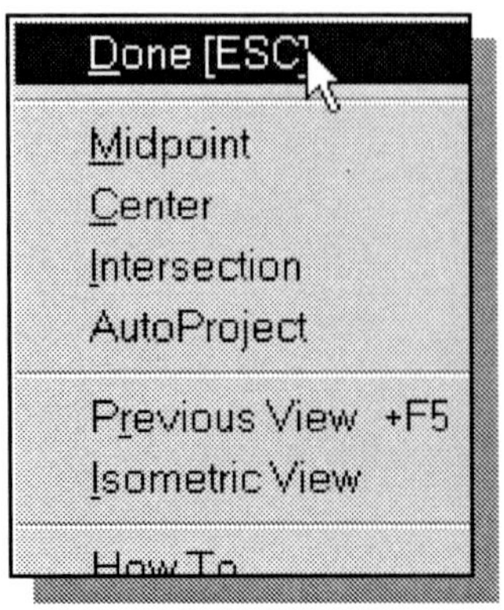

3. Inside the graphics window, click once with the right-mouse-button to bring up the option menu.

4. Select **Done** to end the *Rectangle* command.

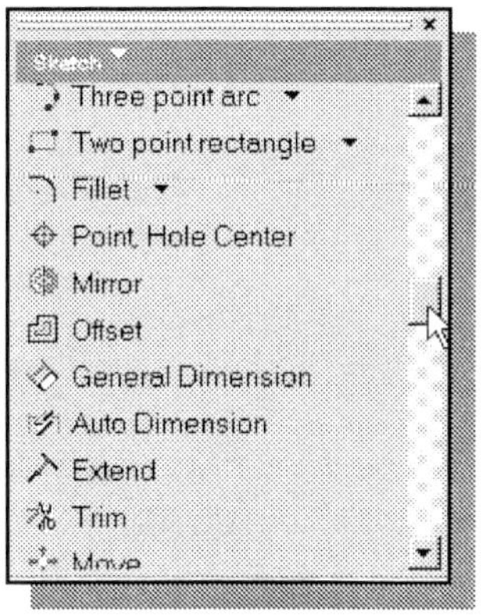

5. Move the cursor to the *Sketch* toolbar area and scroll downward by dragging the *scroll box* with the left-mouse-button.

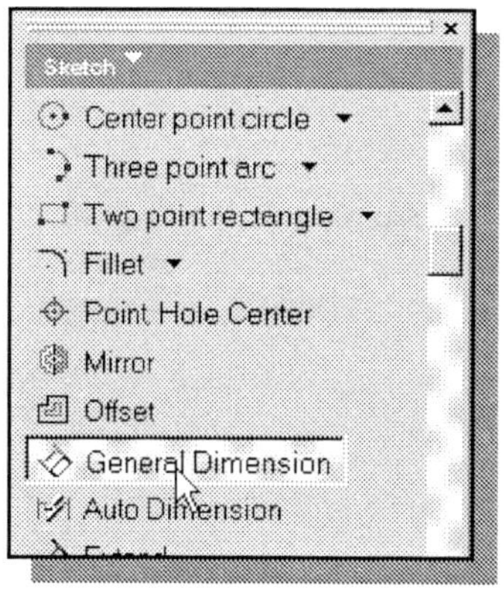

6. Move the cursor on top of the ***General Dimension*** icon. The *General Dimension* command allows us to quickly create and modify dimensions. Left-click once on the icon to activate the *General Dimension* command.

7. The message "*Select Geometry to Dimension*" is displayed in the *Status Bar* area at the bottom of the *Inventor* window. Select the bottom-horizontal line by left-clicking once on the line.

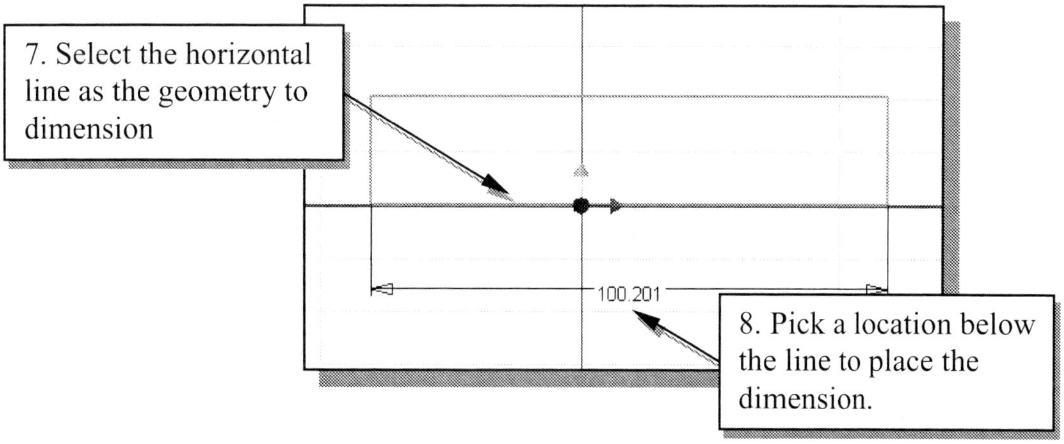

8. Move the graphics cursor below the selected line and left-click to place the dimension. (Note that the value displayed on your screen might be different than what is shown in the above figure.)

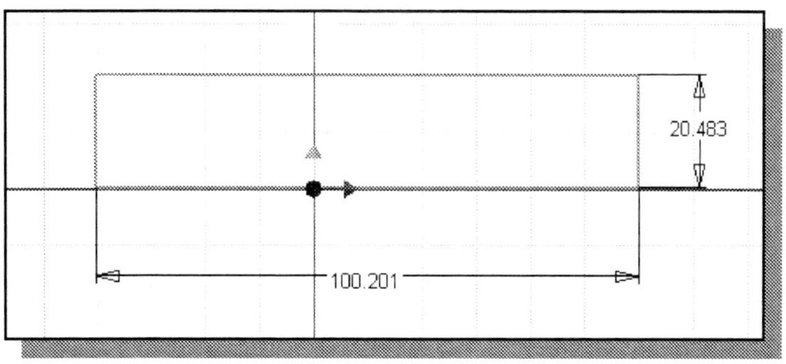

9. On your own, create the vertical size dimension of the sketched rectangle as shown.

Model Dimensions Format

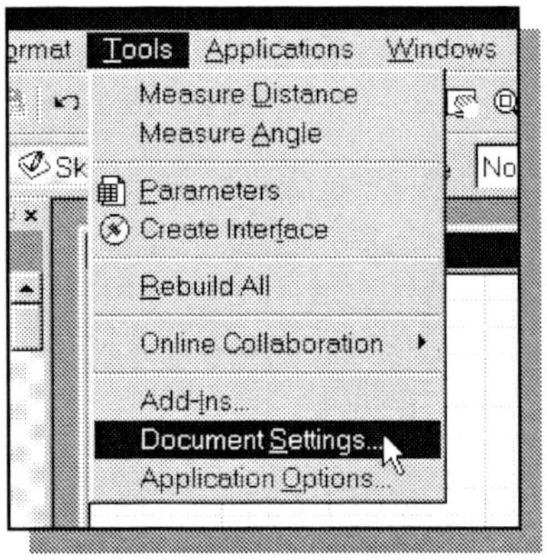

1. In the pull-down menu, select

   Tools → Document Settings

2. In the *Document Settings* dialog box, set the precision to no digits after the decimal point for both the linear dimension display and angular dimension display. Notice the settings that are also available for different *Units* setups.

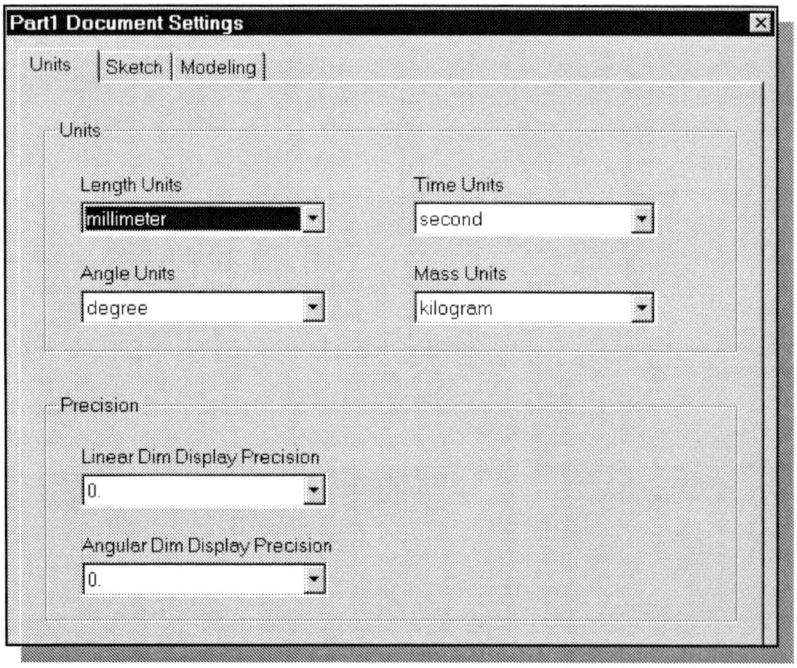

3. Pick **OK** to exit the *Units* dialog box.

Modifying the dimensions of the sketch

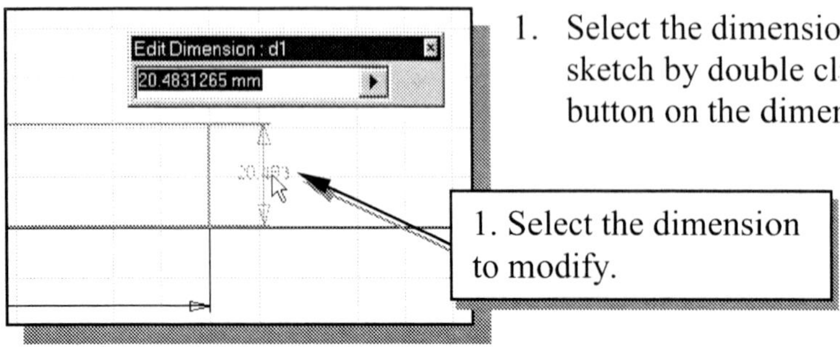

1. Select the dimension that is to the right side of the sketch by double clicking with the left-mouse-button on the dimension text.

2. In the *Edit Dimension* window, the current length of the line is displayed. Enter **50** to set the selected length of the sketch to 50 millimeters.

3. Click on the ***Accept*** icon to accept the entered value.

➤ *Autodesk Inventor* will now update the profile with the new dimension value.

4. On you own, repeat the above steps and adjust the dimensions so that the sketch appears as shown below.

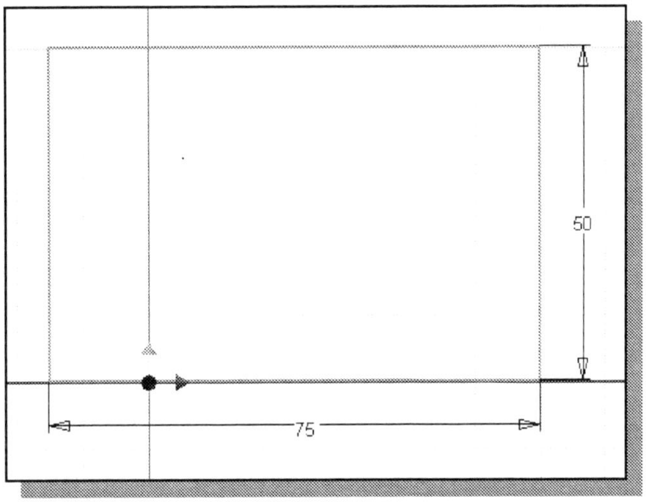

Repositioning Dimensions

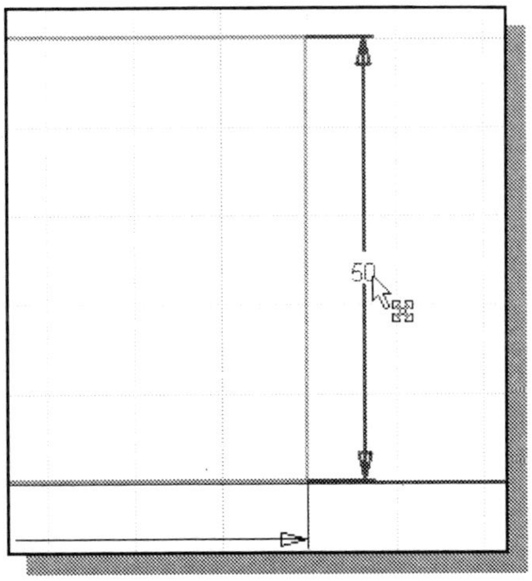

1. Move the cursor near the vertical dimension; note that the dimension is highlighted. Move the cursor slowly until a small marker appears next to the cursor, as shown below.

2. Drag with the left-mouse-button to reposition the selected dimension.

3. Repeat the above steps to reposition the horizontal dimension.

4. Inside the graphics window, click once with the **right-mouse-button** to display the option menu. Select **Finish Sketch** in the popup menu to end the *Sketch* option.

Completing the Base Solid Feature

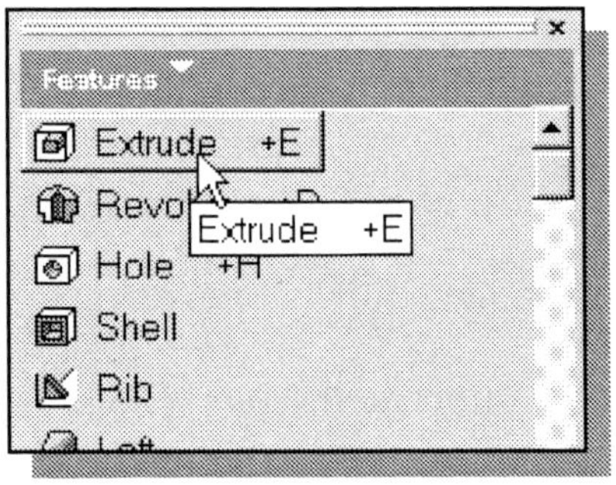

1. In the *Feature* toolbar (the toolbar that is located to the left side of the graphics window), select the ***Extrude*** command by releasing the left-mouse-button on the icon.

2. In the *Extrude* popup window, enter **15** as the extrusion distance. Notice that the sketch region is automatically selected as the extrusion profile.

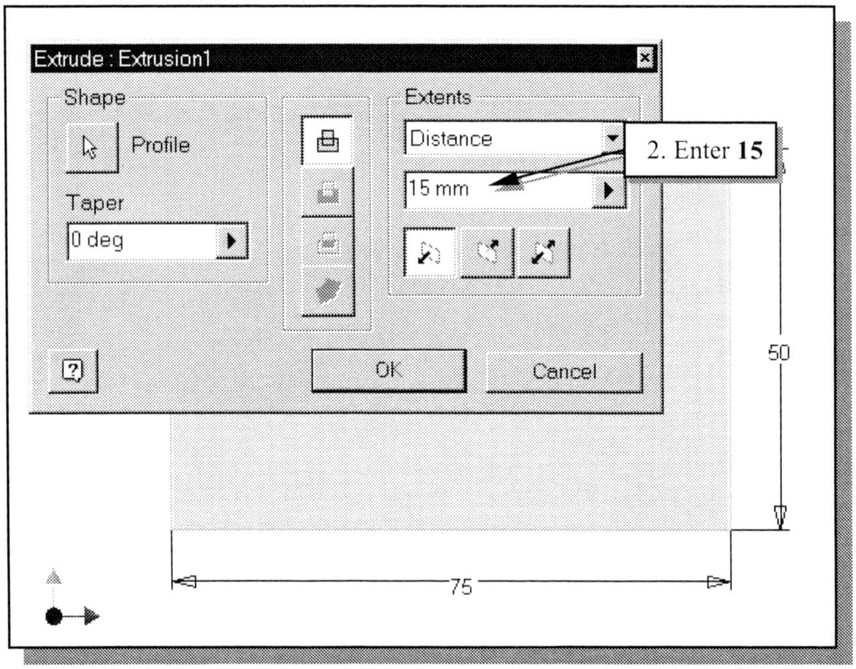

3. Click on the **OK** button to proceed with creating the 3D part.

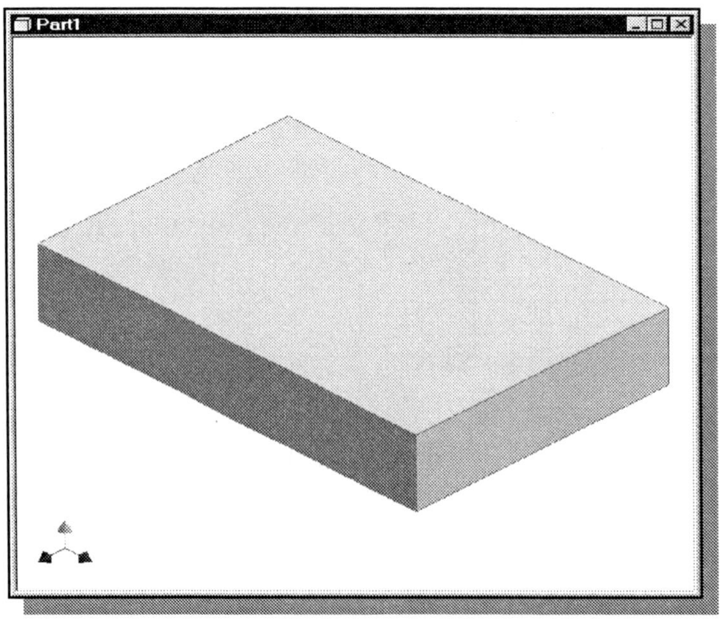

Creating the next solid feature

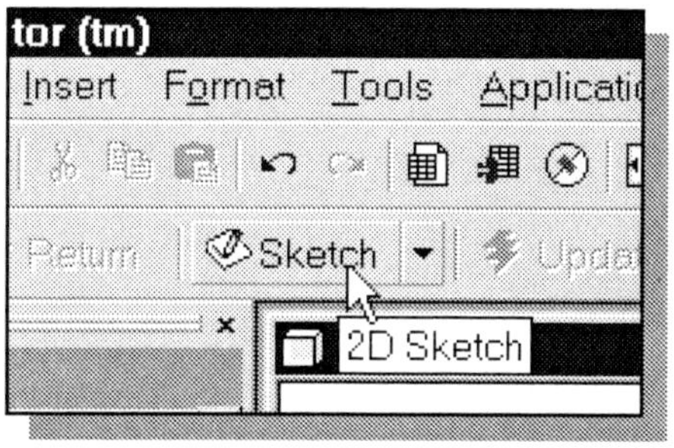

1. In the *Standard* toolbar select the ***Sketch*** command by left-clicking once on the icon.

2. In the *Status Bar* area, the message: "*Select face, workplane, sketch or sketch geometry.*" is displayed. *Autodesk Inventor* expects us to identify a planar surface where the 2D sketch of the next feature is to be created. Move the graphics cursor on the 3D part and notice that *Autodesk Inventor* will automatically highlight feasible planes and surfaces as the cursor is on top of the different surfaces.

3. Use the dynamic rotate function to display the bottom face of the solid model as shown below.

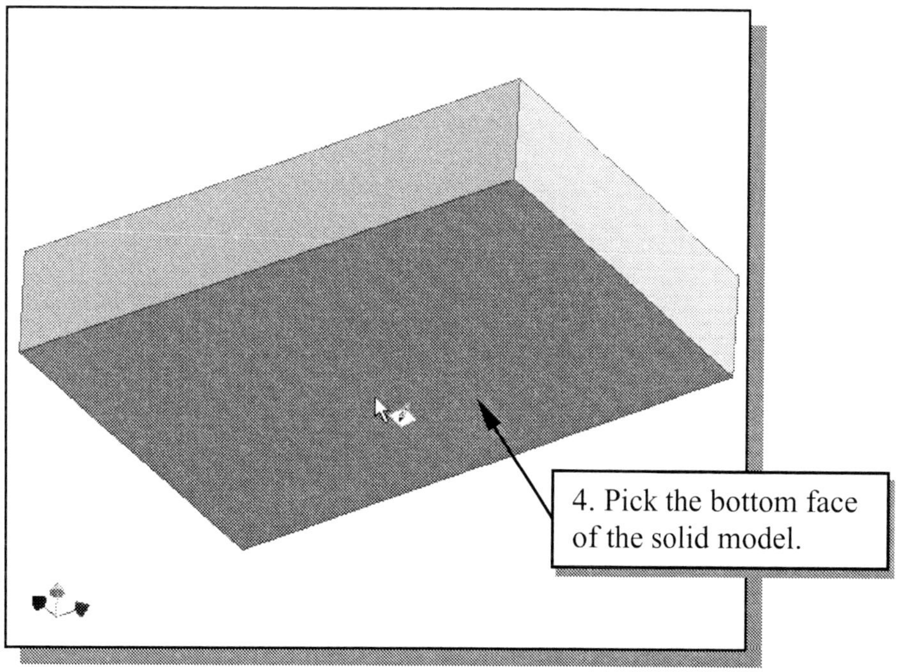

4. Pick the bottom face of the 3D model as the sketching plane.

➢ Note that the sketching plane is aligned to the selected face. *Autodesk Inventor* automatically establishes a User-Coordinate-System (UCS) and records its location with respect to the part on which it was created.

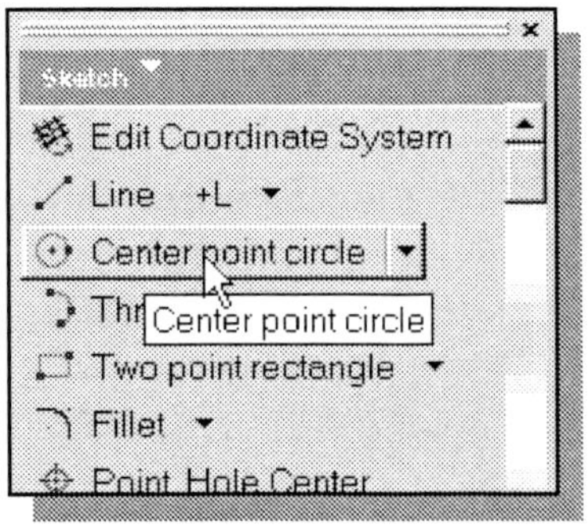

5. Select the ***Center point circle*** command by clicking once with the left-mouse-button on the icon in the *Sketch* toolbar.

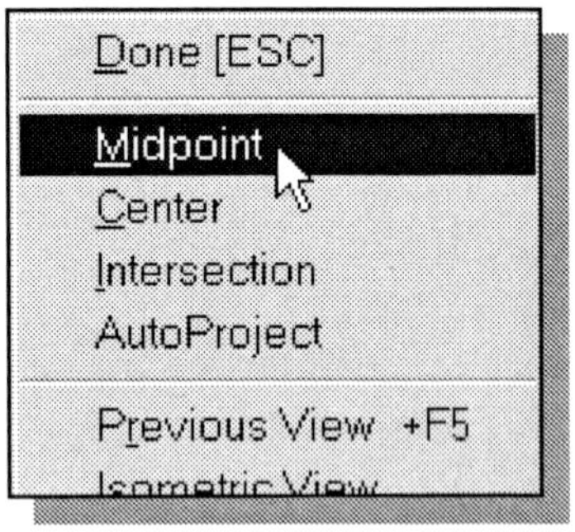

6. Inside the graphics window, click once with the right-mouse-button to display the option menu. Select the **Midpoint** option in the popup menu.

➢ We will align the center of the circle to the midpoint of the base feature.

7. Select the shorter edge of the base feature and then select the corner of the base feature to create a circle as shown below.

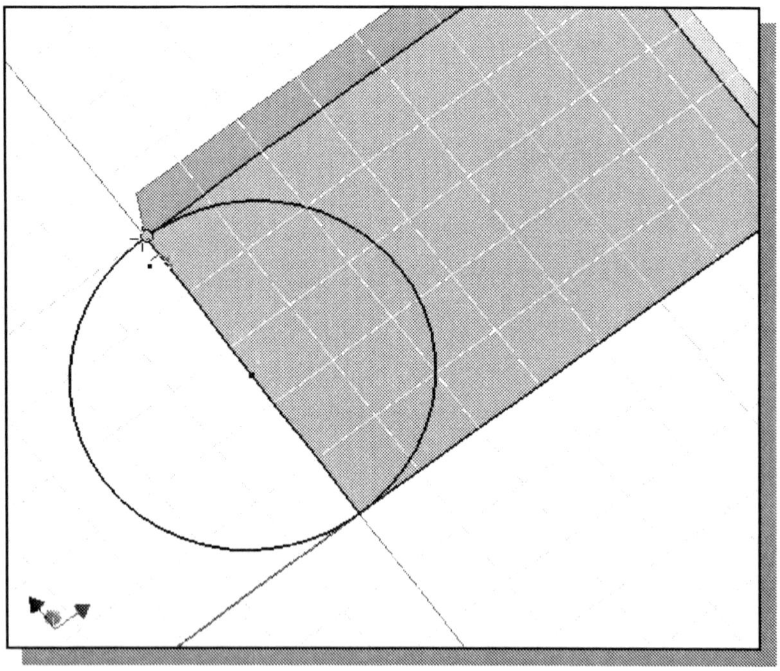

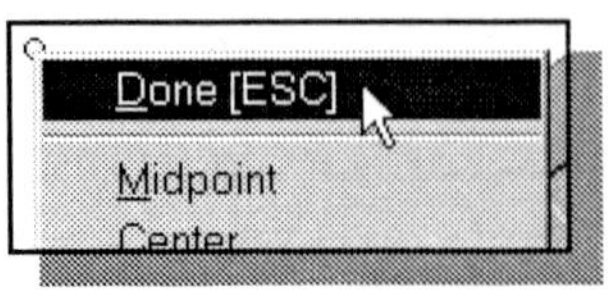

8. Inside the graphics window, click once with the right-mouse-button to display the option menu. Select **Done** in the popup menu to end the *Circle* command.

9. Inside the graphics window, click once with the right-mouse-button to display the option menu. Select **Finish Sketch** in the popup menu to end the *Sketch* option.

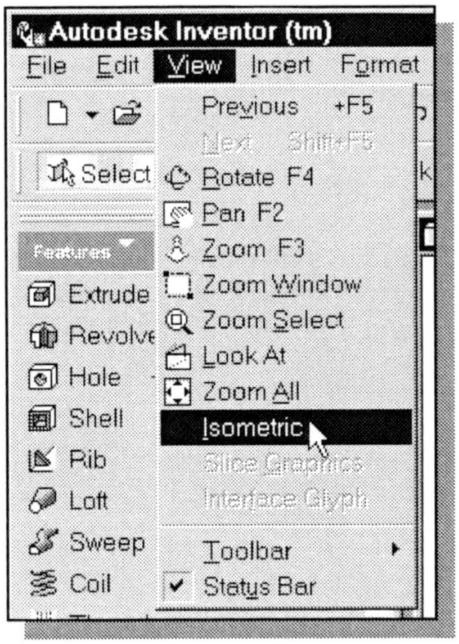

10. Select ***Isometric*** in the **View** pull-down menu to change the display to the isometric view as shown.

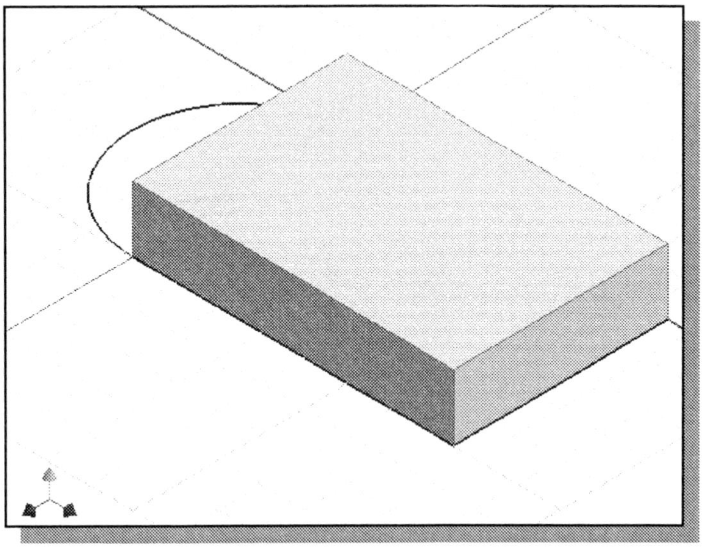

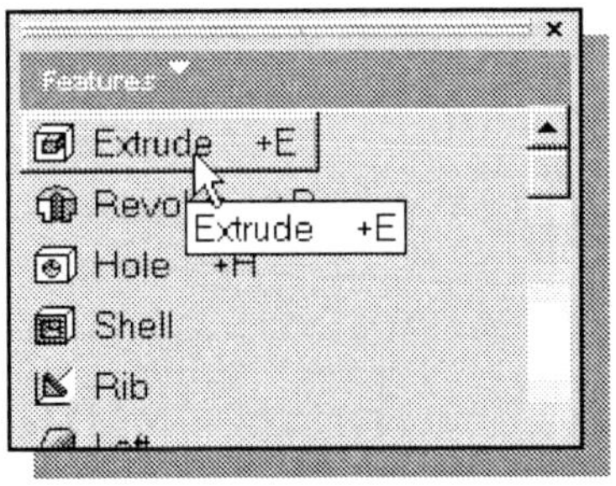

11. In the *Feature* toolbar (the toolbar that is located to the left side of the graphics window), select the ***Extrude*** command by releasing the left-mouse-button on the icon.

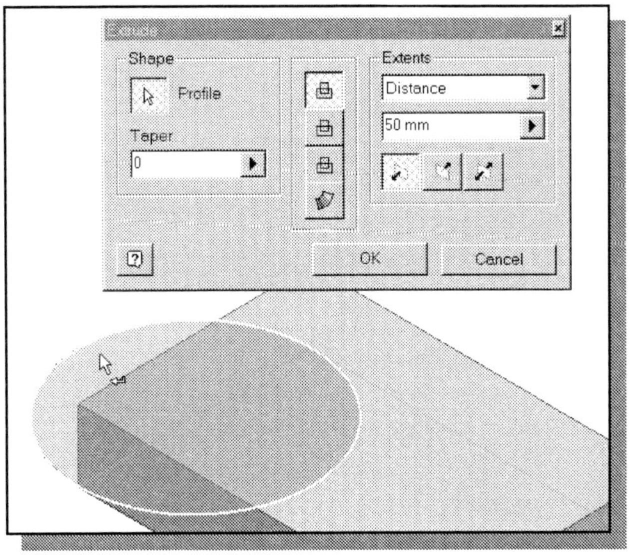

12. In the *Extrude* popup window, the **Profile** button is pressed down; *Autodesk Inventor* expects us to identify the profile to be extruded. Move the cursor inside the circle we just created and left-click once to select the region as the profile to be extruded.

13. In the *Extrude* popup window, enter **40** as the blind extrusion distance as shown below. Confirm the operation option is set to ***Join.*** Click on the **Flip** button to reverse the direction of extrusion (upward) as shown below.

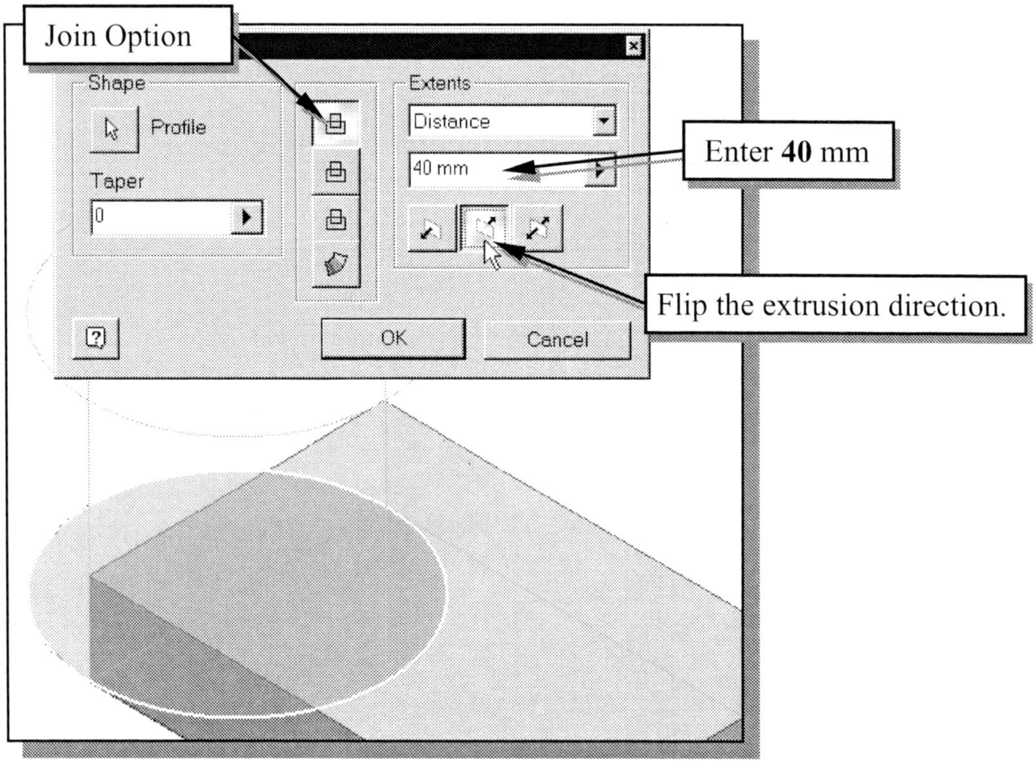

14. Click on the **OK** button to proceed with the *Join* operation.

- The two features are joined together into one solid part; the ***CSG-Union*** operation was performed.

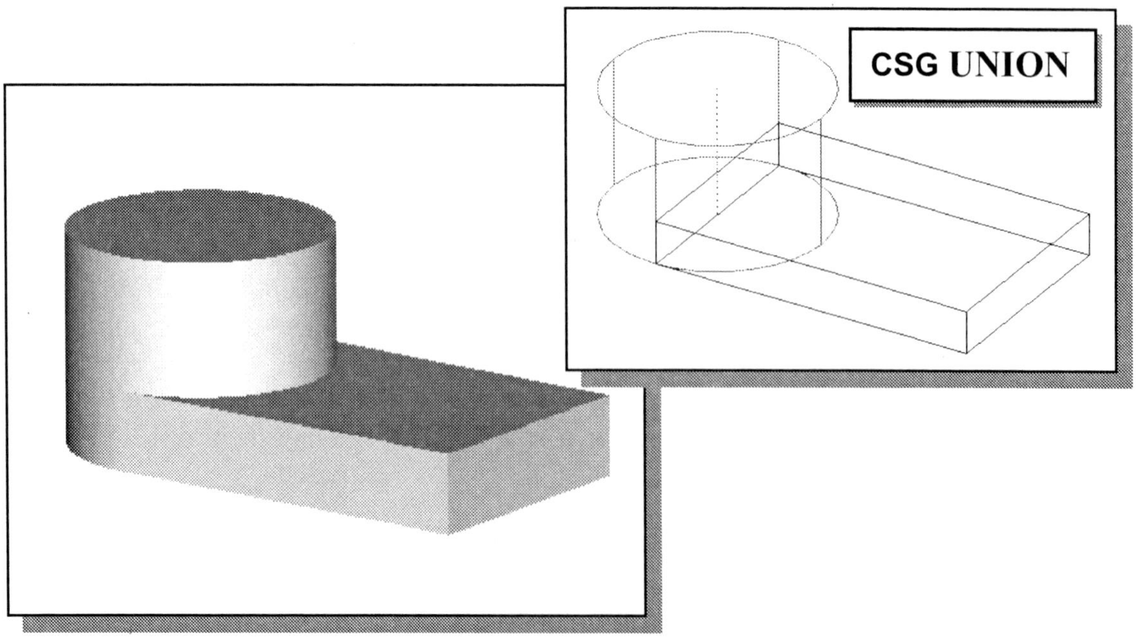

Creating a CUT Feature

- We will create a circular cut as the next solid feature of the design. We will align the sketch plane to the top of the last cylinder feature.

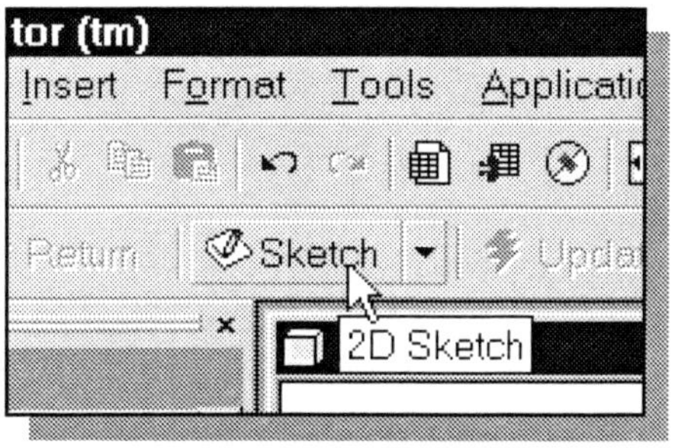

1. In the *Standard* toolbar select the ***Sketch*** command by left-clicking once on the icon.

2. Pick the top face of the cylinder as shown.

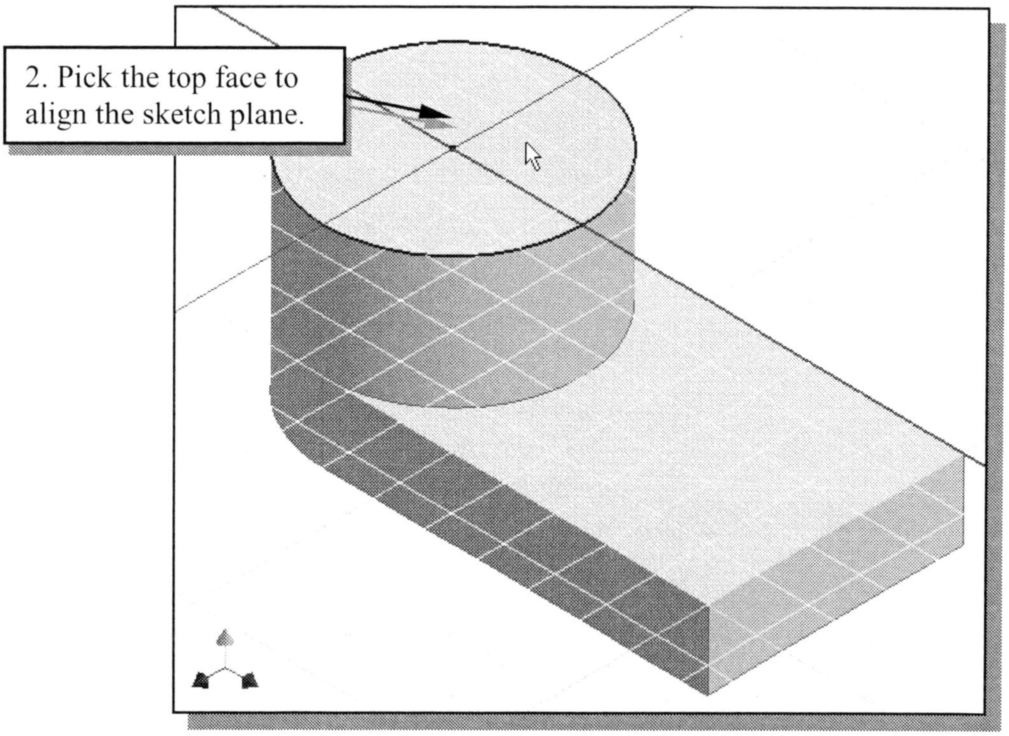

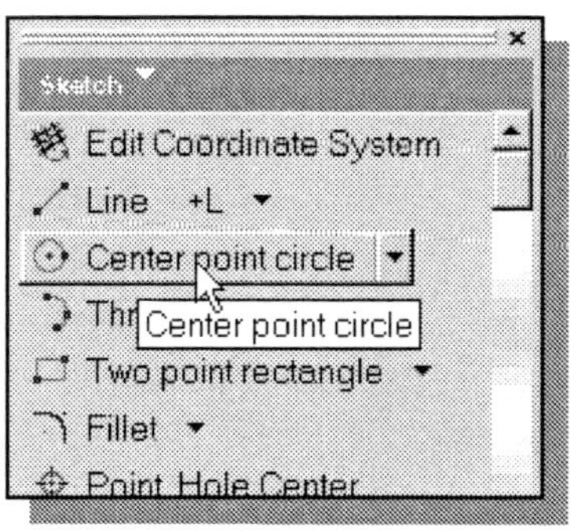

3. Select the ***Center point circle*** command by clicking once with the **left-mouse-button** on the icon in the *Sketch* toolbar.

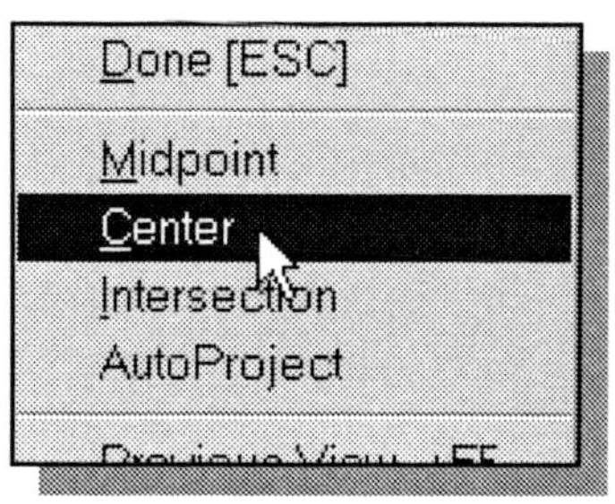

4. Inside the graphics window, click once with the right-mouse-button to display the option menu. Select the **Center** option in the popup menu.

5. Select the top circular edge of the solid feature.

6. Sketch a circle of arbitrary size inside the top face of the cylinder as shown below.

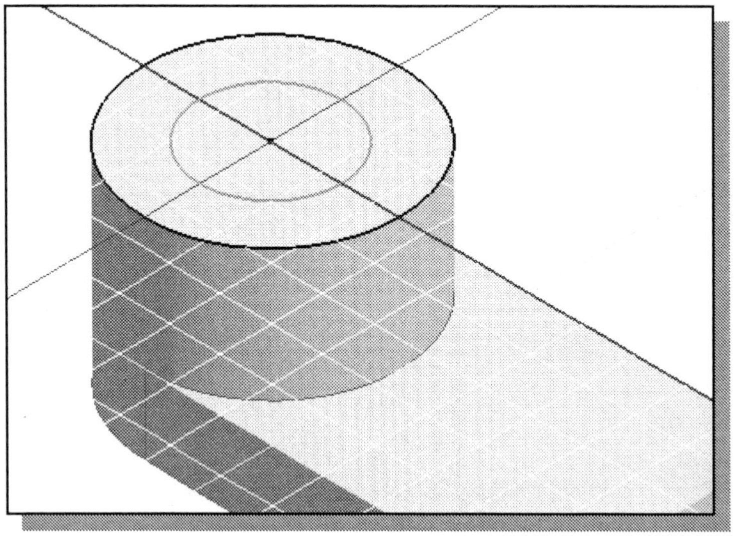

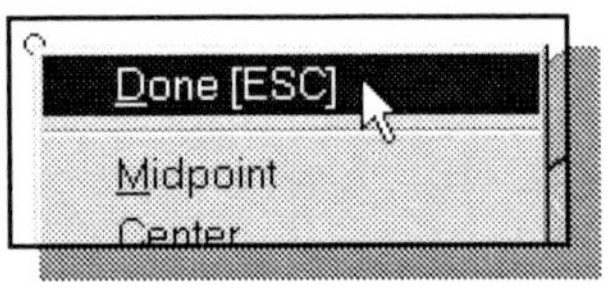

7. Inside the graphics window, click once with the right-mouse-button to display the option menu. Select **Done** in the popup menu to end the *Circle* command.

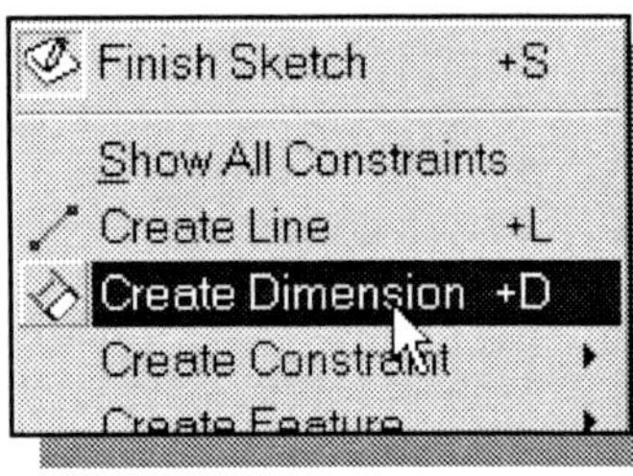

8. Inside the graphics window, click once with the right-mouse-button to display the option menu. Select the **Create Dimension** option in the popup menu.

9. Create a dimension to describe the size of the circle and set it to **30**mm.

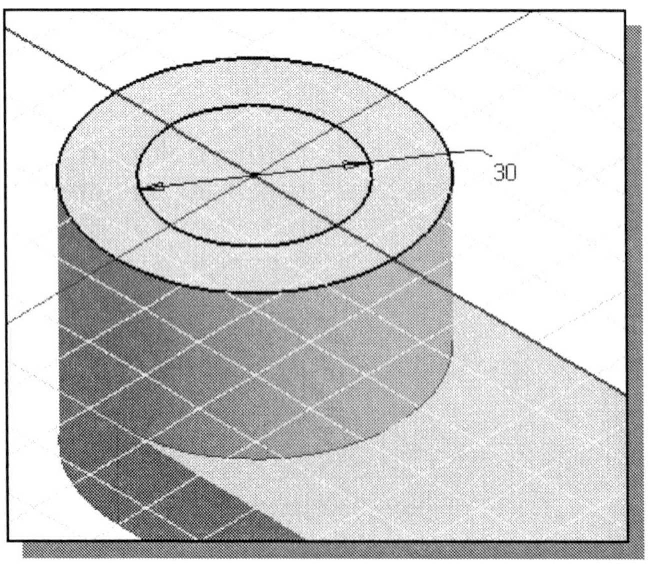

10. Inside the graphics window, click once with the right-mouse-button to display the option menu. Select **Done** in the popup menu to end the *Circle* command.

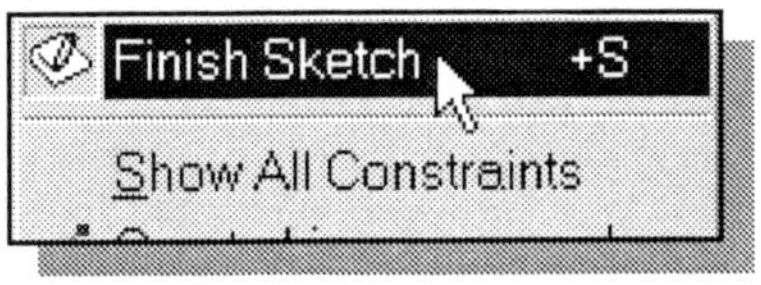

11. Inside the graphics window, click once with the right-mouse-button to display the option menu. Select **Finish Sketch** in the popup menu to end the *Sketch* option.

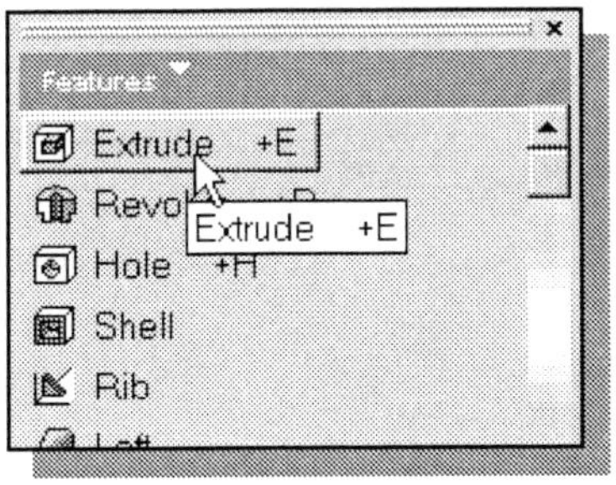

12. In the *Feature* toolbar (the toolbar that is located to the left side of the graphics window), select the ***Extrude*** command by releasing the left-mouse-button on the icon.

13. In the *Extrude* popup window, the **Profile** button is pressed down; *Autodesk Inventor* expects us to identify the profile to be extruded. Move the cursor inside the circle we just created and left-click once to select the region as the profile to be extruded.

14. In the *Extrusion* popup window, set the operation option to ***Cut.*** Select ***All*** as the *Extents* option as shown below. Confirm the arrowhead points downward.

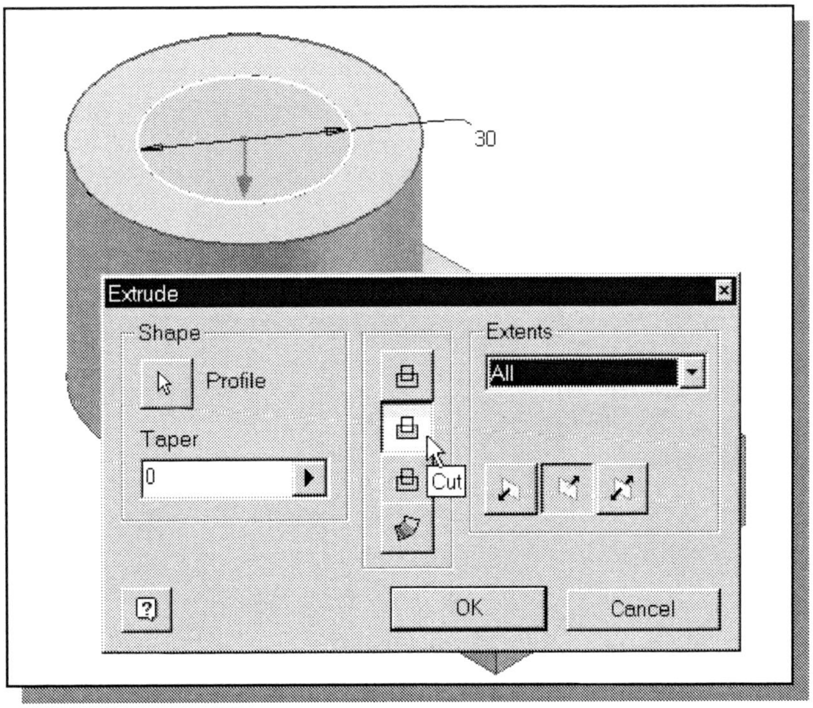

15. Click on the **OK** button to proceed with the ***Cut*** operation.

- The circular volume is removed from the solid model; the *CSG-Cut* operation resulted in a single solid.

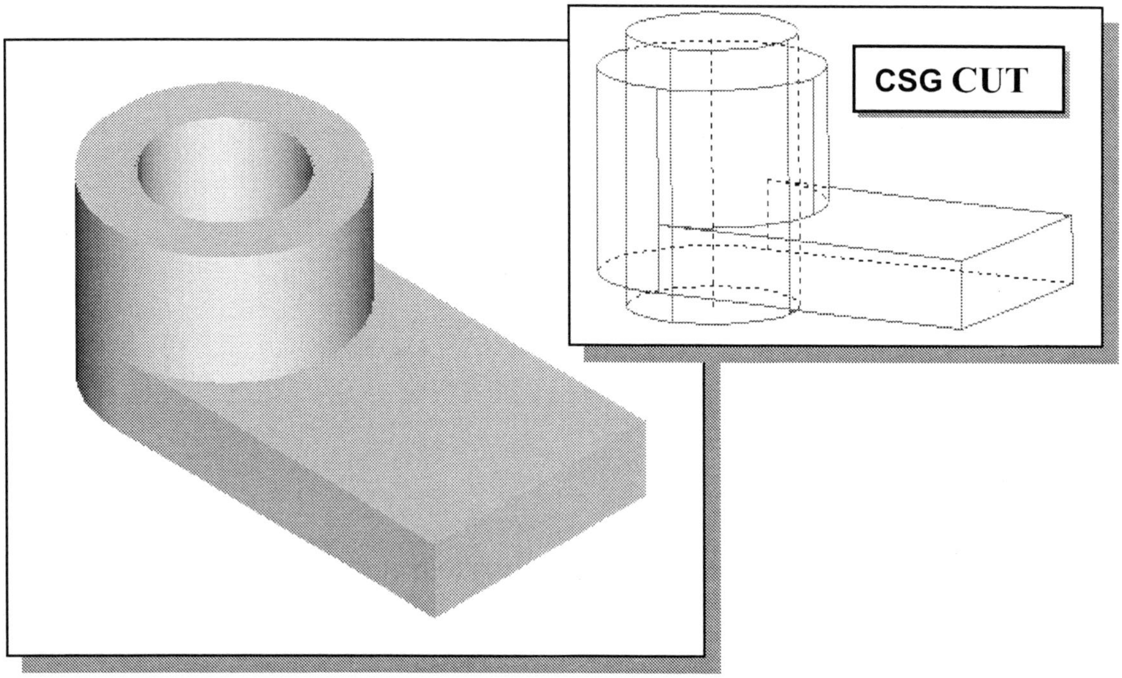

Creating a PLACED FEATURE

- In *Autodesk Inventor*, there are two types of geometric features: **placed features** and **sketched features**. The last cut feature we created is a *sketched feature*, where we created a rough sketch and performed an extrusion operation. We can also create a hole-feature, which is a placed feature. A *placed feature* is a feature that does not need a sketch and can be created automatically. Holes, fillets, chamfers, and shells are all placed features.

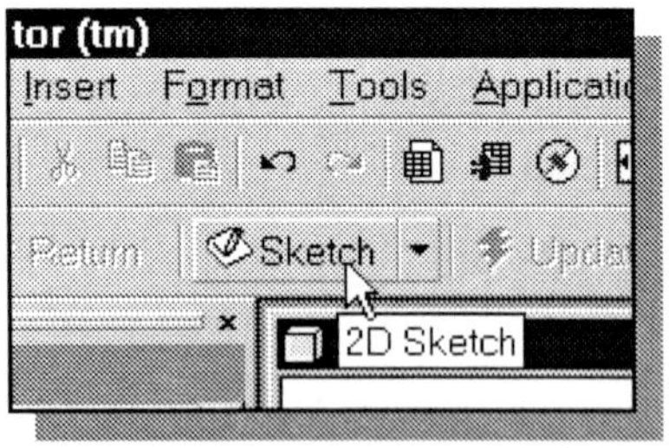

1. In the *Standard* toolbar select the ***Sketch*** command by left-clicking once on the icon.

2. Pick the top face of the base feature as shown.

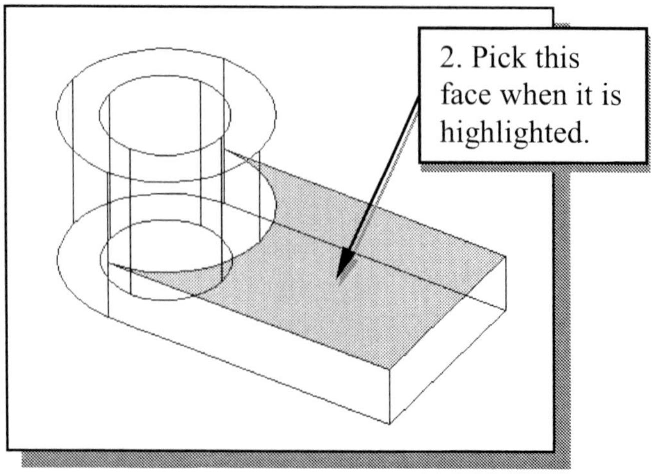

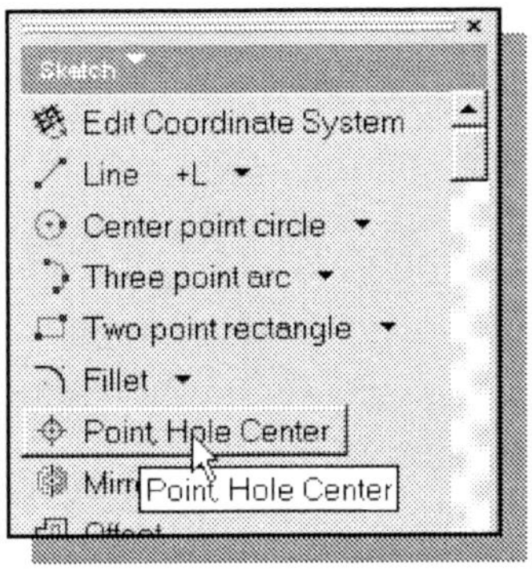

3. Select the ***Point, Hole Center*** command by clicking once with the left-mouse-button on the icon in the *Sketch* toolbar.

4. Pick a location near the center of the top face of the base feature as shown.

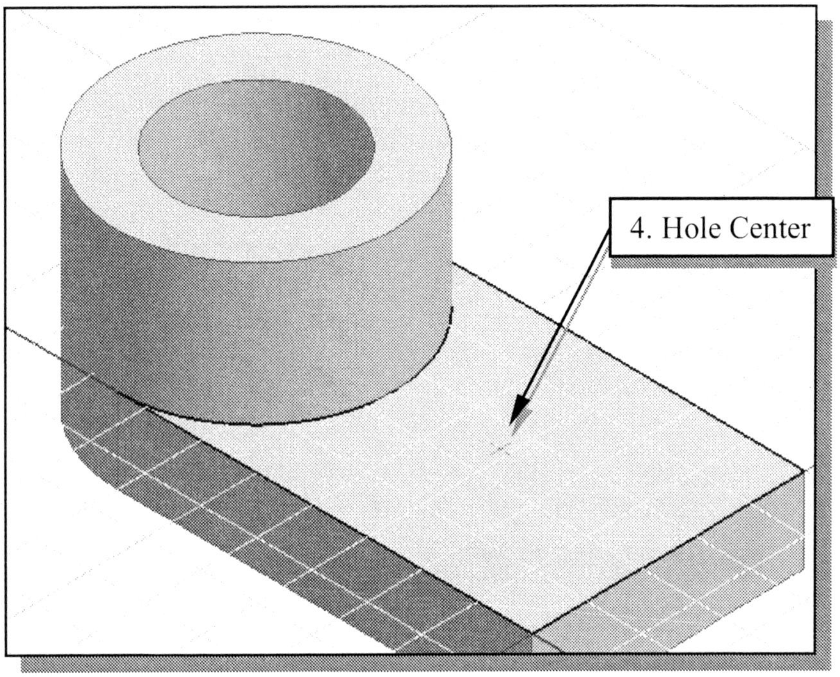

5. On your own, create and modify the two dimensions as shown (location dimensions to position the hole center point.)

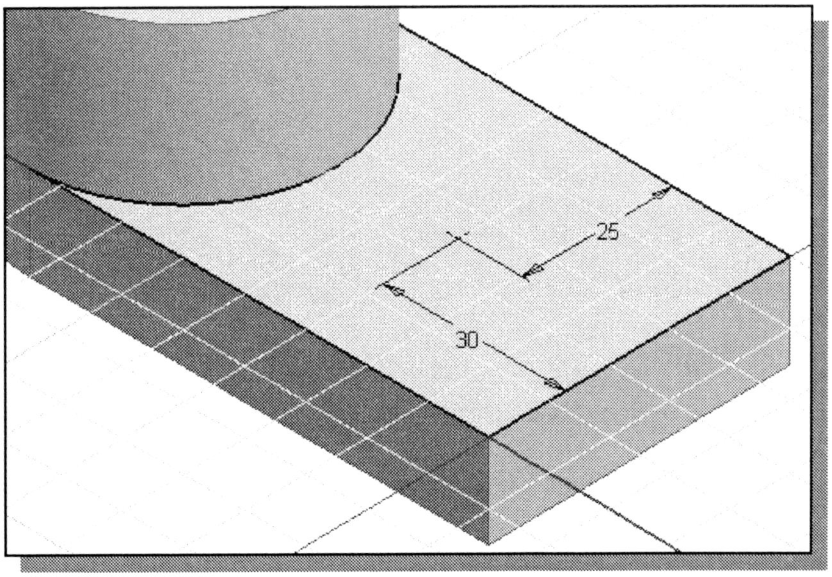

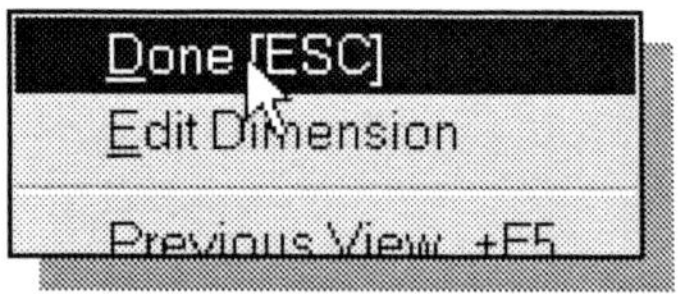

6. Inside the graphics window, click once with the right-mouse-button to display the option menu. Select **Done** in the popup menu to end the *General Dimension* command.

7. Inside the graphics window, click once with the right-mouse-button to display the option menu. Select **Finish Sketch** in the popup menu to end the *Sketch* option.

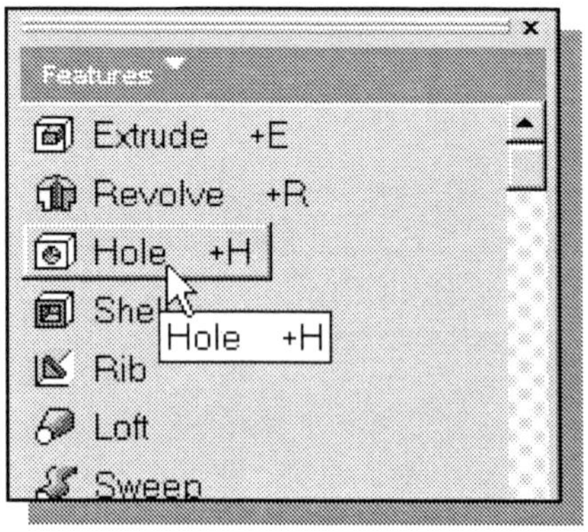

8. In the *Feature* toolbar (the toolbar that is located to the left side of the graphics window), select the ***Hole*** command by releasing the left-mouse-button on the icon.

9. In the *Holes* window, the **Centers** button is pressed down; *Autodesk Inventor* allows us to identify as many centers as we like to create the same feature. Set the *Termination* option to ***Through All***.

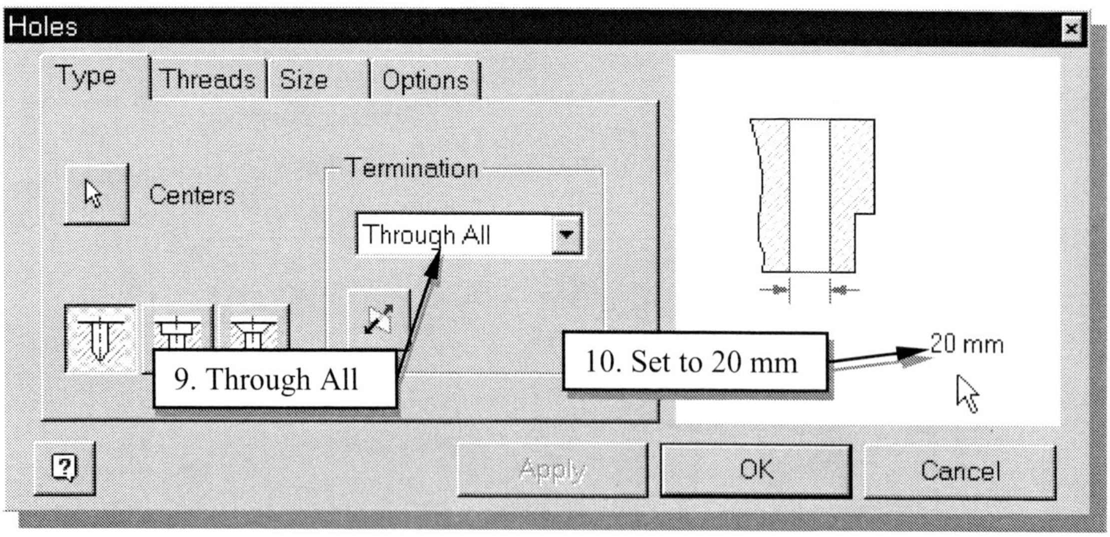

10. In the ***Drill Size*** option window, click on the displayed diameter and change the displayed value to **20** mm as the new diameter of the drill.

11. Click on the **OK** button to proceed with the ***Hole*** feature.

- The circular volume is removed from the solid model; the *CSG-Cut* operation resulted in a single solid.

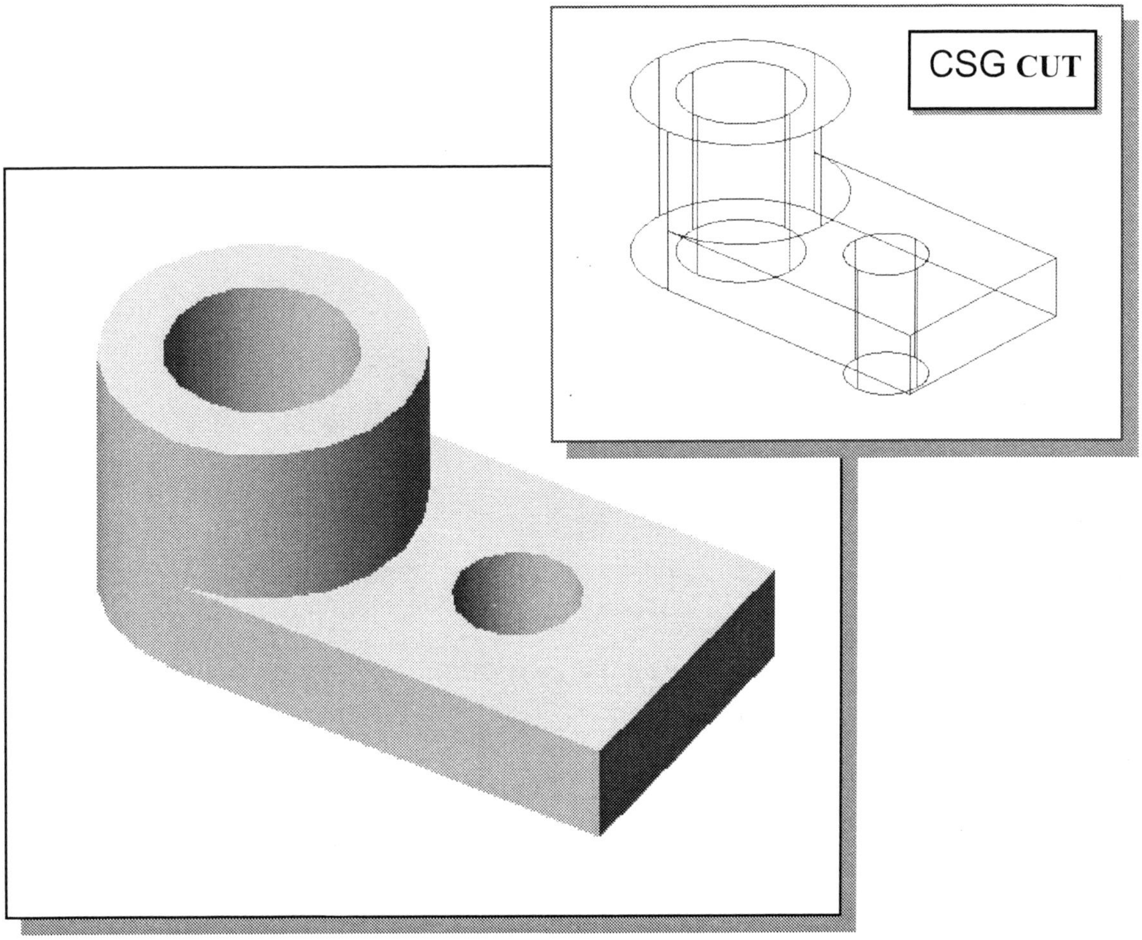

➢ The last two features we created produced the same result even though they are accomplished by using two different approaches. The sketched cut feature approach is more flexible in the shape that can be used. The placed feature approach uses a different procedure to accomplish the same task, but its use is restricted to certain types of geometry.

Creating a Rectangular Cut Feature

- We will create a rectangular cut as the last solid feature of the ***Locator***.

1. In the *Standard* toolbar, select the ***Sketch*** command by left-clicking once on the icon.

2. Pick the right face of the base feature as shown.

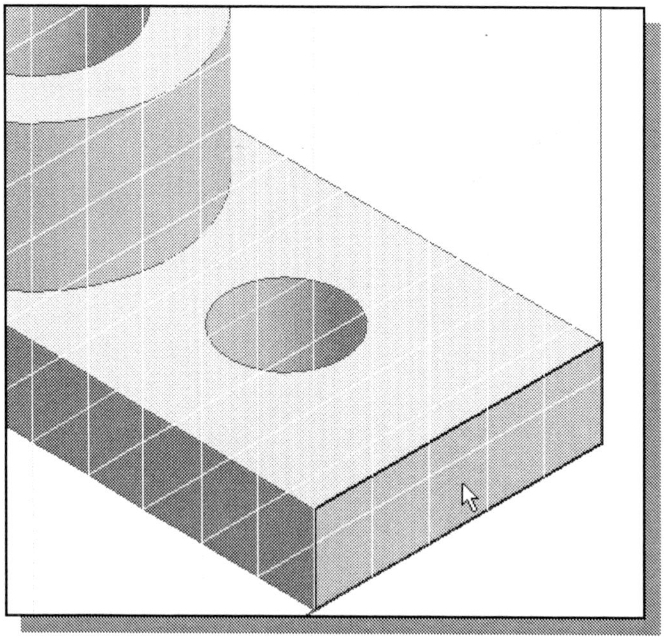

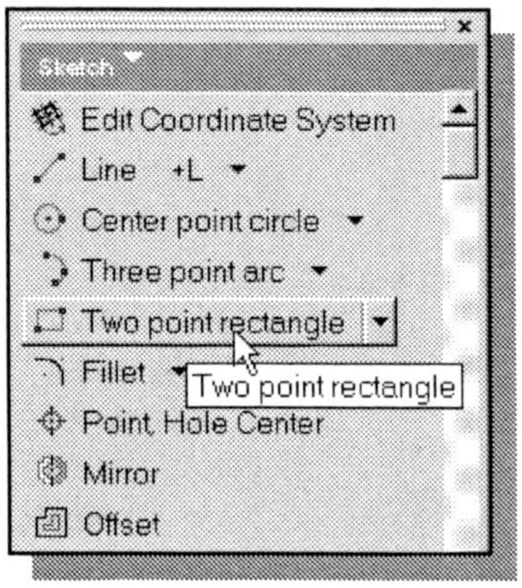

3. Select the ***Two point rectangle*** command by clicking once with the left-mouse-button on the icon in the *Sketch* toolbar.

4. Create a rectangle that is aligned to the top and bottom edges of the base feature as shown below.

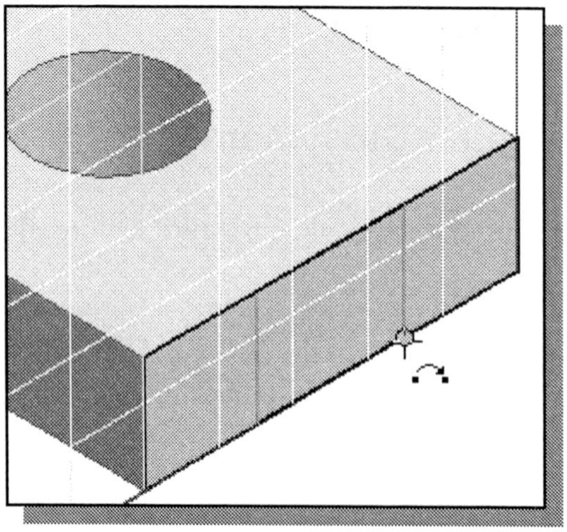

5. On your own, create and modify the two dimensions as shown below.

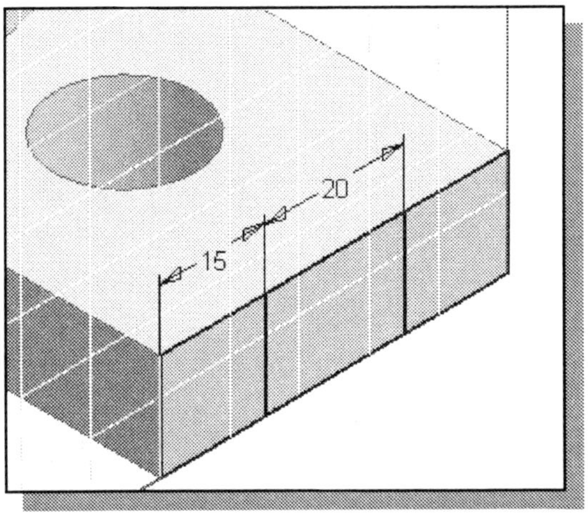

6. Inside the graphics window, click once with the **right-mouse-button** to display the option menu. Select **Finish Sketch** in the popup menu to end the *Sketch* option.

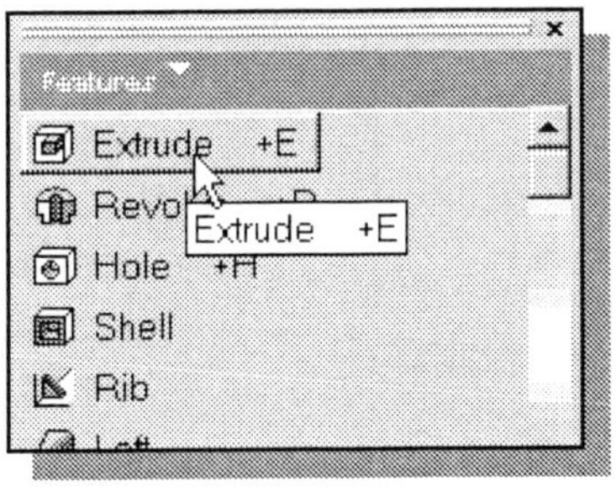

7. In the *Feature* toolbar (the toolbar that is located to the left side of the graphics window), select the ***Extrude*** command by releasing the left-mouse-button on the icon.

8. In the *Extrude* popup window, the **Profile** button is pressed down; *Autodesk Inventor* expects us to identify the profile to be extruded. Move the cursor inside the rectangle we just created and left-click once to select the region as the profile to be extruded.

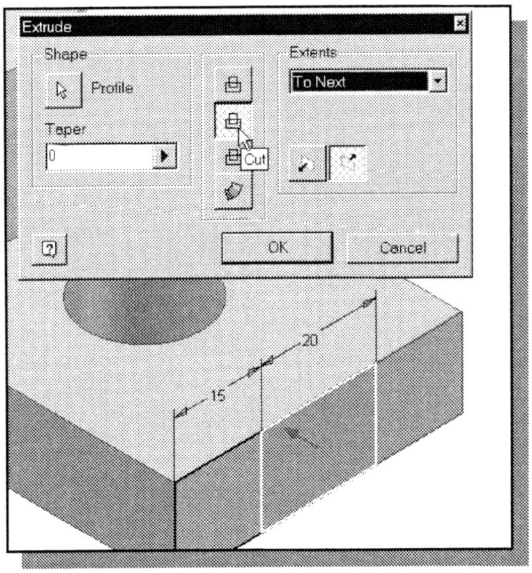

9. In the *Extrude* popup window, set the operation option to ***Cut.*** Select ***To Next*** as the *Extents* option as shown. Confirm the arrowhead points toward the center of the solid model.

10. Click on the **OK** button to create the *cut feature* and complete the design.

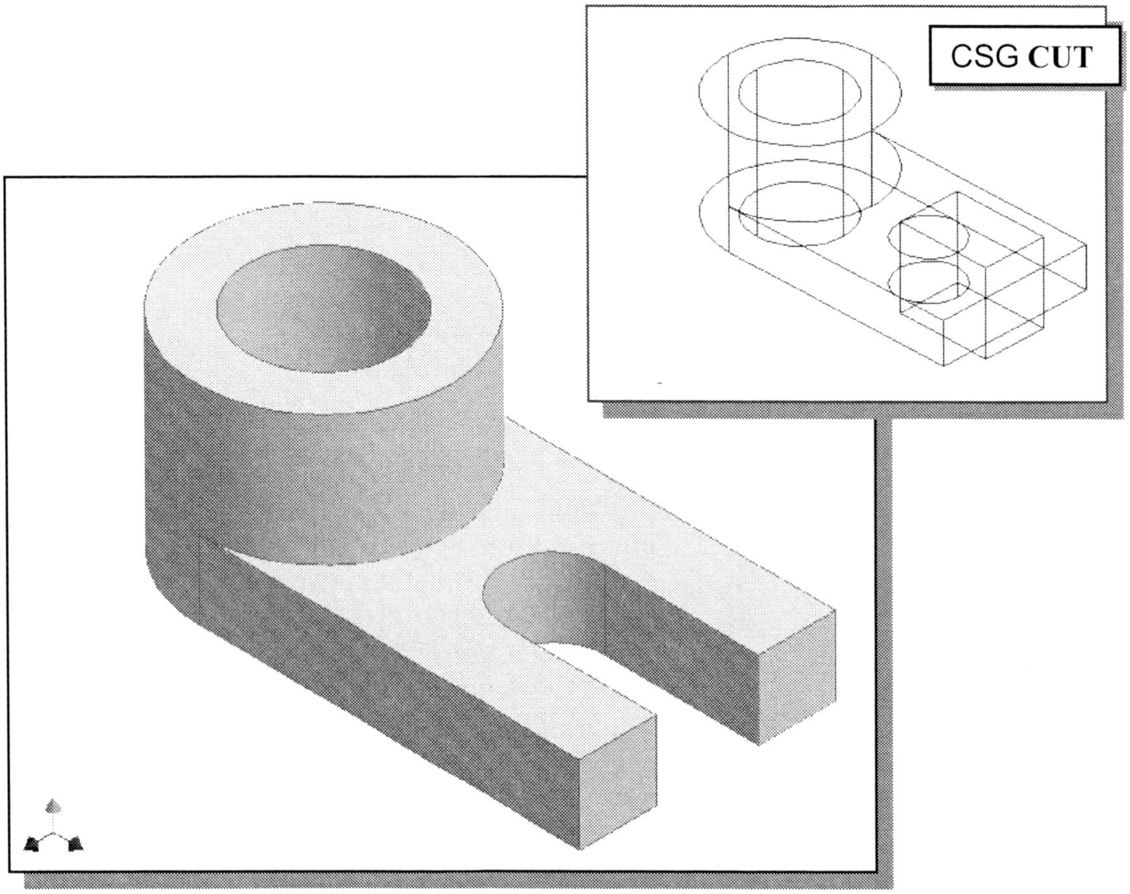
CSG CUT

Questions:

1. What are the three basic *Boolean operations* commonly used in computer geometric modeling software?

2. What is a *primitive solid*?

3. What does *CSG* stand for?

4. Which *Boolean operation* keeps only the volume common to the two solid objects?

5. What is the difference between a *CUT feature* and a *HOLE feature* in *Autodesk Inventor*?

6. Using the CSG concepts, create *Binary Tree* sketches showing the steps you plan to use to create the two models shown on the next page:

Ex.1)

Ex.2)

Exercises:

1.

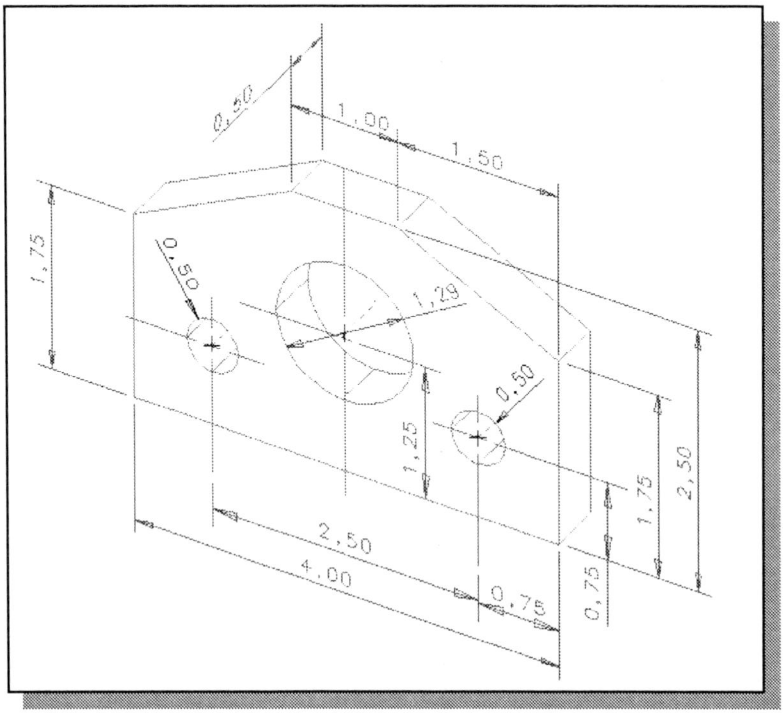

2.

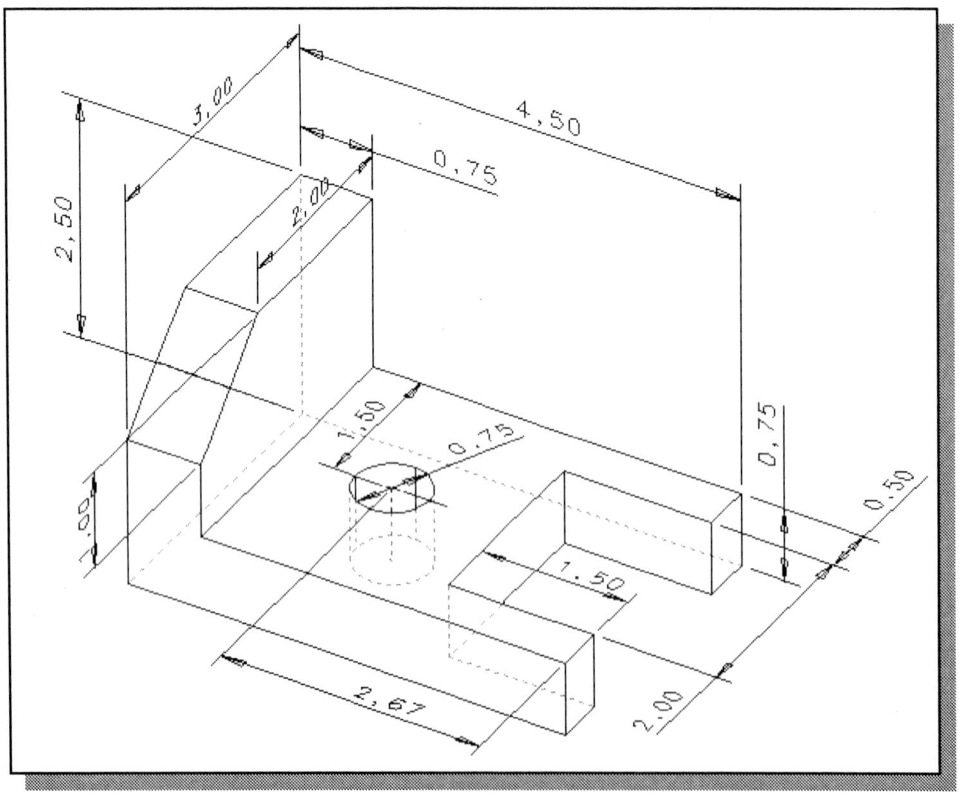

Lesson 3
Model History Tree

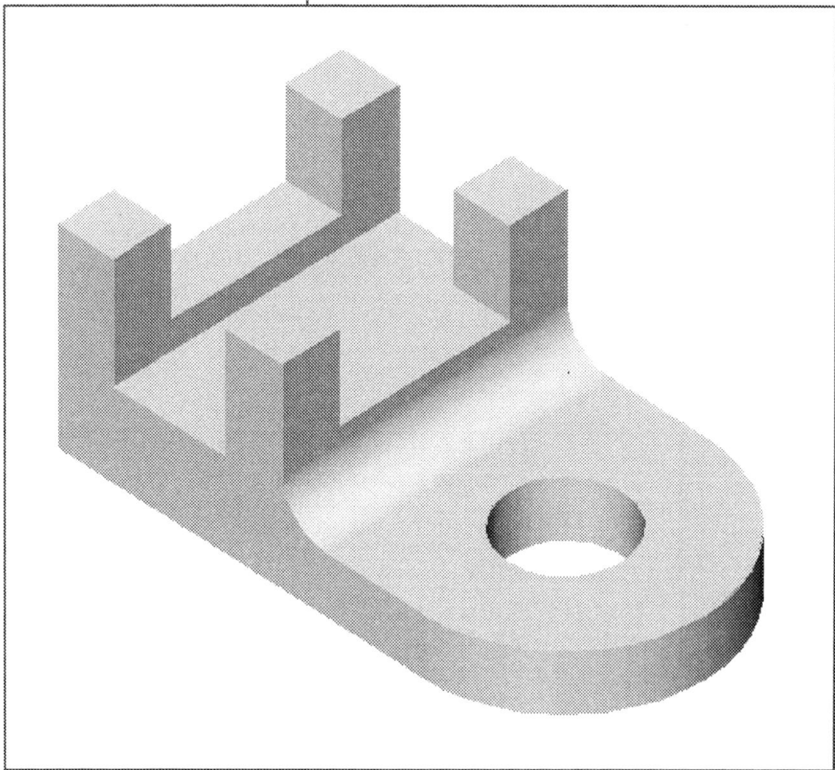

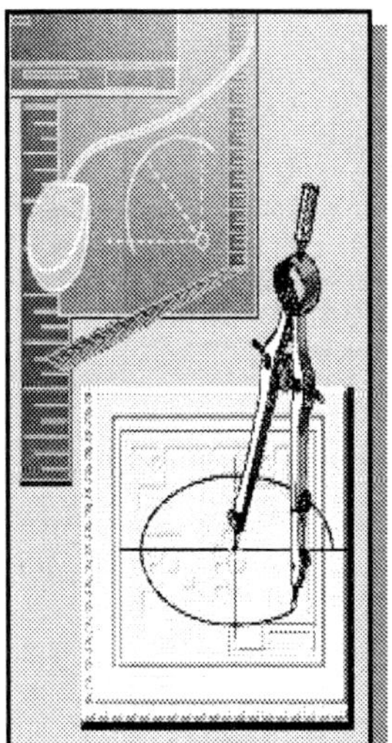

Learning Objectives

When you have completed this lesson, you will be able to:

- ♦ Understand the Feature Interactions.
- ♦ Use the Part Browser.
- ♦ Modify and Update Feature Dimension
- ♦ Perform History-Based Part Modifications.
- ♦ Change the Names of created Features.
- ♦ Perform Basic Design Changes.

Introduction

In *Autodesk Inventor*, the **design intents** are embedded into features in the **history tree**. The structure of the model history tree resembles that of a **CSG binary tree**. A CSG binary tree contains only *Boolean relations*, while the ***Autodesk Inventor*** **history tree** contains all features, including *Boolean relations*. A history tree is a sequential record of the features used to create the part. This history tree contains the construction steps, plus the rules defining the design intent of each construction operation. In a history tree, each time a new modeling event is created, previously defined features can be used to define information such as size, location, and orientation. It is therefore important to think about your modeling strategy before you start creating anything. It is important, but also difficult, to plan ahead for all possible design changes that might occur. This approach in modeling is a major difference of **FEATURE-BASED CAD SOFTWARE**, such as *Autodesk Inventor*, from previous generation CAD systems.

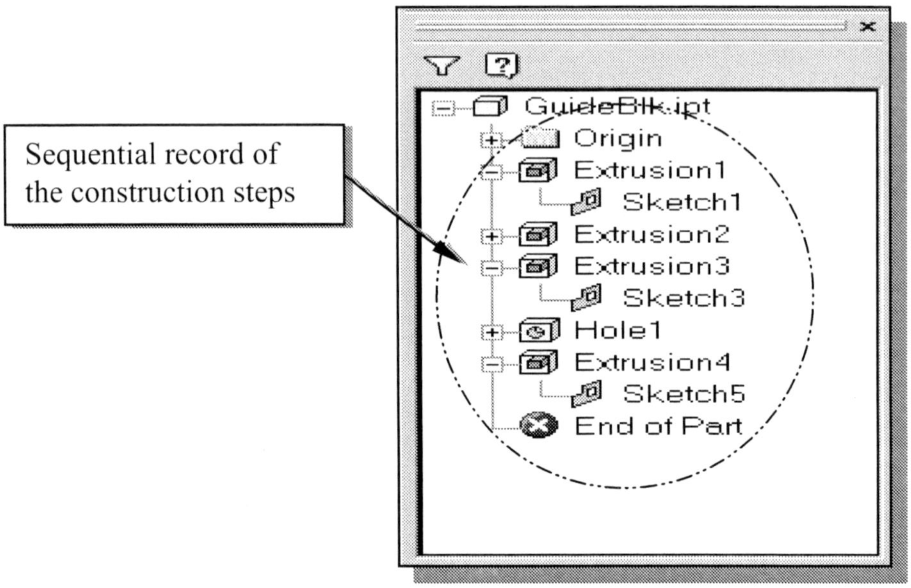

Feature-based parametric modeling is a cumulative process. Every time a new feature is added, a new result is created and the feature is also added to the history tree. The database also includes parameters of features that were used to define them. All of this happens automatically as features are created and manipulated. At this point, it is important to understand that all of this information is retained, and modifications are done based on the same input information.

In *Autodesk Inventor*, the history tree gives information about modeling order and other information about the feature. Part modifications can be accomplished by accessing the features in the history tree. It is therefore important to understand and utilize the feature history tree to modify designs. *Autodesk Inventor* remembers the history of a part, including all the rules that were used to create it, so that changes can be made to any operation that was performed to create the part. In *Autodesk Inventor*, to modify a feature, we access the feature by selecting the feature in the ***Browser*** window.

The *L-Support* Design

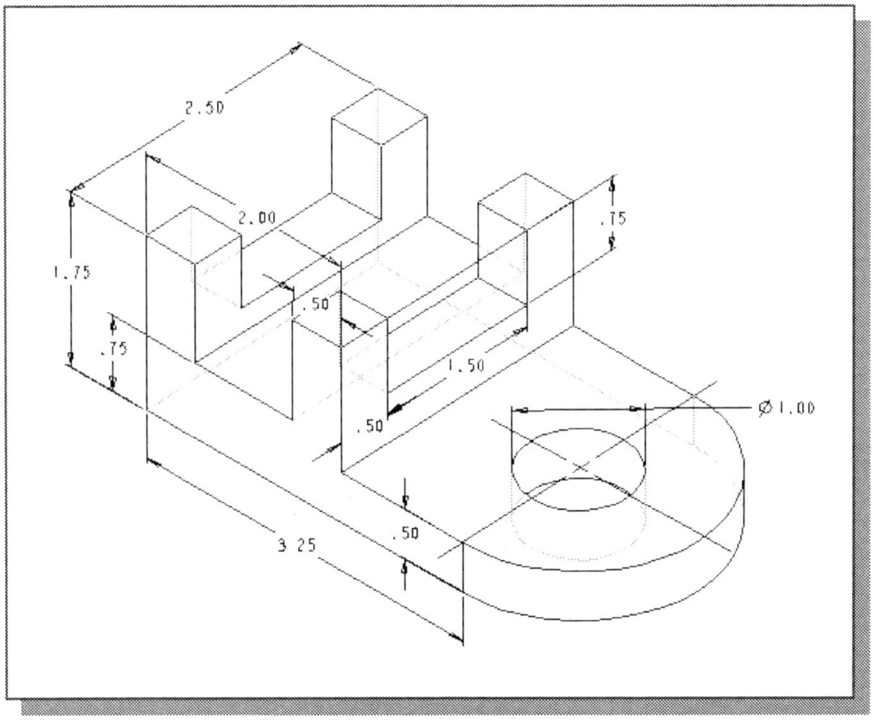

❖ Based on your knowledge of *Autodesk Inventor* so far, how many features would you use to create the design? Which feature would you choose as the **BASE FEATURE**, the first solid feature, of the model? What is your choice in arranging the order of the features? Would you organize the features differently if additional fillets were to be added in the design? Take a few minutes to consider these questions and do preliminary planning by sketching on a piece of paper. You are also encouraged to create the model on your own prior to following through the tutorial.

Starting *Autodesk Inventor*

1. Select the ***Autodesk Inventor*** option on the *Start* menu or select the ***Autodesk Inventor*** icon on the desktop to start *Autodesk Inventor*. The *Autodesk Inventor* main window will appear on the screen.

2. Once the program is loaded into the memory, the *Startup* dialog box appears at the center of the screen.

3. Select the ***New*** icon with a single click of the left-mouse-button in the *What to Do* dialog box.

4. Select the **English** tab and in the *New - Choose Template* area, select **Standard(in).ipt**.

5. Pick **OK** in the *Startup* dialog box to accept the selected settings.

Modeling Strategy

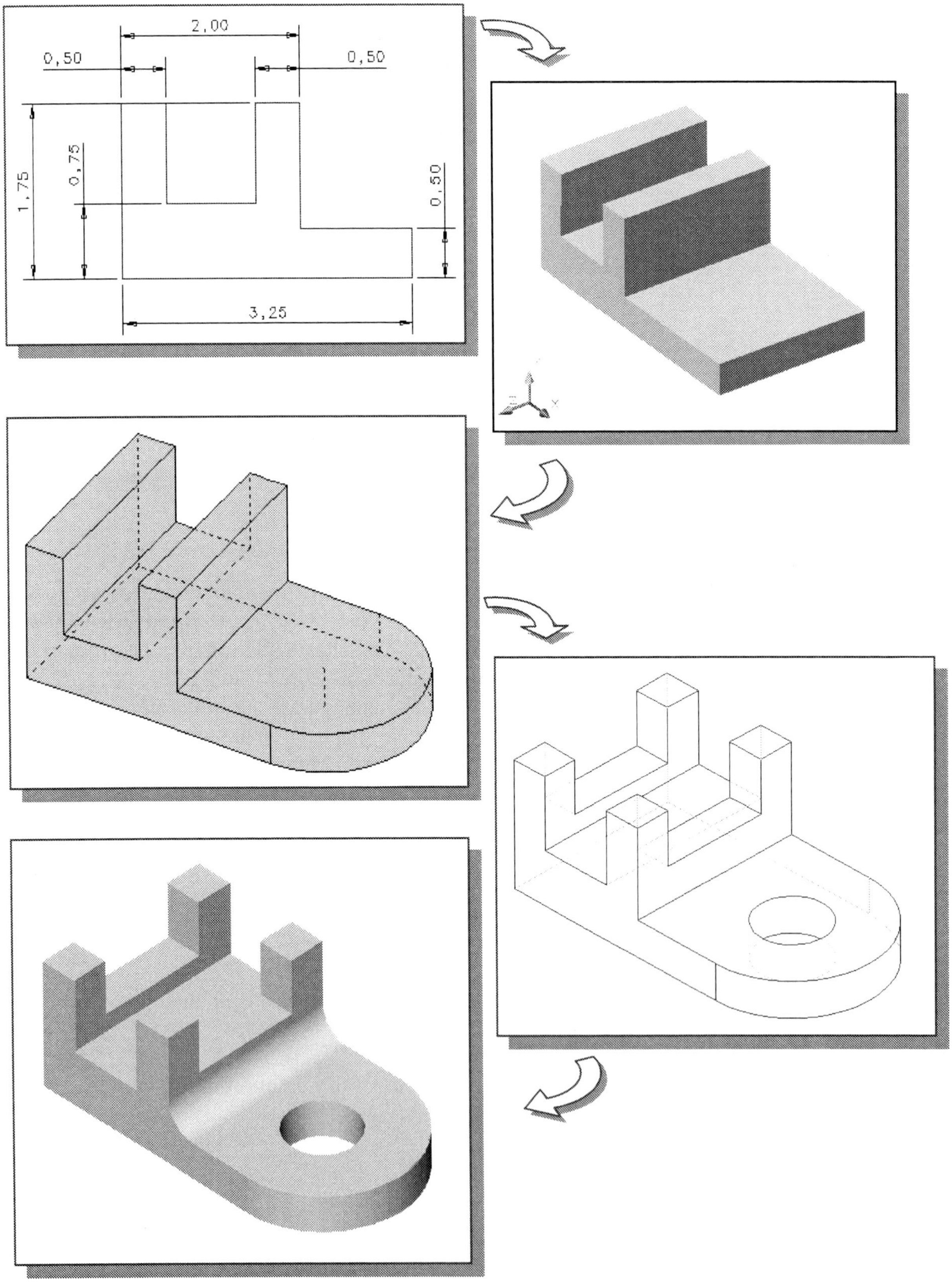

The *Autodesk Inventor Browser*

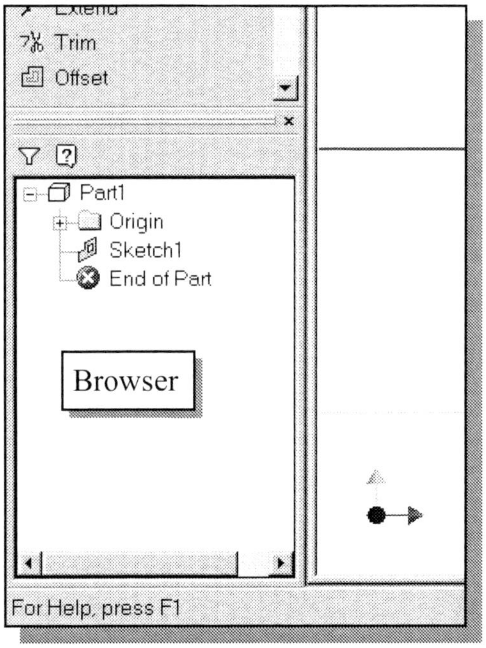

- In the *Autodesk Inventor* screen layout, the *Browser* is located to the left of the graphics window. *Autodesk Inventor* can be used for part modeling, assembly modeling, part drawings, and assembly presentation. The ***Browser*** window provides a visual structure of the features, constraints, and attributes that are used to create the part, assembly, or scene. The *Browser* also provides right-click menu access for tasks associated specifically with the part or feature, and it is the primary focus for executing many of the *Autodesk Inventor* commands.

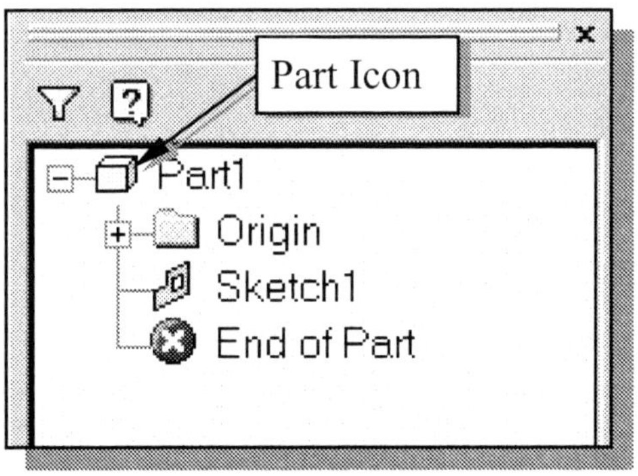

- The first item displayed in the *Browser* is the name of the part, which is also the file name. By default, the name "Part1" is used when we first started *Autodesk Inventor*. The *Browser* can also be used to modify parts and assemblies by moving, deleting, or renaming items within the hierarchy. Any changes made in the *Browser* directly affect the part or assembly and the results of the modifications are displayed on screen instantly. The *Browser* also reports any problems and conflicts during the modification and updating procedure.

Creating the Base Feature

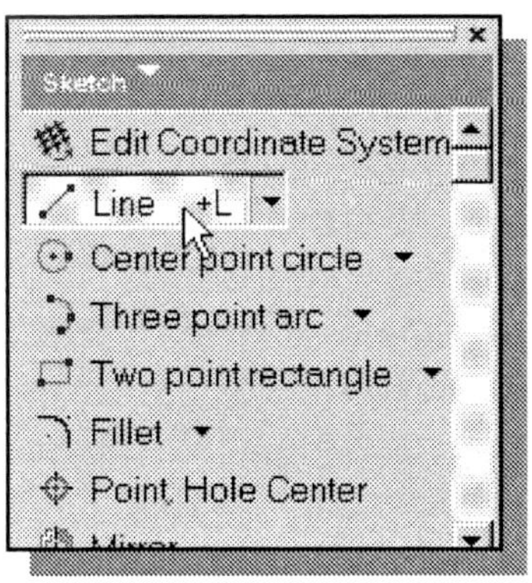

1. Move the graphics cursor to the ***LINE*** icon in the *Sketch* toolbar. A *Help-tip box* appears next to the cursor and a brief description of the command is displayed at the bottom of the drawing screen: *"Creates Straight line segments and tangent arcs."*

2. Select the icon by clicking once with the left-mouse-button; this will activate the ***LINE*** command. In the *Status Bar* area, near the bottom of the *Autodesk Inventor* drawing screen, the message *"Specify start point, drag off endpoint for tangent arcs"* is displayed. *Autodesk Inventor* expects us to identify the starting location of a straight line.

3. On your own, create and adjust the geometry by adding and modifying dimensions as shown below. (Hint: Modify the larger dimensions first.)

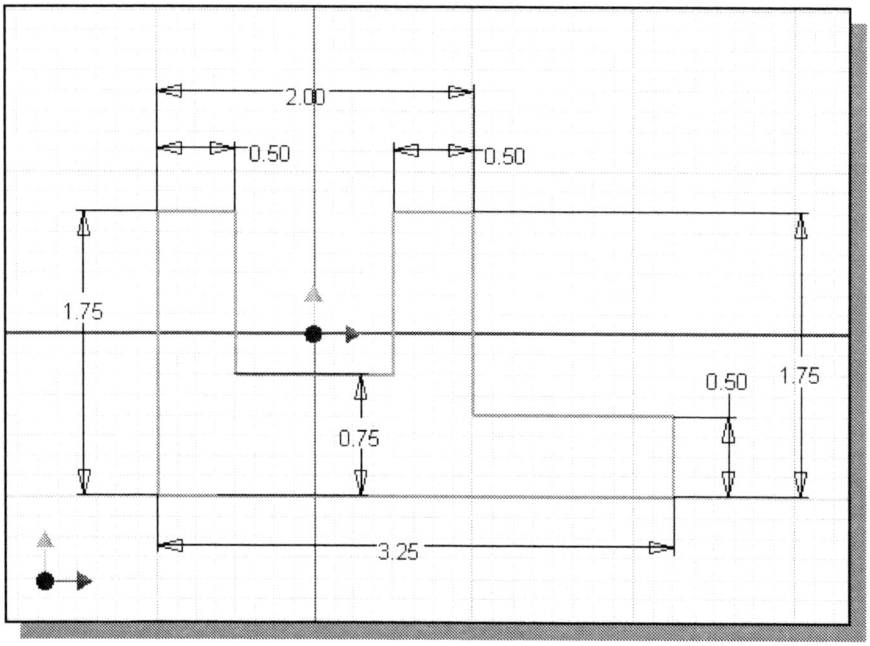

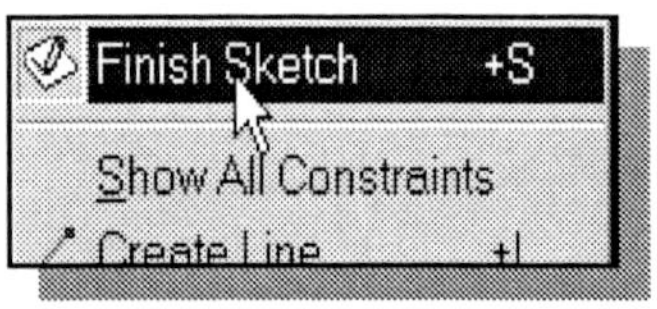

4. Inside the graphics window, click once with the right-mouse-button to display the option menu. Select **Finish Sketch** in the popup menu to end the *Sketch* option.

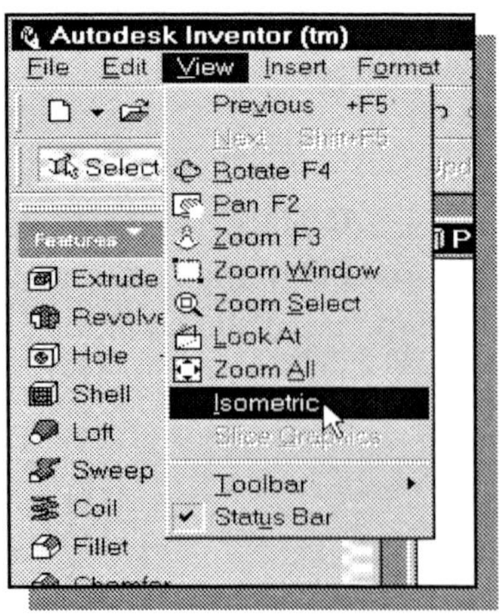

5. Select **Isometric** in the *View* pull-down menu to change the display to the isometric view

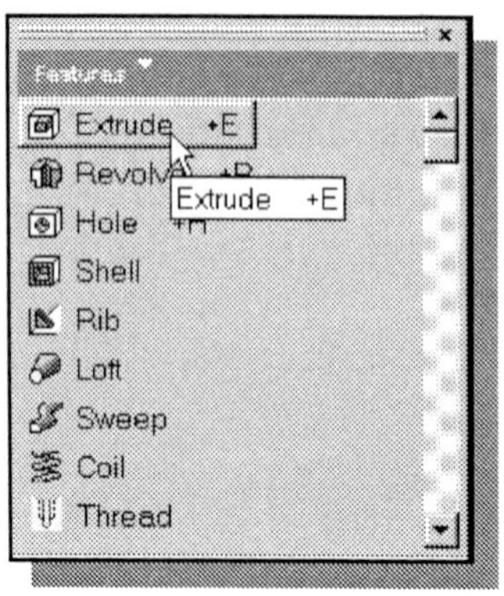

6. In the *Feature* toolbar (the toolbar that is located to the left side of the graphics window), select the ***Extrude*** command by releasing the left-mouse-button on the icon.

7. In the *Distance* option box, enter **2.5** as the extrusion distance.

8. In the *Extrude* popup window, left-click once the ***Mid-plane*** icon. The ***Mid-plane*** option allows us to extrude in both directions of the sketched profile.

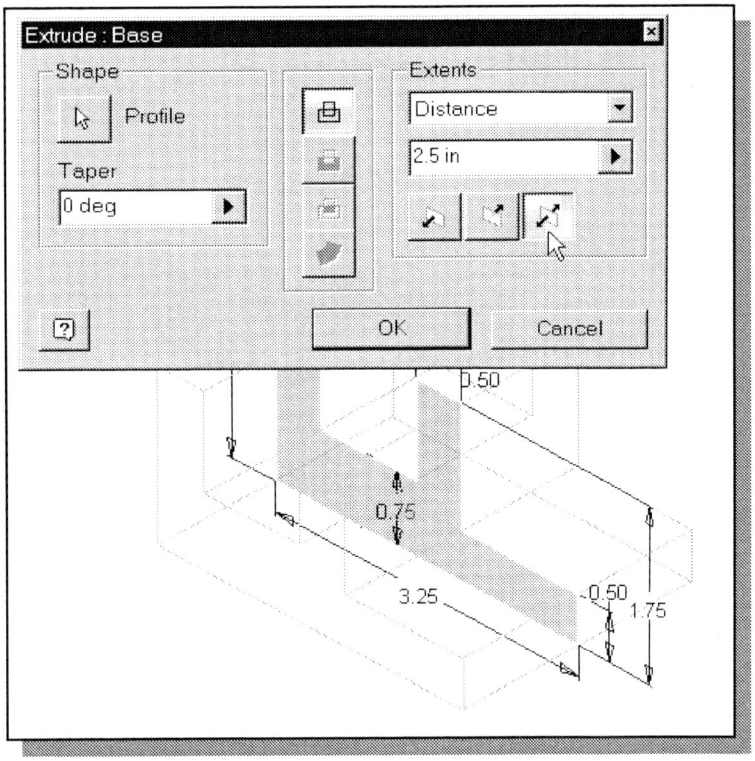

9. Click on the **OK** button to accept the settings and create the base feature.

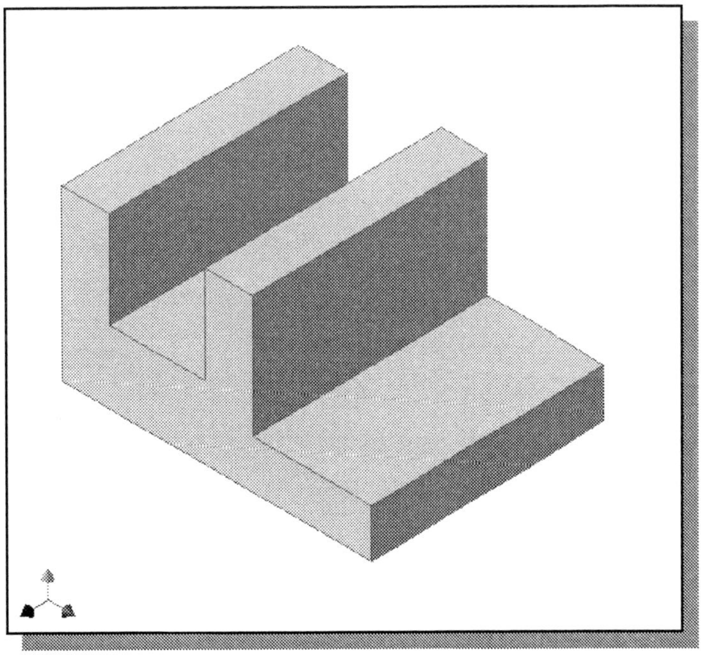

➤ On your own, use the *dynamic viewing functions* to view the 3D model. Also notice the extrusion feature is added to the *Model Tree.*

Add the Second Solid Feature

1. In the *Standard* toolbar select the ***Sketch*** command by left-clicking once on the icon.

2. In the *Status Bar* area, the message: "*Select face, workplane, sketch or sketch geometry.*" is displayed. *Autodesk Inventor* expects us to identify a planar surface, where the 2D sketch of the next feature is to be created. Move the graphics cursor on the 3D part and notice that *Autodesk Inventor* will automatically highlight feasible planes and surfaces as the cursor is on top of the different surfaces. Move the cursor inside the upper horizontal face of the 3D object as shown below.

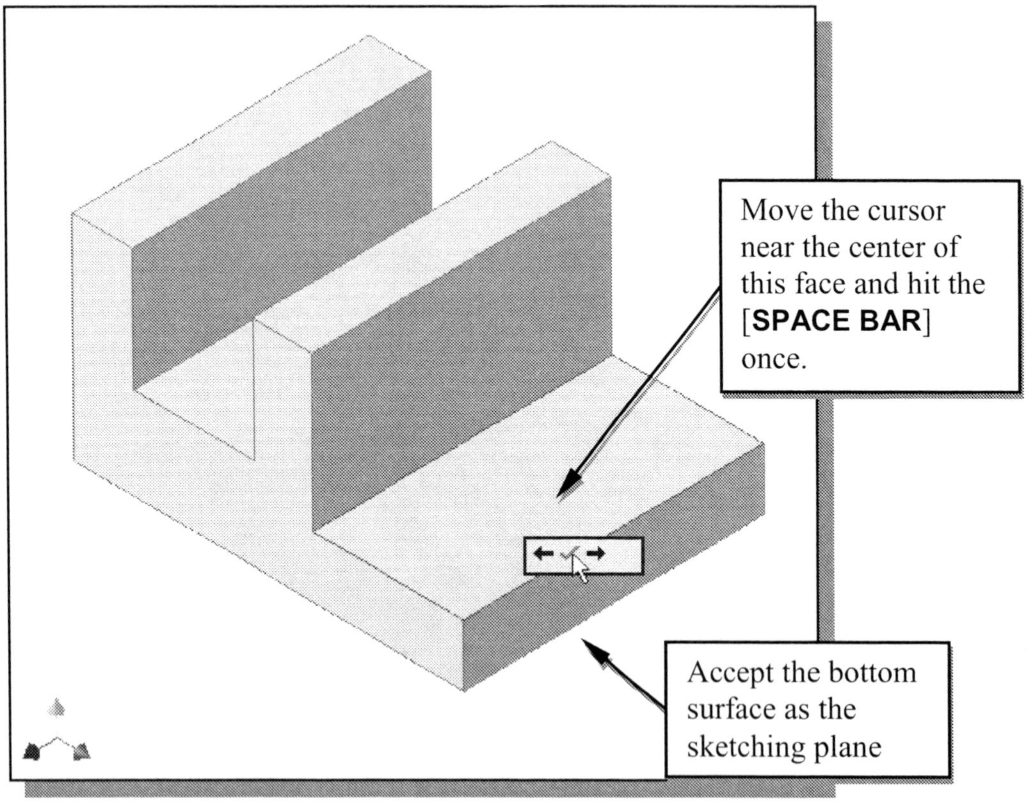

3. Hit the [**SPACE BAR**] once and notice the bottom face of the base feature is highlighted.

4. On your own, click on the left and/or the right arrows to examine all possible selections of surfaces.

5. Click on the check mark to select the bottom-horizontal face of the solid model when it is highlighted.

Creating a 2D sketch

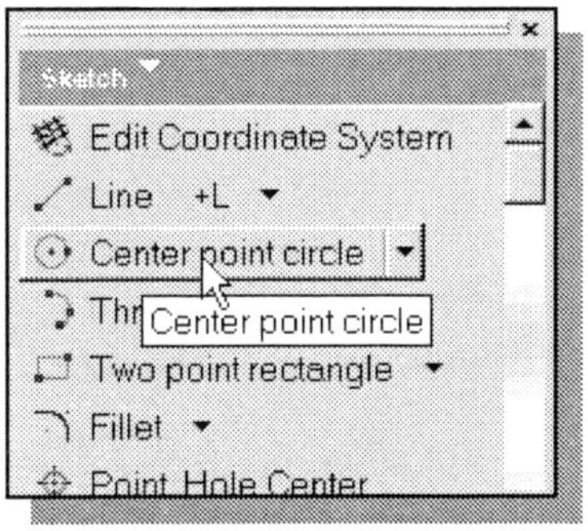

1. Select the ***Center point circle*** command by clicking once with the left-mouse-button on the icon in the *Sketch* toolbar.

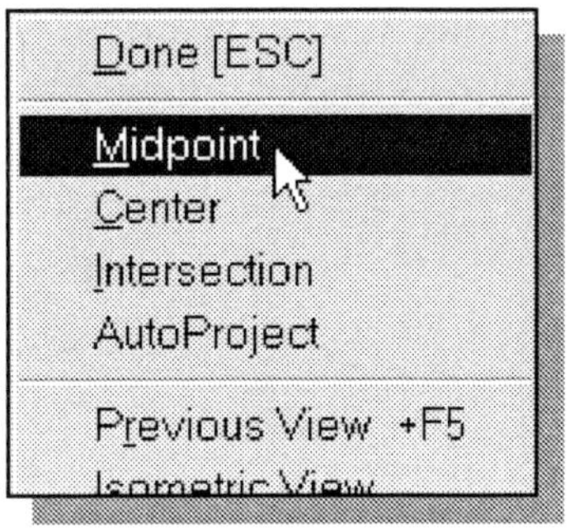

2. Inside the graphics window, click once with the right-mouse-button to display the option menu. Select the ***Midpoint*** option in the popup menu.

➢ Using the ***Midpoint*** option allows us to align the center of the circle to the midpoint of any edges of existing geometry.

3. Select the shorter edge of the base feature and locate the midpoint of the edge as shown in the below figure.

4. Select the corner of the base feature to create a circle as shown below.

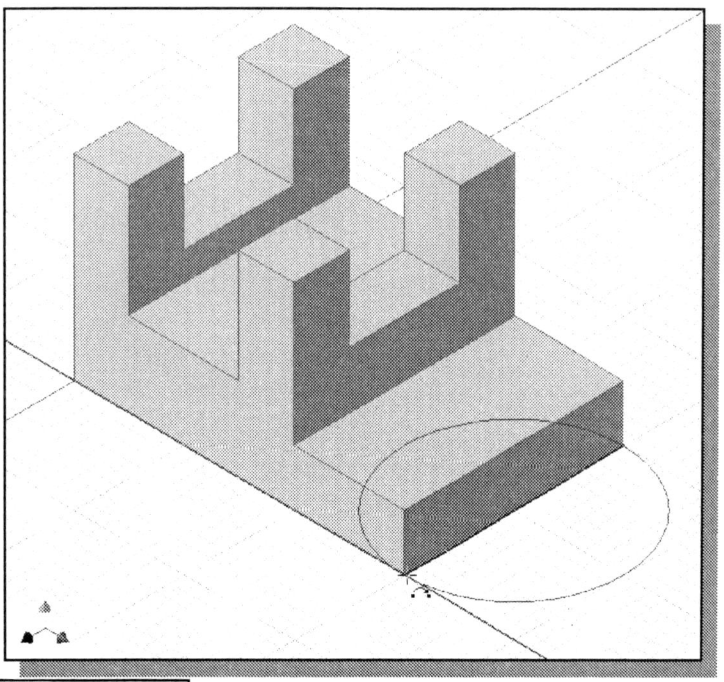

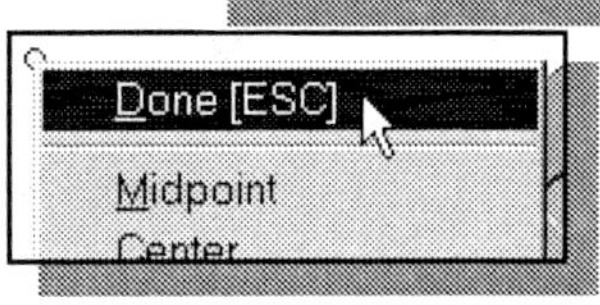

5. Inside the graphics window, click once with the right-mouse-button to display the option menu. Select **Done** in the popup menu to end the *Circle* command.

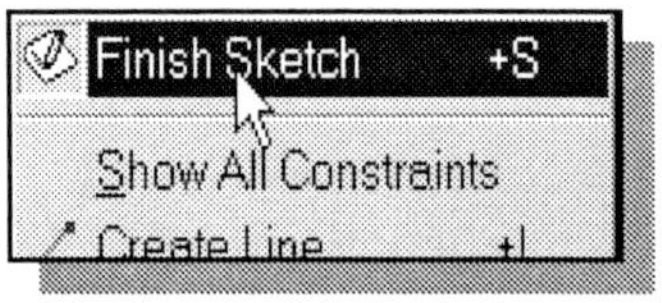

6. Inside the graphics window, click once with the right-mouse-button to display the option menu. Select **Finish Sketch** in the popup menu to end the *Sketch* option.

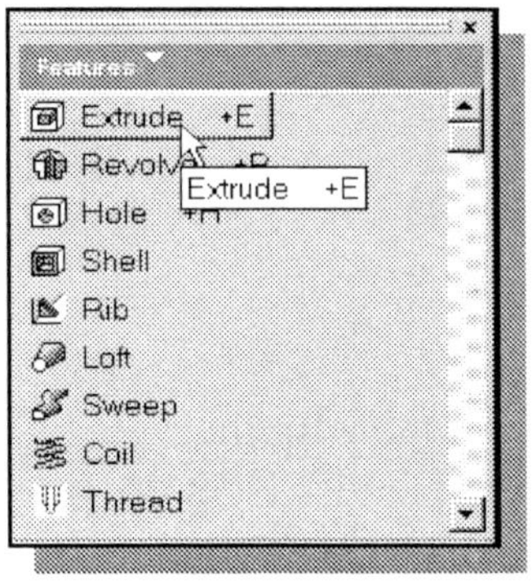

7. In the *Feature* toolbar (the toolbar that is located to the left side of the graphics window), select the ***Extrude*** command by releasing the left-mouse-button on the icon.

8. In the *Extrude* popup window, the ***Profile*** button is pressed down; *Autodesk Inventor* expects us to identify the profile to be extruded. Move the cursor inside the circle we just created and left-click once to select the region as the profile to be extruded.

9. In the *Extrude* popup window, set the *Extents* option to ***To*** as shown below. Confirm the operation option is set to ***Join.***

10. Select the top face of the base feature as the termination surface for the extrusion.

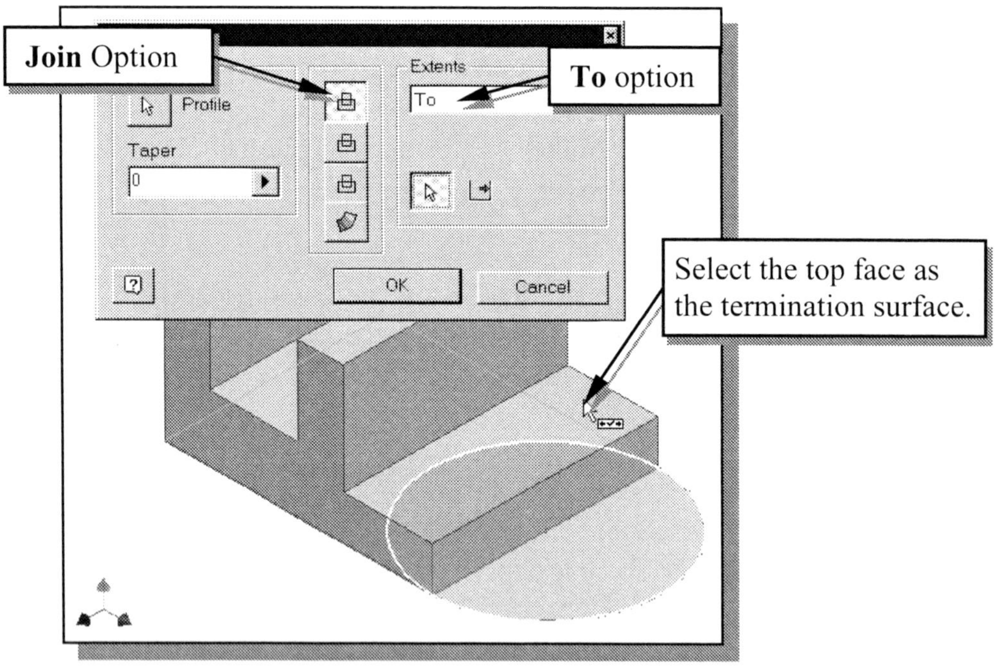

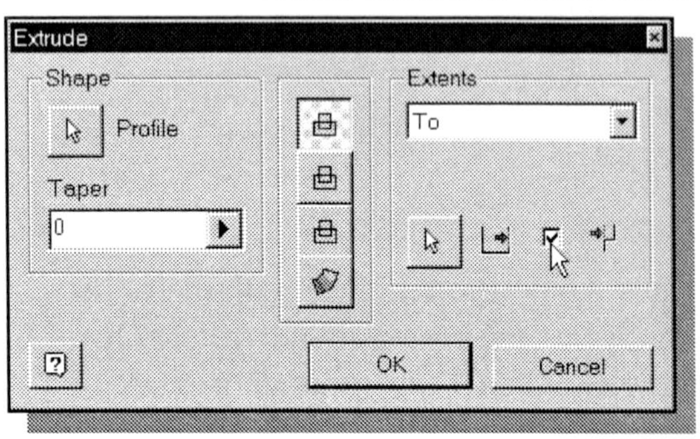

11. Click on the **option box** located in the *Extents* option area; the selected surface will be used as the termination surface.

12. Click on the **OK** button to proceed with the *Join* operation.

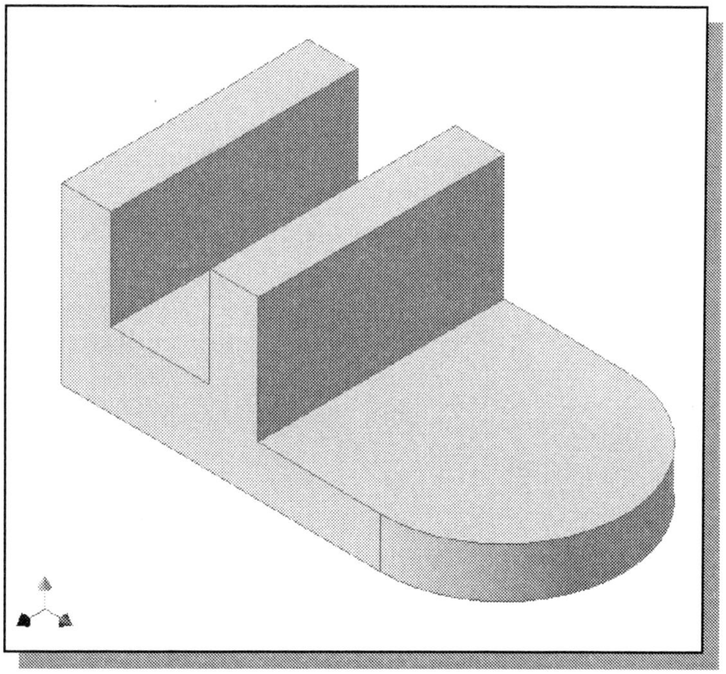

Renaming the Part Features

- Currently, our model contains two extruded features. The feature is highlighted in the display area when we select the feature in the *Browser* window. Each time a new feature is created, the feature is also displayed in the *Model Tree* window. By default, *Autodesk Inventor* will use generic names for part features. However, when we begin to deal with parts with a large number of features, it will be much easier to identify the features using more meaningful names.

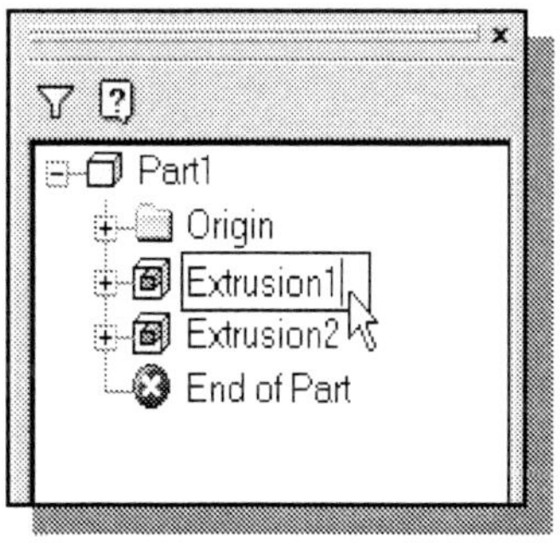

1. Select the first extruded feature in the *Browser* area by left-clicking once on the name of the feature, ***Extrusion1***. Notice the selected feature is highlighted in the graphics window.

2. Inside the *Browser* area, left-mouse-click on the first extruded feature name again to enter the editing mode.

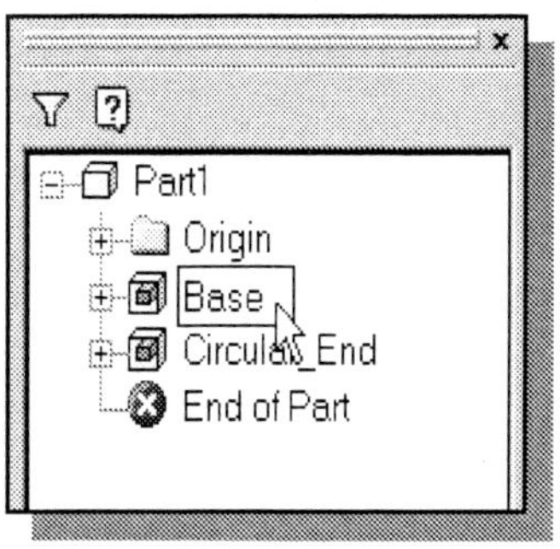

3. Enter ***Base*** as the new name for the first extruded feature.

4. On your own, rename the second extruded feature to ***Circular_End***.

Adjusting the Width of the Base Feature

❖ One of the main advantages of parametric modeling is the ease of performing part modifications at any time in the design process. Part modifications can be done through accessing the features in the history tree. *Autodesk Inventor* remembers the history of a part, including all the rules that were used to create it, so that changes can be made to any operation that was performed to create the part. For our *L-Support* design, we will reduce the size of the base feature from 3.25 inches to 3.0 inches, and the extrusion distance to 2.25 inches.

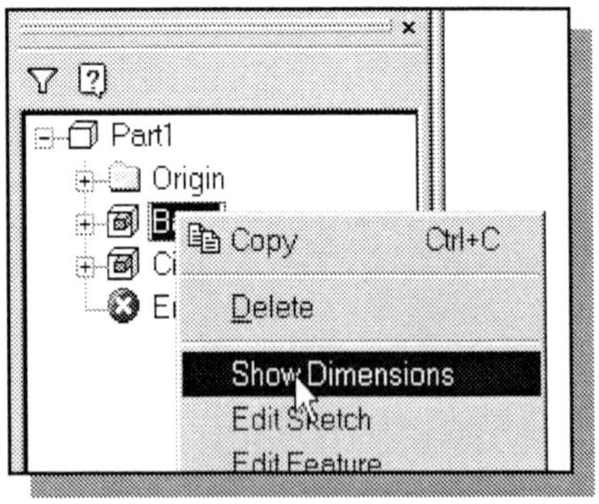

1. Select the first extruded feature, ***Base***, in the *Browser* area. Notice the selected feature is highlighted in the graphics window.

2. Inside the *Browser* area, **right-mouse-click** on the first extruded feature to bring up the option menu and select **Show Dimensions** option in the pop-up menu.

3. All dimensions used to create the ***Base*** feature are displayed on the screen. Select the overall-width of the ***Base*** feature, the **3.25** dimension value, by double-clicking on the dimension text as shown below.

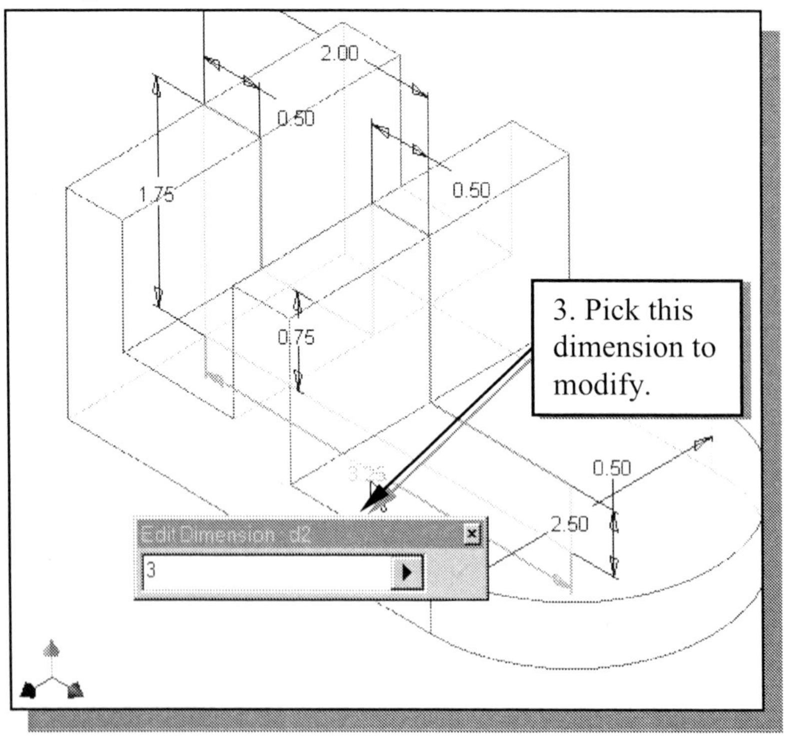

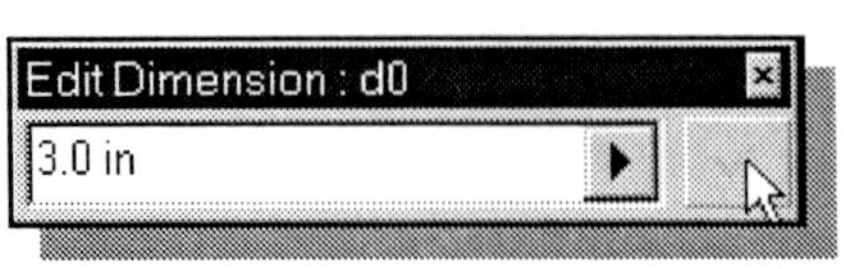

4. Enter **3.0** in the *Edit Dimension* window.

5. On your own, repeat the above steps and modify the extruded distance from **2.5** to **2.0**.

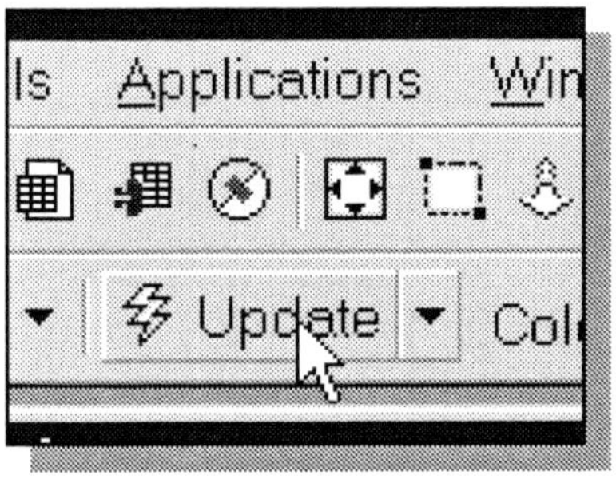

6. Click on the **Update** button in the *Standard* toolbar area as shown.

➢ Note that *Autodesk Inventor* updates the model by re-linking all elements used to create the model. Any problems or conflicts that occur will also be displayed during the updating process. Once a feature has been created, it is very easy to modify its dimensional values in a feature-based parametric solid modeling software, such as *Autodesk Inventor*.

Adding a Placed Feature

1. In the *Standard* toolbar select the ***Sketch*** command by left-clicking once on the icon.

2. Pick the **bottom face** of the ***Base*** feature as shown.

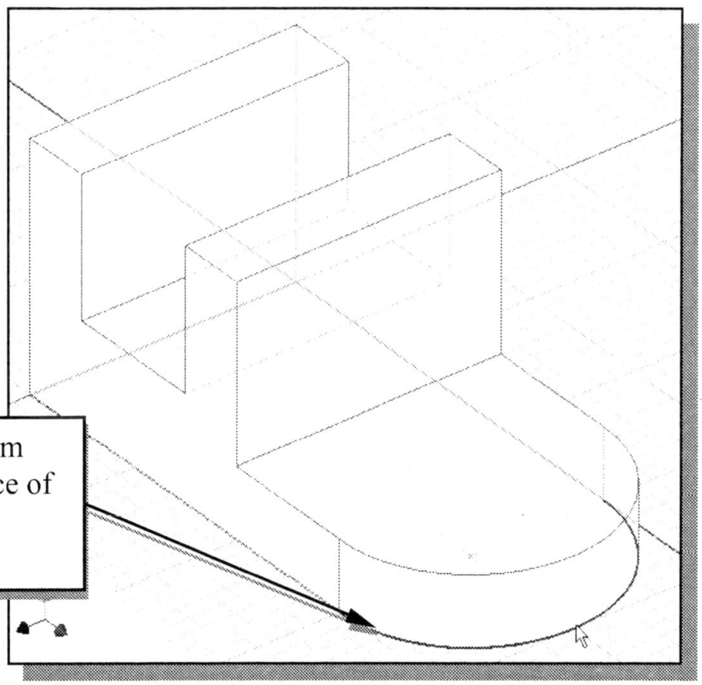

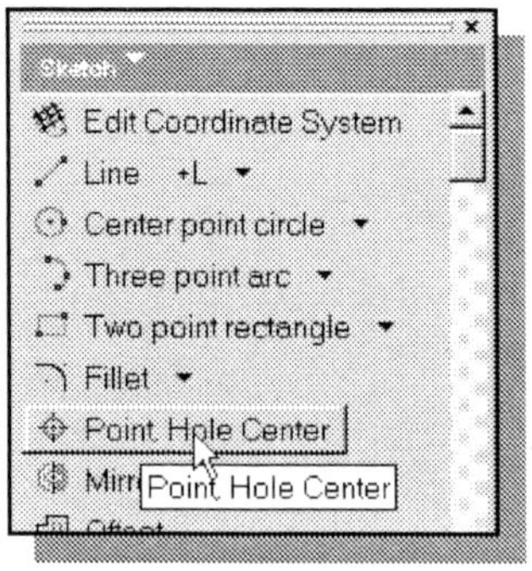

3. Select the ***Point, Hole Center*** command by clicking once with the **left-mouse-button** on the icon in the *Sketch* toolbar.

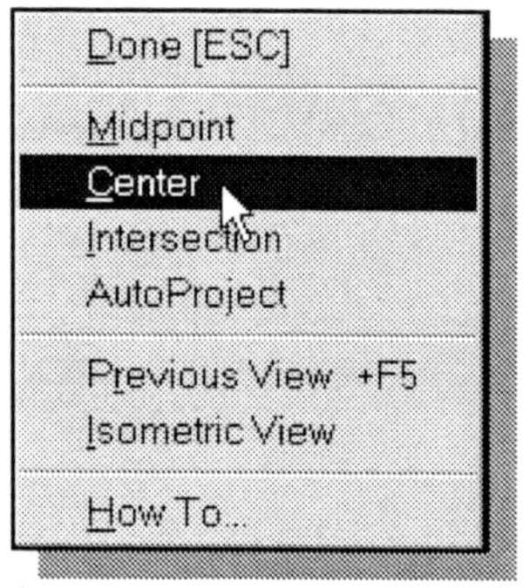

4. Inside the graphics window, click once with the **right-mouse-button** to display the option menu. Select the **Center** option in the popup menu.

5. We will align the center of the circle to the center point of the ***Circular_End*** feature. Select the **top arc** of the circular feature. A *hole center* is placed at the center of the selected *arc*.

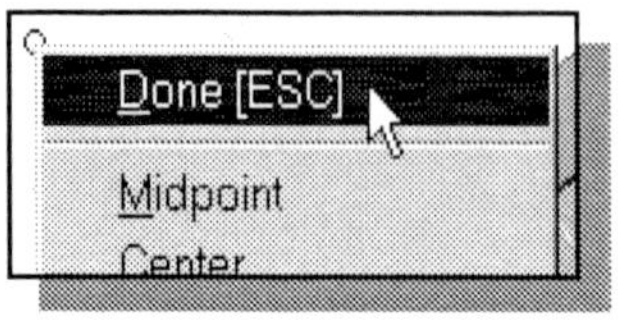

6. Inside the graphics window, click once with the **right-mouse-button** to display the option menu. Select **Done** in the popup menu to end the *Hole Center* command.

7. Inside the graphics window, click once with the **right-mouse-button** to display the option menu. Select **Finish Sketch** in the popup menu to end the ***Sketch*** option.

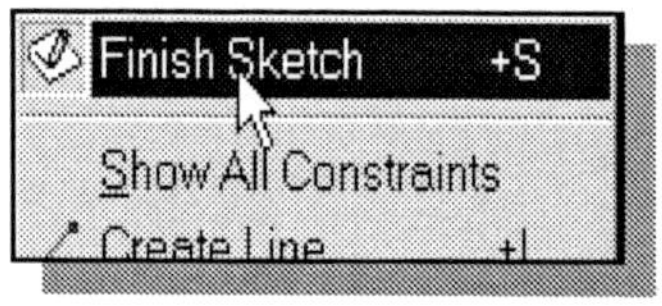

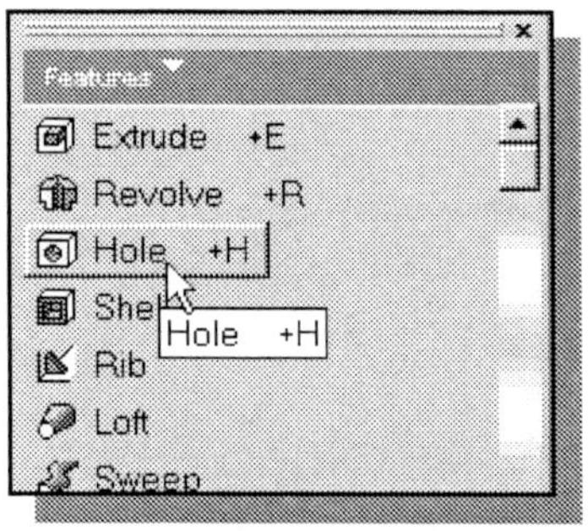

8. In the *Feature* toolbar (the toolbar that is located to the left side of the graphics window), select the ***Hole*** command by releasing the left-mouse-button on the icon.

9. In the *Holes* window, the **Centers** button is pressed down; *Autodesk Inventor* allows us to identify as many centers as we like to create the same feature. Set the *Termination* option to ***Through All***.

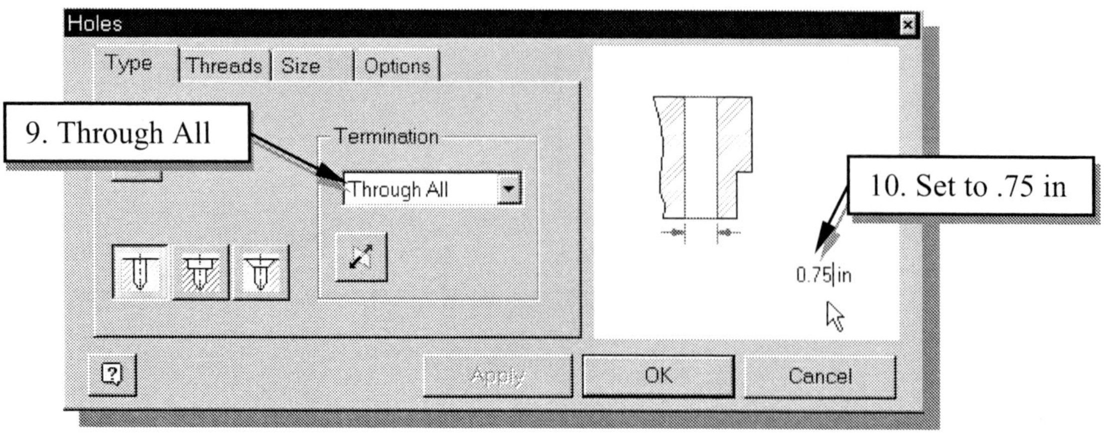

10. In the ***Drill Size*** option window, enter **.75** as the diameter of the drill.

11. Click on the **OK** button to proceed with the ***Hole*** feature.

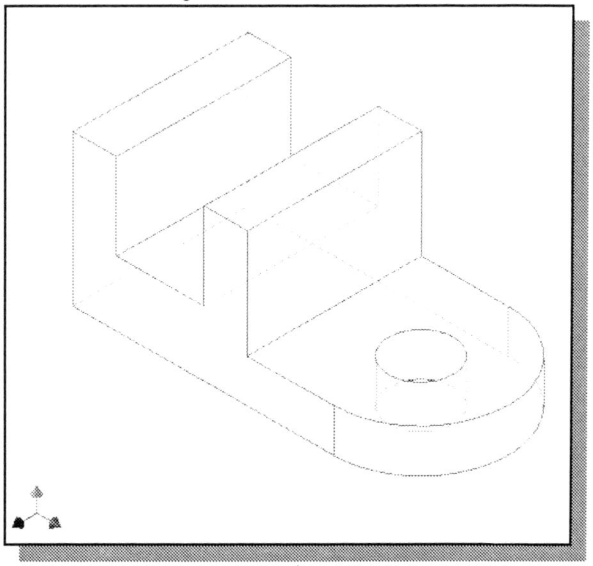

Creating a Rectangular Cut Feature

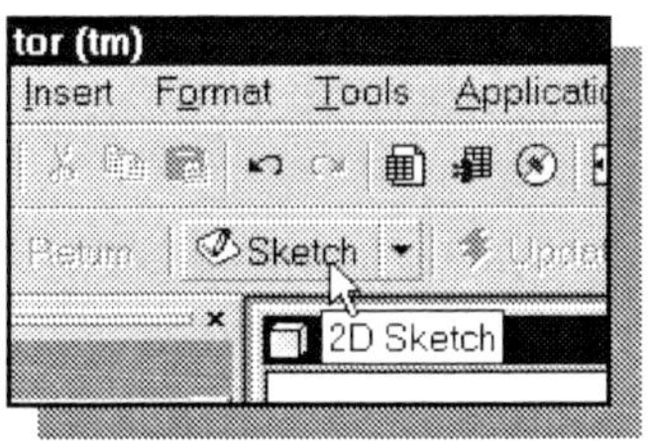

1. In the *Standard* toolbar select the ***Sketch*** command by left-clicking once on the icon.

2. Pick the **vertical face** of the solid as shown. (Note the alignment of the origin of the sketch plane.)

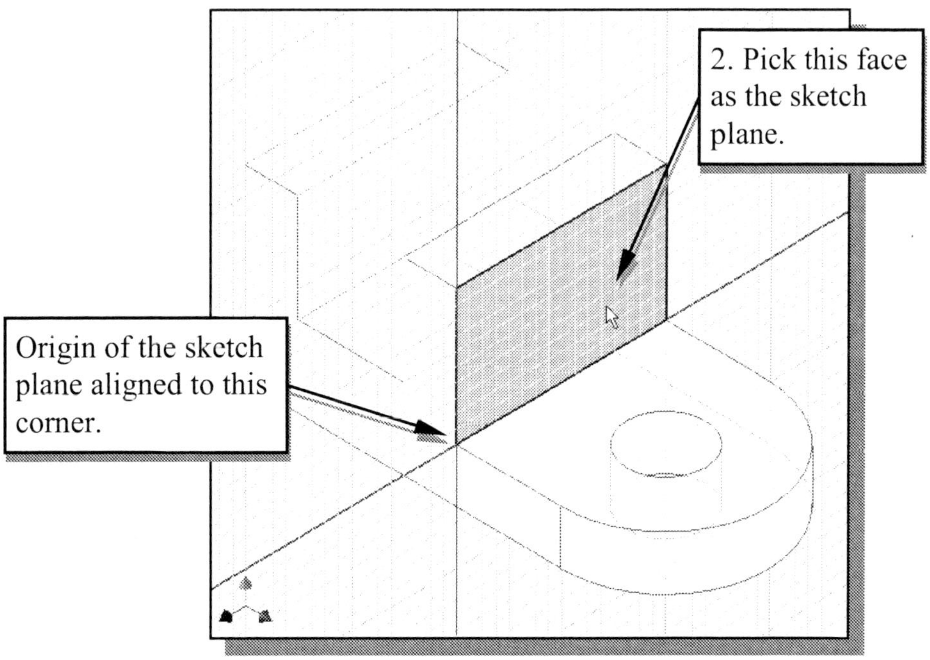

➢ On your own, create a rectangular cut (**1.0 x 0.75**) feature (***To Next*** option) as shown and rename the feature to ***Rect_Cut***.

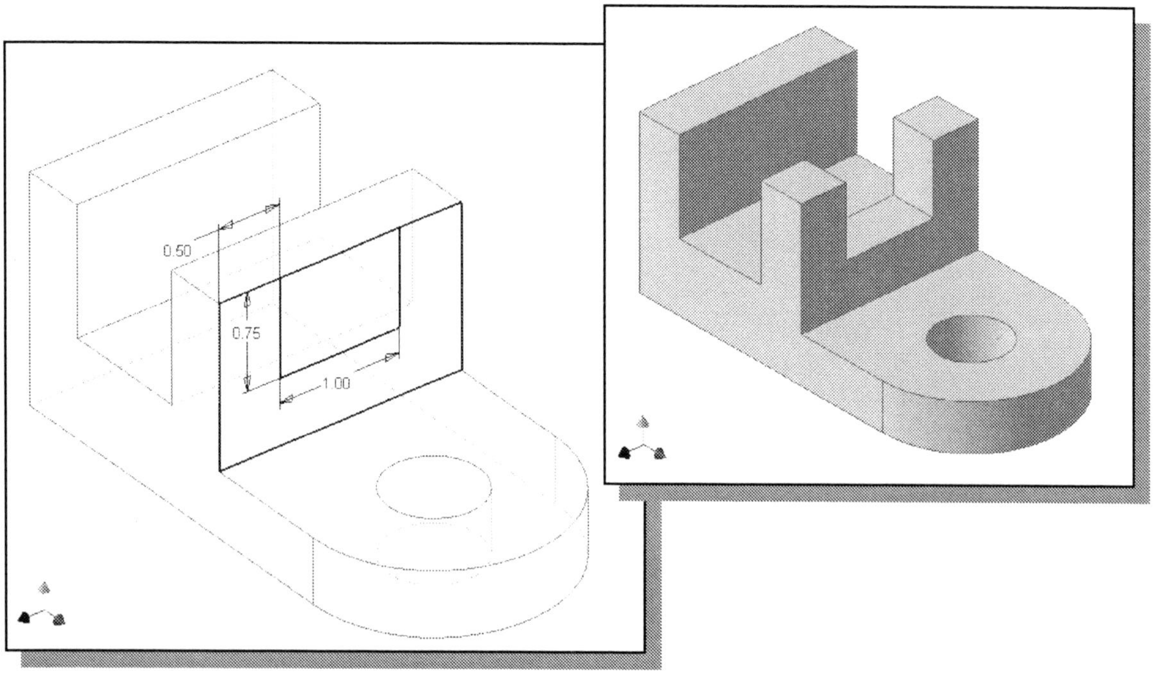

History-based Part Modifications

- *Autodesk Inventor* uses the *history-based part modification* approach, which enables us to make modifications to the appropriate features and re-link the rest of the history tree without having to reconstruct the model from scratch. We can think of it as going back in time and modifying some aspects of the modeling steps used to create the part. We can modify any feature that we have created. As an example, we will adjust the depth of the rectangular cutout.

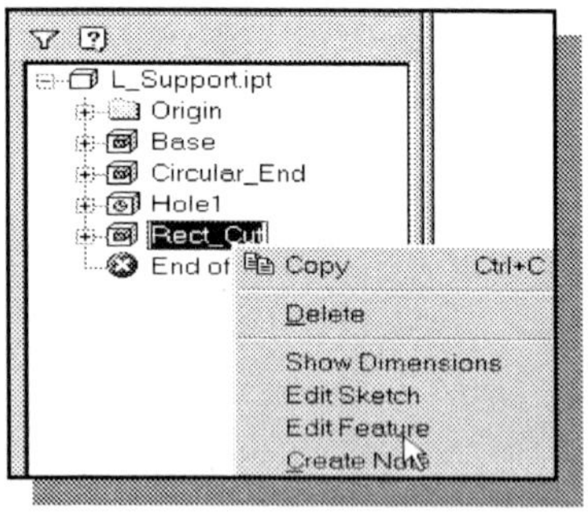

1. In the *Browser* window, select the last cut feature, ***Rect_Cut,*** by left-clicking once on the name of the feature.

2. In the *Browser* window, **right-mouse-click** once on the ***Rect_Cut*** feature.

3. Select **Edit Feature** in the pop-up menu. Notice the *Extrude* dialog box appears on the screen.

4. In the *Extrude* dialog box, set the *Termination* method to the ***All*** option.

5. Click on the **OK** button to accept the settings.

- As can been seen, the history-based modification approach is very straightforward and it only took a few seconds to adjust the cut feature to the ***Through All*** option.

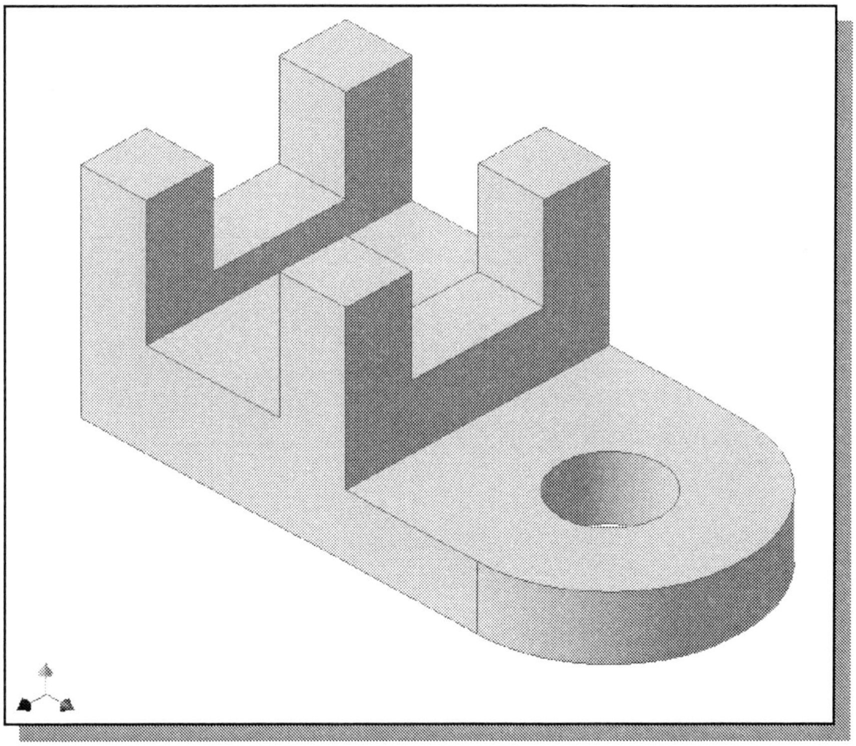

A Design Change

❖ Engineering designs usually go through many revisions and changes. *Autodesk Inventor* provides an assortment of tools to handle design changes quickly and effectively. We will demonstrate some of the tools available by changing the ***Base*** feature of the design.

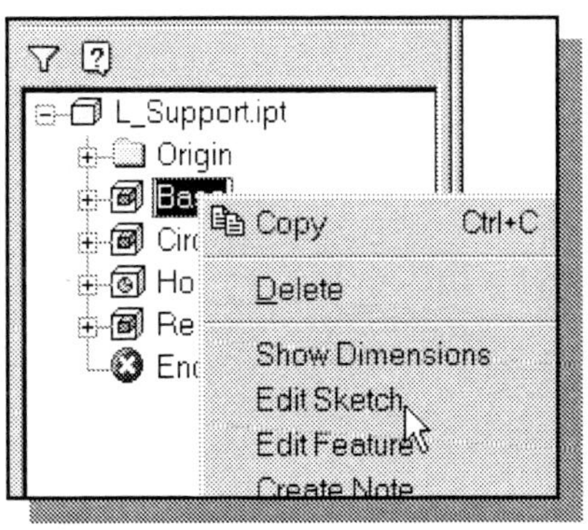

1. In the *Browser* window, select the ***Base*** feature by left-clicking once on the name of the feature.

2. In the *Browser*, **right-mouse-click** once on the ***Base*** feature to bring up the option menu, then pick **Edit Sketch** in the pop-up menu.

❖ *Autodesk Inventor* will now display the original 2D sketch of the selected feature in the graphics window. We have literally gone back in time to the point where we first created the 2D sketch. Notice the feature being modified is also highlighted in the desktop *Browser*.

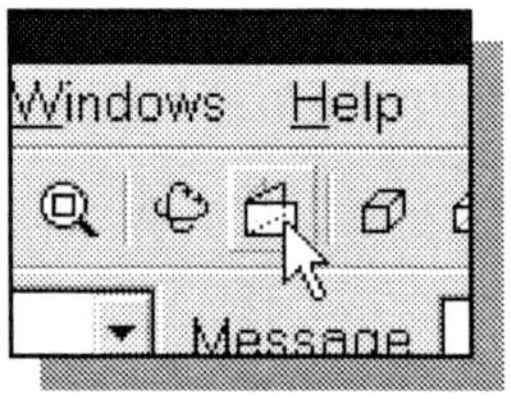

3. Click on the ***Look At*** icon in the *Standard* toolbar area.

- The ***Look At*** command automatically aligns the *sketch plane* of a selected entity to the screen.

4. Select any line segement of the 2D sketch. We have literally gone back in time to the point where we first created the 2D sketch.

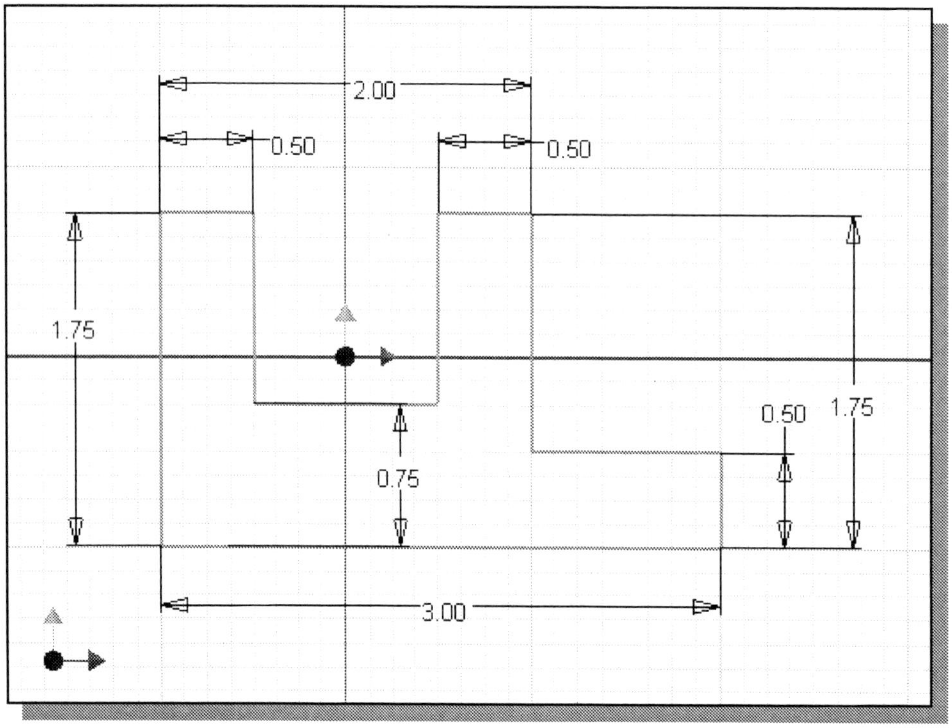

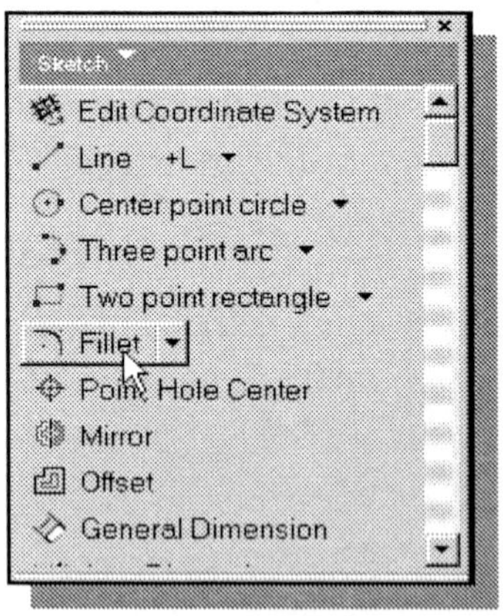

5. Select the ***Fillet*** command in the *Sketch* toolbar.

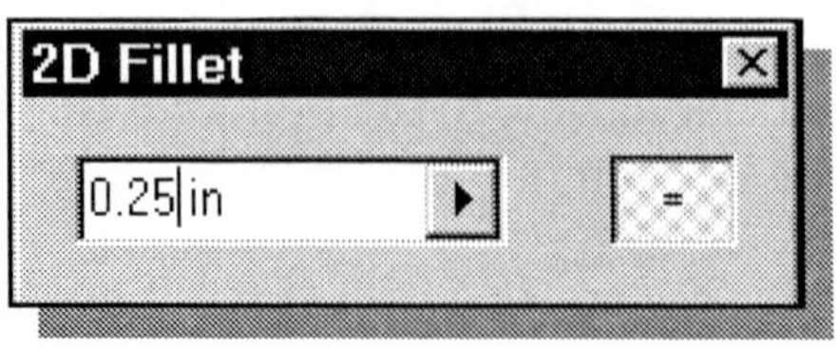

6. In the graphics window, enter **0.25** as the new radius of the fillet.

7. Select the two edges as shown to create the fillet.

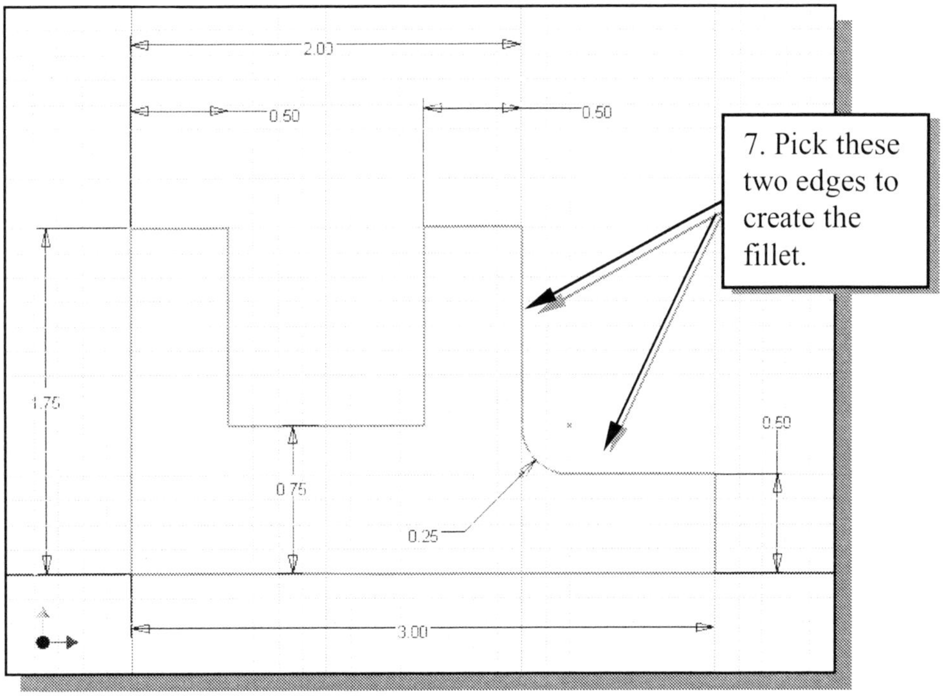

- Note that the fillet is created automatically with the dimension attached. The attached dimension can also be modified through the history tree.

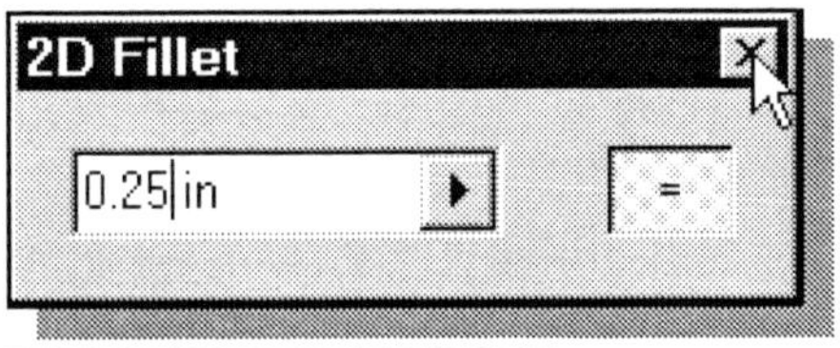

8. Click on the [**X**] icon in the *Radius* window to end the *Fillet* command.

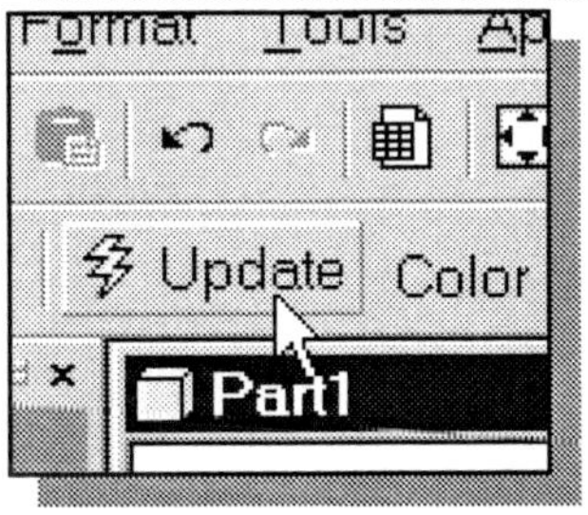

9. Click on the **Update** button in the *Standard* toolbar area as shown.

- The system will attempt to rebuild the part with the updated feature. A warning dialogue box appears on the screen.

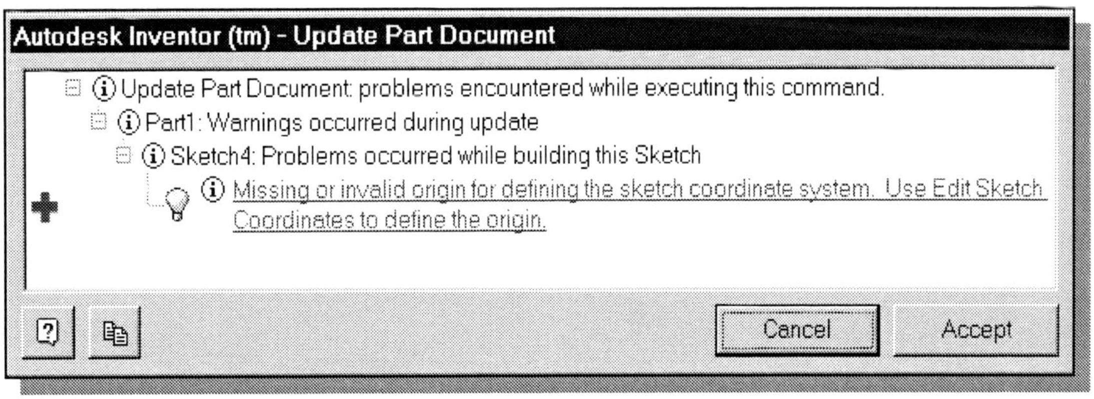

What Happened?

- The message inside the *Update Part Document* window reveals the problems that *Autodesk Inventor* encountered while rebuilding all the features with the modifications that were made.

  ❖ For our example, *Autodesk Inventor* identified the problem occurred while rebuilding ***Sketch4***. The problem is "*Missing or invalid origin for defining the sketch coordinate system.*" *Autodesk Inventor* also suggested a possible solution to this problem: "*Use Edit Sketch Coordinates to define the Origin.*"

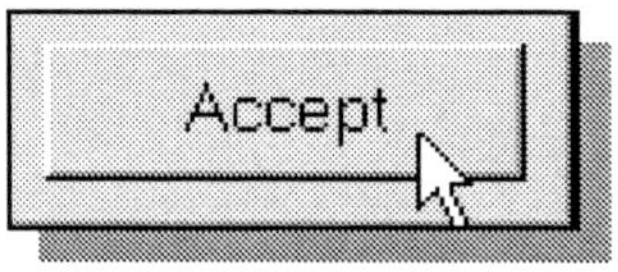

1. Click on the **Accept** button to proceed with the modification. Notice in the *Browser* window, a special marker is displayed next to the feature where problems were encountered.

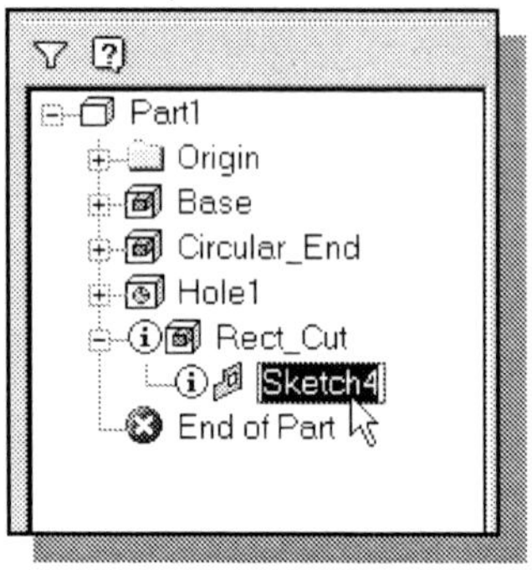

2. Click on the [+] symbol in front of the ***Rect_Cut*** feature to display more information on the feature.

➢ The 2D sketch, ***Sketch4***, is one of the elements of the ***Rect_Cut*** feature.

3. Select the 2D sketch, ***Sketch4***, in the *Browser* area. Notice the selected feature, along with its dimensions, is highlighted in the graphics window.

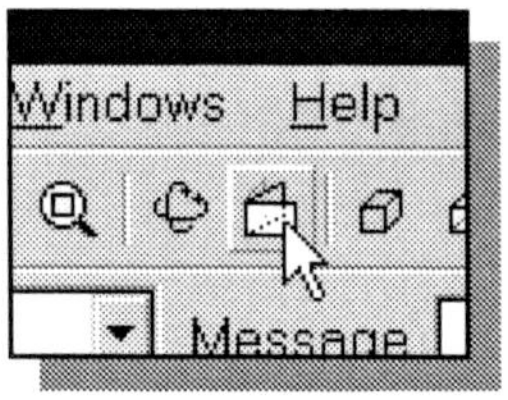

4. Click on the ***Look At*** icon in the *Standard* toolbar area.

- The ***Look At*** command automatically aligns the *sketch plane* of the selected entity to the screen.

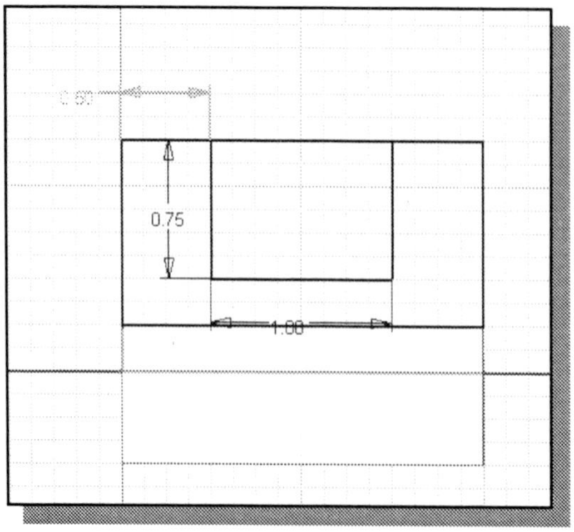

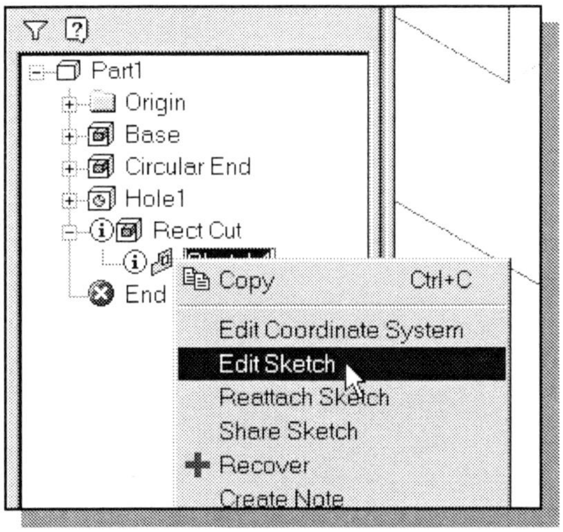

5. In the *Browser*, **right-mouse-click** once on the ***Sketch4*** feature to bring up the option menu, then pick **Edit Sketch** in the pop-up menu.

6. On your own, switch to the ***Isometric* view** to examine the alignment of the origin of the sketch plane.

➢ The origin of ***Rect_Cut*'s** sketch plane is aligned to the lower left corner of the vertical face as shown. This corner no long exists after we added the fillet to the 2D sketch of the ***Base*** feature. The *Rect_Cut* feature is referencing a non-existing corner, which caused the error during the update process.

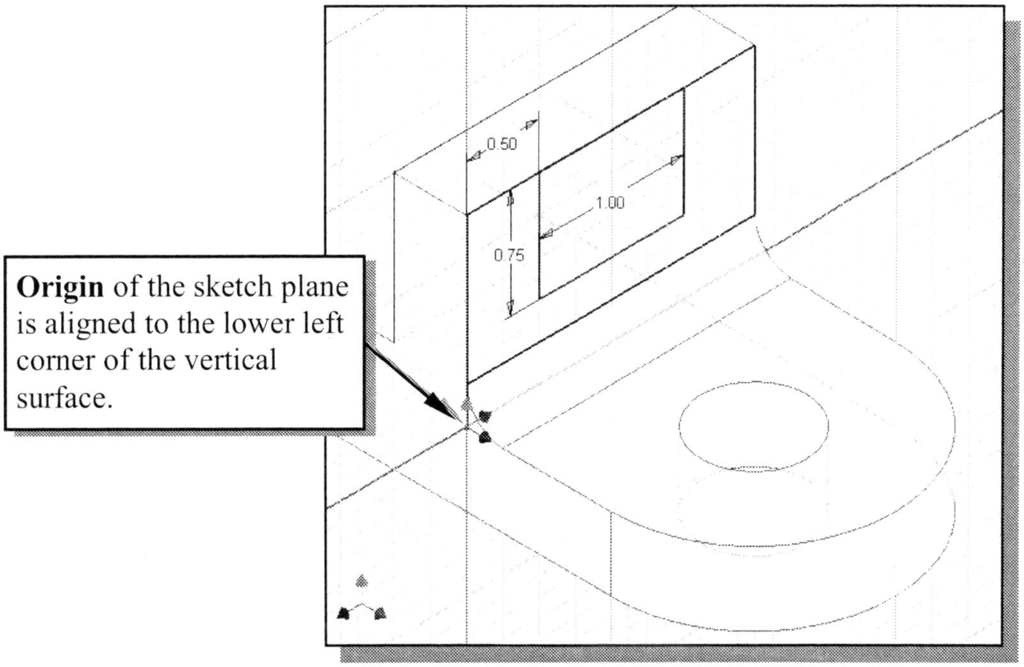

❖ Now that we have identified the source of the problem, we can proceed to correct this problem by aligning the origin of the sketch plane to another location. To modify the sketch coordinate system, we will first exit the Edit Sketch option.

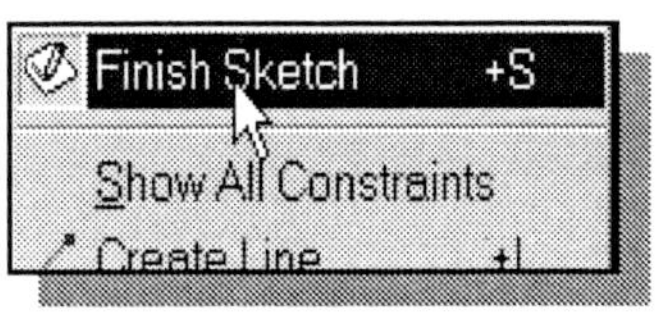

7. Inside the graphics window, click once with the **right-mouse-button** to display the option menu. Select **Finish Sketch** in the popup menu to end the ***Edit Sketch*** option.

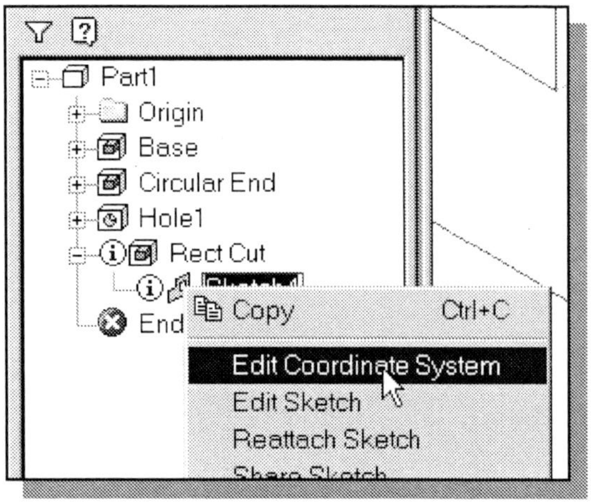

8. Select the **Edit Coordinate System** option by clicking once with the **right-mouse-button** on ***Sketch4*** in the *Sketch* toolbar.

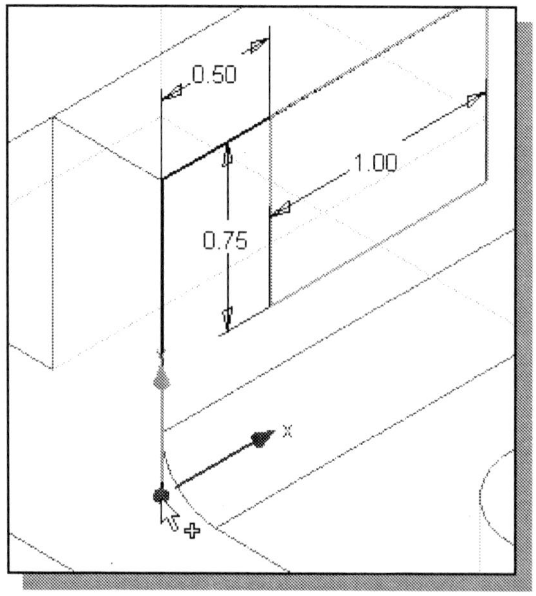

9. In the *Status Bar* area, near the bottom of the *Autodesk Inventor* drawing screen, the message "*Select origin, X-axis or Y-axis for alignment*" is displayed. Click on the origin as shown in the figure.

10. In the *Status Bar* area, near the bottom of the *Autodesk Inventor* drawing screen, the message "*Select a Vertex, Circular Edge, Workpoint or SketchPoint*" is displayed. Click on the **top-left corner** of the vertical face of the solid model as shown below. The origin of the sketch plane coordinate system is moved to the new location.

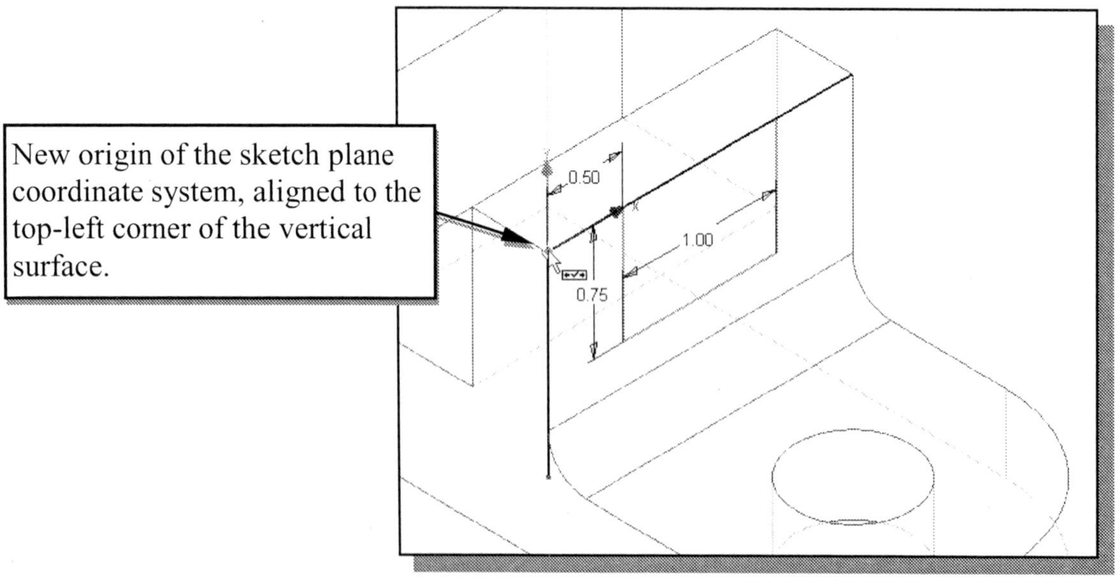

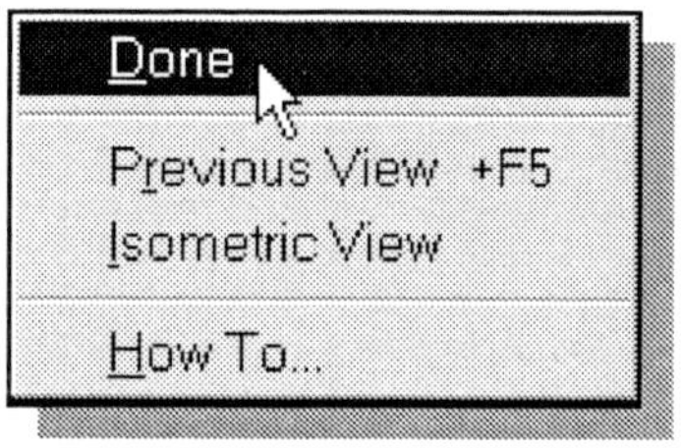

11. Inside the graphics window, click once with the **right-mouse-button** to display the option menu. Select **Finish Sketch** in the popup menu to end the ***Edit Coordinate System*** option.

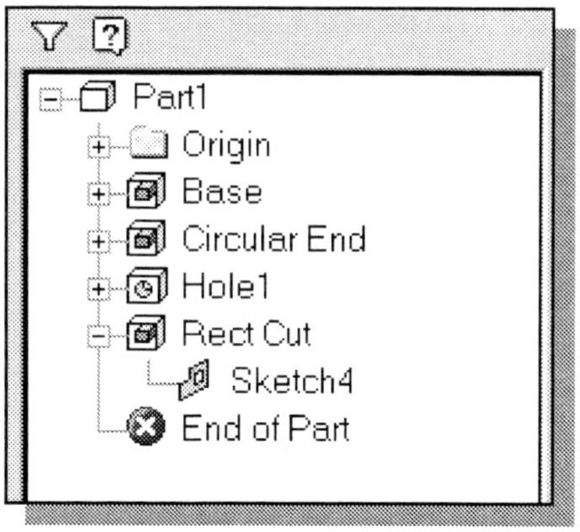

- By modifying the sketch coordinate system, the system updates the part automatically with the updated feature. This time, no warning dialogue box appeared and the special marker is also removed from the part browser area. We have successfully corrected the problem encountered during the base sketch modification.

❖ In a typical design process, the initial design will undergo many analyses, testing, and reviews. The *history-based part modification* approach is an extremely powerful tool that enables us to quickly update the design. At the same time, it is quite clear that PLANNING AHEAD is also important in doing feature-based modeling.

Questions:

1. What are stored in the *Autodesk Inventor History Tree*?

2. When extruding, what is the difference between *Distance* and *All*?

3. What is the *history-based part modification* approach?

4. What determines how a model reacts when other features in the model change?

5. Describe the steps to modify the coordinate system of existing sketches?

6. Describe two methods available in *Autodesk Inventor* to *modify the dimension value* of the parametric sketch.

7. Create *History Tree sketches* showing the steps you plan to use to create the two models shown on the next page:

Ex.1)

Ex.2)

Exercises:

1.

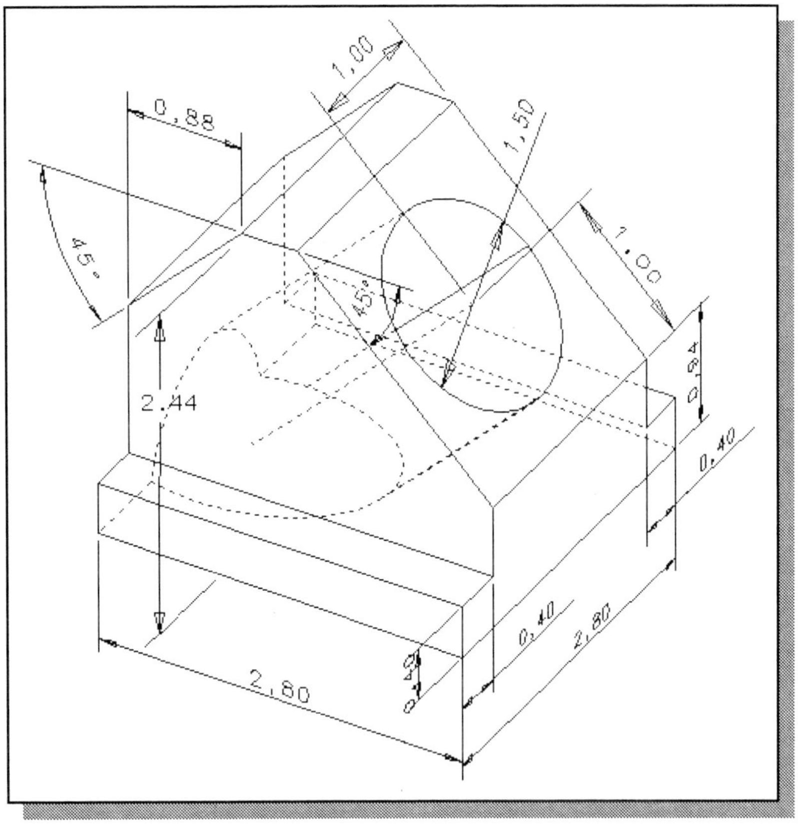

2.

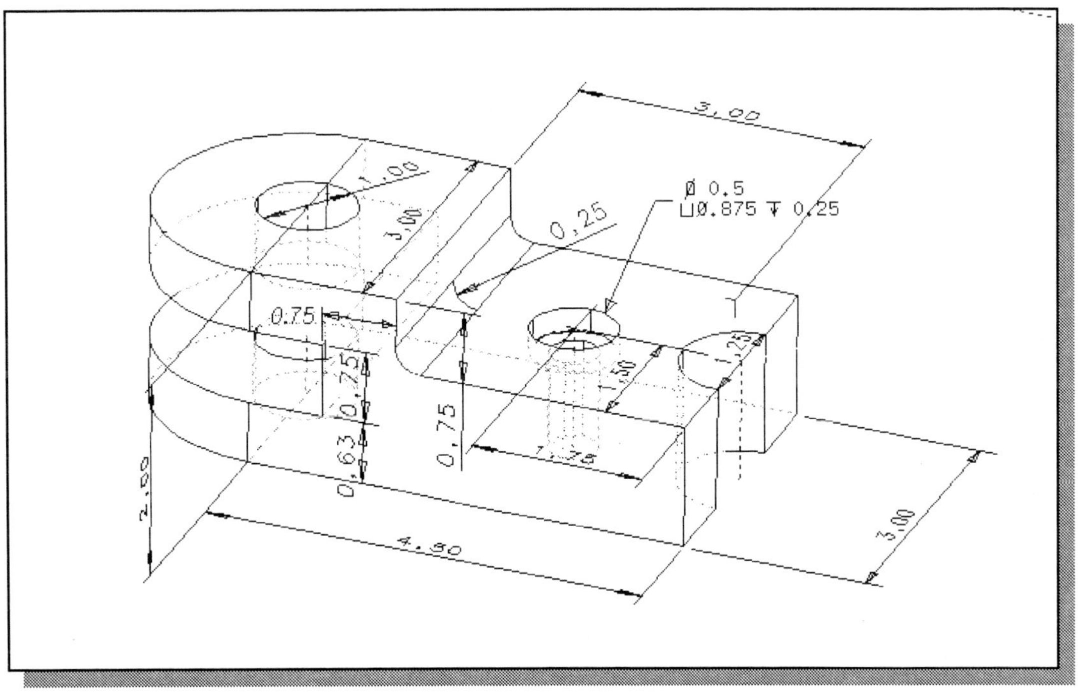

Notes:

Lesson 4
Parametric Constraints Fundamentals

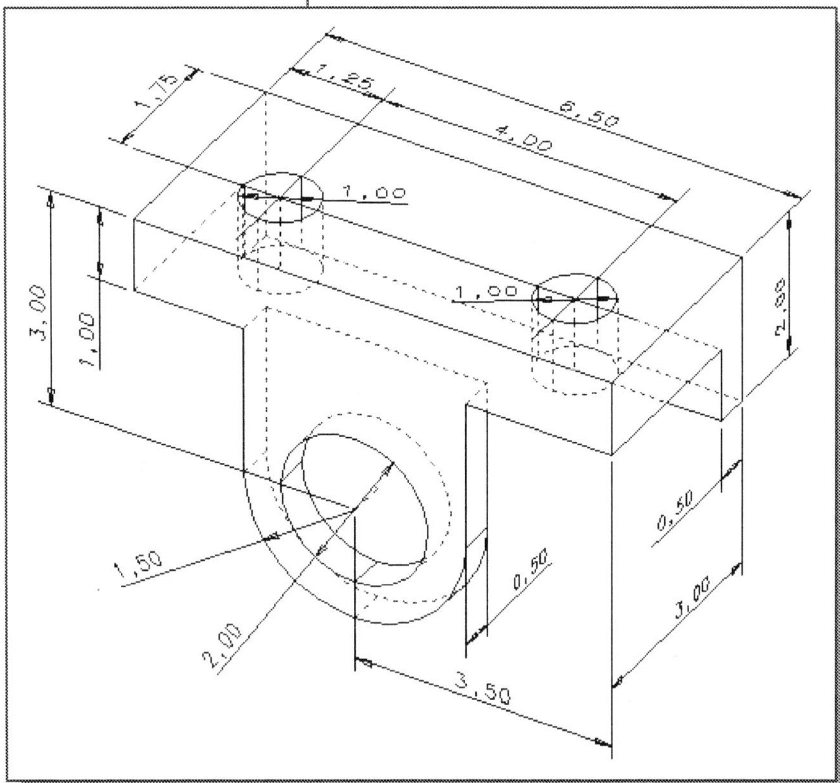

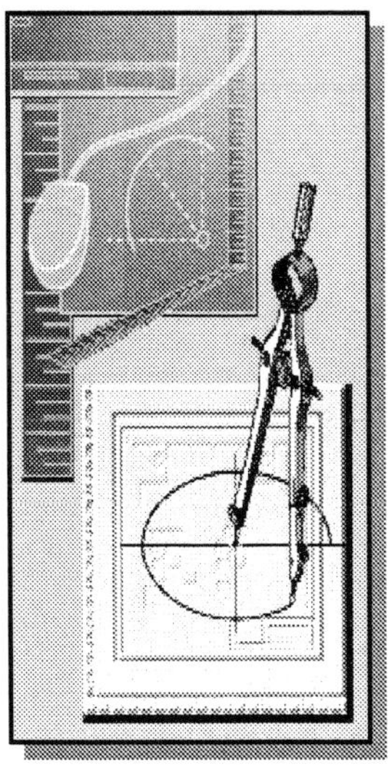

Learning Objectives

When you have completed this lesson, you will be able to:

- **Create Parametric Relations.**
- **Use Dimensional Variables.**
- **Display, Add, and Delete Geometric Constraints.**
- **Understand and Apply Different Geometric Constraints.**
- **Display and Modify Parametric Relations.**
- **Create Fully Constrained Sketches.**

CONSTRAINTS and RELATIONS

A primary and essential difference between parametric modeling and previous generation computer modeling is that parametric modeling captures the *design intent*. In the previous lessons, we have seen that the design philosophy of "*shape before size*" is implemented through the use of *Autodesk Inventor's* *Profile* and *Dimension* commands. In performing geometric constructions, dimensional values are necessary to describe the **SIZE** and **LOCATION** of constructed geometric entities. Besides using dimensions to define the geometry, we can also apply geometric rules to control geometric entities. More importantly, *Autodesk Inventor* can capture design intent through the use of **geometric constraints**, **dimensional constraints**, and **parametric relations.** In *Autodesk Inventor*, there are two types of constraints: **geometric constraints** and **dimensional constraints**. For part modeling in *Autodesk Inventor*, constraints are applied to *2D sketches*. **Geometric constraints** are **geometric restrictions** that can be applied to geometric entities; for example, *horizontal*, *parallel*, *perpendicular*, and *tangent* are commonly used *geometric constraints* in *parametric modeling*. **Dimensional constraints** are used to describe the SIZE and LOCATION of individual geometric shapes. In *Autodesk Inventor*, **parametric relations** are user-defined mathematical equations composed of dimensional variables and/or *design variables*. In parametric modeling, features are made of geometric entities with both relations and constraints describing individual design intent. In this lesson, we will discuss the fundamentals of parametric relations and geometric constraints.

Create a Simple Plate Design

- In parametric modeling, dimensions are design parameters that are used to control the sizes and locations of geometric features. Dimensions are more than just values; they can also be used as feature control variables. This concept is illustrated by the following example.

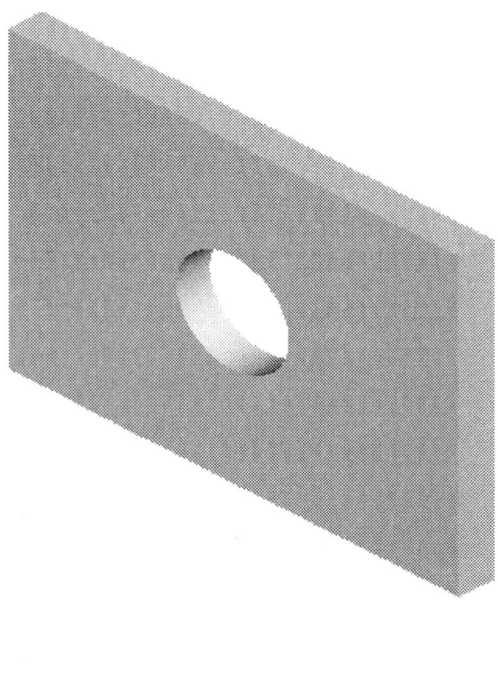

Starting Autodesk Inventor

1. Select the ***Autodesk Inventor*** option on the *Start* menu or select the ***Autodesk Inventor*** icon on the desktop to start *Autodesk Inventor*. The *Autodesk Inventor* main window will appear on the screen.

2. Once the program is loaded into the memory, the *Startup* dialog box appears at the center of the screen.

3. Select the ***New*** icon with a single click of the left-mouse-button in the *What to Do* dialog box.

4. Select the **English** tab and in the *New - Choose Template* area and then select **Standard(in).ipt**.

5. Pick **OK** in the *Startup* dialog box to accept the selected settings.

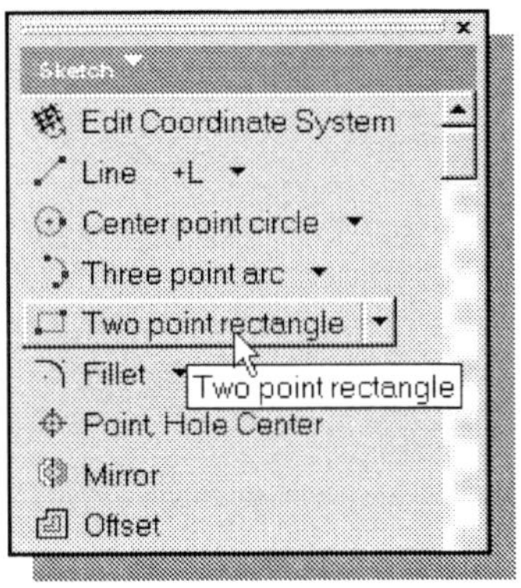

6. Select the ***Two point rectangle*** command by clicking once with the left-mouse-button on the icon in the *Sketch* toolbar.

7. Create a rectangle of arbitrary size positioned near the center of the screen.

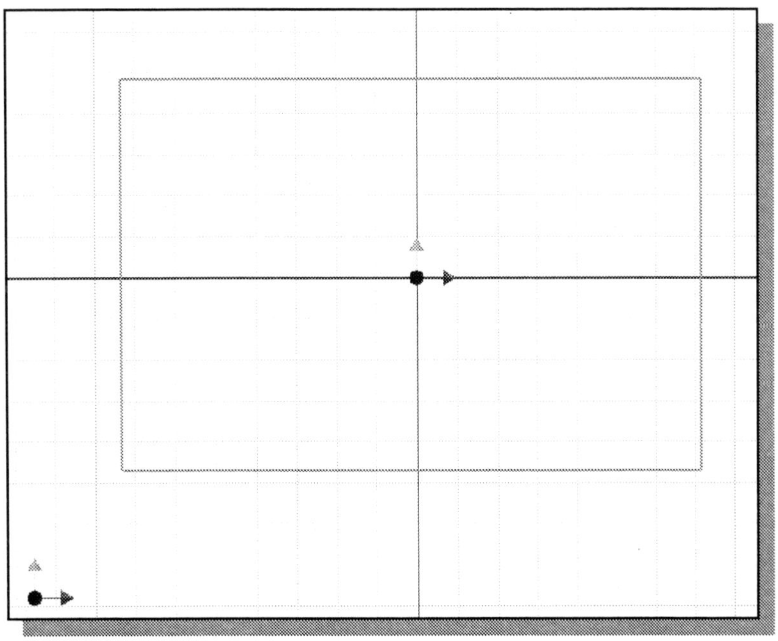

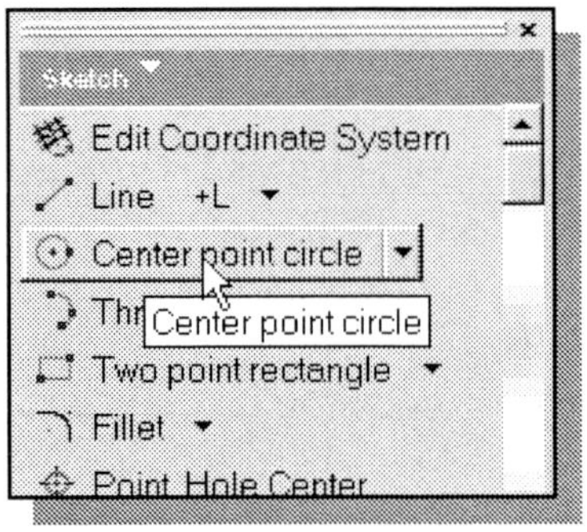

8. Select the ***Center point circle*** command by clicking once with the left-mouse-button on the icon in the *Sketch* toolbar.

9. Create a circle of arbitrary size inside the rectangle as shown below.

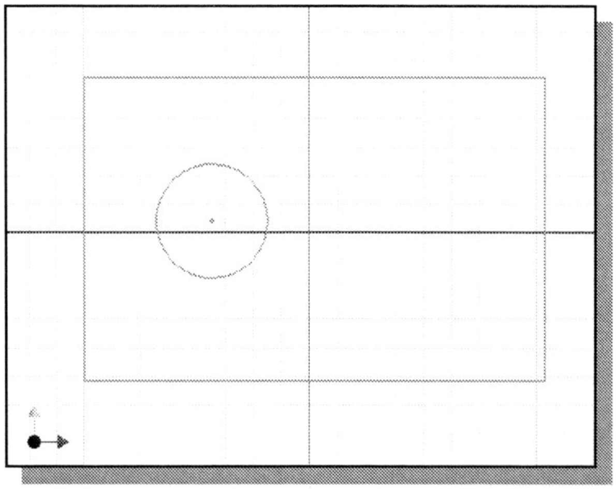

10. On your own, adjust the geometry by adding and modifying dimensions as shown below. (Note: Create and modify the overall width and height of the rectangle first. These two dimensions will be used as the control variables for the rest of the dimensions.)

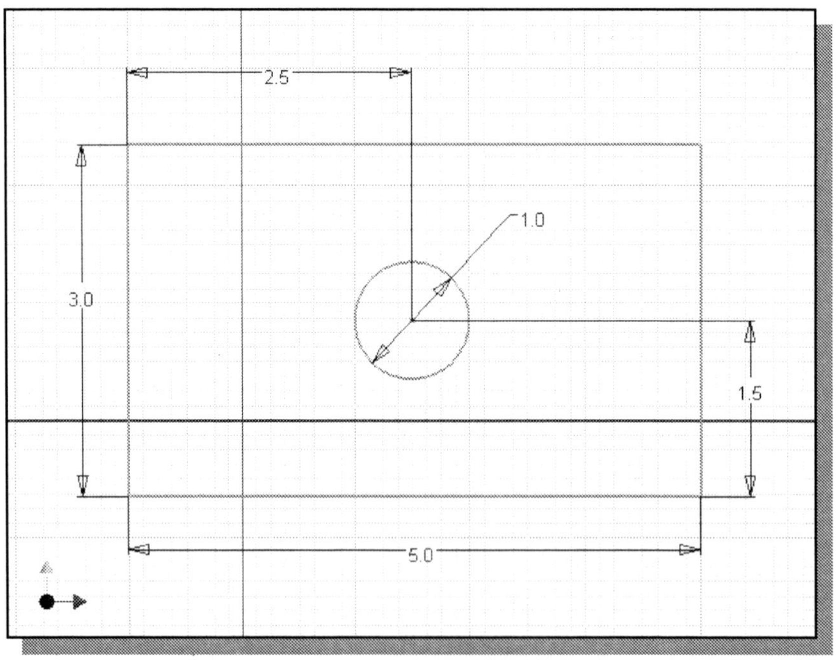

- On your own, change the overall width of the rectangle to **6.0** and the overall height of the rectangle to **3.6** and observe the location of the circle in relation to the edges of the rectangle. Adjust the dimensions back to **5.0** and **3.0** as shown in the above figure before continuing.

Dimensional Values and Dimensional Variables

Initially in *Autodesk Inventor*, values are used to create different geometric entities. The text created by the *Dimension* command also reflects the actual location or size of the entity. Each dimension is also assigned a name that allows the dimension to be used as a control variable. The default format is "dxx," where the "xx" is a number that *Autodesk Inventor* increments automatically each time a new dimension is added.

Let us look at our current design, which represents a plate with a hole at the center. The dimensional values describe the size and/or location of the plate and the hole. If a modification is required to change the width of the plate, the location of the hole will remain the same as described by the two location dimensional values. This is okay if that is the design intent. On the other hand, the *design intent* may require (1) keeping the hole at the center of the plate and (2) maintaining the size of the hole to be one-third of the height of the plate. We will establish a set of parametric relations using the dimensional variables to capture the design intent described in statements (1) and (2) above.

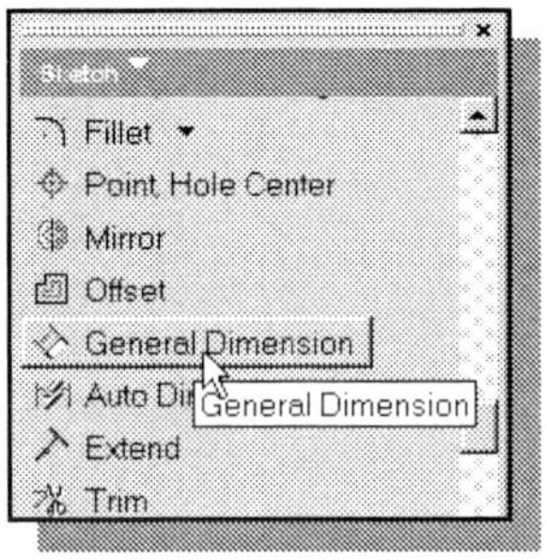

1. Move the cursor on top of the ***General Dimension*** icon. The *General Dimension* command allows us to quickly create and modify dimensions. Left-click once on the icon to activate the *General Dimension* command.

2. Click on the **width dimension** of the rectangle to display the *Edit Dimension* window.

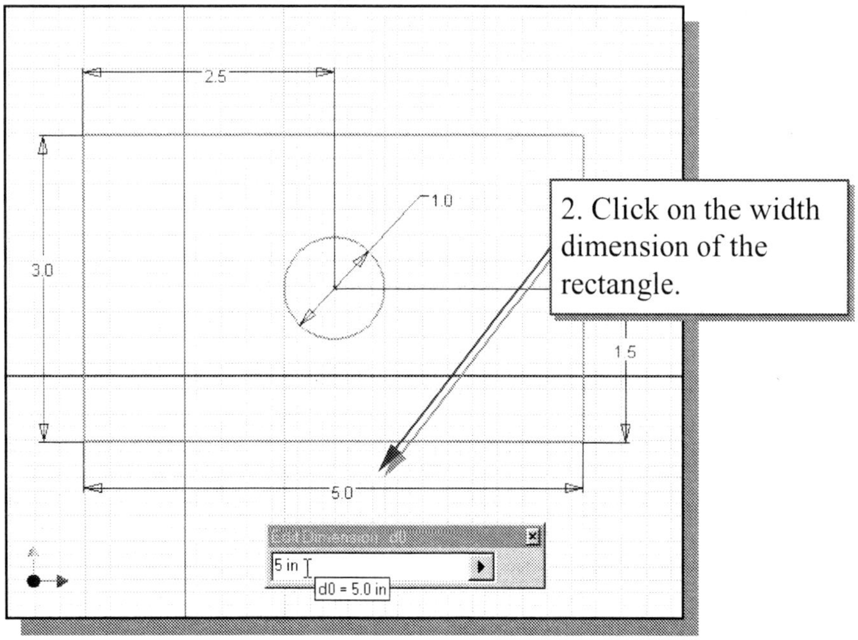

- Notice the ***variable name*** **d0** is displayed in the title area of the *Edit Dimension* window and also in the cursor box when the cursor is moved near the text box.

3. Click on the ***check mark*** button to close the *Edit Dimension* window.

Parametric Equations

- Each time we add a dimension to a model, that value is established as a parameter for the model. We can use parameters in equations to set the values of other parameters.

1. Click on the **horizontal location dimension** of the circle to display the *Edit Dimension* window.

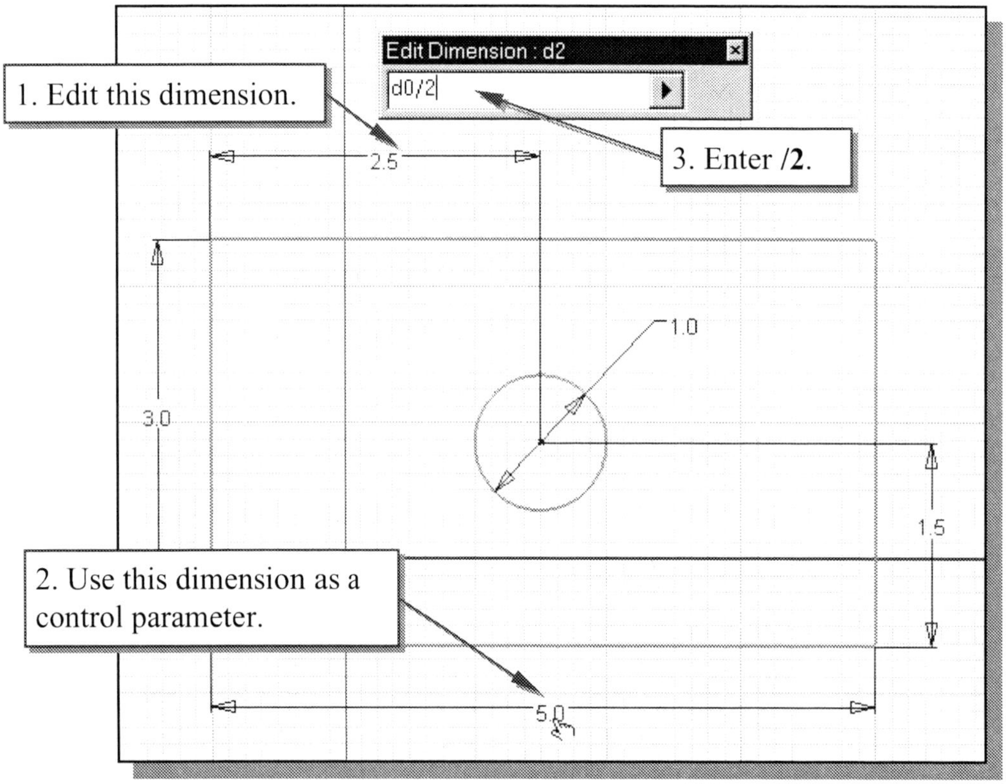

2. Click on the width dimension of the rectangle **d0** (value of **5.0**). Notice the variable name is automatically entered in the *Edit Dimension* window.

3. In the *Edit Dimension* window, enter **/2** to set the horizontal location dimension of the circle to be one-half of the width of the rectangle.

4. Click on the ***check mark*** button to close the *Edit Dimension* window.

5. On your own, repeat the above steps and set the vertical location dimension to one-half of the height of the rectangle.

❖ Notice, at this point, the dimension values displayed appear to be identical to what they were before we added the parametric relation. The parametric relations we entered are used to control the location of the circle; the location is based on the height and width of the rectangle.

➢ On your own, change the overall width of the rectangle to **6.0** and the height of the rectangle to **3.6** and observe the modified location of the circle. Adjust the dimensions back to **5.0** and **3.0** as shown in the above figure before continuing.

Viewing the Established Parameters and Relations

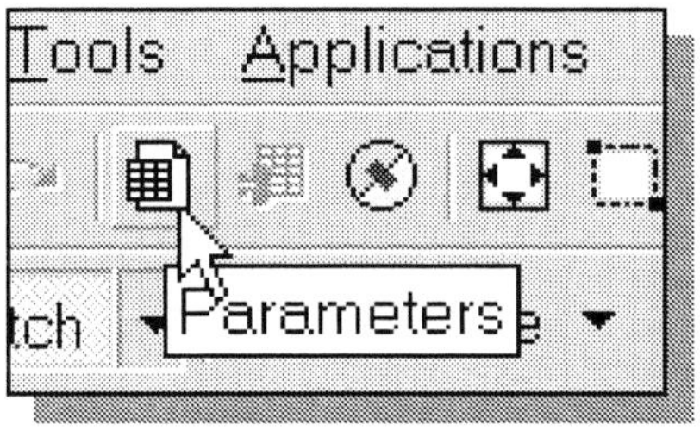

1. In the *Standard* toolbar select the ***Parameters*** command by left-clicking once on the icon. The ***Parameters*** popup window appears.

- The *Parameters* command can be used to display all dimensions used to define the model. We can also create additional parameters as design variables, which are called ***User Parameters***.

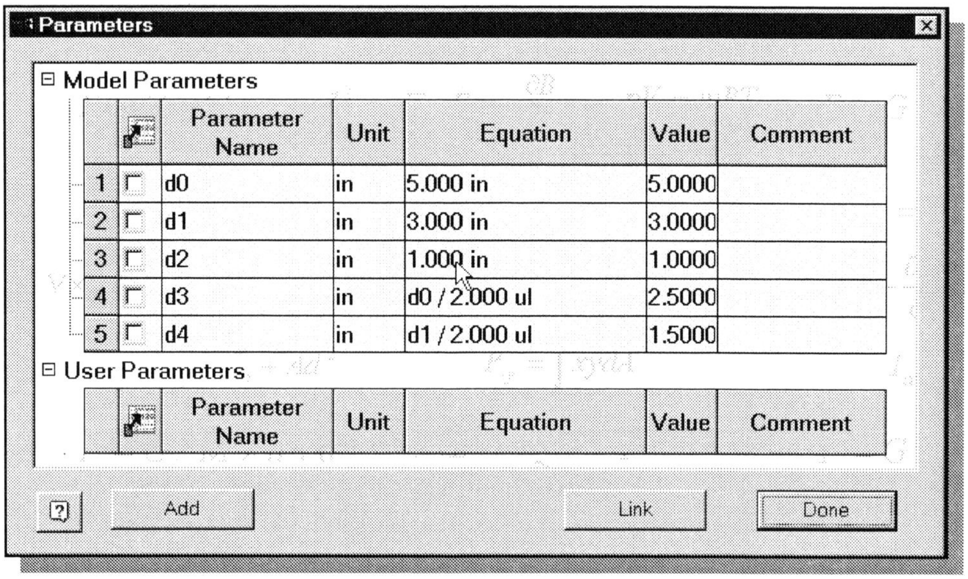

2. Click on the **1.0** value in the equation section of the *Parameters* window. Enter **d1/3** as the parametric relation to set the size of the circle to be one-third of the height of the rectangle as shown below.

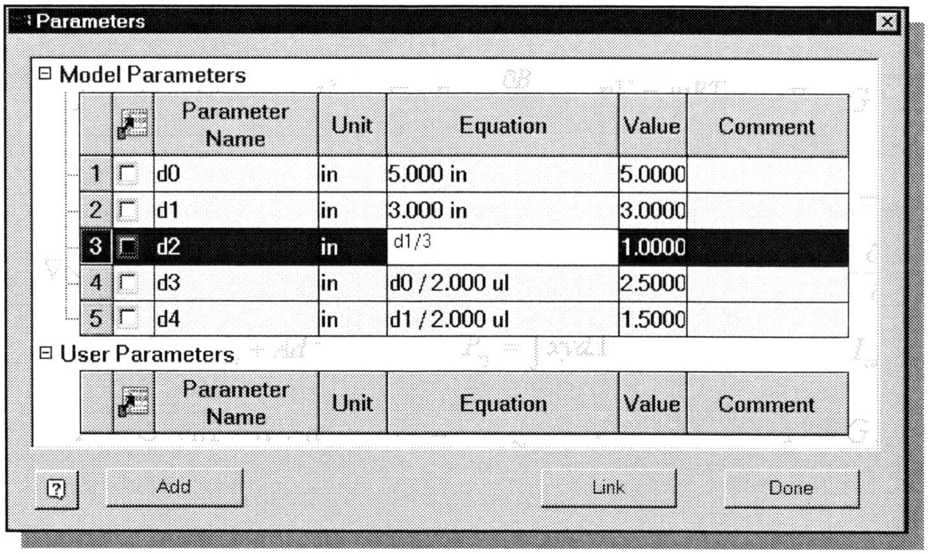

3. Click on the **Done** button to accept the settings.

4. On your own, change the dimensions of the rectangle to **6.0 x 3.6** and observe the changes to the location and size of the circle. (Hint: Double-click the dimension text to bring up the *Edit Dimension* window.)

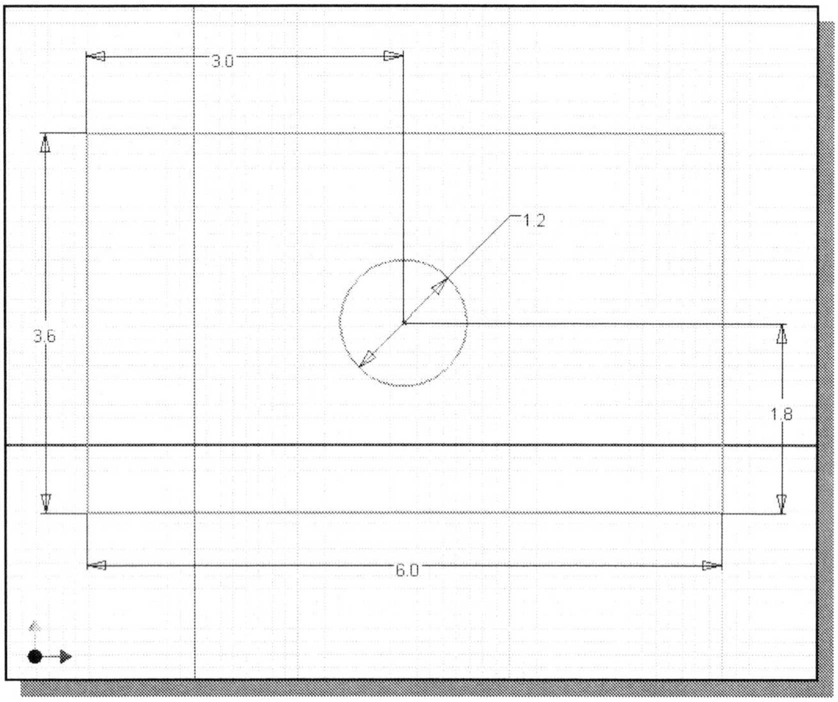

❖ *Autodesk Inventor* automatically adjusts the dimensions of the design, and the parametric relations we entered are also applied and maintained. The dimensional constraints are used to control the size and location of the hole. The design intent, previously expressed by statements (1) and (2) at the beginning of this section, is now embedded into the model.

➢ On your own, use the ***Extrude*** command and create a 3D solid model with a plate-thickness of **0.25**. Also, experiment with modifying the parametric relations and dimensions through the *Part Browser*.

Saving the Model File

1. Select **Save** in the *Standard* toolbar. We can also use the "**Ctrl-S**" combination (press down the "Ctrl" key and hit the "S" key once) to save the part.

2. In the popup window, enter ***Plate*** as the name of the file.

3. Click on the **SAVE** button to save the file.

Fully Constrained Geometry

In *Autodesk Inventor*, as we create 2D sketches, geometric constraints such as *horizontal* and *parallel* are automatically added to the sketched geometry. In most cases, additional constraints and dimensions are needed to fully describe the sketched geometry beyond the geometric constraints added by the system. Although we can use *Autodesk Inventor* to build partially constrained or totally unconstrained solid models, the models may behave unpredictably as changes are made. In most cases, it is important to consider the design intent and to add proper constraints to geometric entities. In the following sections, a simple triangle is used to illustrate the different tools that are available in *Autodesk Inventor* to create/modify geometric and dimensional constraints.

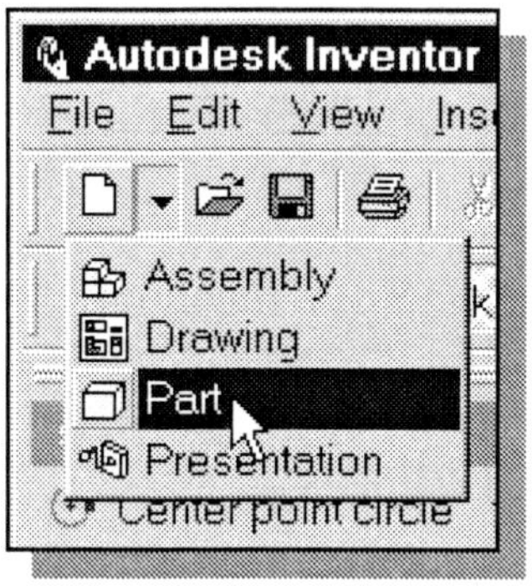

1. Start a new drawing by left-clicking once on the ***New → Part*** icon in the *Standard* toolbar.

- Another graphics window appears on the screen. We can switch between the two models by clicking on the different graphics windows.

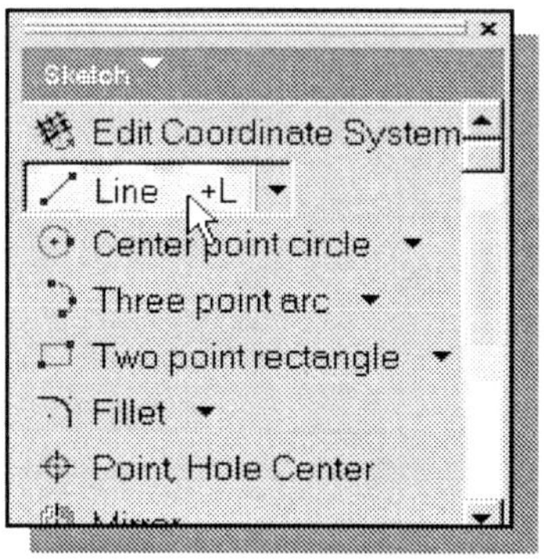

2. Move the graphics cursor to the ***LINE*** icon in the *Sketch* toolbar. A *Help-tip box* appears next to the cursor and a brief description of the command is displayed at the bottom of the drawing screen: *"Creates Straight line segments and tangent arcs."*

3. Create a triangle of arbitrary size positioned near the center of the screen as shown below. (Note that the base of the triangle is horizontal.)

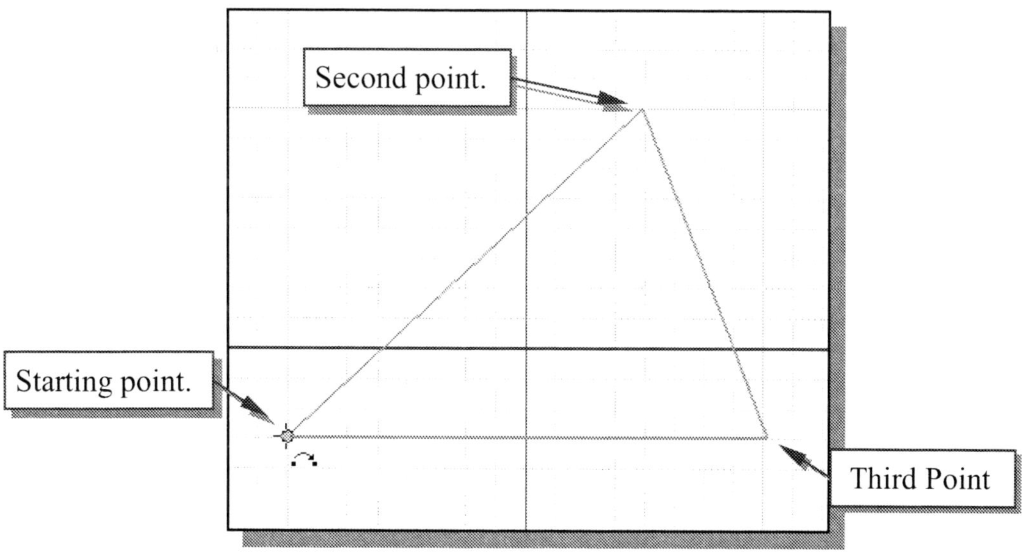

Displaying existing constraints

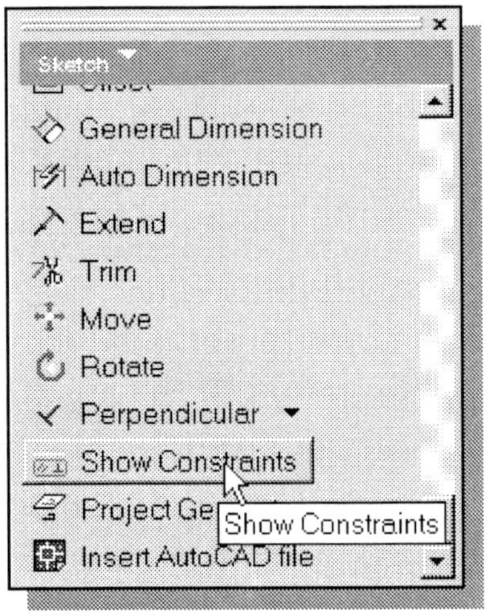

1. Select the ***Show Constraints*** command in the *Sketch* toolbar. This icon allows us to display constraints that are already applied to the 2D profiles. Left-click once on the icon to display the **Show Constraints**.

➢ In *Autodesk Inventor*, constraints are applied as geometric entities are created. *Autodesk Inventor* will attempt to add proper constraints to the geometric entities based on the way we create the entities. Constraints are displayed as symbols next to the entities as they are created. The current profile consists of three line entities, three straight lines. The horizontal line has three constraints applied to it, two coincident constraints and a horizontal constraint.

2. Move the cursor on top of the horizontal line and notice the ***active constraint*** box appears, showing three constraints are applied to the line.

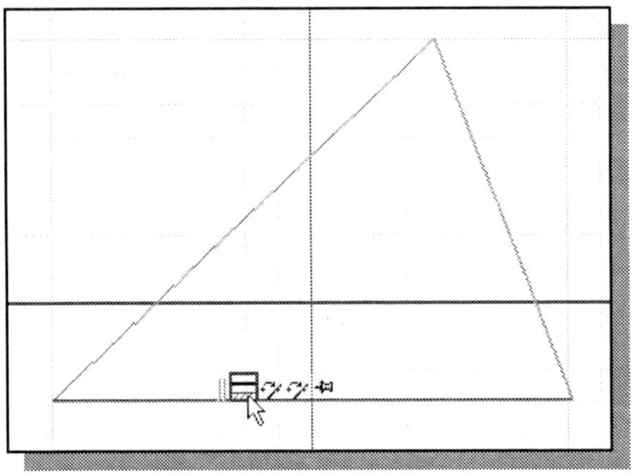

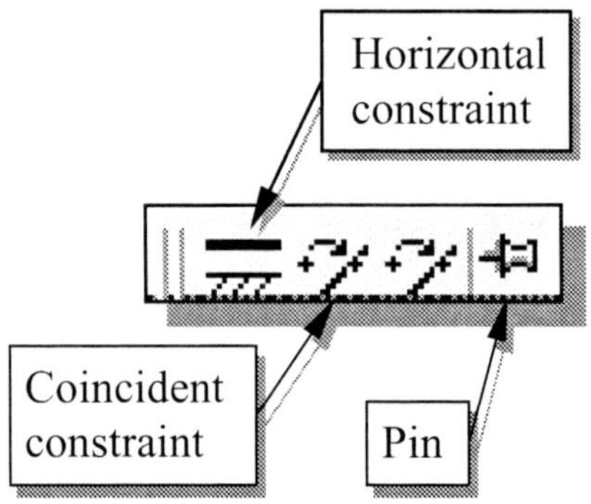

3. Click on the ***Pin*** icon, the last icon in the active constraint box, to lock the display of the *Active Constraints* at its current location.

4. On your own, move the cursor on top of the other two lines and display the active constraint box of the other two entities.

5. Move the cursor on top of the constraints displayed and notice the highlighted endpoint/line indicating the location/entities where the constraints are applied.

6. Click on the ***Pin*** icon, the last icon in the active constraint box, to unlock the display of the constraints.

7. Inside the graphics window, right-mouse-click to bring up the option menu and select **Done** to end the *Show Constraints* command.

Applying Geometric/Dimensional Constraints

- In *Autodesk Inventor*, ten types of constraints are available. Depending upon the way the constraints are applied, the same results can be accomplished by applying different constraints to the geometric entities.

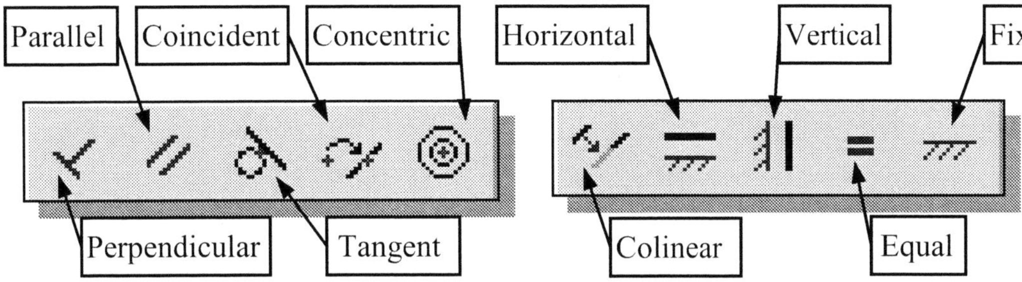

Perpendicular constraint: Causes selected curves or ellipse axes to lie at right angles to one another.

Parallel constraint: Causes selected lines or ellipse axes to lie parallel to one another.

Tangent constraint: Constrains two curves to be tangent to one another

Coincident constraint: Constrains two points together or one point to a curve.

Concentric constraint: Constrains two arcs, circles, or ellipses to the same center point.

Colinear constraint: Causes two lines or ellipse axes to lie along the same line.

Horizontal constraint: Causes lines, ellipse axes, or pairs of points to lie parallel to the X-axis of the sketch coordinate system.

Vertical constraint: Causes lines, ellipse axes, or pairs of points to lie parallel to the Y-axis of the sketch coordinate system.

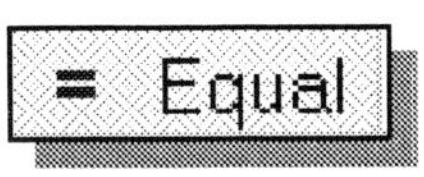

Equal constraint: Selected arcs/circles constrained to the same radius or selected lines to the same length.

Fixed location constraint: Constrains points or curves to a fixed location relative to the sketch coordinate system.

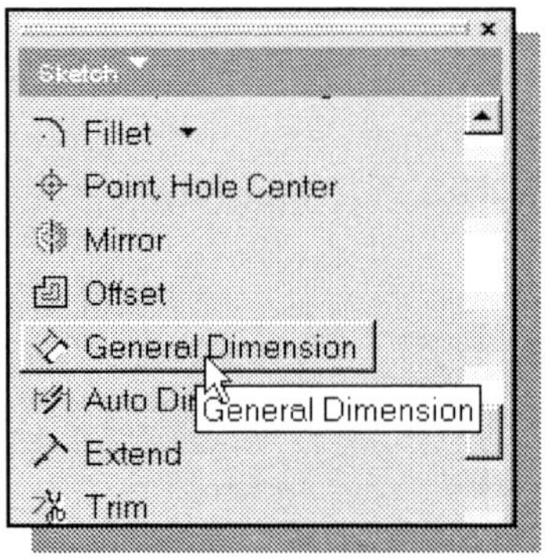

1. Select the ***General Dimension*** command in the *Sketch* toolbar. The *General Dimension* command allows us to quickly create and modify dimensions. Left-click once on the icon to activate the *General Dimension* command.

2. The message "*Select Geometry to Dimension*" is displayed in the *Status Bar* area, at the bottom of the *Inventor* window. Create the dimension as shown in the figure below. (The displayed value might be different on your screen.)

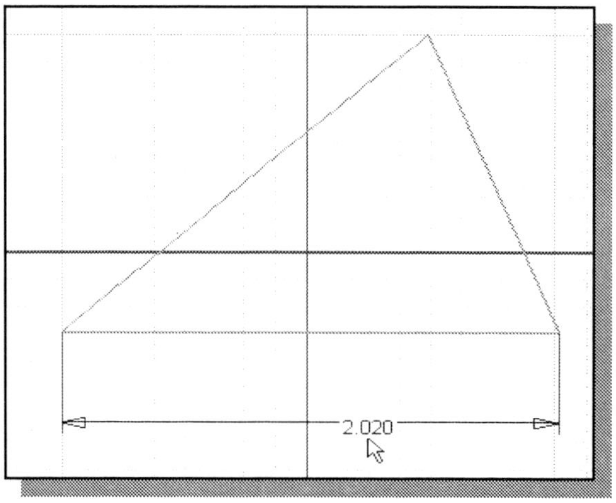

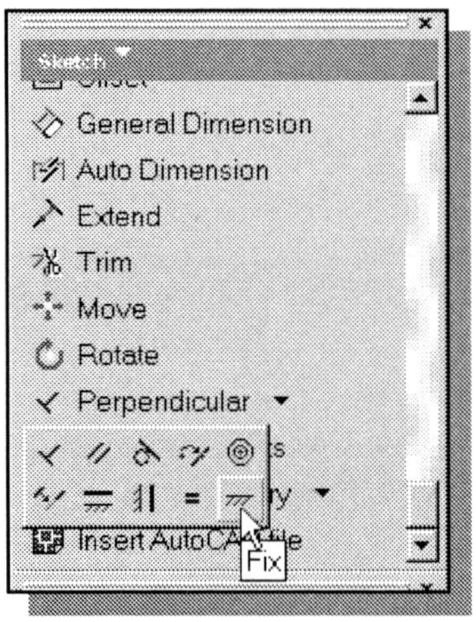

3. Move the cursor to the ***Constraint*** icon, the icon that is below the *General Dimension* icon, in the *Sketch* toolbar. Click on the triangle icon to display additional options available. A *Help-tip box* appears next to the cursor and a brief description of the command is displayed at the bottom of the drawing screen as the cursor is moved over the different icons.

4. Click on the ***Fix*** constraint icon to activate the command.

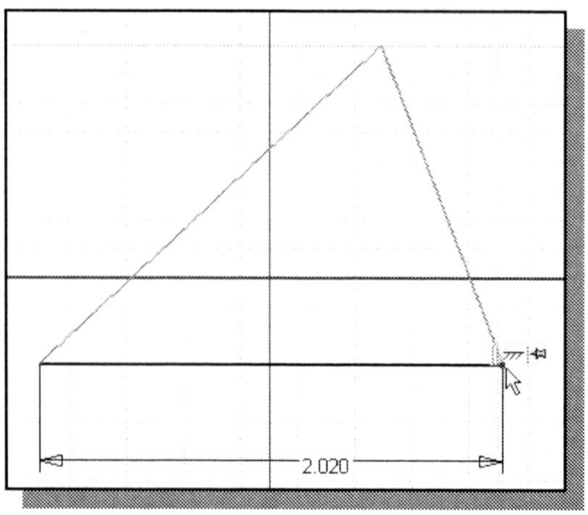

5. Pick the lower-right corner of the triangle to make the corner a fixed point.

6. On your own, use the *Show Constraints* command to confirm the *Fix Constraint* is properly applied.

➢ Geometric constraints can be used to control the direction in which changes can occur. For example, in the current design we are adding a horizontal dimension to control the length of the horizontal line. If the length of the line is modified to a greater value, *Autodesk Inventor* will lengthen the line toward the left side. This is due to the fact that the *Fix* constraint will restrict any horizontal movement of the horizontal line toward the right side

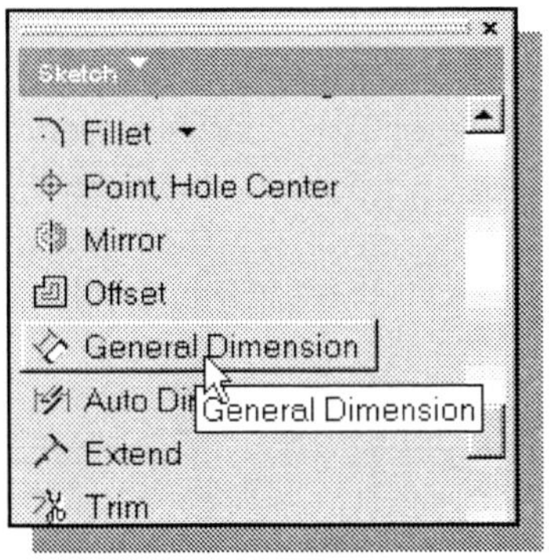

7. Select the ***General Dimension*** command in the *Sketch* toolbar.

8. Click on the dimension text to open the *Edit Dimension* window.

9. Enter a value that is greater than the displayed value to observe the effects of the modification. (For example, the above figure shows a value of 2.02, so enter **3.0** in the text box area.)

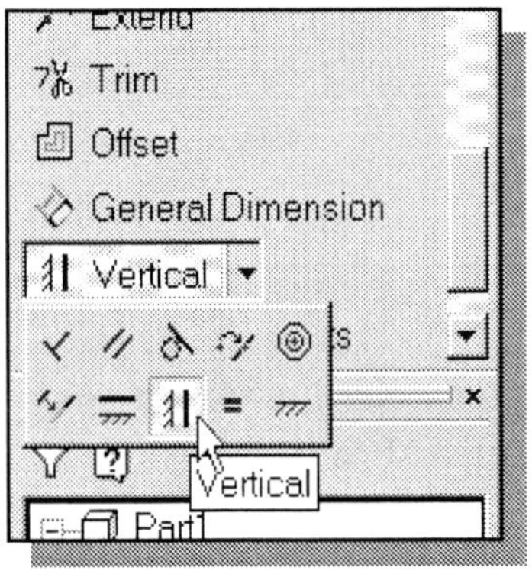

10. On your own, use the ***Undo*** command to reset the dimension value to the previous value.

11. Select the ***Vertical*** constraint icon in the *2D Constraints* toolbar.

12. Pick the inclined line on the right to make the line vertical.

13. Hit the [**Esc**] key once to end the vertical constraint command.

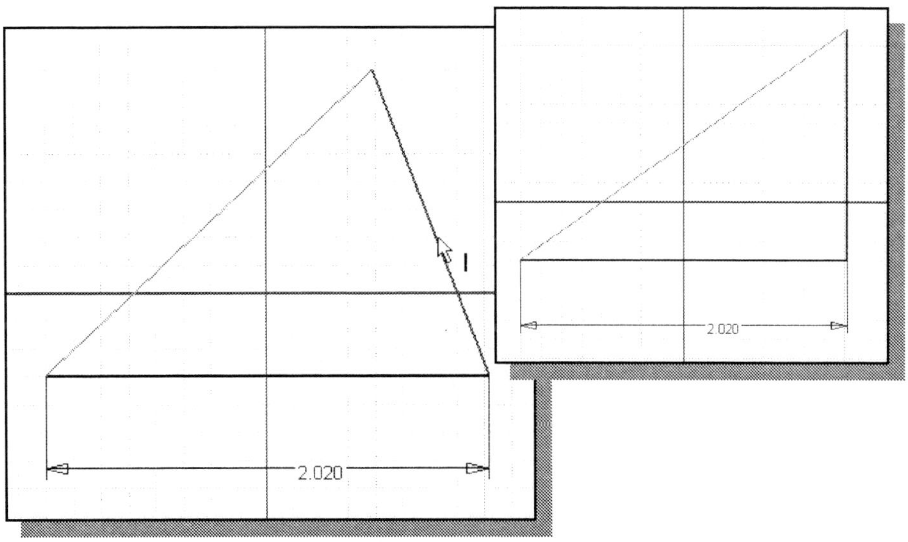

➢ Think of the constraints and dimensions as defining elements of the geometric entities. How many more constraints or dimensions do you think will be necessary to fully constrain the sketched geometry? Which constraints or dimensions would you use to fully constrain the geometry?

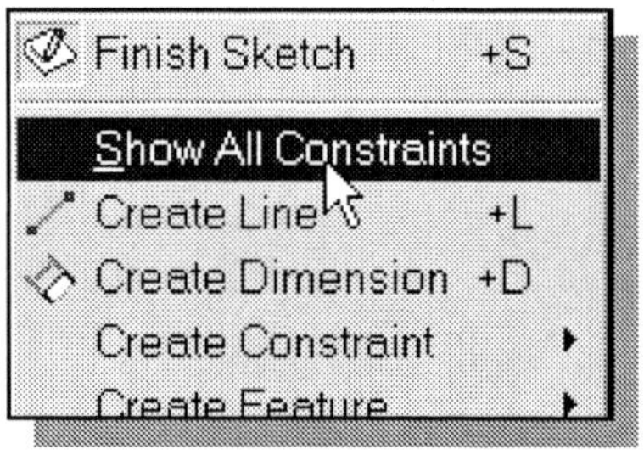

14. Inside the graphics window, click once with the right-mouse-button to display the option menu. Select **Show All Constraints** in the popup menu to all the applied constraints.

15. Move the cursor on top of the top corner of the triangle, then press and hold down the left-mouse-button when the selection-options symbol is displayed.

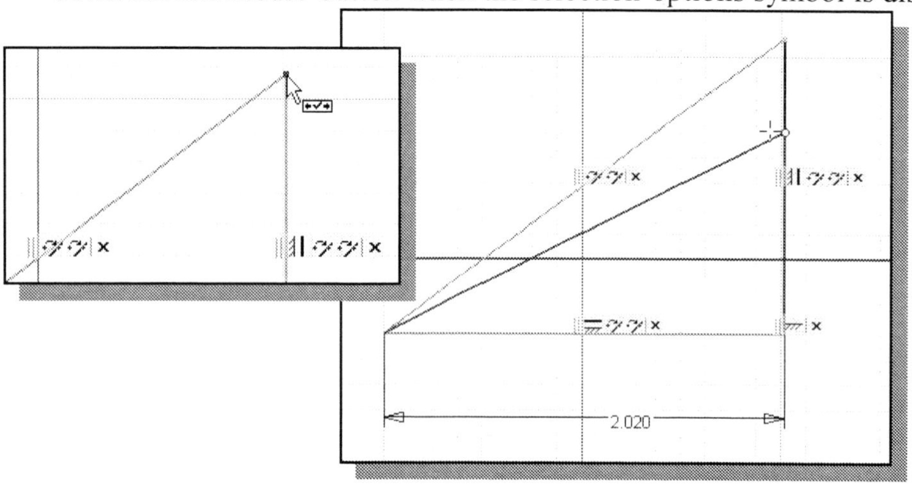

16. Drag the top corner of the triangle and note that the corner is free to move only in an upward or downward direction. Release the mouse button at a new location and note that the lines are automatically adjusted to the new location.

17. On your own, experiment with dragging the other corners to new locations.

- The three constraints that are applied to the geometry provide a full description to the location of the two lower corners of the triangle. The vertical constraint, along with the fix constraint at the lower-right corner, does not fully describe the location of the top corner of the triangle. We will need to add additional information, such as the length of the vertical line or an angle dimension.

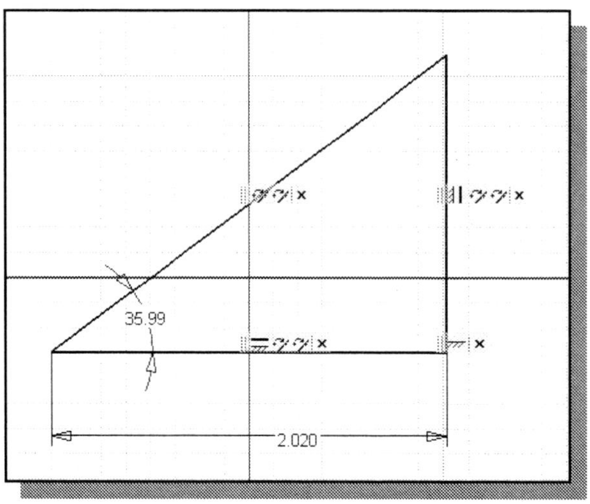

18. On your own, add an angle dimension to the left corner of the triangle.

19. Press the [**Esc**] key once to exit the *General Dimension* command.

20. On your own, modify the angle to 45° and then experiment with dragging the top corner of the triangle to a new location.

- The geometry is fully constrained with the added dimension.

Over-constraining and Driven Dimensions

- We can use *Autodesk Inventor* to build partially constrained or totally unconstrained solid models. In most cases, these types of models may behave unpredictably as changes are made. *Autodesk Inventor* will not let us over-constrain a sketch; additional dimensions can still be added to the sketch, but they will be used for reference only. These additional dimensions are called ***driven dimensions***. *Driven dimensions* do not constrain the sketch; they only reflect the values of the dimensioned geometry. They are enclosed in parentheses to distinguish them from normal (parametric) dimensions. A *driven dimension* can be converted to a normal dimension only if another dimension or geometric constraint is removed.

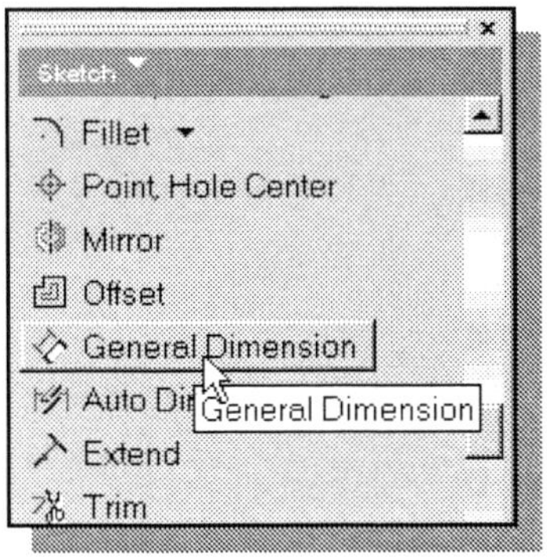

1. Select the ***General Dimension*** command in the *Sketch* toolbar.

2. Select the vertical line.

3. Pick a location that is to the right side of the triangle to place the dimension text.

4. A warning dialogue box appears on the screen stating that the dimension we are trying to create will over-constrain the sketch. Click on the **Accept** button to proceed with the creation of a driven dimension.

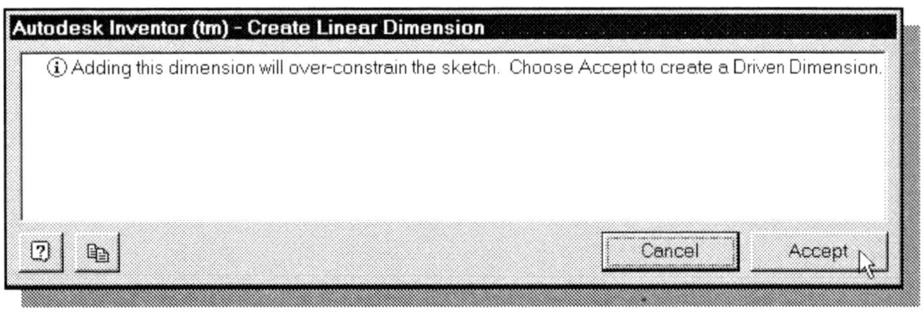

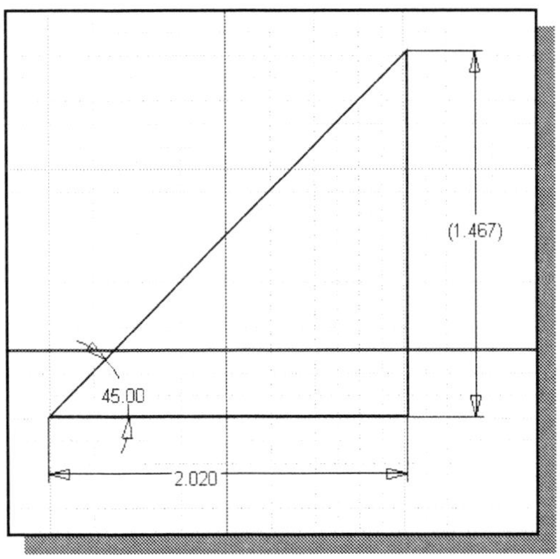

5. On your own, modify the angle dimension to **35°** and observe the changes of the 2D sketch and the driven dimension.

Deleting existing constraints

1. On your own, display all the active constraints. (Hint: Use the *Show Constraints* command in the *Sketch* toolbar or the *Show All Constraints* in the option menu.)

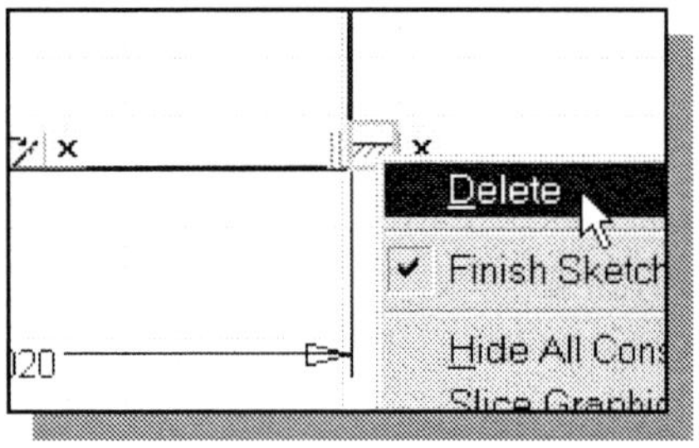

2. Move the cursor on top of the ***Fix*** constraint icon and right-mouse-click once to bring up the option menu.

3. Select **Delete** to remove the *Fix* constraint that is applied to the lower-right corner of the triangle.

4. On your own, delete the driven dimension we created in the last section.

5. Move the cursor on top of the top corner of the triangle, and then press down the left-mouse button when the selection options symbol is displayed.

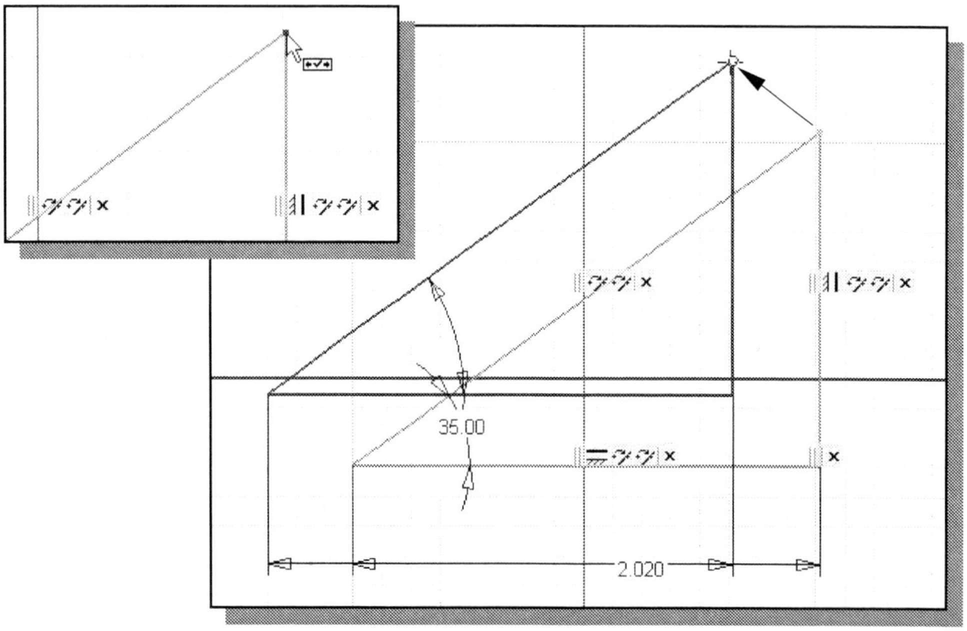

6. Drag the top corner of the triangle and note that the entire triangle is free to move in all directions. Drag the corner toward the top-right corner of the graphics window as shown in the above figure. Release the mouse button to move the triangle to the new location.

7. On your own, experiment with dragging the other corners and/or the three line segments to new locations on the screen.

❖ **Dimensional constraints** are used to describe the SIZE and LOCATION of individual geometric shapes. **Geometric constraints** are **geometric restrictions** that can be applied to geometric entities. The constraints applied to the triangle are sufficient to maintain its size and shape, but the geometry can be moved around; its location definition isn't complete.

Adding Additional Geometry

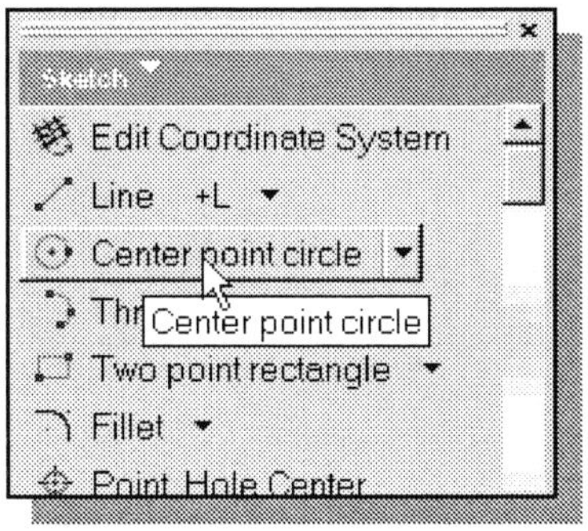

1. Select the ***Center point circle*** command by clicking once with the left-mouse-button on the icon in the *Sketch* toolbar.

2. On your own, create a circle of arbitrary size inside the triangle as shown below.

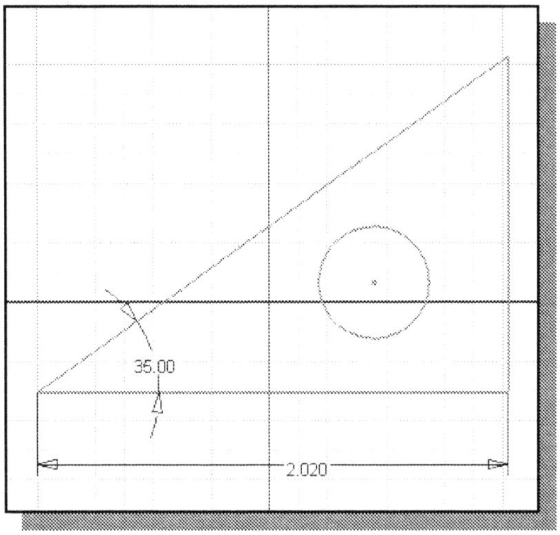

3. Click on the ***Tangent*** constraint icon in the *Sketch* toolbar.

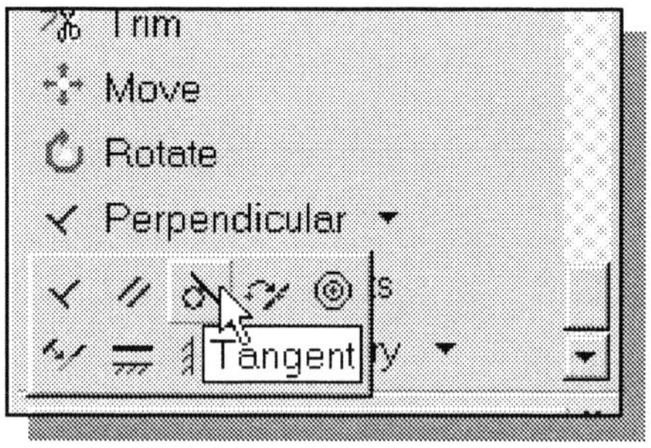

4. Pick the circle by left-mouse-clicking once on the geometry.

5. Pick the inclined line. The sketched geometry is adjusted as shown below.

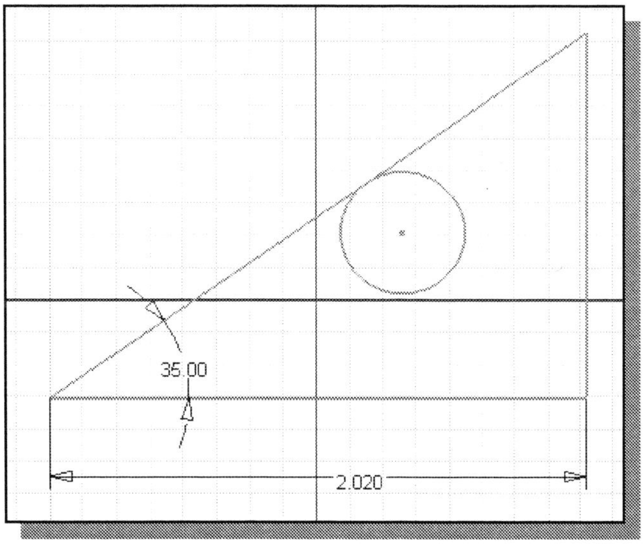

- How many more constraints or dimensions do you think will be necessary to fully constrain the circle? Which constraints or dimensions would you use to fully constrain the geometry?

6. Move the cursor on top of the right side of the circle, drag the circle toward the right edge of the graphics window. Notice the arrow symbol next to the circle indicating the size of the circle is not defined.

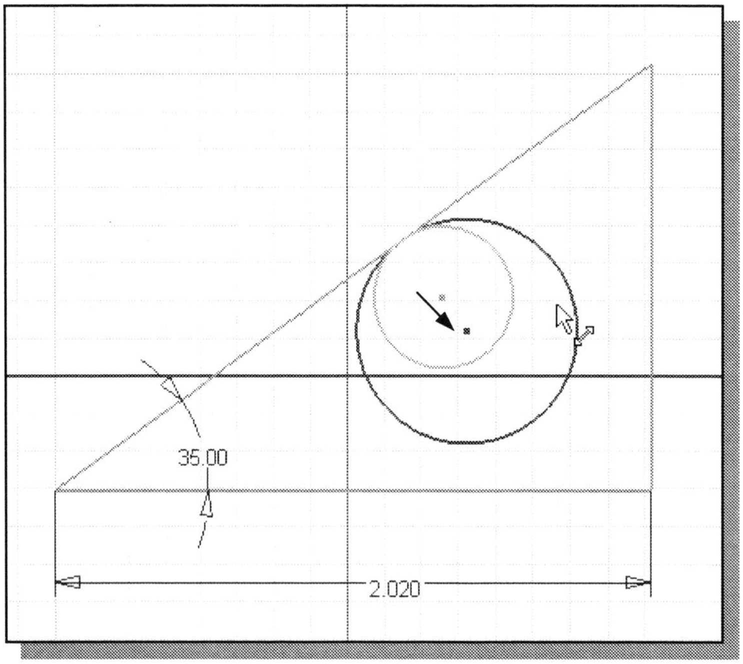

7. Drag the center of the circle to a different location. Notice the *Tangent* constraint is always maintained by the system.

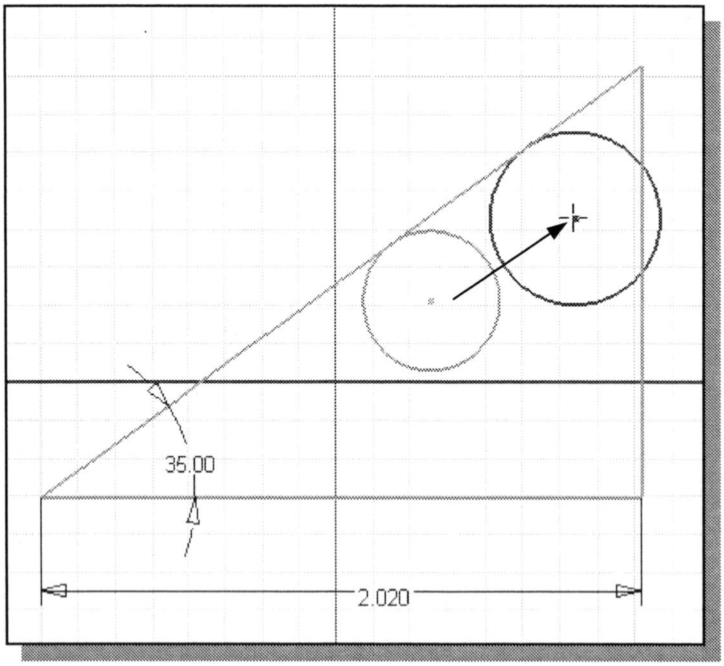

➢ On your own, experiment with adding additional constraints and/or dimensions to fully constrain the sketched geometry. Use the *Undo* command to undo any changes before proceeding to the next section.

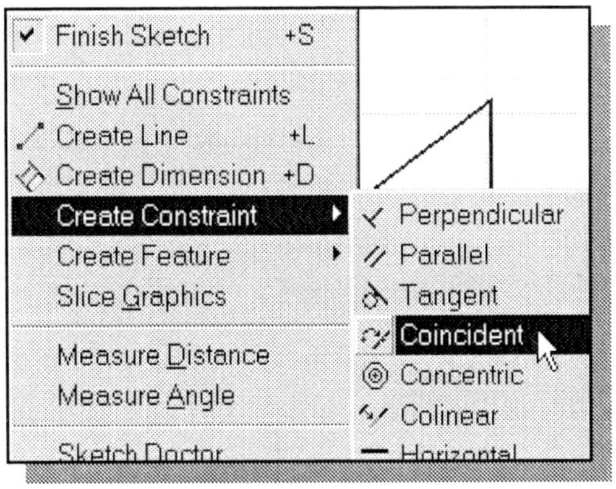

8. Inside the graphics window, click once with the **right-mouse-button** to display the option menu. Select **Create Constraint → Conincident** in the popup menus.

- The option menu is a quick way to access many of the commonly used commands in *Autodesk Inventor*.

9. Pick the vertical line.

10. Pick the center of the circle to align the center of the circle and the vertical line.

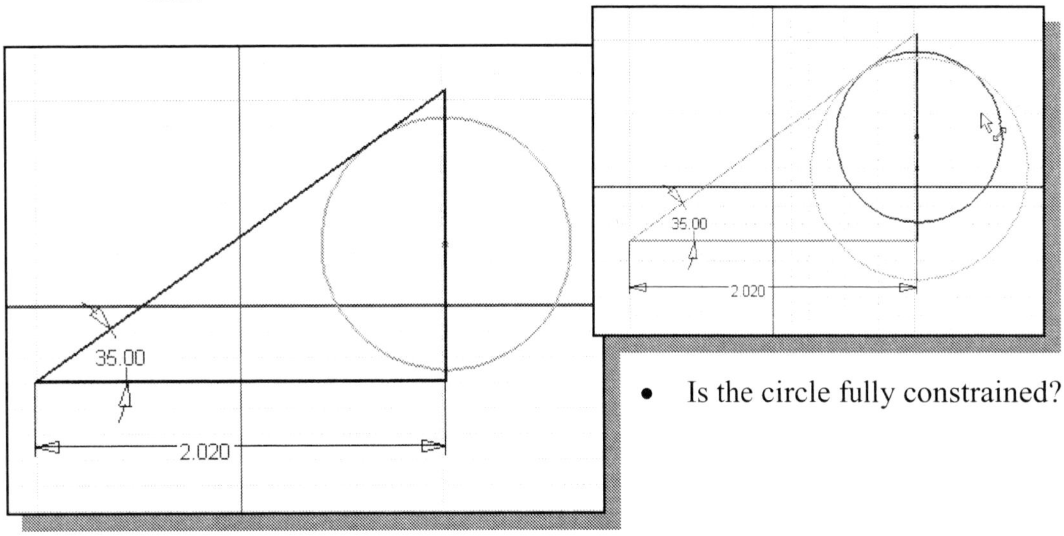

- Is the circle fully constrained?

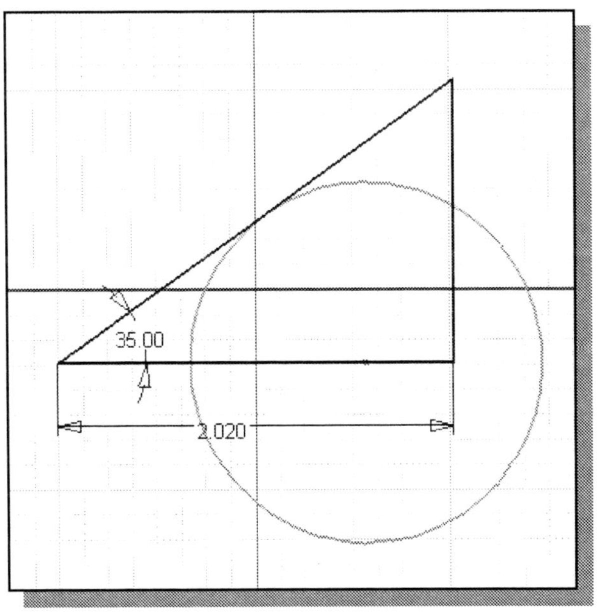

11. On your own, delete the *Coincident* constraint we just applied and add a ***Coincident*** constraint in between the center of the circle and the horizontal line.

- How many more constraints or dimensions do you think will be necessary to fully constrain the circle? Which constraints or dimensions would you use to fully constrain the geometry?

❖ The application of different constraints affects the geometry differently. The design intent is maintained in the CAD model's database and thus allows us to create very intelligent CAD models that can be modified/revised fairly easily. On your own, experiment and observe the results of applying different constraints to the triangle. For example: (1) adding another *Fix* constraint to the top corner of the triangle; (2) deleting the horizontal dimension and adding another *Fix* constraint to the left corner of the triangle; and (3) adding another *Tangent* constraint and adding the size dimension to the circle.

12. On your own, modify the 2D sketch as shown below.

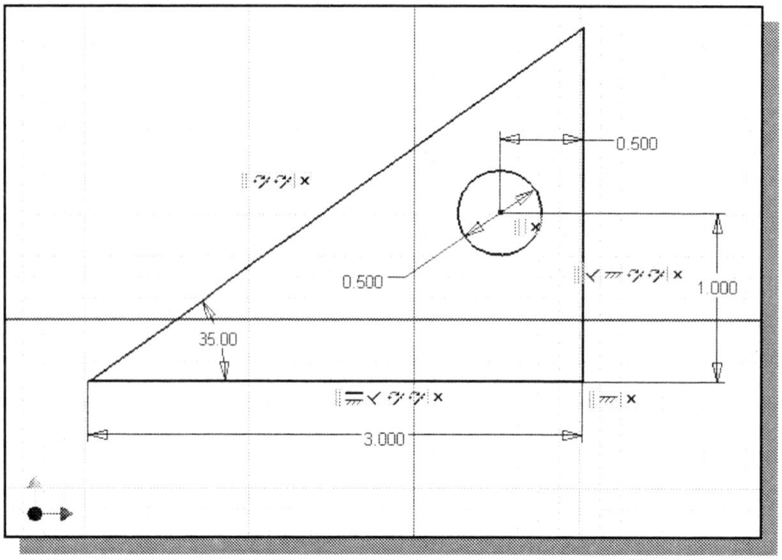

➢ On your own, use the ***Extrude*** command and create a 3D solid model with a plate-thickness of **0.25**. Also experiment with modifying the parametric relations and dimensions through the *Part Browser*.

Constraint Settings

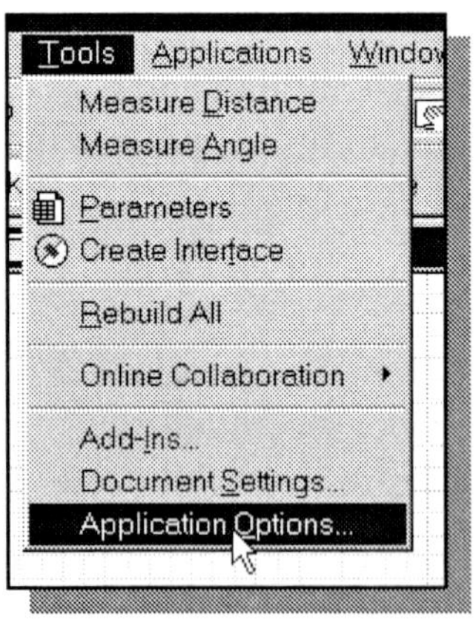

- Select **Application Options** in the **Tools** pull-down menu. Click on the **Sketch** tab to display and/or modify the constraint settings. On your own, adjust the settings and experiment with the effects of the different settings.

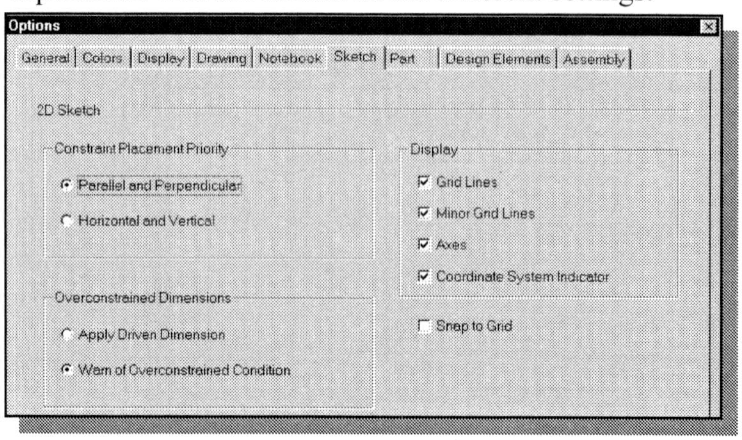

Questions:

1. What is the difference between *dimensional* constraints and *geometric* constraints?

2. How can we confirm that a sketch is fully constrained?

3. How do we access the *Constraints* commands?

4. Describe the procedure to display user-defined equations.

5. List and describe three different geometric constraints available in *Autodesk Inventor*.

6. How do we add constraints manually?

7. Does *Autodesk Inventor* allow us to build partially constrained or totally unconstrained solid models? What are the advantages and disadvantages of building these types of models?

8. Identify and describe the following commands.

(a)

(b)

(c)

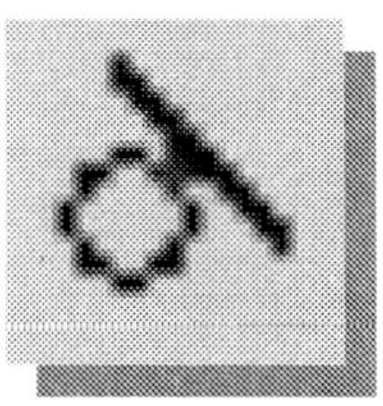

(d)

Exercises:

(Create and establish three parametric relations for each of the following designs.)

1.

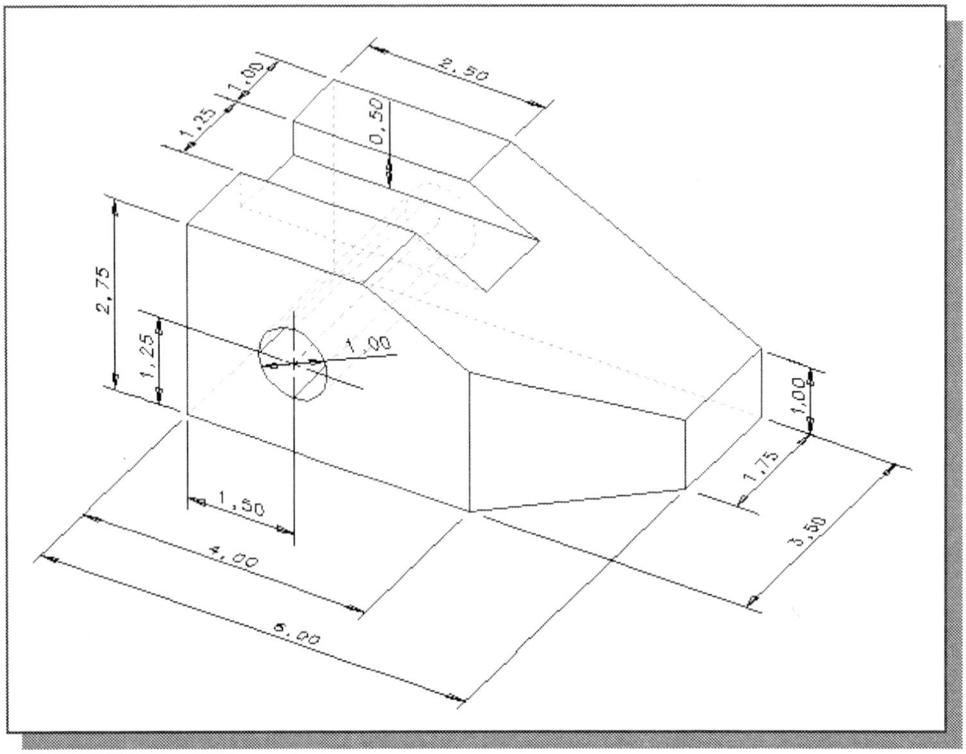

2.

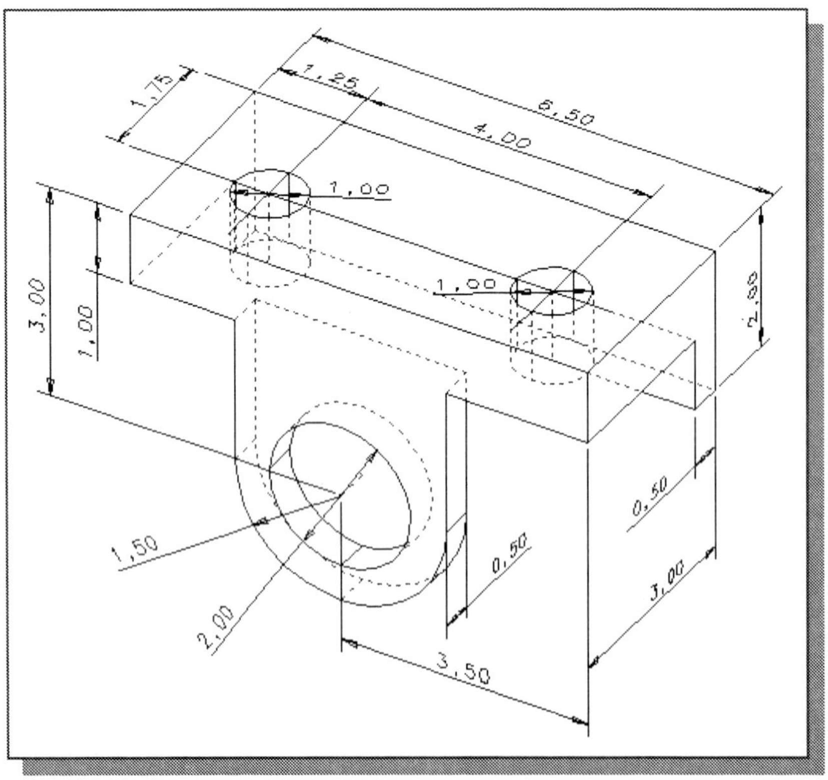

Lesson 5
The BORN Technique and Work Features

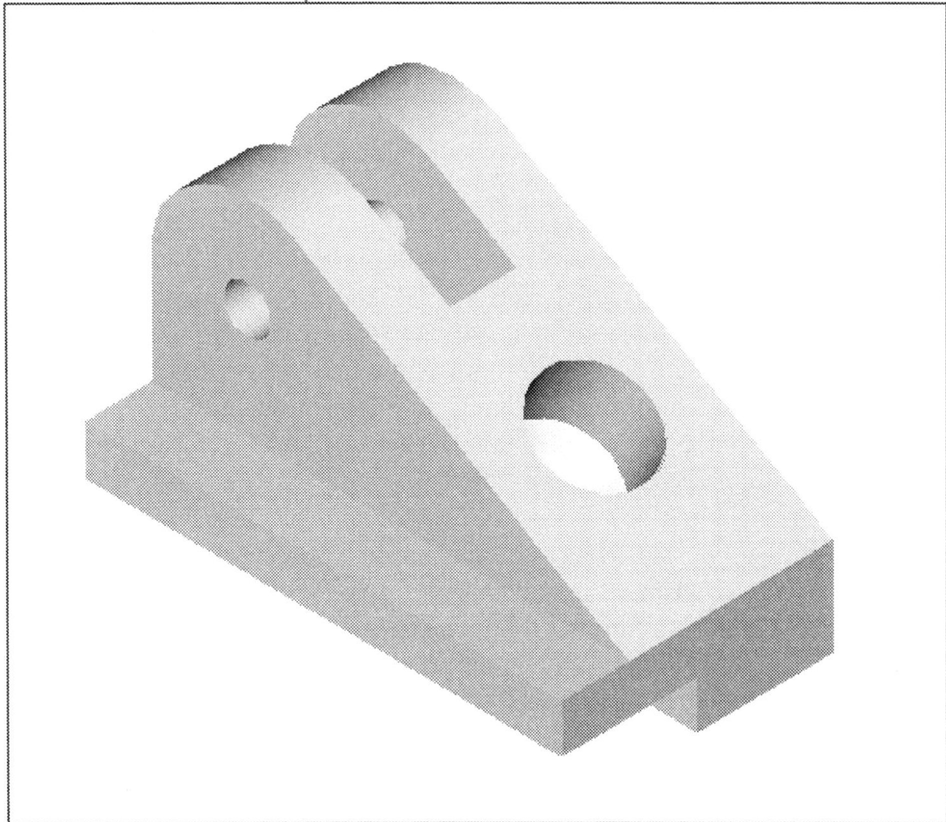

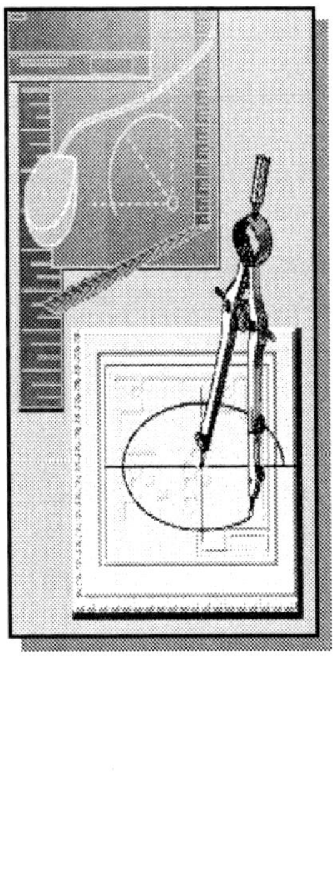

Learning Objectives

When you have completed this lesson, you will be able to:
- ♦ Understand the BORN technique.
- ♦ Create Reference Geometry.
- ♦ Create Placed Features.
- ♦ Create an OFFSET Work Plane.
- ♦ Understand the Importance of Feature Interactions.

The BORN Technique

In the previous lessons, we have chosen the *first feature* to be an extruded solid object. All subsequent features, therefore, are built by referencing the first feature, or ***base feature***. The *base feature* is the center of all features and is considered as the key-feature of the design. This approach to creating solid models places more emphasis on the selection of the *base feature*. In most cases, this approach is quite adequate and proper in creating the solid models for different types of designs.

A more advanced technique of creating solid models is what is known as the "**Base Orphan Reference Node**" (**BORN**) technique. The basic concept of the BORN technique is to use a *Cartesian coordinate system* as the first feature prior to creating any solid features. With the *Cartesian coordinate system* established, we then have three mutually perpendicular datum planes (namely the *XY*, *YZ*, and *ZX planes*) available to use as sketching planes. The three datum planes can also be used as references for dimensions and geometric constructions. Using this technique, the first node in the history tree is called an "orphan," meaning that it has no history to be replayed. The technique of creating the reference geometry in this "base node" is therefore called the "Base Orphan Reference Node" (BORN) technique.

Autodesk Inventor automatically establishes a set of reference geometry when we start a new part, namely a *Cartesian coordinate system* with three work planes, three work axes, and a work point. We can also add additional reference geometry without referencing any solid features. All subsequent solid features can then use the coordinate system and/or reference geometry as sketching planes. The *base feature* is still important, but the *base feature* is no longer the ONLY choice for selecting the sketching plane for subsequent solid features. This approach provides us with more options while we are creating parametric solid models. More importantly, this approach provides greater flexibility for part modifications and design changes. This approach is also very useful in creating assembly models, which will be illustrated in *Lesson 10*.

Reference Geometry I – Work Features

Feature-based parametric modeling is a cumulative process. The relationships that we define between features determine how a feature reacts when other features are changed. Because of this interaction, certain features must, by necessity, precede others. A new feature can use previously defined features to define information such as size, shape, location and orientation. *Autodesk Inventor* provides several tools to automate this process. This lesson demonstrates the use of work features, projected geometry, and the BORN technique. Work features can be thought of as user-definable datum, which are updated with the part geometry. We can create work planes, axes, or points that do not already exist. Work features can also be used to align features or to orient parts in an assembly. This lesson demonstrates the use of the ***Offset*** option to create a new work plane, a surface that does not already exist, to help geometric construction. By creating parametric work features, the established feature interactions in the CAD database assure the capturing of the design intent.

Reference Geometry II - Projected Geometry

❖ **Projected geometry** is another type of *reference geometry*. The *Project Geometry* tool can be used to project geometry from previously defined sketches or features onto the sketch plane. The position of the projected geometry is fixed to the feature from which it was projected. We can use the *Project Geometry* tool to project geometry from a sketch or feature onto the active sketch plane.

Typical usage of projected geometry include:

- Project a silhouette of a 3D feature onto the sketch plane for use in a 2D profile.
- Project the default center point onto the sketch plane to constrain a sketch to the origin of the coordinate system.
- Project a sketch from a feature onto the sketch plane so that the projected sketch can be used to constrain a new sketch.

The *Guide Block* Design

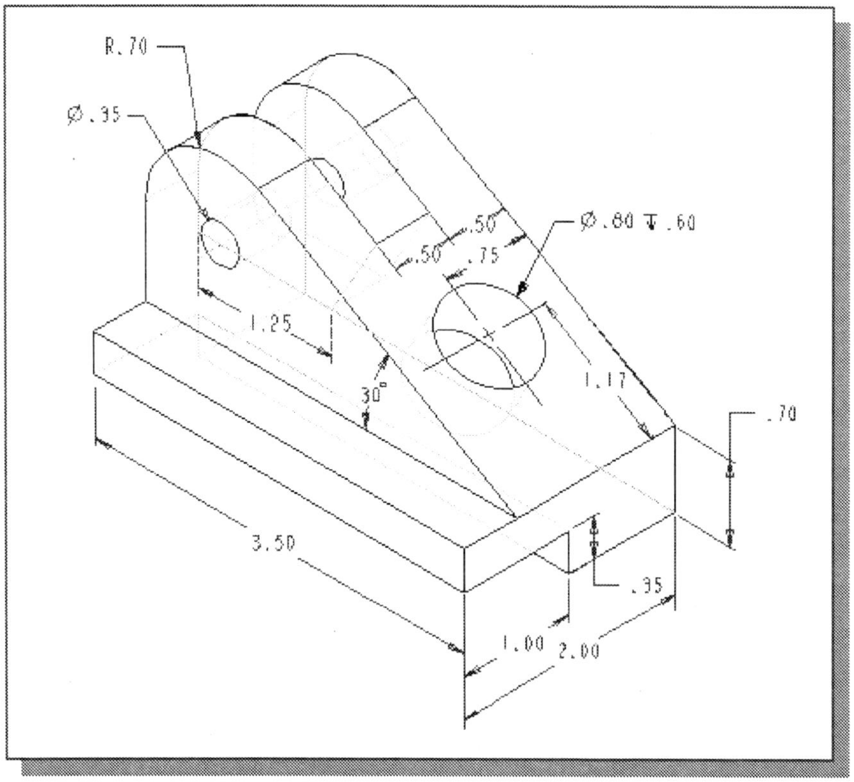

❖ Based on your knowledge of *Autodesk Inventor* so far, how many features would you use to create the design? Which feature would you choose as the first feature, the **BASE FEATURE,** of the model? What is your choice in arranging the order of the features? What are the more difficult features involved in the design? What tools do you think would be helpful in constructing the model? Take a few minutes to consider these questions and do preliminary planning by sketching on a piece of paper. You are also encouraged to create the model on your own prior to following through the tutorial.

Modeling Strategy

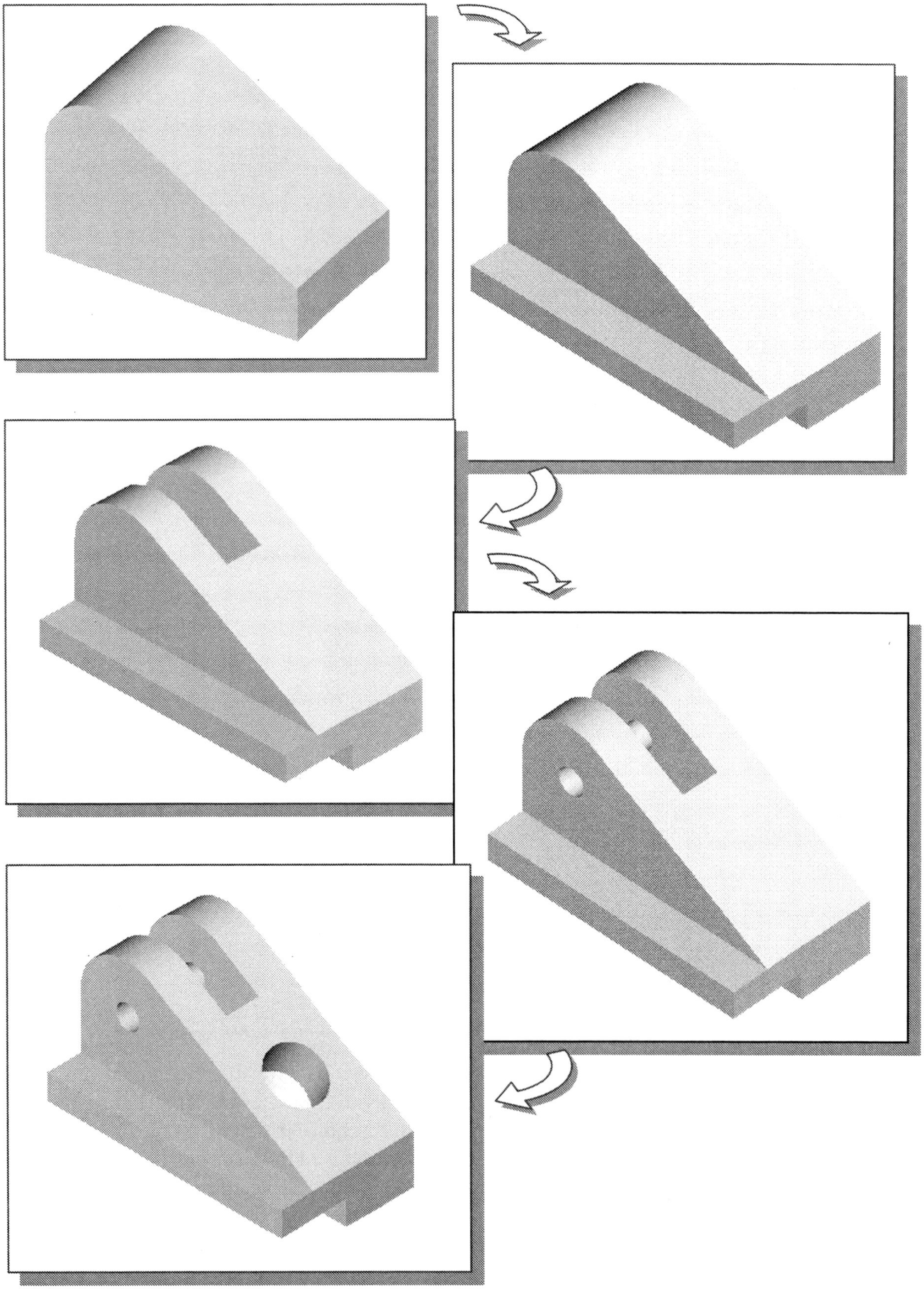

Starting Autodesk Inventor

1. Select the *Autodesk Inventor* option on the *Start* menu or select the *Autodesk Inventor* icon on the desktop to start *Autodesk Inventor*. The *Autodesk Inventor* main window will appear on the screen.

2. Once the program is loaded into the memory, the ***Startup*** dialog box appears at the center of the screen.

3. Select the ***New*** icon with a single click of the left-mouse-button in the *What to Do* dialog box.

4. Select the **English** tab and in the *New - Choose Template* area, select **Standard(in).ipt**.

5. Pick **OK** in the *Startup* dialog box to accept the selected settings.

Default sketch plane setting

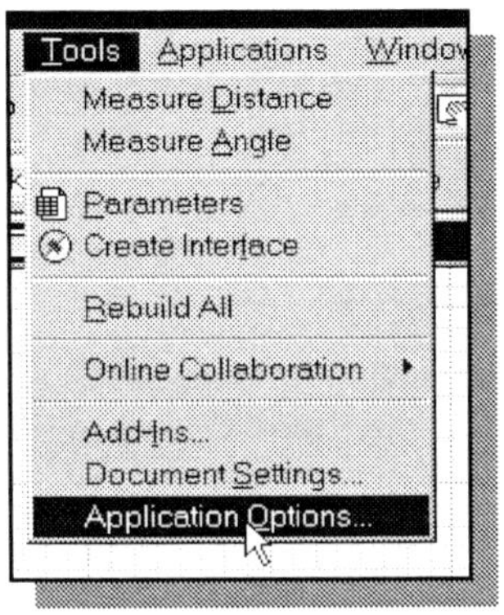

1. Select **Application Options** in the **Tools** pull-down menu.

- The **Application Options** menu allows us to set behavioral options, such as *color*, *file locations*, etc.

2. Click on the **Part** tab to display and/or modify the default sketch plane settings.

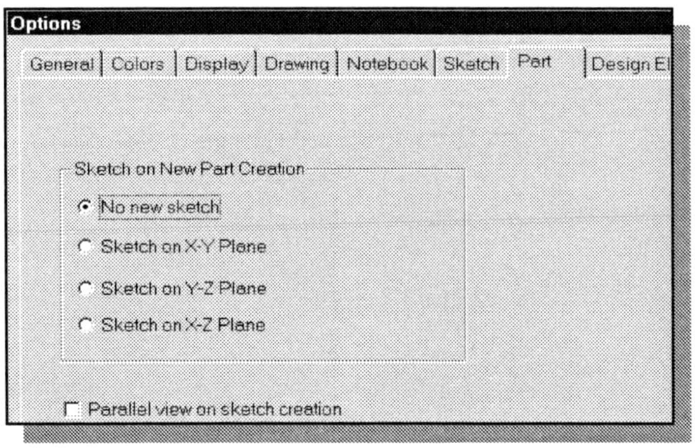

3. Click on the ***No new sketch*** option to set the setting on which sketch plane is used during new part creation.

4. Click on the **OK** button to accept the setting.

- Note that the new setting does not change the current part file; the setting will take effect when a new part file is opened.

5. On your own, **close** the current part file.

6. Click on the ***New*** icon in the *Standard* toolbar and open a new part file.

❖ Note the new part file, *PART2*, is no longer set up with a default sketching plane.

Applying the BORN Technique

1. In the *Part Browser* window, click on the [**+**] symbol in front of the ***Origin*** feature to display more information on the feature.

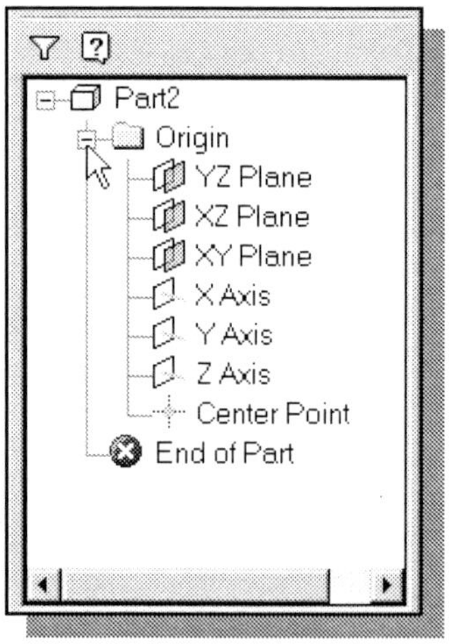

❖ In the *Browser* window, notice a new part name appeared with seven work features established. The seven work features include three *work-planes*, three *work-axes*, and a *work-point*. By default, the three work-planes and work-axes are aligned to the **world coordinate system** and the work-point is aligned to the *origin* of the **world coordinate system**.

2. Inside the *Browser* window, move the cursor on top of the third work-plane, the ***XY Plane***. Notice a rectangle, representing the work-plane, appears in the graphics window.

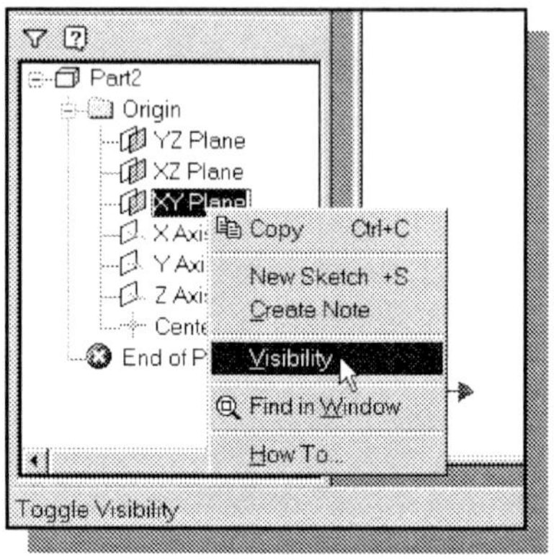

3. Inside the *Browser* window, click once with the **right-mouse-button** on *XY Plane* to display the option menu. Click on **Visibility** to toggle on the display of the plane.

4. On your own, repeat the above steps and toggle ***ON*** the display of all of the *work-planes*, *work-axes*, and the *center-point* on the screen.

5. On your own, use the *dynamic viewing* options (*3D orbit*, *Zoom* and *Pan*) to view the work features established.

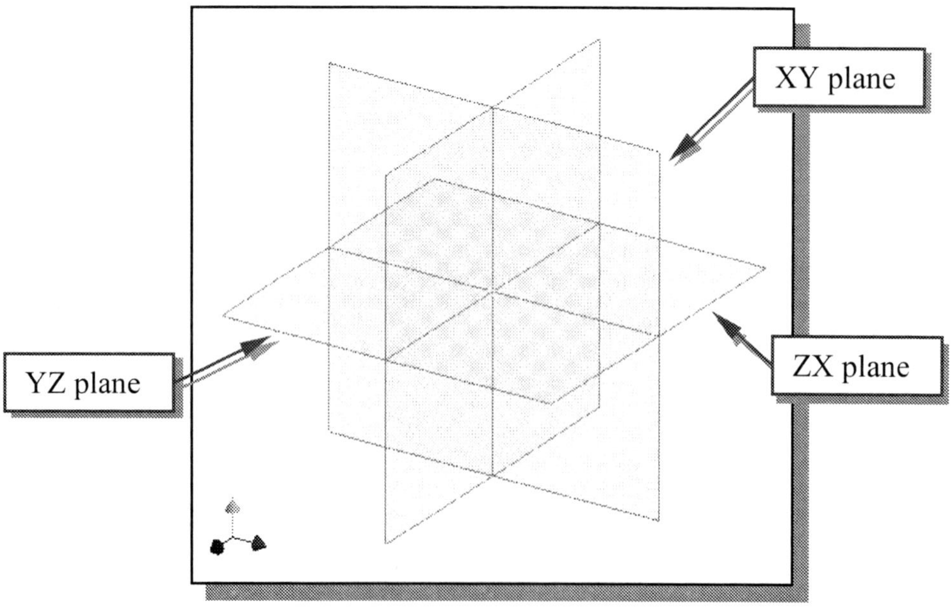

❖ By default, the basic set of work-planes is aligned to the world coordinate system; the work-planes are the first features of the part. We can now proceed to create solid features referencing the three mutually perpendicular datum planes. Instead of using only the default sketching-plane as the starting point, we can now select any of the work-planes as the sketching planes for subsequent solid features.

1. In the *Standard* toolbar select the ***Sketch*** command by left-clicking once on the icon.

2. In the *Status Bar* area, the message: "*Select face, workplane, sketch or sketch geometry.*" is displayed. *Autodesk Inventor* expects us to identify a planar surface where the 2D sketch of the next feature is to be created. Move the graphics cursor on top of ***XY Plane***, inside the *Browser* window as shown, and notice that *Autodesk Inventor* will automatically highlight the corresponding plane in the graphics window. Left-click once to select the *XY Plane* as the sketching plane.

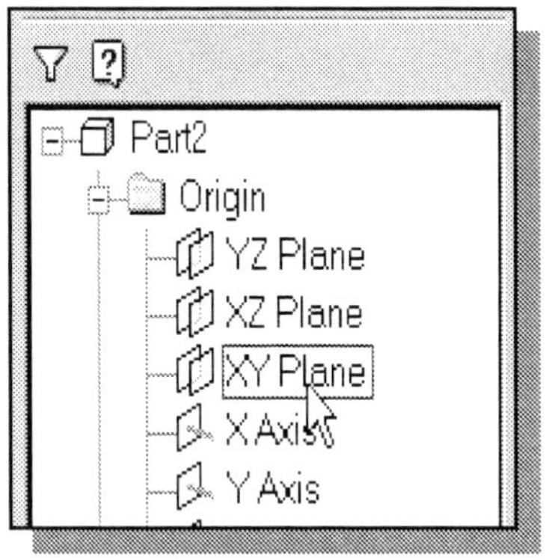

❖ *Autodesk Inventor* allows us to identify and select features in the graphics window and also in the *Browser* window.

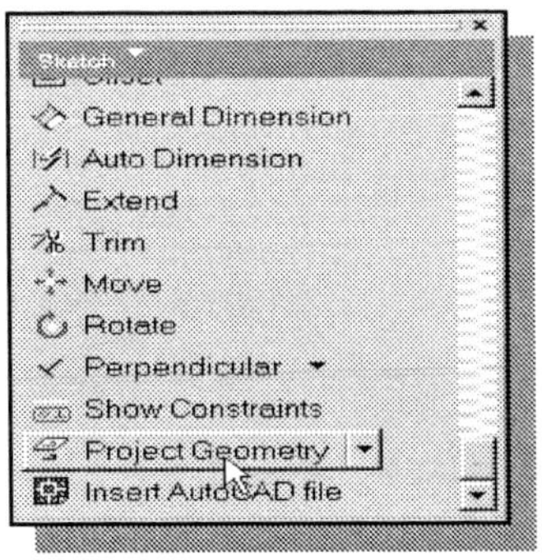

3. Select the ***Project Geometry*** command in the *Sketch* toolbar. The *Project Geometry* command allows us to project existing features to the active sketching plane. Left-click once on the icon to activate the *Project Geometry* command.

4. In the *Status Bar* area, the message: "*Select edge, vertex, work geometry or sketch geometry to project.*" is displayed. *Autodesk Inventor* expects us to select any existing geometry, which will be projected onto the active sketching plane. Inside the *Browser* window, move the graphics cursor on top of ***Center Point*** as shown, and notice that *Autodesk Inventor* will automatically highlight the corresponding feature in the graphics window. Left-click once to project the center point onto the sketching plane.

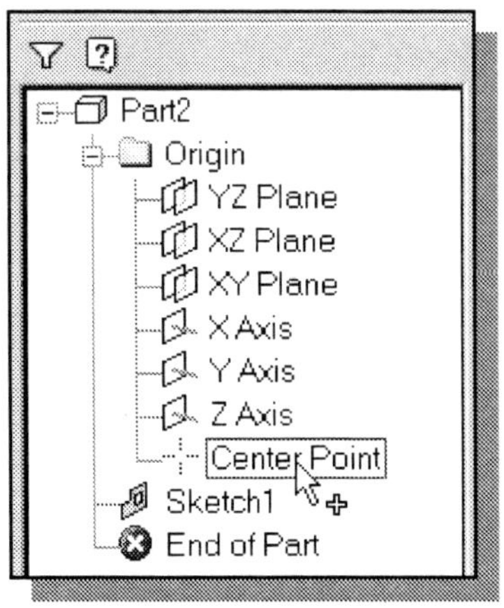

Creating the 2D Sketch for the Base Feature

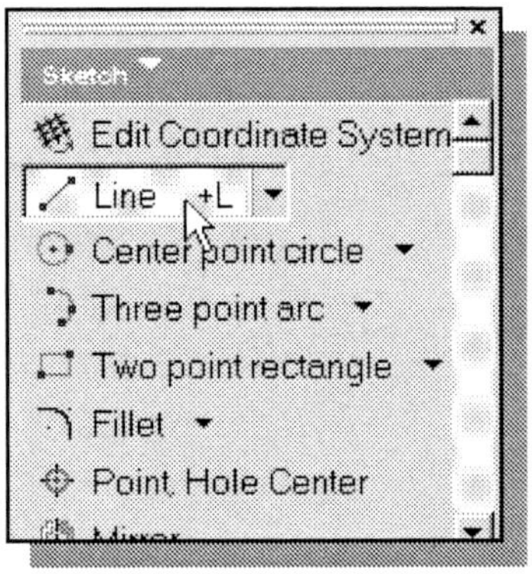

1. Move the graphics cursor to the ***Line*** icon in the *Sketch* toolbar. A *Help-tip box* appears next to the cursor and a brief description of the command is displayed at the bottom of the drawing screen: *"Creates Straight line segments and tangent arcs."*

2. Pick the **center point**, the point that was projected onto the sketching plane. Note the *alignment symbol* as the cursor is moved next to the center point.

3. Create a horizontal line by selecting a location toward the right and then a vertical line as shown below.

4. For the next point, move the cursor directly above the starting point and select a point when the *alignment symbol* is displayed.

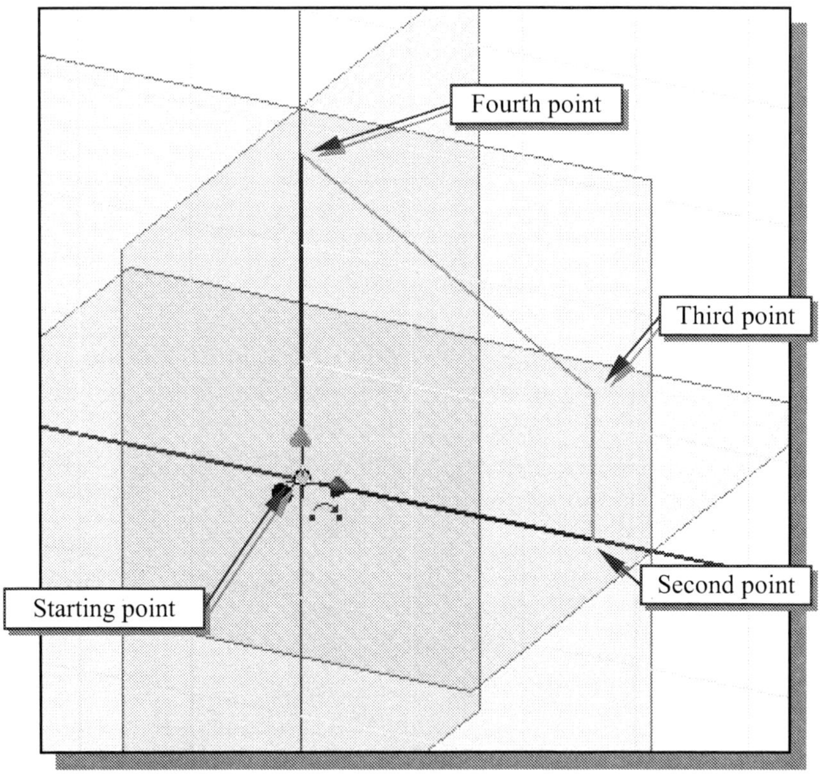

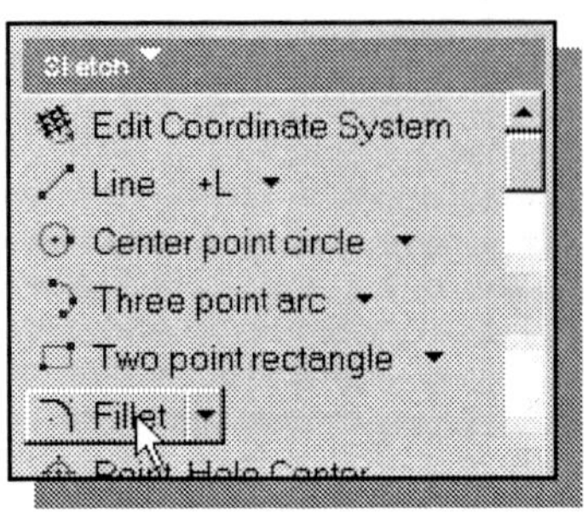

5. Select the ***Fillet*** command in the *Sketch* toolbar.

- We will use the default radius to create a rounded corner at the top corner of the current sketch.

6. Select the two edges as shown below and create a fillet of arbitrary radius.

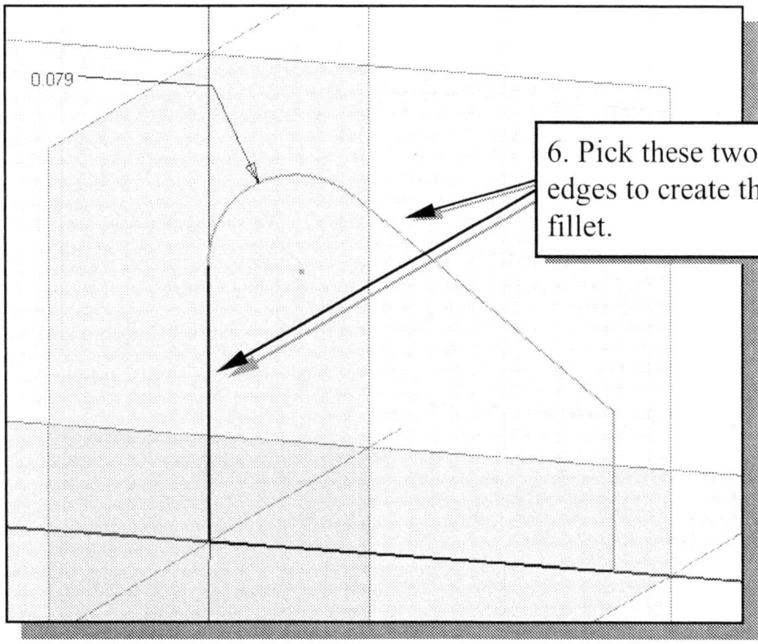

7. Click on the [**X**] icon to close the fillet *Radius* popup window.

Apply/modify constraints and dimensions

➢ How many more constraints or dimensions would be necessary to fully describe the sketched geometry?

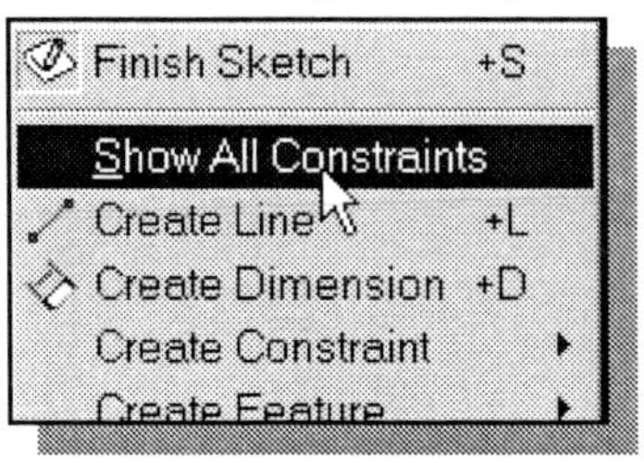

1. Inside the graphics window, click once with the **right-mouse-button** to display the option menu. Select **Show All Constraints** in the popup menu to display all the applied constraints.

➢ On your own, examine the constraints that have been applied to the 2D sketch. Notice the different constraints applied to the sketch: the *vertical*, *horizontal*, and *tangent* constraints. Also note in the above figure, the *Fix* constraint is applied to the upper right corner of the sketch.

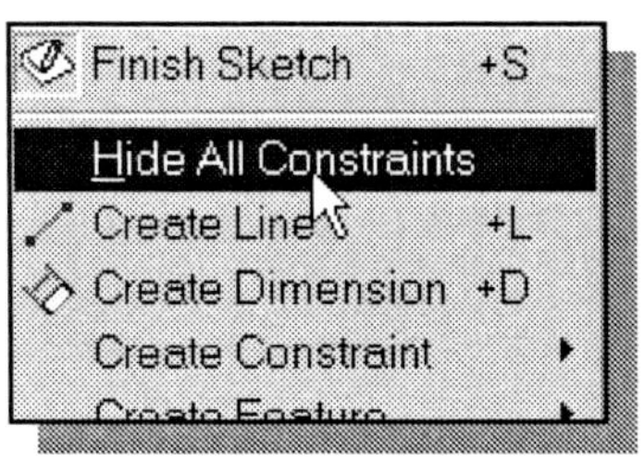

2. Inside the graphics window, **right-mouse-click** once to bring up the option menu and select **Hide All Constraints** to proceed with hiding the constraints.

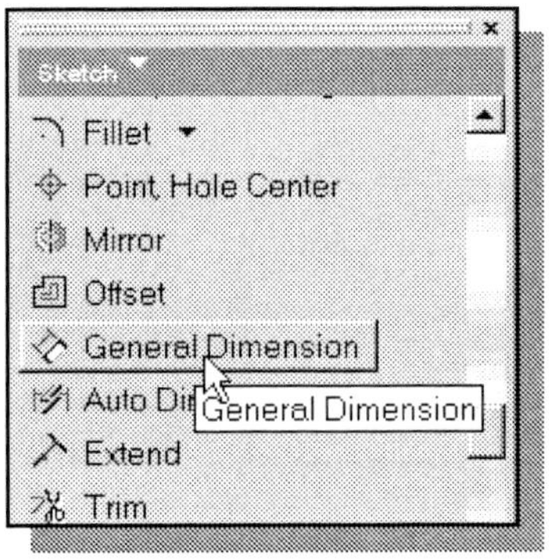

3. Select the ***General Dimension*** command in the *Sketch* toolbar.

4. Pick the horizontal line as the first entity to dimension as shown below.

5. Place the dimension text below the horizontal line. The dimension value displayed below might be different than the display on your screen.

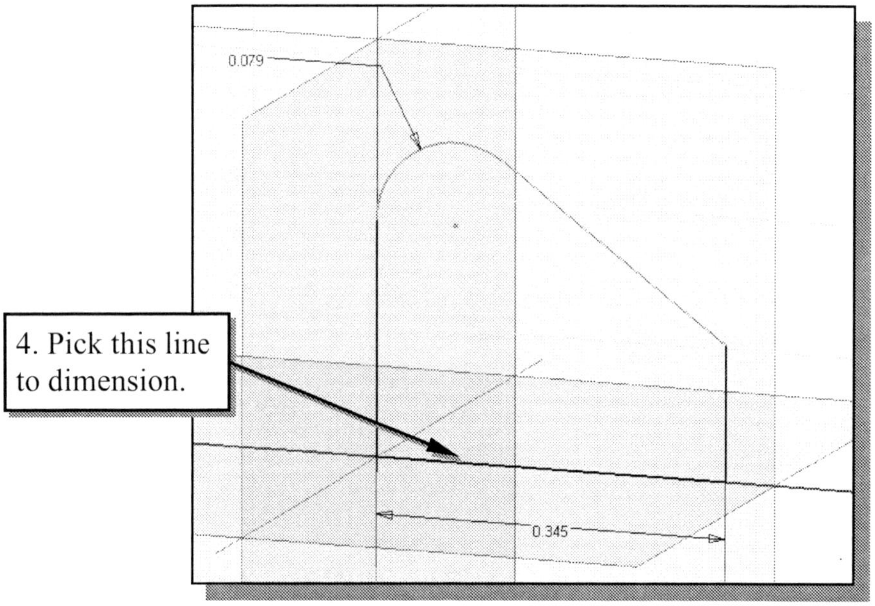

6. On your own, create the angle dimension and the height dimension as shown. (Hint: Selecting two non-parallel lines will create an angle dimension.)

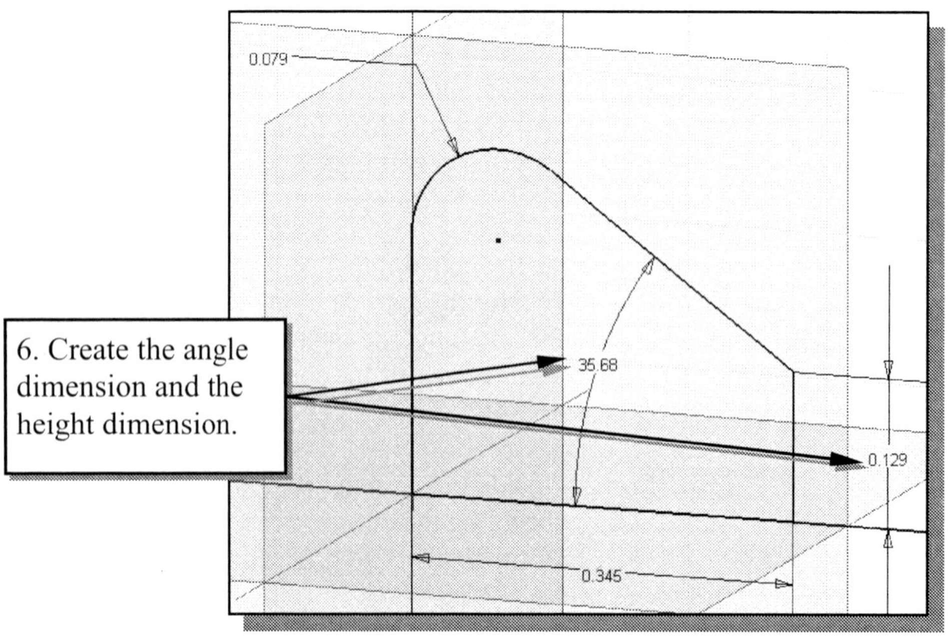

Parametric Relations

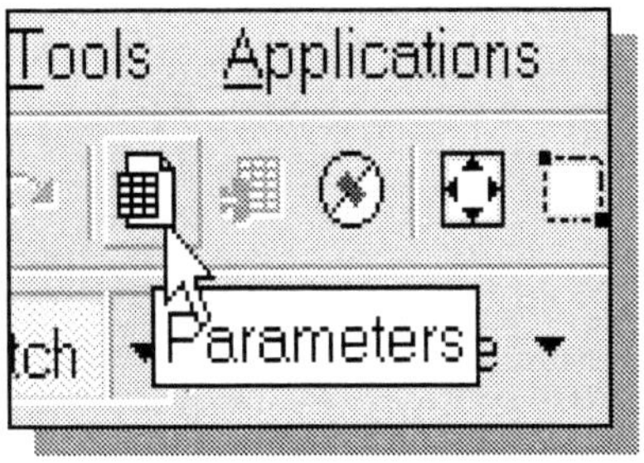

1. In the *Standard* toolbar select the ***Parameters*** command by left-clicking once on the icon. The *Parameters* popup window appears.

2. On your own, create two parametric relations defining the ***size*** of the *Round* and the ***length*** of the *right-edge* as one-fifth of the width dimension as shown below. (Both refer to the width dimension **d1**.)

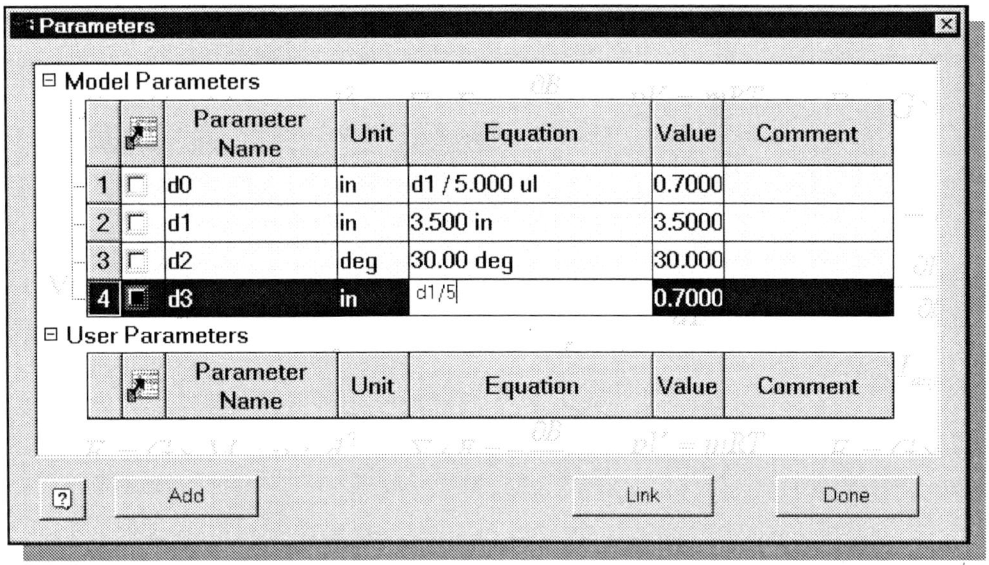

3. Modify the overall width of the sketch to **3.5** and the angle to **30** as shown in the above figure.

4. Click on the **Done** button to accept the settings.

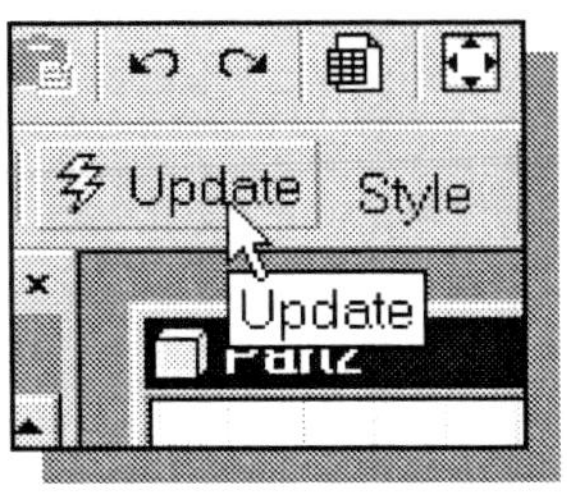

5. Click on the **Update** button in the *Standard* toolbar area to proceed with updating the 2D sketch.

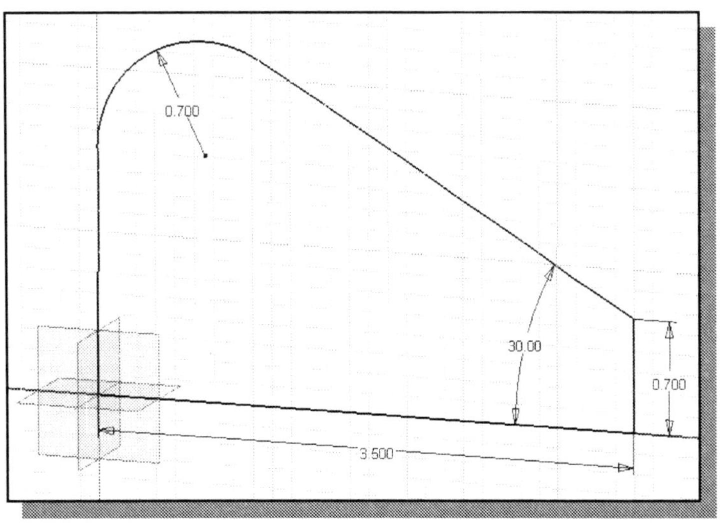

Create the First Extrude Feature

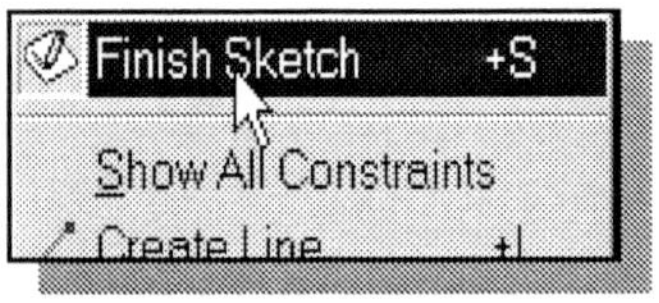

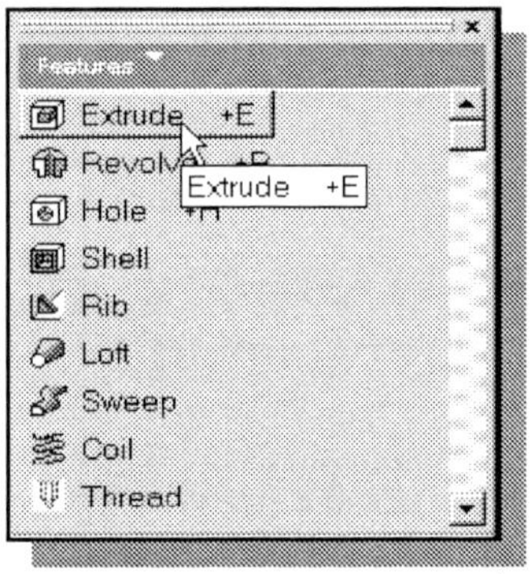

1. Inside the graphics window, click once with the right-mouse-button to display the option menu. Select **Finish Sketch** in the popup menu to end the *Sketch* option.

2. In the *Feature* toolbar (the toolbar that is located to the left side of the graphics window), select the ***Extrude*** command by clicking once with the left-mouse-button on the icon.

3. In the *Distance* option box, enter **2.0** as the extrusion distance.

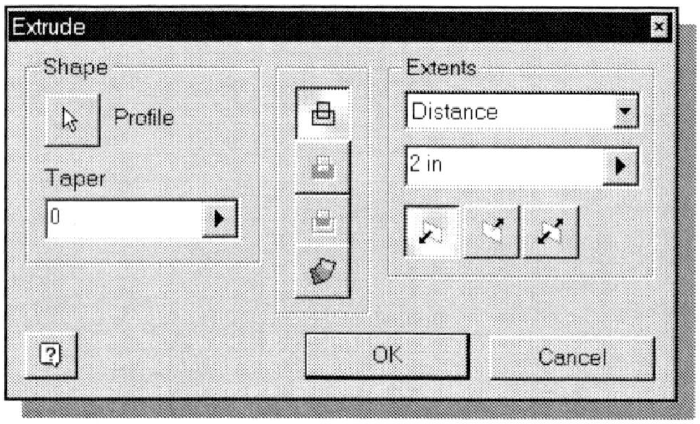

4. In the *Extrude* popup window, click on the **OK** button to proceed with the *Extrude* command.

❖ Now is a good time to save the model (Quick key: [Ctrl] + [S]). It is a good habit to save your model periodically, just in case something might go wrong while you are working on the model. You should also save the model after you have completed any major constructions.

Creating an Offset Work Plane

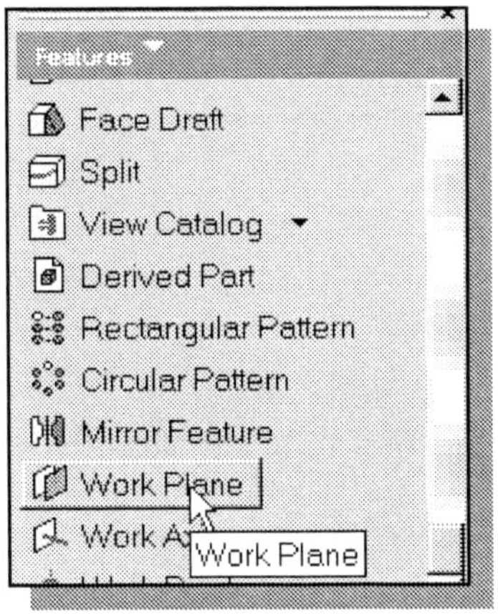

1. In the *Feature* toolbar (the toolbar that is located to the left side of the graphics window), select the ***Work Plane*** command by left-mouse-clicking the icon.

2. In the *Status Bar* area, the message: "*Define work plane by highlighting and selecting geometry*" is displayed. *Autodesk Inventor* expects us to select any existing geometry, which will be used as a reference to create the new work plane.

3. Inside the graphics window, move the graphics cursor next to the edges of the ***XY Plane***, until it is highlighted as shown below. Left-click once to select the *XY Plane* as the reference of the new work plane.

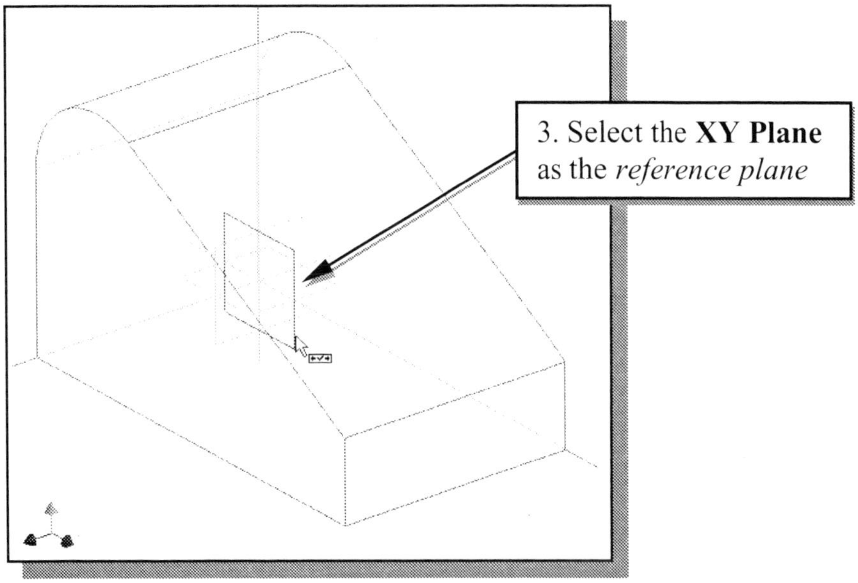

4. Use the left-mouse-button and drag toward the lower-left corner of the graphics window. The *Offset* popup window is displayed.

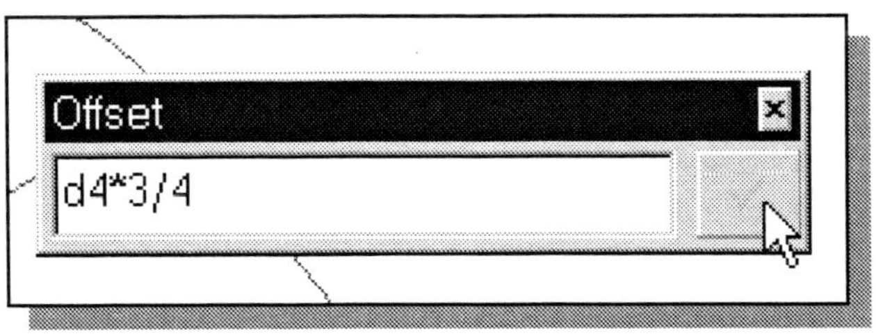

5. In the *Offset* popup window, enter **d4*3/4** as the offset distance for the new work plane.

❖ Note that **d4** is the variable name of the extrusion distance for the base solid.

6. Click on the **check mark** button to accept the setting.

Creating a 2D sketch on the work plane

1. In the *Standard* toolbar select the ***Sketch*** command by left-clicking once on the icon.

2. In the *Status Bar* area, the message: "*Select face, work plane, sketch or sketch geometry.*" is displayed. Pick the work plane by clicking on the lower edge of the work plane as shown below.

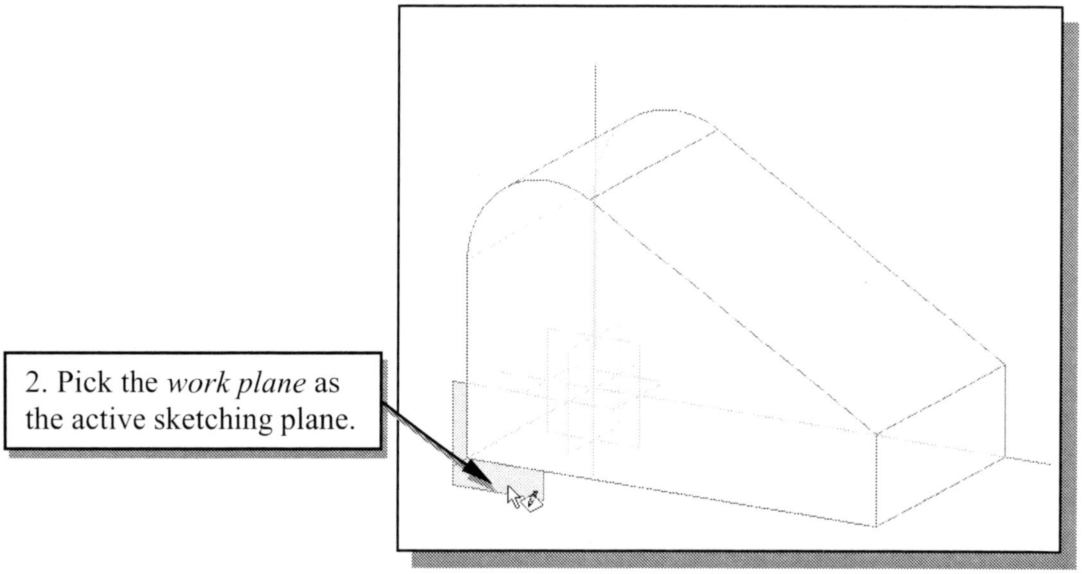

3. On your own, use the *dynamic viewing* options (*3D orbit*, *Zoom* and *Pan*) to view the alignment of the sketching plane. Adjust the display to view the left-vertical surface of the model, as shown below, before proceeding to the next section.

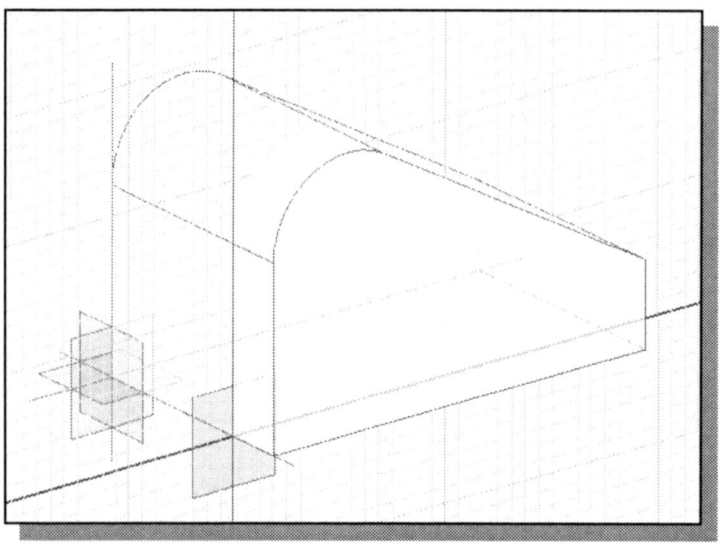

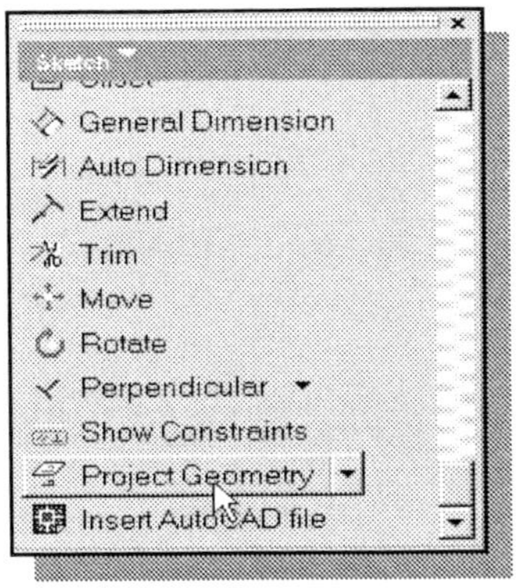

4. Select the ***Project Geometry*** command in the *Sketch* toolbar. The *Project Geometry* command allows us to project existing features to the active sketching plane. Left-click once on the icon to activate the *Project Geometry* command.

5. In the *Status Bar* area, the message: "*Select edge, vertex, work geometry or sketch geometry to project.*" is displayed. Left-click once on ***Center Point*** to project the center point onto the sketching plane.

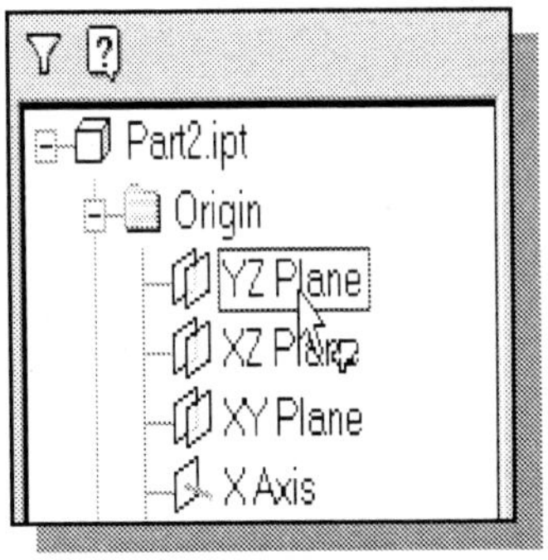

6. In the *Status Bar* area, the message: "*Select edge, vertex, work geometry or sketch geometry to project.*" is displayed. Inside the *Browser* window, select ***YZ Plane*** to create a projected geometry onto the sketching plane.

❖ Note a dark line appears along the vertical axis. The projection of a plane appears as a line on the sketching plane.

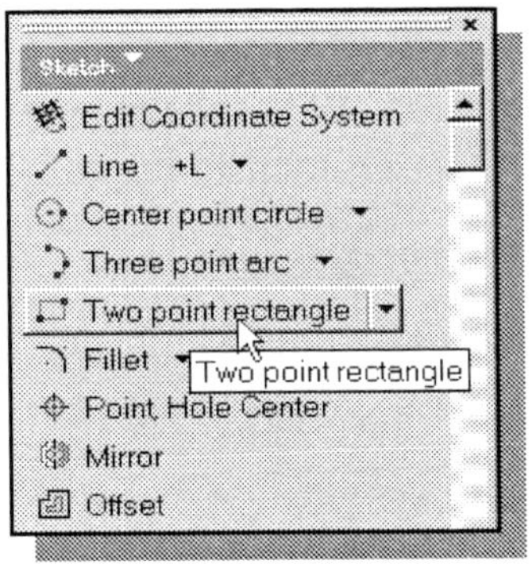

7. Select the ***Two point rectangle*** command by clicking once with the left-mouse-button on the icon in the *Sketch* toolbar.

8. On your own, create a rectangle of arbitrary size, with one corner aligned to the vertical axis, above the projected center point, as shown below.

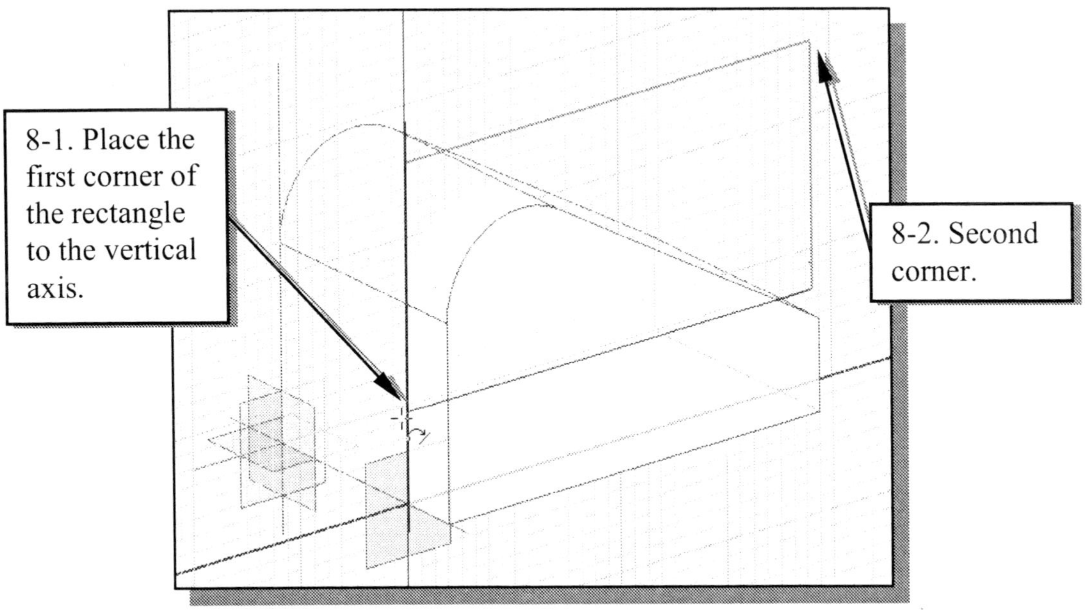

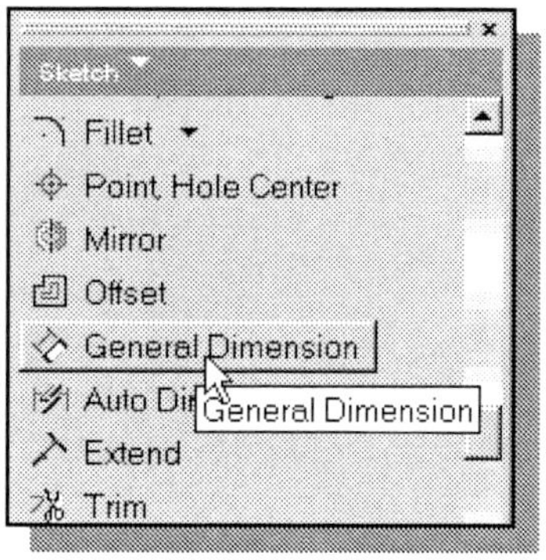

9. Move the cursor on top of the ***General Dimension*** icon. Left-click once on the icon to activate the *General Dimension* command.

10. Select the projected center point as the first entity to dimension.

11. Select the bottom horizontal edge of the rectangle as the second entity to dimension.

12. Place the dimension text toward the right side of the graphics window as shown below.

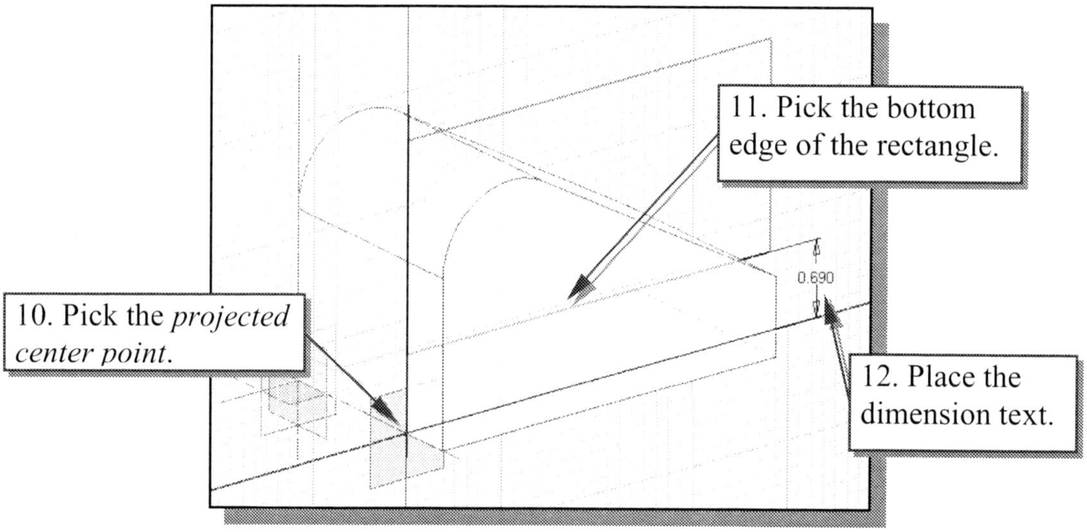

13. On your own, create the two size-dimensions of the rectangle as shown below.

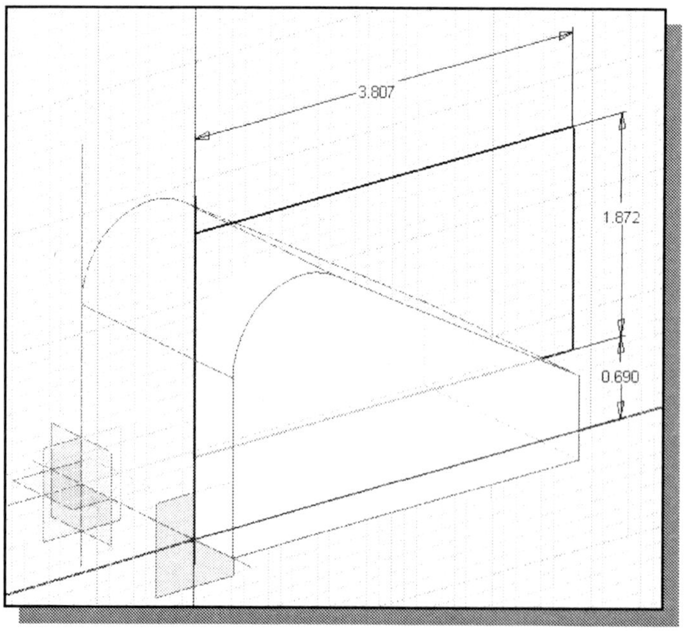

14. On your own, modify the size-dimensions of the rectangle to match the width dimension (**d1**) of the base feature and set the location-dimension of the rectangle to be one-fifth of the width dimension (**d1**) as shown below.

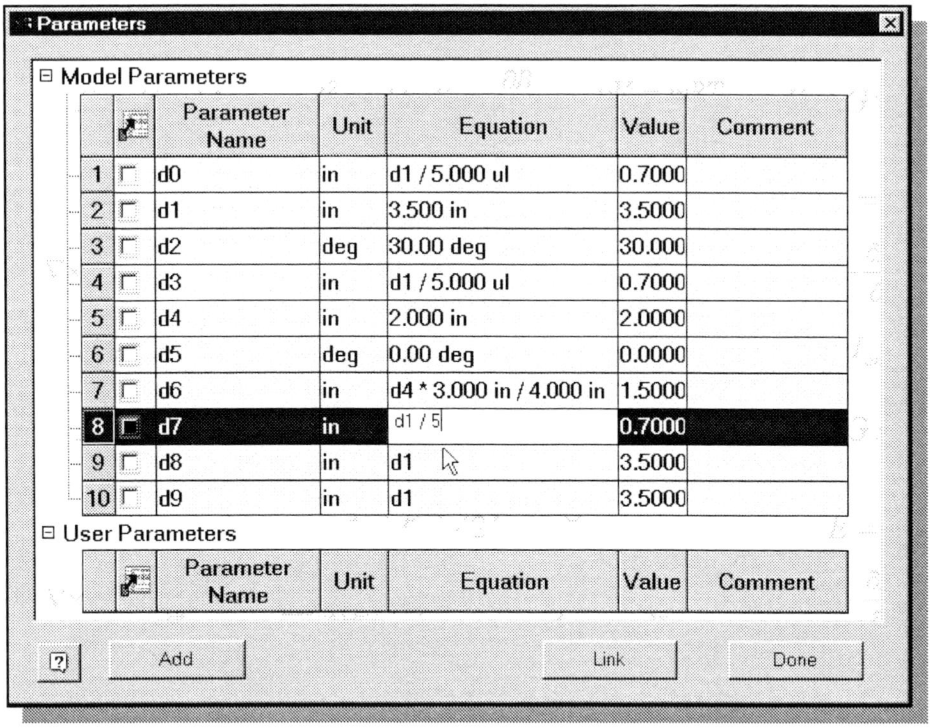

	Parameter Name	Unit	Equation	Value	Comment
1	d0	in	d1 / 5.000 ul	0.7000	
2	d1	in	3.500 in	3.5000	
3	d2	deg	30.00 deg	30.000	
4	d3	in	d1 / 5.000 ul	0.7000	
5	d4	in	2.000 in	2.0000	
6	d5	deg	0.00 deg	0.0000	
7	d6	in	d4 * 3.000 in / 4.000 in	1.5000	
8	d7	in	d1 / 5	0.7000	
9	d8	in	d1	3.5000	
10	d9	in	d1	3.5000	

15. Click on the **Done** button to exit the *Parameters* dialog box.

16. Click on the **Update** button in the *Standard* toolbar area to proceed with updating the 2D sketch.

Completing the Second Extrude Feature

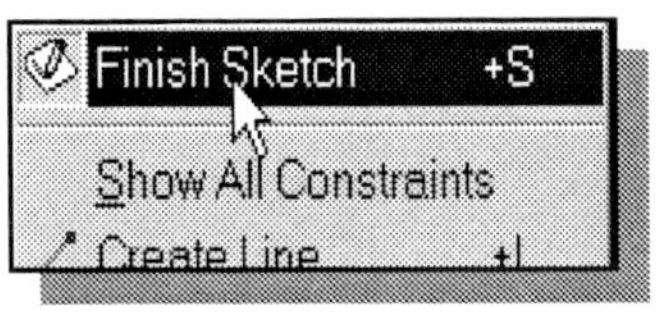

1. Inside the graphics window, click once with the right-mouse-button to display the option menu. Select **Finish Sketch** in the popup menu to end the *Sketch* option.

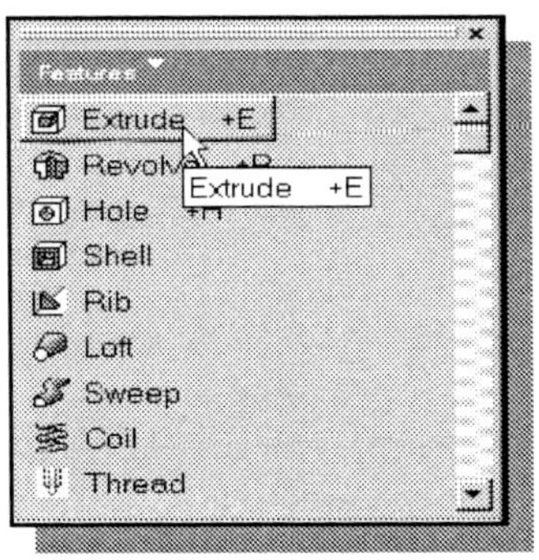

2. In the *Feature* toolbar (the toolbar that is located to the left side of the graphics window), select the ***Extrude*** command by clicking once with the left-mouse-button on the icon.

3. In the *Extrude* dialog box, click on the ***Cut*** operation button.

4. In the *Distance* option box, set the extrusion *Extents* to ***All***.

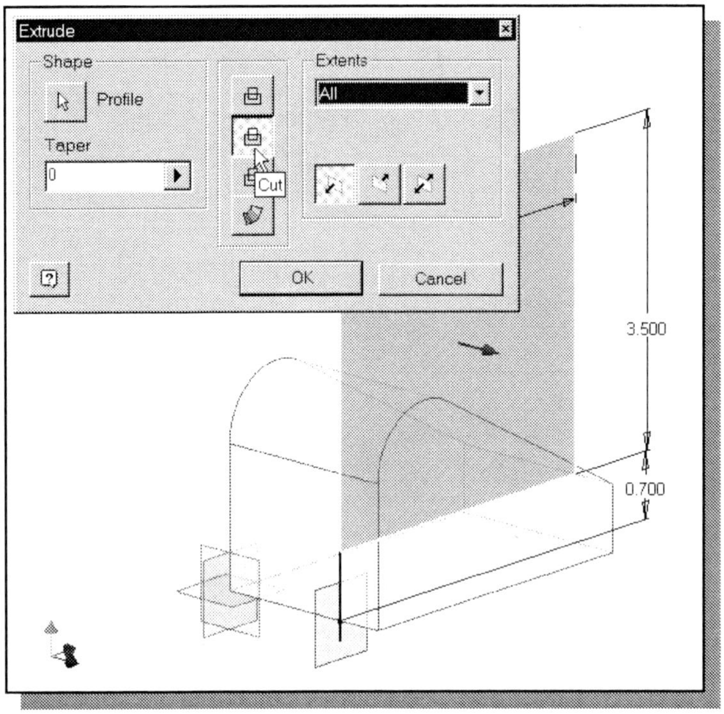

5. Confirm the arrow is pointing toward the front side of the solid model as shown in the above figure.

6. Click on the **OK** button to proceed with the *Cut* operation.

Creating the next Cut feature

1. In the *Standard* toolbar select the ***Sketch*** command by left-clicking once on the icon.

2. In the *Status Bar* area, the message: "*Select face, work plane, sketch or sketch geometry.*" is displayed. Pick the right-vertical face of the solid model shown below.

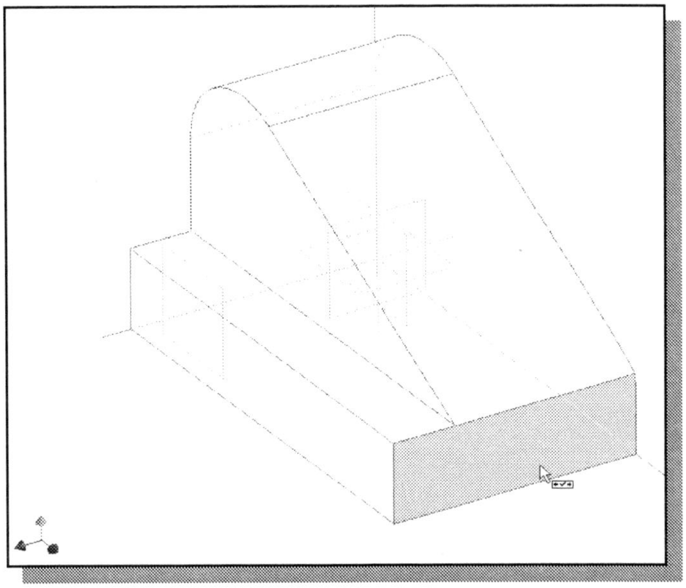

3. On your own, create a rectangle and apply the dimensions as shown below. (Note that **d1** is the overall width of the base feature and **d4** is the extrusion distance of the base feature. The bottom-left corner of the rectangle is aligned to bottom corner of the solid model.)

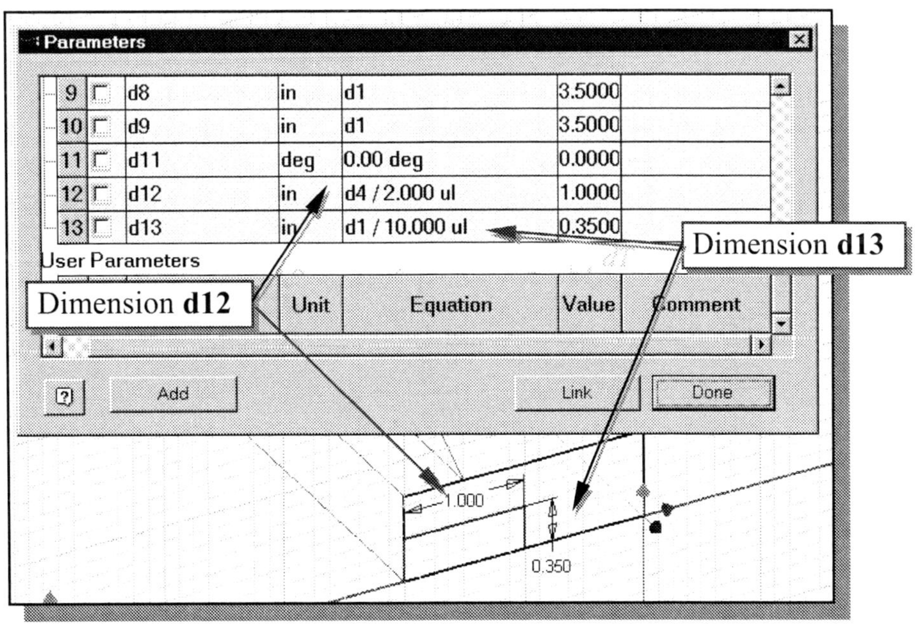

4. On your own, use the ***Extrude*** command and create a cutout that cuts through the entire 3D solid model as shown below.

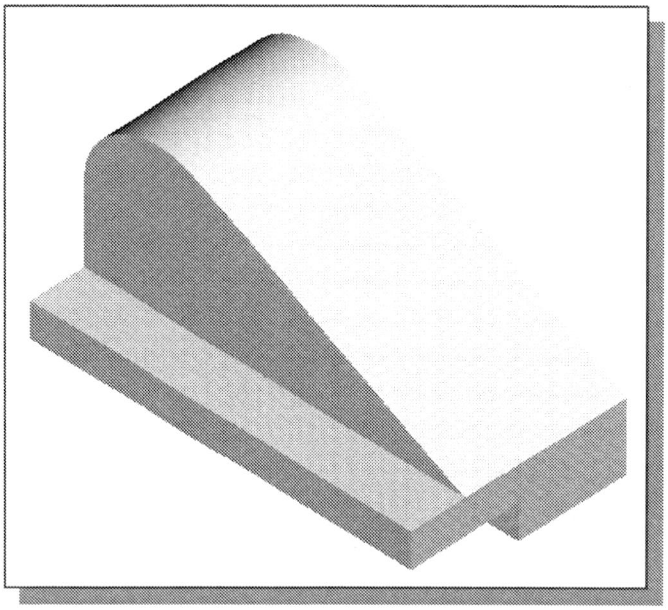

➢ What are the differences between the methods we used to create the last two cut-features? Which method is faster to do for our design? What are the advantages and disadvantages of the two approaches?

Third Cutout - Using Another Work Plane

- A **work plane** is a tool that can be used to help construct features that must reside on a part where there is no existing 2D surface to sketch on. A *work plane* can be used to create an artificial 2D surface for feature construction. If the *work plane* is moved, by adjusting dimensions or constraints, the plane and any features attached to it are also moved.

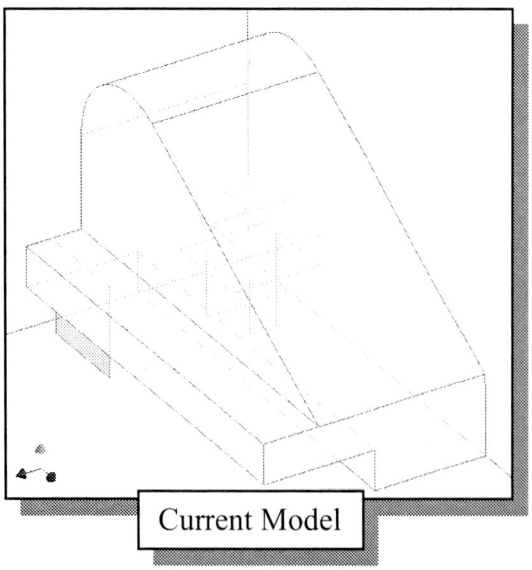

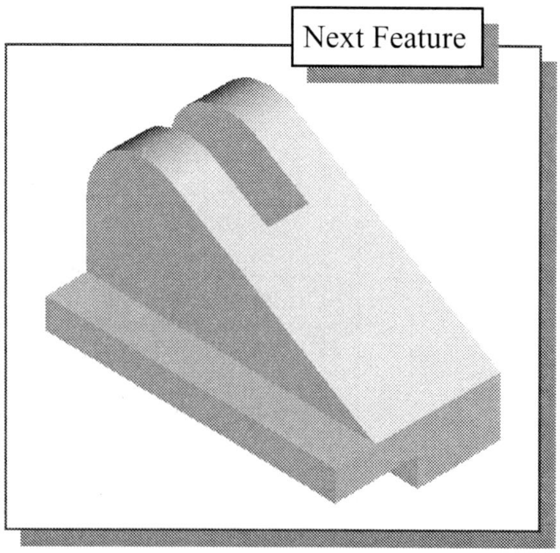

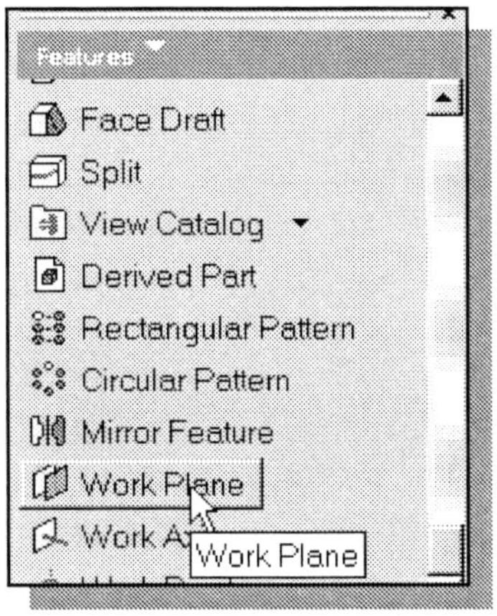

1. In the *Feature* toolbar (the toolbar that is located to the left side of the graphics window), select the ***Work Plane*** command by left-clicking once on the icon.

2. In the *Status Bar* area, the message: "*Define work plane by highlighting and selecting geometry*" is displayed. *Autodesk Inventor* expects us to select any existing geometry, which will be used as a reference to create the new work plane.

3. Inside the graphics window, move the cursor next to any edge of the ***XY Plane*** so that it is highlighted as shown below. Left-click once to select the *XY Plane* as the reference of the new work plane.

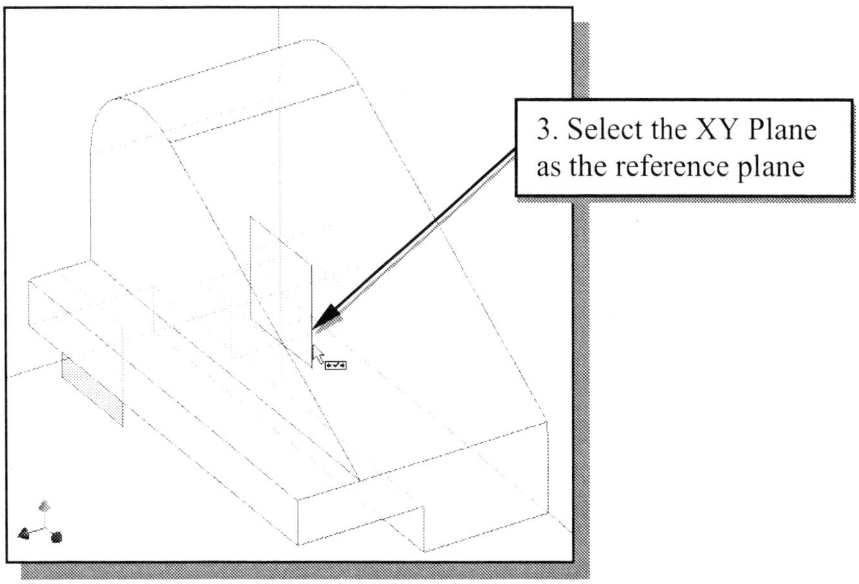

4. Use the left-mouse-button and drag toward the lower-left corner of the graphics window.

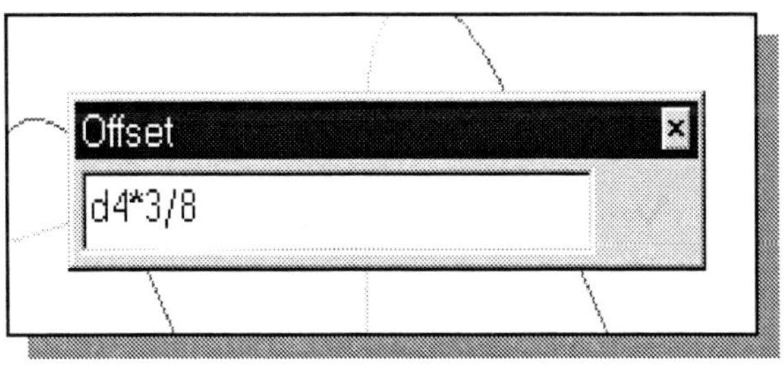

5. In the *Offset* popup window, enter **d4*3/8** as the offset distance for the new work plane.

❖ Note that **d4** is the variable name of the extrusion distance for the base solid.

6. Click on the check-mark button to accept the setting and proceed to create the new work plane.

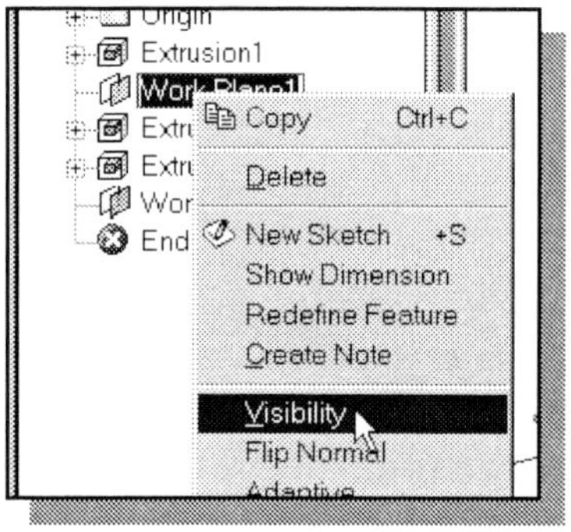

7. Inside the *Browser* window, right-mouse-click on ***Work Plane1*** to bring up the option menu.

8. Click on the *Visibility* box to turn ***OFF*** the display of the work plane.

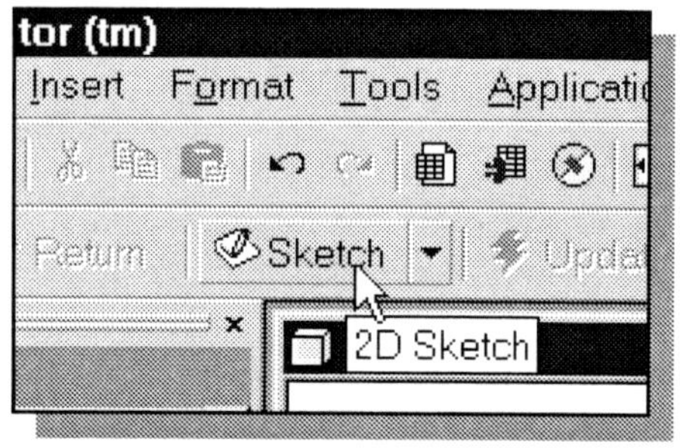

9. In the *Standard* toolbar select the ***Sketch*** command by left-clicking once on the icon.

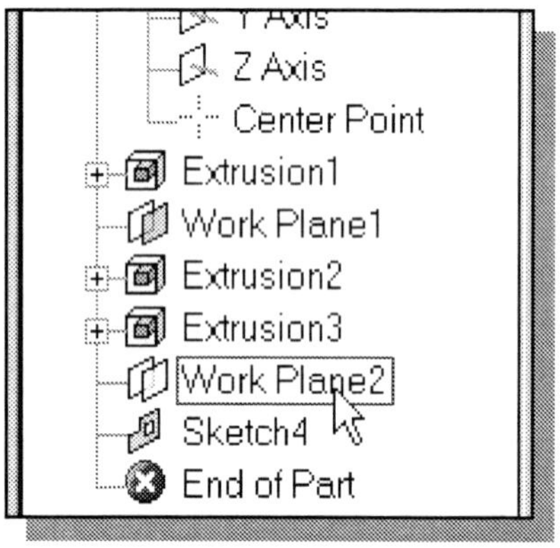

10. In the *Status Bar* area, the message: *"Select face, work plane, sketch or sketch geometry."* is displayed. Inside the *Browser* window, select ***Work Plane2*** by clicking on the name of the work plane as shown.

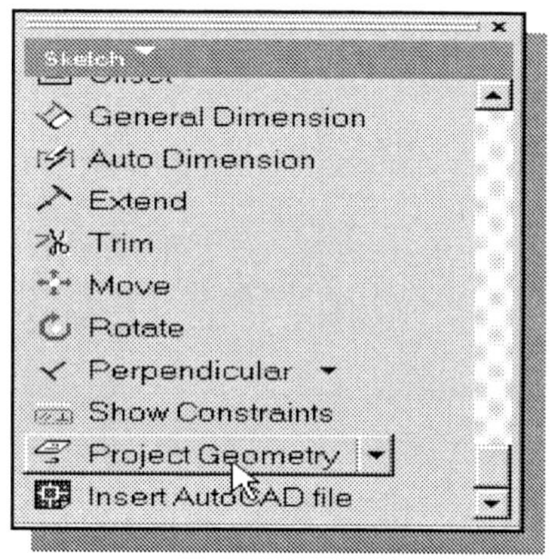

11. Select the ***Project Geometry*** command in the *Sketch* toolbar. The *Project Geometry* command allows us to project existing features to the active sketching plane. Left-click once on the icon to activate the *Project Geometry* command.

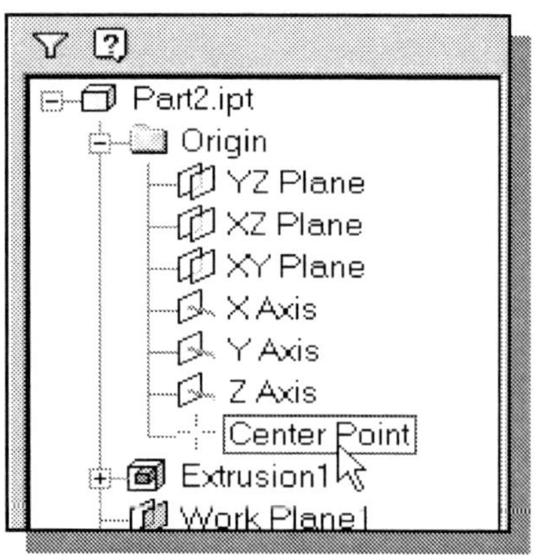

12. In the *Status Bar* area, the message: "*Select edge, vertex, work geometry or sketch geometry to project.*" is displayed. Left-click once on ***Center Point*** to project the center point onto the sketching plane.

13. In the *Status Bar* area, the message: "*Select edge, vertex, work geometry or sketch geometry to project.*" is displayed. On your own, inside the *Browser* window, select ***YZ Plane*** to create a projected geometry onto the sketching plane.

14. Select the back-edge of the inclined face to create a projected geometry onto the sketching plane as shown below.

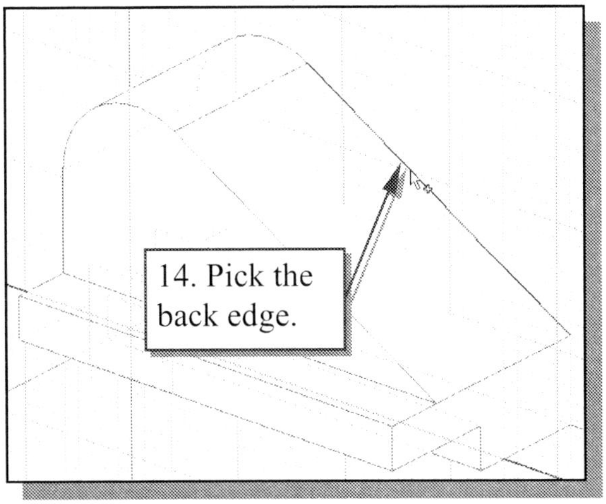

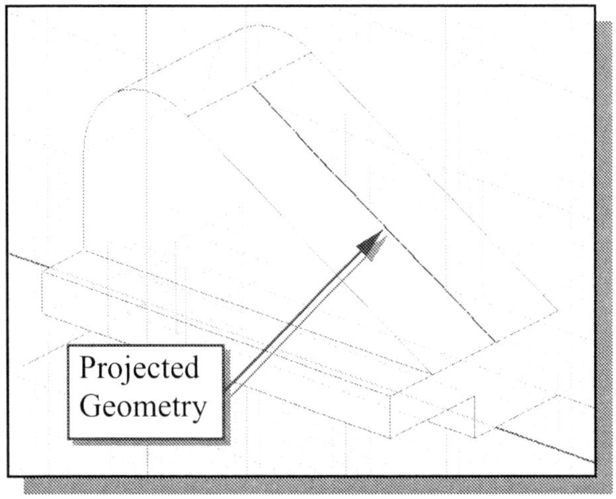

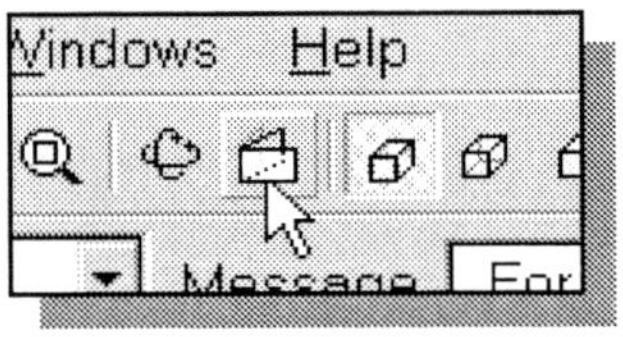

15. In the *Standard* toolbar area, click on the ***Look At*** button.

❖ The *Look At* command allows us to switch to a 2D view of a selected surface.

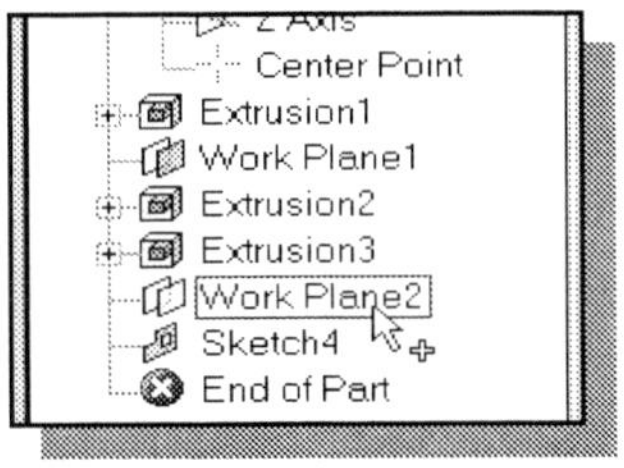

16. Inside the *Browser* window, select ***Work Plane2***.

17. On your own, create a closed-region sketch by starting at the ***starting point*** as shown below. Note that the first line created is perpendicular to the inclined line and the ***third point*** and the ***fourth point*** are aligned vertically with the **projected center point** and **vertical axis**.

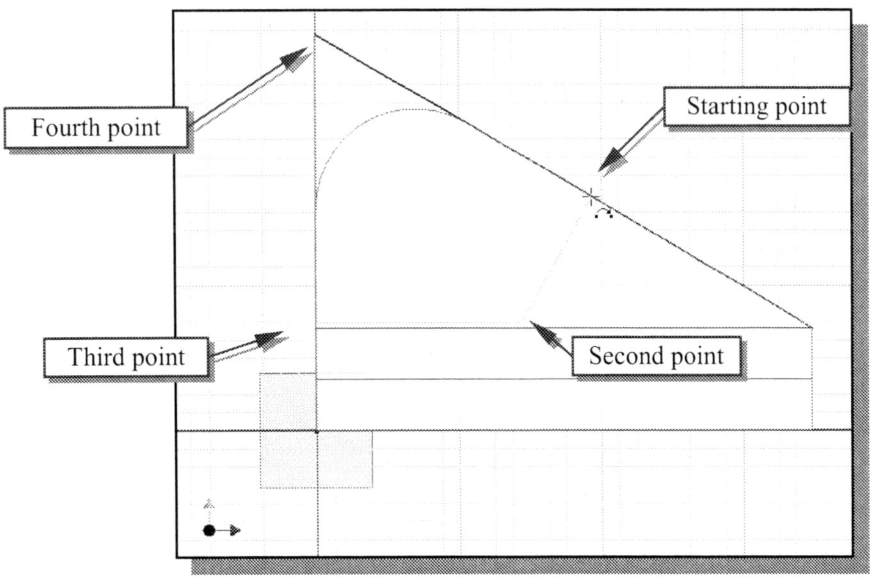

18. On your own, complete the profile by examining the active constraints and create/modify the two dimensions as shown below. (Hint: select the project center point and the horizontal line of the sketch for the vertical dimension.)

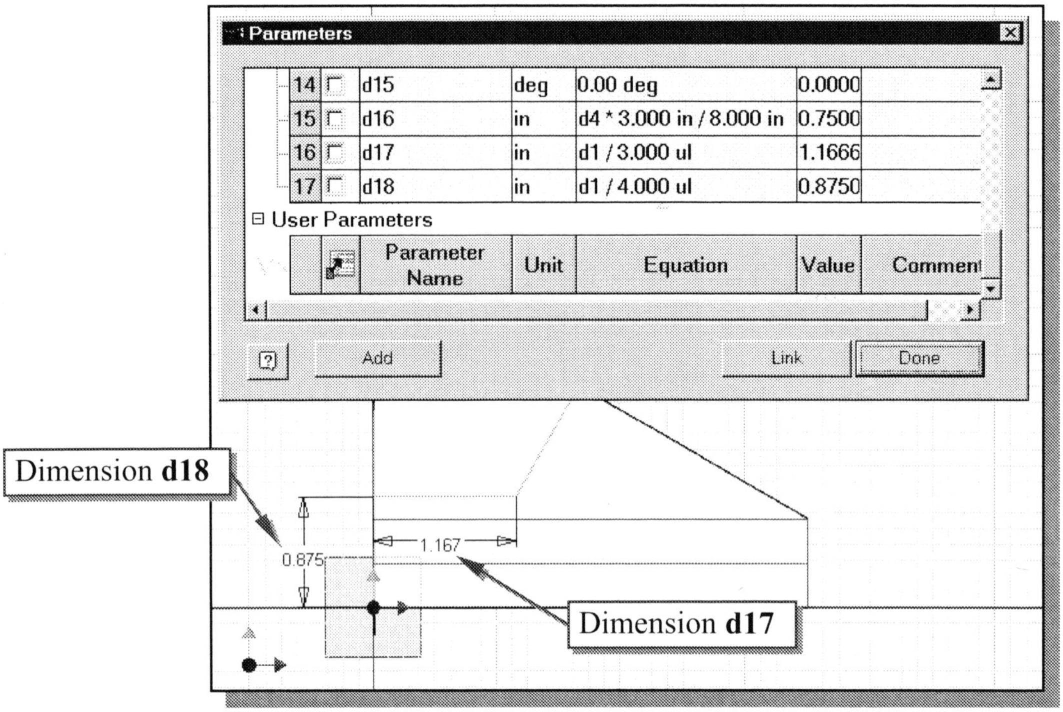

19. On your own, create a ***CUT*** extrusion using the ***MidPlane*** option**,** with a distance of **d4/4**.

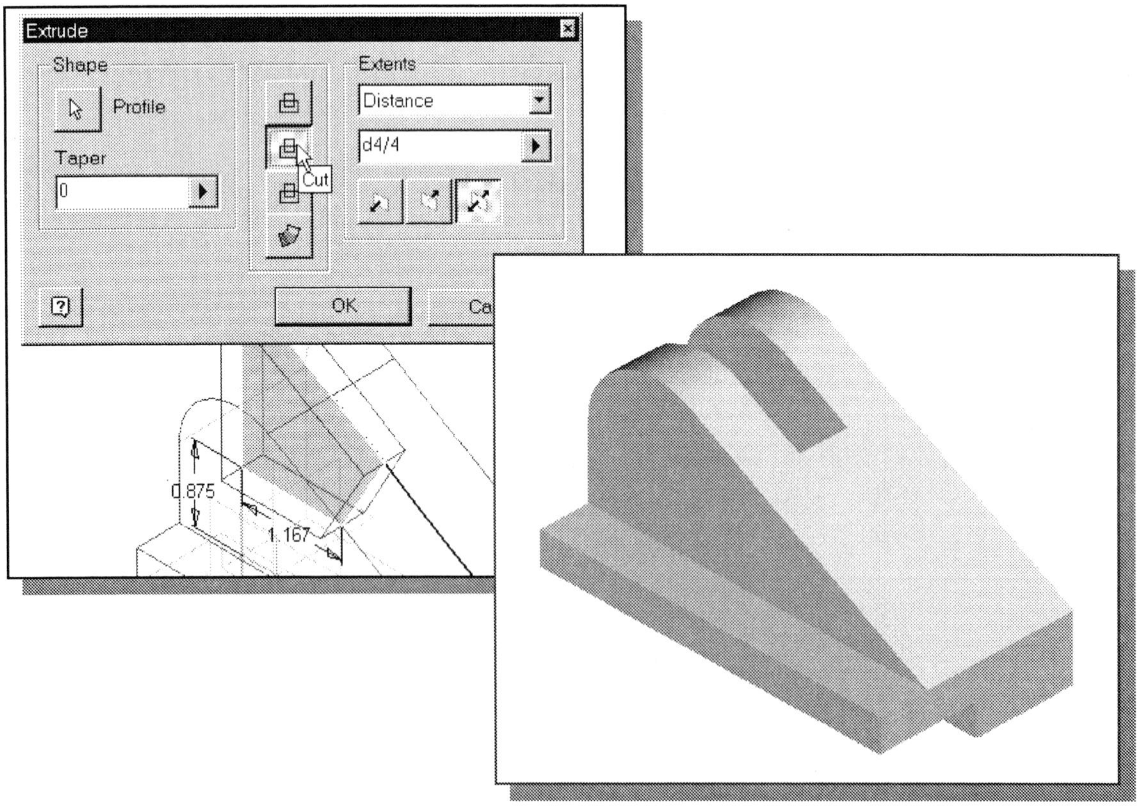

Adding additional geometry to the 2D sketch of the base feature

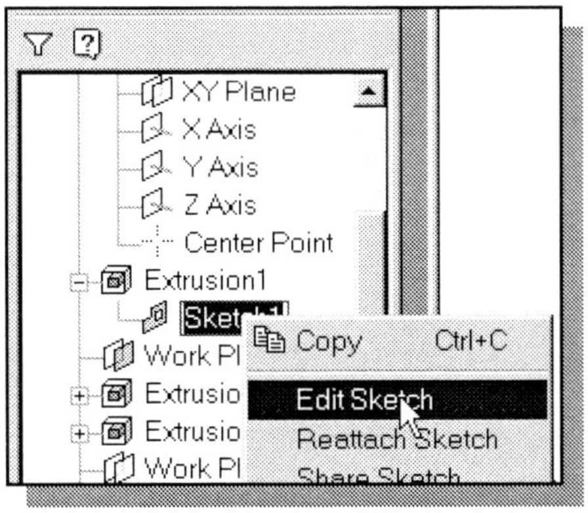

1. In the *Browser* window, click on the [**+**] icon in front of ***Extrusion1***.

2. Right-click once on ***Sketch1*** to bring up the option menu.

3. Select **Edit Sketch** in the popup option menu.

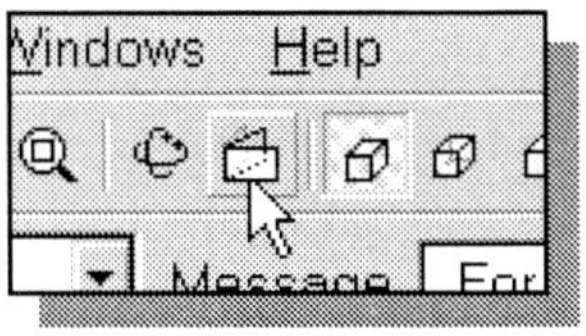

4. In the *Standard* toolbar area, click on the ***Look At*** button.

5. Select any edge of the 2D sketch to orient the sketching plane to the screen.

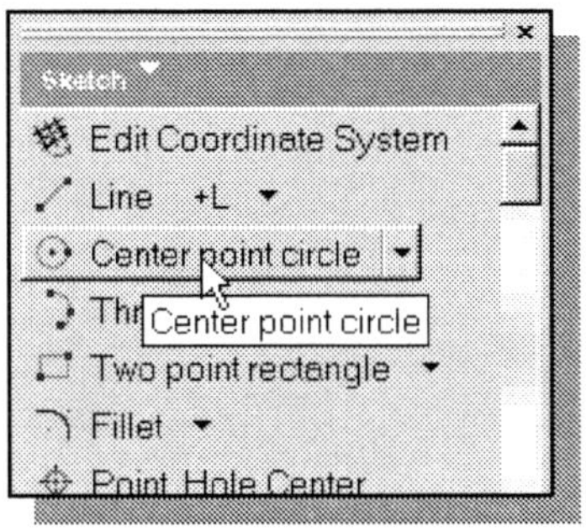

6. Select the ***Center point circle*** command by clicking once with the **left-mouse-button** on the icon in the *Sketch* toolbar.

7. Pick the center of the arc to align the center of the new circle.

8. Create a circle of arbitrary size as shown below.

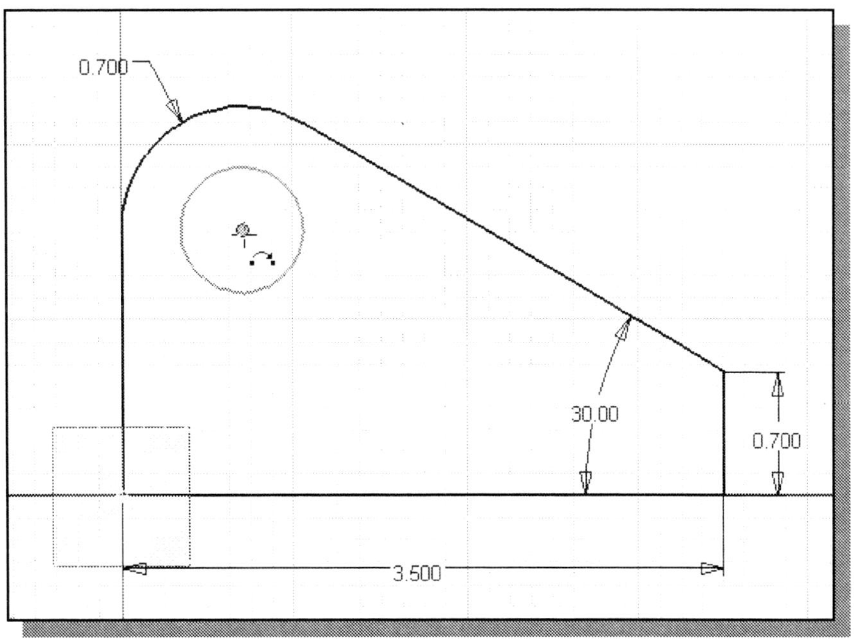

9. On your own, add the size dimension of the circle and set the dimension to **d1/10**.

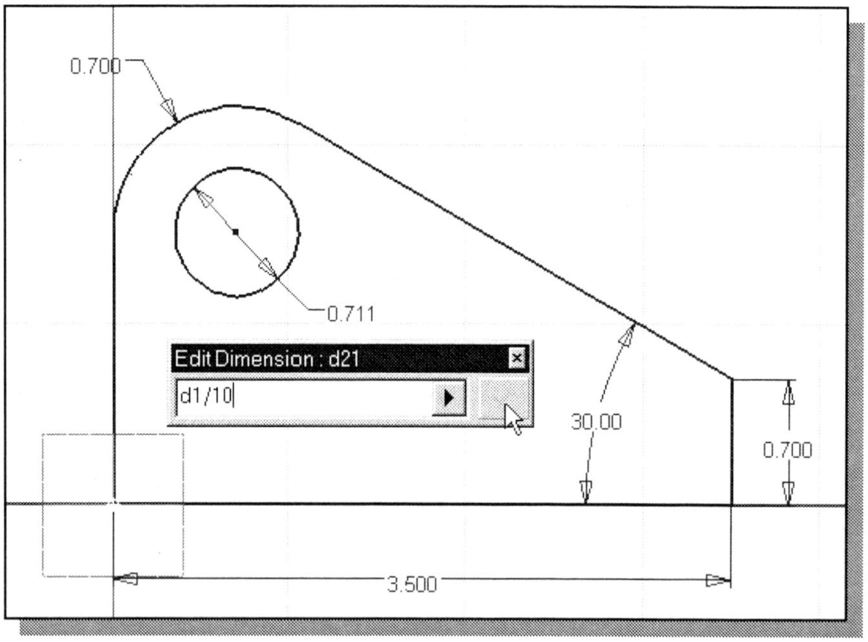

10. Click on the **Update** button in the *Standard* toolbar area to proceed with updating the solid model.

❖ The circular hole does not appear in the solid model. The solid model appears to be the same as if we never added the additional geometry to the base feature. The outline of the 2D sketch used to create the base feature is unchanged; we will need to update the **profile** used to complete the feature.

❖ In *Autodesk Inventor*, **profiles** are closed loops that define a cross section of a sketched feature. In an *Extrude*, *Revolve*, *Sweep*, or *Loft* operation, we are required to select one or more loops to form a profile. The profile must be a closed region and must not contain self-intersecting geometry. To create a profile, we can create single or multiple loops or select existing edges that join together to form a closed loop. All loops selected in a single operation are treated as a single profile. We will next update the profile used to generate the base feature.

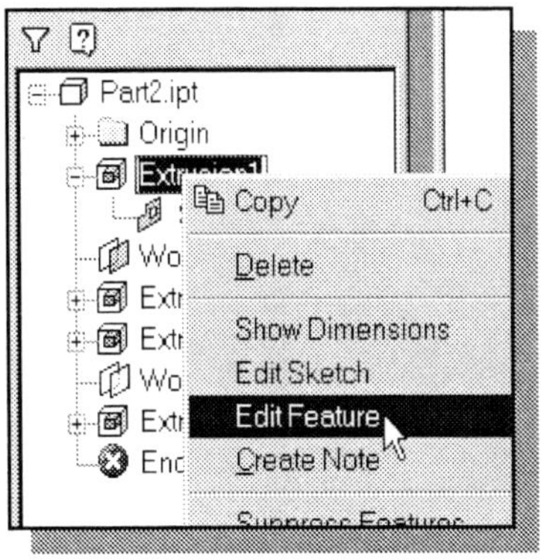

11. In the *Browser* window, right-click once on ***Extrusion1*** to bring up the option menu.

12. Select **Edit Feature** in the popup option menu.

13. In the *Extrude* dialogue box, click on the *Profile* icon as shown below.

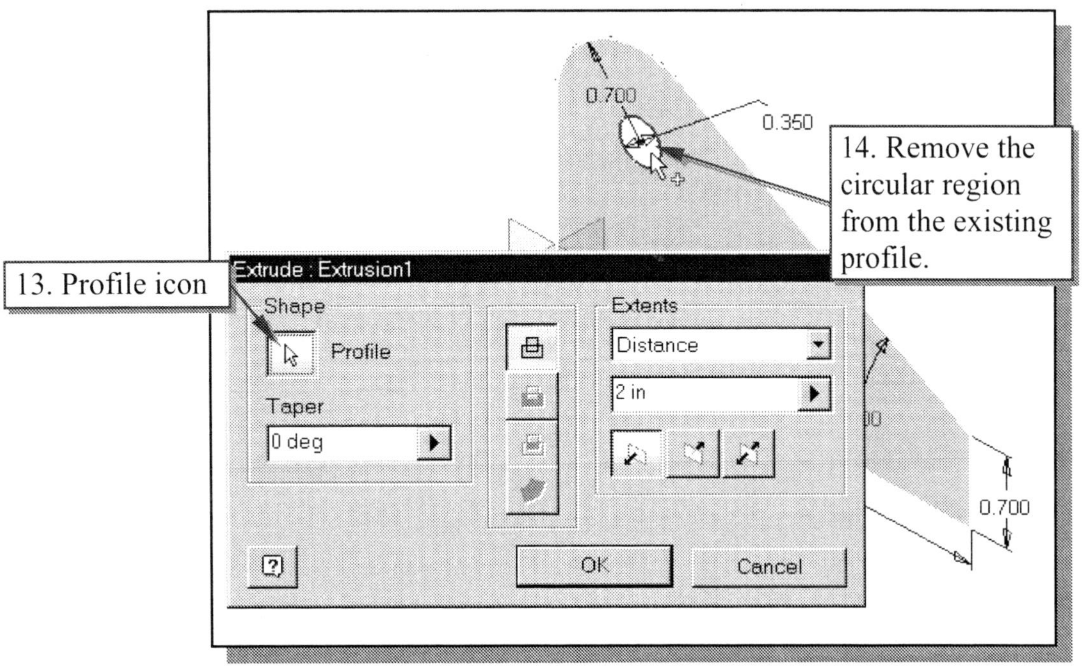

14. Hold down the [**Ctrl**] key and left-click inside the circular region as shown in the above figure.

➢ The shaded region represents the Profile region, which is used to create the solid feature.

15. Click on the **OK** button to accept the modification of the profile and proceed to update the solid model.

Placed Feature – Distance option

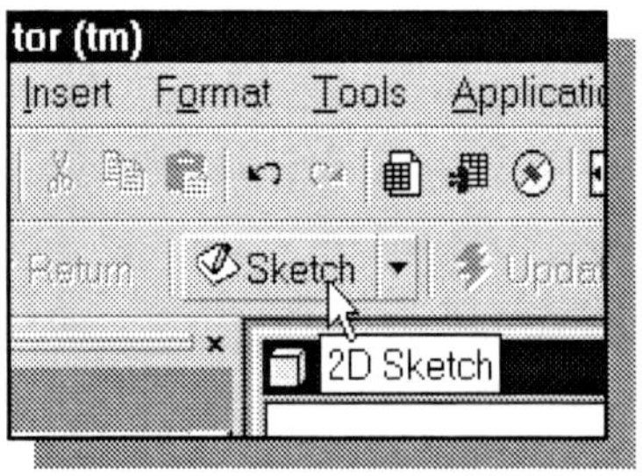

1. In the *Standard* toolbar select the ***Sketch*** command by left-clicking once on the icon.

2. In the *Status Bar* area, the message: "*Select face, work plane, sketch or sketch geometry.*" is displayed. Pick the inclined face of the solid model as shown below.

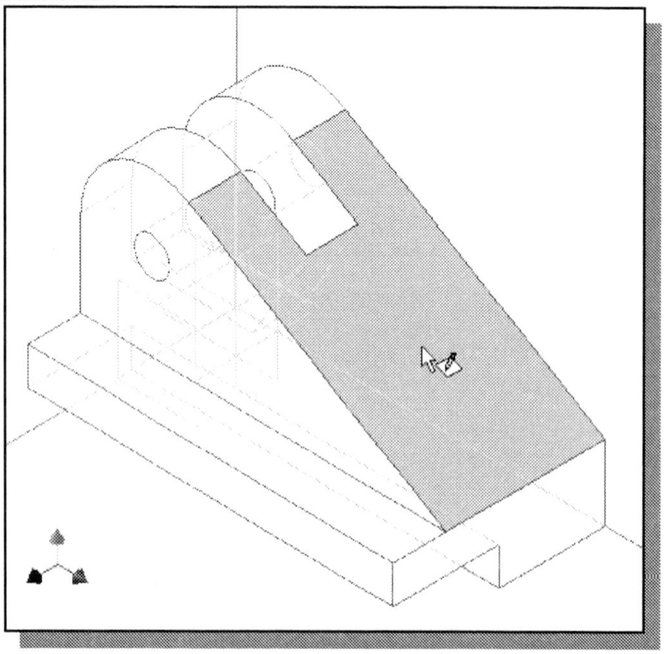

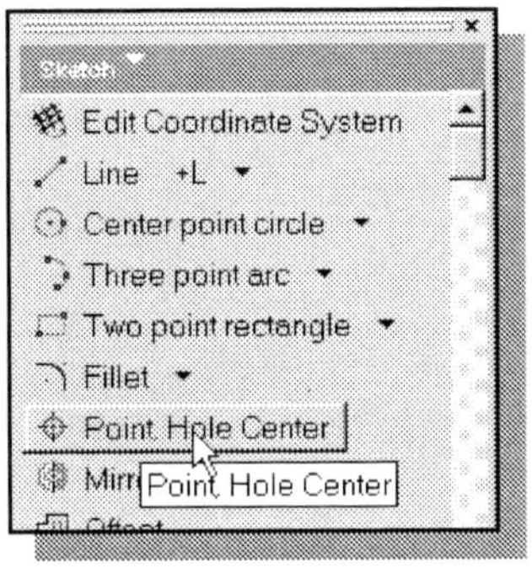

3. Select the ***Point, Hole Center*** command by clicking once with the left-mouse-button on the icon in the *Sketch* toolbar.

4. Place the *hole's center* near the center of the inclined face as shown.

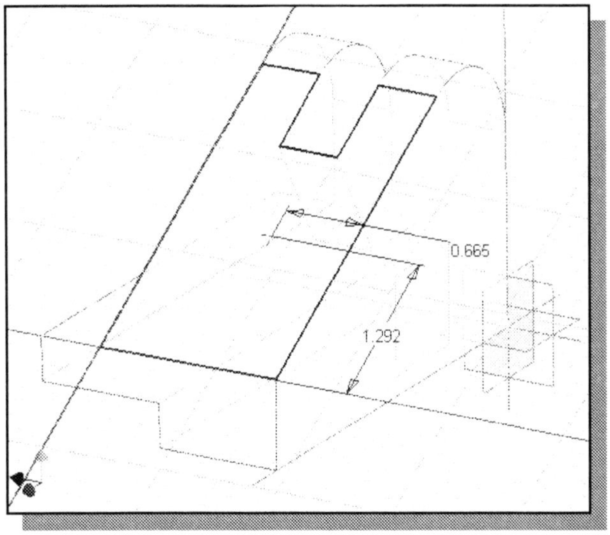

5. On your own, create the two dimensions as shown in the above figure.

6. On your own, adjust and *update* the two location dimensions as shown below.

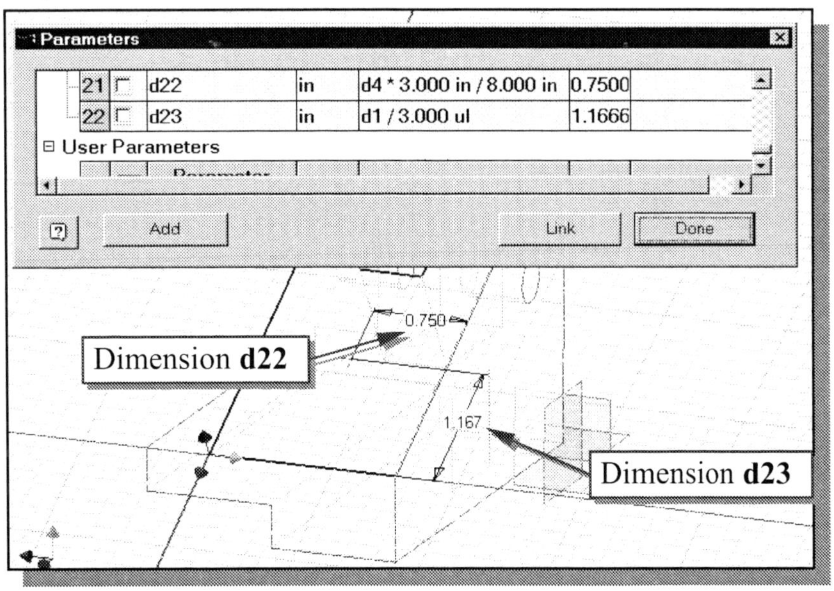

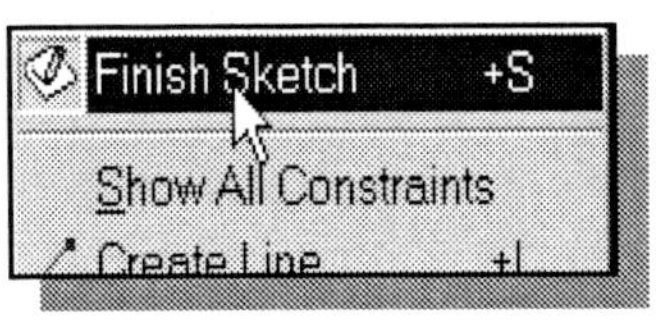

7. Inside the graphics window, click once with the right-mouse-button to display the option menu. Select **Finish Sketch** in the popup menu to end the *Sketch* option.

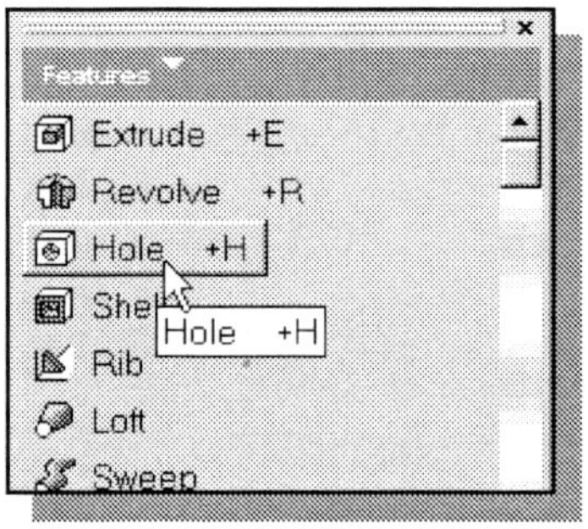

8. In the *Feature* toolbar (the toolbar that is located to the left side of the graphics window), select the ***Hole*** command by clicking once with the left-mouse-button on the icon.

9. In the *Holes* window, the **Centers** button is pressed down; *Autodesk Inventor* allows us to identify as many centers as we like to create the same feature.

10. Click on the **Options** tab and confirm the drill point is set to **118** degrees.

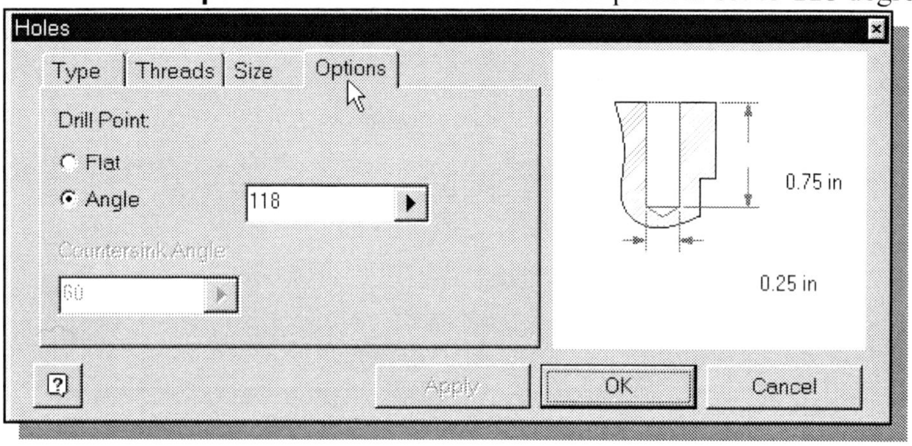

11. Click on the **OK** button to accept the default settings and create the placed hole feature.

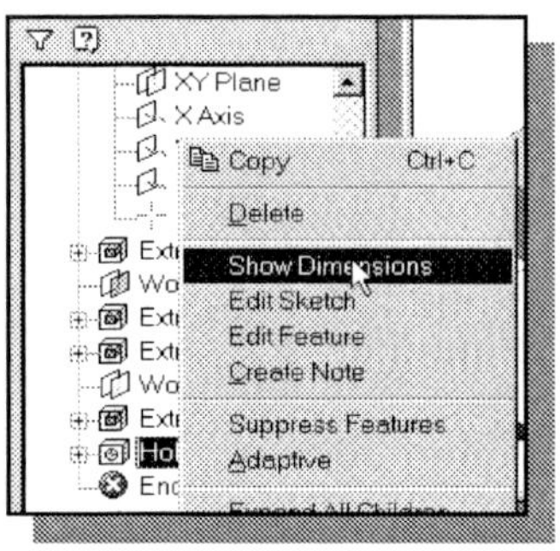

12. Inside the *Browser* window, right-mouse-click on the *hole feature* we just created.

13. Select **Show Dimensions** in the option menu.

14. Inside the graphics window, double-click on the diameter of the hole to bring up the *Hole Dimensions* dialog box as shown below.

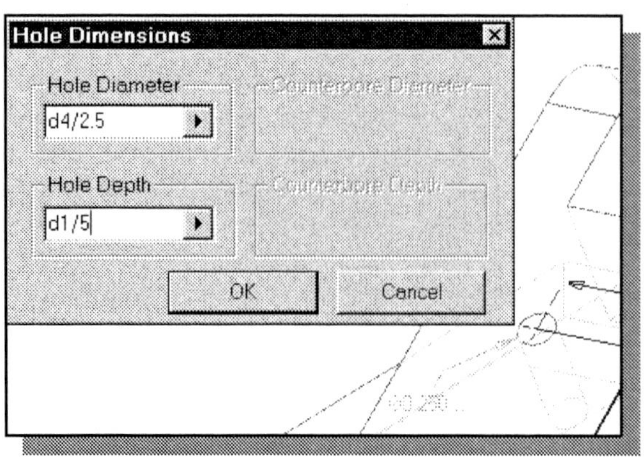

15. In the *Hole Dimensions* dialog box, enter **d4/2.5** as the new *Hole Diameter*.

16. In the *Hole Dimensions* dialog box, enter **d1/5** as the new *Hole Depth*.

17. Click on the **OK** button to accept the settings.

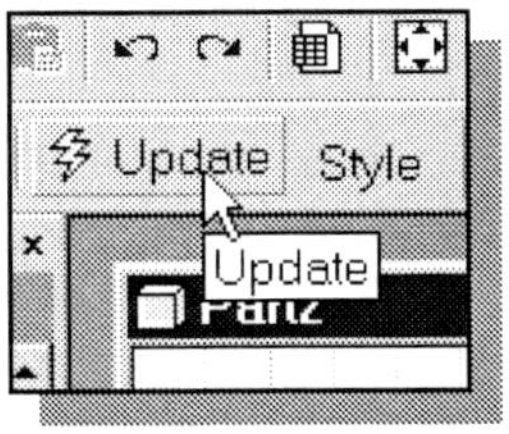

18. Click on the **Update** button in the *Standard* toolbar area to proceed with updating the solid model.

A Design Change

In a typical design process, the initial design will undergo many analyses, testing, and reviews. *Autodesk Inventor* allows us to update the initial design fairly easily throughout the design process.

The model we constructed contains four controlling dimensions: the overall width, the extrude-distance of the base, the angle of the incline surface, and the drill angle. The *history-based part modification* approach enables us to quickly update the design. For example, you can access the *Model History Tree* and *Edit* the overall width of the part to **4.5** inches and the extrusion distance of the base feature to **1.75**. With parametric modeling, design changes such as finalizing the established parametric equations can be done quickly and effortlessly.

Questions:

1. Describe the procedure and advantages of using the *BORN* technique?

2. What are the advantages of using *work features*?

3. Describe the procedure to create an *offset work plane*.

4. Why use *parametric relations*?

5. What is the result of the parametric expression *Width*3/4+0.25*?

6. How do we create geometry on a surface that does not already exist?

7. Identify and describe the following commands:

(a)

(b)

(c)

(d)

Exercises:

1.

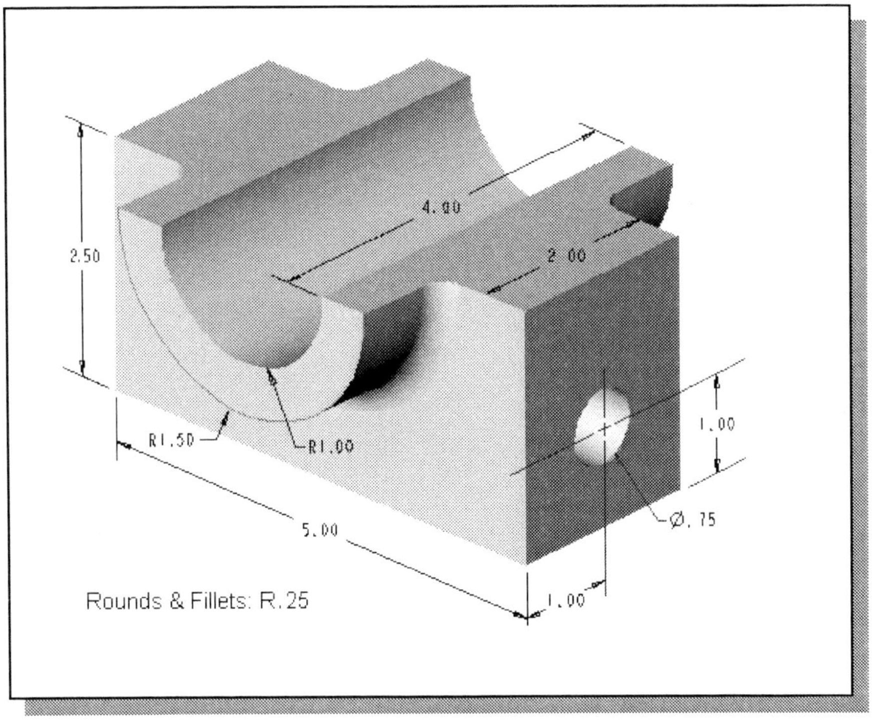

2.

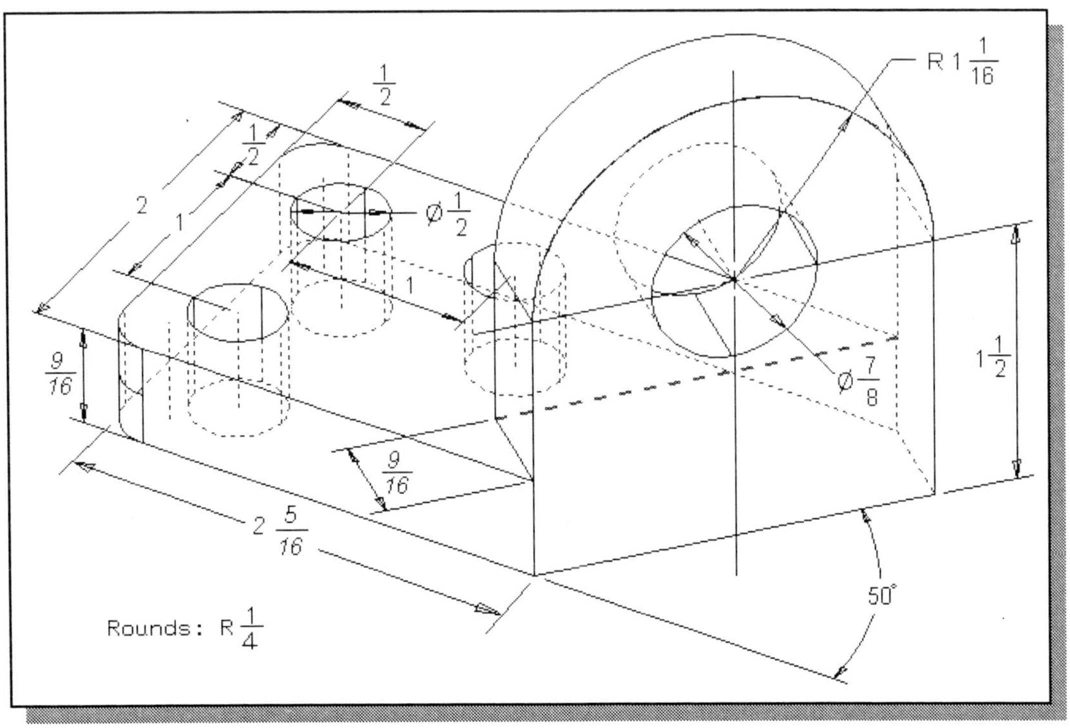

Notes:

Lesson 6
Part Drawings and Associative Functionality

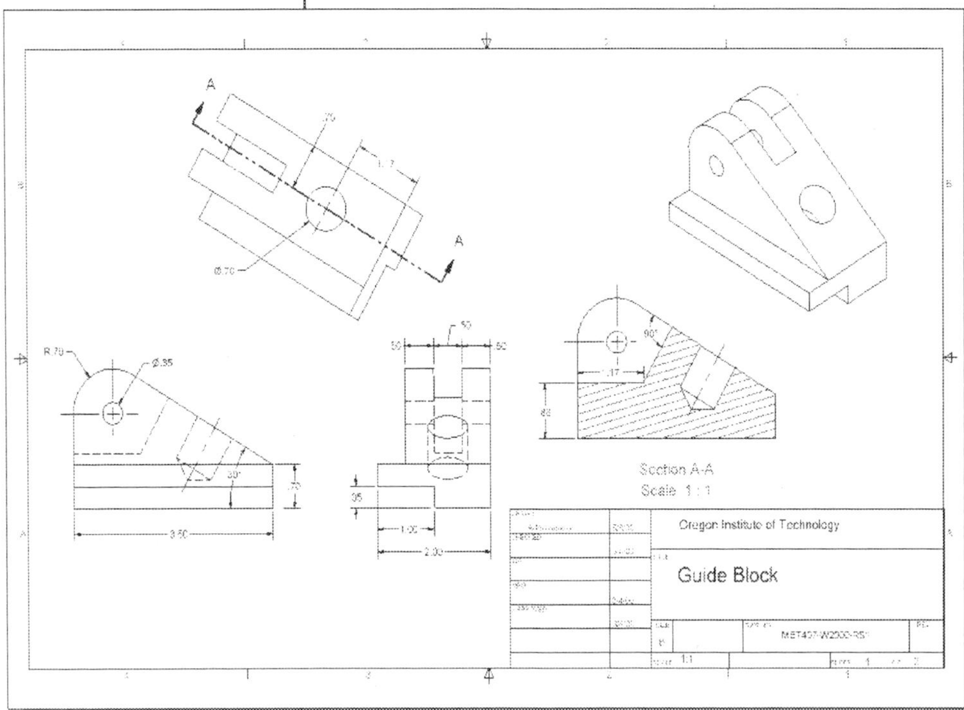

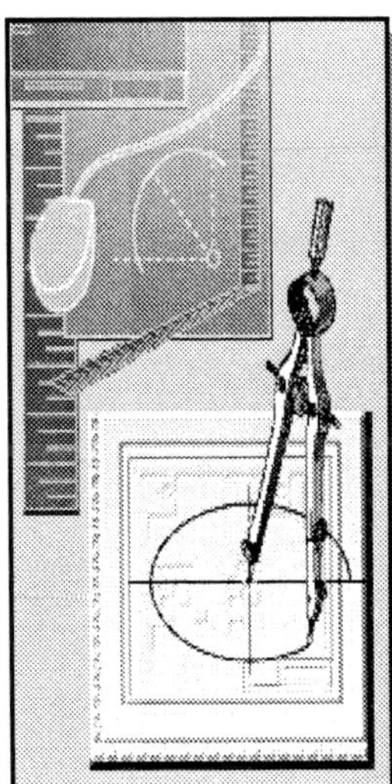

Learning Objectives

When you have completed this lesson, you will be able to:

- ♦ **Create Drawing Layouts from Solid Models.**
- ♦ **Understand Associative Functionality.**
- ♦ **Add Borders and Title Block in the Layout Mode**
- ♦ **Arrange and Manage 2-D Views in Drawing Mode.**
- ♦ **Create Sectioned Orthogonal Views.**
- ♦ **Display and Hide Feature Dimensions.**
- ♦ **Create Reference Dimensions.**

Drawings from Parts and Associative Functionality

With the software/hardware improvements in solid modeling, the importance of two-dimensional drawings is decreasing. Drafting is considered one of the downstream applications of using solid models. In many production facilities, solid models are used to generate machine tool paths for *computer numerical control* (CNC) machines. Solid models are also used in *rapid prototyping* to create 3D physical models out of plastic resins, powdered metal, etc. Ideally, the solid model database should be used directly to generate the final product. However, the majority of applications in most production facilities still require the use of two-dimensional drawings. Using the solid model as the starting point for a design, solid modeling tools can easily create all the necessary two-dimensional views. In this sense, solid modeling tools are making the process of creating two-dimensional drawings more efficient and effective.

Autodesk Inventor provides associative functionality in the different *Autodesk Inventor* modes. This functionality allows us to change the design at any level, and the system reflects it at all levels automatically. For example, a solid model can be modified in the *Part Modeling Mode* and the system automatically reflects that change in the *Drawing Mode*. And we can also modify a feature dimension in the *Drawing Mode*, and the system automatically updates the solid model in all modes.

In this lesson, the general procedure of creating multi-view drawings is illustrated. The *Guide_Block* design from last chapter is used to demonstrate the associative functionality between the model and drawing views.

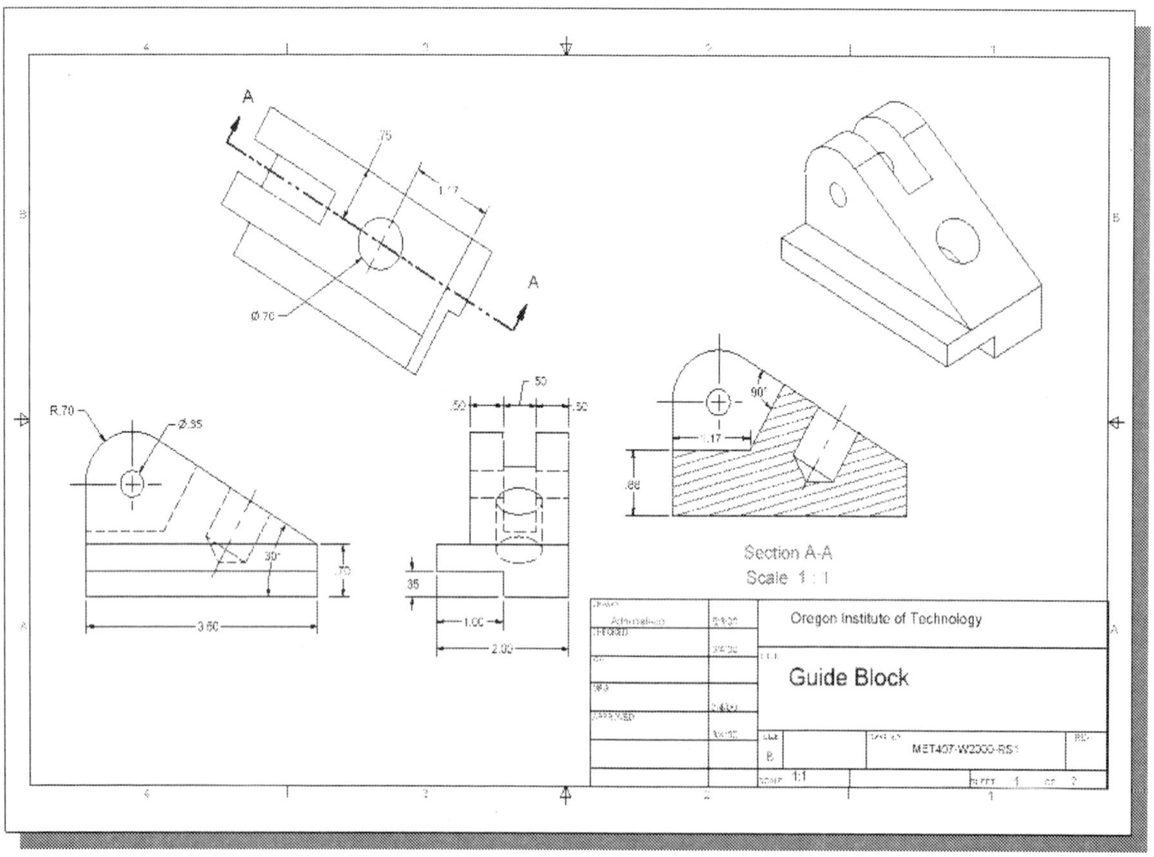

Starting Autodesk Inventor

1. Select the ***Autodesk Inventor*** option on the *Start* menu or select the ***Autodesk Inventor*** icon on the desktop to start *Autodesk Inventor*. The *Autodesk Inventor* main window will appear on the screen.

2. Once the program is loaded into the memory, the ***Startup*** dialog box appears at the center of the screen.

3. Select **Open** with a single click of the left-mouse-button in the *What to Do* dialog box.

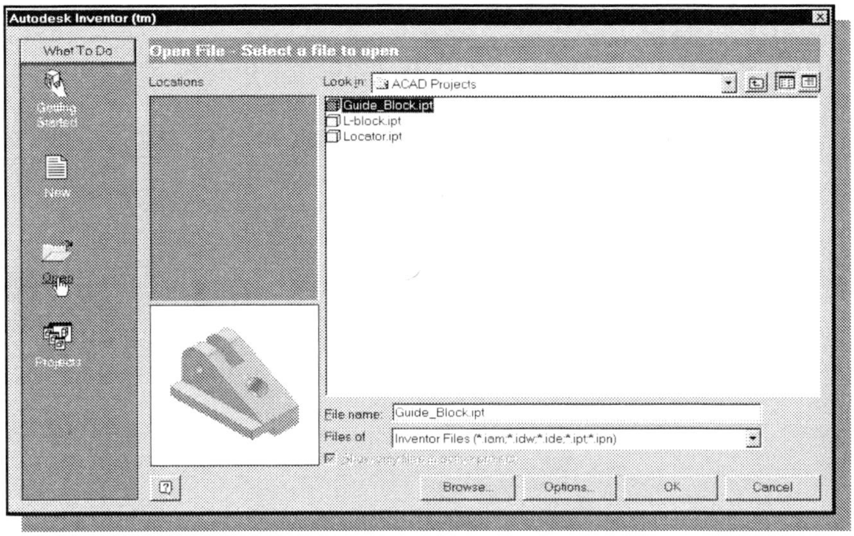

4. In the *File* list box, select the ***Guide_Block.ipt*** file. Use the *Browse* option to locate the file if it is not displayed in the *File* list box.

5. Click on the **OK** button in the *Startup* dialog box to accept the selected settings.

Drawing Mode – 2D Paper Space

- *Autodesk Inventor* allows us to generate 2D engineering drawings from solid models so that we can plot the drawings to any exact scale on paper. An engineering drawing is a tool that can be used to communicate engineering ideas/designs to manufacturing, purchasing, service, and other departments. Until now we have been working in ***model space*** to create our design in ***full size***. We can arrange our design on a two-dimensional sheet of paper so that the plotted hardcopy is exactly what we want. This two-dimensional sheet of paper is known as the ***paper space*** in *AutoCAD* and *Autodesk Inventor*. We can place borders and title blocks, objects that are less critical to our design, on *paper space*. In general, each company uses a set of standards for drawing content, based on the type of product and also on established internal processes. The appearance of an engineering drawing varies depending on when, where, and for what it is produced. However, the general procedure for creating an engineering drawing from a solid model is fairly well defined. In *Autodesk Inventor*, creation of 2D engineering drawings from solid models consists of four basic steps: drawing sheet formatting, creating/positioning views, annotations, and printing/plotting.

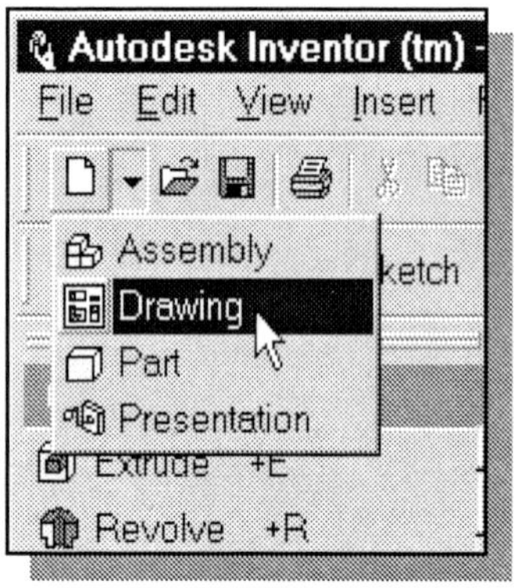

1. Click on the **drop-down arrow** next to the ***New File*** button in the *Standard* toolbar area to display the available *New File* options.

2. Select **Drawing** from the option list.

➢ Note that a new graphics window appears on the screen. We can switch between the solid model and the drawing by clicking the corresponding graphics windows.

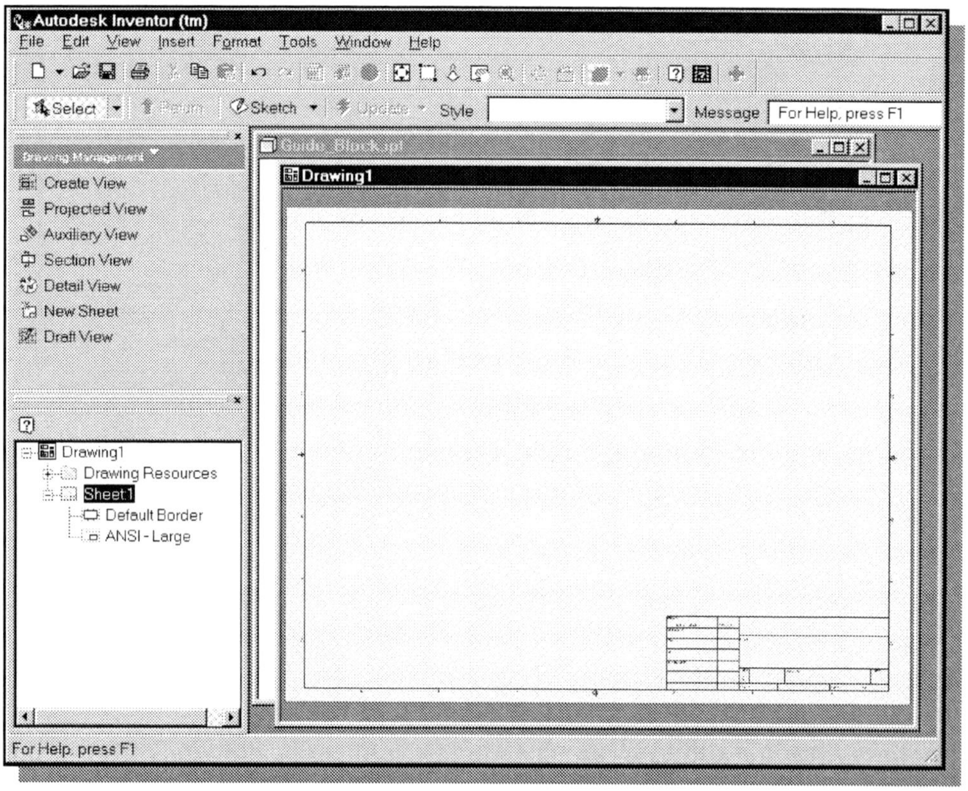

❖ In the graphics window, *Autodesk Inventor* displays a default drawing sheet that includes a title block. The drawing sheet is placed on the 2D paper space, and the title block also indicates the paper size being used.

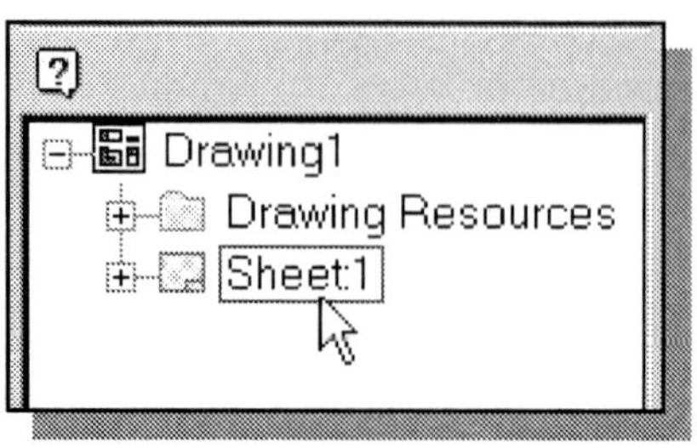

➢ In the *Browser* area, the *Drawing1* icon is displayed at the top, which indicates that we have switched to **Drawing Mode.** ***Sheet1*** is the current drawing sheet that is displayed in the graphics window. Note that all items created in the Drawing Mode are placed on a 2D paper space.

Drawing Sheet Format

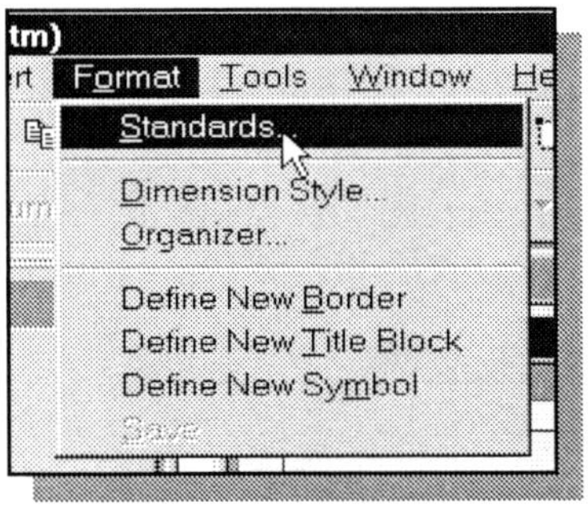

1. Choose **Format** in the pull-down menu.

2. Select **Standards** in the options list.

3. In the *Drafting Standards* dialog box, confirm that the *Current Standard* is set to ***ANSI***.

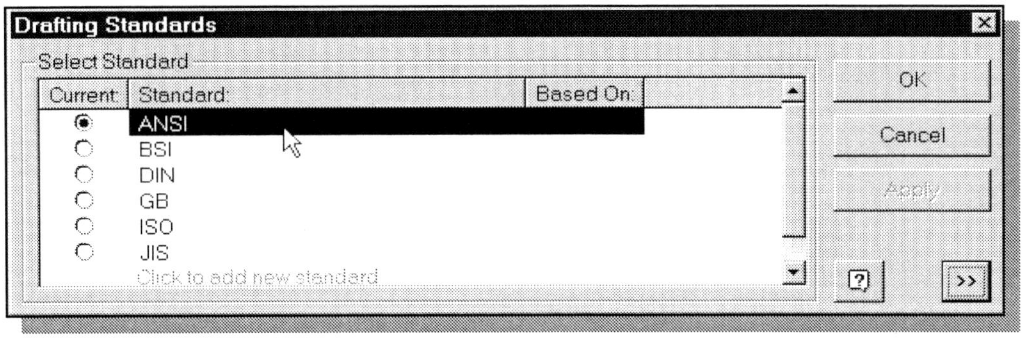

❖ In this tutorial, we will demonstrate creating the part drawing using the ANSI drafting standard. *Autodesk Inventor* provides several settings for use with different standards, such as ISO, GB, BSI, DIN, and JIS.

4. In the *Drafting Standards* dialog box, click on the **arrow** button to show more detailed settings of the current standard.

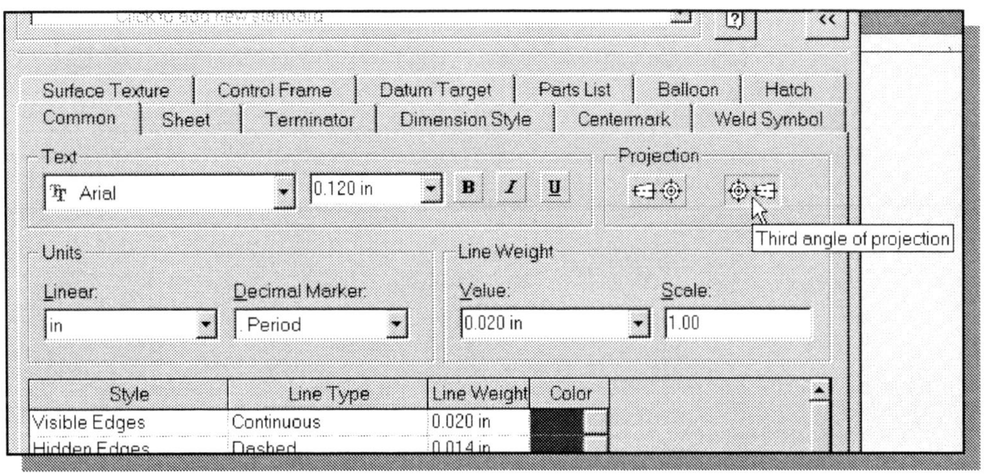

5. In the *Common Settings* page, confirm that the *Projection Type* is set to ***Third Angle***.

❖ Notice the different settings available in the *Drafting Standards* window, such as the *Units* setting and the *Line Weight* setting.

6. Click on the **OK** button to accept the settings.

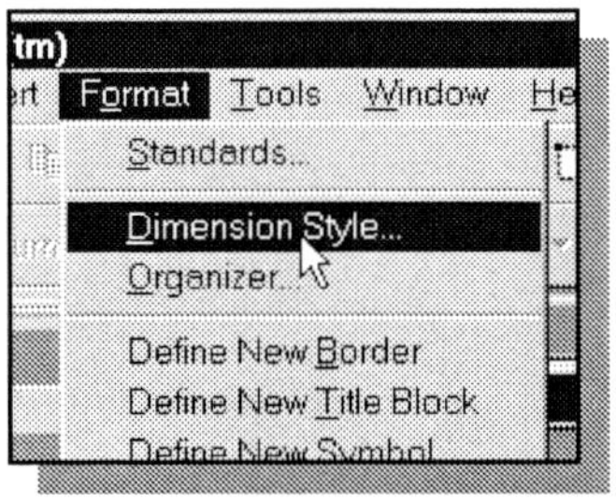

7. Choose **Format** in the pull-down menu.

8. Select **Dimension Style** in the options list.

9. Click on the **Dimension Value** tab to display and examine the settings for linear/angular dimension values.

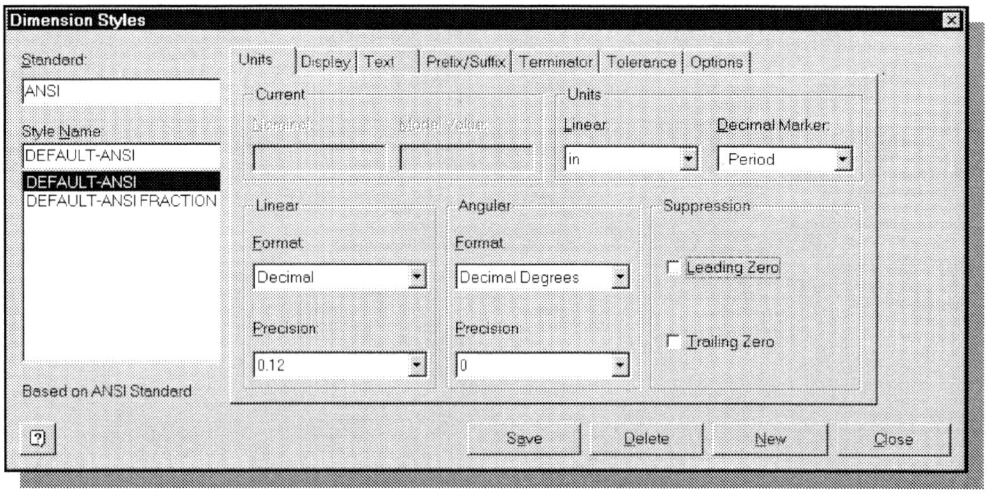

- Note that the *Linear* units is set to inches and the precision for linear dimensions is set to two digits after the decimal point.

10. Click on the **Text** tab to display and examine the settings for dimension text. Note that the default *Autodesk Inventor* ***Dimension Styles*** settings are based on the ANSI Y14.5-1994 standard.

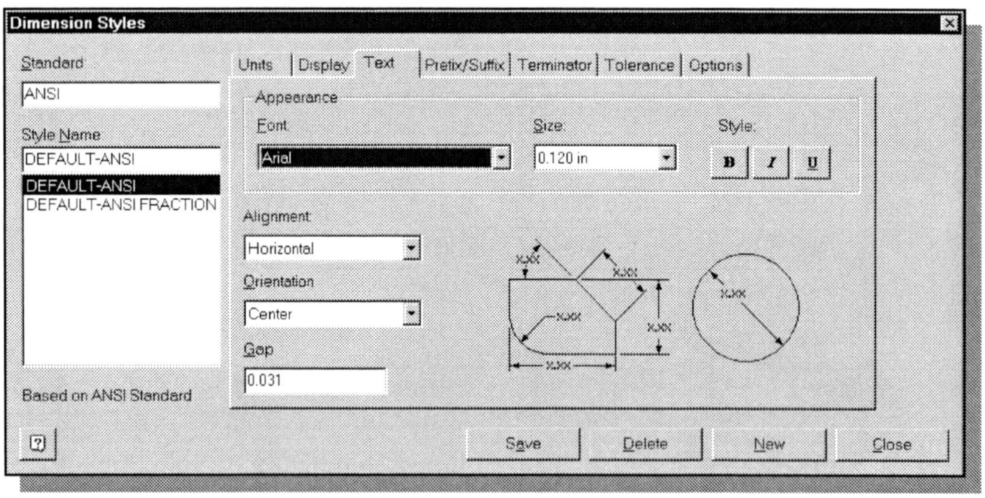

- On your own, display and examine the other settings available under the *Dimension Styles* dialog box.

11. Click on the **Close** button to exit the *Drafting Standards* dialog box.

Using the Pre-defined Drawing Sheet Formats

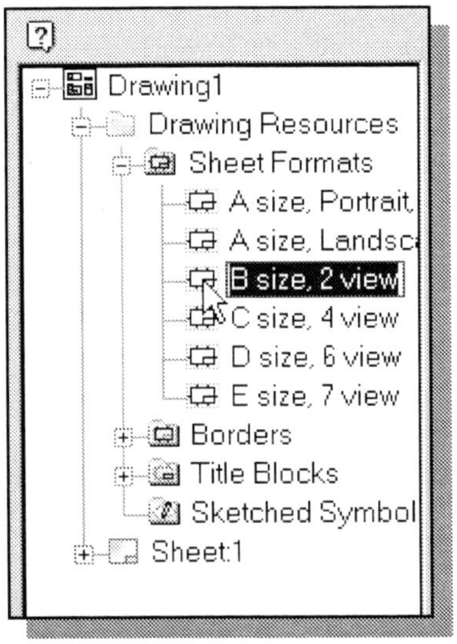

1. Inside the *Drawing Browser* window, click on the [**+**] symbol in front of ***Drawing Resources*** to display the available options.

2. Click on the [**+**] symbol in front of ***Sheet Formats*** to display the available pre-defined sheet formats.

❖ Notice several pre-defined *sheet formats*, each with a different view configuration, are available in the *Browser* window.

3. Inside the *Browser* window, double-click on the ***B size, 2 view*** sheet format.

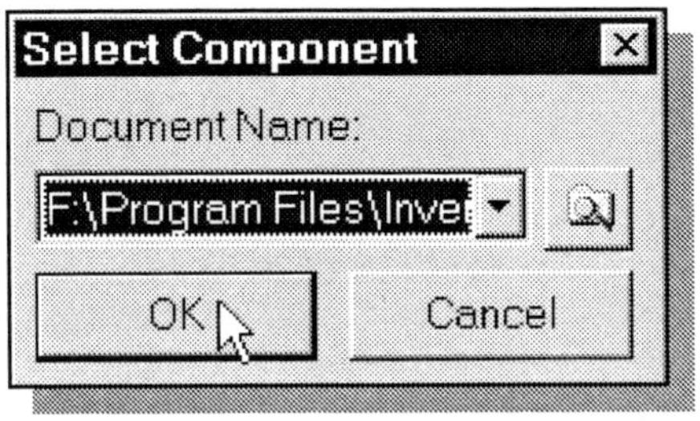

4. Click on the **OK** button to accept the default part file and generate the 2D views.

➢ The ***Guide_Block*** model is the only model opened. By default, all of the 2D drawings will be generated from this model file.

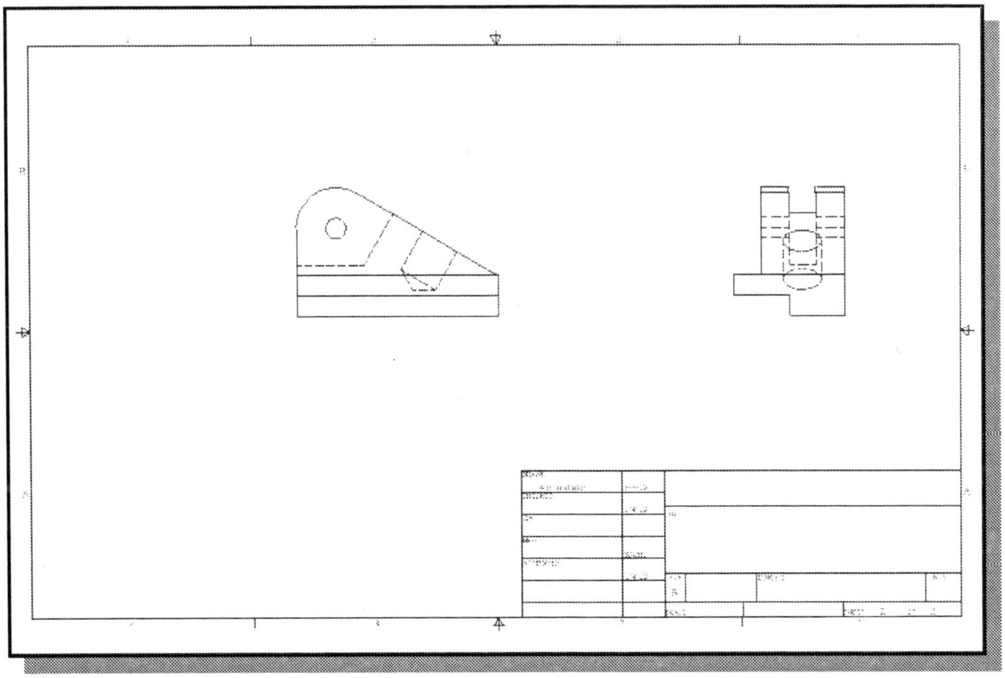

❖ We have created a B-size drawing of the *Guide_Block* model. *Autodesk Inventor* automatically generates and positions the front-view and side-view of the model inside the title block.

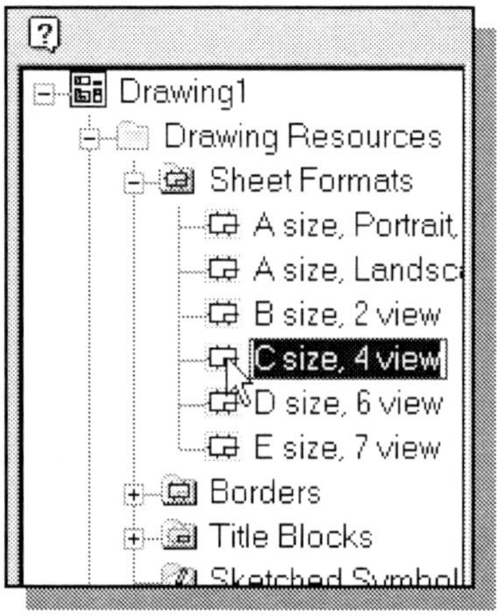

5. Inside the *Browser* window, double-click on the ***C size, 4 view*** sheet format.

6. Click on the **OK** button to use the default part file, *guide_block.ipt*, to generate the 2D views.

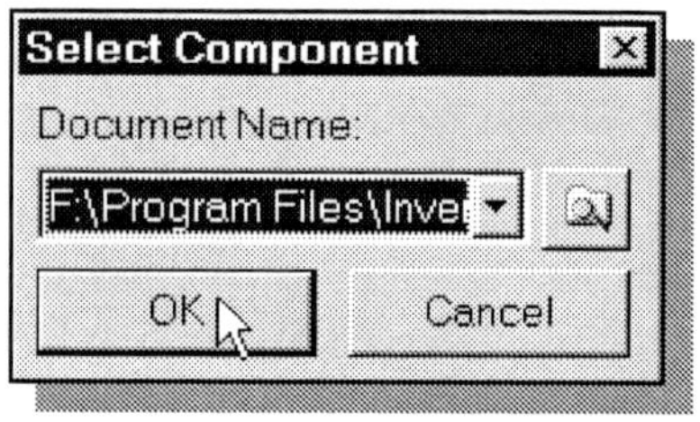

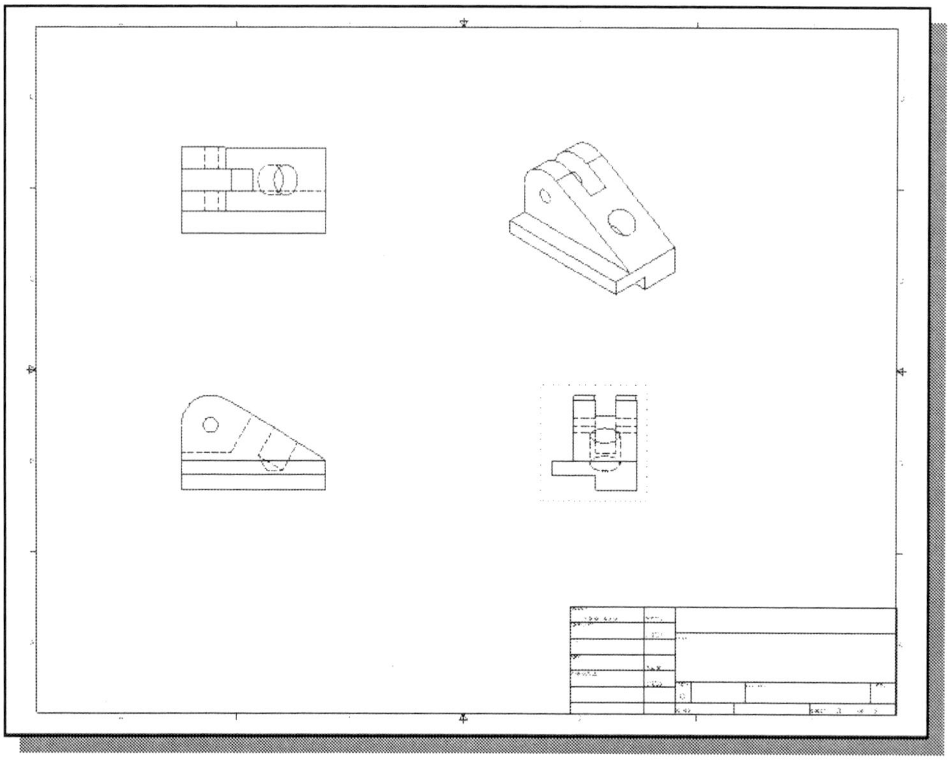

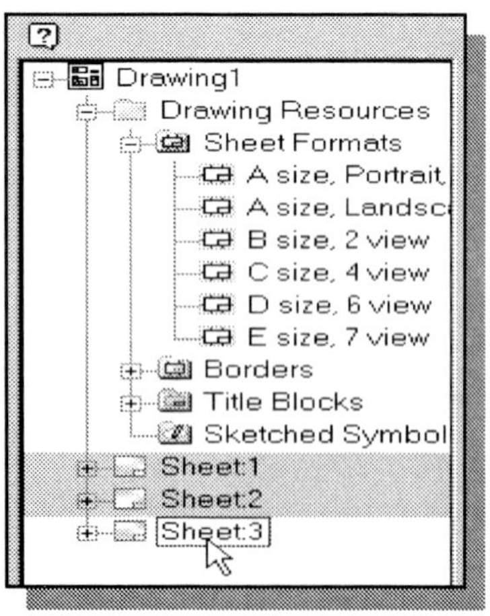

❖ Note that we have created three drawing sheets, displayed in the *Drawing Browser* window as *Sheet1*, *Sheet2*, and *Sheet3*. *Autodesk Inventor* allows us to create multiple 2D drawings from the same model file, which can be used for different purposes.

Deleting, Activating, and Editing a Drawing Sheet

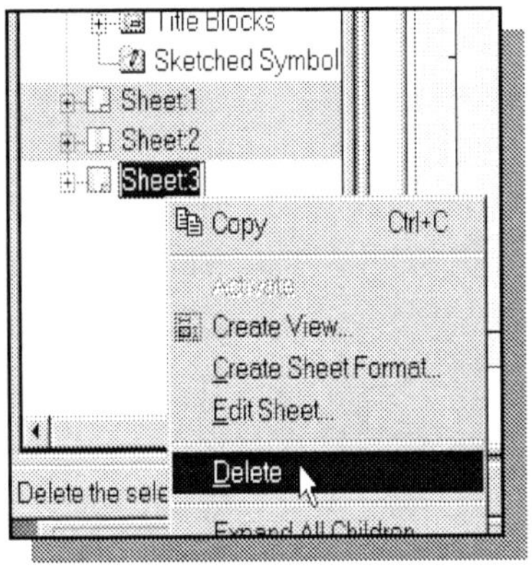

1. Inside the *Drawing Browser* window, right-mouse-click on ***Sheet3*** to display the option menu.

2. Select **Delete** in the option menu to remove the *Sheet3* drawing.

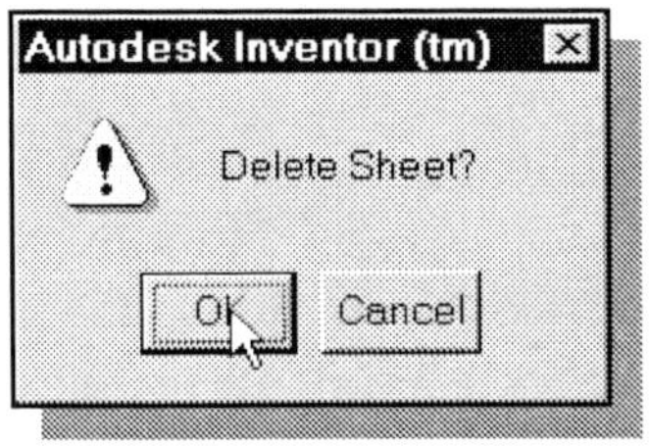

3. In the *warning window*, click on the **OK** button to proceed with deleting the drawing.

❖ Note that ***Sheet3*** is removed and ***Sheet2*** now becomes the active drawing sheet.

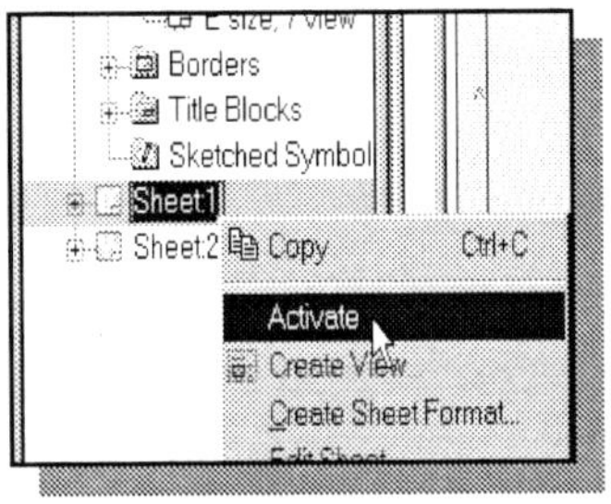

4. Inside the *Drawing Browser* window, right-mouse-click on ***Sheet1*** to display the option menu.

5. Select **Activate** in the option menu to set the *Sheet1* drawing as the active drawing sheet.

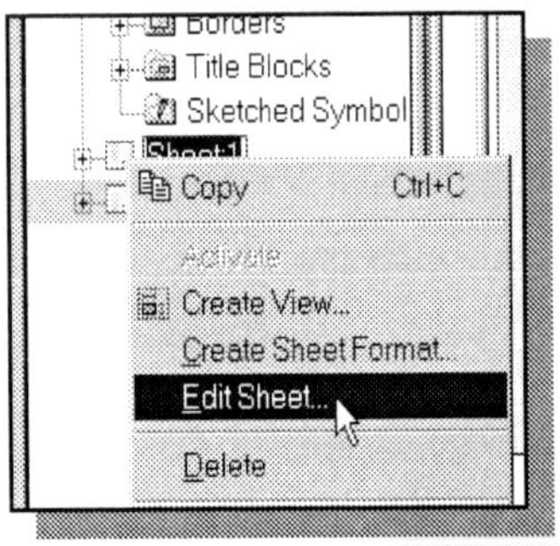

6. Inside the *Drawing Browser* window, right-mouse-click on ***Sheet1*** to display the option menu.

7. Select **Edit Sheet** in the option menu to display the settings for *Sheet1* drawing.

8. Set the sheet size to ***B-size*** and click on the **OK** button to exit the *Edit Sheet* dialog box.

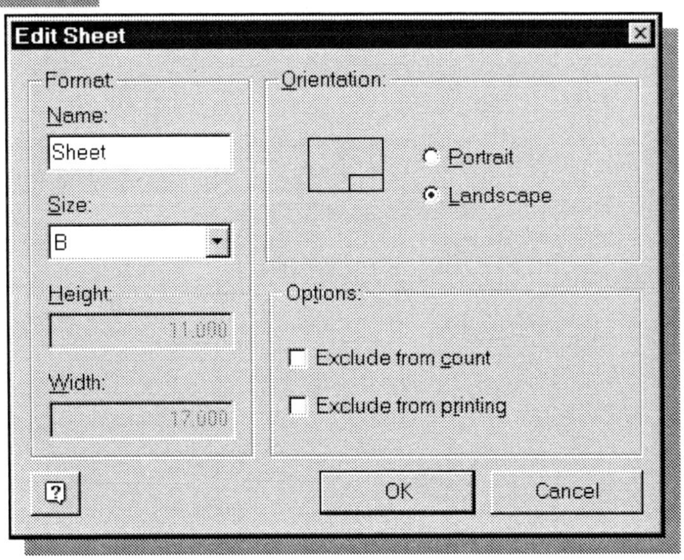

Adding a Base View

❖ In *Autodesk Inventor Drawing Mode*, the first drawing view we create is called a **base view**. A *base view* is the primary view in the drawing; other views can be derived from this view. When creating a *base view*, *Autodesk Inventor* allows us to specify the view to be shown. By default, *Autodesk Inventor* will treat the *world XY plane* as the front view of the solid model. Note that there can be more than one *base view* in a drawing.

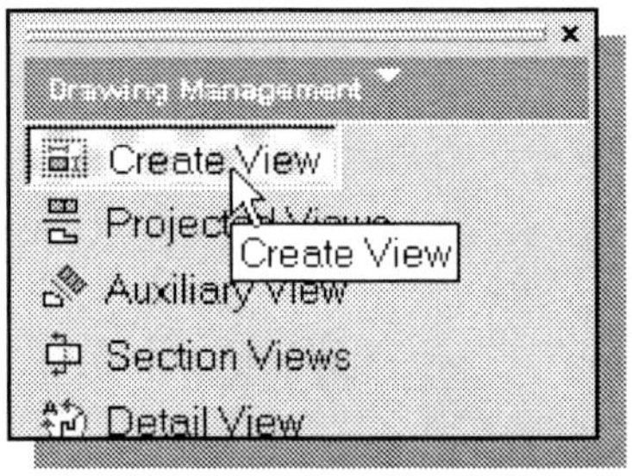

1. Click on the **Create View** in the *Drawing Management* window to create a base view.

2. In the *Create View* dialog box, confirm that the settings are set to ***Front View*** and **Hidden Line** as shown in the figure below. (**DO NOT** click on the **OK** button at this point.)

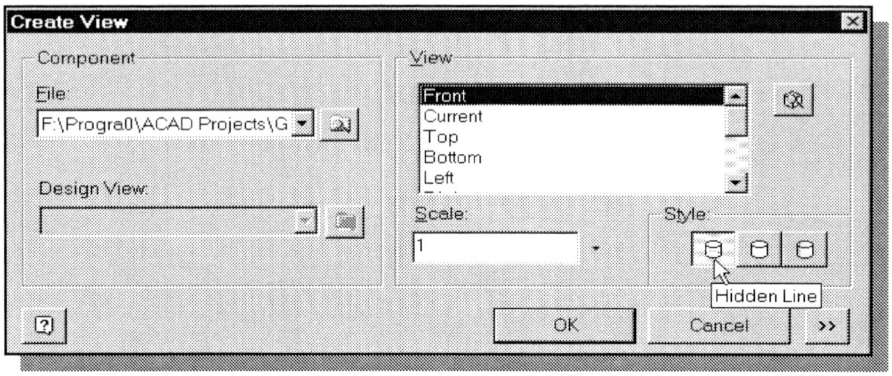

3. Move the cursor inside the graphics window and place the **base view** near the center of the graphics window as shown below. (If necessary, drag the *Create View* dialog box to another location on the screen.) Note that once the *base view* is placed, the *Create View* dialog box is closed automatically.

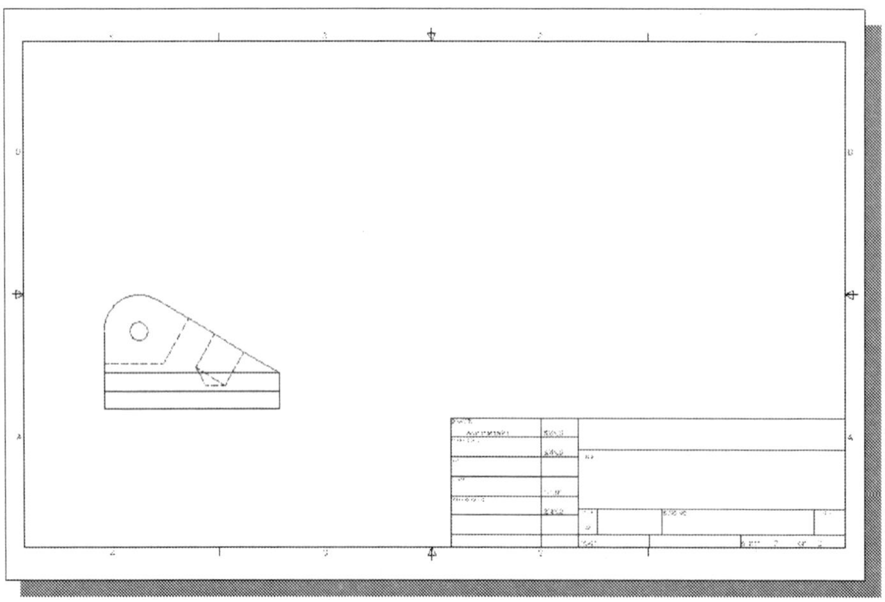

Creating Projected Views

❖ In *Autodesk Inventor Drawing Mode*, **projected views** can be created with a first-angle or third-angle projection, depending on the drafting standard used for the drawing. We must have a base view before a projected view can be created. Projected views can be orthographic projections or isometric projections. Orthographic projections are aligned to the base view and inherit the base view's scale and display settings. Isometric projections are not aligned to the base view.

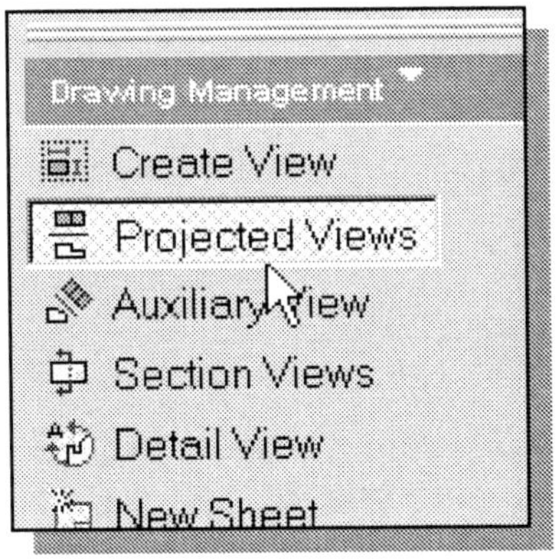

1. Click on the **Projected View** button in the *Drawing Management* window to create a projected view.

2. Click on the base view to select the base view for the projection.

3. Move the cursor toward the right side of the base view and select a location to position the projected side-view of the model.

4. Move the cursor toward the upper-right corner of the title block and select a location to position the isometric view of the model as shown below.

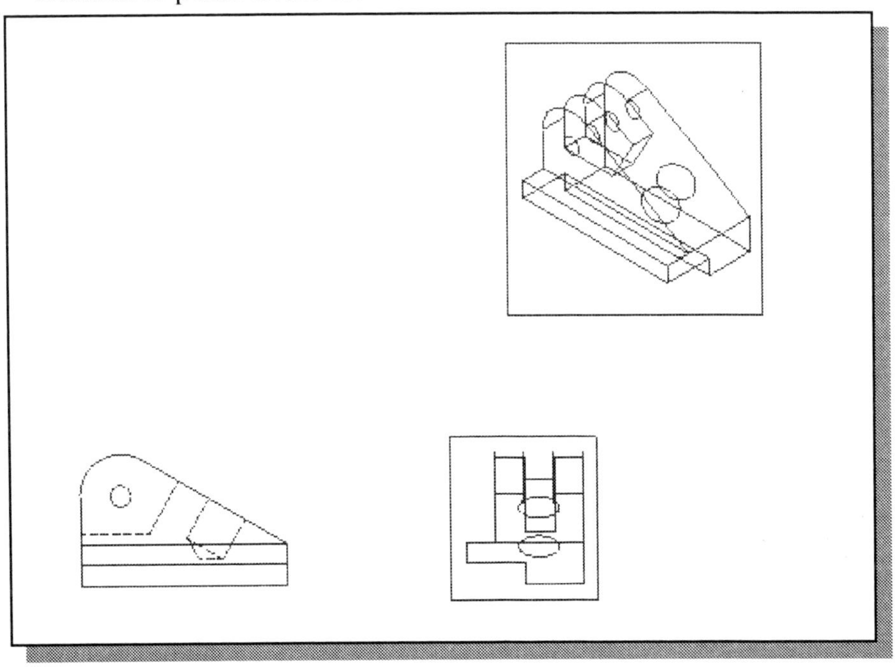

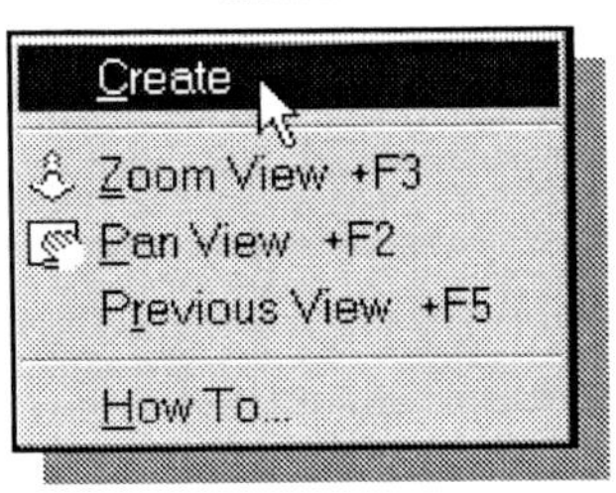

5. Inside the graphics window, right-mouse-click once to bring up the option menu.

6. Select **Create** to proceed with creating the two projected views.

Adding an Auxiliary View

❖ In *Autodesk Inventor*, we can create an *auxiliary view* by projecting from an edge or line in a base view. The resulting view is very similar to a *projected view* except that an auxiliary view can be at any angle to the base view. The resulting view is also aligned to the base view.

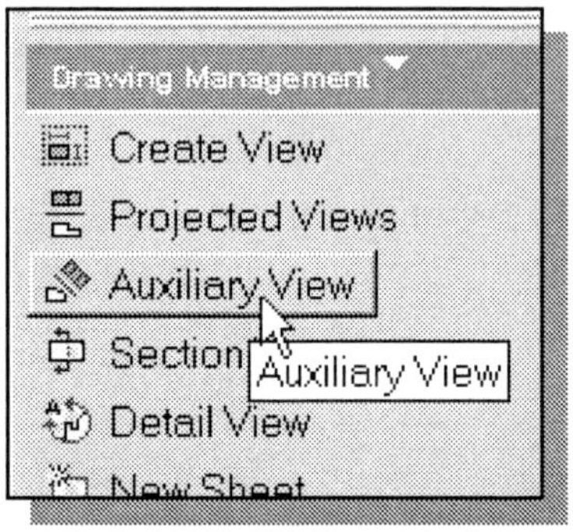

1. Click on the **Auxiliary View** button in the *Drawing Management* window to create an auxiliary view.

2. Click on the base view to select the base view for the projection.

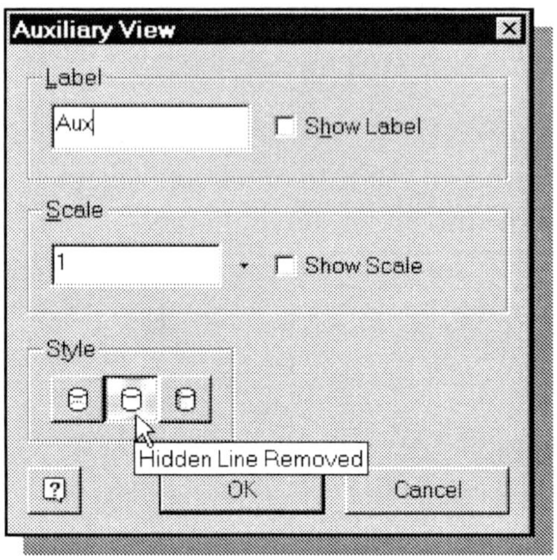

3. In the *Auxiliary View* dialog box, change the label name to ***Aux*** and the display *Style* to **Hidden Line Removed**, as shown in the figure. (**DO NOT** click on the **OK** button.)

4. *Autodesk Inventor* expects us to define the direction of the projection. Select an edge that is perpendicular to the inclined surface of the model as shown below.

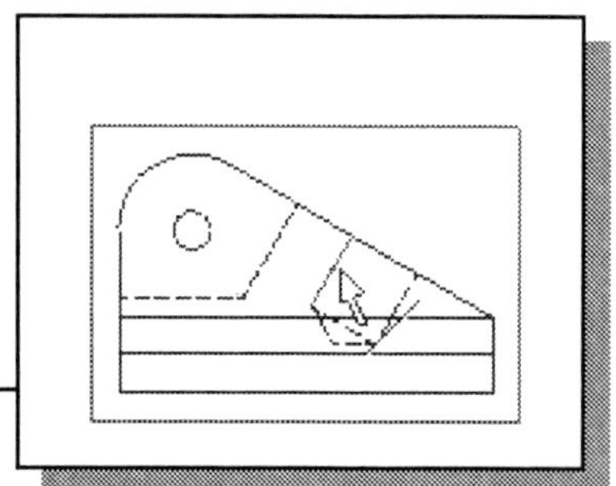

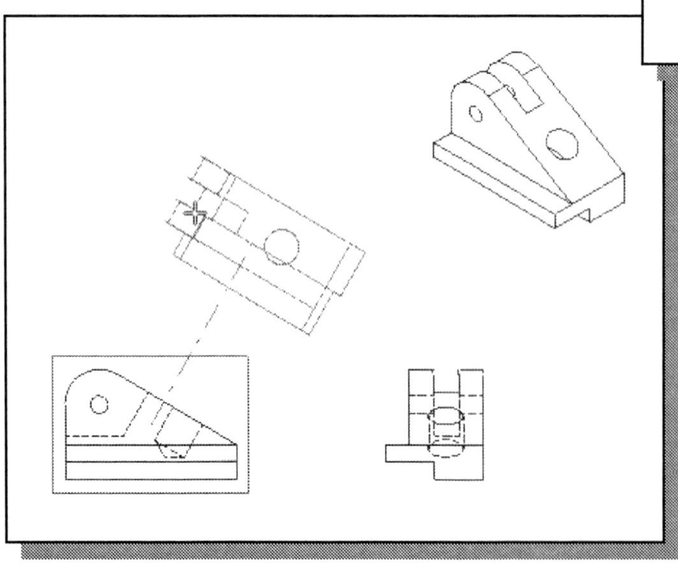

5. Move the cursor toward the upper-right side of the base view and select a location to position the projected auxiliary view of the model. (If necessary, drag the *Create View* dialog box to another location on the screen.) Note that once the view is placed, the *Auxiliary View* dialog box is closed automatically.

Adding a Sectioned Orthogonal View

❖ To create a section view, a view projection line is required. The **view projection line**, also known as the **cutting plane line**, defines a cutting line for the section view. Depending upon how a view projection line is drawn, the line can be used to define the type of section view or define a boundary for a partial view. If the view projection line is created outside the base view, it defines a plane from which to project an auxiliary view.

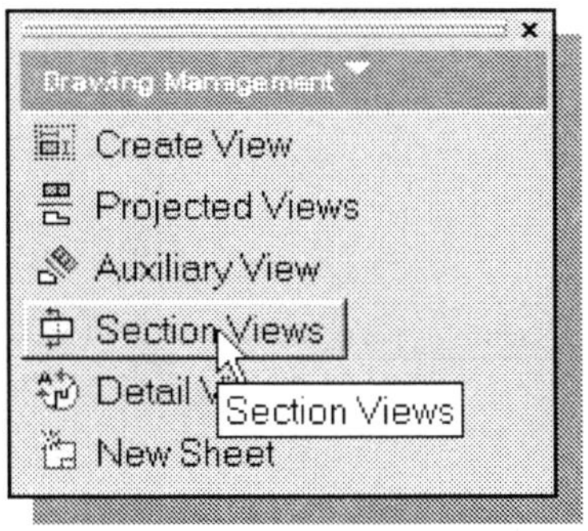

1. Click on the **Section Views** button in the *Drawing Management* window to create a section view.

2. Inside the graphics window, click on the *auxiliary view* to select the view where the view projection line is to be created.

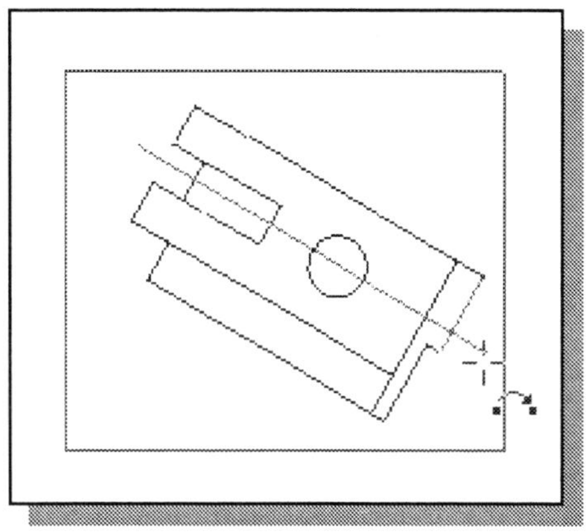

3. Create a line that passes through the center of the hole feature as shown. Note the different alignment symbols displayed as the cursor is moved to different locations.

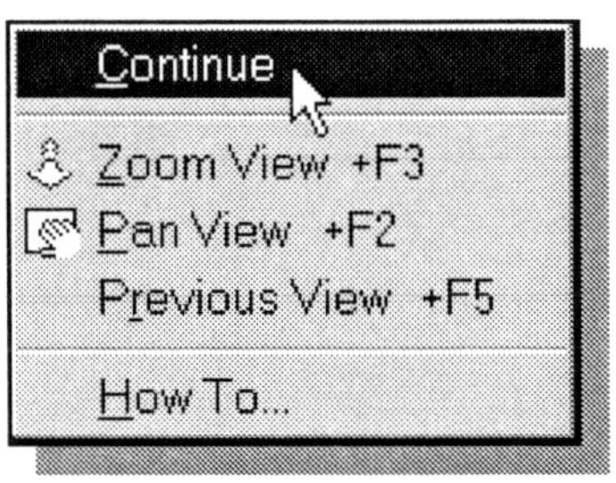

4. Inside the graphics window, right-mouse-click once to bring up the option menu.

5. Select **Continue** to proceed with the *Section View* command.

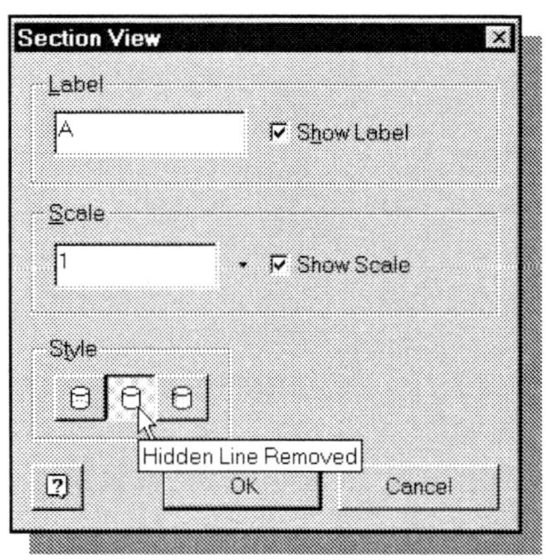

6. In the *Section View* dialog box, set the display *Style* to **Hidden Line Removed**, as shown in the figure. (**DO NOT** click on the **OK** button.)

7. Next, *Autodesk Inventor* expects us to place the projected section. Select a location in between the auxiliary view and the base view as shown below. Do not be overly concerned if the views overlap with each other, we will reposition the section view in the next step.

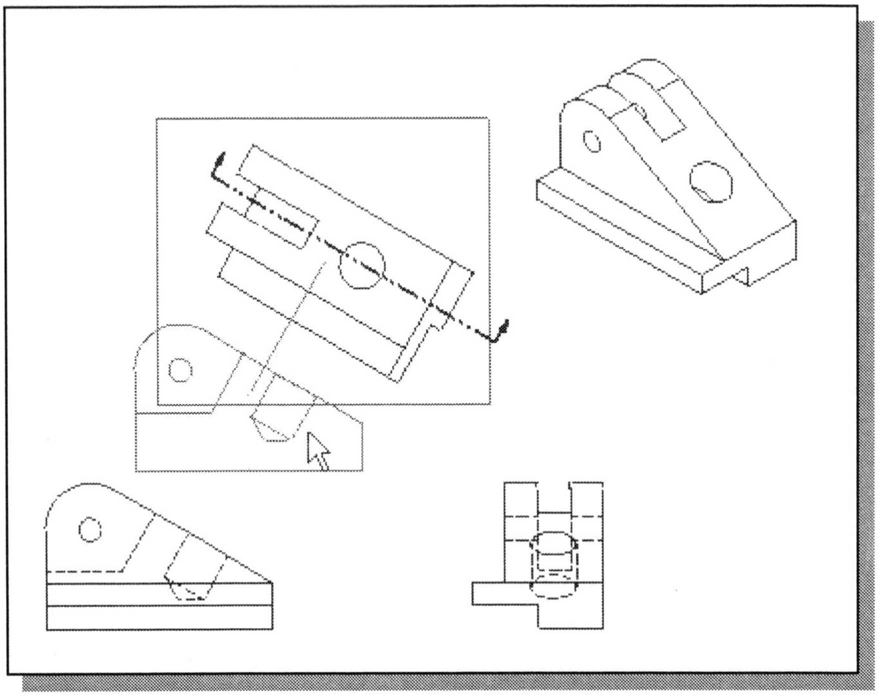

8. Move the cursor on top of the section view and watch for the box around the entire view indicating the view is selectable as shown in the figure.

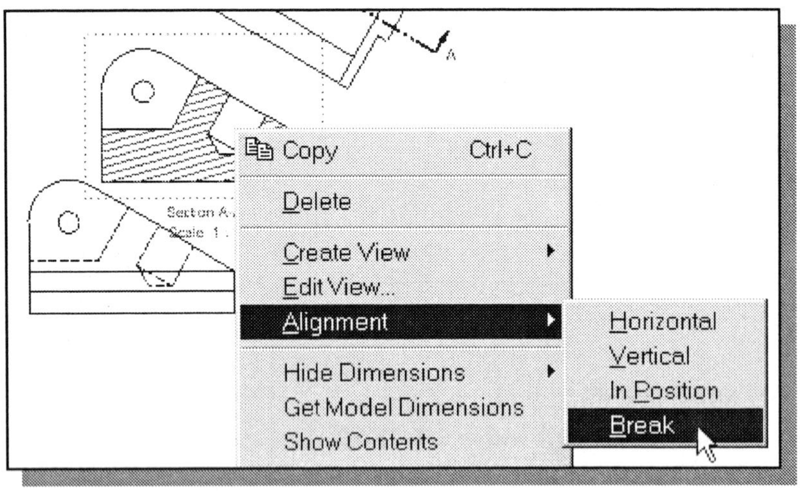

9. Right-mouse-click once to bring up the option menu.

10. Select **Alignment** → **Break** in the option menu.

❖ By default, a section view is aligned to the reference view where the projection was generated. The *Break* option allows us to release the alignment and move the view to an arbitrary location.

Repositioning Views

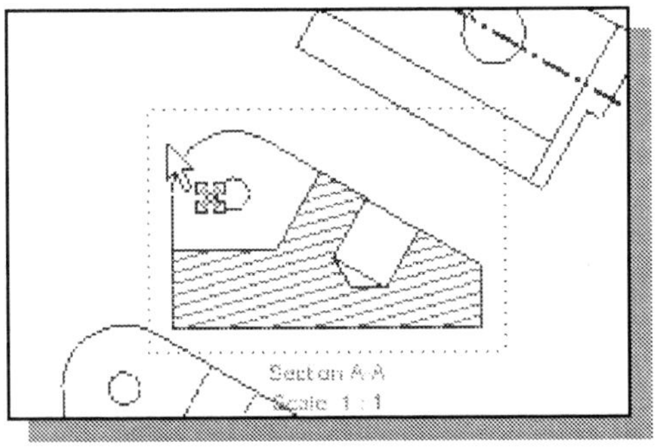

1. Move the cursor on top of the section view and watch for the box around the entire view indicating the view is selectable as shown in the figure.

❖ Note the four-arrows *Move* symbol indicating we can drag the view to any location in the graphics window.

2. Press and hold down the left-mouse-button and reposition the section view near the right side of the title block as shown below.

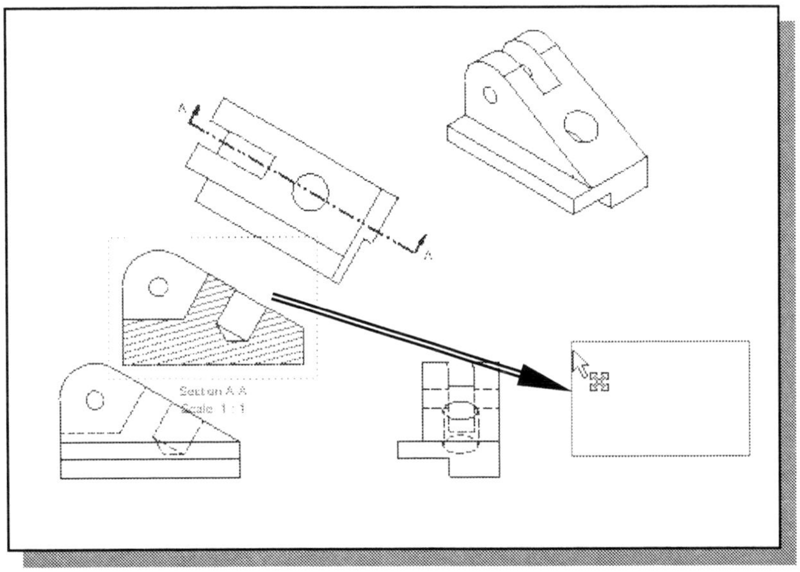

3. On your own, reposition the views we have created so far. Note that the front view, side-view, and the auxiliary view are all aligned to each other.

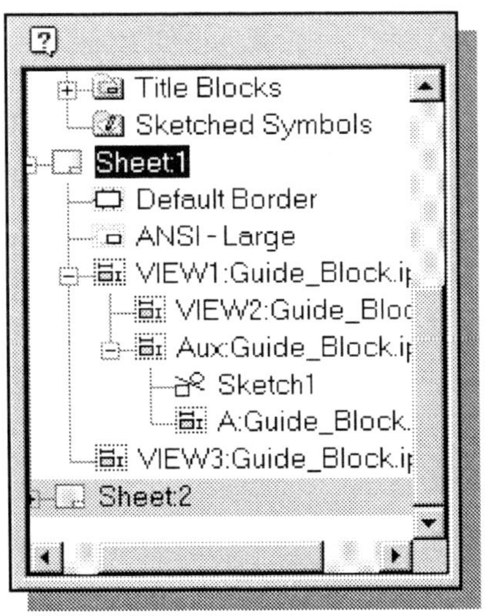

➢ Note that in the *Drawing Browser* area, a hierarchy of the created views is displayed under *Sheet1*. The base view, *View1*, is listed as the first view created, with *View2* and *Aux* linked to it. The section view, *View A*, is projected from the *Aux* view. The **view projection line** is placed under *Sketch1*, which can be modified if necessary. Drawing views are associated with the model and the drawing sheets. As we create views from the base view, they are nested beneath the base view in the *Browser*.

Displaying Feature Dimensions

- By default, feature dimensions are not displayed in 2D views in *Autodesk Inventor*. We can change the default settings while creating the views or switch on the display of the parametric dimensions using the option menu.

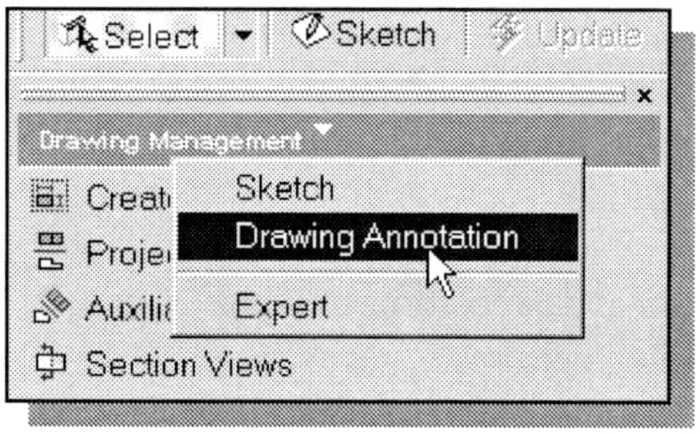

1. Left-mouse-click in the *title* area of the *Drawing Management* window.

2. Select **Drawing Annotation** by left-clicking once in the drop-down list.

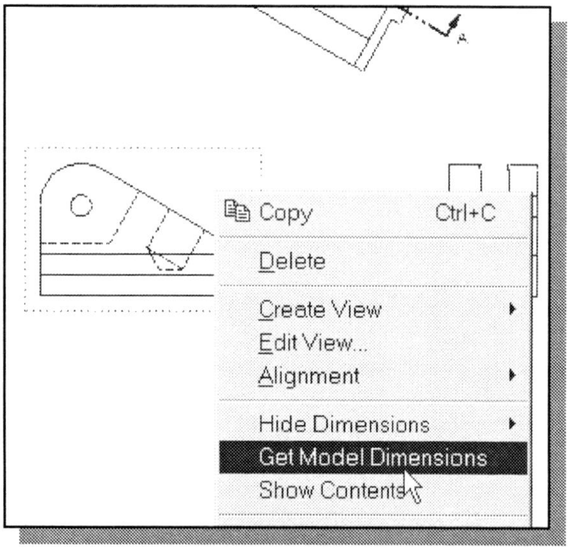

3. Move the cursor on top of the front-view of the model and watch for the box around the entire view indicating the view is selectable as shown in the figure.

4. Inside the graphics window, right-mouse-click once to bring up the option menu.

5. Select **Get Model Dimension** to display the parametric dimensions used to create the model.

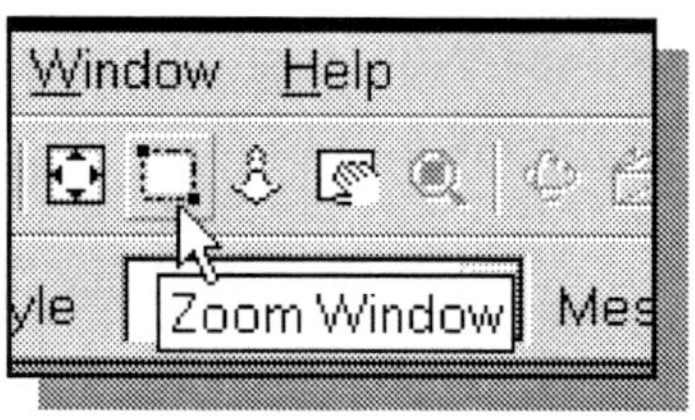

6. Click on the **Zoom Window** button in the *Standard* toolbar.

7. Pick two locations on the screen to enclose the front view of the model to proceed with the **Zoom** command.

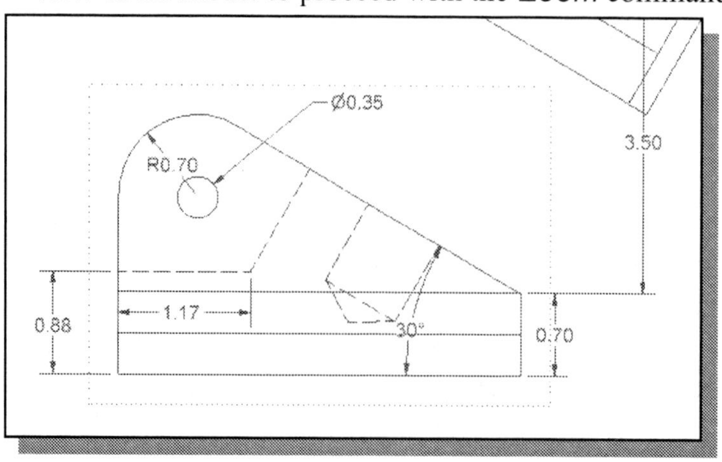

Hiding and Repositioning Feature Dimensions

- *Autodesk Inventor* automatically displays the parametric dimensions used to create the individual feature in the appropriate views, the views aligned to the sketching planes. We have full control of the visibility of all the parametric dimensions.

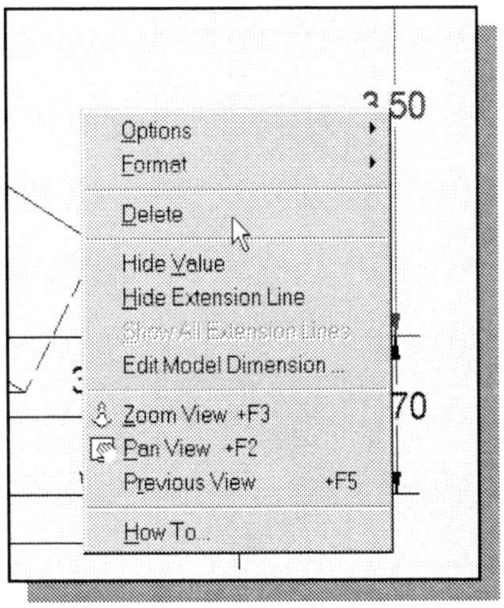

1. Move the cursor on top of the vertical dimension **3.50** and watch for when the dimension text becomes highlighted indicating the dimension is selectable.

2. Inside the graphics window, right-mouse-click once to bring up the option menu.

3. Select **Delete** to hide the highlighted parametric dimension.

❖ Note that the dimension is only deleted from the associated view; it is not deleted from the solid model.

4. On your own, hide the unwanted dimensions so that the display on your screen appears as shown below.

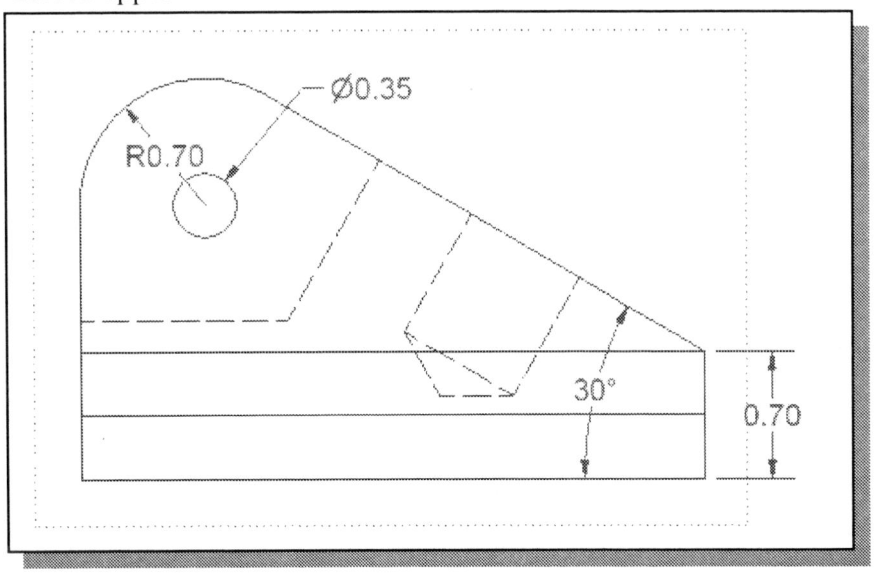

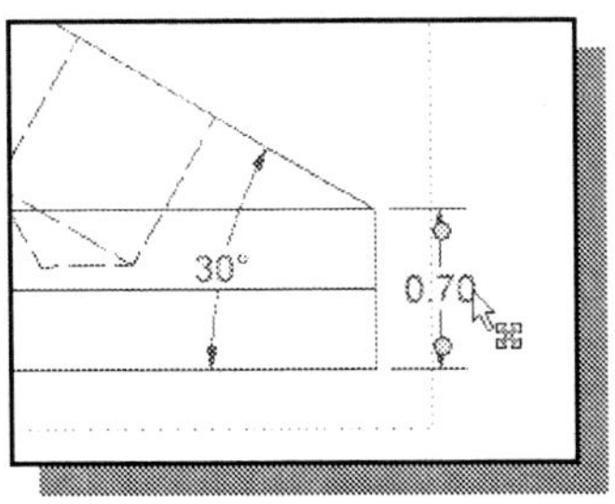

5. Move the cursor on top of the height dimension text **0.70** and watch for when the dimension text becomes highlighted with the four-arrows symbol indicating the dimension is selectable.

6. Reposition the dimension to a new location by using the left-mouse-button and drag the dimension text.

7. Move the cursor on top of the diameter dimension **.35** and right-mouse-click once to bring up the option menu.

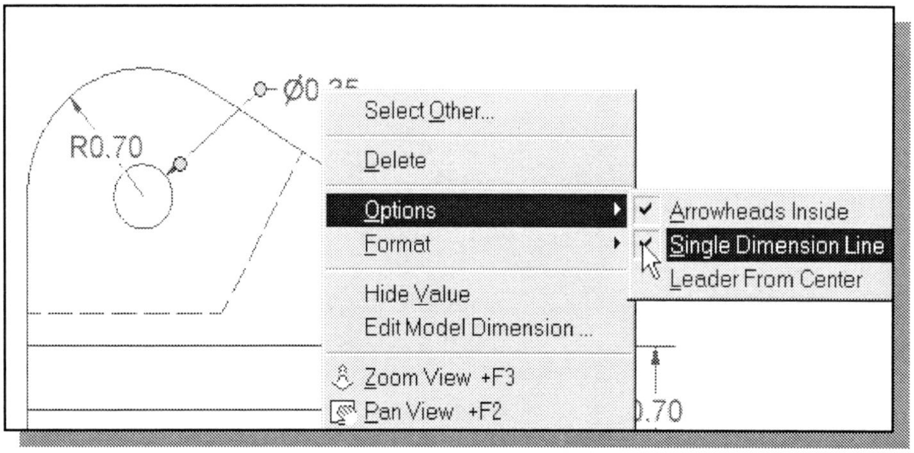

8. Select **Options → Single Dimension Line** to toggle off the single arrow option for the selected dimension. Note the displayed arrows inside the circle.

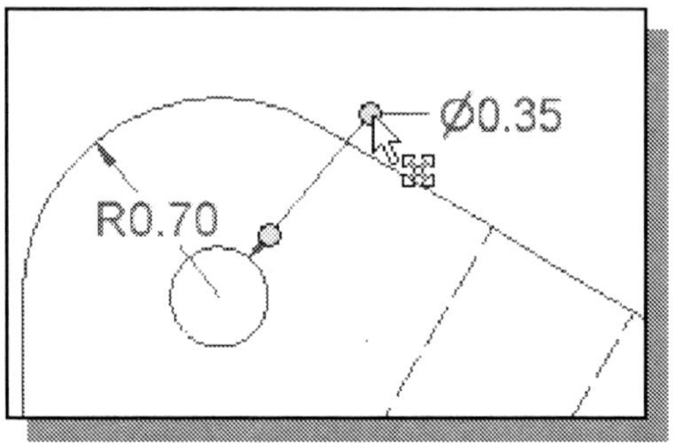

9. Use the left-mouse-button and drag on the grip point displayed of the **0.35** diameter dimension to reposition the entire dimension. Note that we can also drag on the dimension text, which only repositions the text.

10. On your own, reposition the dimensions as shown in the below figure.

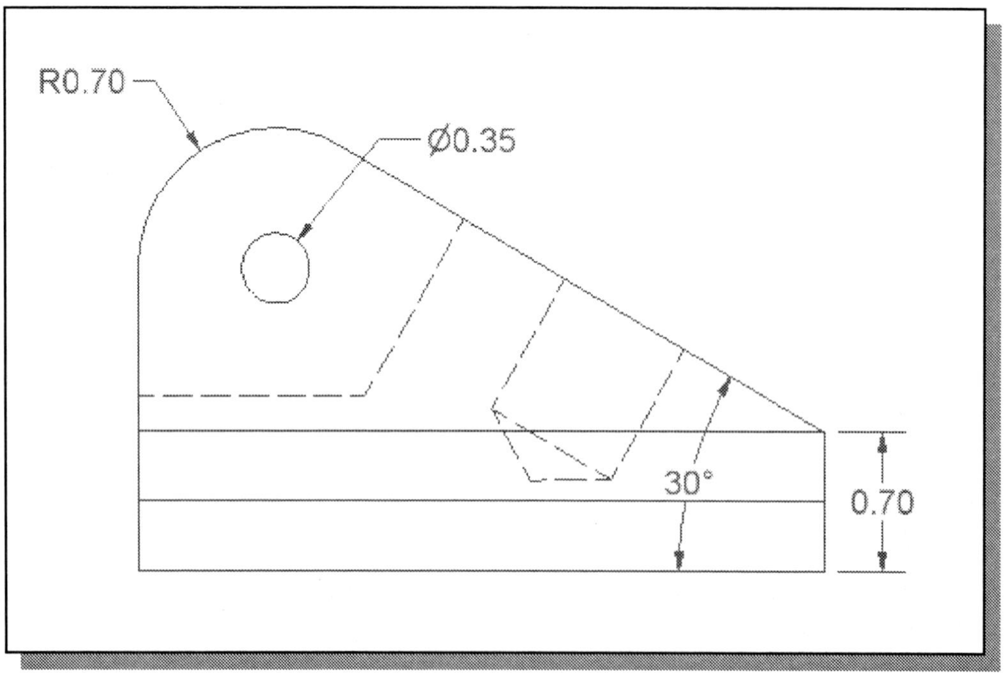

Adding Center Mark and Center Lines

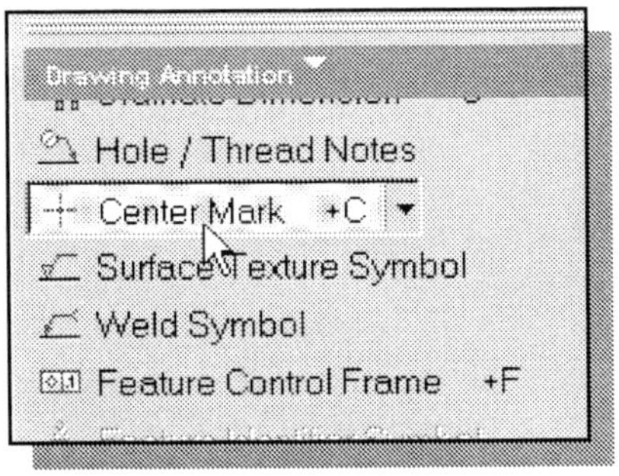

1. Click on the **Center Mark** button in the *Drawing Annotation* window.

2. Click on the circle in the front view to add the center mark.

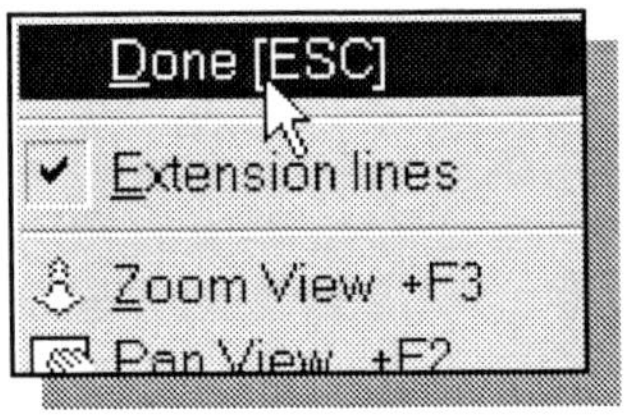

3. Inside the graphics window, click once with the right-mouse-button to display the option menu. Select **Done** in the popup menu to end the *Center Mark* command.

4. Use the left-mouse-button and drag the left-endpoint of the horizontal centerline toward the left.

5. Repeat the last step and adjust the vertical centerline as shown below.

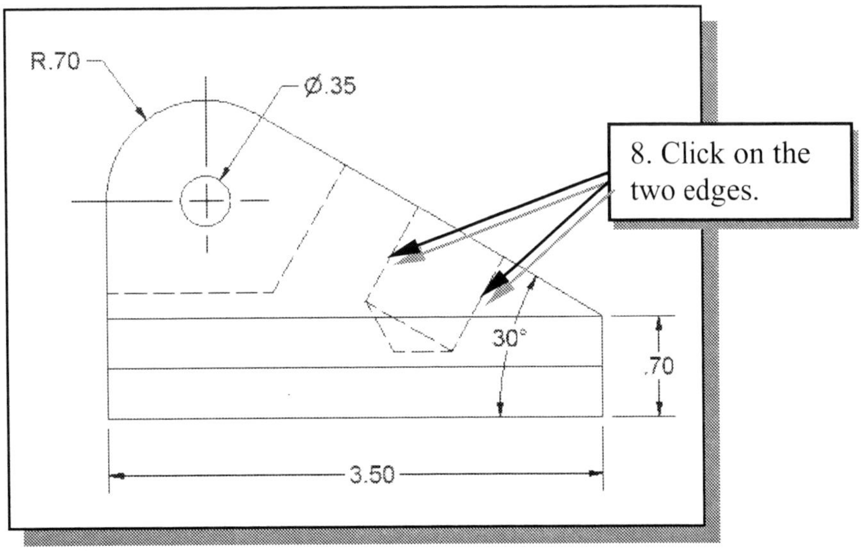

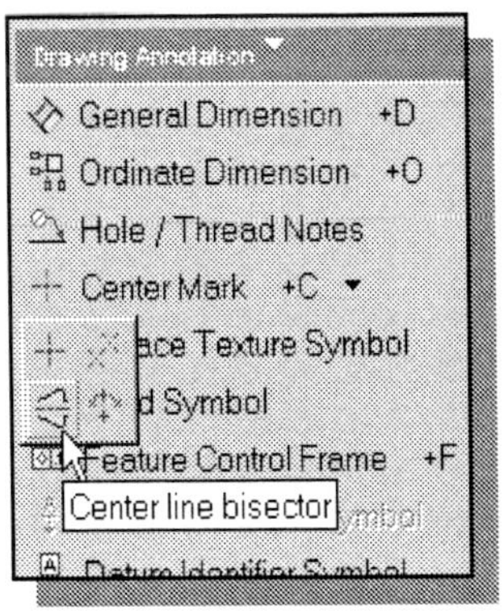

6. Click on the **drop-down arrow** next to the ***New File*** button in the *Drawing Annotation* window to display the available options.

7. Select **Center line bisector** from the option list.

8. Inside the graphics window, click on the two edges of the *Drill* feature on the inclined surface as shown in the above figure.

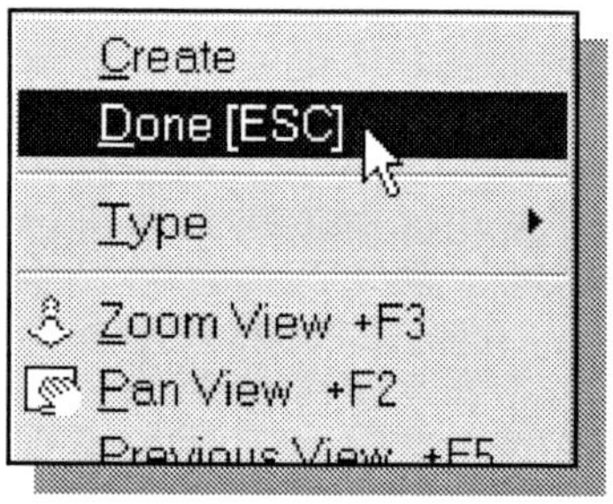

9. Inside the graphics window, click once with the right-mouse-button to display the option menu. Select **Done** in the popup menu to end the *Center line bisector* command.

10. On your own, adjust the length of the centerline as shown below.

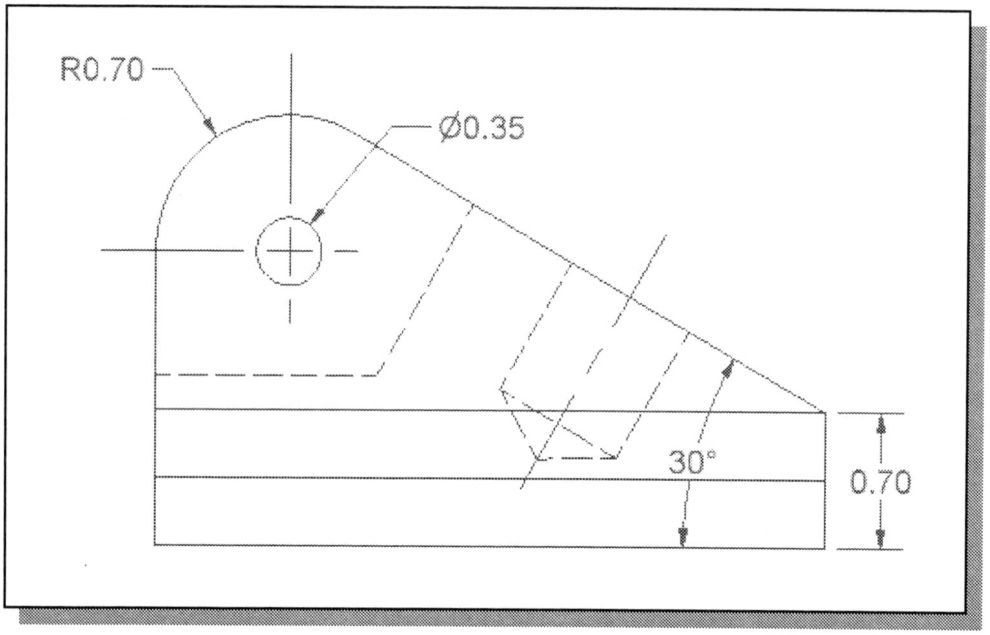

11. Click on the ***Pan*** button in the *Standard* toolbar.

12. On your own, adjust the display to view the *Auxiliary* view as shown below.

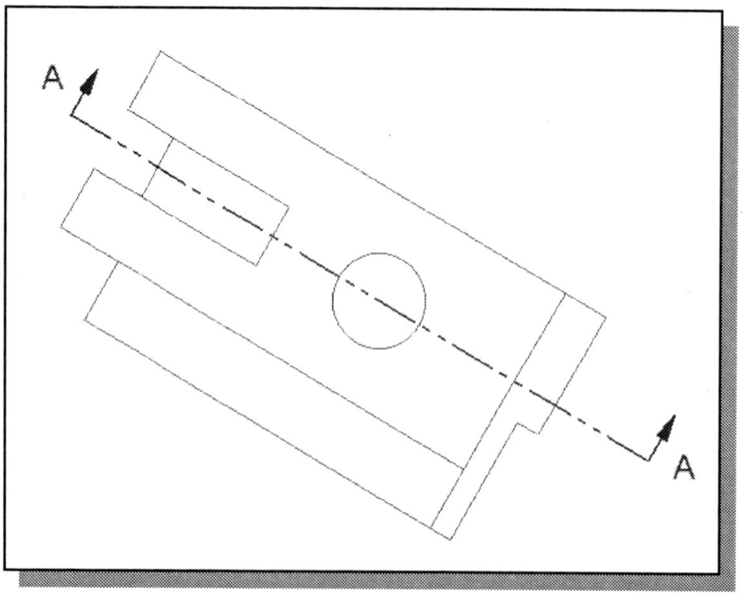

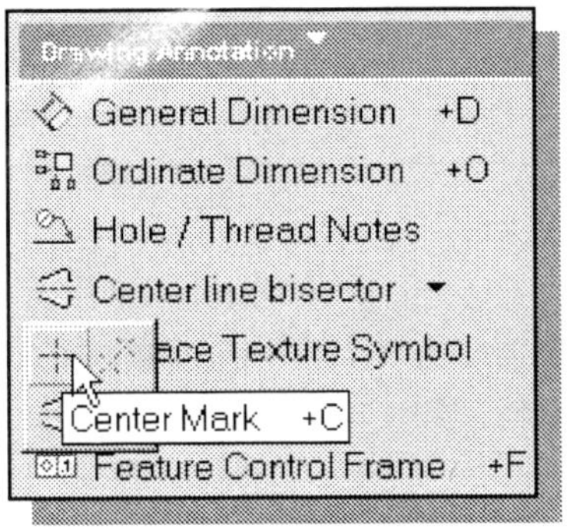

13. Click on the **drop-down arrow** next to the ***Center line bisector*** button in the *Drawing Annotation* window to display the available options.

14. Select **Center Mark** from the option list.

15. Inside the graphics window, click on the circle to create the center mark.

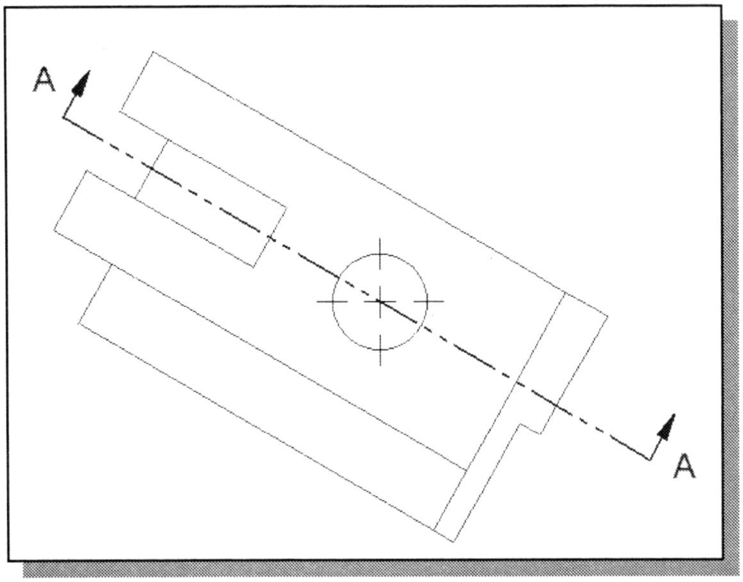

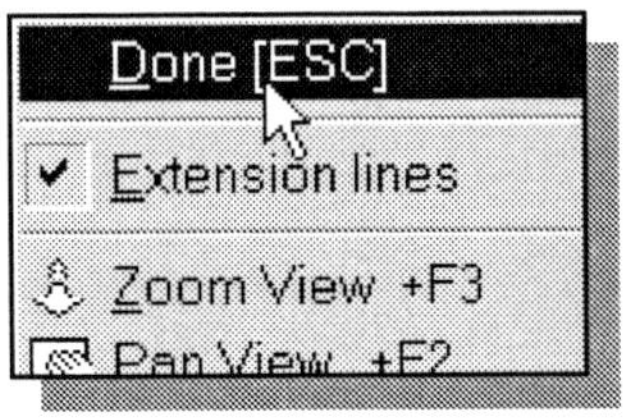

16. Inside the graphics window, click once with the right-mouse-button to display the option menu. Select **Done** in the popup menu to end the *Center Mark* command.

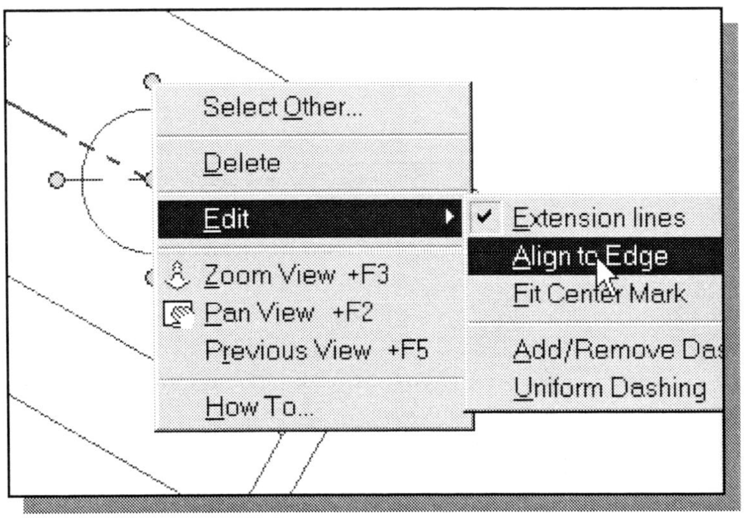

17. Move the cursor on top of the center mark and right-mouse-click once to bring up the option menu.

18. Select **Edit** → **Align to Edge** in the option menu.

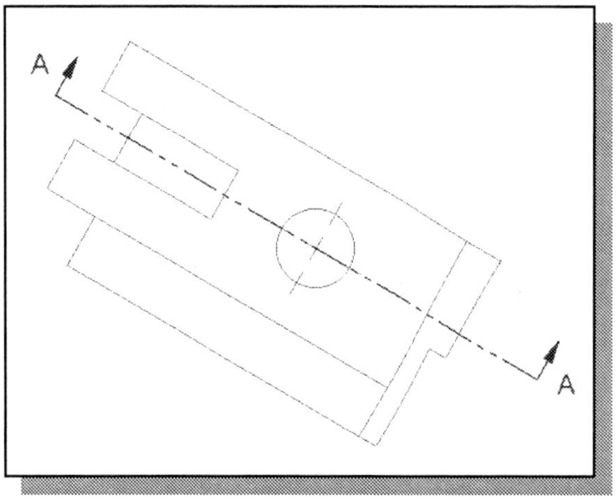

19. Click on any edges of the auxiliary view to align the centerlines as shown below.

20. Move the cursor on top of the *Auxiliary* view of the model, and watch for the box around the entire view indicating the view is selectable.

21. Inside the graphics window, right-mouse-click once to bring up the option menu.

8. Select **Get Model Dimension** to display the parametric dimensions used to create the model.

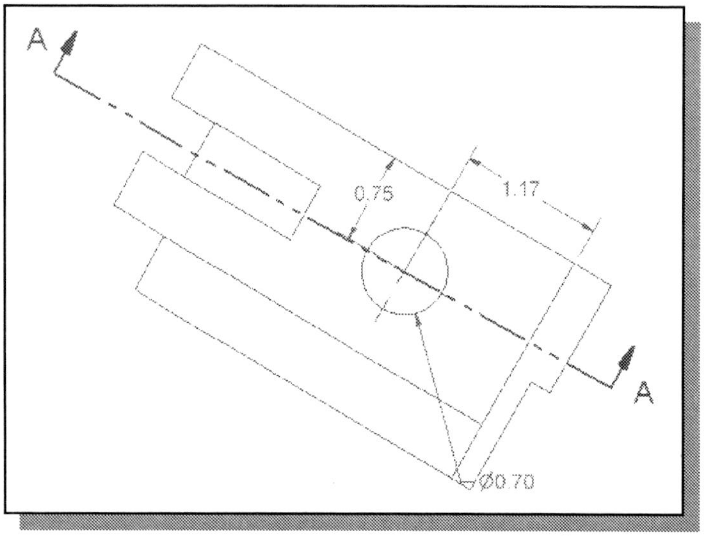

22. On your own, adjust the dimensions as shown below.

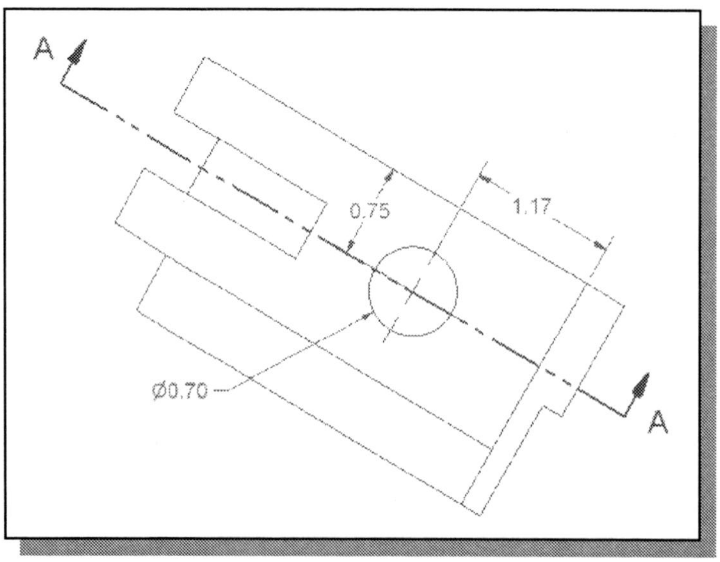

Adding Additional Dimensions – Reference Dimensions

- Besides displaying the **feature dimensions**, dimensions used to create the features, we can also add additional **reference dimensions** in the drawing. *Feature dimensions* are used to control the geometry, whereas *reference dimensions* are controlled by the existing geometry. In the drawing layout, therefore, we can *delete* the *reference dimensions* but we can only *hide* the *feature dimensions.* One should try to use as many *feature dimensions* as possible and add *reference dimensions* only if necessary. It is also more effective to use *feature dimensions* in the drawing layout since they are created when the model was built. Note that additional *Drawing Mode* entities, such as lines and arcs, can be added to drawing views. Before *Drawing Mode* entities can be used in a reference dimension, they must be associated to a *drawing view*.

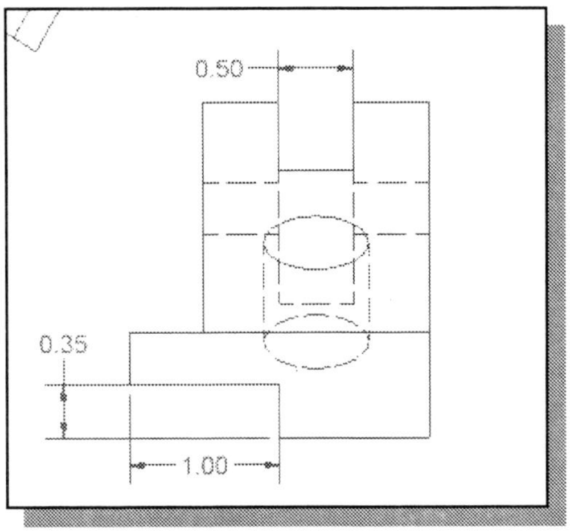

1. On your own, adjust the display to view the side-view of the model as shown.

2. On your own, use the **Get Model Dimension** option to display the parametric dimensions in the side-view as shown in the figure.

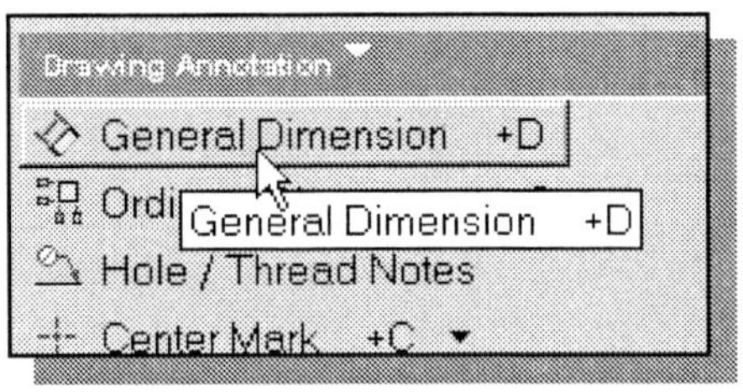

3. In the *Drawing Annotation* window, click on the **General Dimension** button.

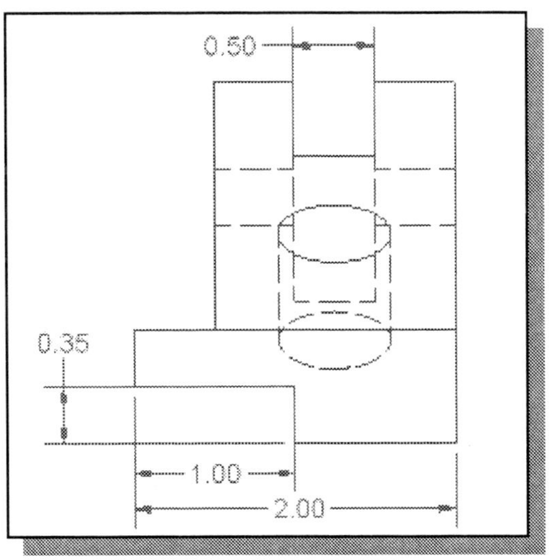

4. In the prompt area, the message "*Select first object*:" is displayed. Select the right-vertical edge of the model.

5. In the prompt area, the message "*Select second object or place dimension*:" is displayed. Select the left-vertical edge of the side view.

6. Pick a location that is below the side-view to place the overall-width dimension text as shown.

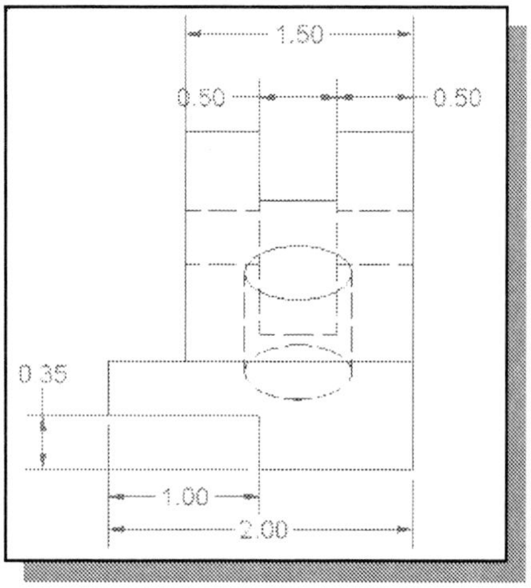

7. On your own, create the two dimensions showing the cut feature located at the top of the model.

8. Inside the graphics window, move the cursor on top of the center dimension and right-mouse-click to bring up the option menu.

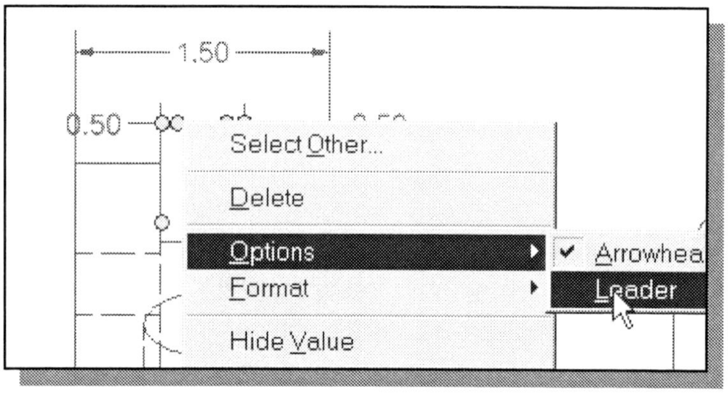

9. Select **Options** → **Leader** in the option menu as shown in the above figure.

10. On your own, reposition the dimension as shown below.

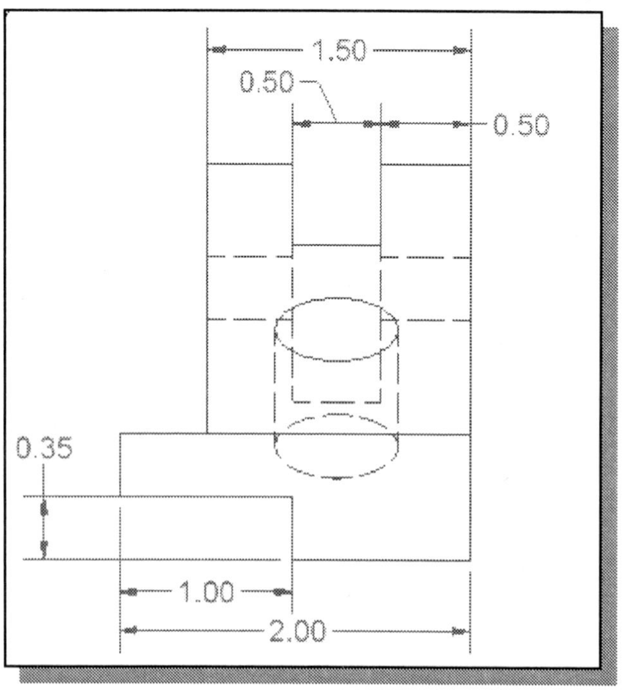

Completing the Drawing Sheet

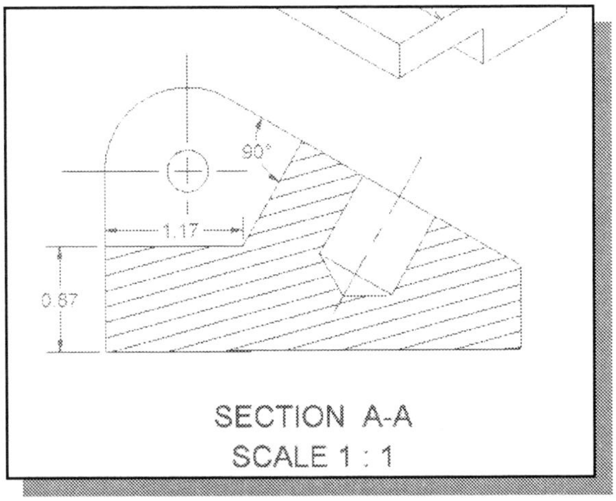

1. On your own, create the necessary centerlines and dimensions for the section view as shown.

2. On your own, use the ***Zoom*** and ***Pan*** commands to adjust the display and concentrate in the title block area.

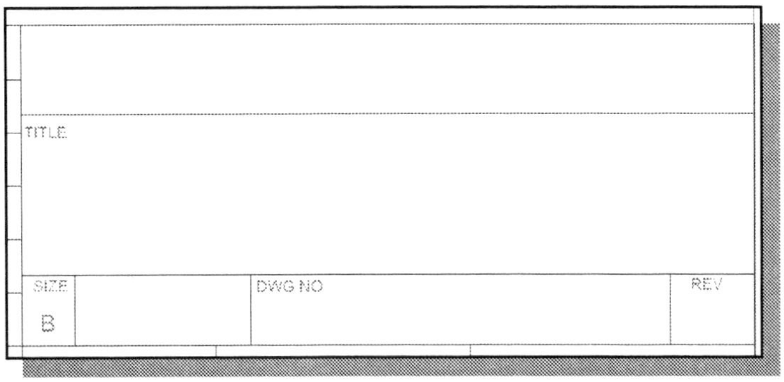

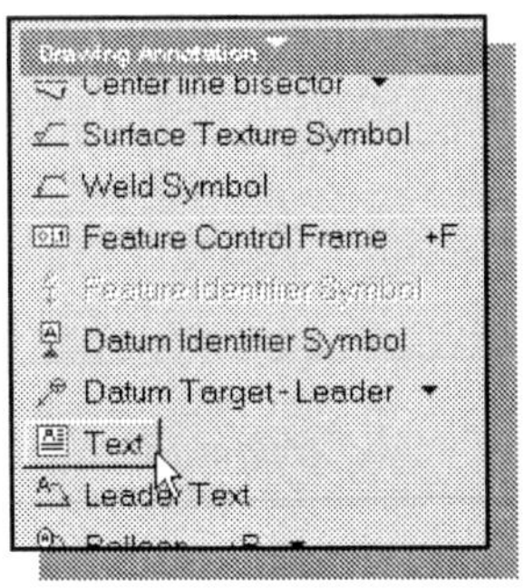

3. In the *Drawing Annotation* window, click on the **Text** button.

4. Pick a location that is inside the title block area as the location for the new text to be entered.

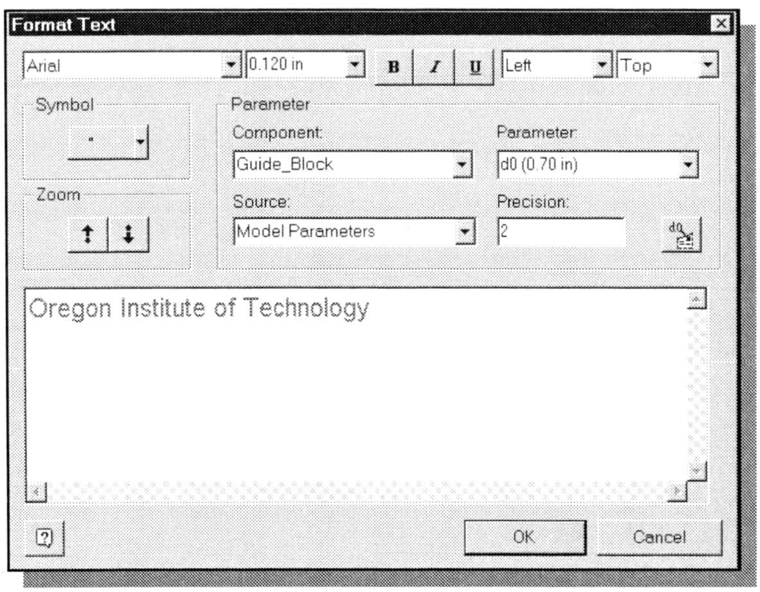

5. In the *Format Text* dialog box, enter the name of your organization as shown. Also note the different settings available. (**DO NOT** click on the **OK** button.)

6. On your own, enter the text as shown below.

➢ On your own, complete the 2D drawing as shown in the below figure.

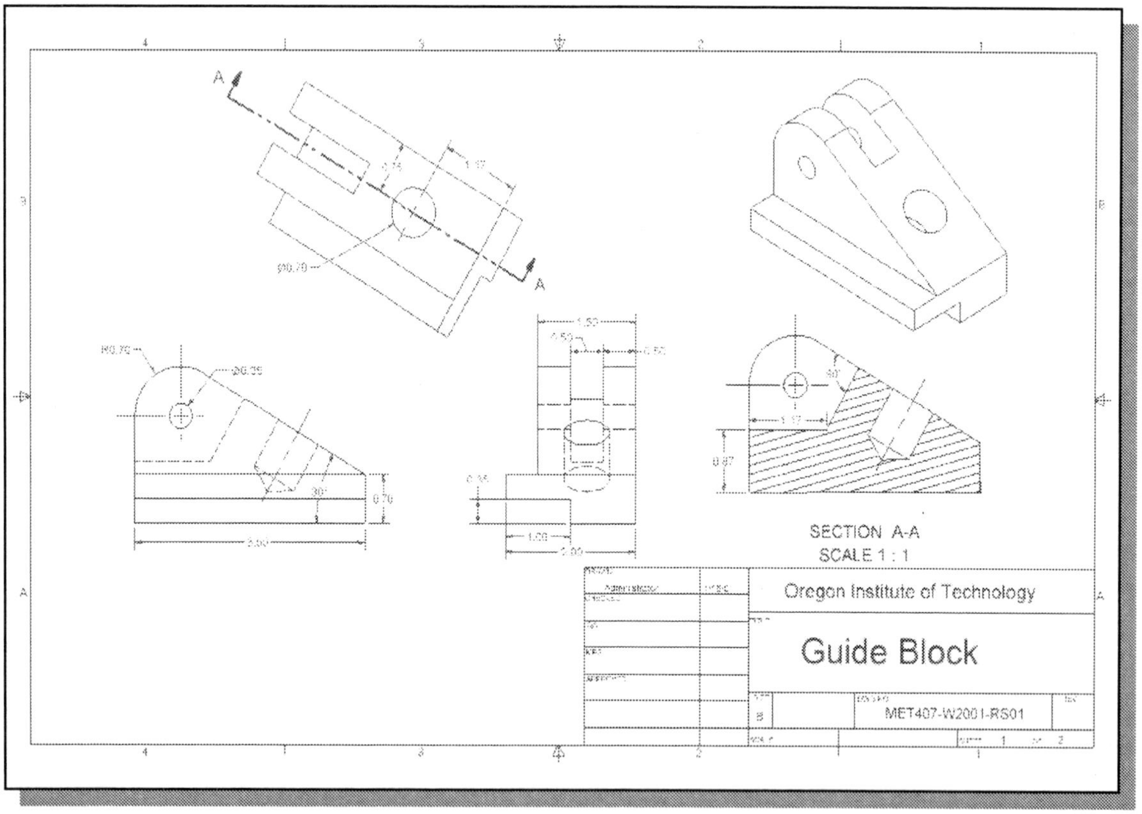

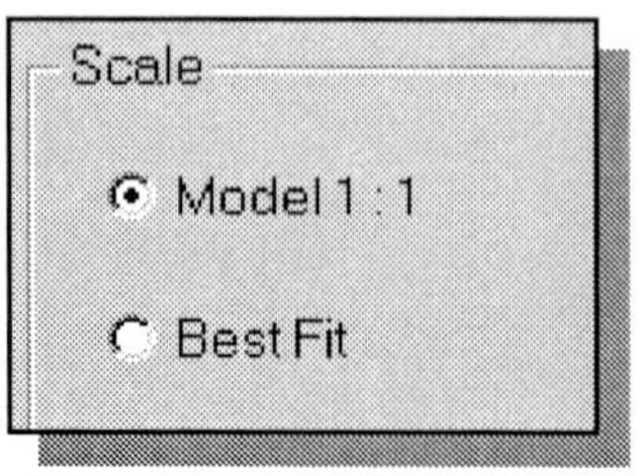

♦ The completed drawing can now be printed. On your own, print out a copy of the drawing using the **File → Print** option. (Hint: In the print dialog box, set the scale factor according to the paper sizes that are available.)

Associative Functionality – Modifying Feature Dimensions

- *Autodesk Inventor's associative functionality* allows us to change the design at any level, and the system reflects the changes at all levels automatically.

1. Click on the ***Guide_Block*** part window to switch to the part modeler mode.

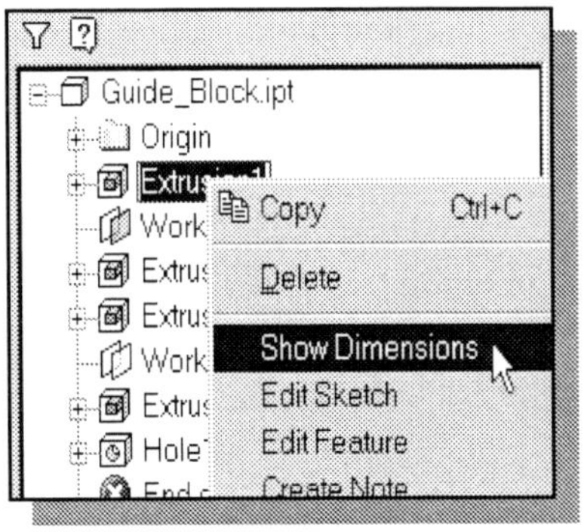

2. In the *Browser* window, right-click once on ***Extrusion1*** to bring up the option menu.

3. Select **Show Dimensions** in the popup option menu.

4. Double-click on the diameter dimension (**0.350**) of the drill feature as shown in the below figure.

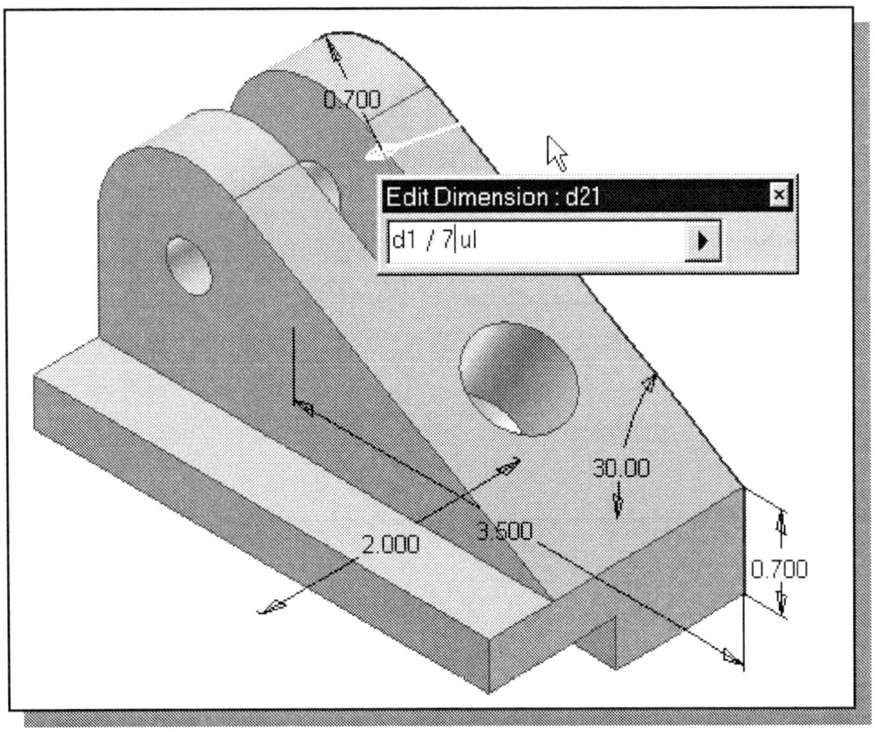

5. In the *Edit Dimension* dialog box, enter **d1/7** as the new diameter dimension.

6. Click on the **check mark** button to accept the setting.

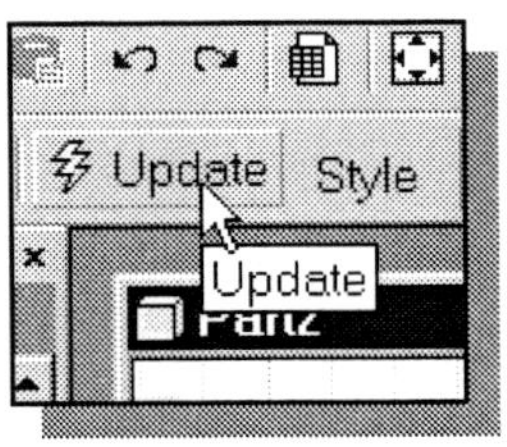

7. Click on the **Update** button in the *Standard* toolbar area to proceed with updating the solid model.

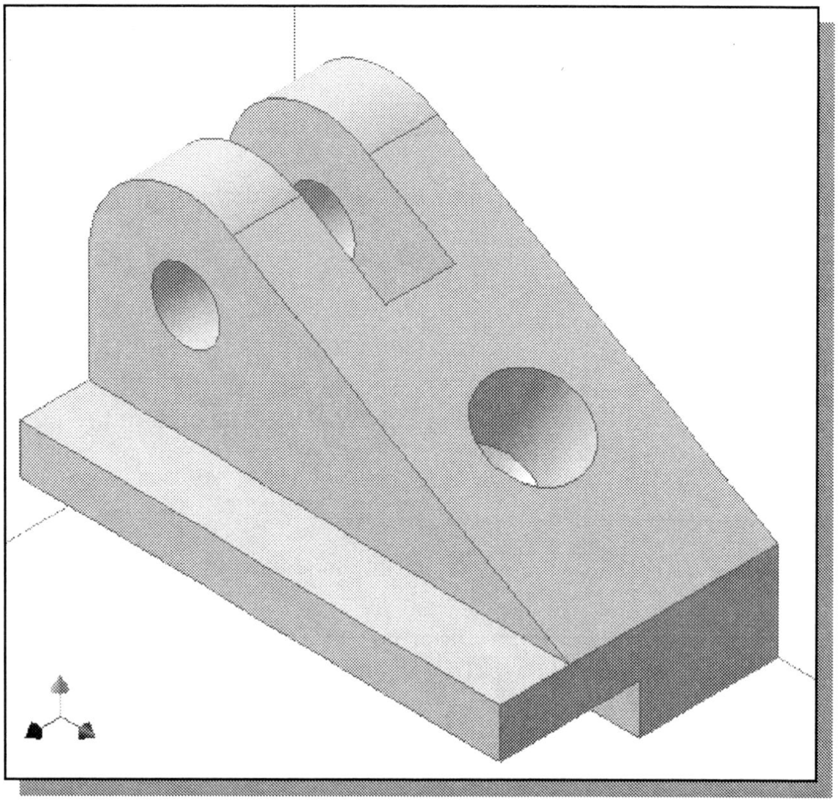

8. Click on the ***Drawing1*** graphics window to switch to the paper space and note that the drawing views are updated automatically.

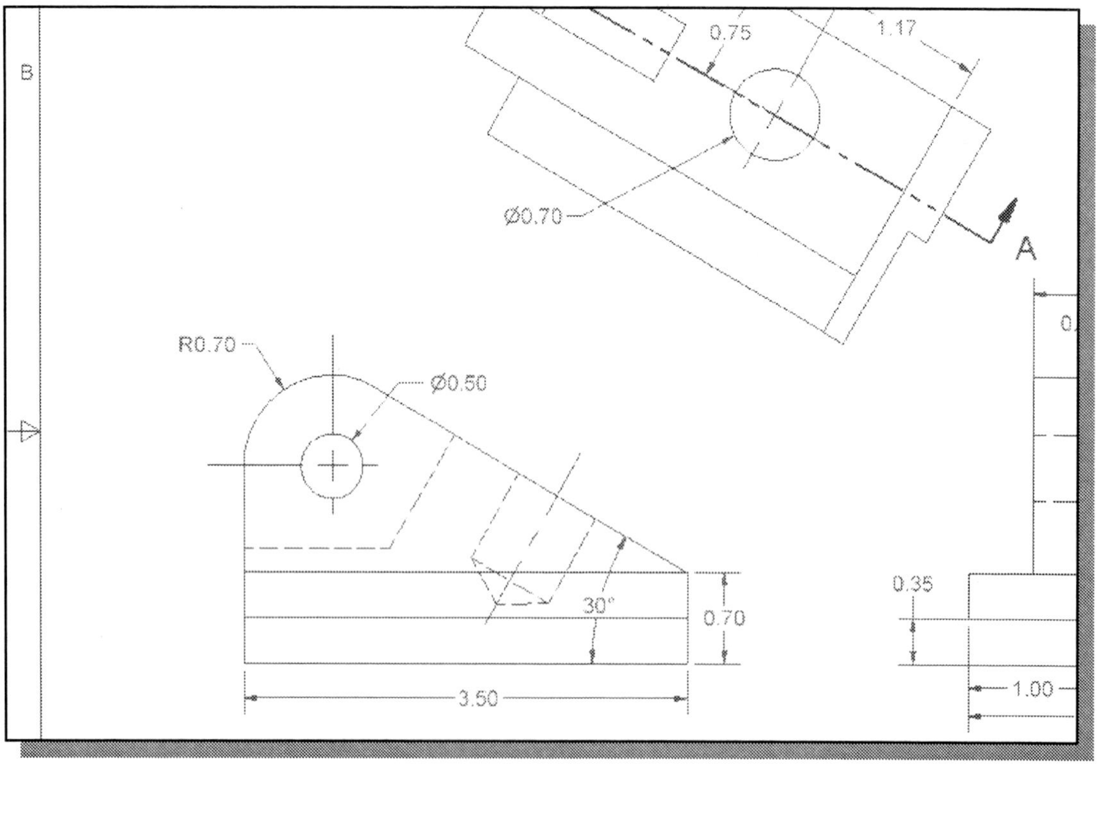

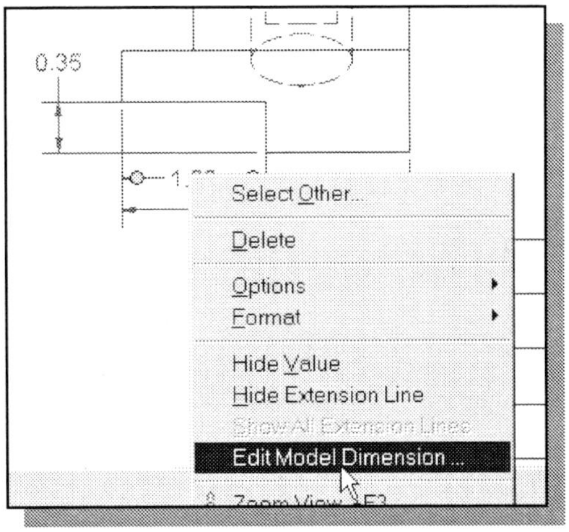

9. Inside the graphics window, right-click on the **1.00** dimension in the *Side* view to bring up the option menu.

10. Select **Edit Model Dimension** in the popup menu.

11. Change the dimension to **0.75**.

12. Click on the **check mark** button to accept the setting.

➢ Note the cut feature is updated in all views automatically.

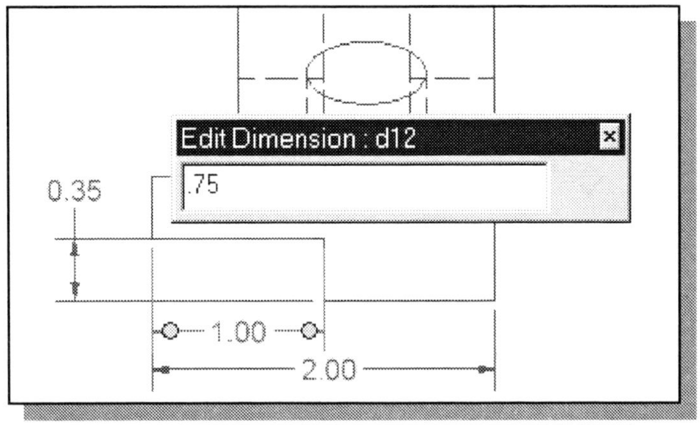

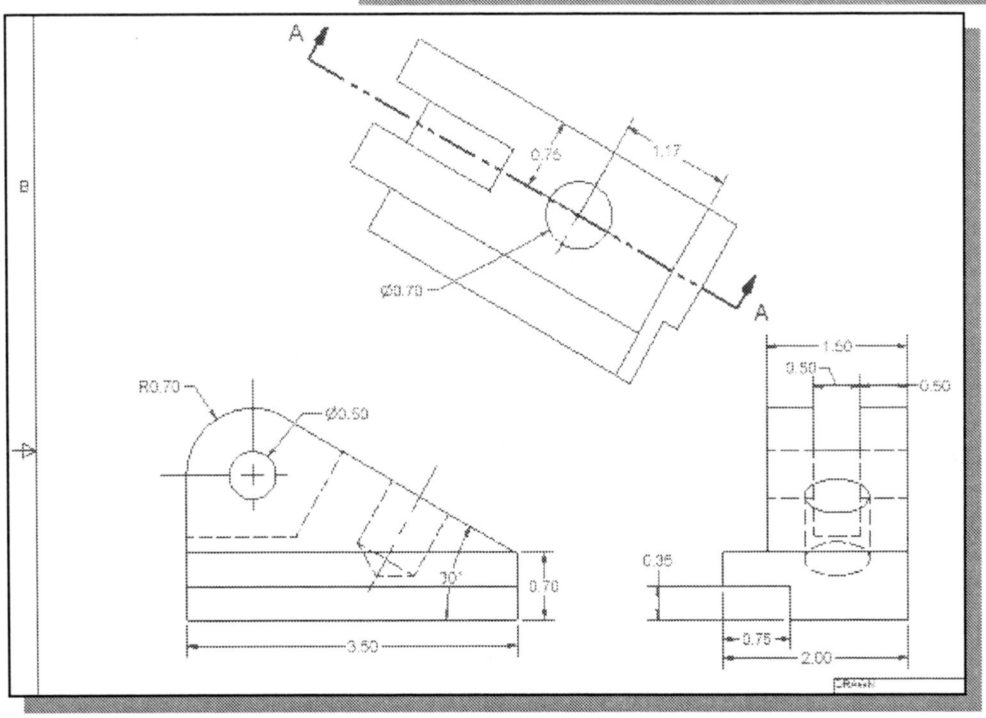

❖ On your own, switch to the *Part Model Mode* and confirm the design is updated as well.

Editing the Isometric view

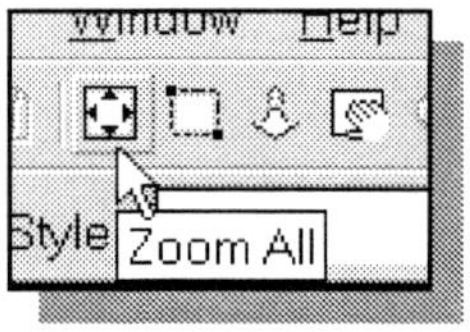

1. Click on the ***Zoom All*** button in the *Standard* toolbar.

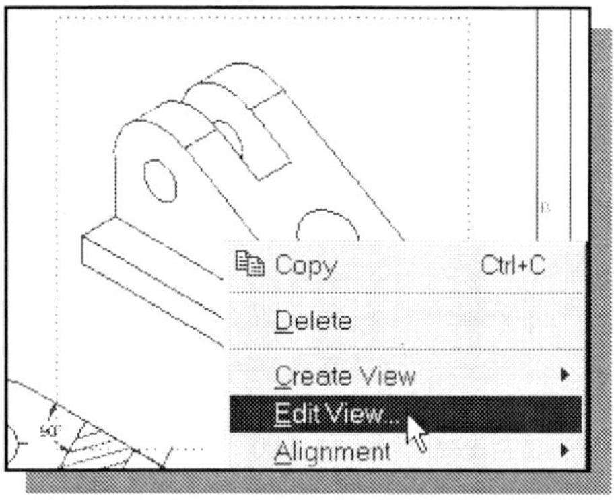

2. Right-mouse-click inside the *Isometric* view to bring up the option menu as shown.

3. Select **Edit View** in the option menu.

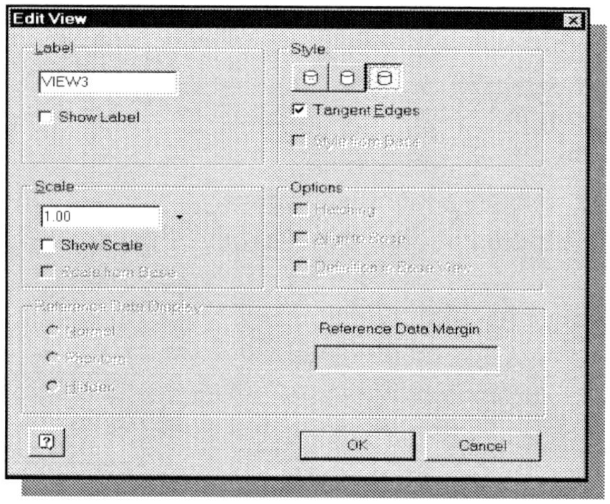

4. In the *Edit View* dialog box, set the display *Style* to **Shaded** and the *Scale* to ***1.0***.

5. Click on the **OK** button to accept the settings.

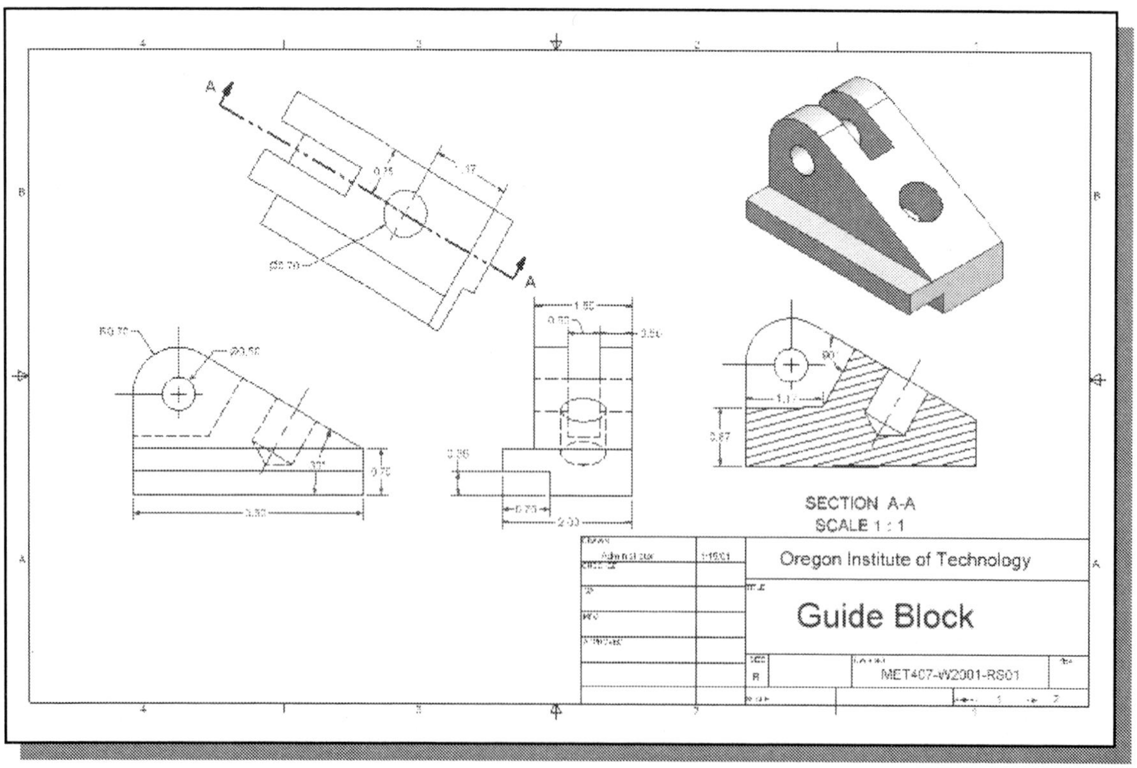

Questions:

1. What does *Autodesk Inventor*'s *associative functionality* allow us to do?

2. How do we move a view on the *Drawing Sheet*?

3. How do we move a dimension from one view to another?

4. What is the difference between a *feature dimension* and a *reference dimension*?

5. How do we reposition dimensions?

6. What are the required elements in order to generate a sectional view?

7. What is a *Base View*?

8. Identify and describe the following commands:

(a)

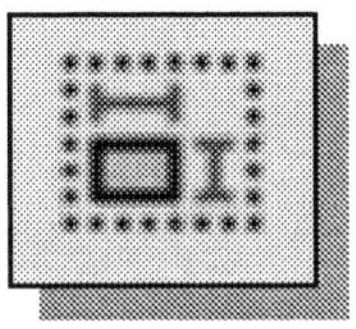

(b)

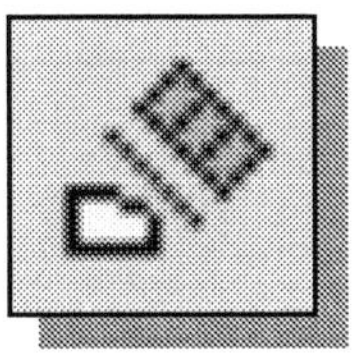

(c)

(d)

Exercises:

1.

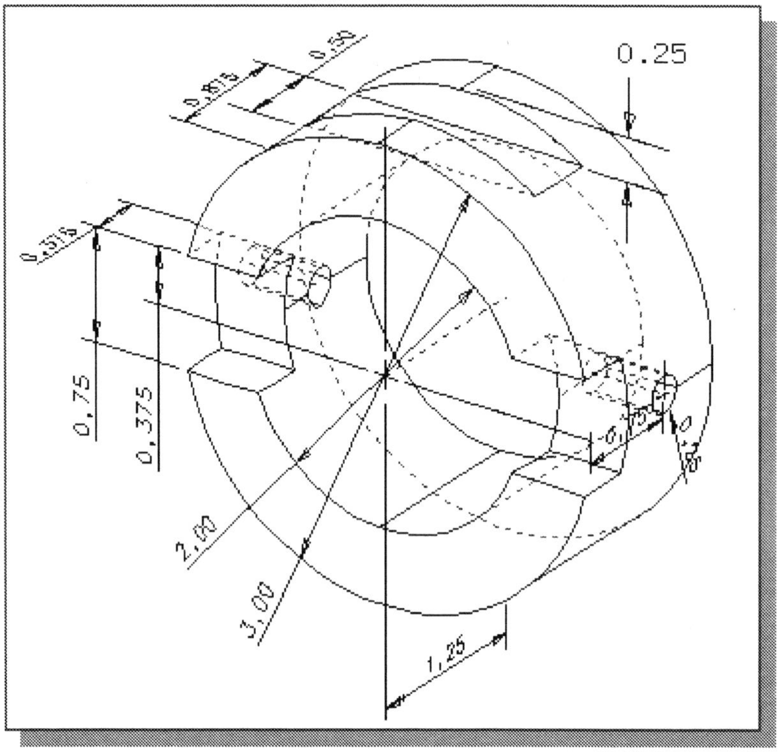

2.

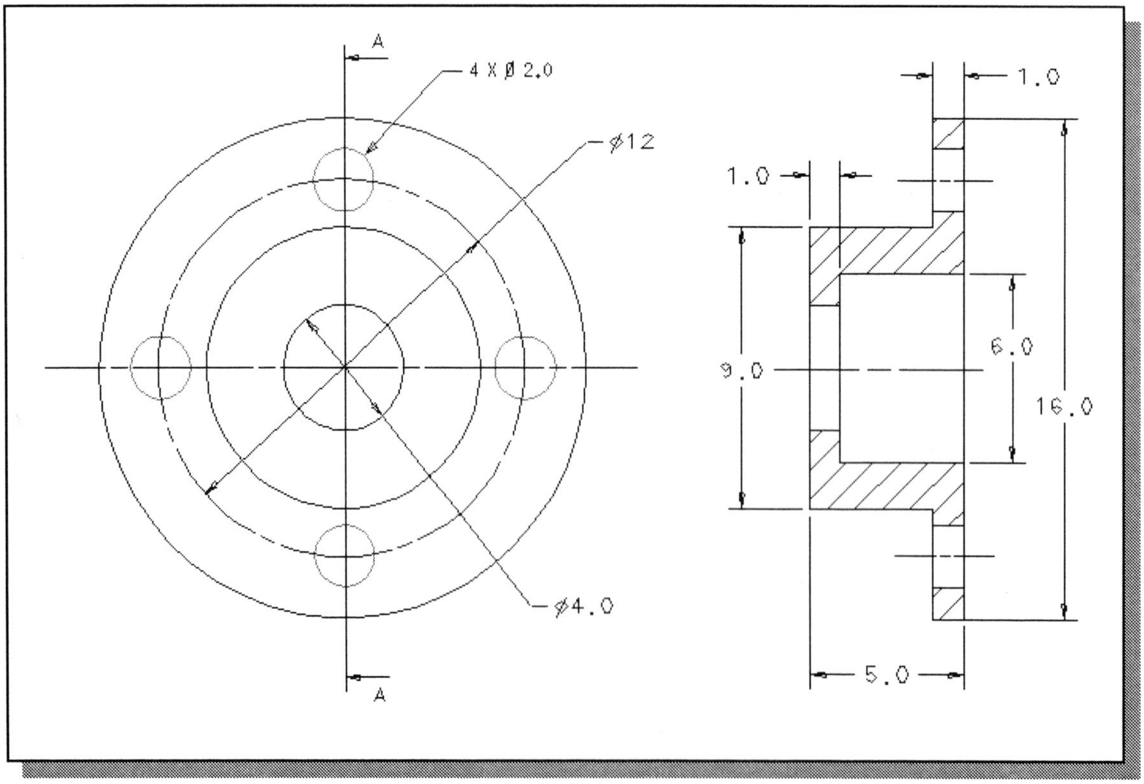

Lesson 7
Symmetrical Features in Designs

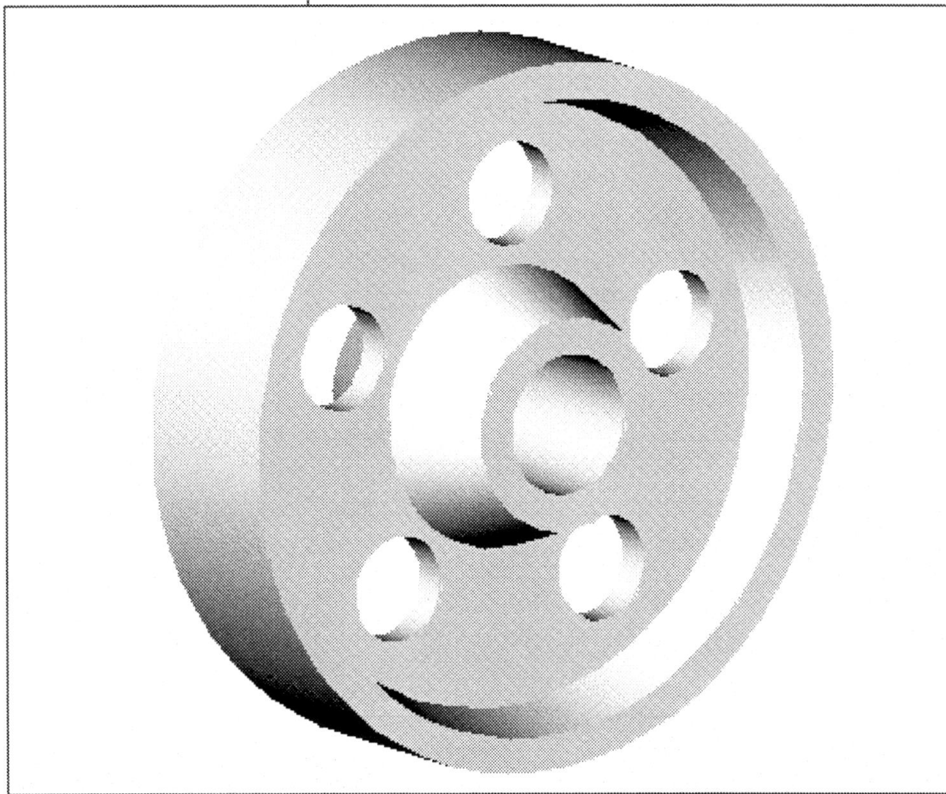

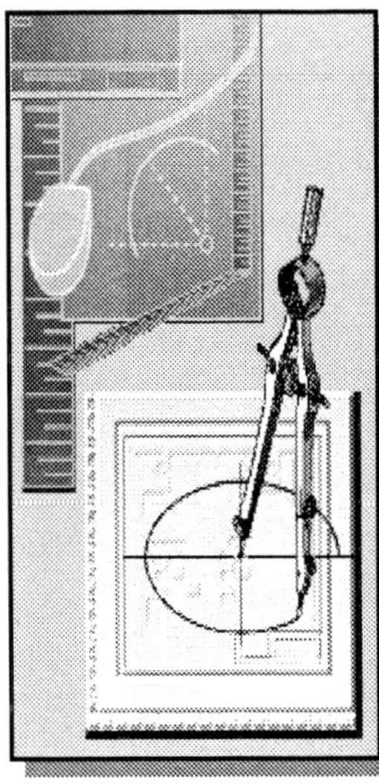

Learning Objectives

When you have completed this lesson, you will be able to:

- ♦ Create Revolved Features.
- ♦ Use the Mirror Feature Command.
- ♦ Create New Borders and Title Blocks.
- ♦ Create Circular Patterns.
- ♦ Create and Modify Linear Dimensions.
- ♦ Use the Autodesk Inventor's Associative functionality
- ♦ Create Symmetrical Features in Designs.

Introduction

In parametric modeling, it is important to identify and determine the features that exist in the design. *Feature-based parametric modeling* enables us to build complex designs by working on smaller and simpler units. This approach simplifies the modeling process and allows us to concentrate on the characteristics of the design. Symmetry is an important characteristic that is often seen in designs. Symmetrical features can be easily accomplished by the assortments of tools that are available in feature-based modeling systems, such as *Autodesk Inventor*.

The modeling technique of extruding two-dimensional sketches along a straight line to form three-dimensional features, as illustrated in the previous chapters, is an effective way to construct solid models. For designs that involve cylindrical shapes, shapes that are symmetrical about an axis, revolving two-dimensional sketches about an axis can form the needed three-dimensional features. In solid modeling, this type of feature is called a ***revolved feature***.

In *Autodesk Inventor*, besides using the *Revolve* command to create revolved features, several options are also available to handle symmetrical features. For example, we can create multiple identical copies of symmetrical features with the ***Feature Array*** command, or create mirror images of models using the ***Mirror Feature*** command. In this lesson, the construction and modeling techniques of these more advanced features are illustrated.

A Revolved Design: *PULLEY*

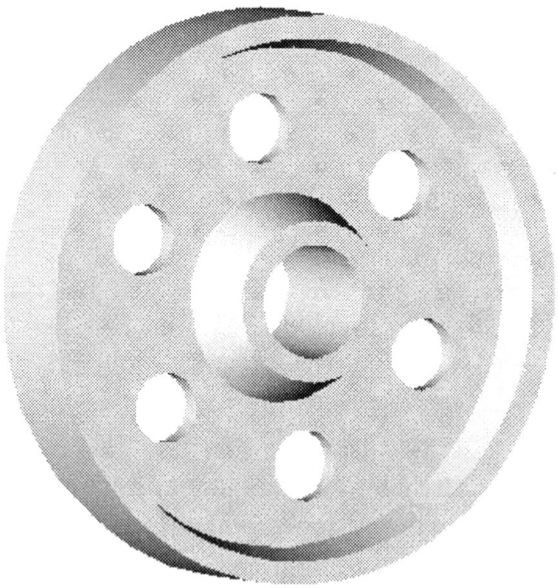

❖ Based on your knowledge of *Autodesk Inventor*, how many features would you use to create the design? Which feature would you choose as the **base feature** of the model? Identify the symmetrical features in the design and consider other possibilities in creating the design. You are encouraged to create the model on your own prior to following through the tutorial.

Modeling Strategy - A Revolved Design

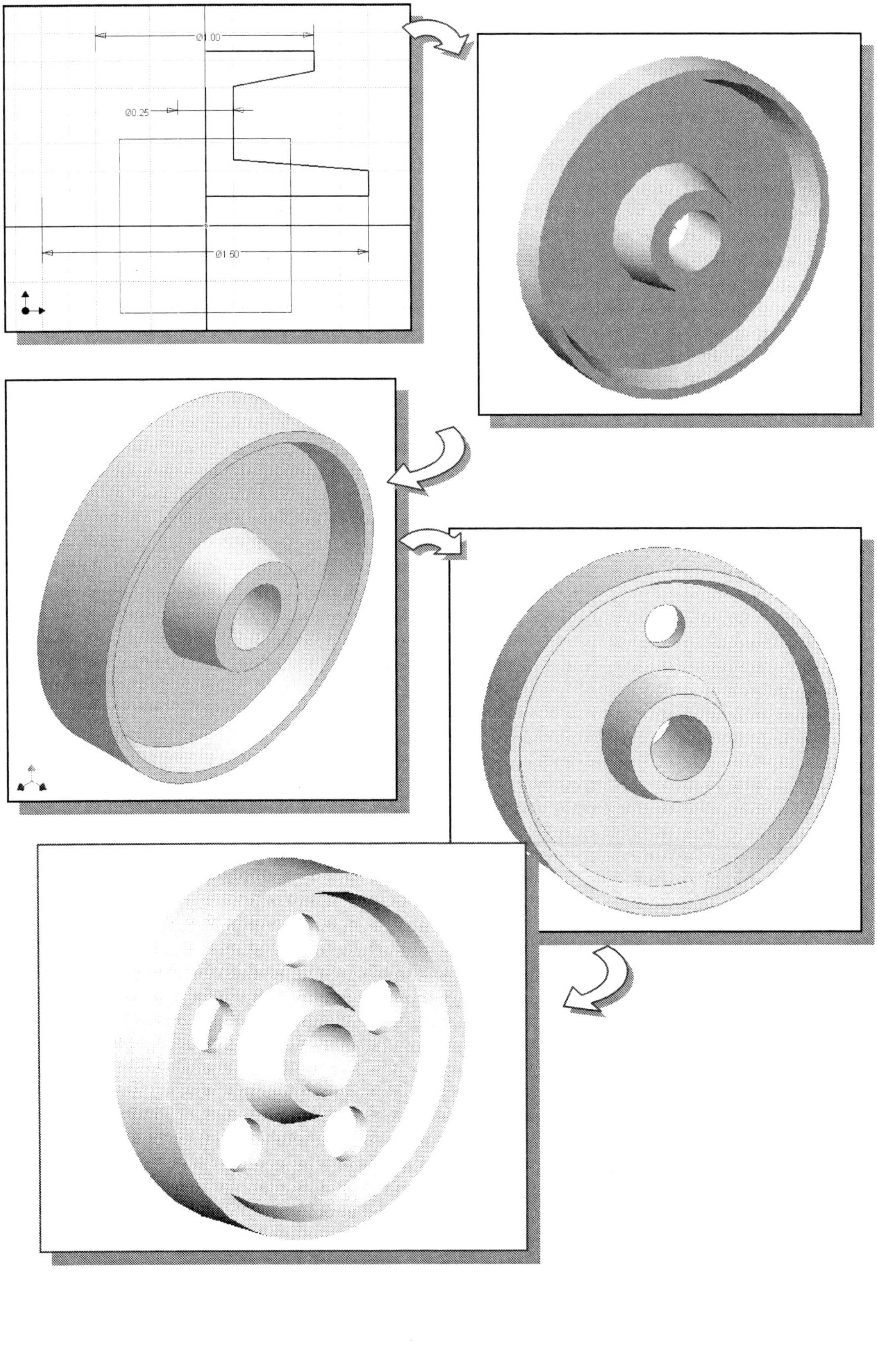

Starting Autodesk Inventor

1. Select the ***Autodesk Inventor*** option on the *Start* menu or select the ***Autodesk Inventor*** icon on the desktop to start *Autodesk Inventor*. The *Autodesk Inventor* main window will appear on the screen.

2. Once the program is loaded into the memory, the *Startup* dialog box appears at the center of the screen.

3. Select the ***New*** icon with a single click of the left-mouse-button in the *What to Do* dialog box.

4. Select the **English** tab and in the *New - Choose Template* area, select **Standard(in).ipt**.

5. Pick **OK** in the *Startup* dialog box to accept the selected settings.

Setup the display of the Sketch Plane

1. In the *Part Browser* window, click on the [+] symbol in front of the ***Origin*** feature to display more information on the feature.

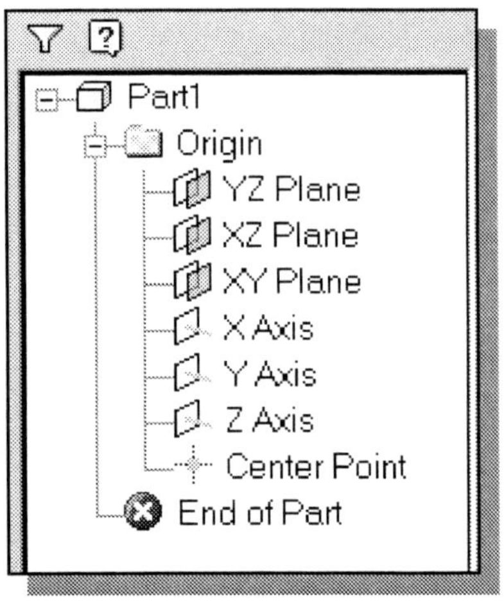

❖ In the *Browser* window, notice a new part name appeared with seven work features established. The seven work features include three *work-planes*, three *work-axes* and a *work-point*. By default, the three work-planes and work-axes are aligned to the **world coordinate system** and the work-point is aligned to the *origin* of the **world coordinate system**.

2. Inside the *Browser* window, move the cursor on top of the third work-plane, ***XY Plane***. Notice a rectangle, representing the work-plane, appears in the graphics window.

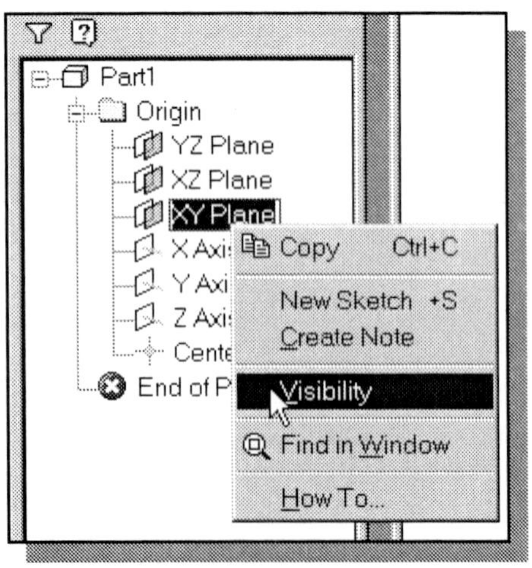

3. Inside the *Browser* window, click once with the right-mouse-button on *XY Plane* to display the option menu. Click on **Visibility** to toggle on the display of the plane.

4. On your own, repeat the above step and toggle ***ON*** the display of the *X* and *Y work-axes* and the *Center Point* on the screen.

Creating the 2D Sketch for the Base feature

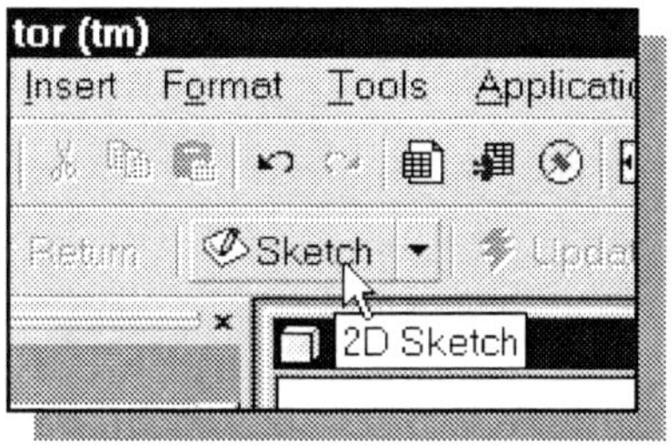

1. In the *Standard* toolbar select the ***Sketch*** command by left-clicking once on the icon.

2. In the *Status Bar* area, the message: "*Select face, workplane, sketch or sketch geometry.*" is displayed. Select the ***XY Plane***, by left-clicking once on any edges of the XY Plane in the graphics window.

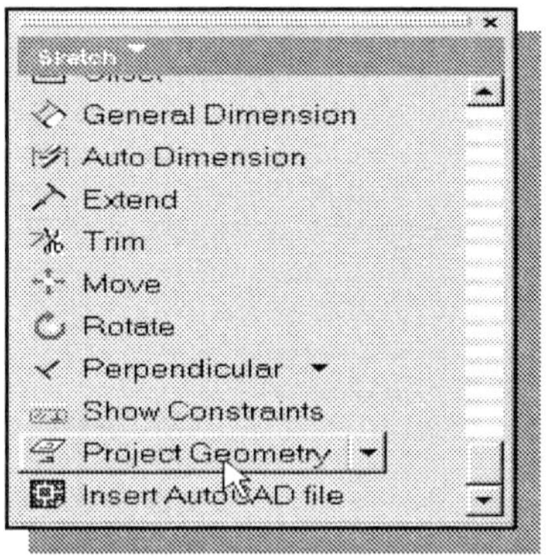

3. Select the ***Project Geometry*** command in the *Sketch* toolbar. The *Project Geometry* command allows us to project existing features to the active sketching plane. Left-click once on the icon to activate the *Project Geometry* command.

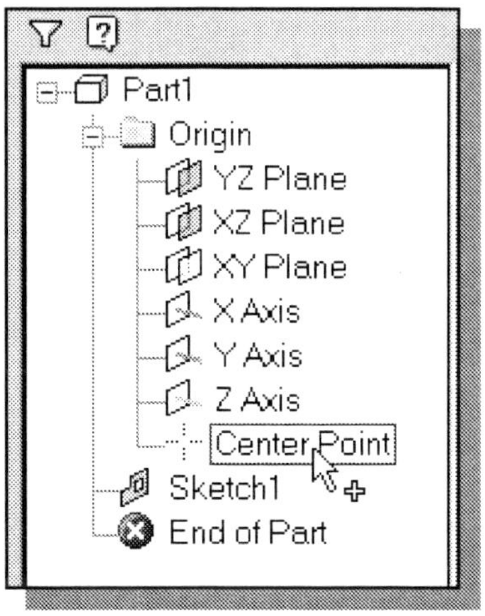

4. In the *Status Bar* area, the message: "*Select edge, vertex, work geometry or sketch geometry to project.*" is displayed. Inside the *Browser* window, select the ***Center Point***, ***X-axis***, ***Y-axis*** and ***Z-axis*** to project these entities onto the sketching plane.

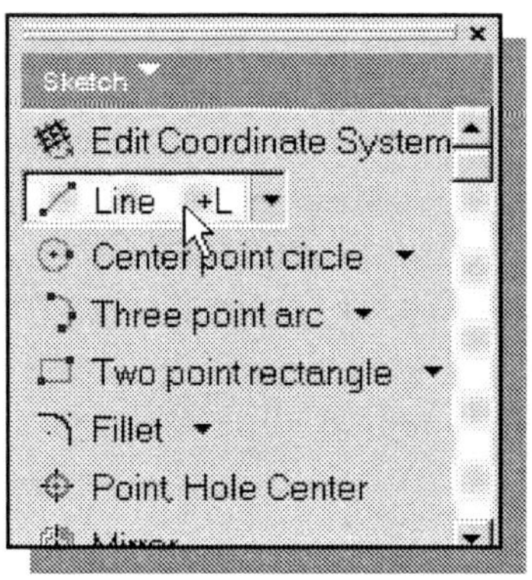

5. Move the graphics cursor to the ***Line*** icon in the *Sketch* toolbar. A *Help-tip box* appears next to the cursor and a brief description of the command is displayed at the bottom of the drawing screen: "*Creates Straight line segments and tangent arcs.*"

6. Create a closed-region-sketch with the starting point aligned to the projected Y-axis as shown below. (Note that the *Pulley* design is symmetrical about a horizontal axis as well as a vertical axis, which allows us to simplify the 2D sketch as shown below.)

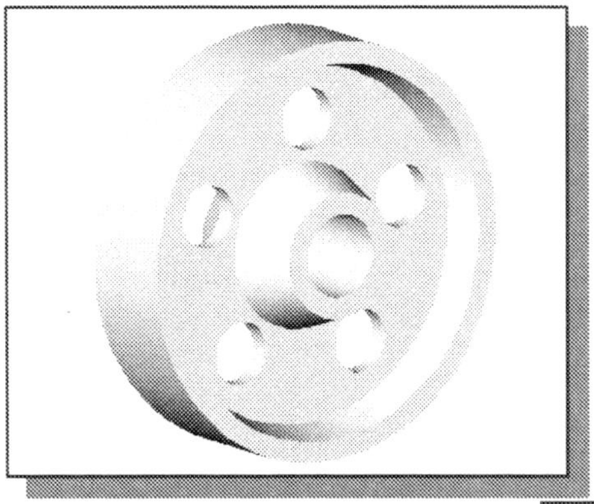

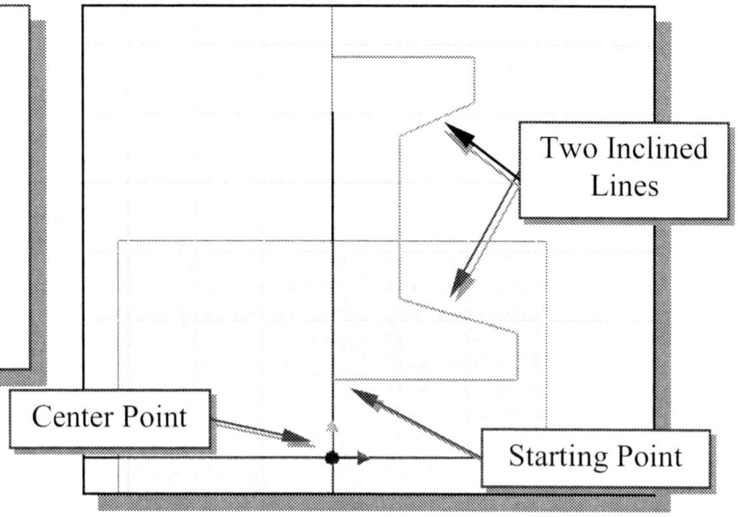

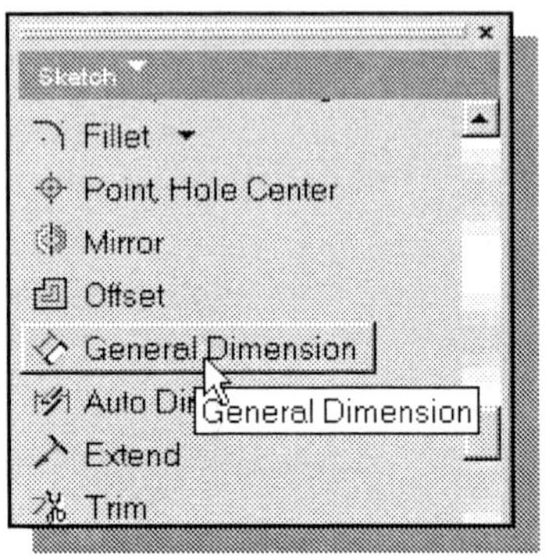

7. Select the ***General Dimension*** command in the *Sketch* toolbar.

8. Pick the ***Y-Axis*** as the first entity to dimension as shown in the below figure.

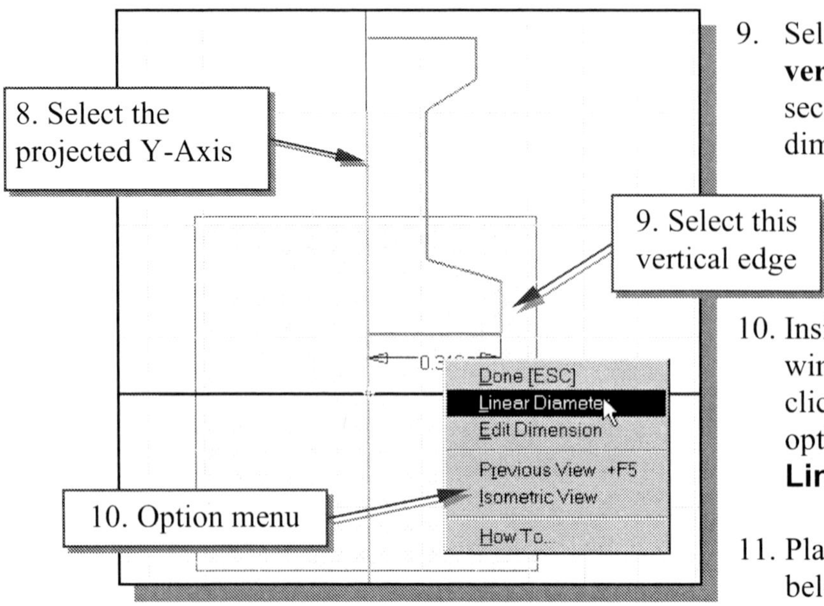

9. Select the lower **right-vertical line** as the second object to dimension.

10. Inside the graphics window, right-mouse-click to bring up the option menu and select **Linear Diameter**.

11. Place the dimension text below the sketch.

- **To create a dimension that will account for the symmetrical nature of the design: pick the axis of symmetry, pick the entity, select Linear diameter in the option menu, and then place the dimension.**

12. On your own, create and adjust the horizontal size dimensions as shown below.

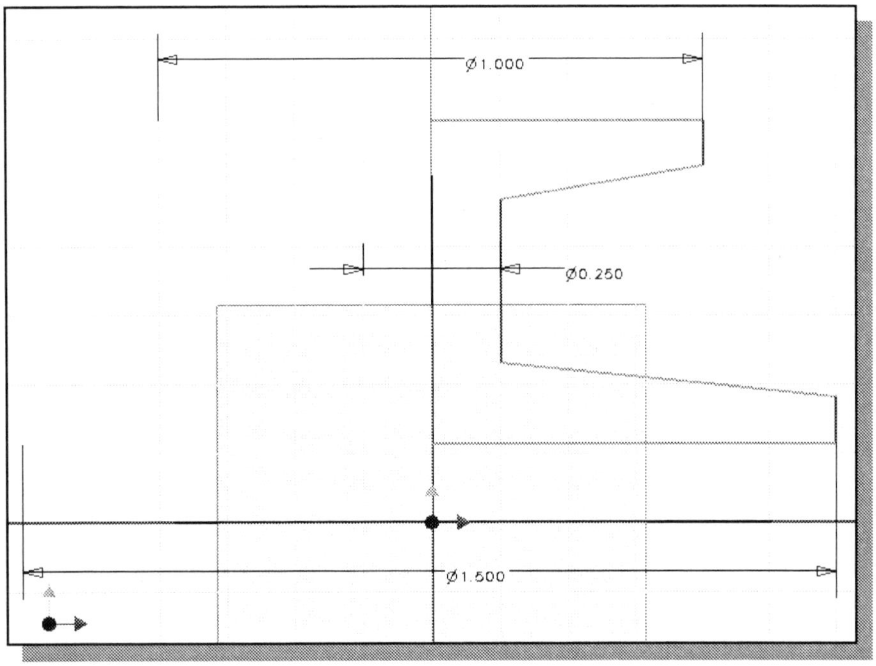

13. Pick the ***X-Axis*** as the first entity to dimension as shown in the figure below.

14. Select the **bottom-horizontal line** as the second object to dimension.

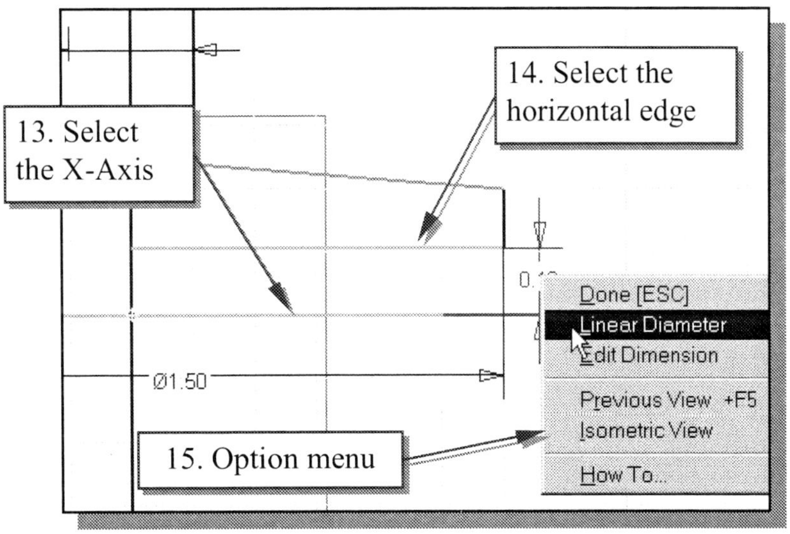

15. Inside the graphics window, right-mouse-click to bring up the option menu and select **Linear Diameter**.

16. Place the dimension text toward the right side of the sketch.

17. On your own, create and adjust the vertical size/location dimensions as shown below. (Hint: Modify the larger dimensions first.)

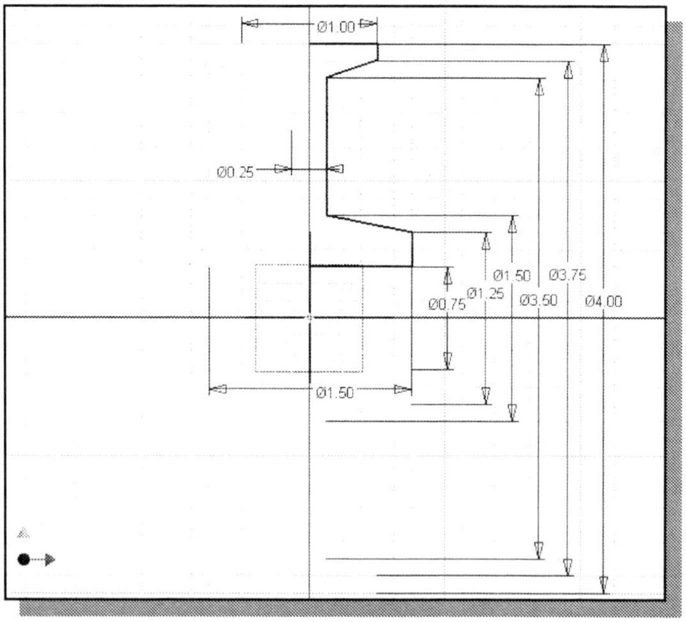

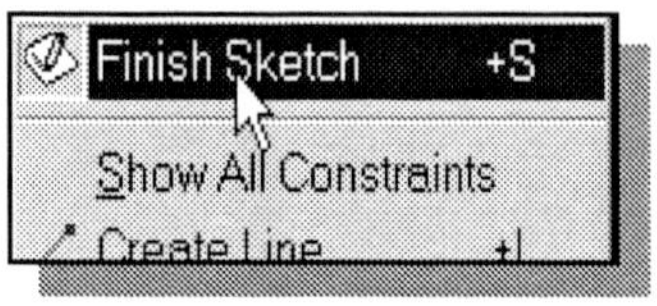

18. Inside the graphics window, click once with the right-mouse-button to display the option menu. Select **Finish Sketch** in the popup menu to end the *Sketch* option.

- On your own, use the ***3D-Rotate*** command to confirm the completed sketch and dimensions are on a 2D plane.

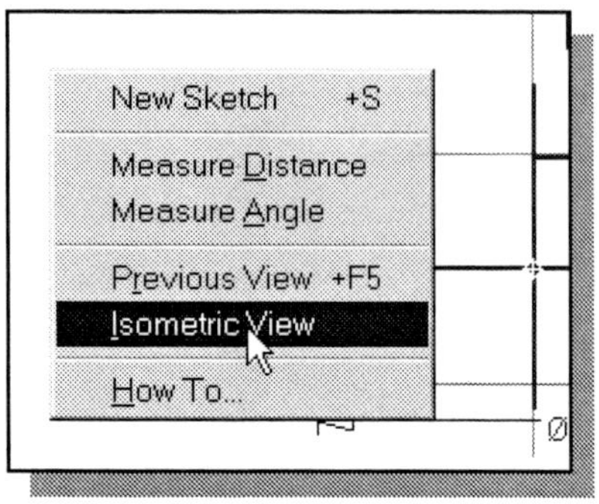

19. Inside the graphics window, right-mouse-click to bring up the option menu.

20. Select **Isometric View** in the option list to adjust the display of the 2D sketch on the screen.

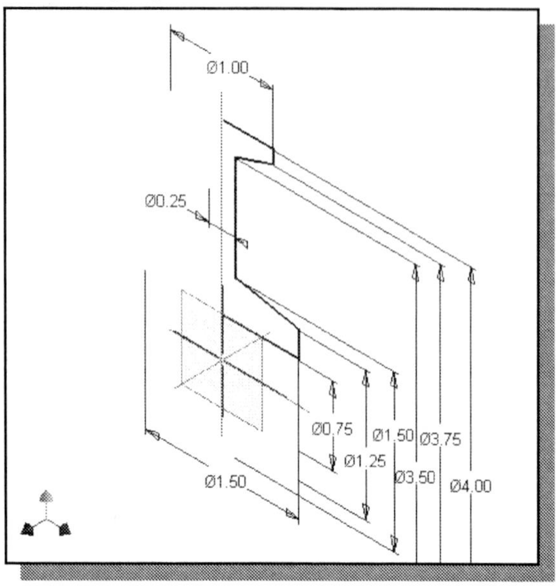

Creating the Revolved Feature

1. In the *Feature* toolbar (the toolbar that is located to the left side of the graphics window), select the ***Revolve*** command by releasing the left-mouse-button on the icon.

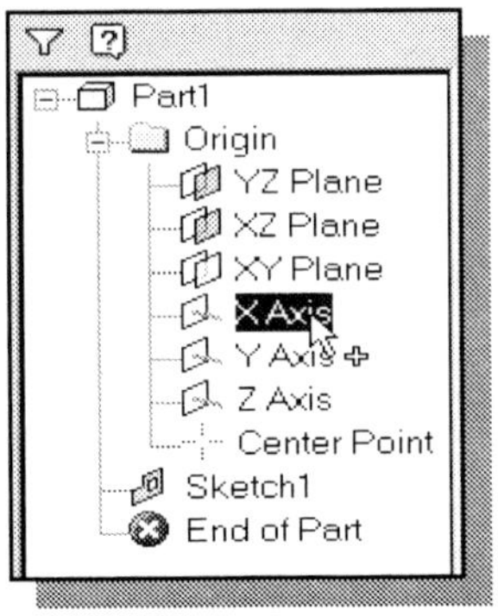

2. In the *Revolve* dialog box, the ***Axis*** button is activated indicating *Autodesk Inventor* expects us to select the revolution axis for the revolved feature. Select ***X-Axis*** as the axis of rotation in the *Browser* window as shown.

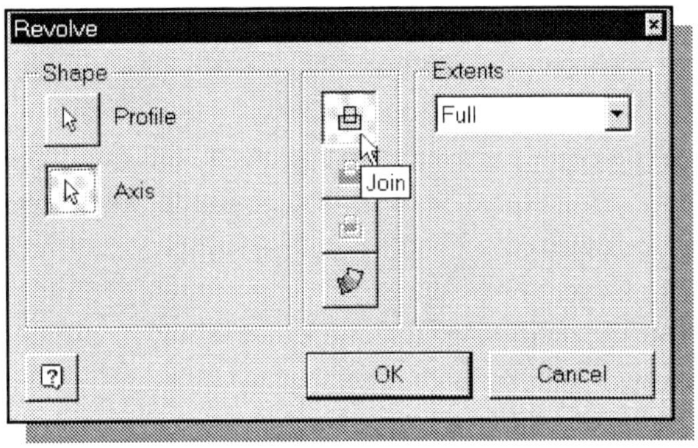

3. In the *Revolve* dialog box, set the termination *Extents* option to ***Full*** as shown.

4. Click on the **OK** button to accept the settings and create the revolved feature.

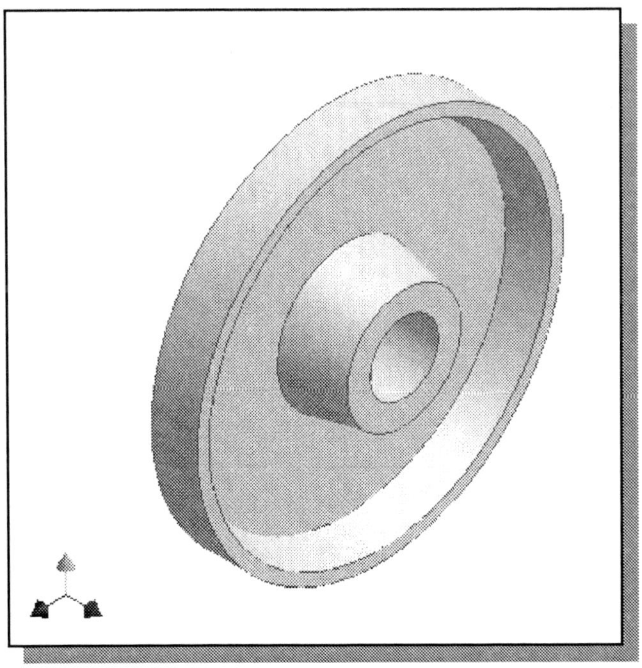

Mirroring Features

- In *Autodesk Inventor*, features can be mirrored to create and maintain complex symmetrical features. We can mirror a feature about a work plane or a specified surface. We can create a mirrored feature while maintaining the original parametric definitions, which can be quite useful in creating symmetrical features. For example, we can create one quadrant of a feature, then mirror it twice to create a solid with four identical quadrants.

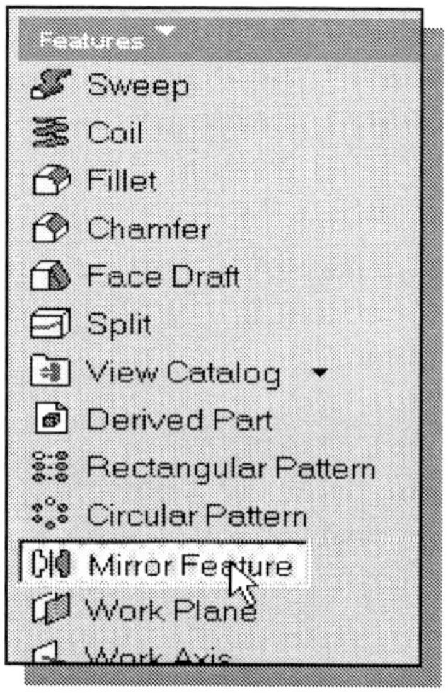

1. In the *Feature* window, select the ***Mirror Feature*** command by releasing the left-mouse-button on the icon.

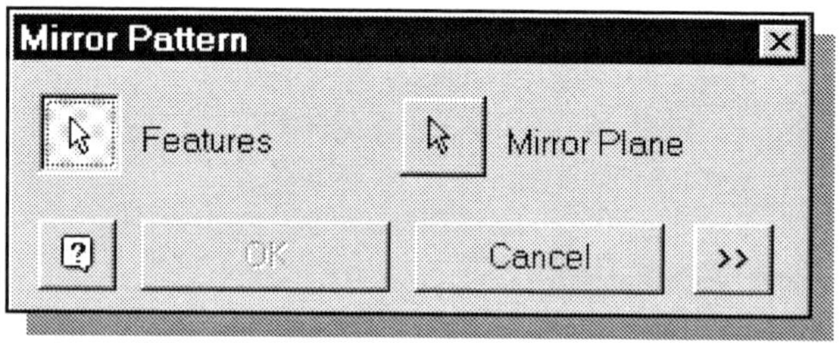

2. In the *Mirror Pattern* dialog box, the ***Features*** button is activated. *Autodesk Inventor* expects us to select features to be mirrored. In the prompt area, the message "*Select feature to pattern*" is displayed. Select any edge of the 3D base feature.

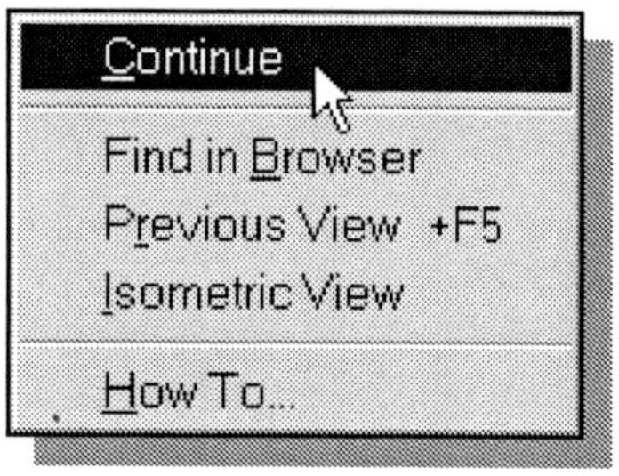

3. Inside the graphics window, right-mouse-click to bring up the option menu.

4. Select **Continue** in the option list to proceede with the *Mirror Feature* command.

5. In the *Mirror Pattern* dialog box, the ***Mirror Plane*** button is activated. *Autodesk Inventor* expects us to select a planar surface about which to mirror. In the prompt area, the message "*Select plane to mirror about*" is displayed.

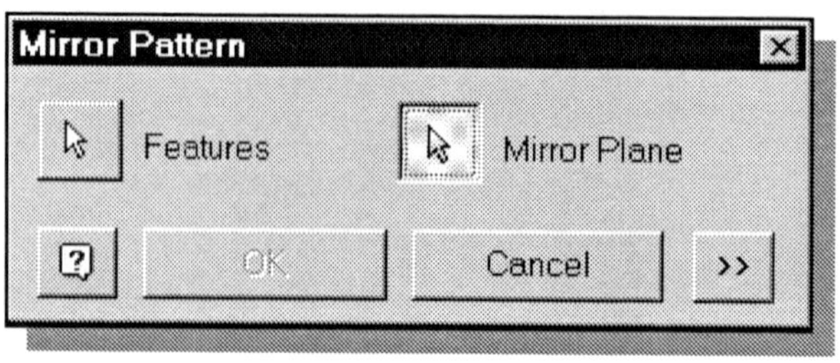

6. On your own, use the *3D-Rotate* function key [**F4**] to dynamically rotate the solid model so that we are viewing the back surface as shown on the next page.

7. Select the surface as shown below as the planar surface about which to mirror.

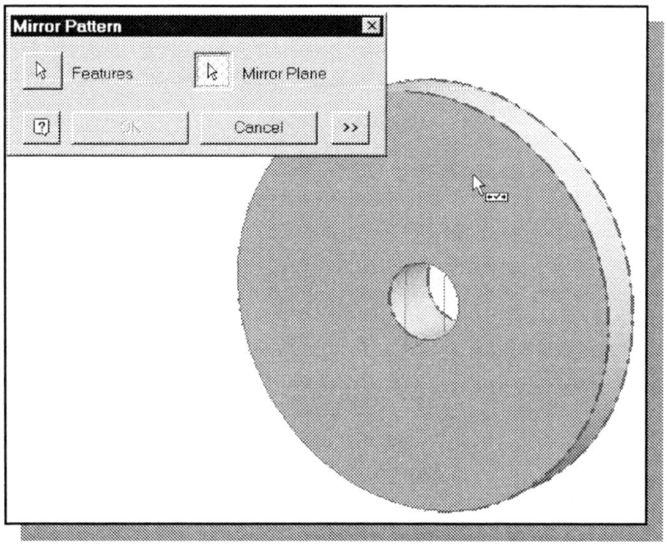

8. Click on the **OK** button to accept the settings and create a mirrored feature.

9. On your own, use the *3D-Rotate* function key [**F4**] to dynamically rotate the solid model and view the resulting solid.

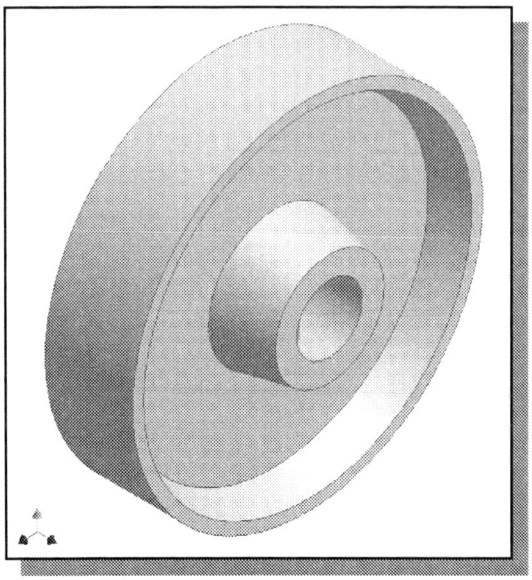

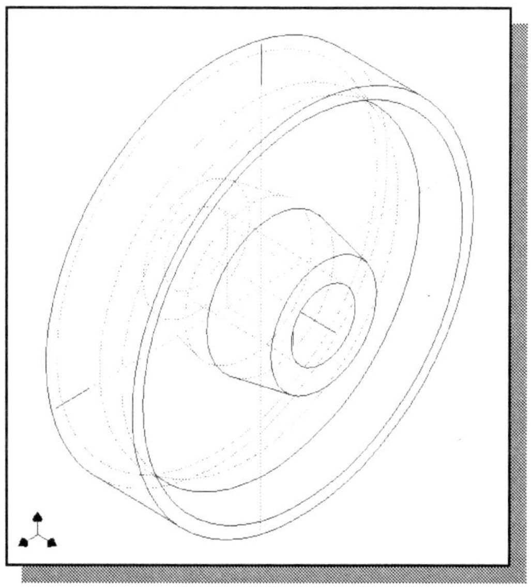

- Now is a good time to save the model (Quick key: [Ctrl] + [S]). It is a good habit to save your model periodically, just in case something might go wrong while you are working on the model. You should also save the model after you have completed any major constructions.

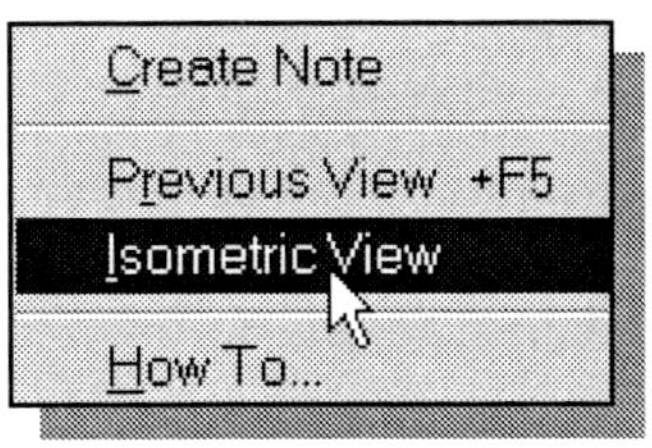

10. Inside the graphics window, right-mouse-click to bring up the option menu.

11. Select **Isometric View** in the option list to adjust the display of the 2D sketch on the screen.

Creating A Pattern Leader

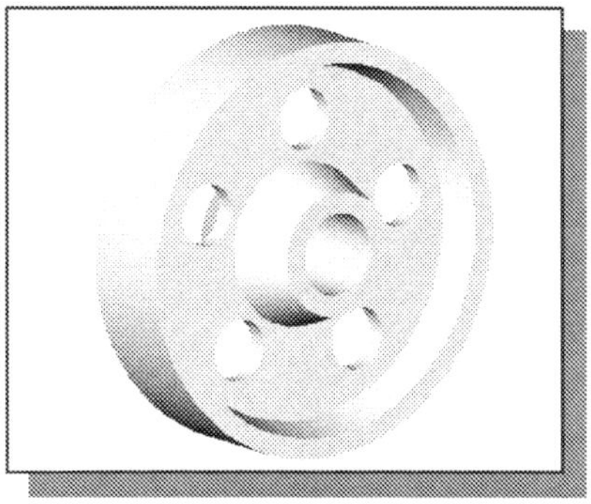

- The pulley design requires the placement of five identical holes on the base solid. Instead of creating the five holes one at a time, we can simplify the creation of these holes by using the ***Pattern*** command, which allows us to create duplicate features. Prior to using the *Pattern* command, we will first create a ***pattern leader***, which is a regular extrude feature.

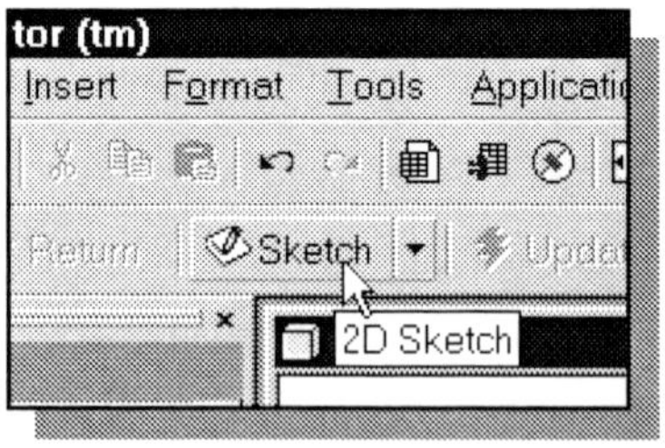

1. In the *Standard* toolbar select the ***Sketch*** command by left-clicking once on the icon.

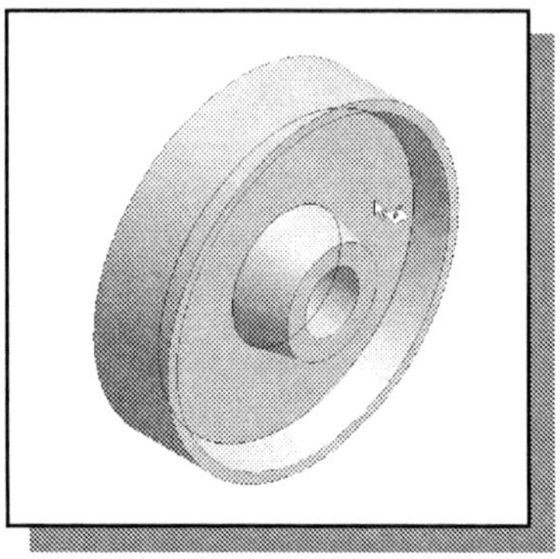

2. In the *Status Bar* area, the message: "*Select face, work plane, sketch or sketch geometry.*" is displayed. Pick the inside vertical plane as shown.

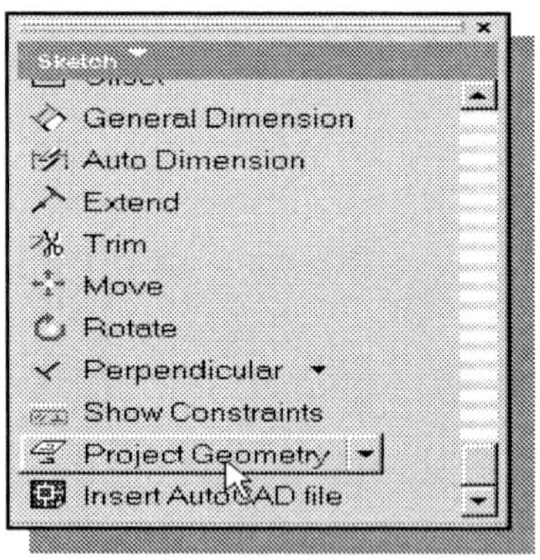

3. Select the ***Project Geometry*** command in the *Sketch* toolbar. The ***Project Geometry*** command allows us to project existing geometry to the active sketching plane. Left-click once on the icon to activate the *Project Geometry* command.

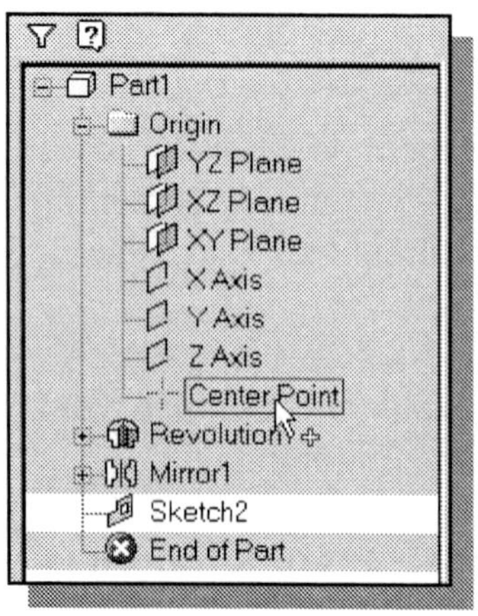

4. In the *Status Bar* area, the message: "*Select edge, vertex, work geometry or sketch geometry to project.*" is displayed. Inside the *Browser* window, select the ***Center Point***, ***X-axis***, ***Y-axis***, and ***Z-axis*** to project these entities onto the sketching plane.

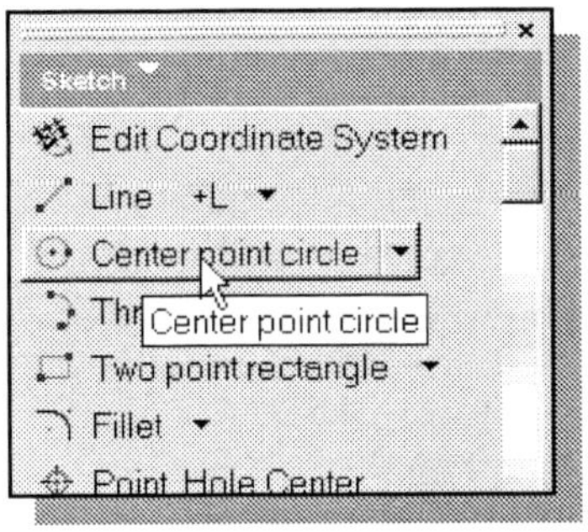

5. Select the ***Center point circle*** command by clicking once with the left-mouse-button on the icon in the *Sketch* toolbar.

6. Pick a point along the vertical Y-axis and create a circle of arbitrary size as shown below.

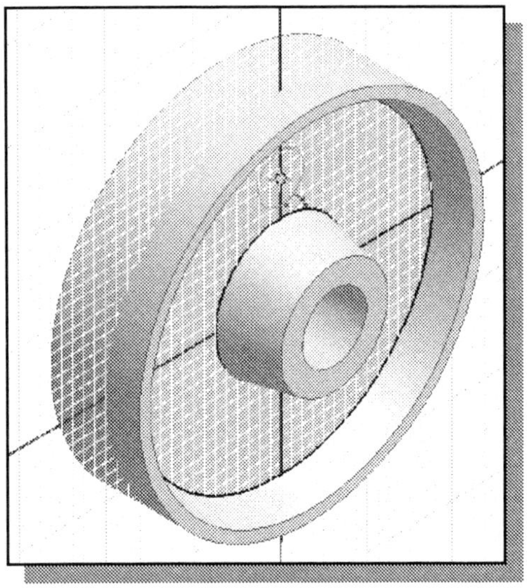

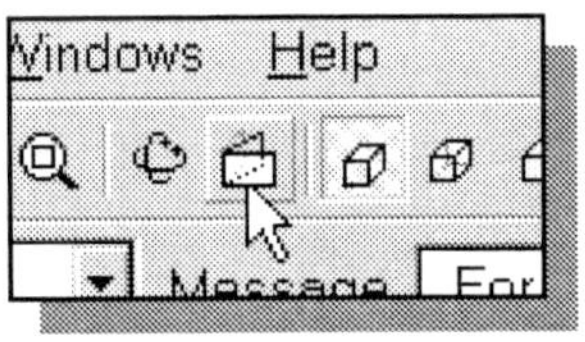

7. In the *Standard* toolbar area, click on the ***Look At*** button.

8. Select the circle we just created to orient the display of the sketching plane on the screen.

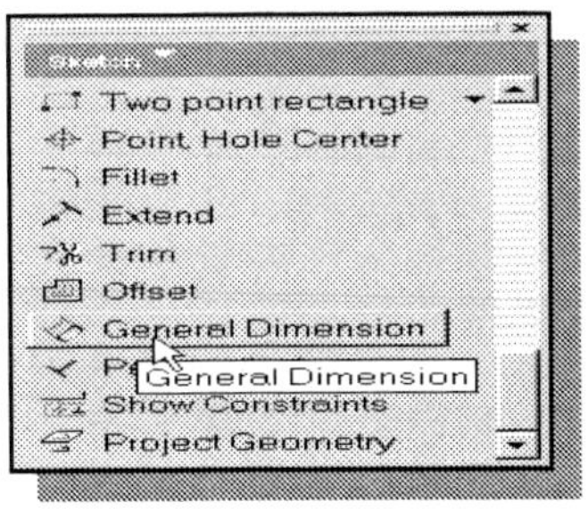

9. Select the ***General Dimension*** command in the *Sketch* toolbar.

10. Pick the ***X-Axis*** as the first entity to dimension as shown in the below figure.

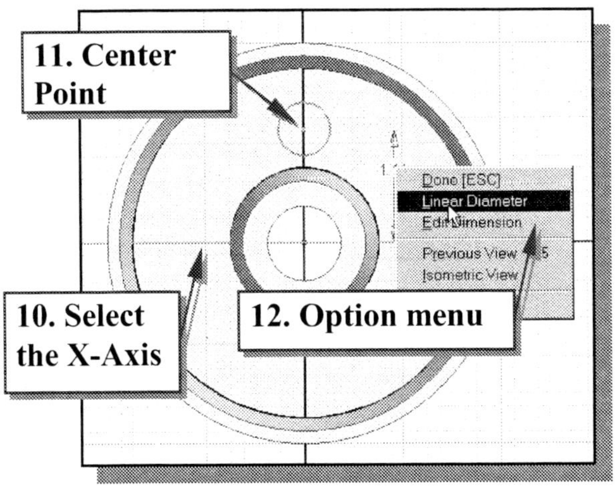

11. Select the ***Center Point*** of the sketched circle as the second object to dimension.

12. Inside the graphics window, right-mouse-click to bring up the option menu and select **Linear Diameter**.

13. Place the dimension text toward the right side of the sketch.

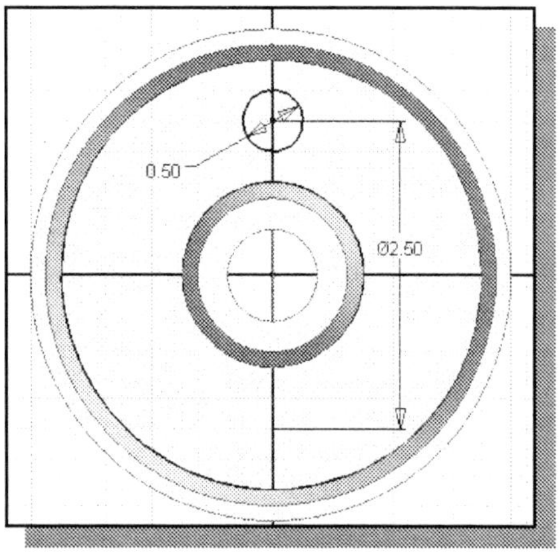

14. On your own, create and modify the dimensions as shown.

15. Inside the graphics window, click once with the right-mouse-button to display the option menu. Select **Finish Sketch** in the popup menu to end the *Sketch* option.

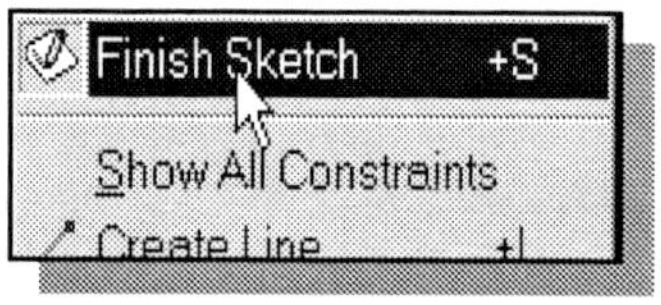

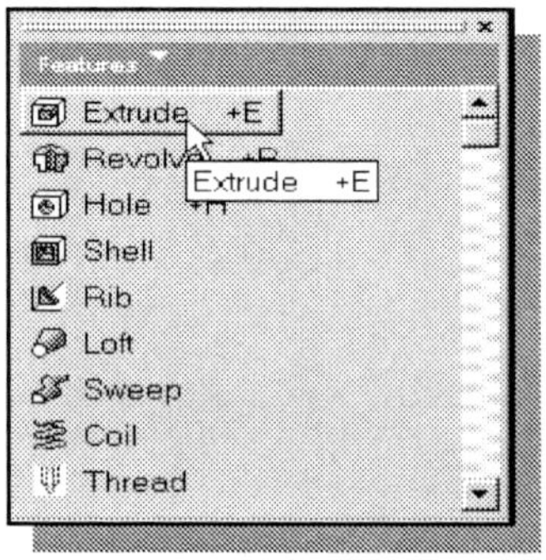

16. In the *Feature* toolbar (the toolbar that is located to the left side of the graphics window), select the ***Extrude*** command by releasing the left-mouse-button on the icon.

17. Select the inside region of the circle as the profile of the extrusion.

18. Inside the *Extrude* dialog box, select the ***Cut*** operation and set the *Extents* to ***All*** as shown.

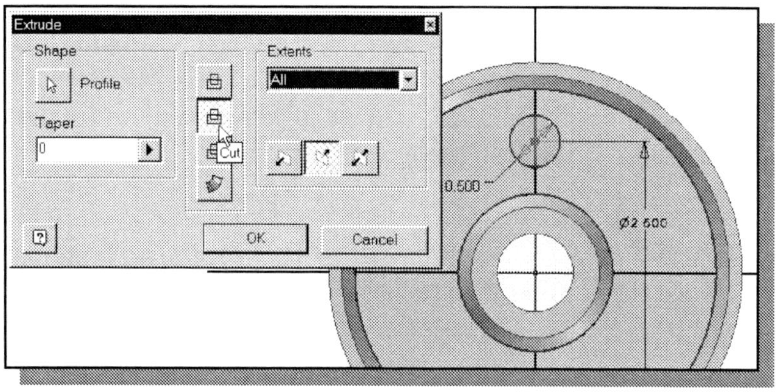

19. Click on the **OK** button to accept the settings and create the cut feature.

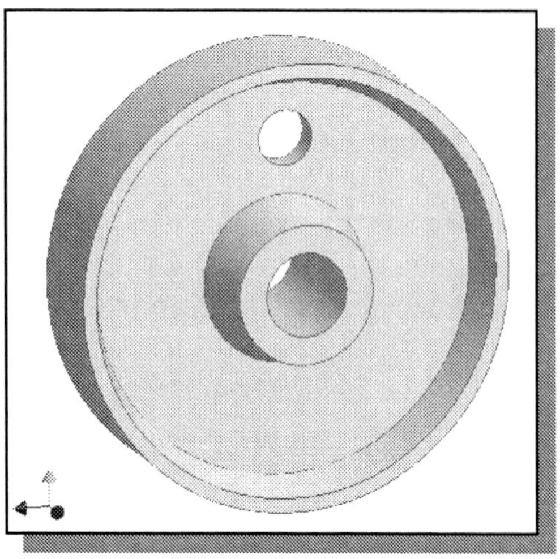

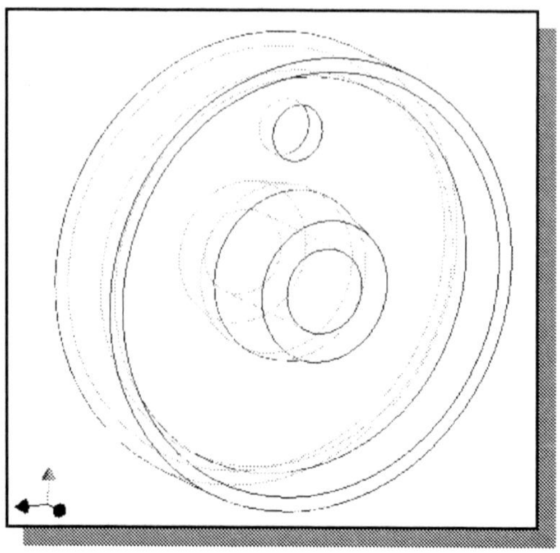

Circular Pattern

- In *Autodesk Inventor*, existing features can be easily duplicated. The ***Pattern*** command allows us to create both rectangular and polar arrays of features. The patterned features are parametrically linked to the original feature; any modifications to the original feature are also reflected in the arrayed features.

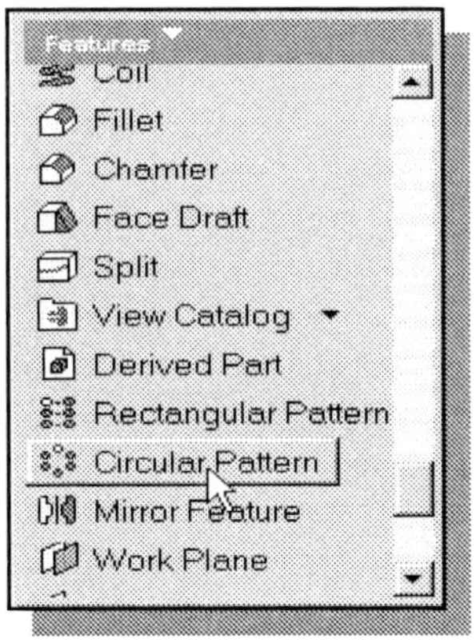

1. In the *Features* toolbar, select the ***Circular Pattern*** command by left-clicking once on the icon.

2. The message "*Select Feature to be arrayed*:" is displayed in the command prompt window. Select the **circular cut feature** when it is highlighted as shown.

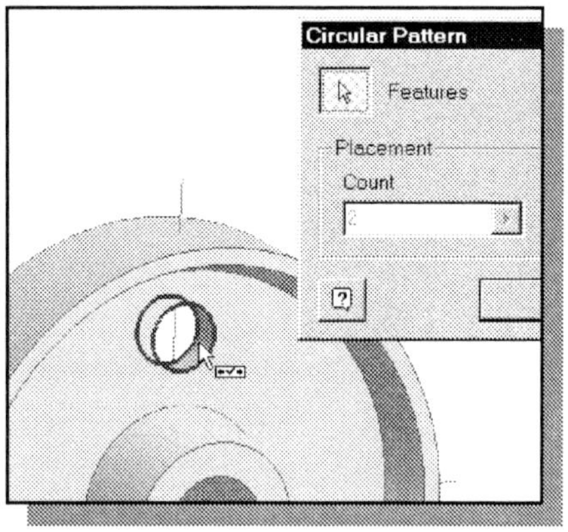

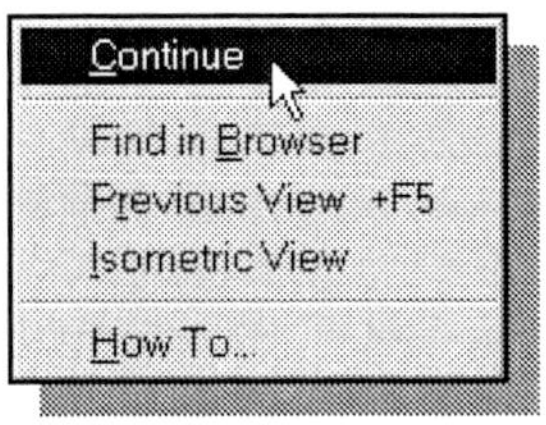

3. Inside the graphics window, right-mouse-click to bring up the option menu.

4. Select **Continue** in the option list to proceed with the *Circular Pattern* command.

5. In the *Circular Pattern* dialog box, the ***Rotation Axis*** button is activated. *Autodesk Inventor* expects us to select an axis to pattern about. In the prompt area, the message "*Define the axis of revolution*" is displayed. Select the ***X-axis*** as shown.

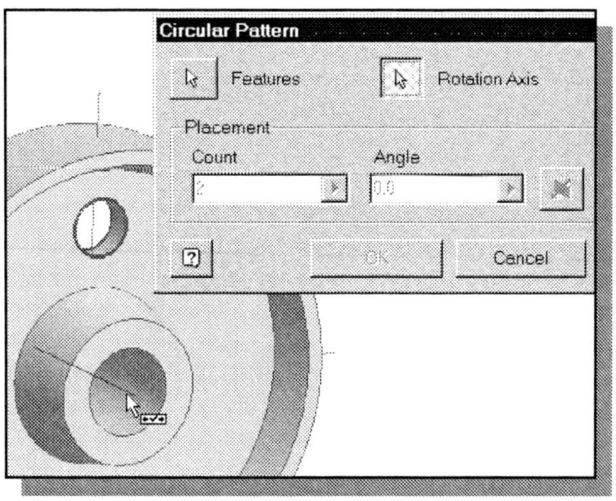

6. In the *Circular Pattern* dialog box, enter **5** in the ***Count*** box and **360** in the ***Angle*** box as shown. (Note the different options available for the *Circular Pattern* command.)

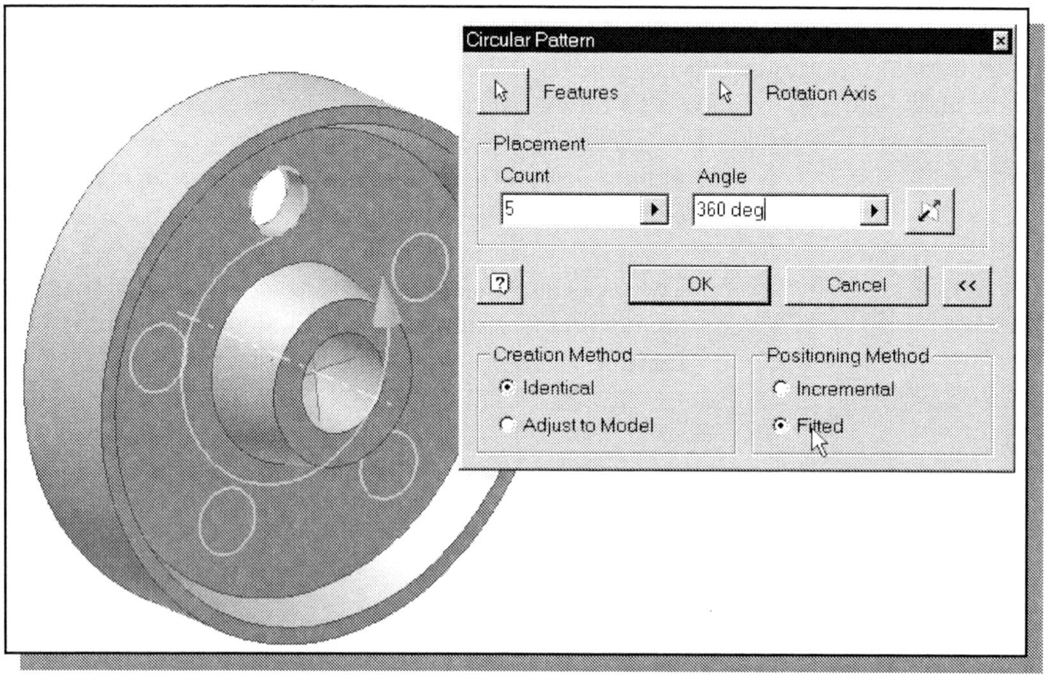

7. Click on the **OK** button to accept the settings and create the *circular pattern*.

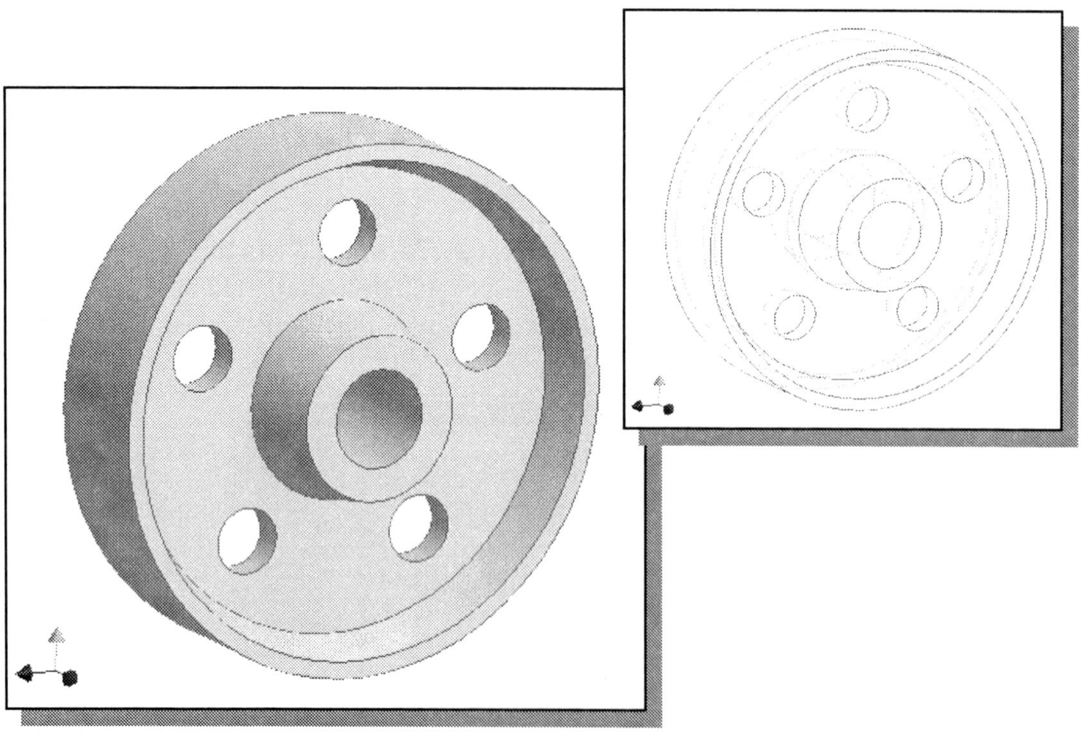

Examining the design parameters

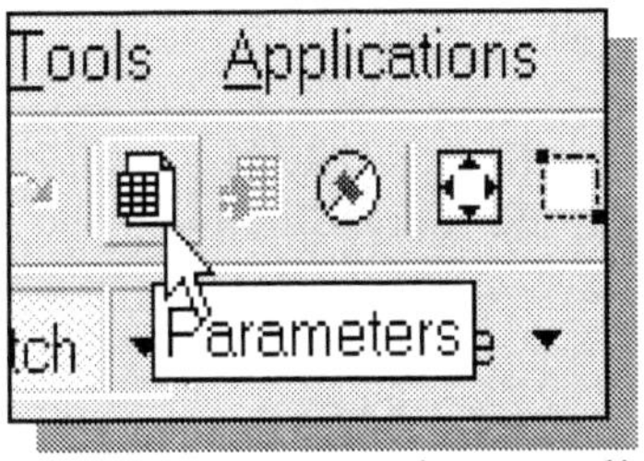

1. In the *Standard* toolbar select the ***Parameters*** command by left-clicking once on the icon. The *Parameters* popup window appears.

2. Note the two dimensions used to create the circular pattern are also listed as shown in the below figure.

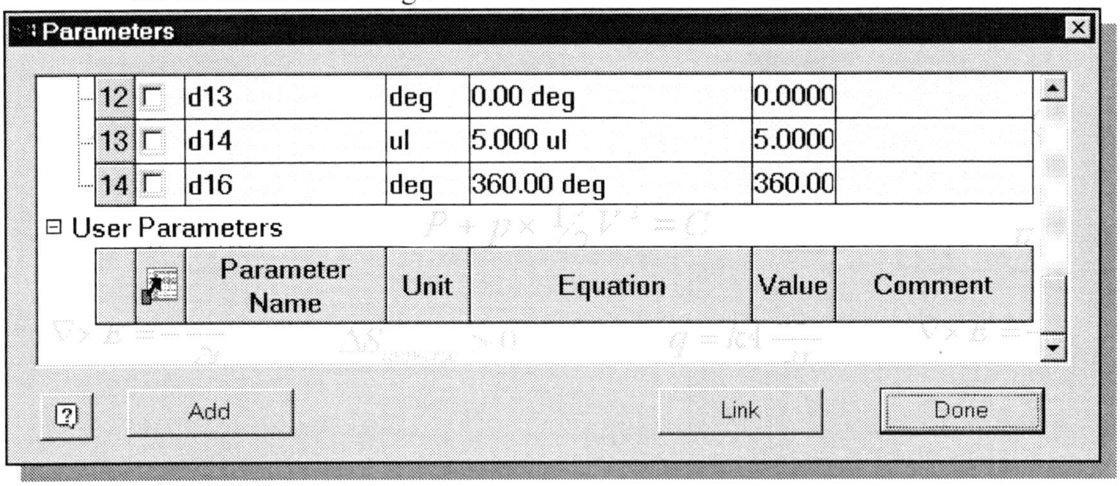

3. Click on the **Done** button to accept the settings.

4. Select **Save** in the *Standard* toolbar; we can also use the "**Ctrl-S**" combination (press down the [Ctrl] key and hit the [S] key once) to save the part.

Drawing Mode – Defining New Border and Title Block

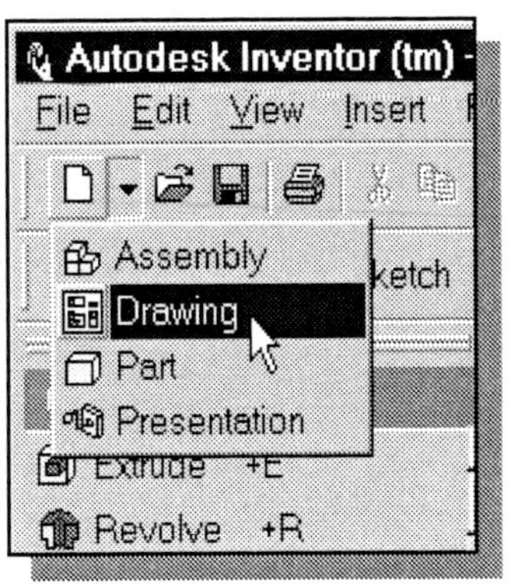

1. Click on the **drop-down arrow** next to the ***New File*** button in the *Standard* toolbar area to display the available new file options.

2. Select **Drawing** from the drop-down list.

➢ Note that a new graphics window appears on the screen. We can switch in between the solid model and the drawing by clicking the corresponding graphics windows.

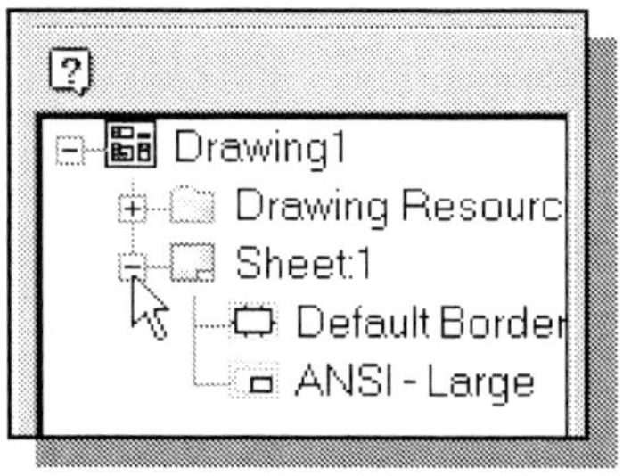

3. Inside the *Drawing Browser* window, click on the [**+**] symbol in front of ***Sheet1*** to display the settings.

4. On your own, **delete** the ***Default Border*** and the ***ANSI title block***. (Hint: right-mouse-click on the names to bring up the option menu.)

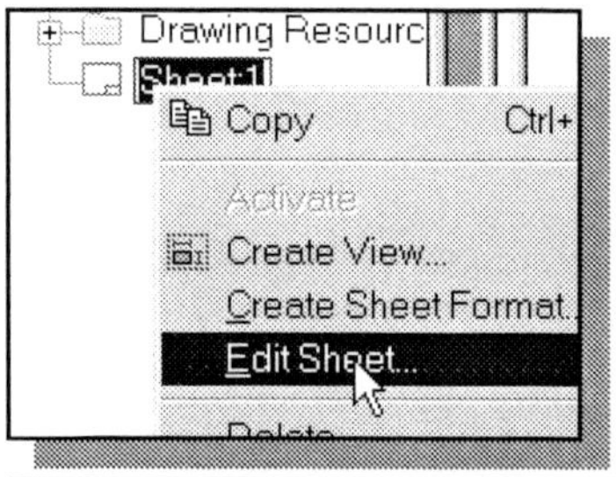

5. Inside the *Drawing Browser* window, right-mouse-click on ***Sheet1*** to bring up the option menu.

6. Select **Edit Sheet** in the option list.

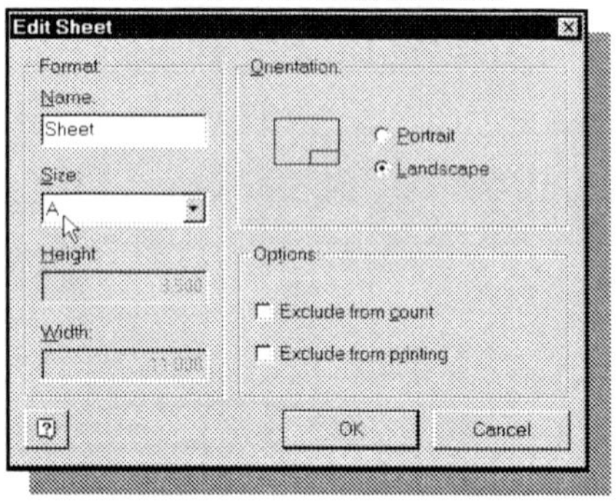

7. In the *Edit Sheet* dialog box, set the sheet size to *A-size (8.5 X 11)*.

8. Confirm the page *Orientation* is set to ***Landscape*** and click on the **OK** button to accept the settings.

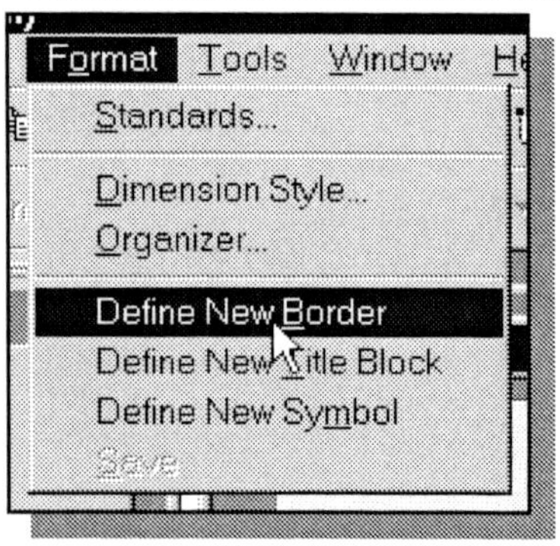

9. In the pull-down menu, select **Format → Define New Border**.

10. On your own, create a rectangle (**7.75 x 10.25**) using the ***Two Point Rectangle*** command and the ***General Dimension*** command.

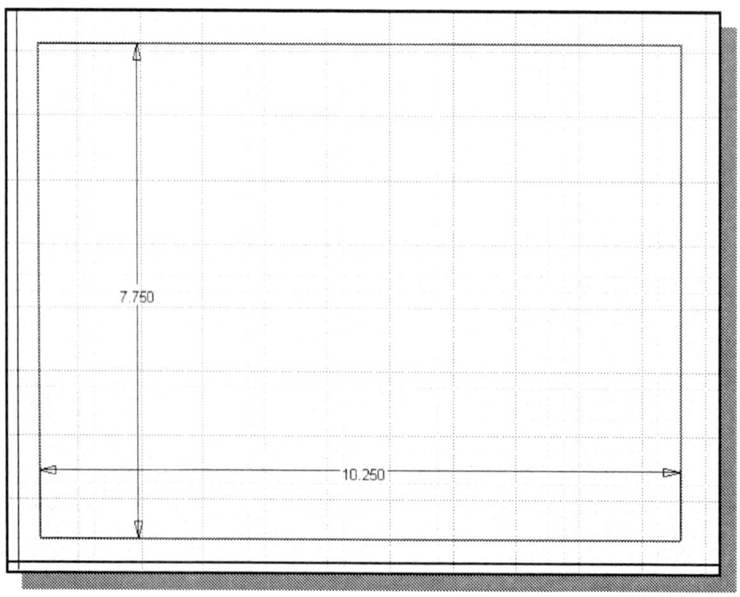

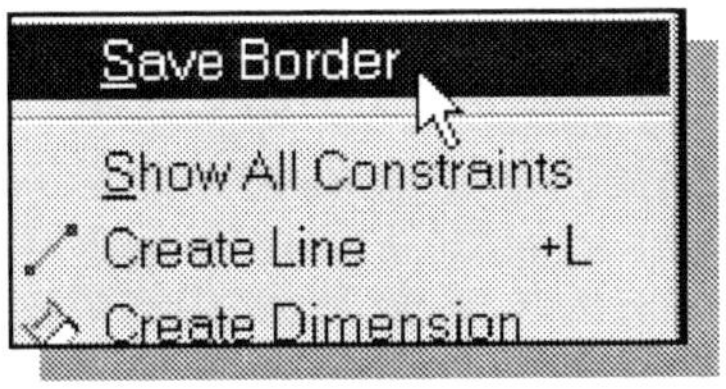

11. Inside the graphics window, right-mouse-click to bring up the option menu.

12. Select **Save Border** in the option list.

13. In the *Border* dialog box, enter **A-Size** as the new border name.

14. Click on the **OK** button to end the *Define New Border* command.

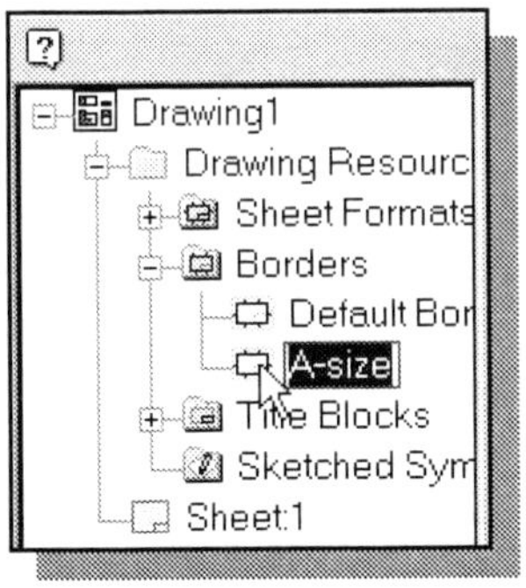

15. Inside the *Browser* window, expand the ***Drawing Resources*** list by clicking on the [+] symbol.

16. Double-click on the ***A-size*** **border**, the border we just created, to place the border in the current drawing. Note that none of the dimensions used to construct the border is displayed.

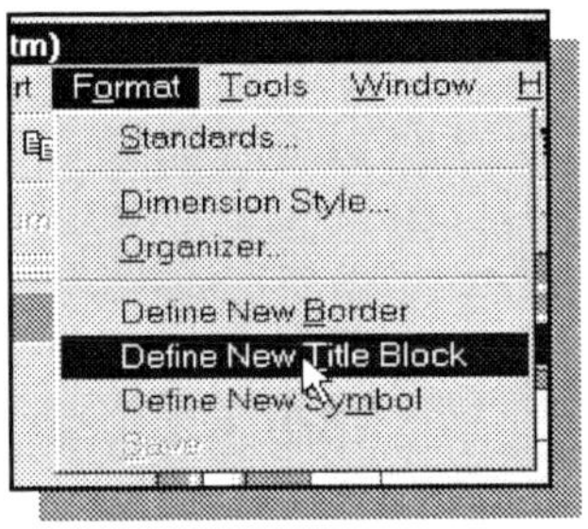

17. In the pull-down menu, select **Format → Define New Title Block**.

18. On your own, create a title block using the ***Two Point Rectangle***, ***Line***, ***General Dimension***, and ***Text*** commands.

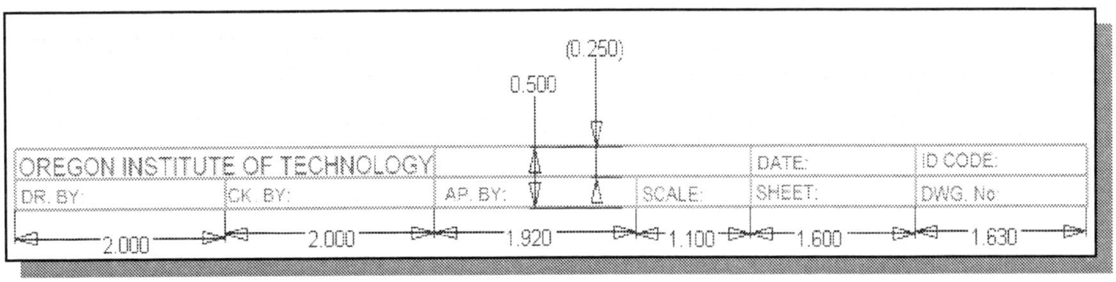

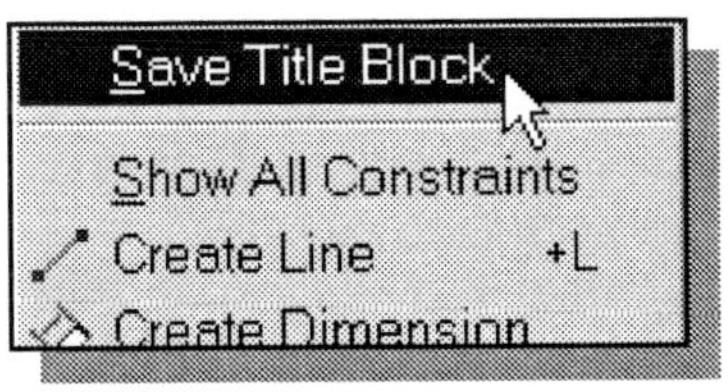

19. Inside the graphics window, right-mouse-click to bring up the option menu.

20. Select **Save Title Block** in the option list.

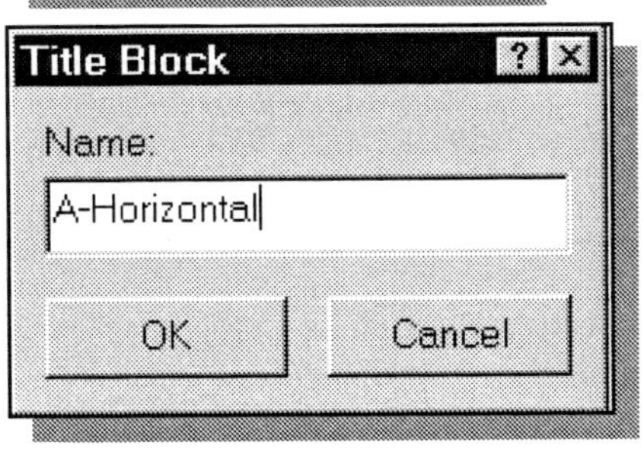

21. In the *Title Block* dialog box, enter **A-Horizontal** as the new title block name.

22. Click on the **OK** button to end the *Define New Title Block* command.

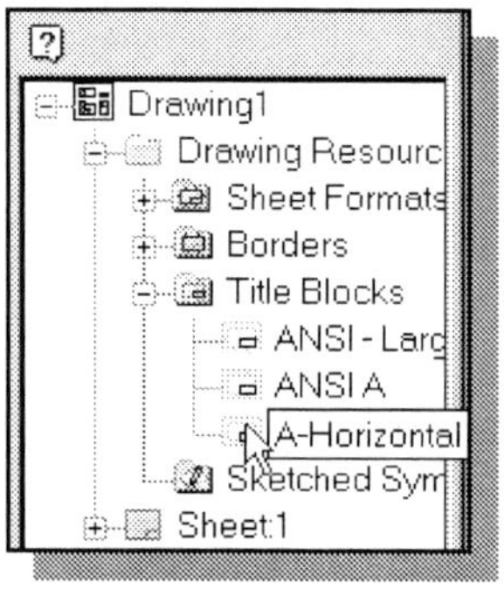

23. Inside the *Browser* window, expand the ***Title Blocks*** list by clicking on the [+] symbol.

24. Double-click on the ***A-Horizontal* title block**, the title block we just created, to place it into the current drawing.

Creating a Drawing Template

➢ In *Autodesk Inventor*, each new drawing is created from a template. During the installation of *Autodesk Inventor*, a default drafting standard was selected which sets the default template used to create drawings. We can use this template or another predefined template, modify one of the predefined templates, or create our own templates to enforce drafting standards and other conventions. Any drawing file can be used as a template; a drawing file becomes a template when it is saved in the *Templates* folder. Once the template is saved, we create a new drawing file using the new template.

1. Select **Save** in the *Standard* toolbar, we can also use the "**Ctrl-S**" combination (press down the [Ctrl] key and hit the [S] key once) to save the part.

2. In the *Save As* dialog box, switch to the **Inventor English Templates** directory.

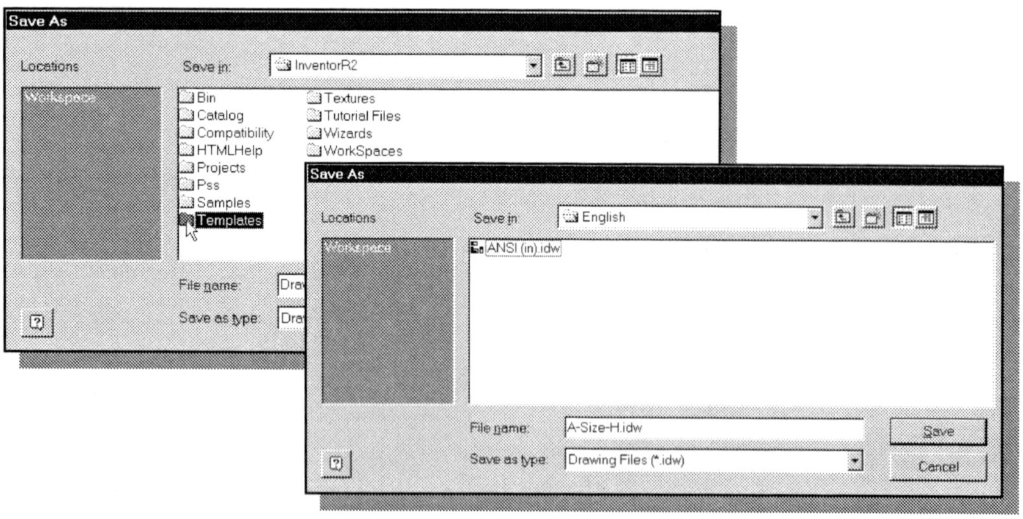

3. Enter **A-Size-H.idw** as the template filename.

4. Click on the **Save** button to create a drawing template file.

Creating Views

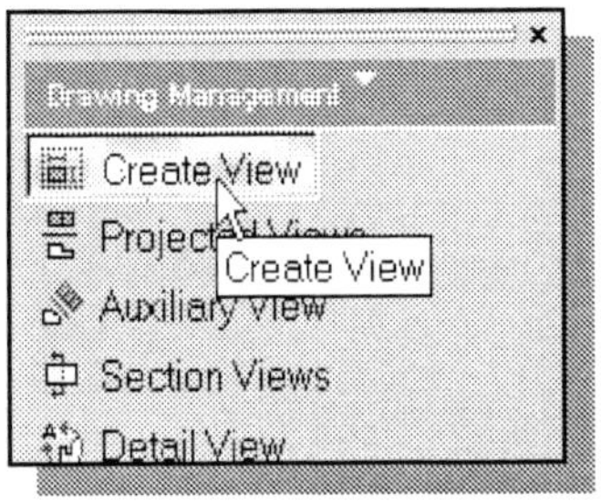

1. Click on **Create View** in the *Drawing Management* toolbar to create a base view.

2. In the *Create View* dialog box, select ***Left View*** and ***Wireframe*** as shown in the figure below. (**DO NOT** click on the **OK** button.)

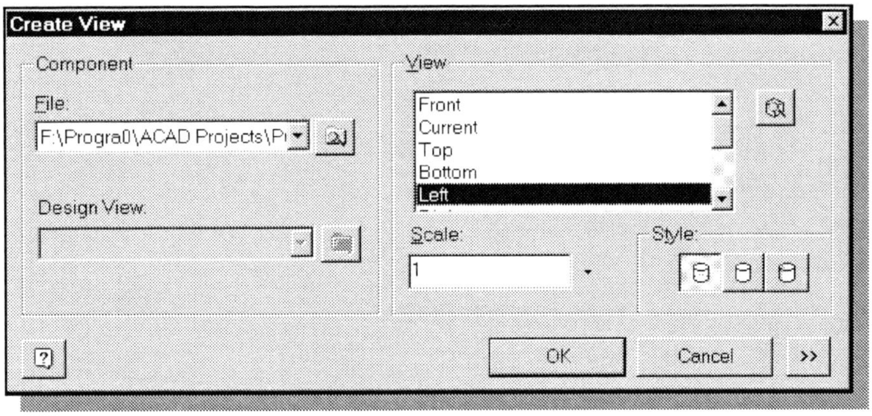

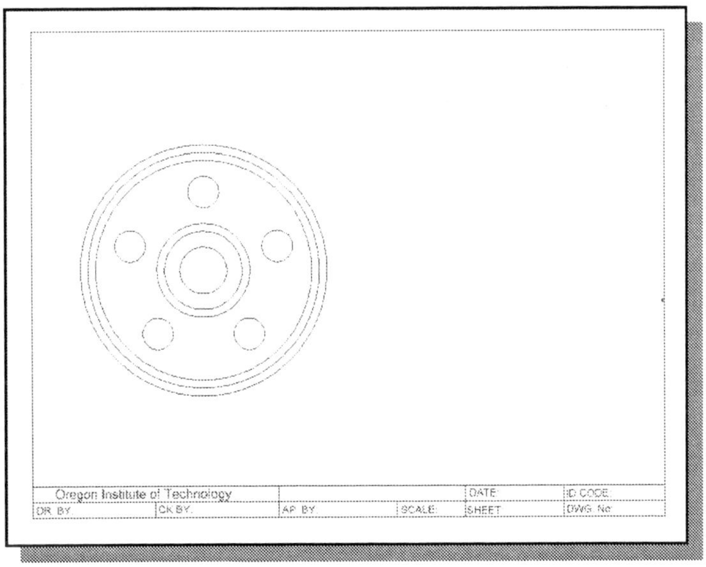

3. Move the cursor inside the graphics window and place the **base view** toward the left side of the border as shown. (If necessary, drag the *Create View* dialog box to another location on the screen.) Note that once the *base view* is placed, the *Create View* dialog box is closed automatically.

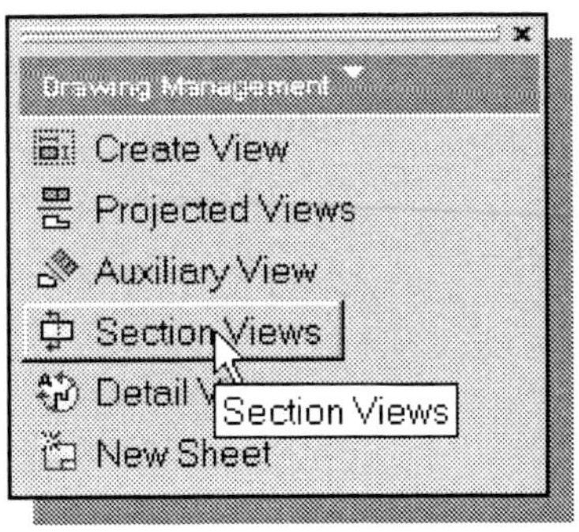

4. Click on the **Section Views** button in the *Drawing Management* window to create a section view.

5. Click on the **base view** to select the view where the section line is to be created.

6. Inside the graphics window, align the cursor to the center of the base view and create the vertical cutting plane line as shown.

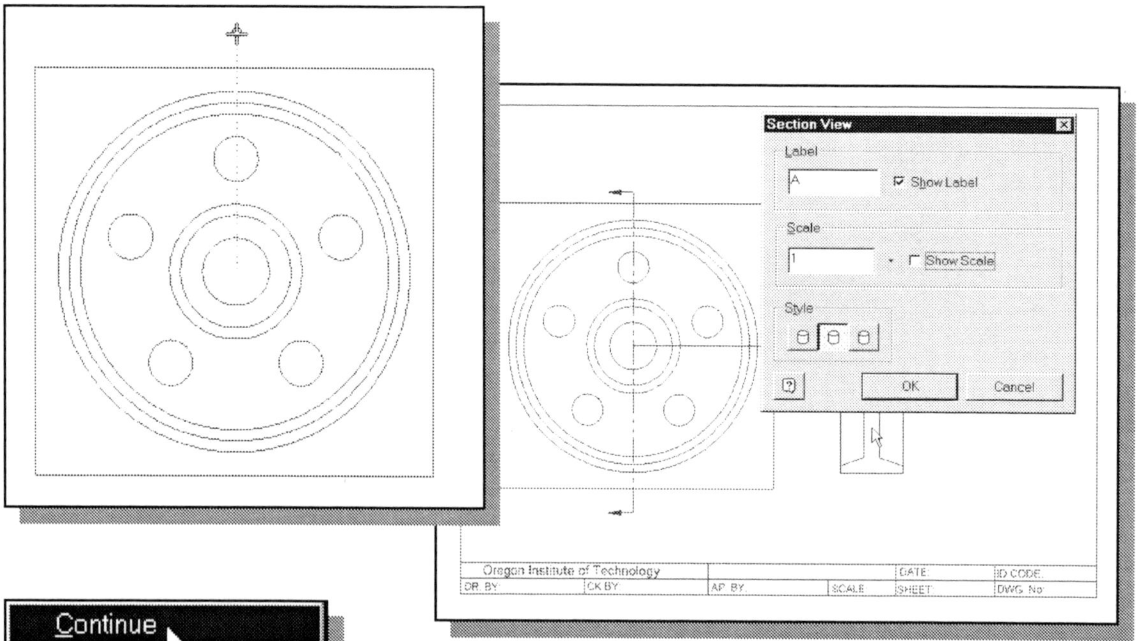

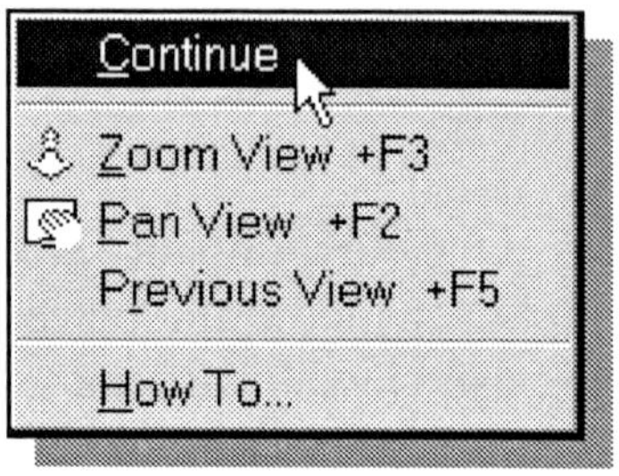

7. Inside the graphics window, right-mouse-click once to bring up the option menu.

8. Select **Continue** to proceed with the *Section View* command.

9. Inside the *Section View* dialog box, turn ***OFF*** the *Show Scale* option.

10. Set the *Display Style* to **Hidden Line Removed**, as shown in the above figure. (**DO NOT** click on the **OK** button.)

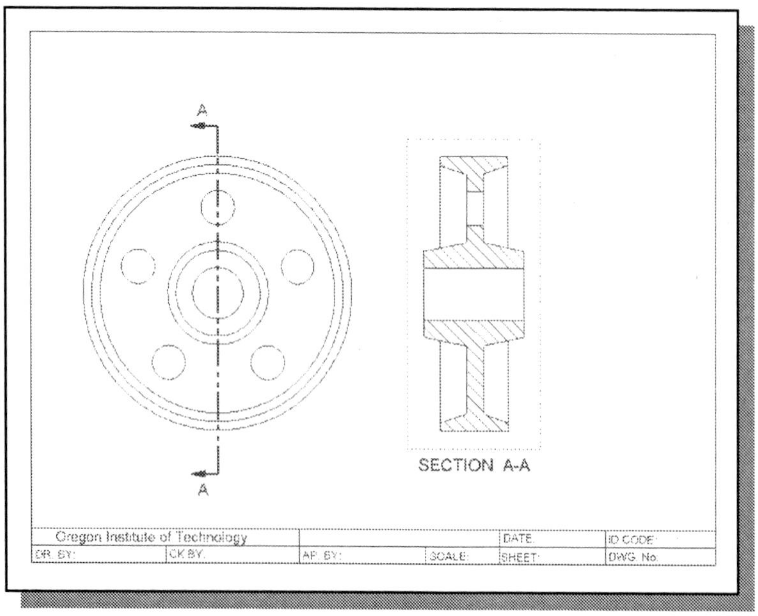

11. Next, *Autodesk Inventor* expects us to place the projected section. Select a location that is toward the right side of the base view as shown in the figure.

Editing Views

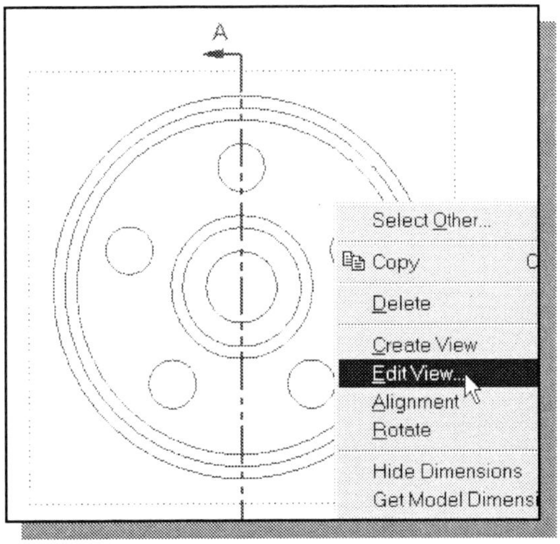

1. Move the cursor on top of the base view and watch for the box around the entire view indicating the view is selectable as shown in the figure. Right-mouse-click once to bring up the option menu.

2. Select **Edit View** in the option menu.

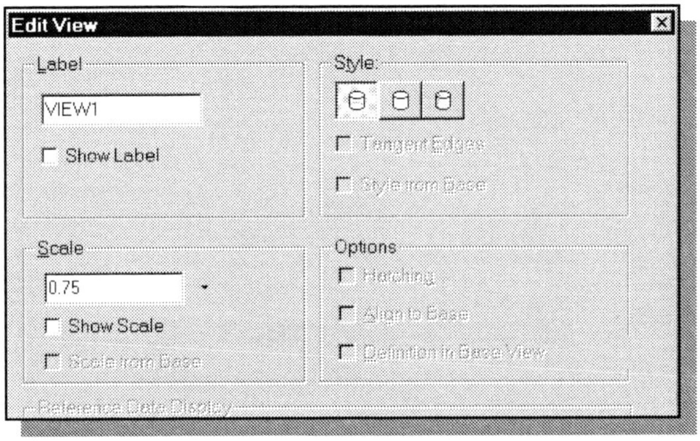

3. Inside the *Edit View* dialog box, set the *Scale* to **0.75** as shown in the figure.

4. Click on the **OK** button to accept the settings and proceed with updating the drawing views.

5. On your own, create an **isometric view** of the design and place the view toward the right side of the section view.

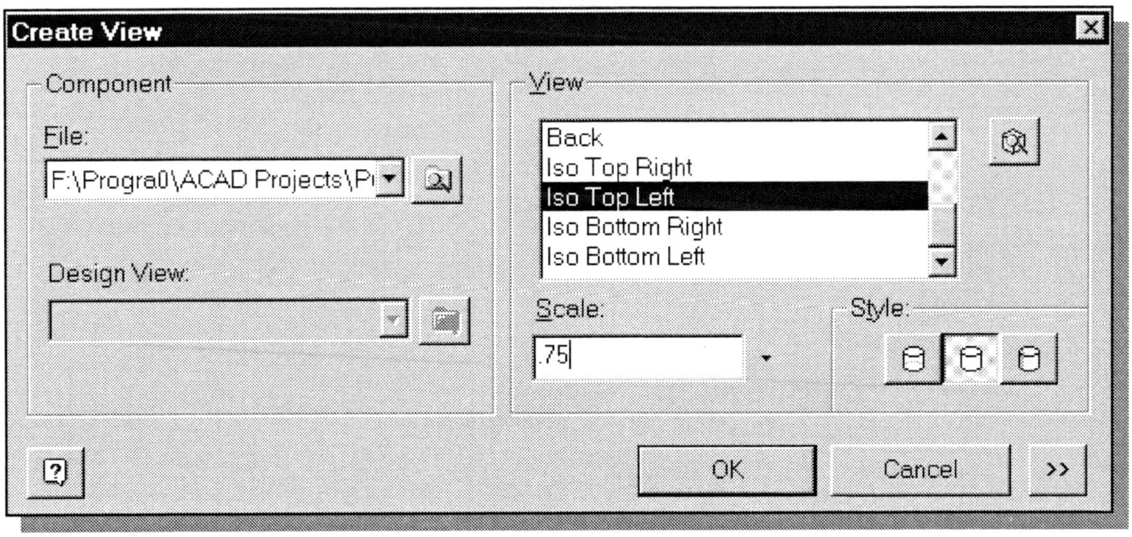

➤ On your own, reposition the views so that they appeared as shown in the figure below.

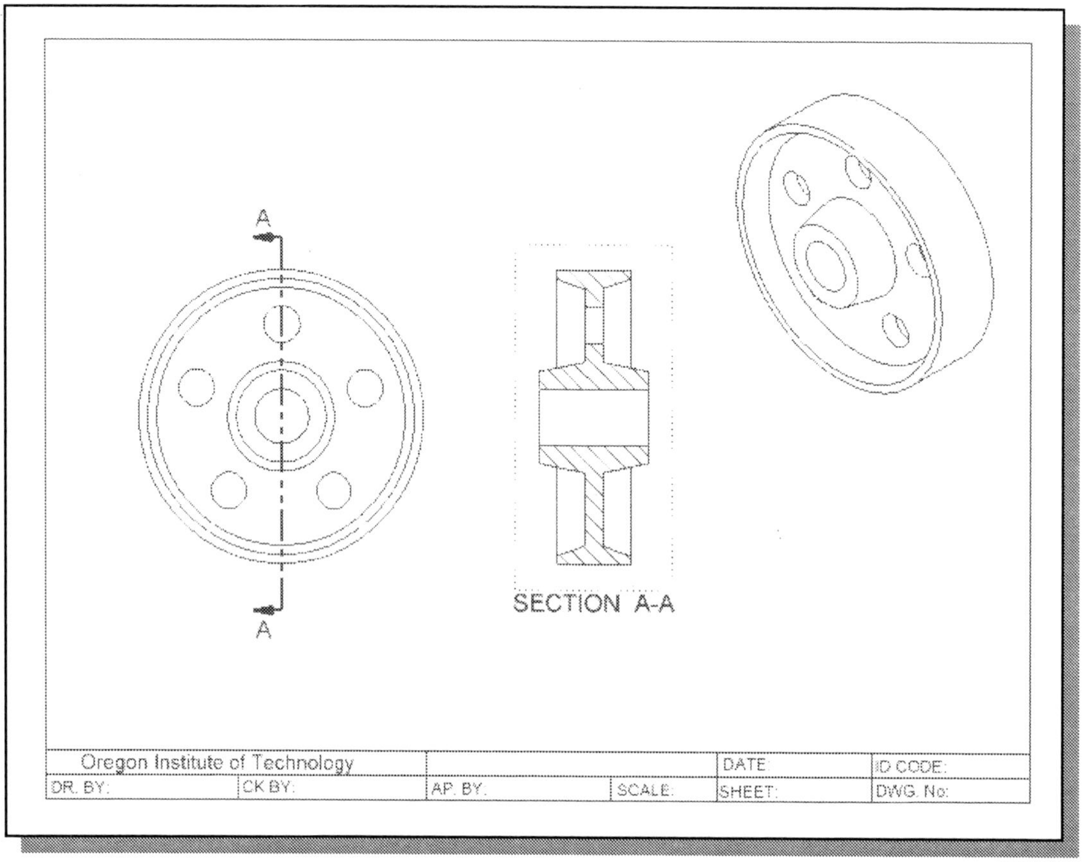

6. Move the cursor on top of the base view of the model and watch for the box around the entire view indicating the view is selectable as shown in the figure.

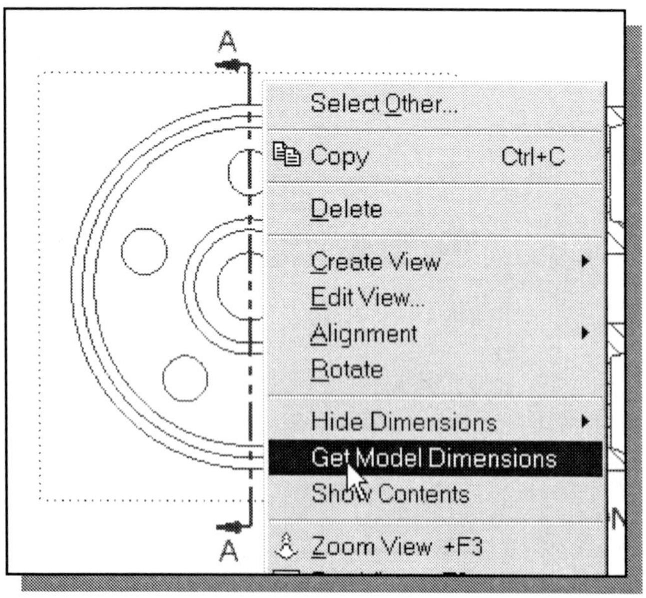

7. Inside the graphics window, right-mouse-click once to bring up the option menu.

8. Select **Get Model Dimensions** to display the parametric dimensions used to create the model.

Associative Functionality – A Design Change

- *Autodesk Inventor's associative functionality* allows us to change the design at any level, and the system reflects the changes at all levels automatically. We will illustrate the associative functionality by changing the circular pattern from five holes to six holes.

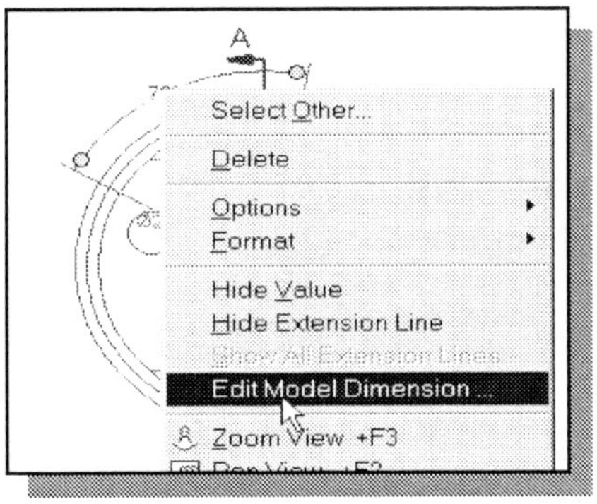

1. Inside the graphics window, right-click on the **72°** dimension in the *base view* to bring up the option menu.

2. Select **Edit Model Dimension** in the popup menu.

3. In the *Edit Dimension* dialog box, change the number to **6** as shown.

4. Click on the **check mark** button to accept the setting.

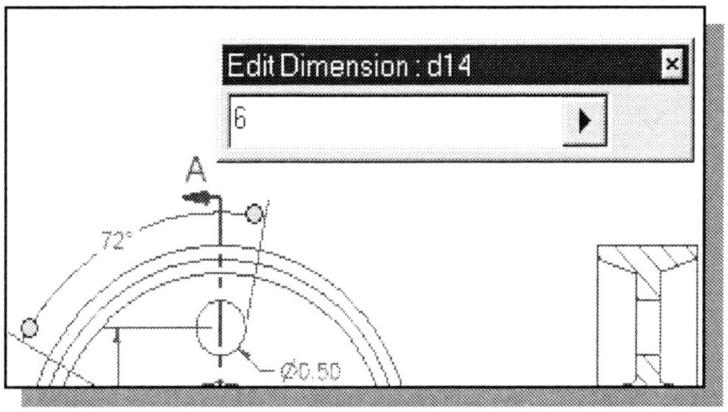

❖ Notice the circular pattern is updated automatically in all views. On your own, switch to the *Part Model* and confirm the design is updated as well.

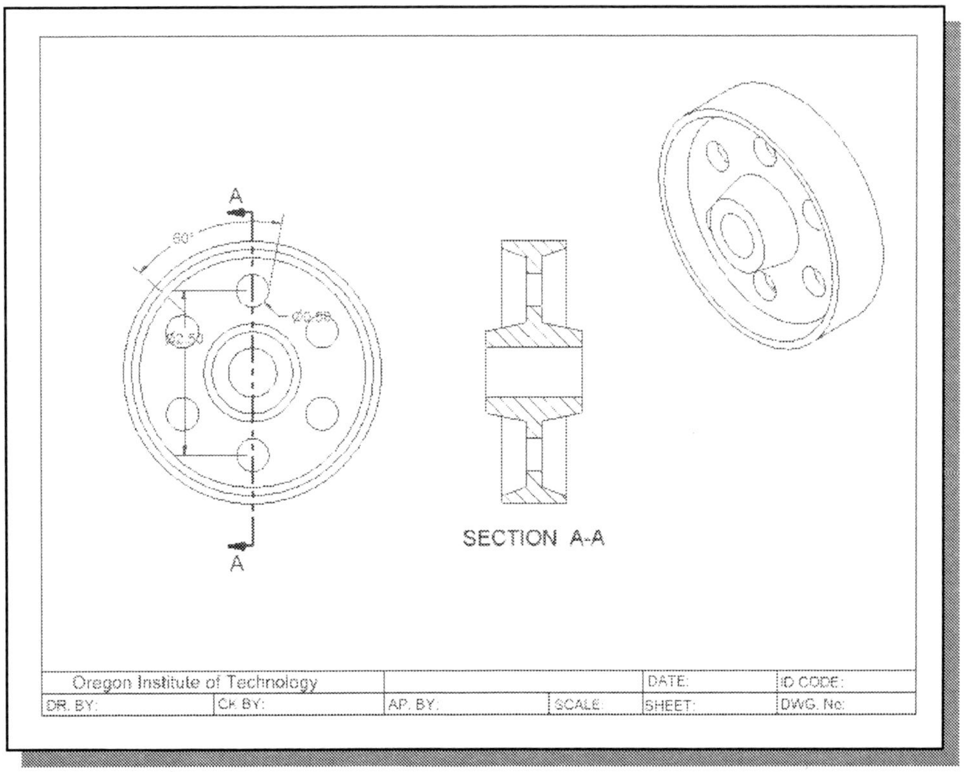

Displaying Feature Dimensions

- By default, feature dimensions are not displayed in 2D views in *Autodesk Inventor*. We can change the default settings while creating the views or switch on the display of the parametric dimensions under the option menu.

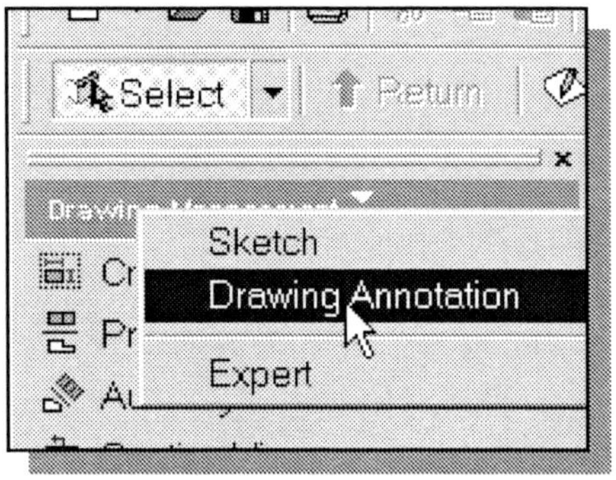

1. Left-mouse-click in the title area of the *Drawing Management* window.

2. Select **Drawing Annotation** by left-clicking once in the drop-down list.

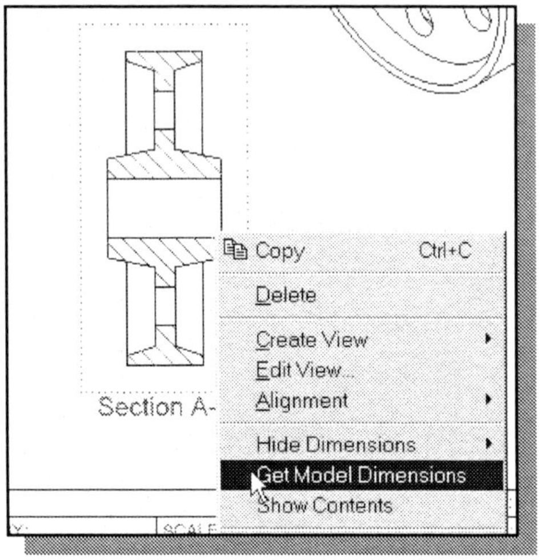

3. Move the cursor on top of the front-view of the model and watch for the box around the entire view indicating the view is selectable as shown in the figure.

4. Inside the graphics window, right-mouse-click once to bring up the option menu.

5. Select **Get Model Dimensions** to display the parametric dimensions used to create the model.

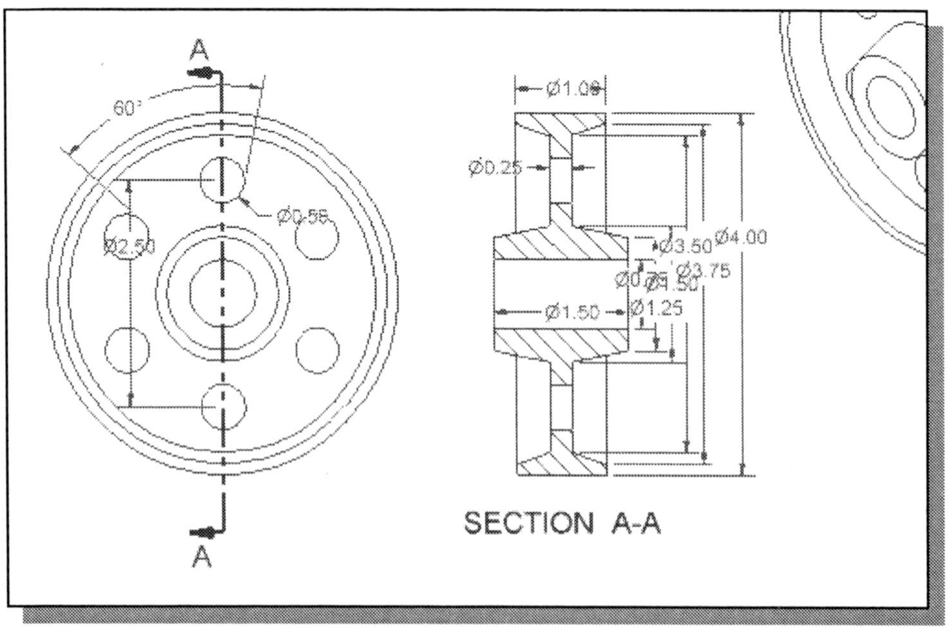

Adding Centerlines to the Pattern feature

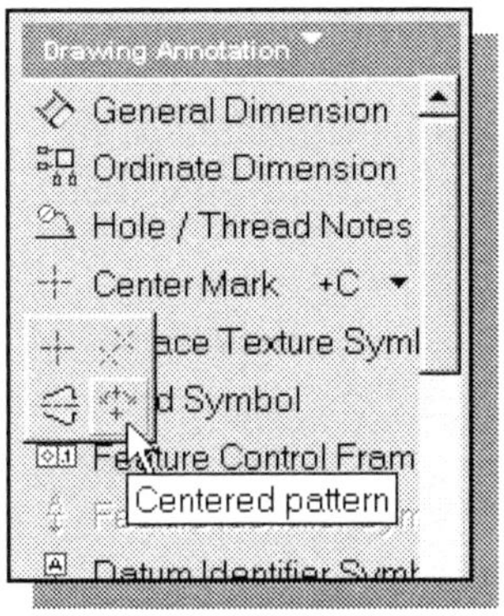

1. Click on the **drop-down arrow** next to the ***Center Mark*** button in the *Drawing Annotation* window to display the available options.

2. Select **Centered pattern** from the option list.

➢ The **Centered pattern** option allows us to add centerlines to a patterned feature.

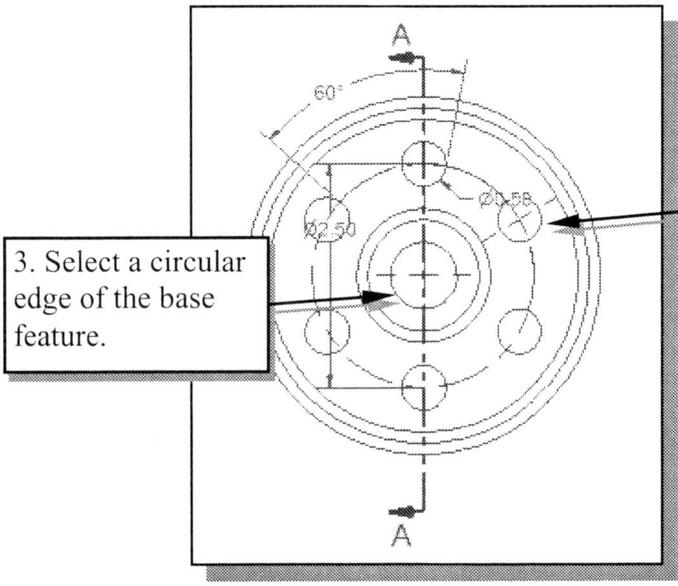

3. Inside the graphics window, click on any circular edge of the base feature.

4. Select any circular edge that is part of the patterned feature.

5. Continue to select the circular edges of the patterned feature, in a counterclockwise manner, until all patterned items are selected.

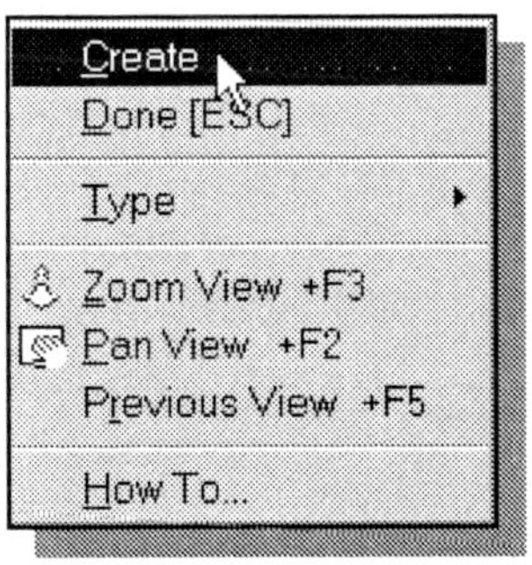

6. Inside the graphics window, right-mouse-click once to bring up the option menu.

7. Select **Create** to create the centerlines around the selected items.

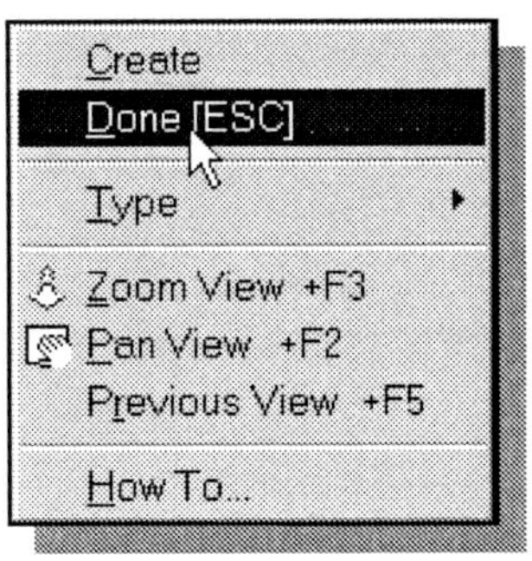

8. Inside the graphics window, right-mouse-click once to bring up the option menu.

9. Select **Done** to end the *Centered Pattern* command.

10. On your own, use the dynamic *Zoom* command to look at the centerlines we just created.

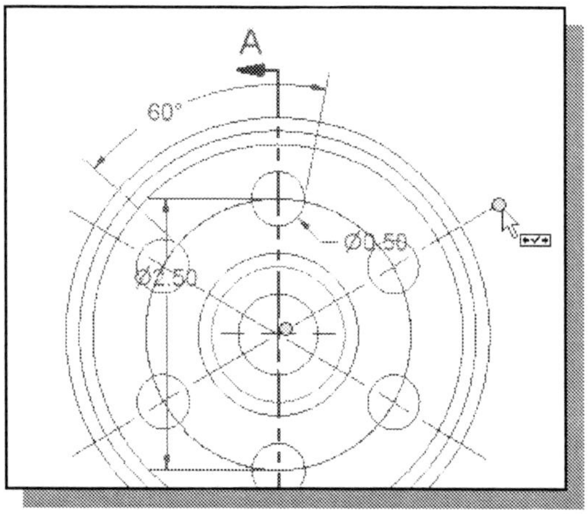

11. On your own, extend the segments of the centerlines so that they pass through the center of the base feature.

Completing the Drawing

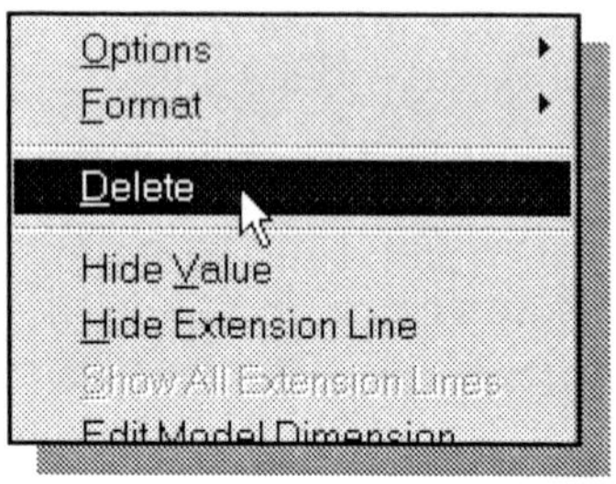

1. On your own, use **Delete** from the option menu to delete unwanted dimensions.

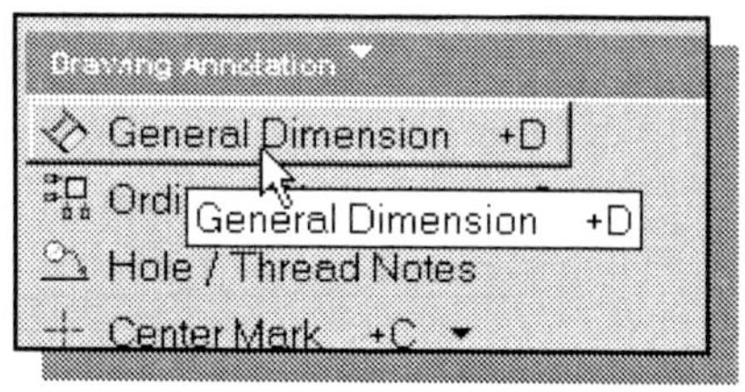

2. Use the ***General Dimension*** command to create additional dimensions as shown below.

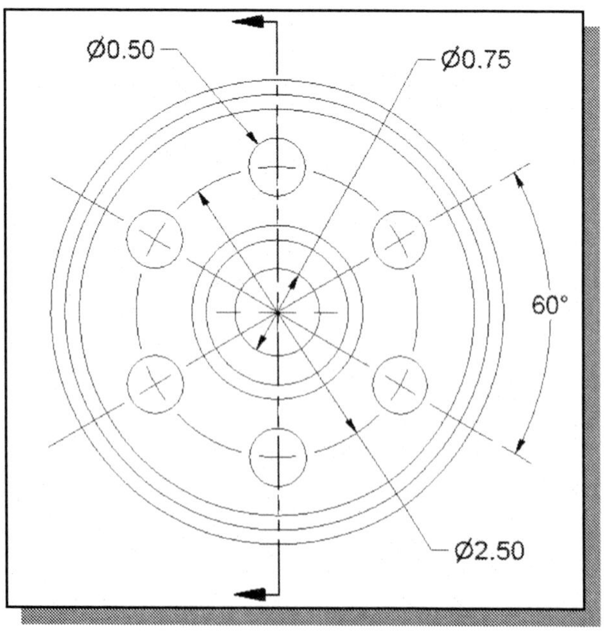

➢ For the circular pattern use the right-mouse-button to set the **Dimension Type** to **Diameter**.

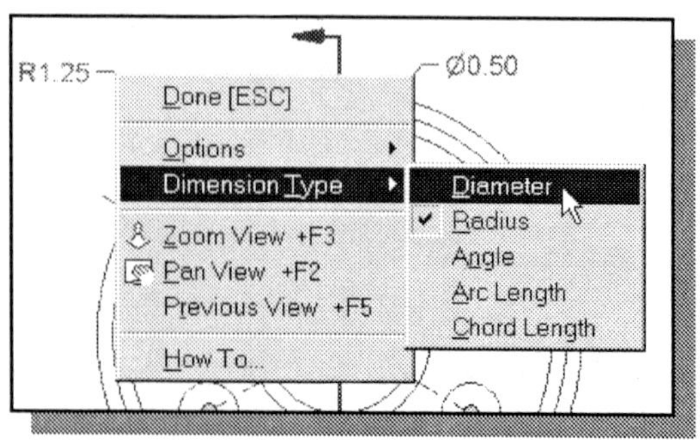

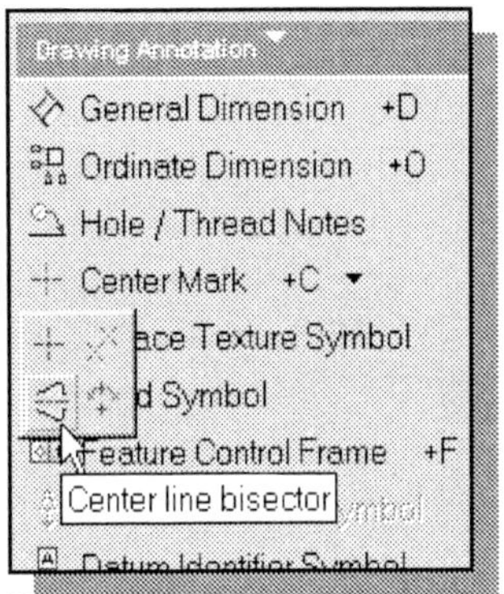

3. Click on the **drop-down arrow** next to the ***Center Mark*** button in the *Drawing Annotation* window to display the available options.

4. Select **Center line bisector** from the option list.

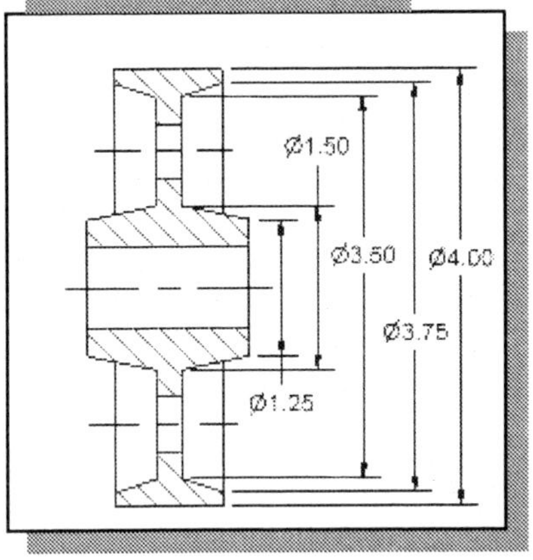

5. Inside the graphics window, click on the two edges of the *section view* as shown in the figure to create a centerline through the view.

6. Repeat the above step and create the centerlines through the patterned holes.

7. On your own, complete the drawing by adding additional text and dimensions.

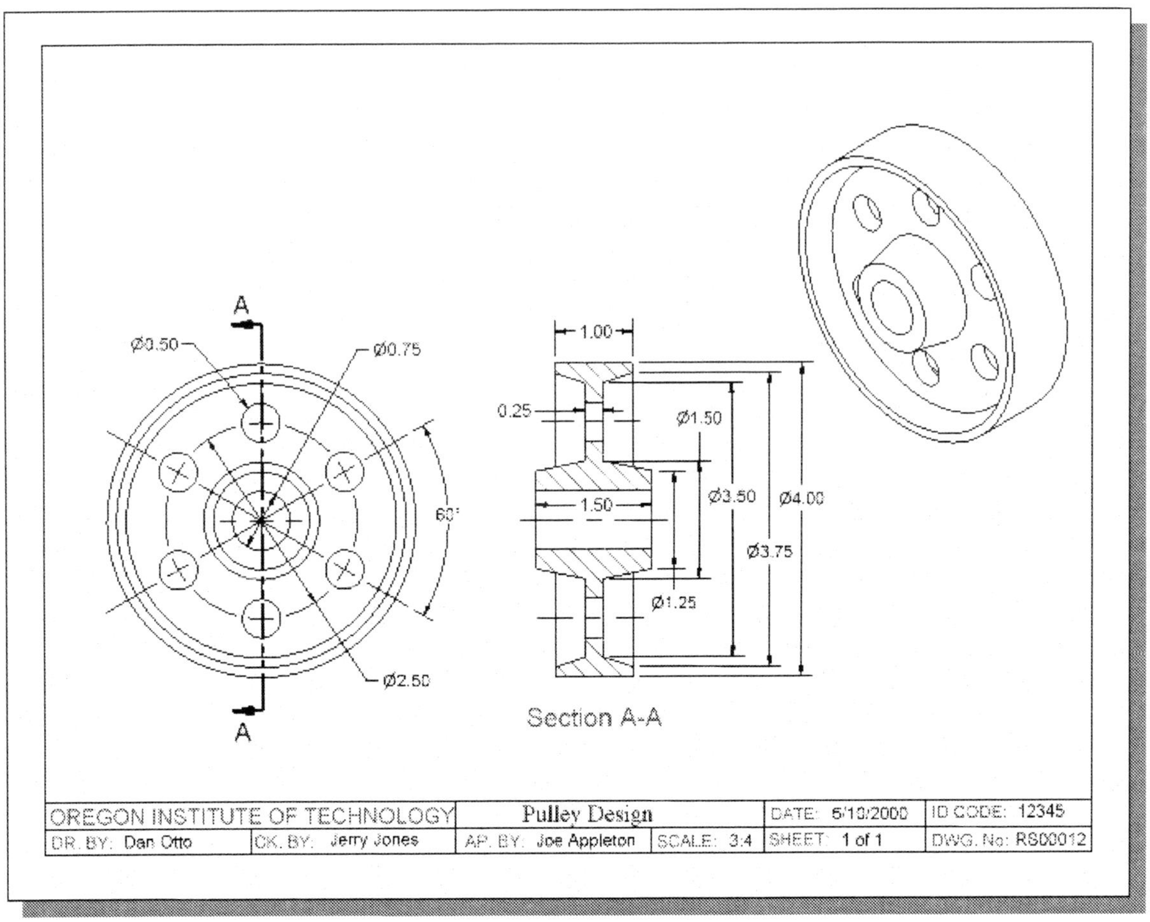

Questions:

1. List the different symmetrical features created in the *Pulley* design.

2. What are the advantages of using *drawing template*?

3. Describe the steps required in using the *Mirror Feature* command.

4. Why is it important to identify symmetrical features in designs?

5. When and why should we use the *Pattern* option?

6. What is the difference between *Rectangular Pattern* and *Circular Pattern*?

7. How do we create a *diameter dimension* for a revolved feature?

8. Identify and describe the following commands:

(a)

(b)

(c)

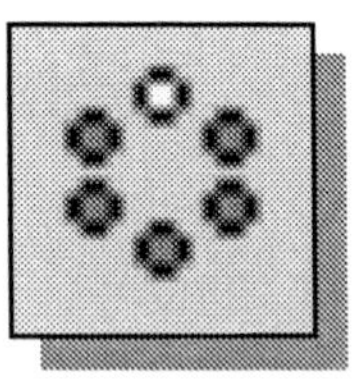

(d)

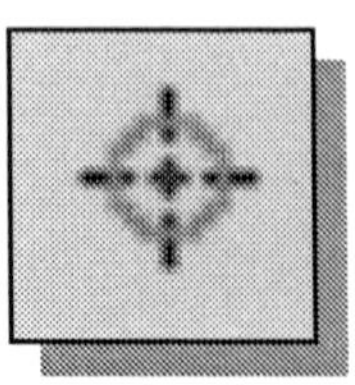

Exercises:

1.

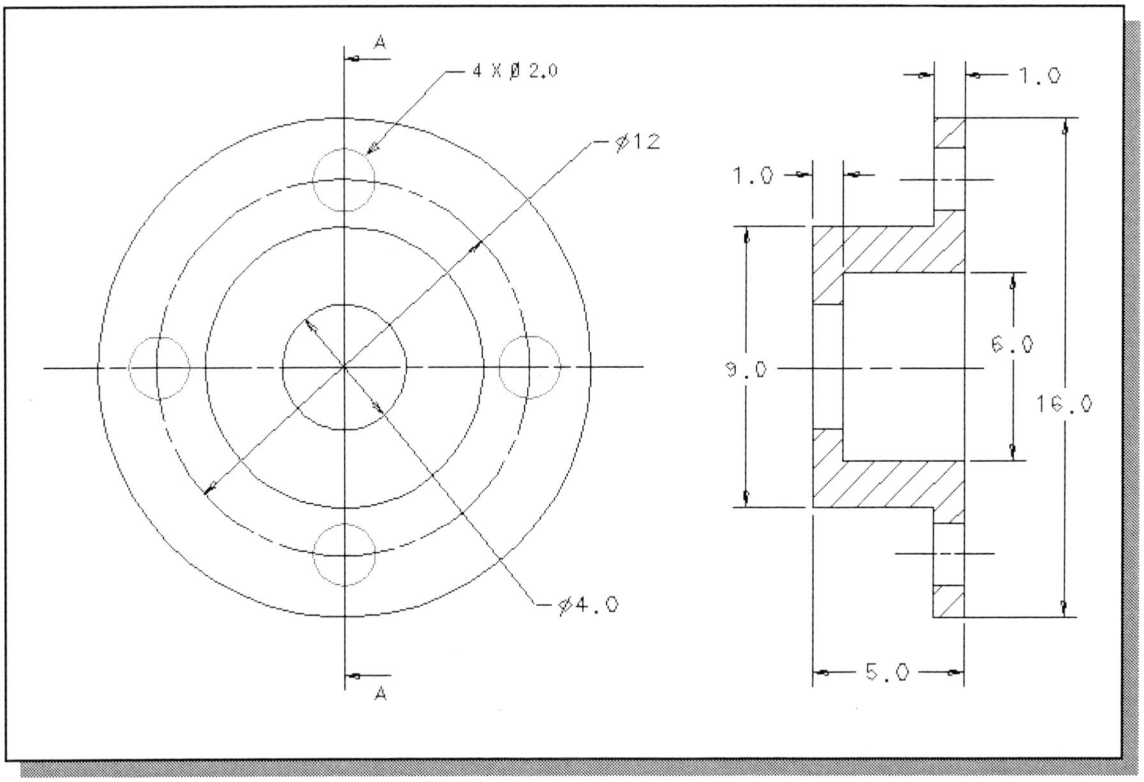

2. Plate thickness: 0.125 inch

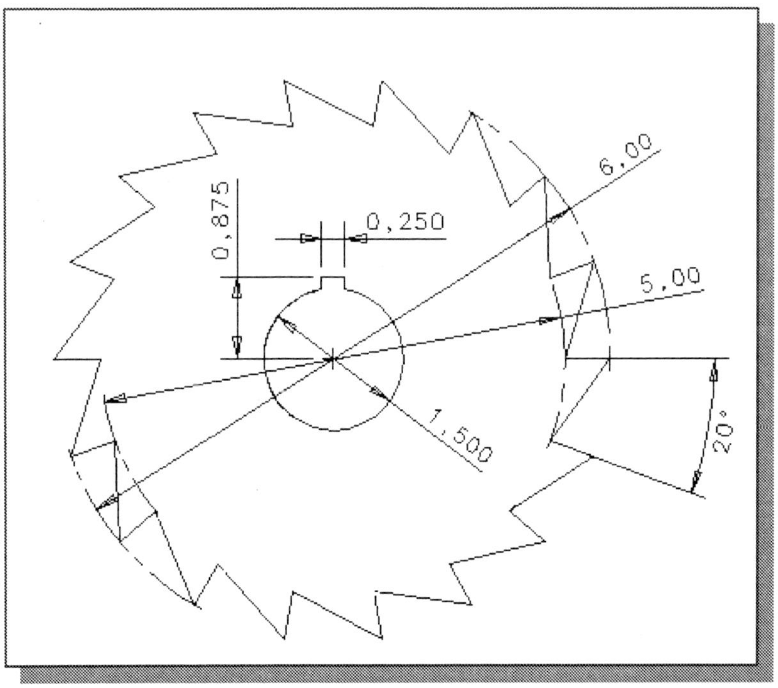

Notes:

Lesson 8
Geometric Construction Tools

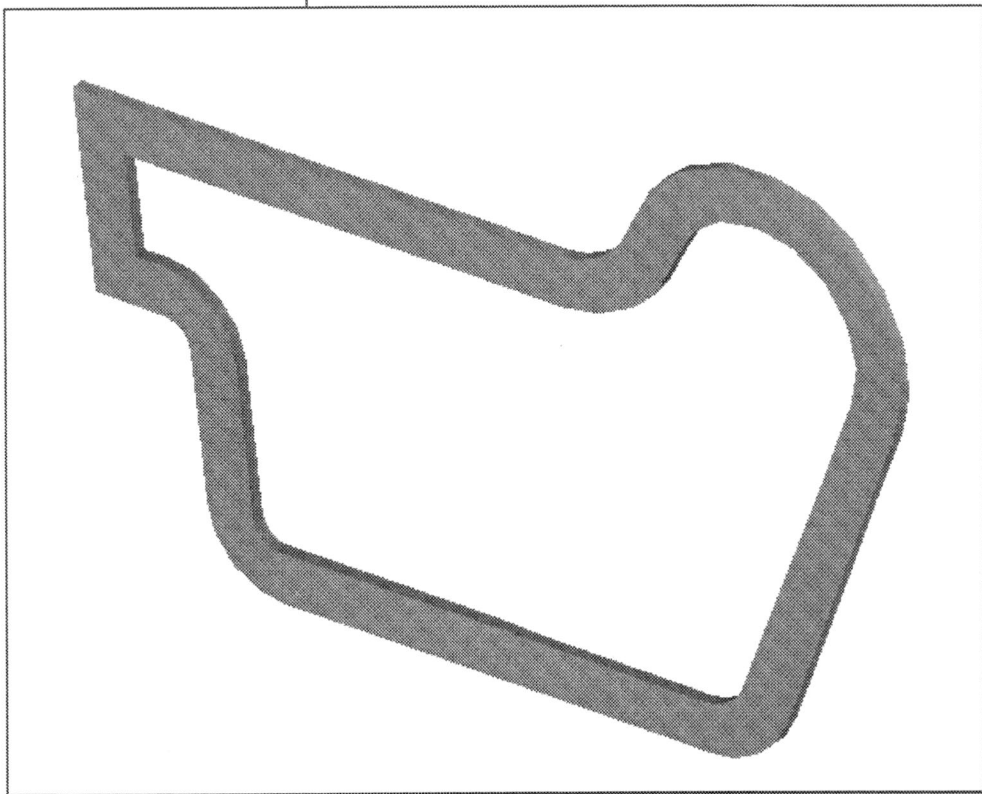

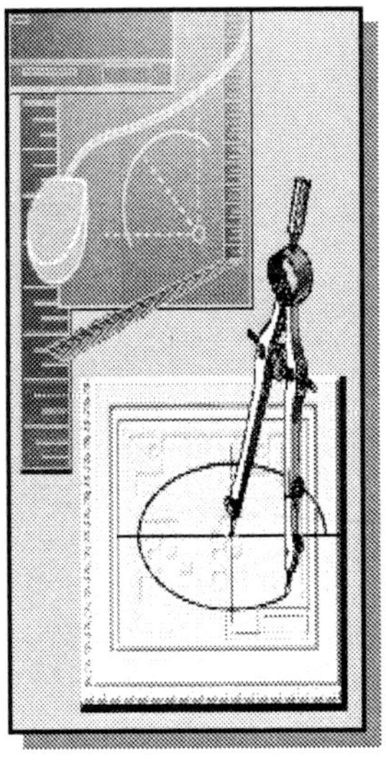

Learning Objectives

When you have completed this lesson, you will be able to:

- ♦ Use the Trim/Extend command.
- ♦ Use the Offset command.
- ♦ Understand the Profile Sketch Approach.
- ♦ Use the 2D Fillet command.
- ♦ Duplicate geometry using the Copy & Paste Option.
- ♦ Use the Projected Geometry Command to Reuse Sketches.
- ♦ Editing with Click and Drag.

Introduction

The main characteristics of solid modeling are the accuracy and completeness of the geometric database of the three-dimensional objects. However, working in three-dimensional space using input and output devices that are largely two-dimensional in nature is potentially tedious and confusing. *Autodesk Inventor* provides an assortment of two-dimensional construction tools to make the creation of wireframe geometry easier and more efficient. *Autodesk Inventor* includes two types of wireframe geometry: **Curves** and **Profiles**. Curves are basic geometric entities such as lines, arcs, etc. Profiles are a group of curves used to define a boundary. A profile is a closed region and can contain other closed regions. Profiles are commonly used to create extruded and revolved features. An *invalid profile* consists of self-intersecting curves or open regions. In this lesson, we will begin with basic geometric construction tools, such as *Trim* and *Extend*, and then introduce the very flexible and powerful *Autodesk Inventor's **Profile Sketch*** approach to create profiles. Mastering the geometric construction tools along with the application of proper constraints and parametric relations is the true essence of *parametric modeling*.

The *Gasket* Design

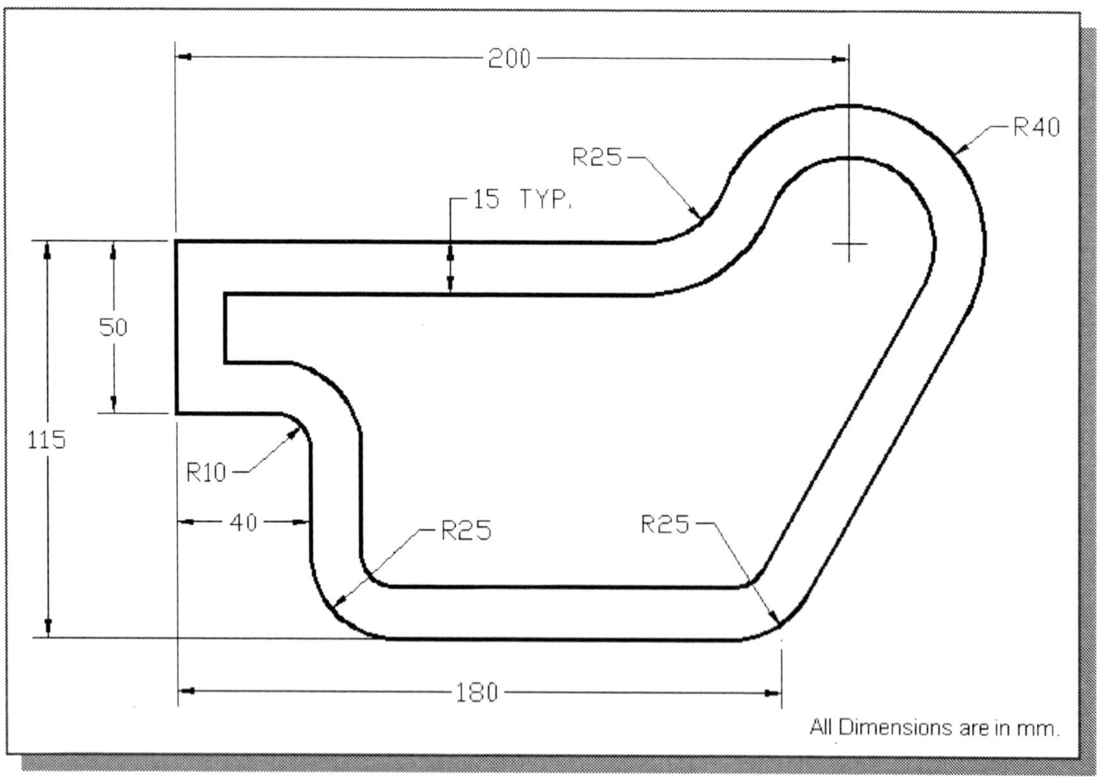

❖ Based on your knowledge of *Autodesk Inventor* so far, how would you create this design? What are the more difficult geometry involved in the design? Take a few minutes to consider a modeling strategy and do preliminary planning by sketching on a piece of paper. You are also encouraged to create the design on your own prior to following through the tutorial.

Modeling Strategy

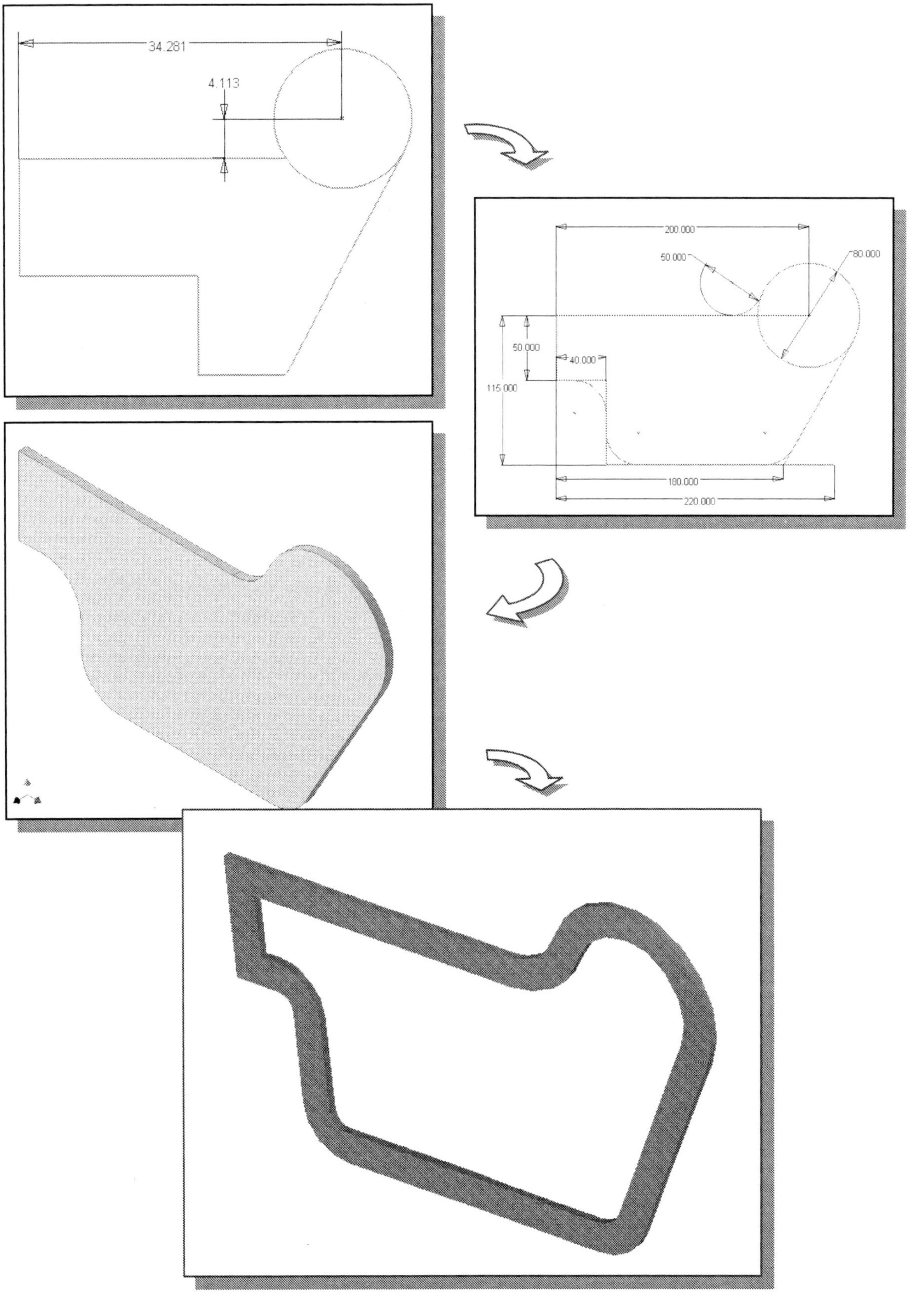

Starting Autodesk Inventor

1. Select the ***Autodesk Inventor*** option on the *Start* menu or select the ***Autodesk Inventor*** icon on the desktop to start *Autodesk Inventor*. The *Autodesk Inventor* main window will appear on the screen.

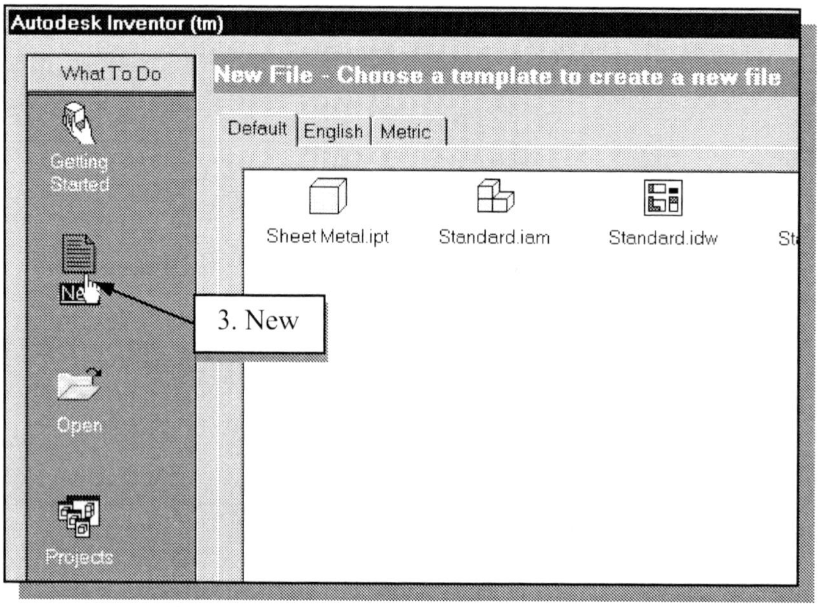

2. Once the program is loaded into the memory, the ***Startup*** dialog box appears at the center of the screen.

3. Select the ***New*** icon with a single click of the left-mouse-button in the *What to Do* dialog box.

4. Select the **Metric** tab as shown below. We will use the millimeter (mm) setting for this example.

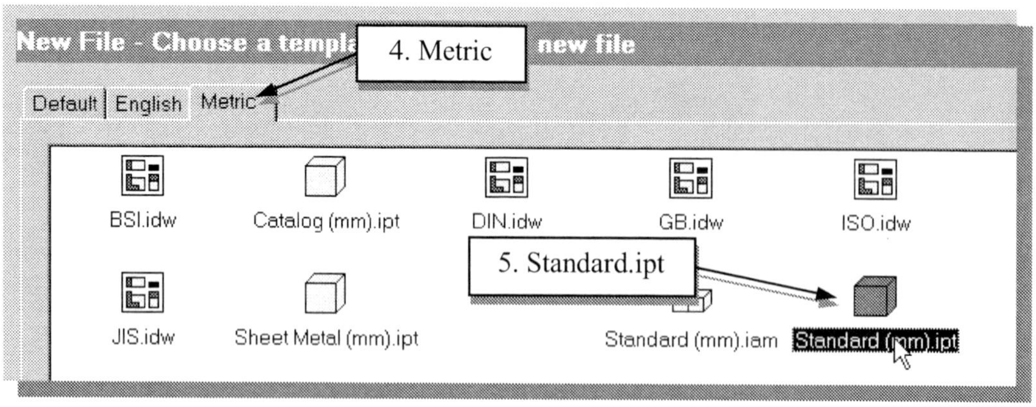

5. In the *New - Choose Template* area, select the **Standard(mm).ipt** icon as shown.

6. Pick **OK** in the *Startup* dialog box to accept the selected settings.

Creating a 2D Sketch

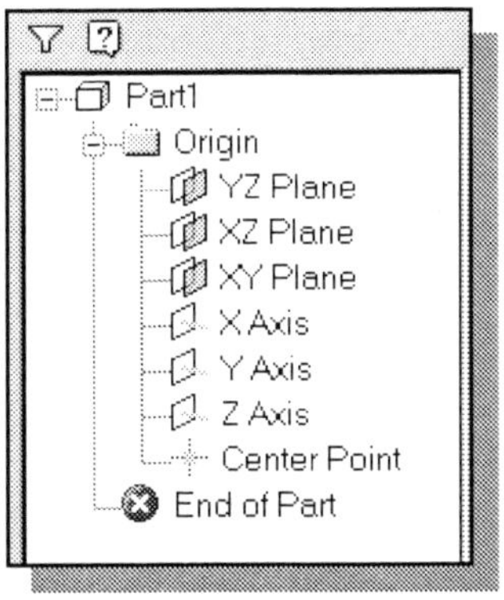

1. In the *Part Browser* window, click on the [+] symbol in front of the ***Origin*** feature to display more information on the feature.

2. In the *Standard* toolbar select the ***Sketch*** command by left-clicking once on the icon.

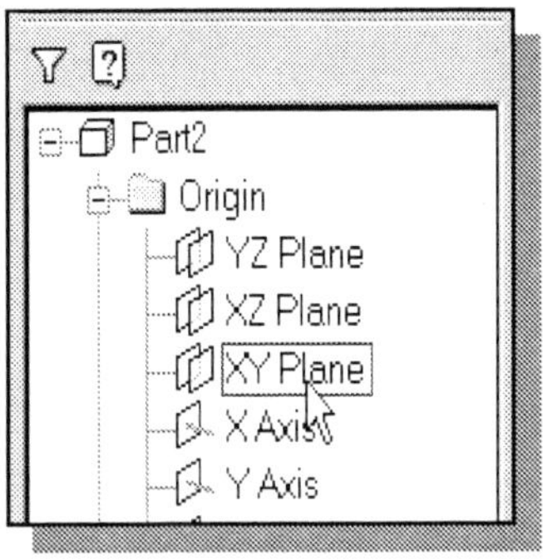

3. In the *Status Bar* area, the message: "*Select face, workplane, sketch or sketch geometry.*" is displayed. Select the ***XY Plane*** in the *Browser* window.

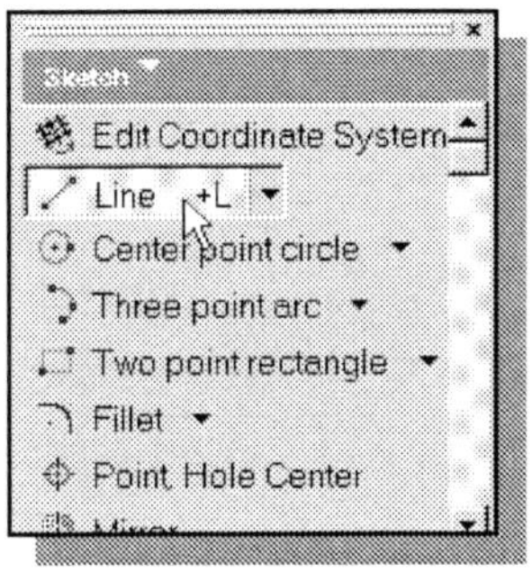

4. Click on the ***Line*** icon in the *Sketch* toolbar.

5. Create a sketch as shown in the below figure. Start the sketch from the top-right corner. The line segments are all parallel and/or perpendicular to each other. We will intentionally make the line segments of arbitrary length, as it is quite common during design stage that not all of the values are determined.

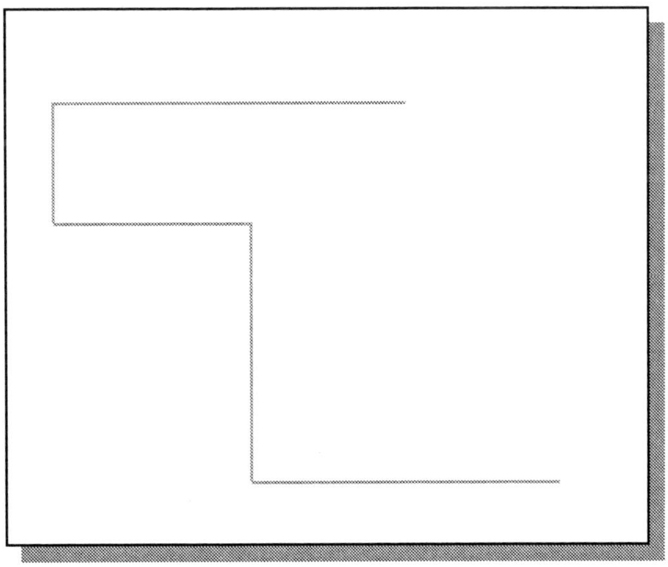

6. Inside the graphics window, right-mouse-click to bring up the option menu and select **Done** to end the *Line* command.

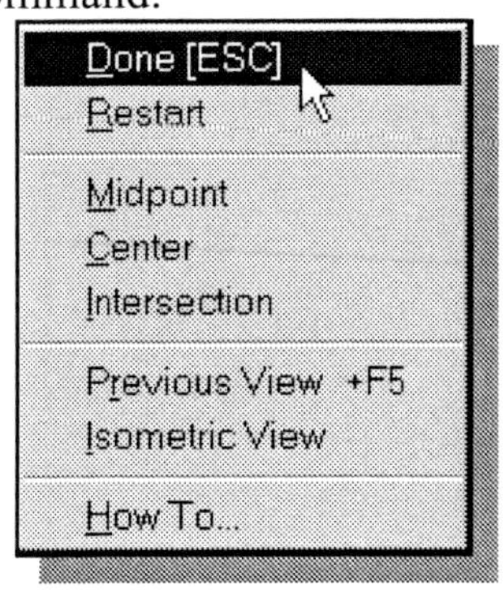

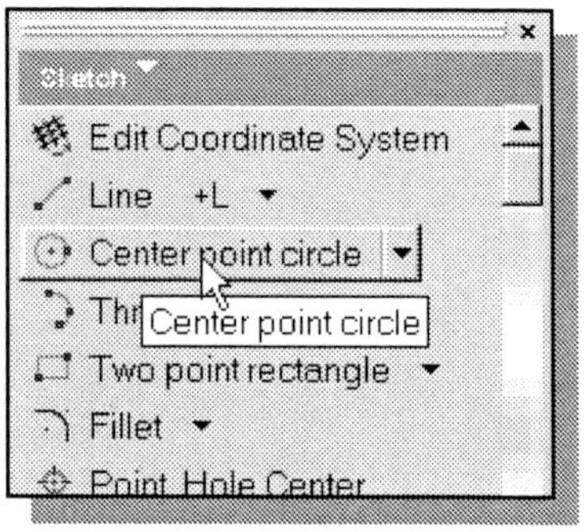

7. Select the ***Center point circle*** command by clicking once with the left-mouse-button on the icon in the *Sketch* toolbar.

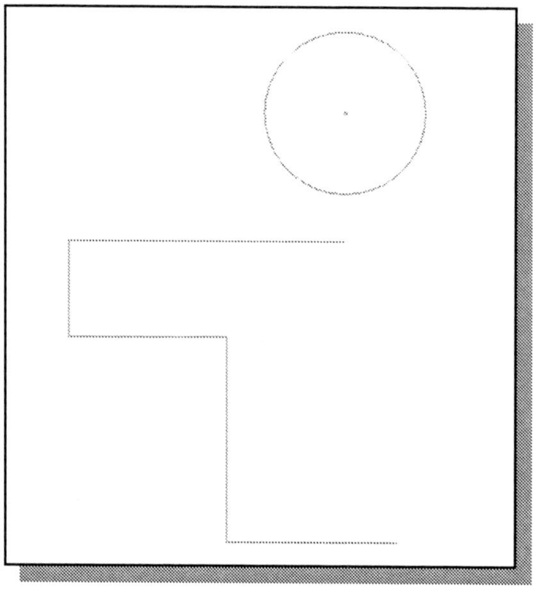

8. Pick a location that is above the top horizontal line as the center location of the circle.

9. Move the cursor toward the left and create a circle of arbitrary size, by clicking once with the left-mouse-button.

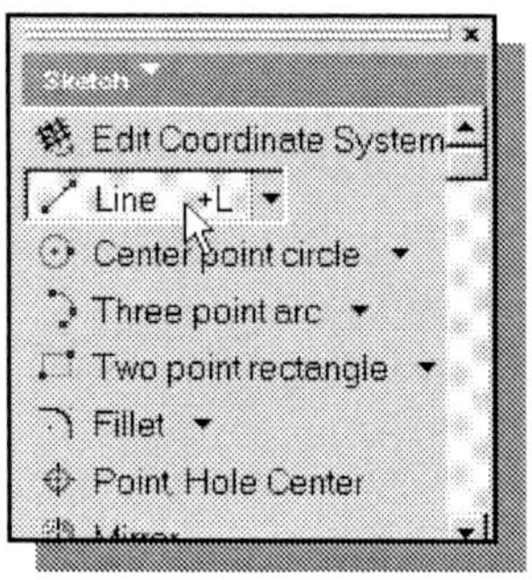

10. Click on the ***Line*** icon in the *Sketch* toolbar.

11. Move the cursor near the upper portion of the circle and pick a location on the circle when the *Coincident* constraint symbol is displayed.

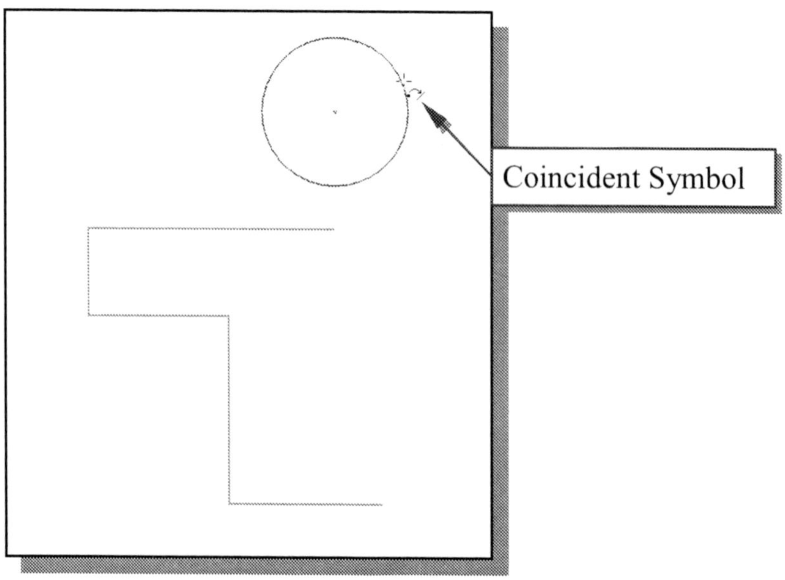

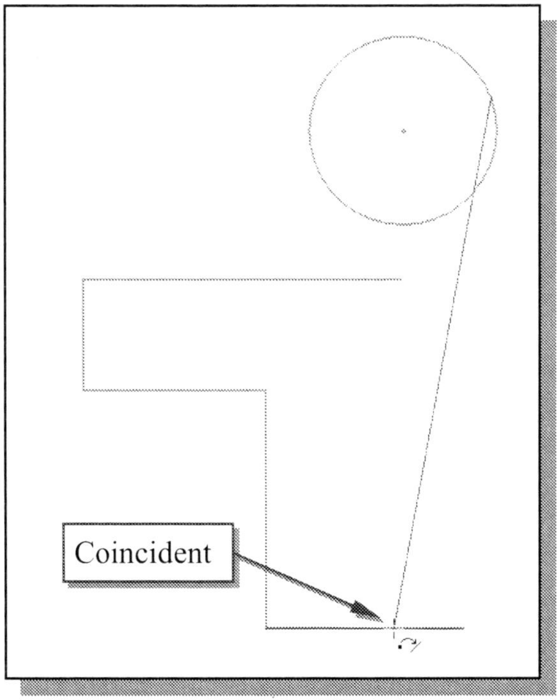

12. For the other end of the line, select a location that is on the lower horizontal line and about one-third from the right endpoint. Notice the coincident constraint symbol is displayed when the cursor is on the horizontal line.

13. Inside the graphics window, right-mouse-click to bring up the option menu.

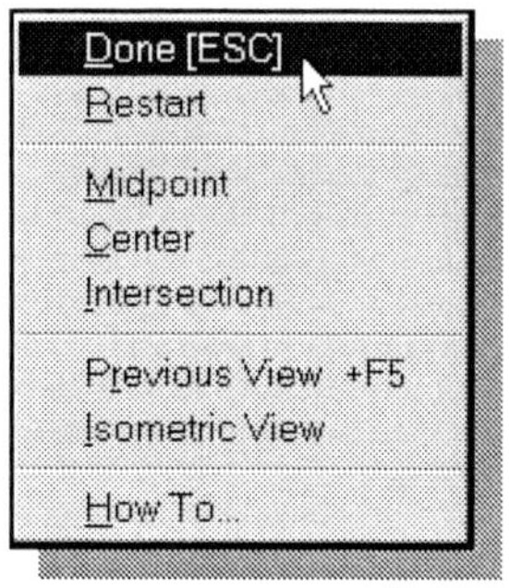

14. In the option menu, select **Done** to end the *Line* command.

Editing the Sketch by Dragging the Entities

❖ In *Autodesk Inventor*, we can click and drag any under-constrained curve or point in the sketch to change the size or shape of the sketched profile.

1. Move the cursor on the left-vertical edge of the sketch. Click and drag the edge to a new location that is toward the left side of the graphics window.

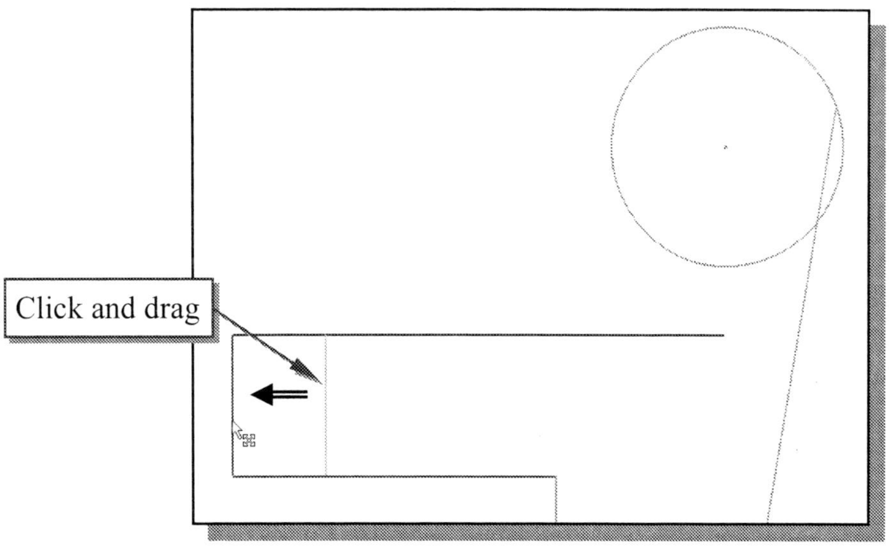

❖ Note that we can only drag the vertical edge horizontally; the connections to the two horizontal lines are maintained while we are moving the geometry.

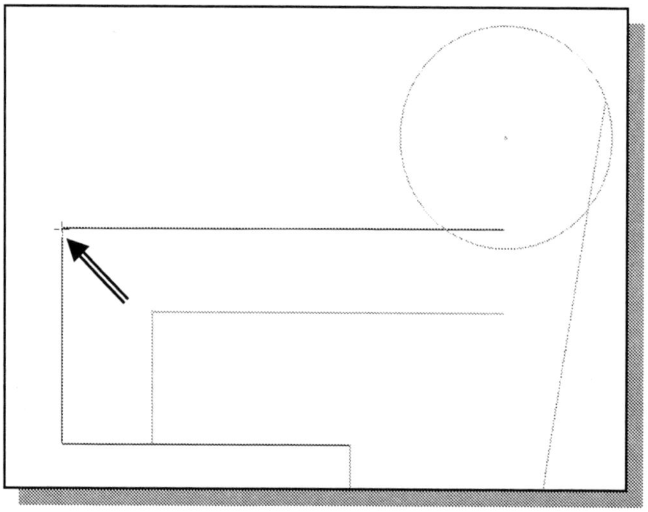

2. Click and drag the top-left corner of the sketch to a new location that is toward the upper-left corner of the graphics window.

❖ Note that all edges connecting to the point are adjusted.

3. Click and drag the circle to a new location.

❖ Note that the connection to the inclined line is maintained as we adjust the size of the circle.

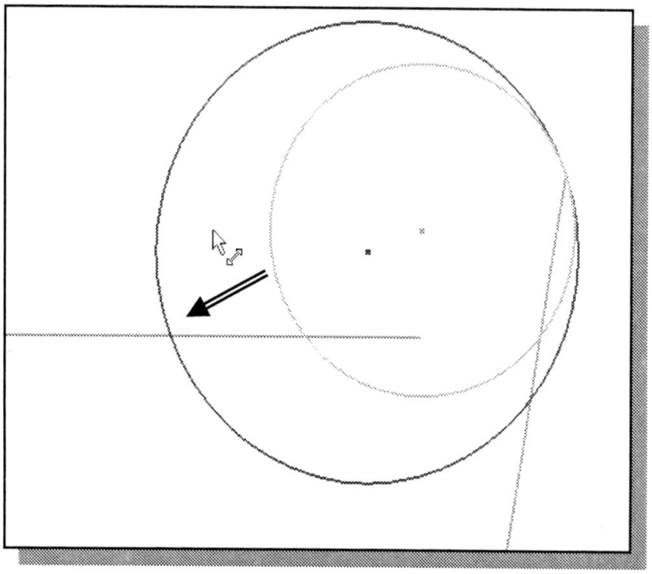

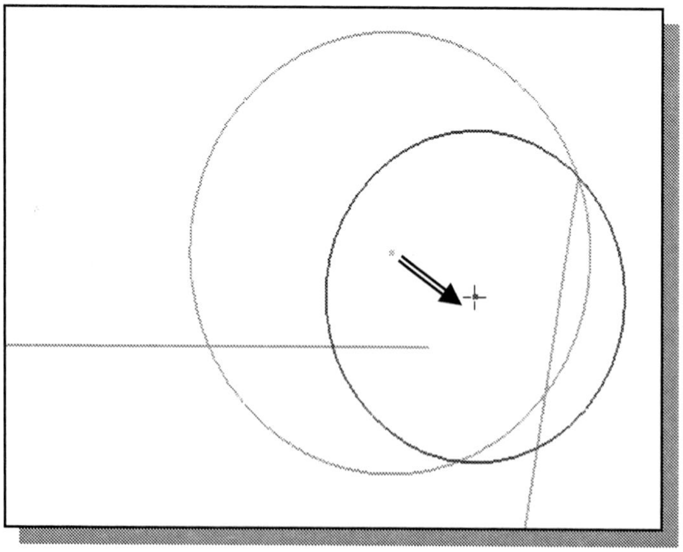

4. Click and drag the center of the circle to a new location.

❖ Note that the connection to the inclined line is maintained as we adjust the size and the location of the circle.

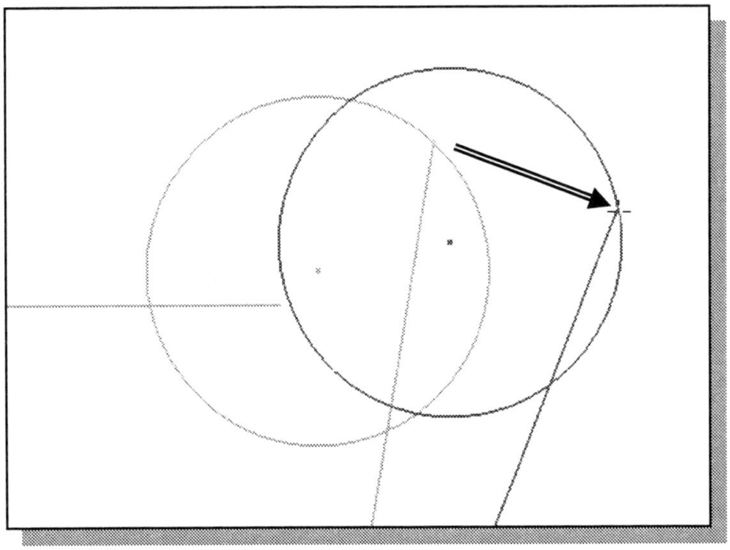

5. Click and drag the top endpoint of the inclined line to a new location.

❖ Note that as we adjust the size and the location of the inclined line, the connection to the circle is maintained.

6. Click and drag the right endpoint of the top-horizontal line to a new location.

❖ Note that as we adjust the size and the location of the horizontal line the connection to the left vertical edge is maintained.

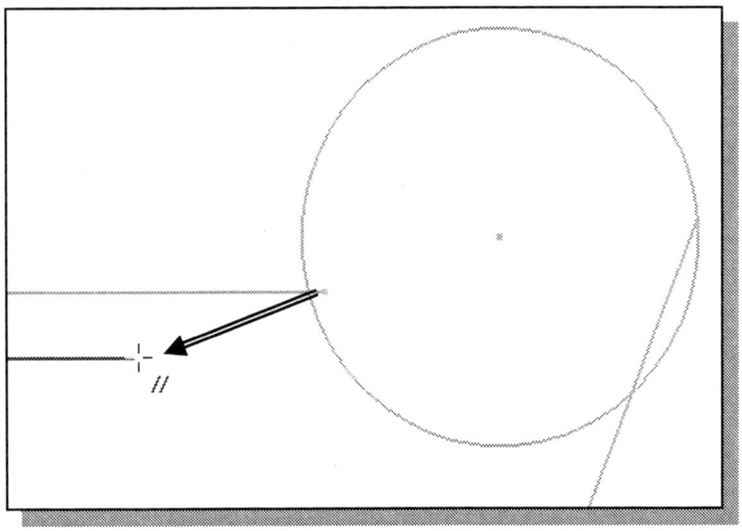

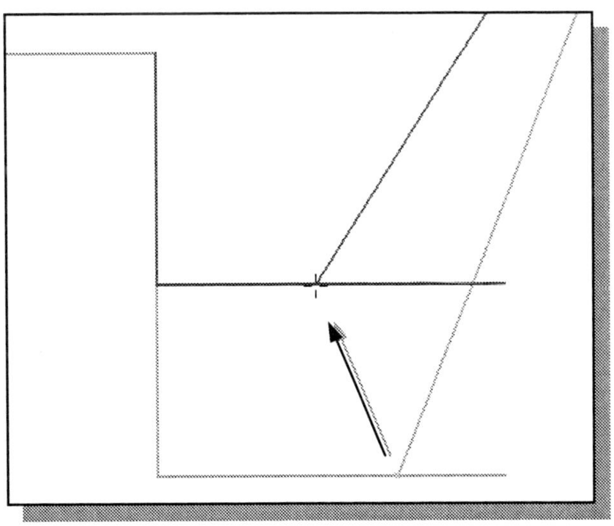

7. Click and drag the lower endpoint of the inclined line to a new location.

❖ Note that several changes occurr as we adjust the size and the location of the inclined line. The location of the bottom horizontal line and the length of the vertical line are adjusted accordingly.

Adding Additional Constraints

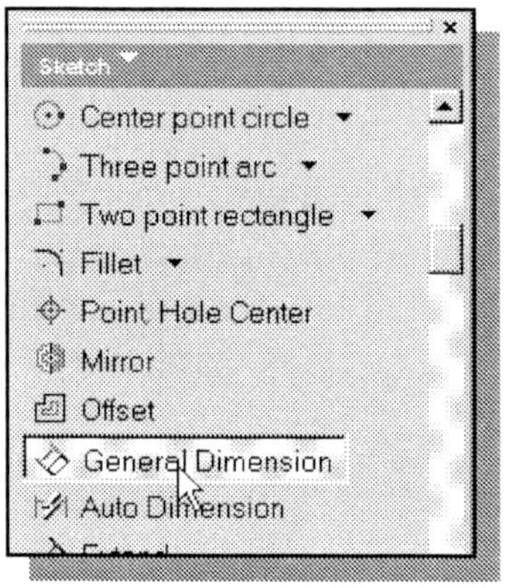

1. Choose **General Dimension** in the *Sketch* toolbar.

2. Add the horizontal location dimension, from the top-left vertical edge to the center of the circle as shown. (Do not be overly concerned with the dimensional value; we are still working on creating a *rough sketch*.)

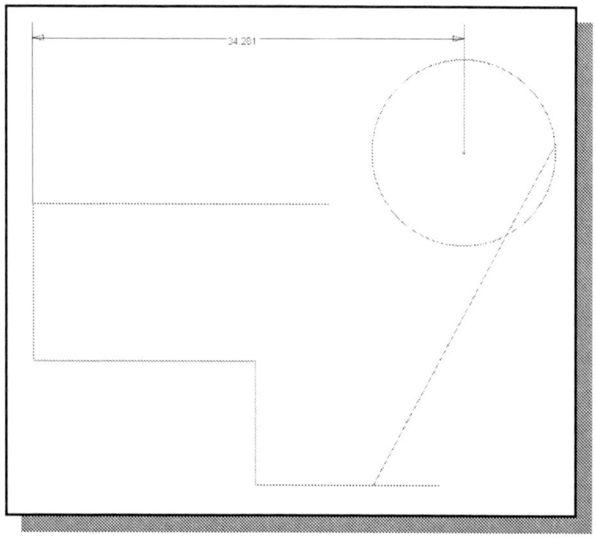

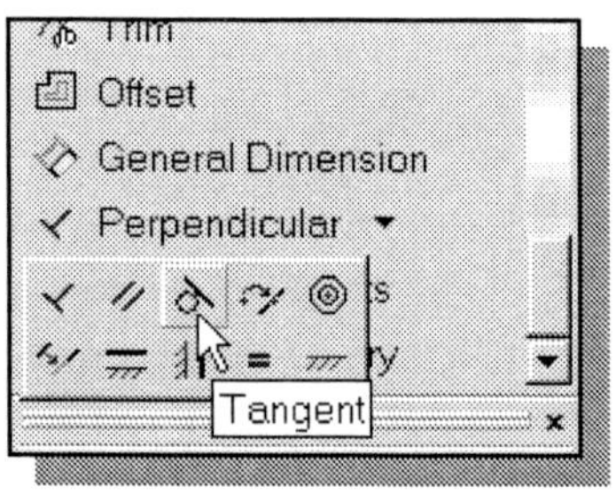

3. Click on the ***Tangent Constraint*** icon in the *Sketch* toolbar.

4. Pick the inclined line by left-mouse-clicking once on the geometry.

5. Pick the circle. The sketched geometry is adjusted as shown below.

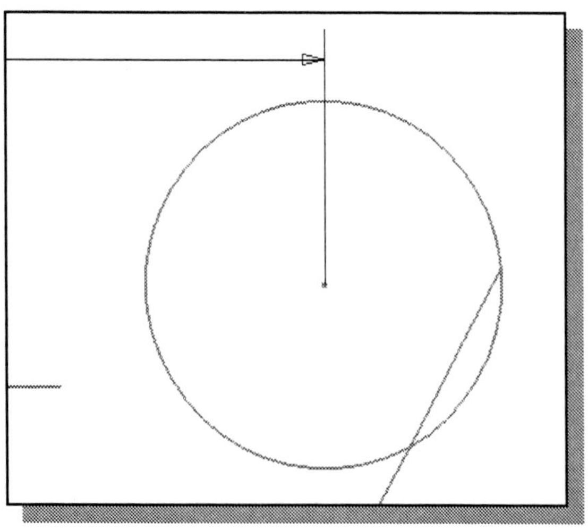

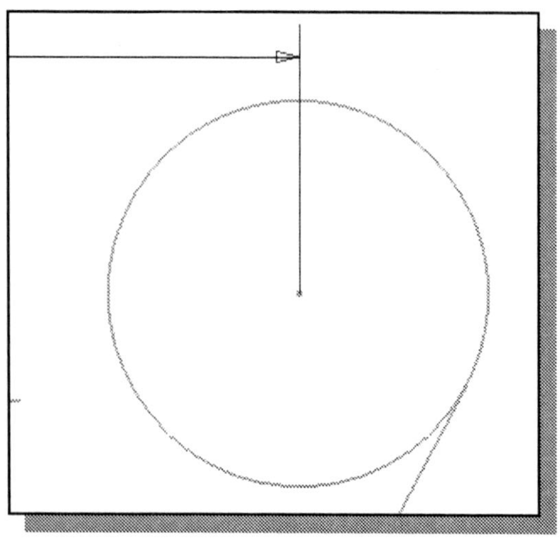

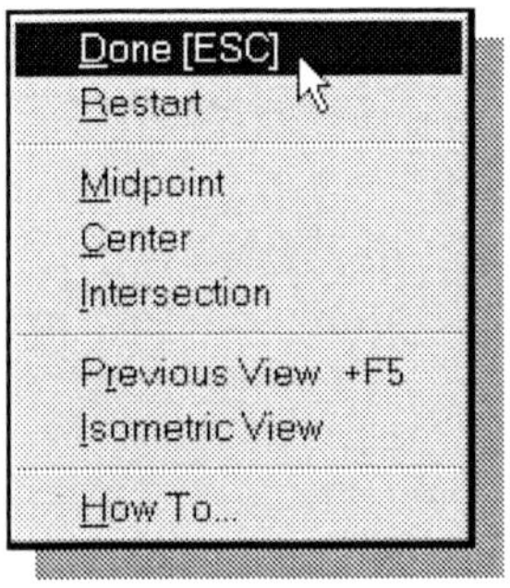

6. Inside the graphics window, right-mouse-click to bring up the option menu.

7. In the option menu, select **Done** to end the *Tangent* command.

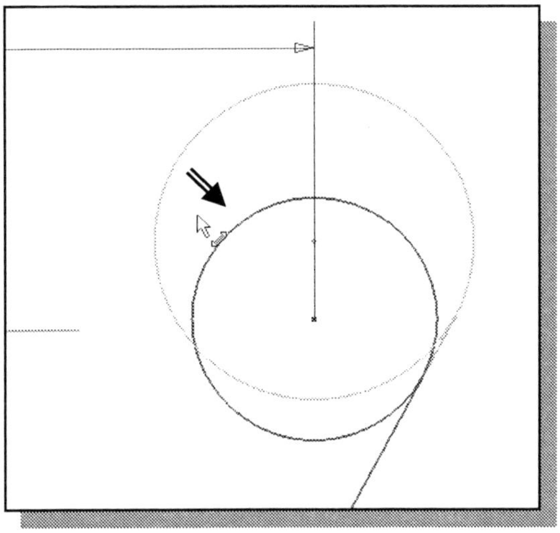

8. Click and drag the circle to a new size.

❖ Note that the dimension we added now restricts the horizontal movement of the center of the circle. The tangent relation to the inclined line is maintained as we adjust the size of the circle.

Copying the Sketched Entities

❖ *Autodesk Inventor* allows us to make copies of objects at several different levels. Copies of features and sketches can be created quickly using the **Copy** and **Paste** options.

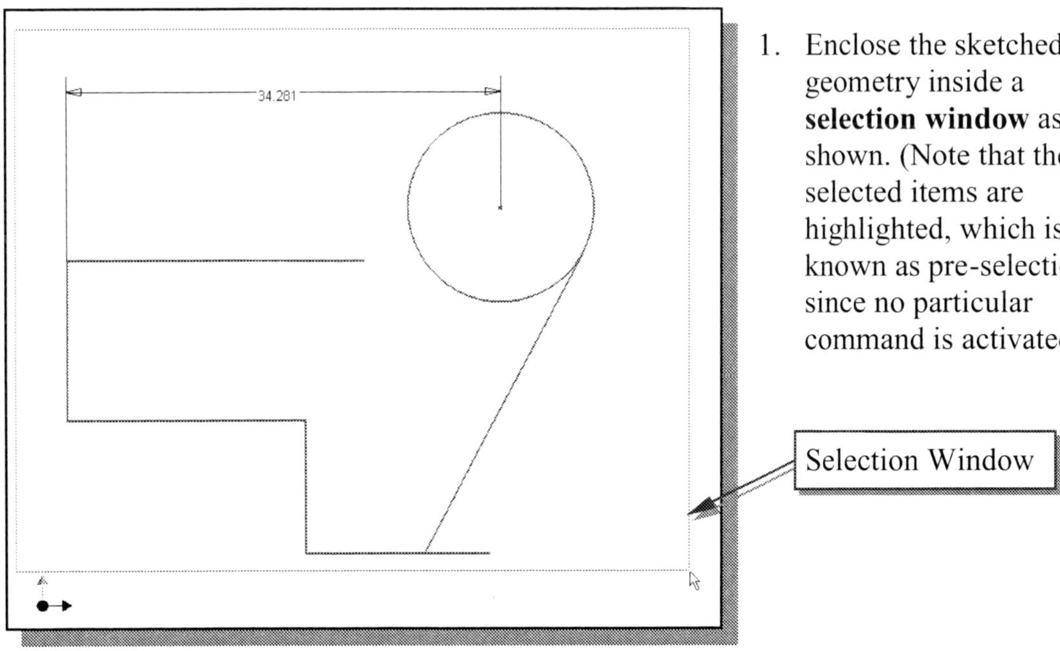

1. Enclose the sketched geometry inside a **selection window** as shown. (Note that the selected items are highlighted, which is also known as pre-selection since no particular command is activated.)

2. Inside the graphics window, right-mouse-click to bring up the option menu.

3. Select **Copy** to copy the selected items into memory. The copy can then be placed into the same graphics window or a different window.

4. Inside the graphics window, right-mouse-click to bring up the option menu.

5. Select **Paste** to place a copy of the selected items on the screen.

❖ Note that the copy of the selected items is placed on the screen at the same location as the original items.

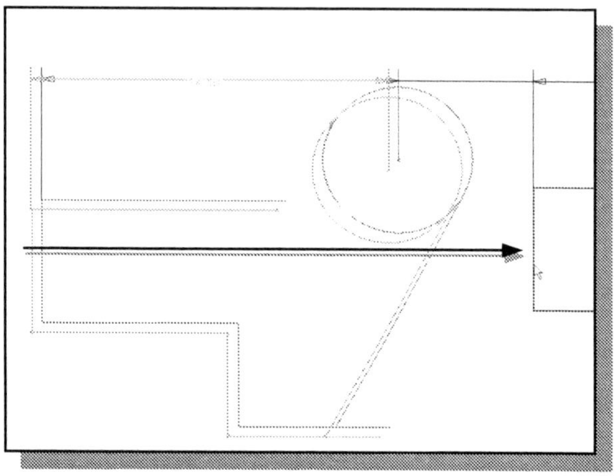

6. The original set is still highlighted, indicating these items are still selected. **Click and drag** the highlighted left vertical edge toward the right side of the copy as shown.

❖ Note that the **click and drag** option acts as a **Move** option when multiple objects are selected.

7. Inside the graphics window, left-mouse-click once in the blank area to release the selected items.

8. **Drag** the dimension text toward the right so that the display appears as shown below.

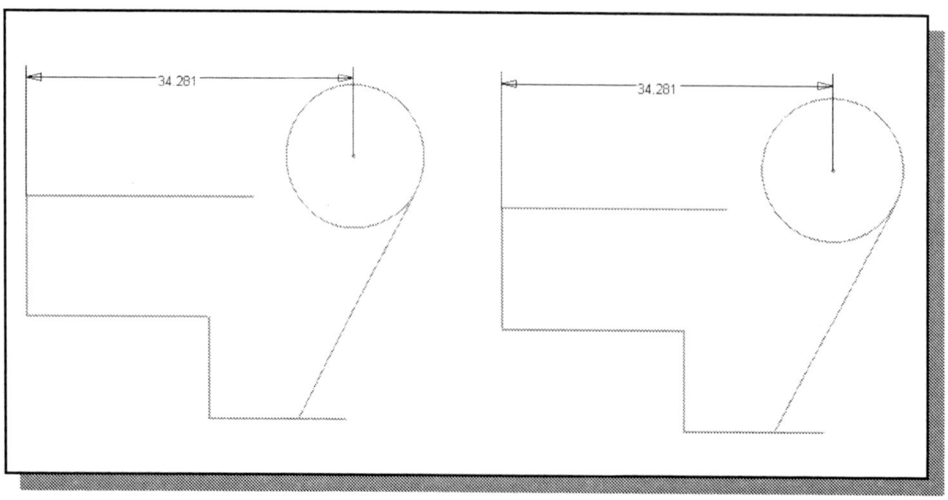

Using the *Trim* and *Extend* Commands

➢ In the following sections, we will illustrate using different approaches to complete the same 2D profile. We will first work on the copy that is on the left side of the graphics window.

❖ The ***Trim*** and ***Extend*** commands can be used to shorten/lengthen an object so that it ends precisely at a boundary. As a general rule, *Autodesk Inventor* will try to clean up sketches by forming a closed region sketch. While we are in either ***Trim*** or ***Extend***, press the [**Shift**] key to switch to the opposite operation.

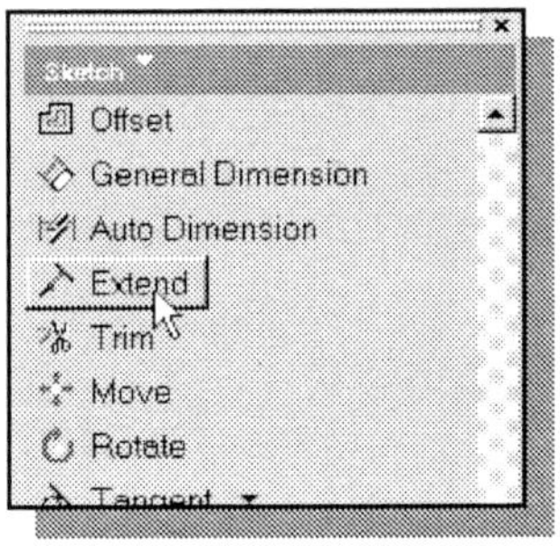

1. Choose ***Extend*** in the *Sketch* toolbar. The message "*Extend curves*" is displayed in the prompt area.

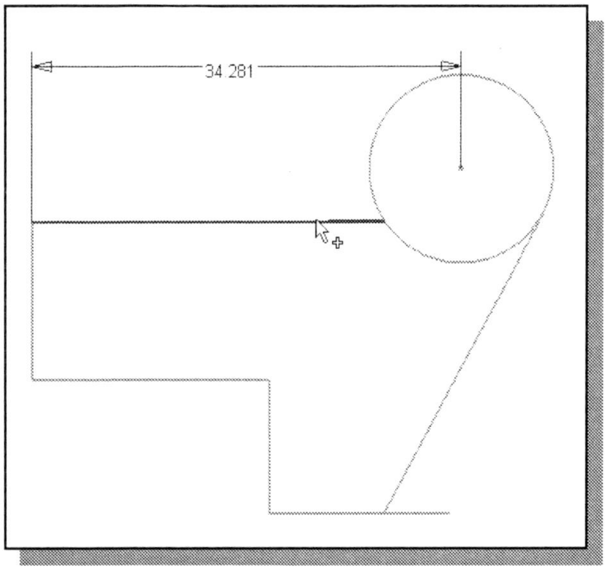

2. We will first extend the top horizontal line to the circle. Move the cursor near the right-hand endpoint of the top horizontal line. *Autodesk Inventor* will automatically display the possible result of the selection.

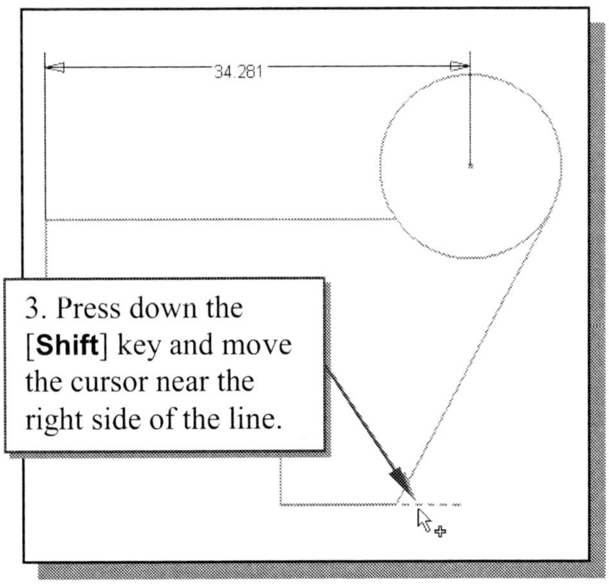

3. We will next trim the bottom horizontal line to the inclined line. The ***Trim*** operation can be activated by selecting the *Trim* icon in the *Sketch* toolbar or by pressing down the [**Shift**] key while we are in the *Extend* command. Move the cursor near the right-hand endpoint of the bottom horizontal line and select the line and press down the [**Shift**] key. *Autodesk Inventor* will display a dashed-line indicating the portion of the line that will be trimmed.

4. **Left-mouse-click** once on the line to perform the *Trim* operation.

5. On your own, create the vertical location dimension as shown below.

6. Adjust the dimension to **0.0** so that the horizontal line and the center of the circle are aligned horizontally.

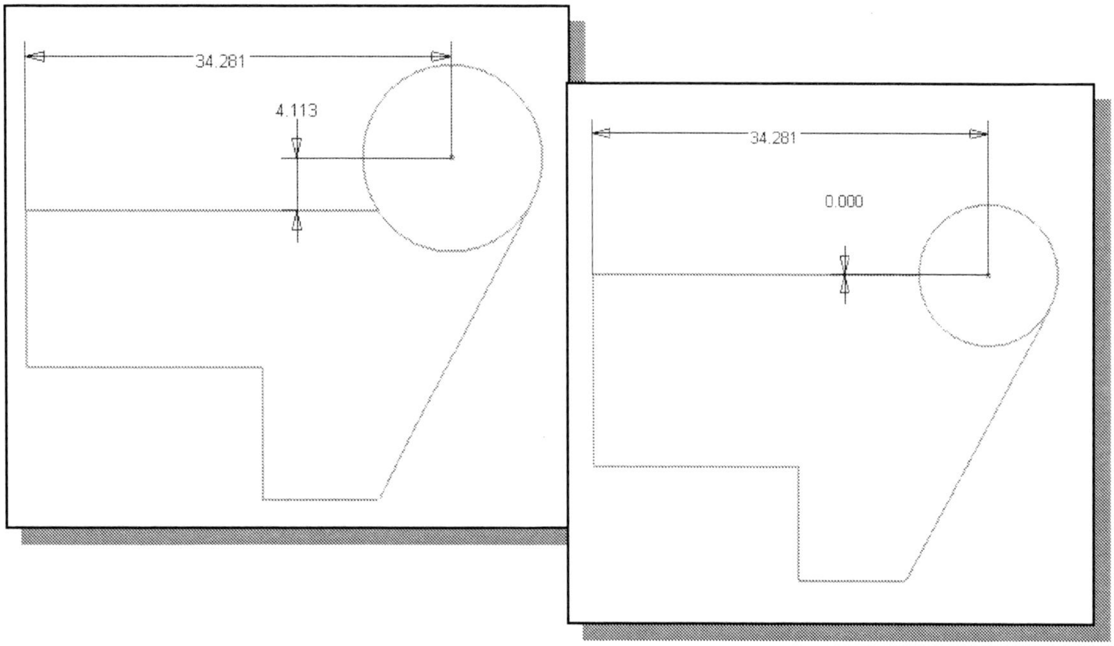

7. On your own, use the ***Show Constraints*** command to examine the applied constraints. Confirm that a ***perpendicular constraint*** is applied to the horizontal and vertical lines as shown.

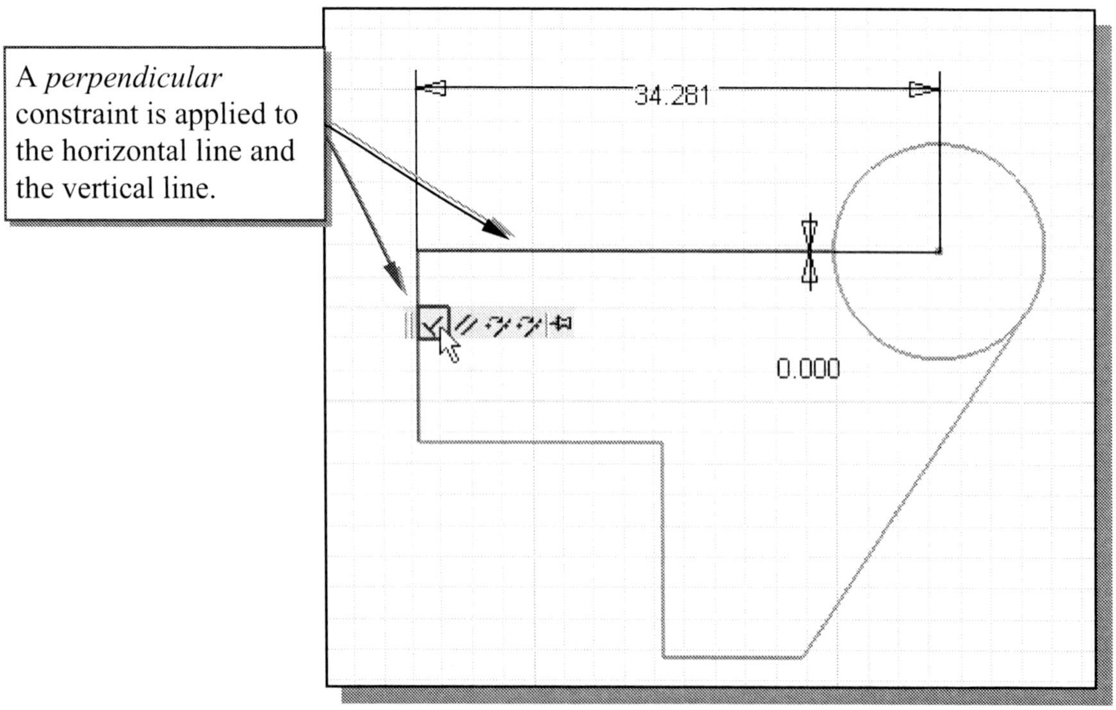

The *Auto Dimension* command

➢ In *Autodesk Inventor*, we can use the ***Auto Dimension*** command to fully constrain a sketch. Fully constrained sketches update predictably as design changes are implemented. The general procedure in applying dimensions to sketches is to use the ***General Dimension*** command to add only the dimensions you need, then use the ***Auto Dimension*** command to calculate all other sketch dimensions. *Autodesk Inventor* remembers which dimensions are added by the user and which are calculated by the system, so that automatic dimensions do not replace the desired dimensions.

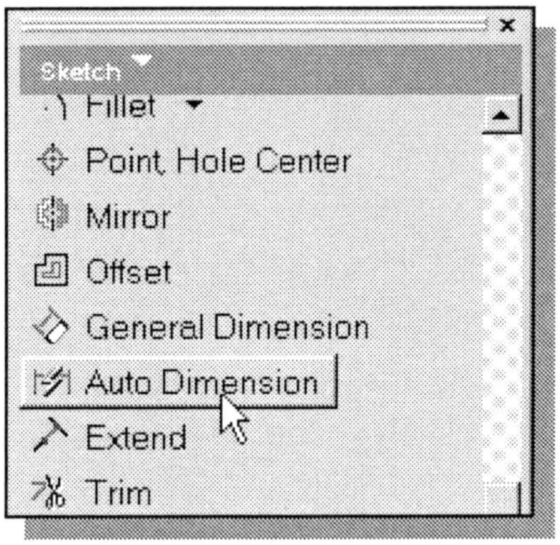

1. Click on the ***Auto Dimension*** icon in the *Sketch* toolbar.

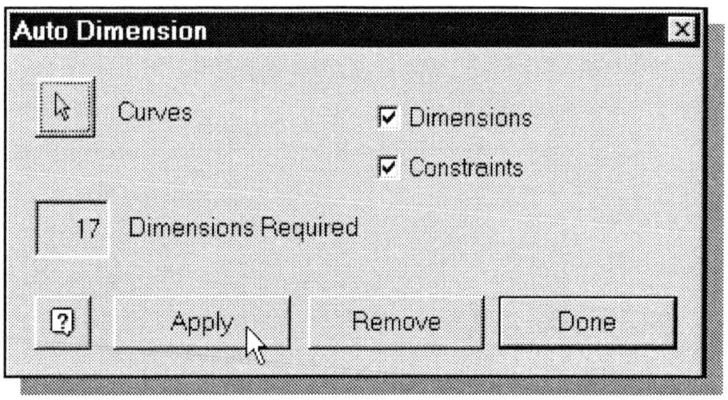

2. The *Auto Dimension* dialog box appears on the screen. Confirm that the *Dimensions* and *Constraints* options are switched *ON* as shown.

3. Click on the **Apply** button to proceed with the *Auto Dimension* command.

   ➢ Note that the system automatically calculates additional dimensions for all created geometric entities. Also note that **four** additional dimensions are still required to fully constrain the sketches as shown in the dialog box. The four dimensions are the location dimensions for the two sketches, to which we will apply proper constraints in the following section.

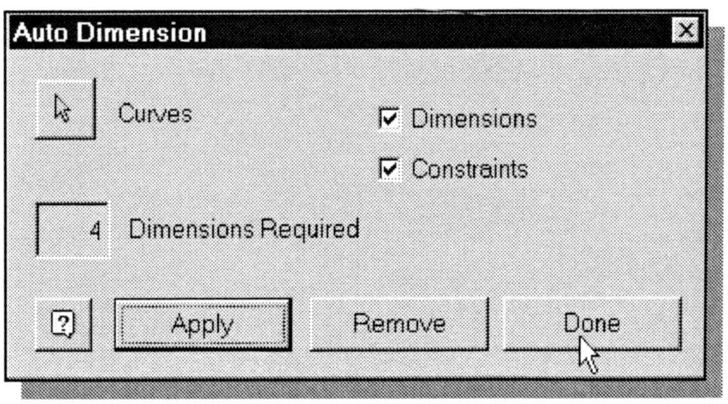

4. Click on the **Done** button to accept the created dimensions.

5. Reposition the displayed dimensions, by click and drag with the left-mouse-button, so that the dimensions can be more easily identified.

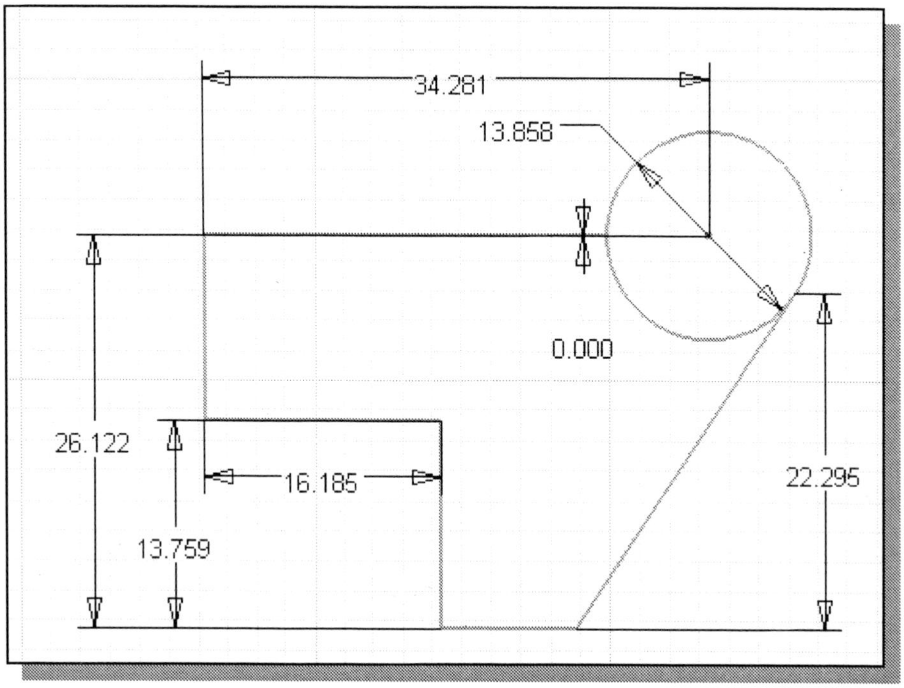

6. On your own, delete the vertical dimension on the inclined line, trim the circle and add the location dimension for the lower right corner of the sketch as shown.

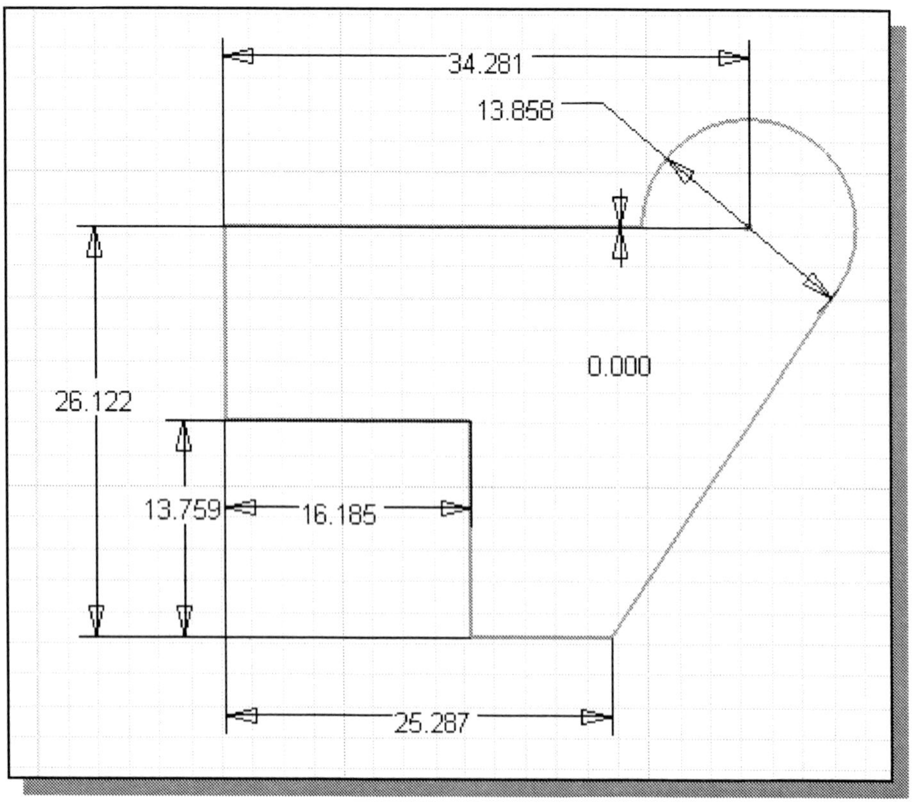

Creating Fillets and Completing the Sketch

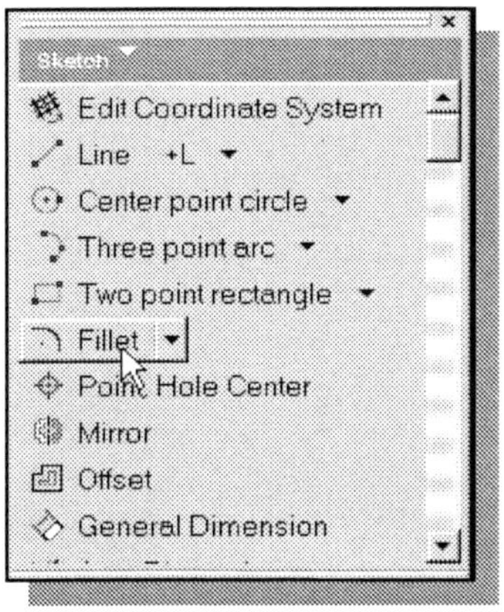

1. Click on the ***Fillet*** icon in the *Sketch* toolbar.

2. The *Radius* dialog box appears on the screen. We will use the default radius value. Click on the top horizontal line and the arc to create a fillet as shown.

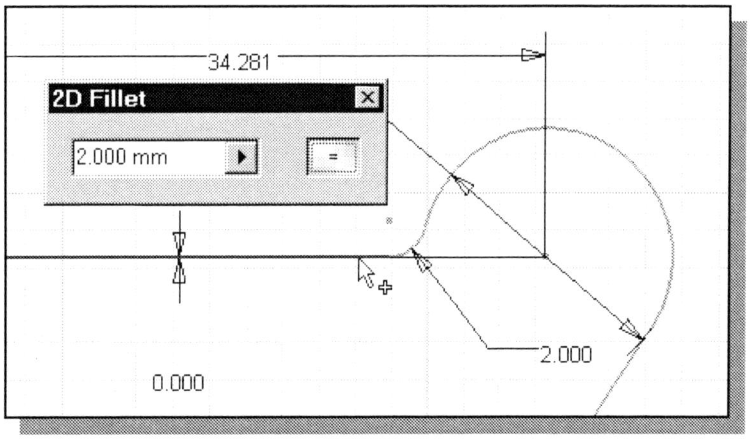

3. On your own, create the additional fillets as shown in the below figure.

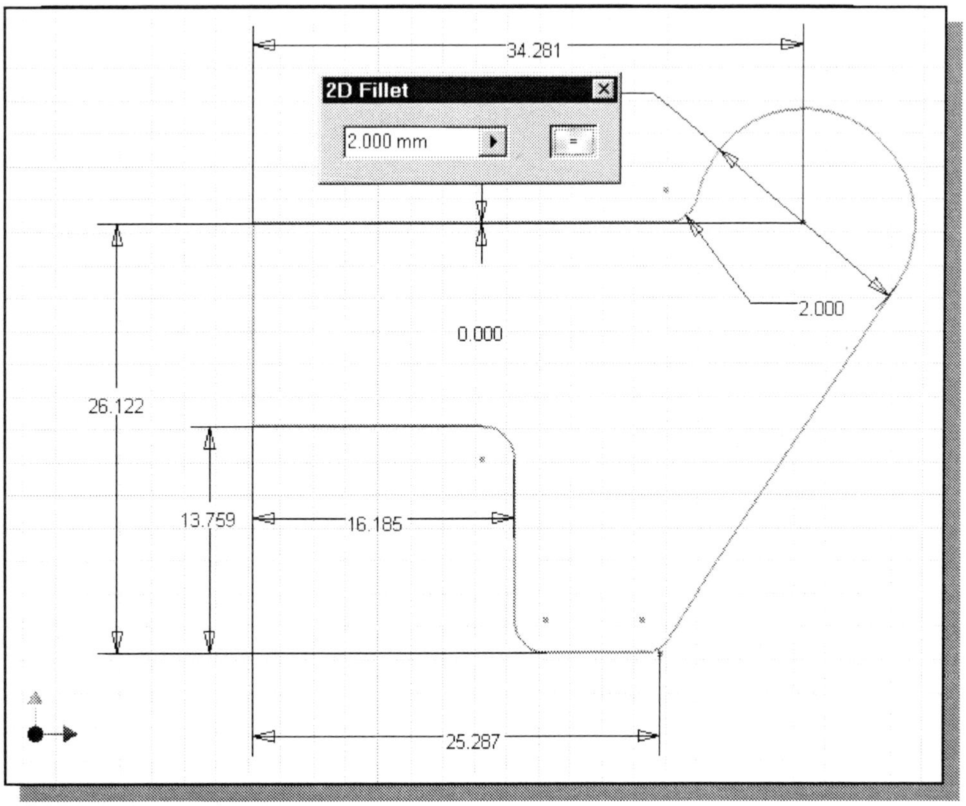

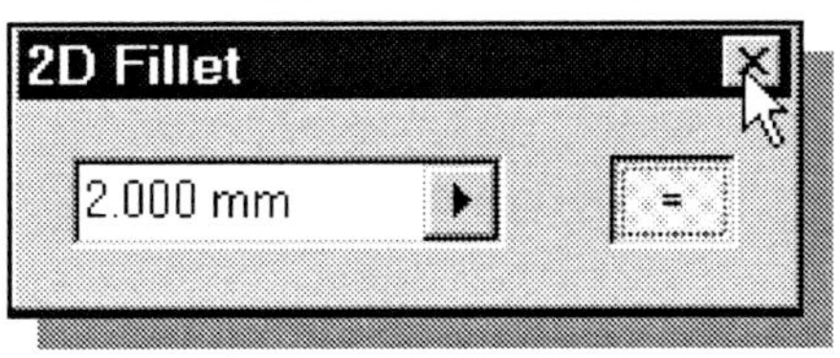

4. Click on the [**X**] icon to close the *2D Fillet* dialog box and end the *Fillet* command.

Adding a Fix constraint and Modify Dimensions

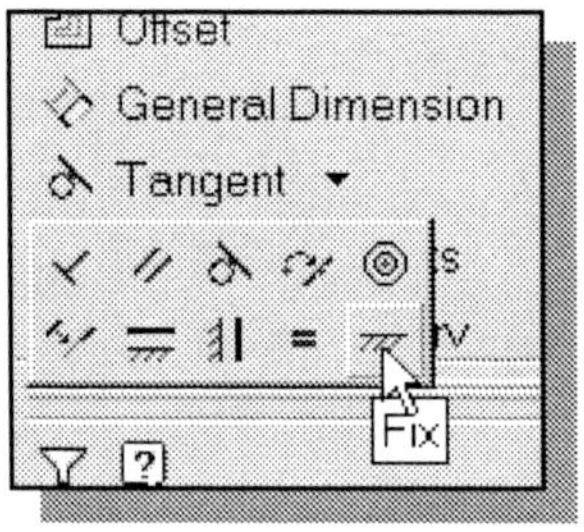

1. Click on the ***Fix*** constraint in the *Sketch* toolbar.

2. Apply the ***Fix*** constraint to the center of the arc as shown below.

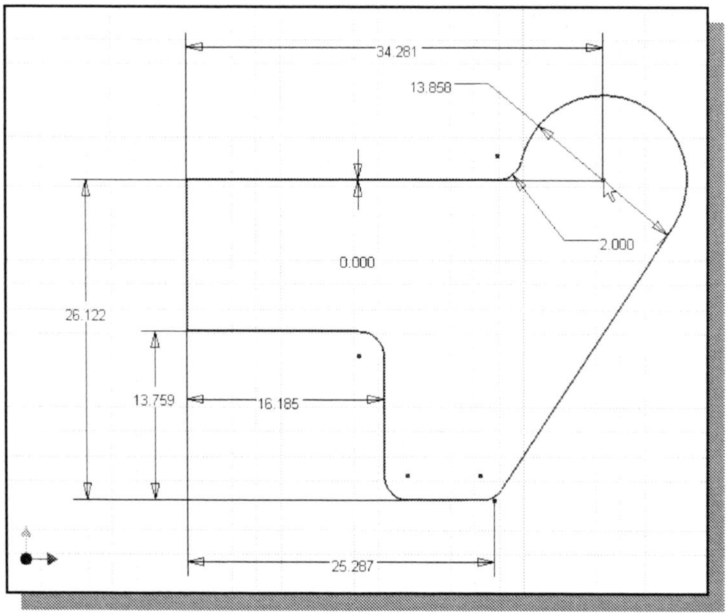

➢ Note that the color of the sketch turned **black** signifying the sketch is fully constrained.

3. On your own, change the dimensions to the desired values as shown below. (Hint: Change the larger values first.)

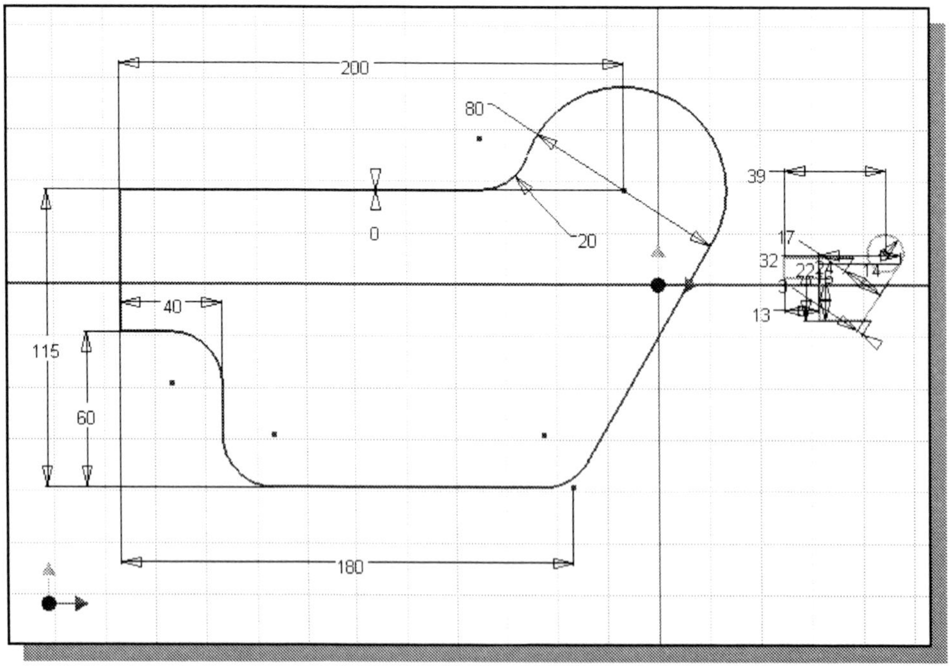

❖ Note that by applying proper constraints to the sketched geometry, a *constraint network* is created that assures the geometry shape behaves predictably as changes are made.

Removing the applied Auto Dimensions

➢ *Autodesk Inventor* remembers which dimensions are specified by the user and which are calculated by the system. The ***Auto Dimension*** command can also be used to confirm the created sketch is fully constrained.

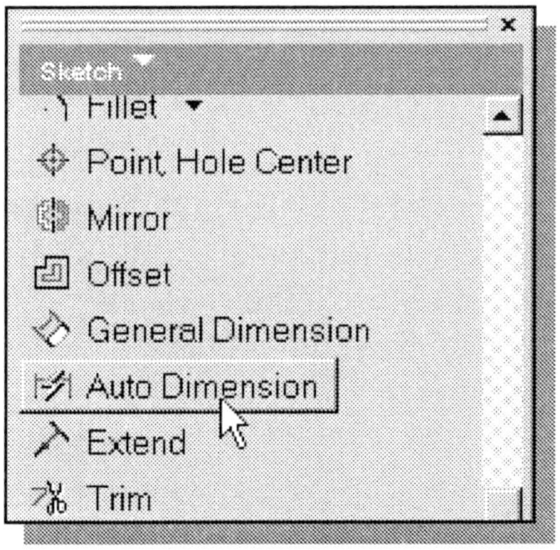

1. Click on the ***Auto Dimension*** icon in the *Sketch* toolbar.

➢ Note that **two** additional dimensions are still required to fully constrain the sketches as shown in the dialog box. The two dimensions are the location dimensions for the sketch to the right, which we will be modifying in the following section.

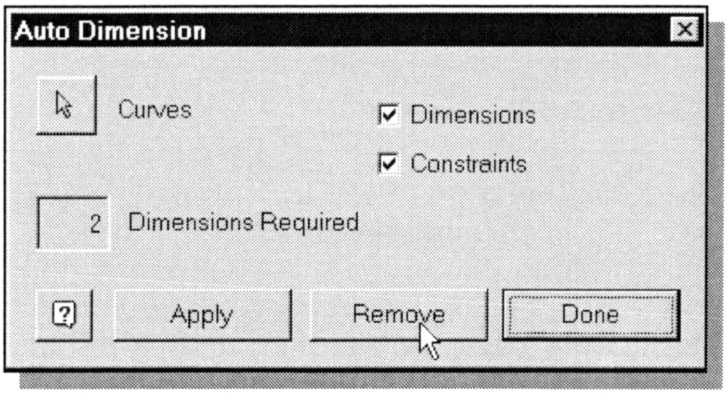

2. Click on the **Remove** button to proceed with the removal of the dimensions calculated by the system.

➢ Note that the system removes only those dimensions that were calculated; all of the dimensions that we created are maintained correctly as shown.

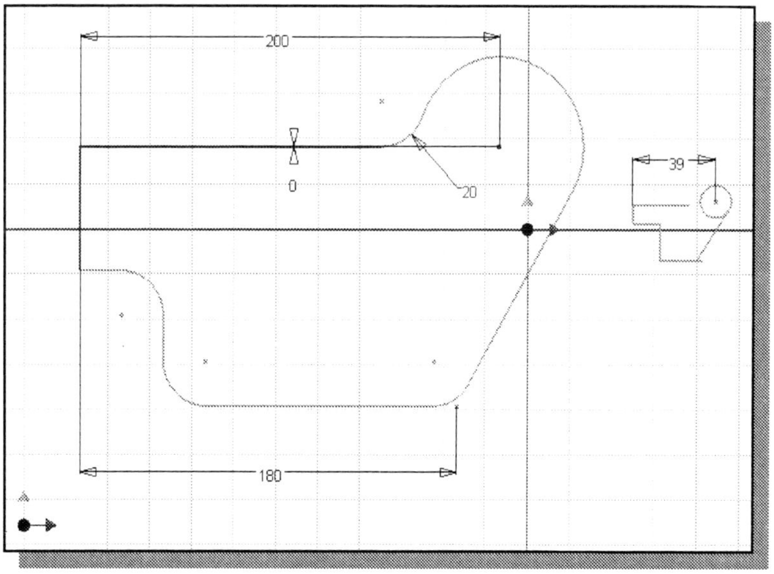

3. Click on the **Done** button to end the *Auto Dimension* command.

Working on the second copy

➢ We will next work on the second copy of the sketched geometry using a slightly different approach.

1. On your own, use a selection window and drag the second copy of the sketched geometry toward the right side of the graphics window.

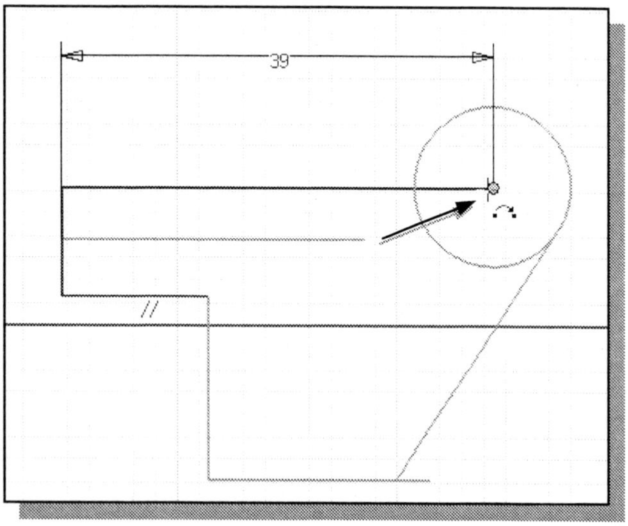

2. Click and drag the **right endpoint** of the top horizontal line to align to the center of the circle as shown. Note the displayed constraint.

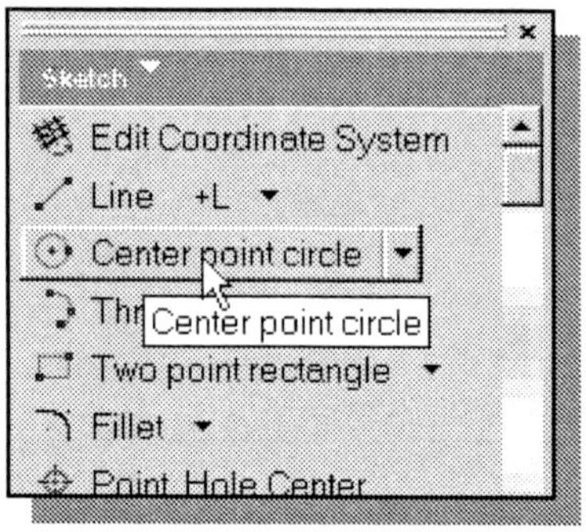

3. Select the ***Center point circle*** command by clicking once with the left-mouse-button on the icon in the *Sketch* toolbar.

4. On your own, create four circles of arbitrary sizes at the locations as shown in the figure below.

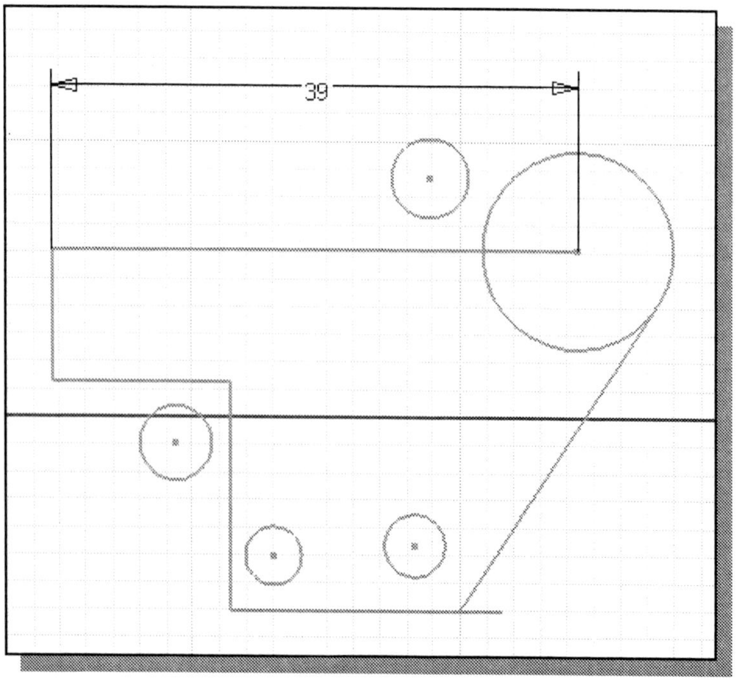

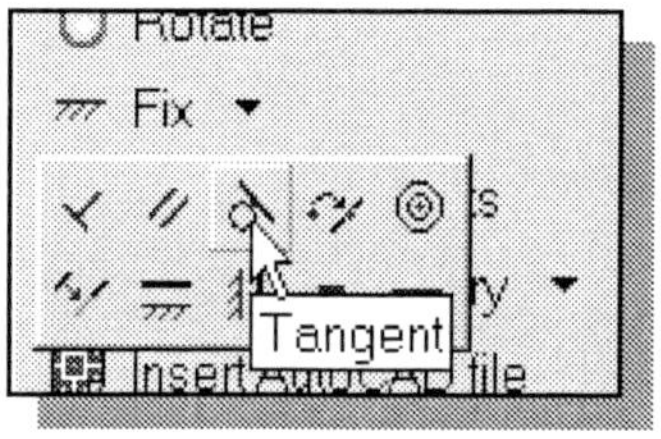

5. On your own, apply the ***Tangent*** constraint to the circles and the adjacent lines as shown below.

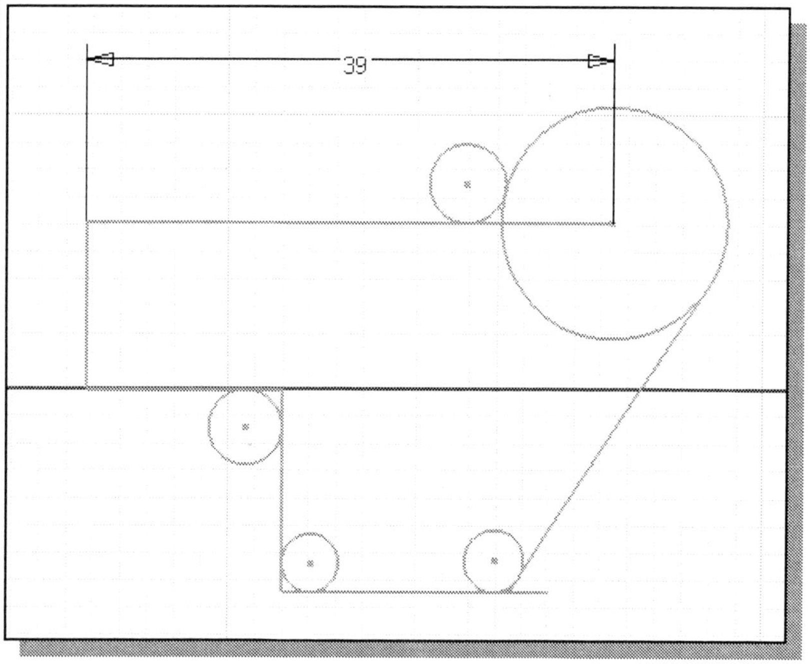

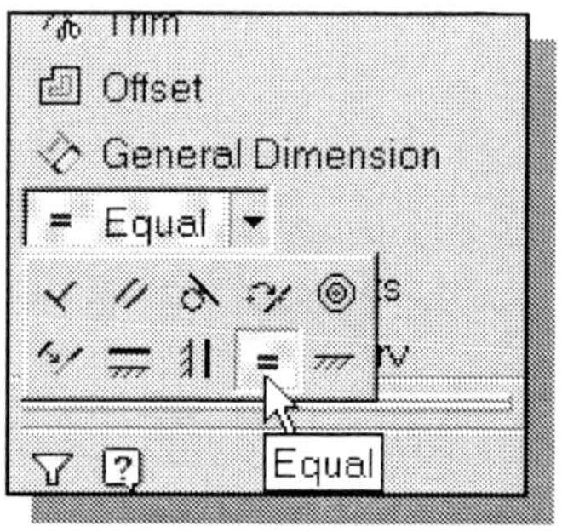

6. On your own, apply the ***Equal*** constraint to the four circles so that they are of the same size.

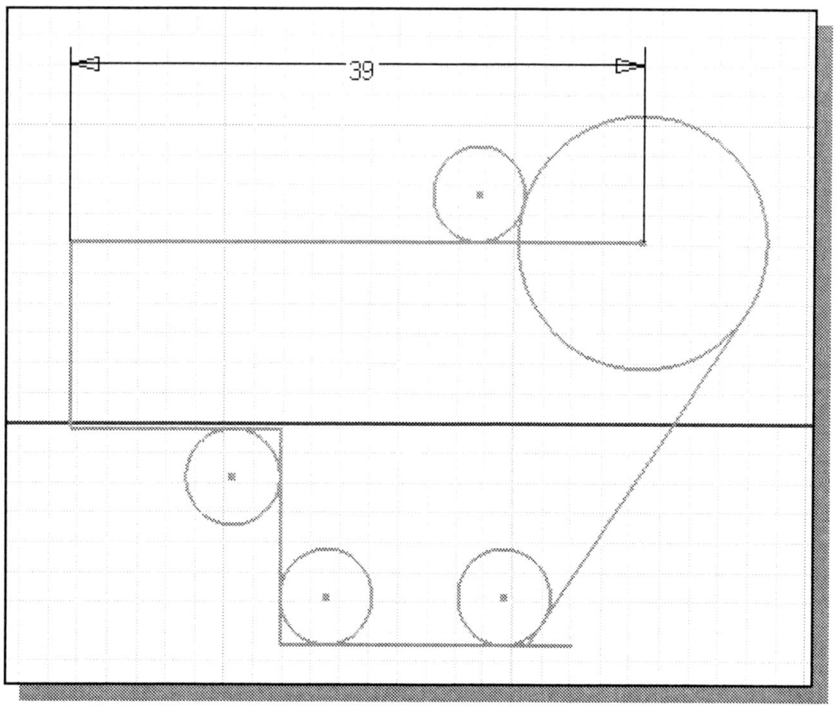

Adding a *Fix* constraint and Dimensions

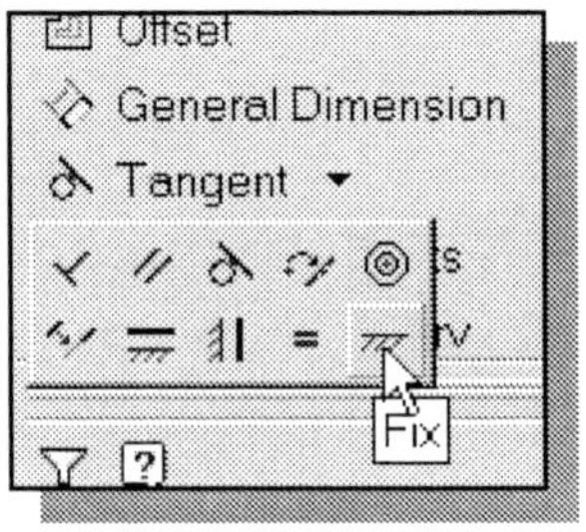

1. Click on the ***Fix*** constraint in the *Sketch* toolbar.

2. Apply the *Fix* constraint to the top left corner as shown below.

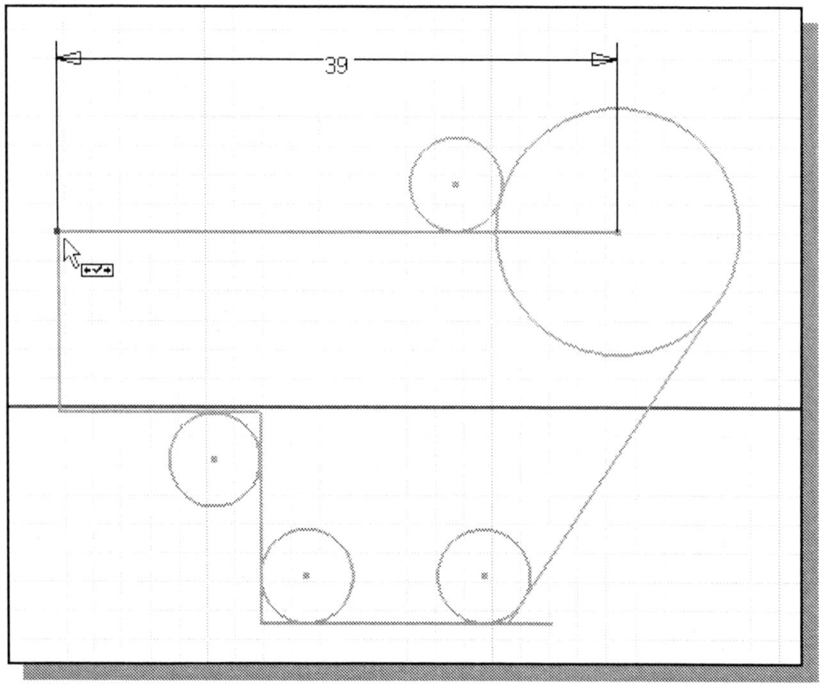

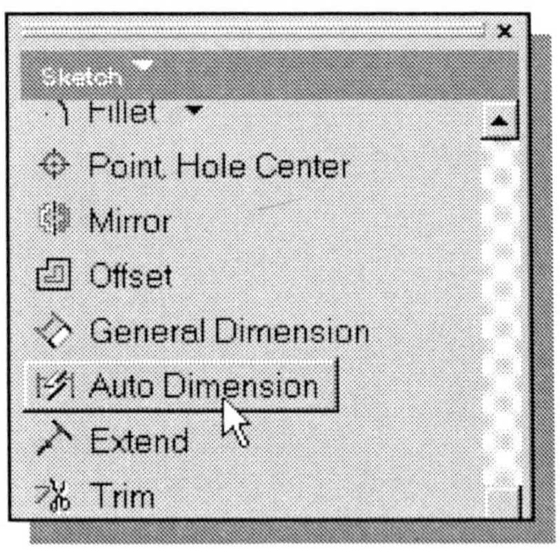

3. Click on the ***Auto Dimension*** icon in the *Sketch* toolbar.

4. The *Auto Dimension* dialog box appears on the screen. Confirm that the *Dimensions* and *Constraints* options are switched *ON* as shown.

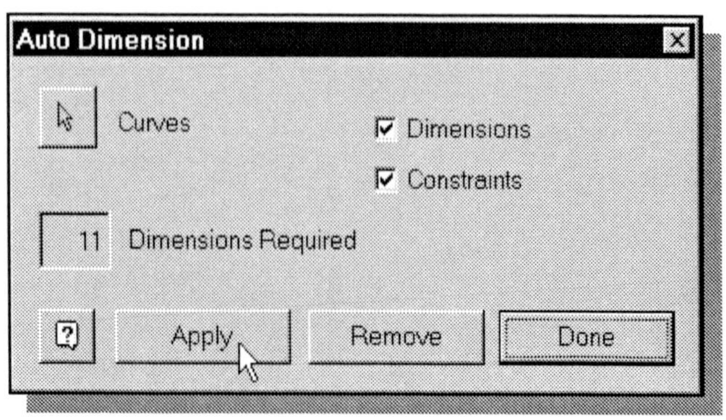

5. Click on the **Apply** button to proceed with *the Auto Dimension* command.

6. Click on the **Done** button to accept the created dimensions.

➢ On you own, reposition the displayed dimensions, by click and drag with the left-mouse-button, so that the dimensions can be more easily identified. Add/delete dimensions so that the sketch appears as shown in the below figure.

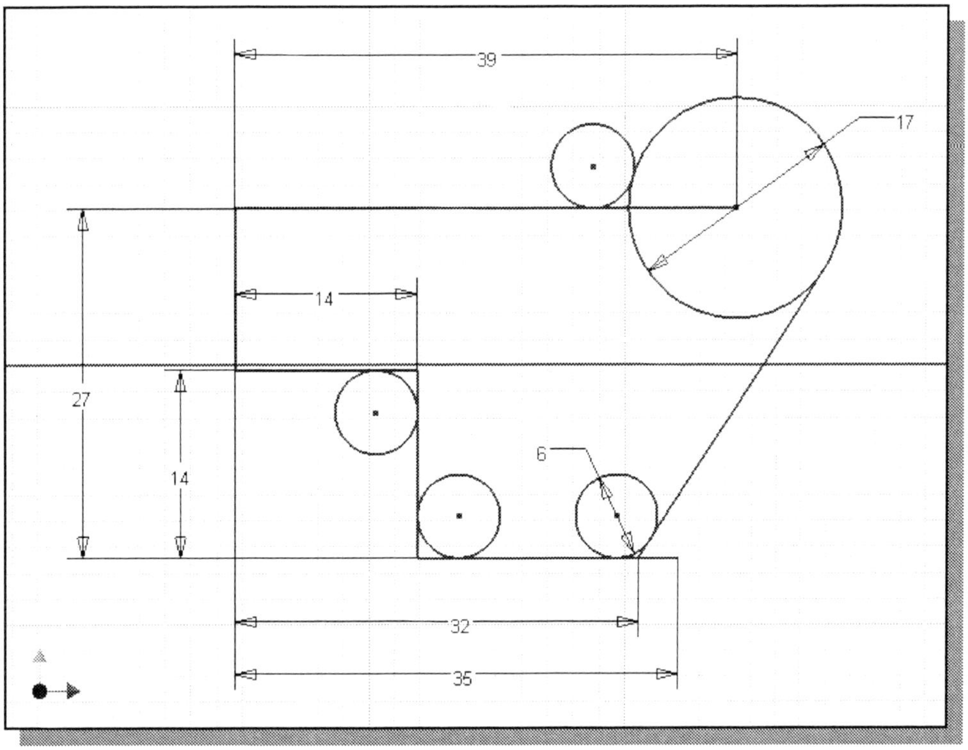

7. On your own, change the dimensions to the desired values as shown below. (Hint: Change the larger values first.)

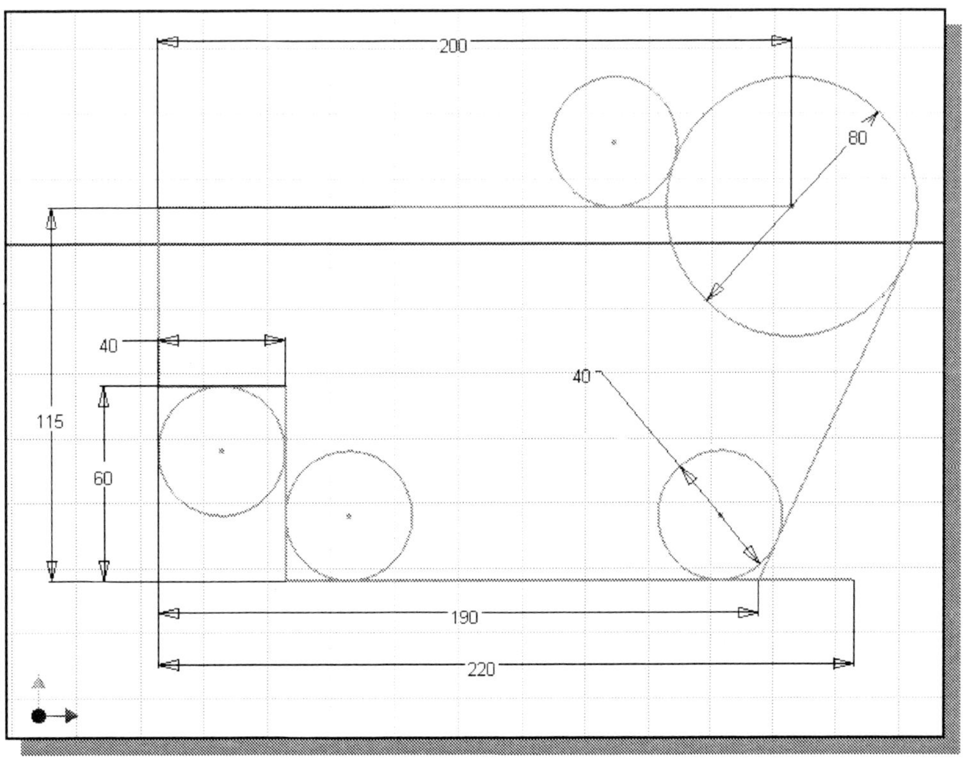

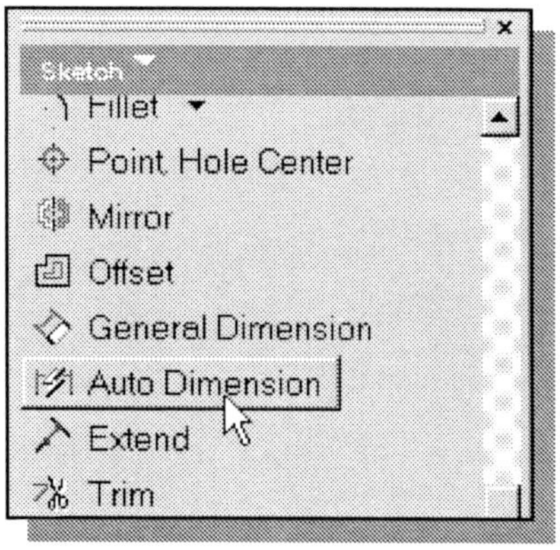

8. On your own, use the ***Auto Dimension*** command to confirm the sketches are fully constrained.

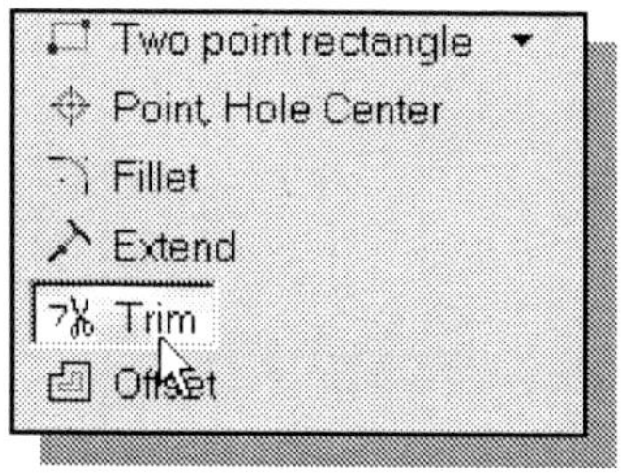

9. Click on the *Trim* command in the *Sketch* toolbar.

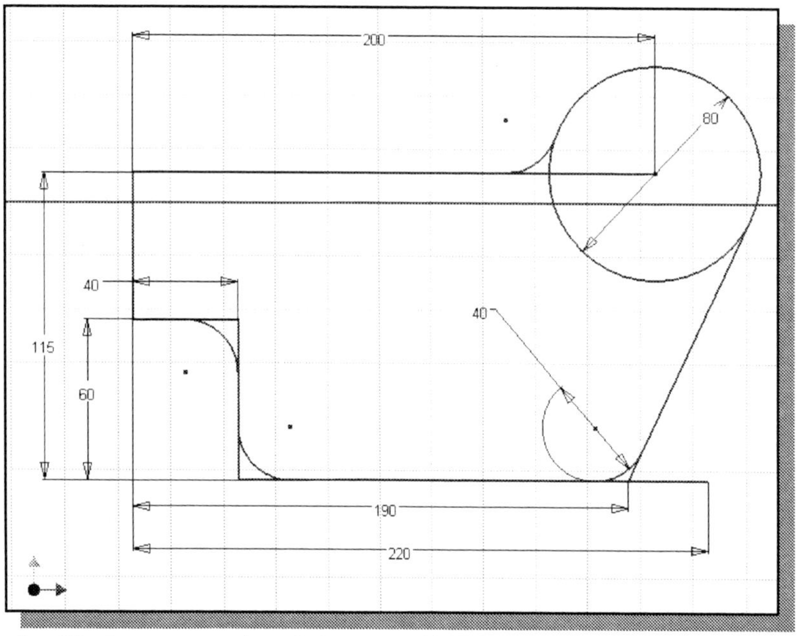

10. On your own, trim the circles as shown. We will intentionally leave the large circle intact.

❖ We have completed the two slightly different sketches and are ready to create solid features from the sketches. At first glance, it may appear that the sketch on the right still requires some editing since it contains extra geometry. In the following sections, it is shown that both sketches can be used to create the same solid feature.

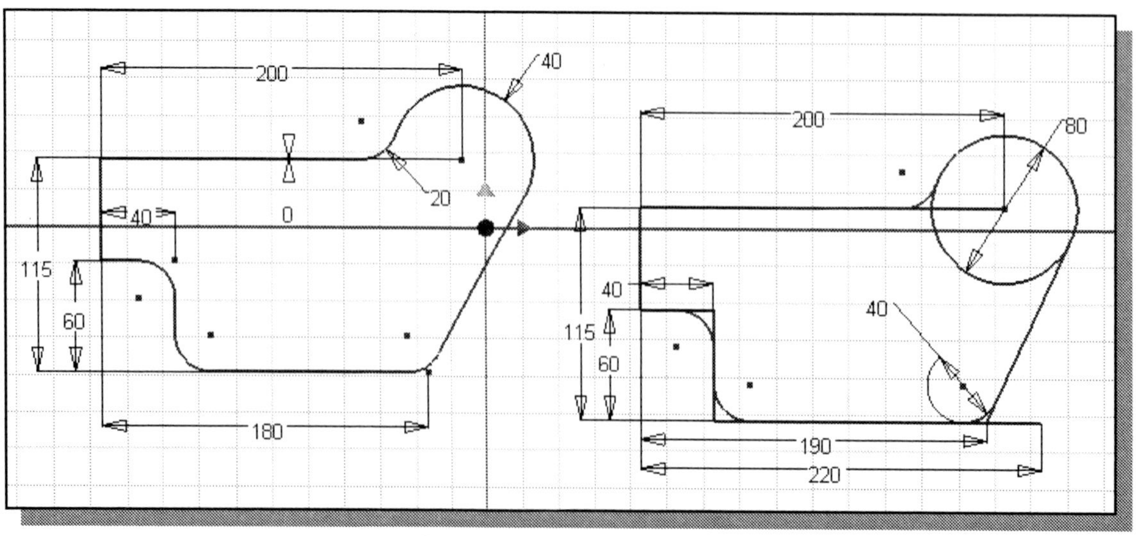

Profile Sketches

❖ In *Autodesk Inventor*, ***profiles*** are closed regions that are defined from sketches. Profiles are used as cross sections to create solid features. For example, ***Extrude***, ***Revolve***, ***Sweep***, ***Loft***, and ***Coil*** operations all require the definition of at least a single profile. The sketches used to define a profile can contain additional geometry since the additional geometry entities are consumed when the feature is created. To create a profile we can create single or multiple closed regions, or we can select existing solid edges to form closed regions. A profile cannot contain self-intersecting geometry; regions selected in a single operation form a single profile. As a general rule, we should dimension and constrain profiles to prevent them from unpredictable size and shape changes. *Autodesk Inventor* does allow us to create under-constrained or non-constrained profiles; the dimensions and/or constraints can be added/edited later.

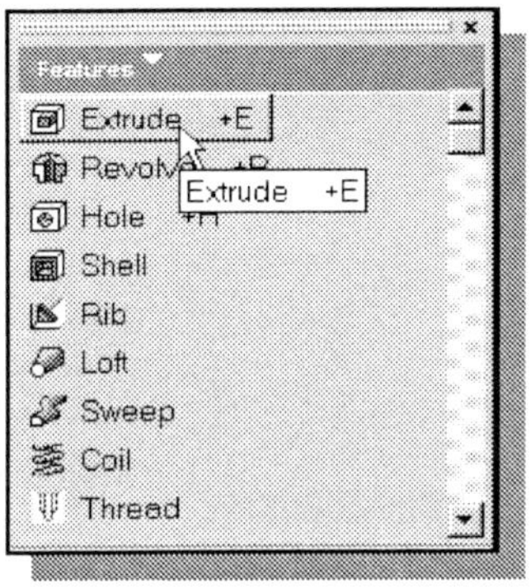

1. In the *Feature* toolbar, select the ***Extrude*** command by left-mouse-clicking once on the icon.

2. Select the inside region of the left sketch to define the profile of the extrusion.

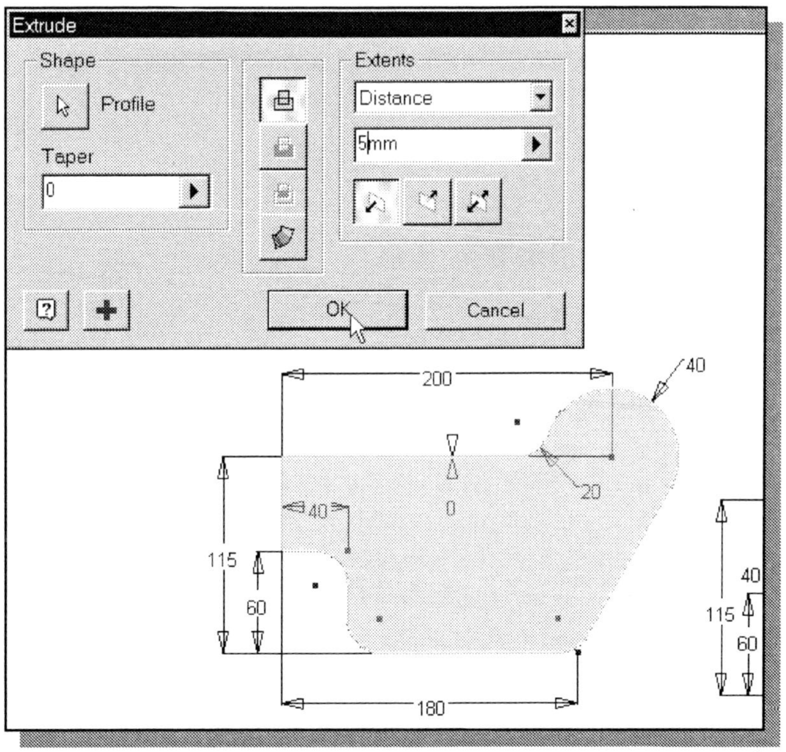

❖ *Autodesk Inventor* automatically highlights the selected closed region and the defining geometry, which forms the profile required for the operation.

3. In the *Extrude* dialog box, enter **5 mm** as the extrusion distance as shown.

4. Click on the **OK** button to accept the settings and create the solid feature.

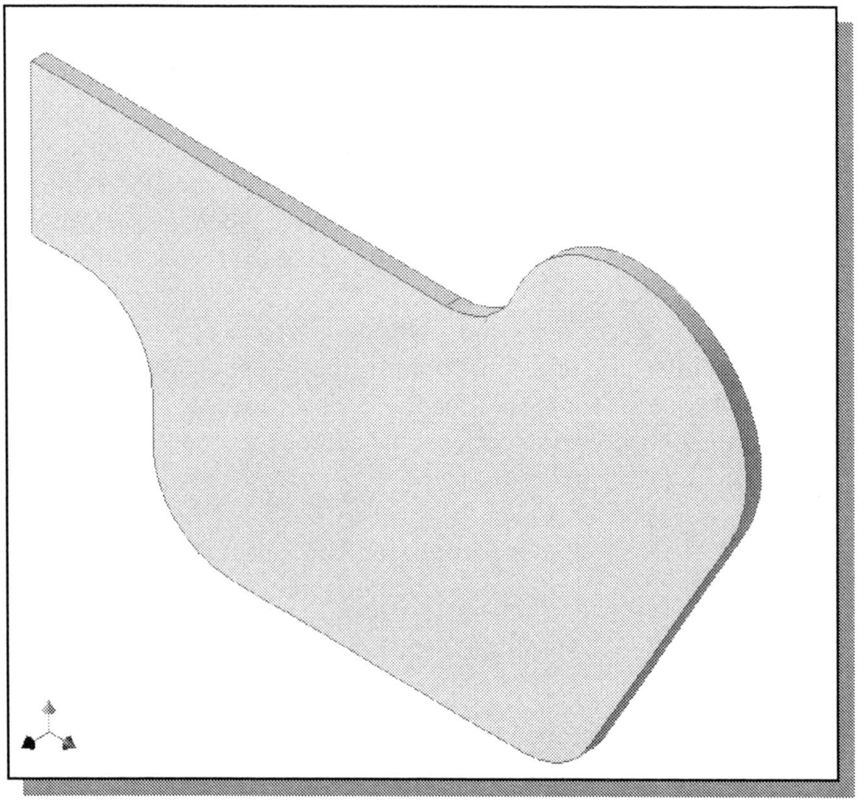

❖ Note that all the sketched geometry entities are consumed and have disappeared from the screen when the feature is created.

Redefining the Profile

- Engineering designs usually go through many revisions and changes. *Autodesk Inventor* provides an assortment of tools to handle design changes quickly and effectively. We will demonstrate some of the tools available by changing the base feature of the design. The profile used to create the extrusion is selected from the sketched geometry entities. In *Autodesk Inventor*, any profile can be edited and/or redefined at any time. It is this type of functionality in parametric solid modeling software that provides designers with greater flexibility and ease to experiment with different design considerations.

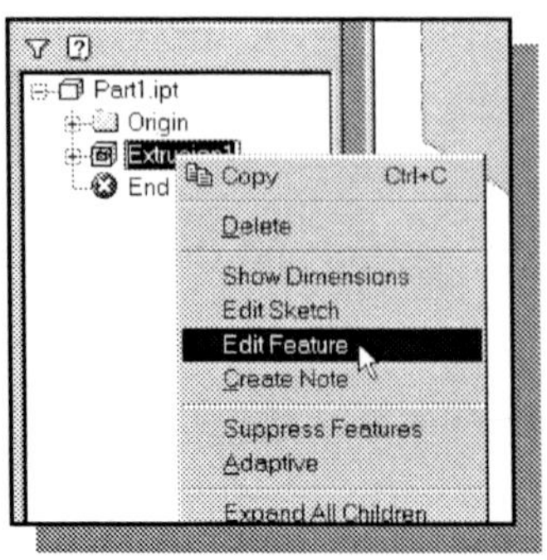

1. In the *Browser*, right-mouse-click once on the *Extrusion1* feature to bring up the option menu, and then pick **Edit Feature** in the pop-up menu.

❖ *Autodesk Inventor* will now display the original 2D sketch of the selected feature in the graphics window. We have literally gone back in time to the point where we first created the 2D sketch. Notice the feature being modified is also highlighted in the *Part Browser*.

2. Click on the ***Look At*** icon in the *Standard* toolbar area.

- The ***Look At*** command automatically aligns the *sketch plane* of a selected entity to the screen.

3. Select any line segement of the 2D sketch.

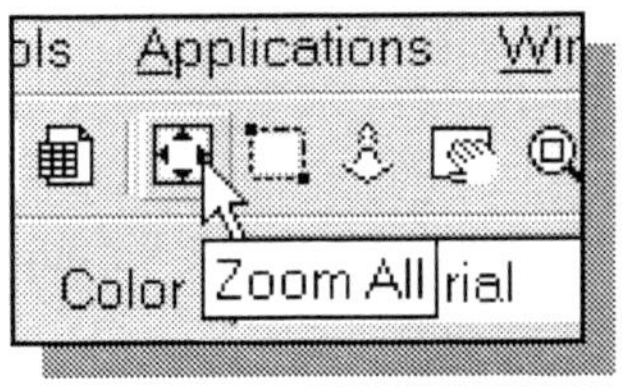

4. Click on the ***Zoom All*** icon in the *Standard* toolbar.

➢ We have literally gone back in time to the point where we first defined the 2D profile.

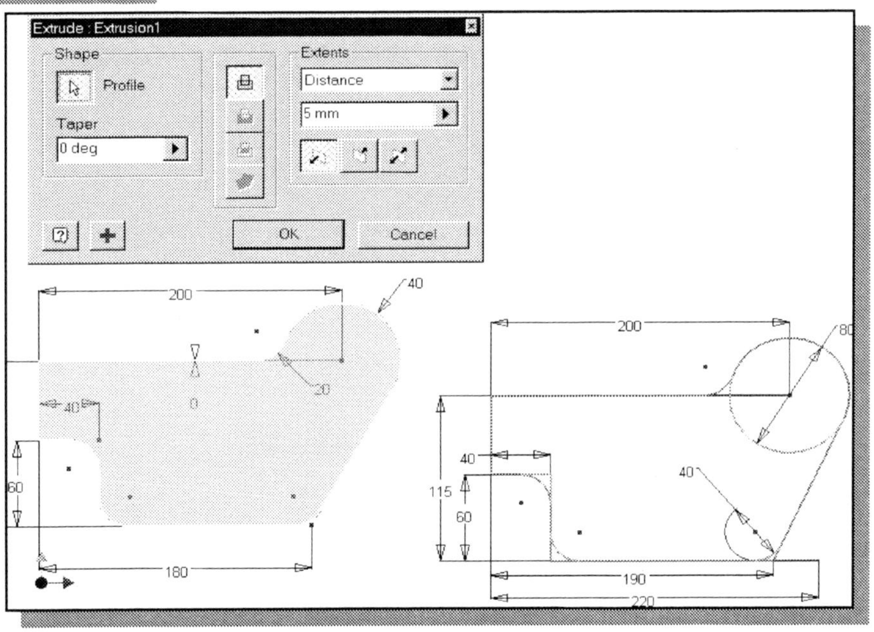

5. In the *Extrude* dialog box, click on the **Profile** button to edit/redefine 2D profile.

6. The geometry entities used to define the profile are highlighted as shown in the above figure. To deselect, move the cursor inside the highlighted region; press the [**Ctrl**] key and left-mouse-click once.

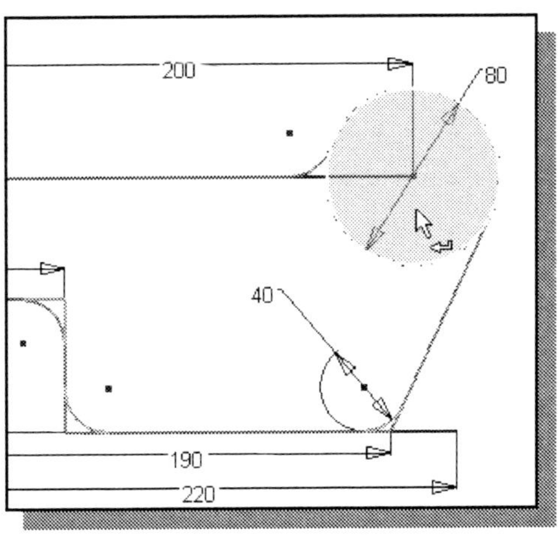

7. Click inside the circle of the sketch on the right side of the graphics window.

➢ *Autodesk Inventor* automatically selects the geometry entities that form a closed region to define the profile.

8. Click on the adjacent areas to complete the profile definition as shown in the below figure.

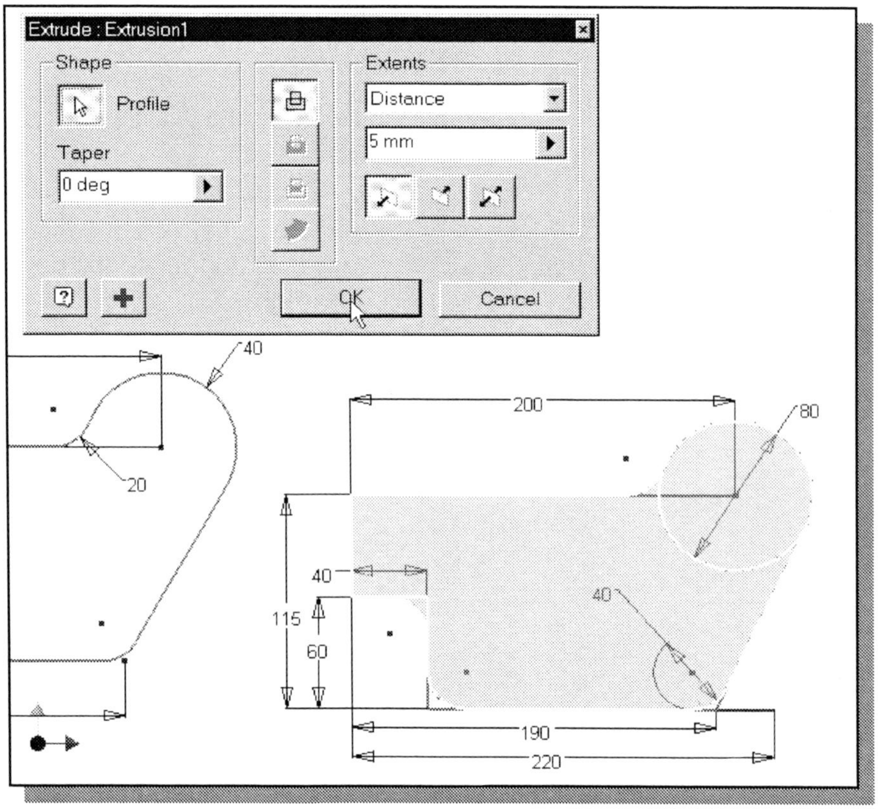

9. In the *Extrude* dialog box, click on the **OK** button to accept the settings and update the solid feature.

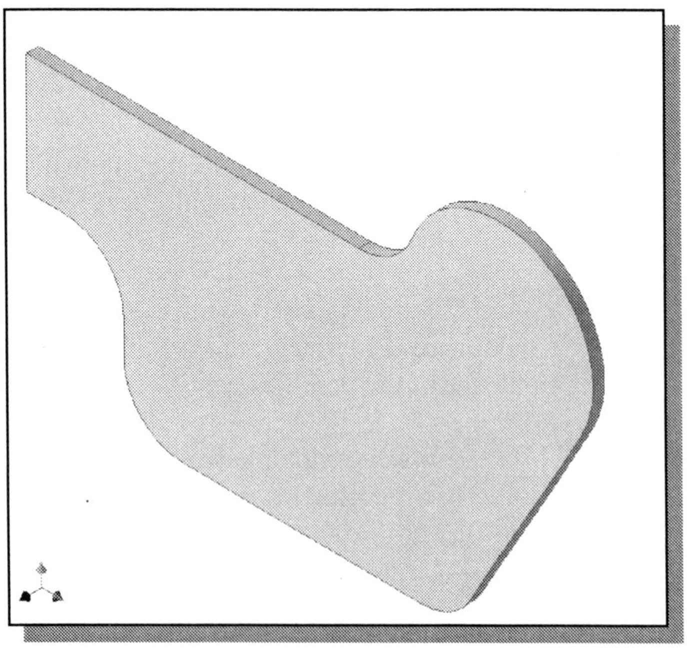

- The feature is recreated using the second copy of the sketched geometry. The profile is created with extra wireframe entities by selecting multiple regions. The extra geometry entities, such as the line segment at the bottom right corner, can be used as construction geometry to help in defining the profile. This approach encourages engineering content over drafting technique, which is one of the key features of *Autodesk Inventor* over other solid modeling software.

Create an OFFSET Cut Feature

➢ To complete the design, we will create a cutout feature by using the *Offset* command. First we will set up the sketching plane to align with the front face of the 3D model.

1. In the *Standard* toolbar select the ***Sketch*** command by left-clicking once on the icon.

2. In the *Status Bar* area, the message: "*Select face, workplane, sketch or sketch geometry.*" is displayed. Select the front face of the 3D model in the graphics window.

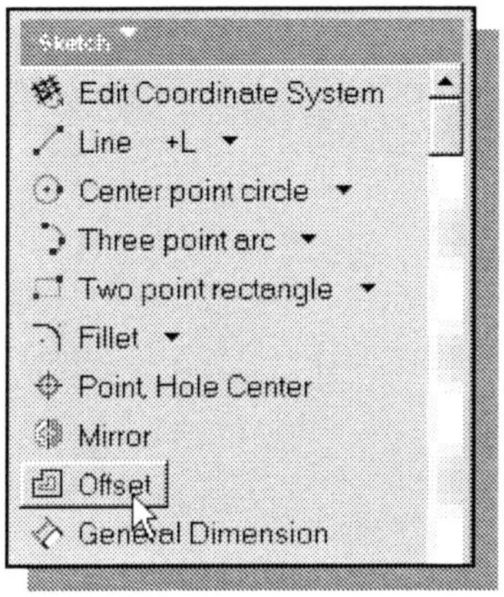

3. Click on the ***Offset*** icon in the *Sketch* toolbar.

4. Select any edge of the front face of the 3D model. *Autodesk Inventor* will automatically select all of the connecting geometry to form a closed region.

5. Move the cursor toward the center of the selected region and notice an offset copy of the outline is displayed.

6. Left-mouse-click once to create the offset profile as shown.

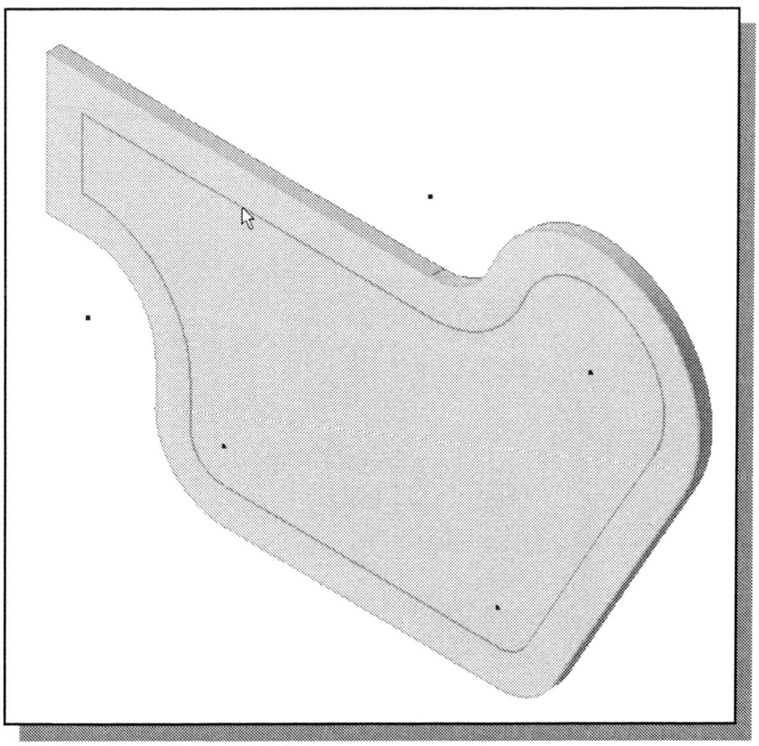

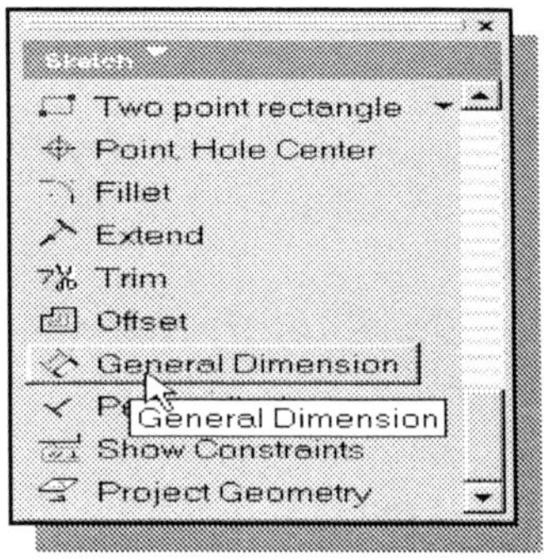

7. On your own, use the ***General Dimension*** command to create the offset dimension as shown in the below figure.

8. Modify the offset dimension to **15 mm** as shown in the figure.

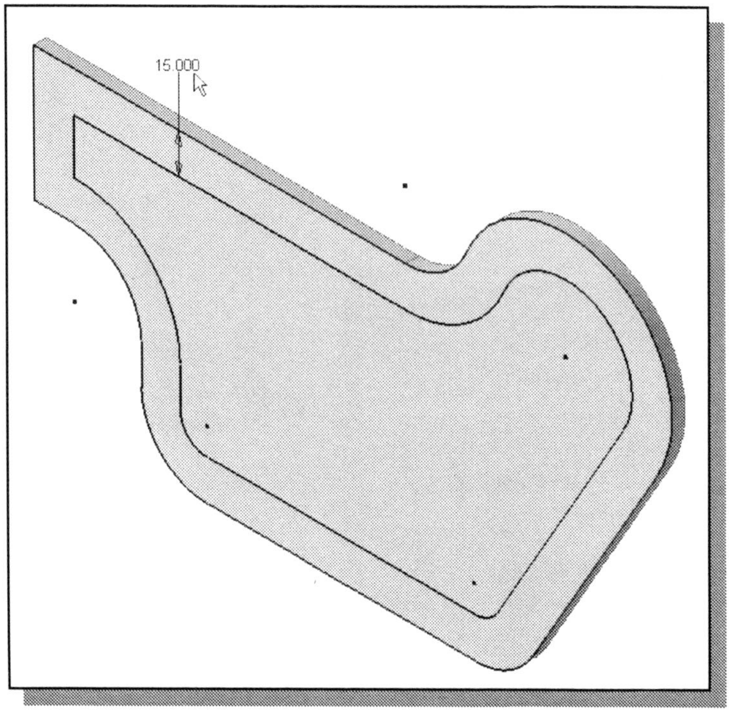

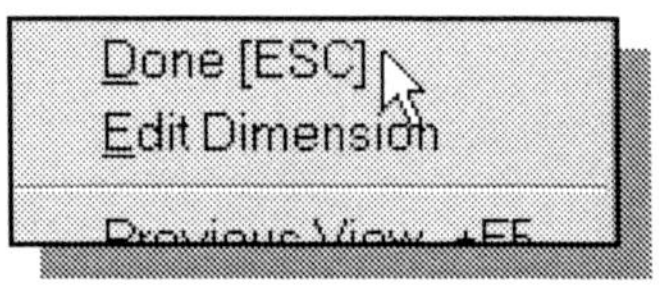

9. Inside the graphics window, click once with the right-mouse-button to display the option menu. Select **Done** in the popup menu to end the *General Dimension* command.

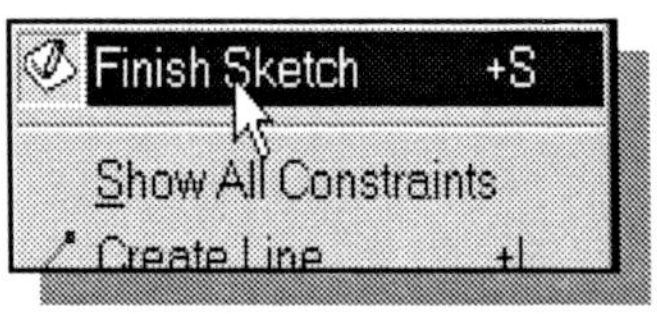

10. Inside the graphics window, click once with the right-mouse-button to display the option menu. Select **Finish Sketch** in the popup menu to end the *Sketch* option.

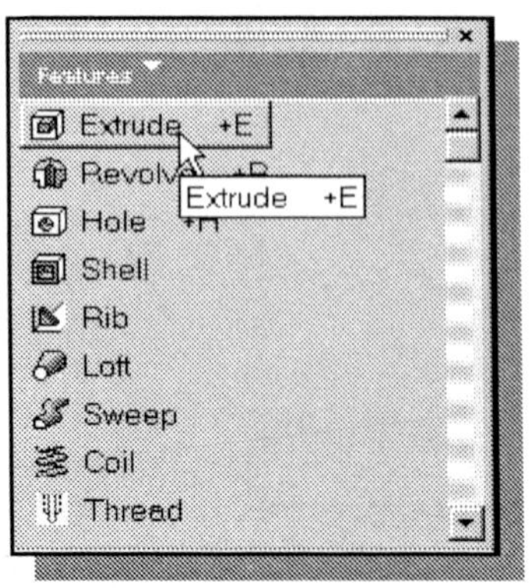

11. In the *Feature* toolbar (the toolbar that is located to the left side of the graphics window), select the ***Extrude*** command by releasing the left-mouse-button on the icon.

12. Select the inside region of the offset geometry as the profile of the extrusion.

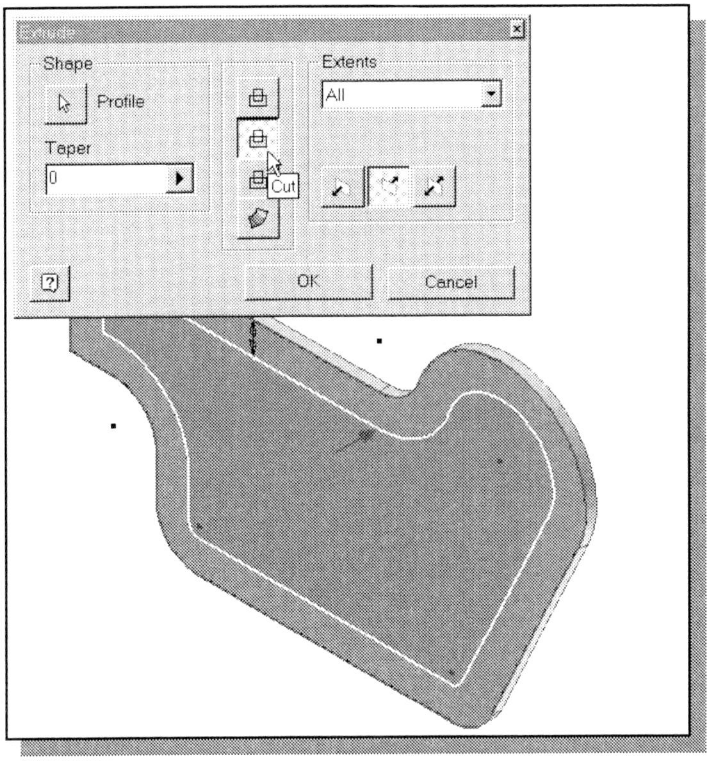

13. Inside the *Extrude* dialog box, select the ***Cut*** operation, set the *Extents* to ***All*** and set the direction of the cutout as shown in the below figure.

14. In the *Extrude* dialog box, click on the **OK** button to accept the settings and create the solid feature.

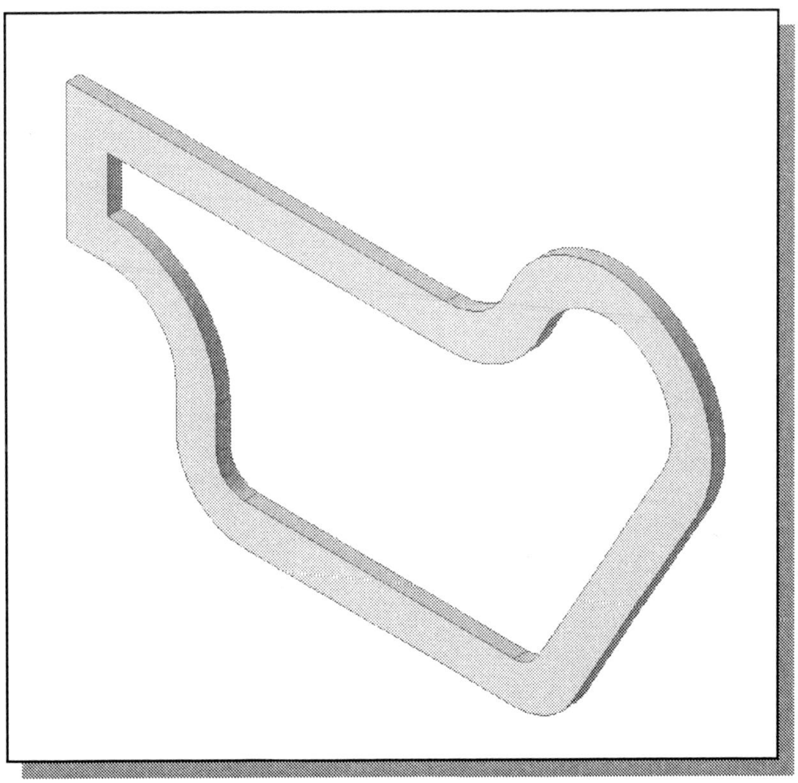

➢ The offset geometry is associated with the original geometry. On your own, adjust the overall height of the design to **150** millimeters and confirm that the offset geometry is adjusted accordingly.

Questions:

1. What are the two types of wireframe geometry available in *Autodesk Inventor*?

2. Can we create a profile with extra 2D geometry entities?

3. How do we access the *Autodesk Inventor's* **Edit Sketch** option?

4. How do we create a *profile*?

5. Can we build a profile that consists of self-intersecting curves?

6. Describe the procedure to create a copy of a sketched 2D wireframe geometry?

7. Identify and briefly describe the following commands:

(a)

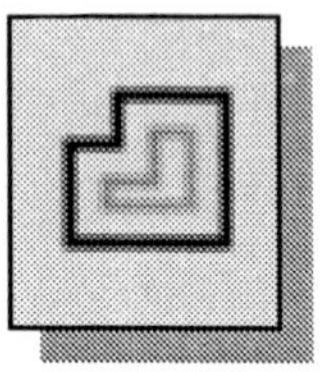

(b)

(c)

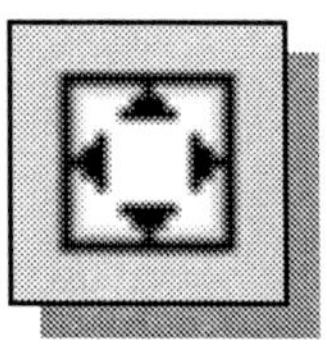

(d)

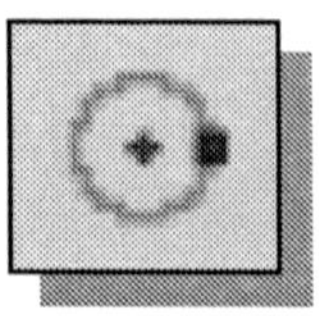

Exercises:

1.

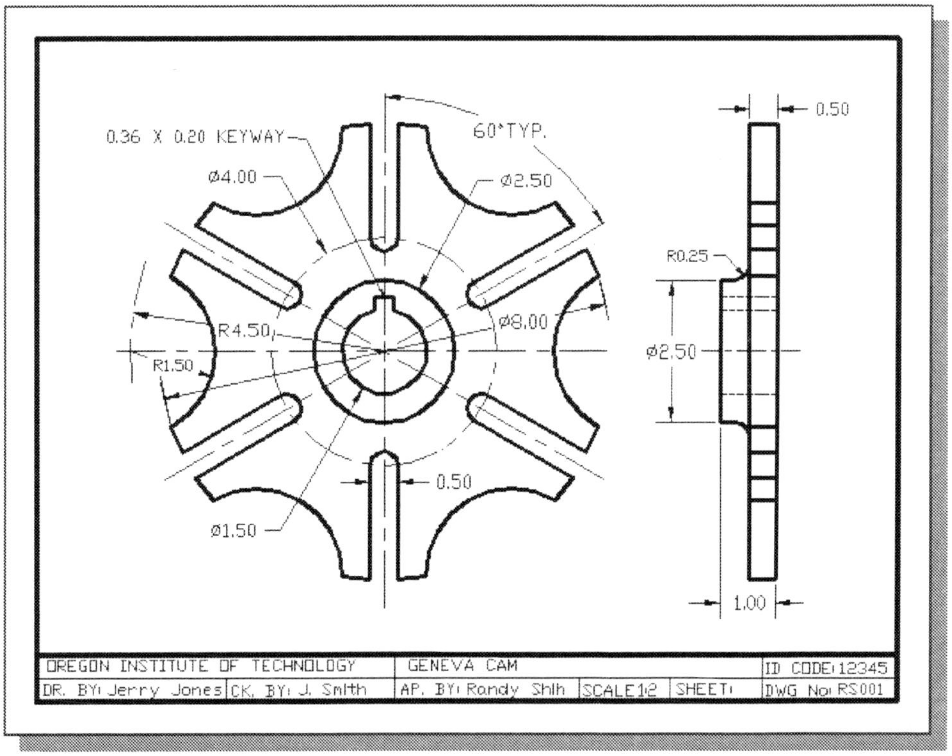

2. Plate Thickness: 0.25

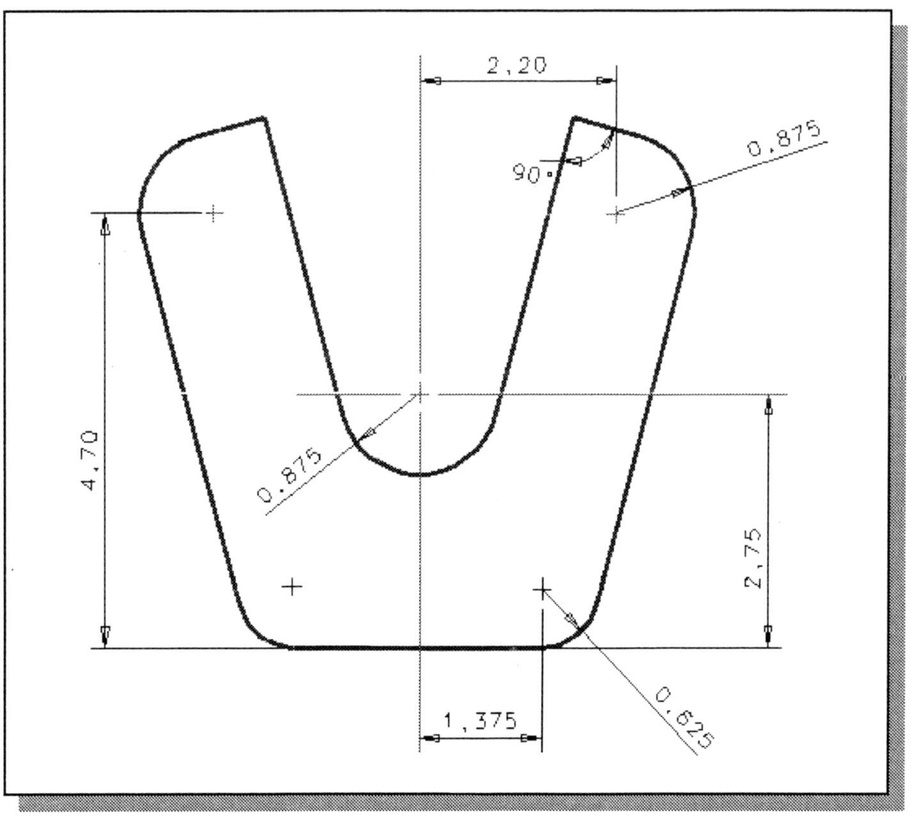

NOTES:

Lesson 9
Parent/Child Relationships

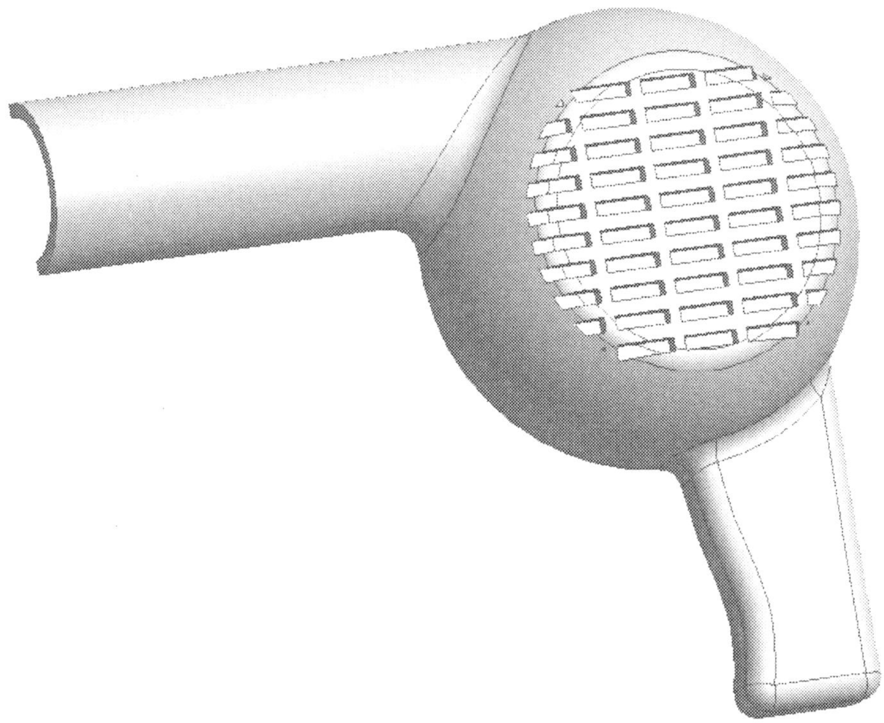

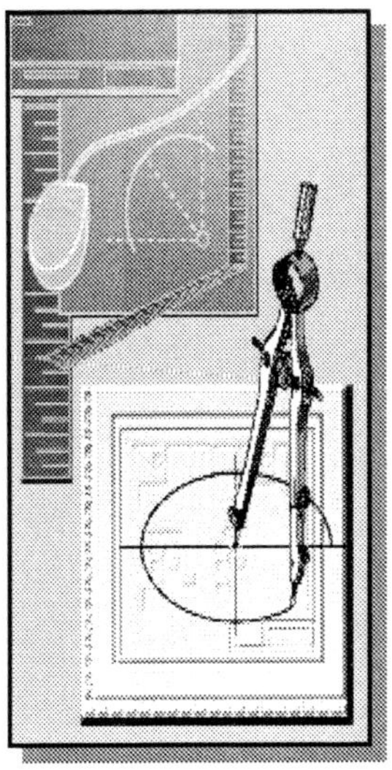

Learning Objectives

When you have completed this lesson, you will be able to:

- ♦ Understand the Parent/Child relations between features.
- ♦ Create Swept Features.
- ♦ Setup Multiple Work planes.
- ♦ Create Lofted Features.
- ♦ Use the Shell Command.
- ♦ Create 3D Rounds & Fillets.

Introduction

The Parent/Child relationship is one of the most powerful aspects of ***parametric modeling***. In *Autodesk Inventor*, each time a new modeling event is created, previously defined features can be used to define information such as size, location, and orientation. The referenced features become **PARENT** features to the new feature, and the new feature is called the **CHILD** feature. The parent/child relationships determine how a model reacts when other features in the model change, thus capturing design intent. It is crucial to keep track of these parent/child relationships. Any modification to a parent feature can change one or more of its children. As one might expect, parent/child relationships can become quite complicated when the features begin to accumulate. It is therefore important to think about modeling strategy before we start to create anything. The main consideration is to try to plan ahead for all possible design changes that might occur which would be affected by the existing parent/child relationships.

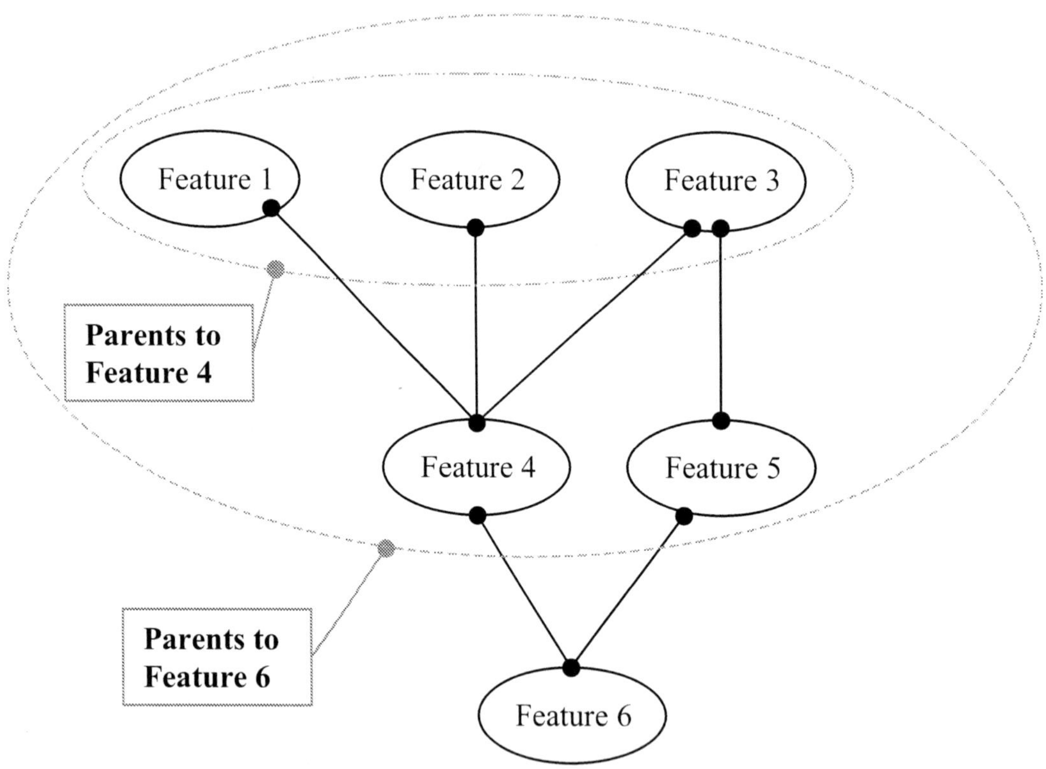

The parent/child relationships can be created *implicitly* or *explicitly*. Implicit relationships are implied by the feature creation method, and explicit relationships are entered manually by the user. In the previous lessons, we have been using implicit parent/child relationships. For example, before creating a 2D sketch in the *Autodesk Inventor Part Mode*, we select a sketching plane. The selected sketching plane became the parent of the new feature. If the sketching plane is moved, the child feature will move with it.

Three-dimensional construction tools

Autodesk Inventor provides an assortment of three-dimensional construction tools to make the creation of solid models easier and more efficient. As demonstrated in the previous lessons, creating **extruded** features and **revolved** features are the two most common methods used to create 3D models. In this next example, we will examine the procedures for using the ***Sweep*** command, the ***Loft*** command, and the ***Shell*** command, and also for creating **3D rounds** and **fillets** along the edges of a solid model. These types of features are common characteristics of molded parts.

The ***Sweep*** option is defined as moving a cross-section through a path in space to form a three-dimensional object. To define a sweep in *Autodesk Inventor*, we define two sections: the trajectory and the cross-section.

The ***Loft*** command allows us to blend multiple profiles with varying shapes on separate planes to create complex shapes. Profiles are usually on parallel planes, but non-perpendicular planes can also be used. We can use as many profiles as we wish but, to avoid twisting the loft shape, we should map points on each profile that align along a straight vector.

The ***Shell*** option is defined as hollowing out the inside of a solid, leaving a shell of specified wall thickness.

A Thin-Walled Part: *Dryer Housing*

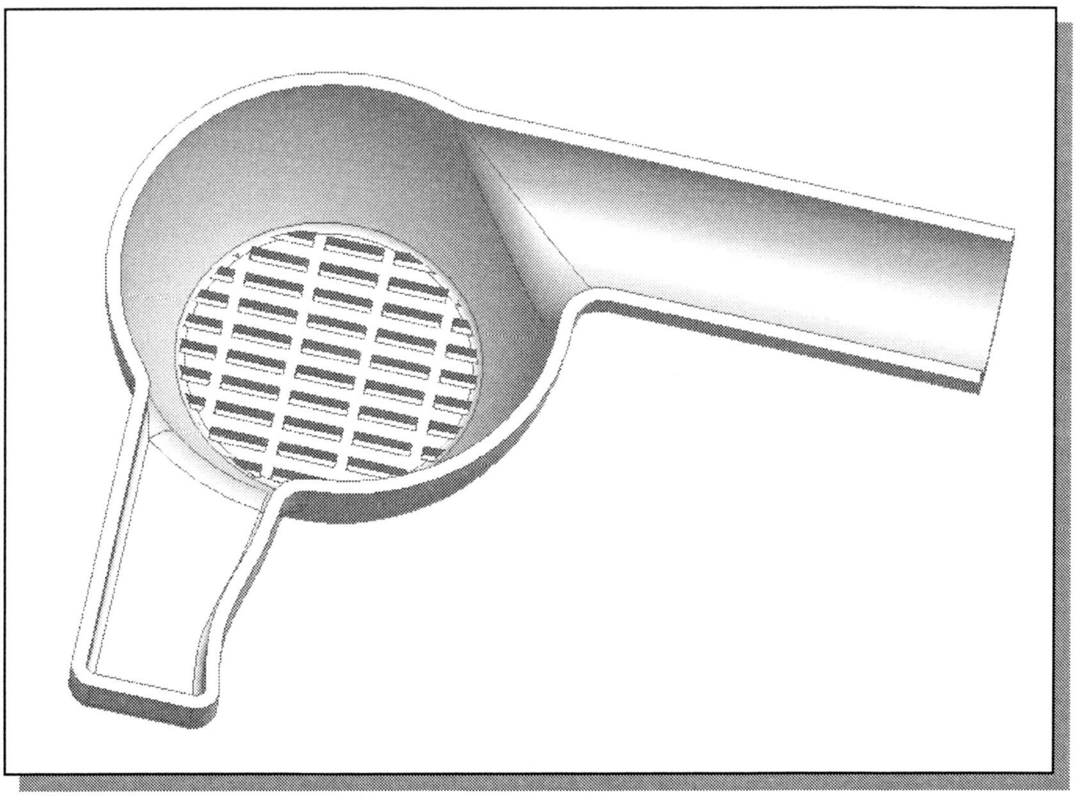

Modeling Strategy

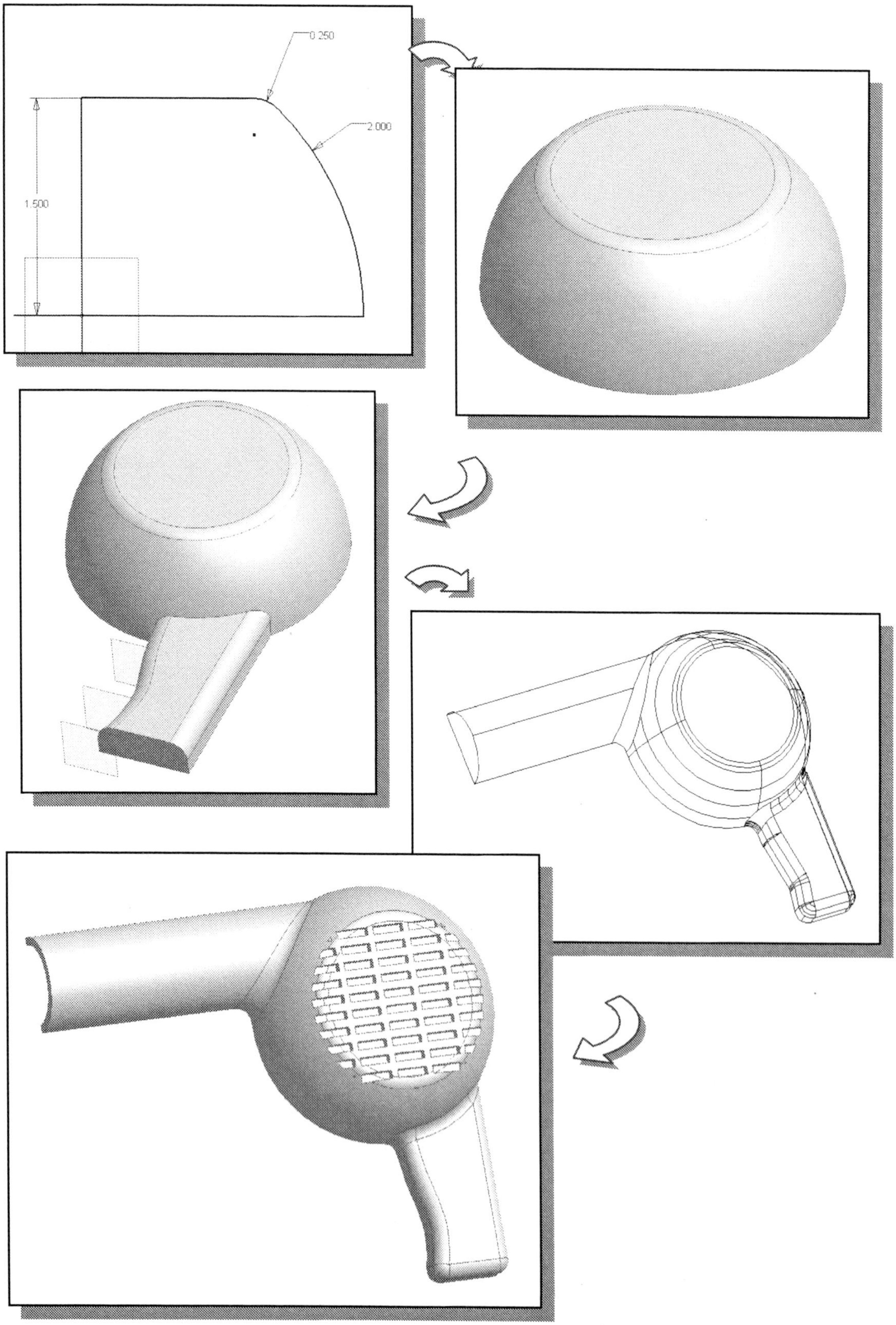

Starting Autodesk Inventor

1. Select the ***Autodesk Inventor*** option on the *Start* menu or select the ***Autodesk Inventor*** icon on the desktop to start *Autodesk Inventor*. The *Autodesk Inventor* main window will appear on the screen.

2. Once the program is loaded into the memory, the ***Startup*** dialog box appears at the center of the screen.

3. Select the ***New*** icon with a single click of the left-mouse-button in the *What to Do* dialog box.

4. Select the **English** tab and in the *New - Choose Template* area, select **Standard(in).ipt**.

5. Pick **OK** in the *Startup* dialog box to accept the selected settings.

Set up the display of the Sketch Plane

1. In the *Part Browser* window, click on the [+] symbol in front of the ***Origin*** feature to display more information on the feature.

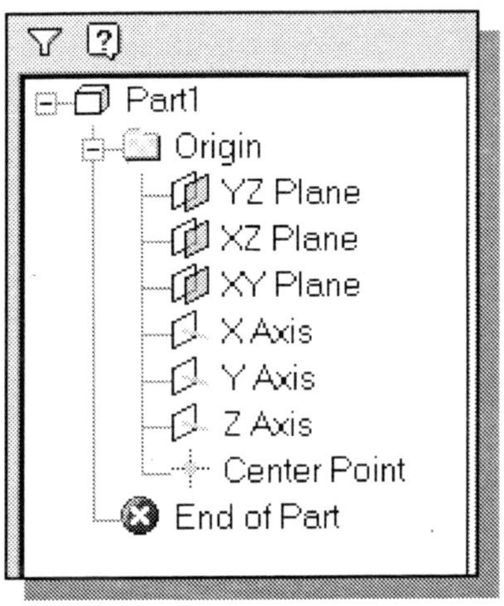

❖ In the *Browser* window, notice a new part name appeared with seven work features established. The seven work features include three *work-planes*, three *work-axes*, and a *work-point*. By default, the three work-planes and work-axes are aligned to the **world coordinate system** and the work-point is aligned to the *origin* of the **world coordinate system**.

2. Inside the *Browser* window, move the cursor on top of the third work-plane, ***XY Plane***. Notice a rectangle, representing the work-plane, appears in the graphics window.

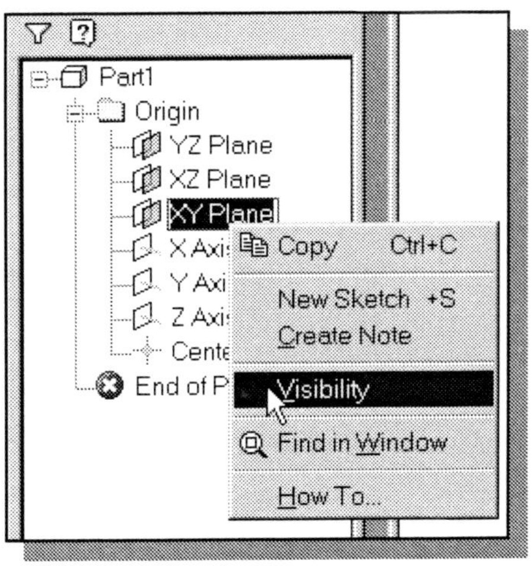

3. Inside the *Browser* window, click once with the right-mouse-button on *XY Plane* to display the option menu. Click on **Visibility** to toggle on the display of the plane.

4. On your own, repeat the above step and toggle ***ON*** the display of the *X* and *Y work-axes* and the *Center Point* on the screen.

Creating the 2D Sketch for the Base feature

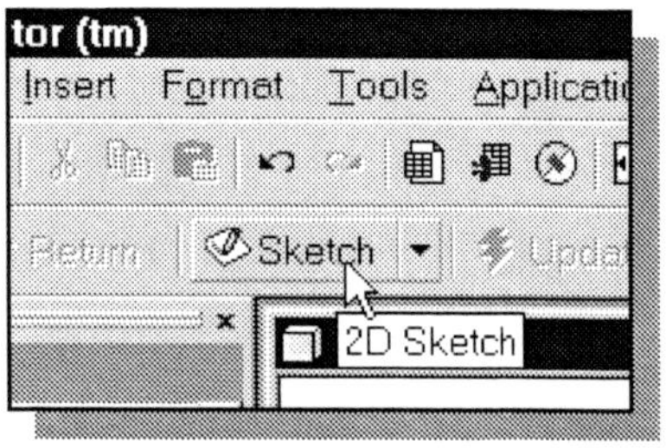

1. In the *Standard* toolbar select the ***Sketch*** command by left-clicking once on the icon.

2. In the *Status Bar* area, the message: "*Select face, workplane, sketch or sketch geometry.*" is displayed. Select the ***XY Plane***, by left-clicking once on any edges of the XY Plane in the graphics window.

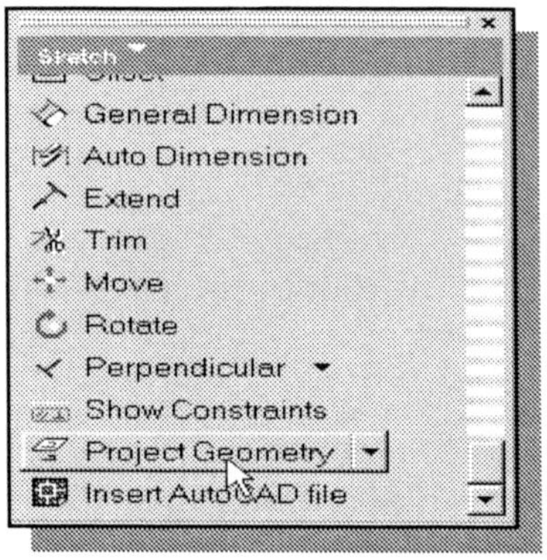

3. Select the ***Project Geometry*** command in the *Sketch* toolbar. The *Project Geometry* command allows us to project existing features to the active sketching plane. Left-click once on the icon to activate the *Project Geometry* command.

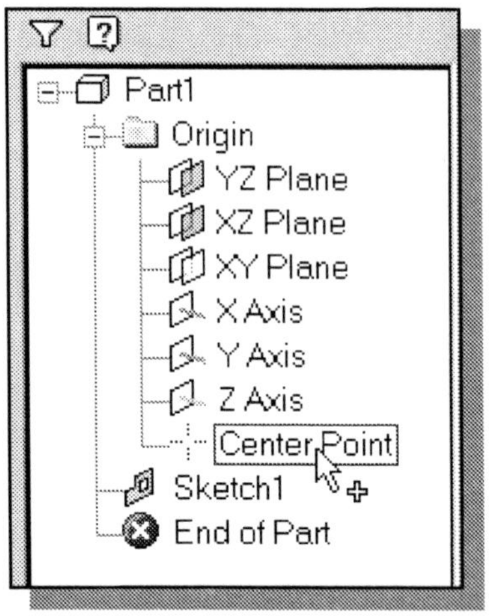

4. In the *Status Bar* area, the message: "*Select edge, vertex, work geometry or sketch geometry to project.*" is displayed. Inside the *Browser* window, select the ***Center Point*** to project the center point onto the sketching plane.

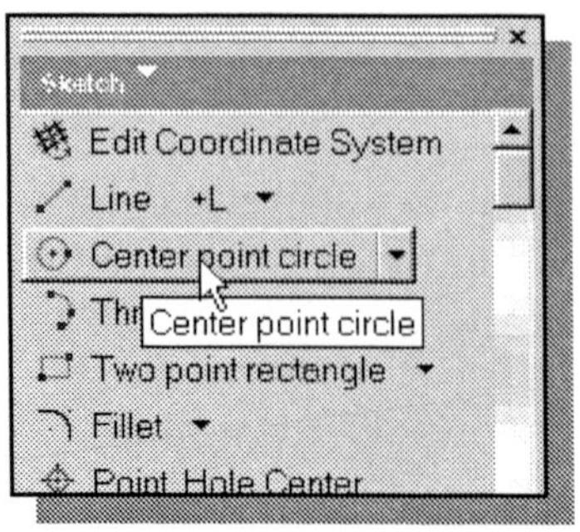

5. Select the ***Center point circle*** command by clicking once with the left-mouse-button on the icon in the *Sketch* toolbar.

6. Pick the **projected *Center Point*** as the center location of the circle.

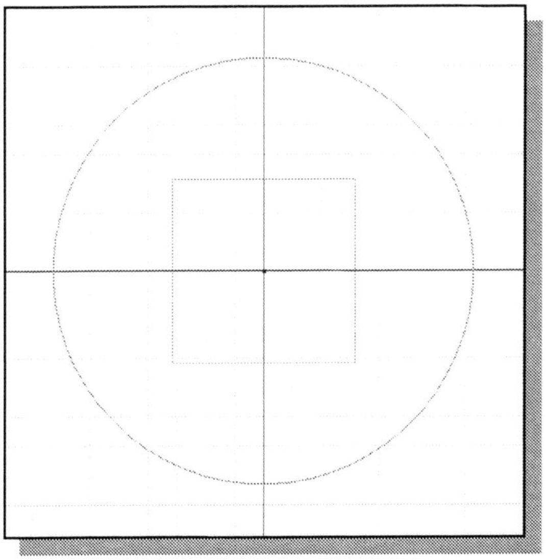

7. Create a **circle** of arbitrary size, with its center aligned to the projected *Center Point* as shown.

8. Click on the ***Line*** icon in the *Sketch* toolbar.

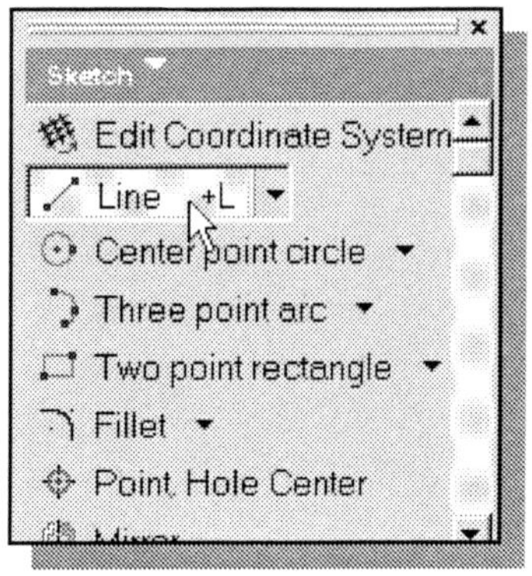

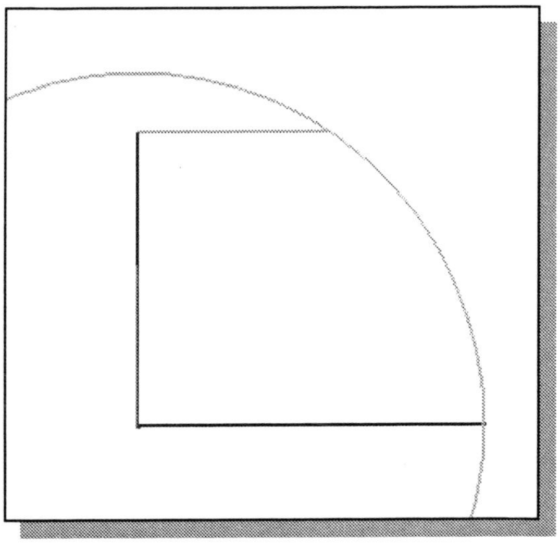

9. Create the three line segments as shown. The lines are either horizontal or vertical with the lower left corner aligned to the projected *Center Point.*

10. Click on the ***Trim*** command in the *Sketch* toolbar.

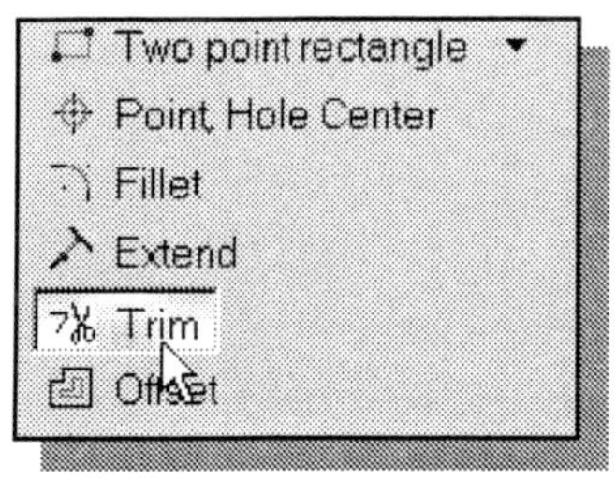

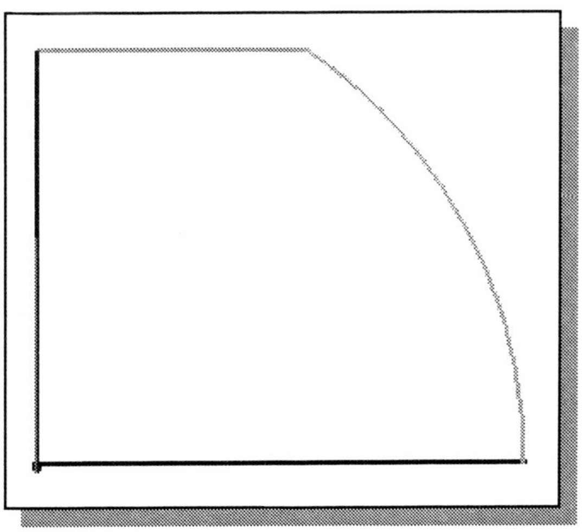

11. Modify the sketch by trimming the circle as shown.

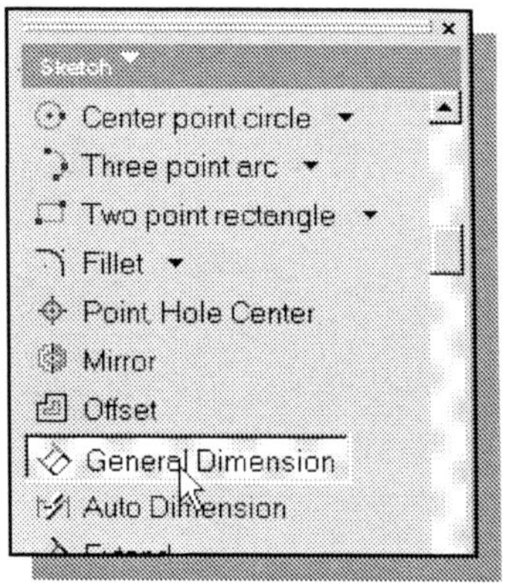

12. On your own, use the ***General Dimension*** command and create/modify the dimensions as shown in the figure below. (Hint: modify the radius dimension first.)

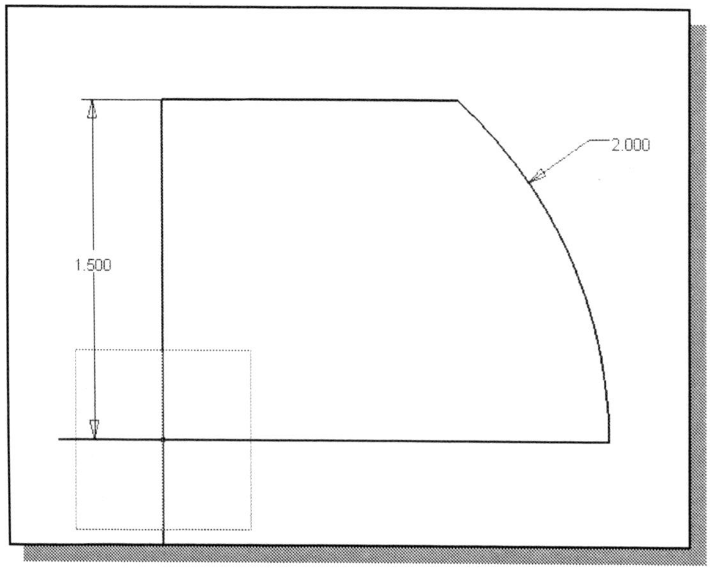

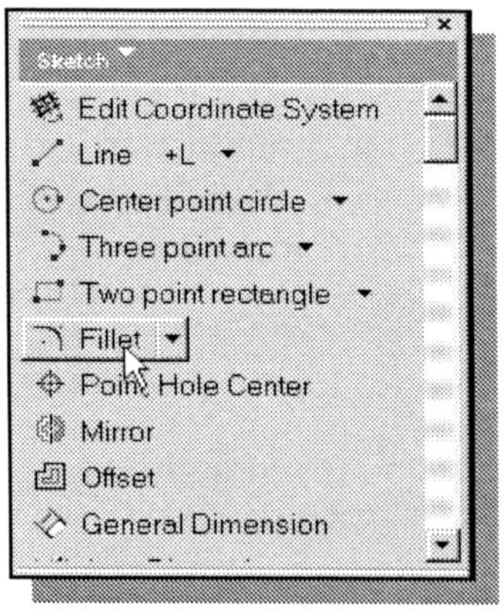

13. Click on the ***Fillet*** icon in the *Sketch* toolbar.

14. In the *2D Fillet* dialog box, set the ***Radius*** to **0.25**.

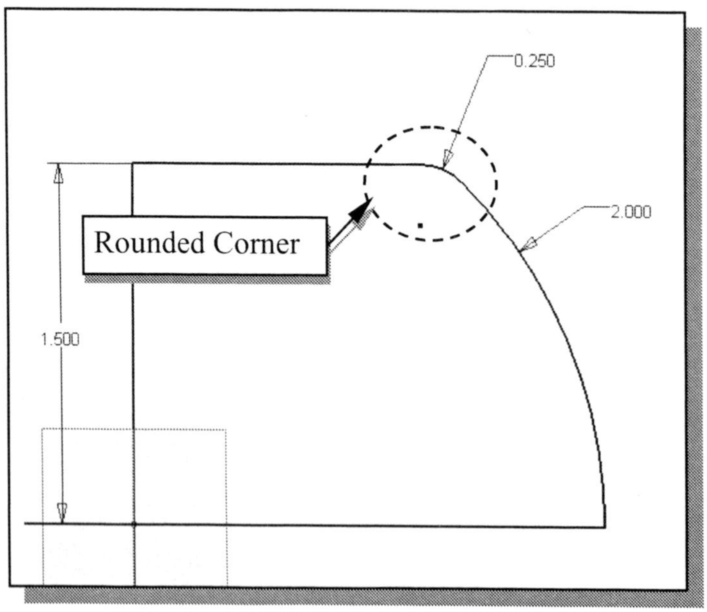

15. Select the top-horizontal line and the arc to create a rounded corner as shown.

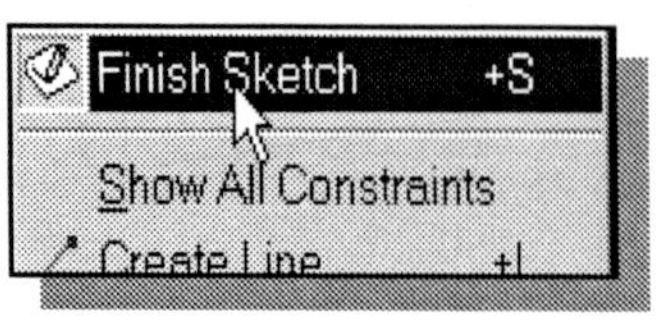

16. Inside the graphics window, click once with the right-mouse-button to display the option menu. Select **Finish Sketch** in the popup menu to end the *Sketch* option.

Create the Revolved Feature

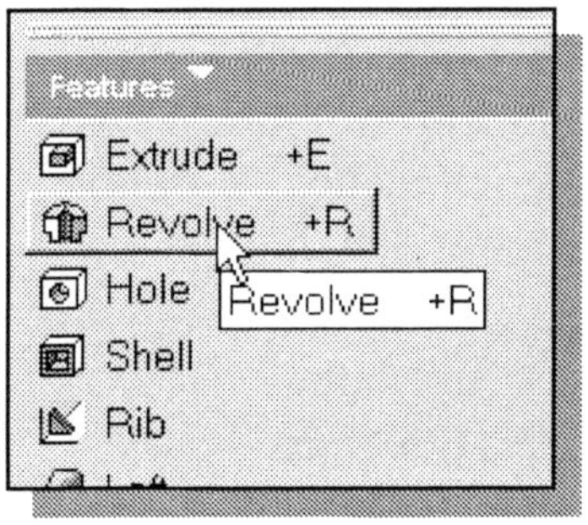

1. In the *Feature* toolbar (the toolbar that is located to the left side of the graphics window), select the ***Revolve*** command by left-mouse-click the icon.

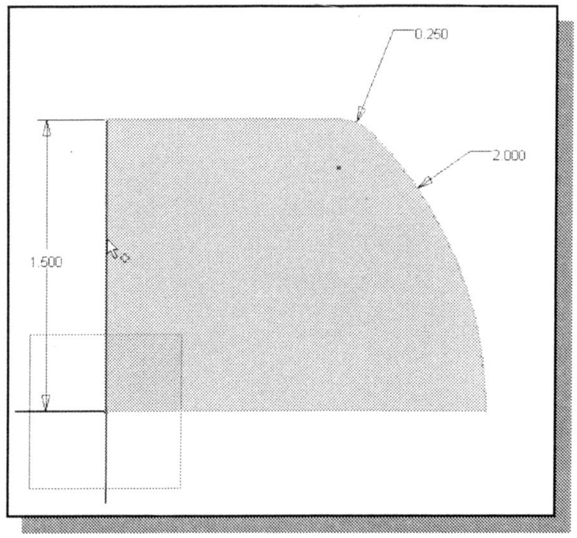

2. In the *Revolve* dialog box, the ***Axis*** button is activated indicating *Autodesk Inventor* expects us to select the revolution axis for the revolved feature. Select the **vertical edge** of the sketch as the axis of rotation as shown.

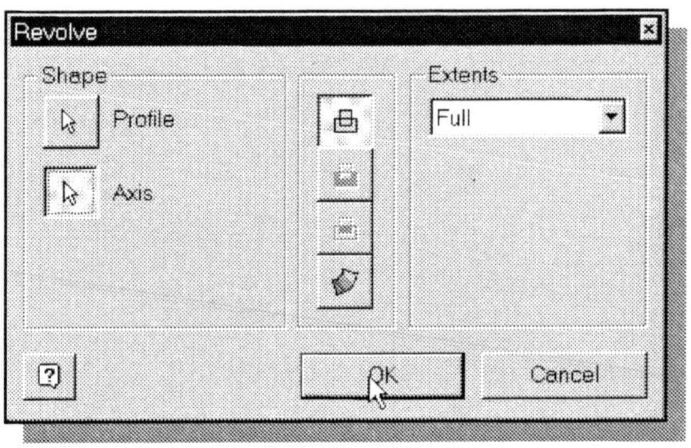

3. In the *Revolve* dialog box, set the termination *Extents* option to **Full** as shown.

4. Click on the **OK** button to accept the settings and create the revolved feature.

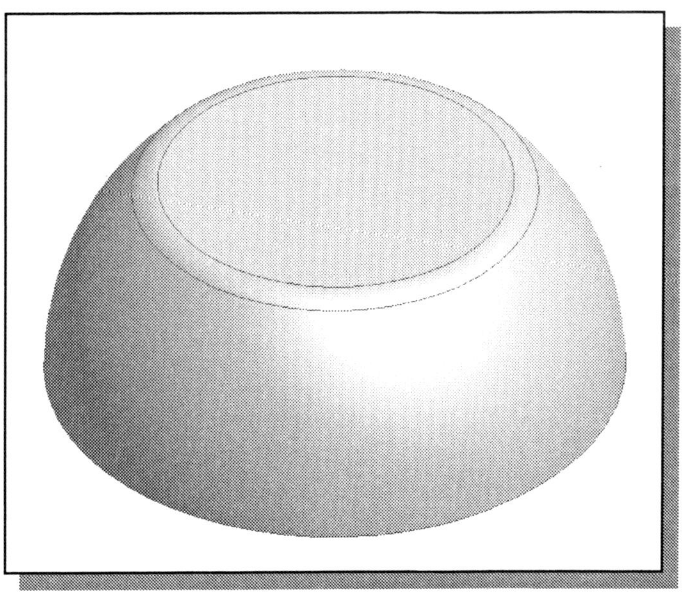

Examining the Parent/Child Relationships

The model history tree shows the work planes, work axes, center point, and the base feature we just created. The parent/child relationships were established implicitly when we created the base feature: (1) ***XY plane*** was selected as the sketch plane; (2) ***Center Point*** was selected as the reference point to constrain the parametric sketch.

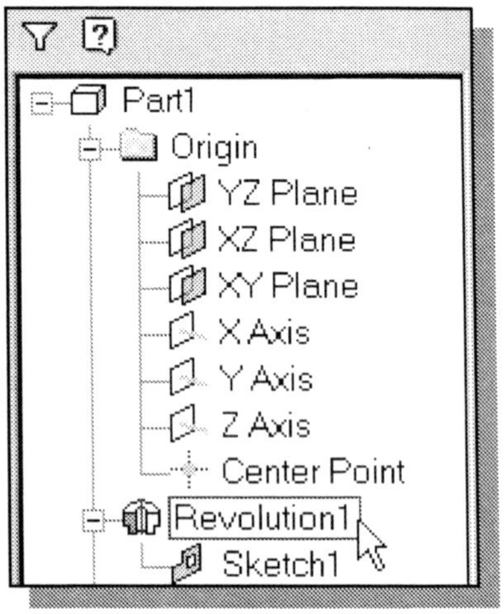

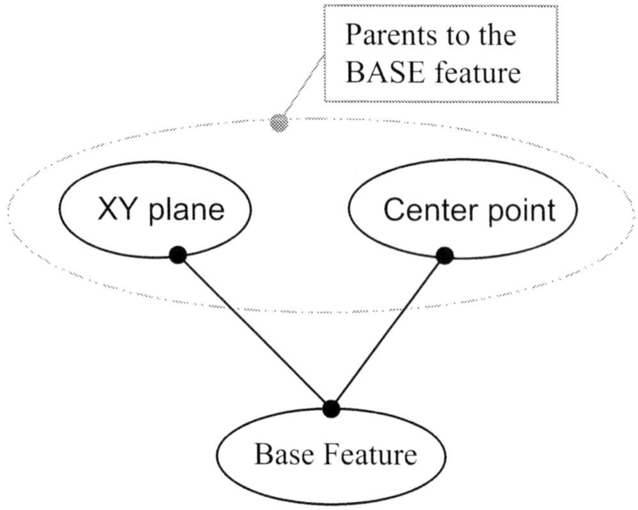

Creating Offset Work Planes

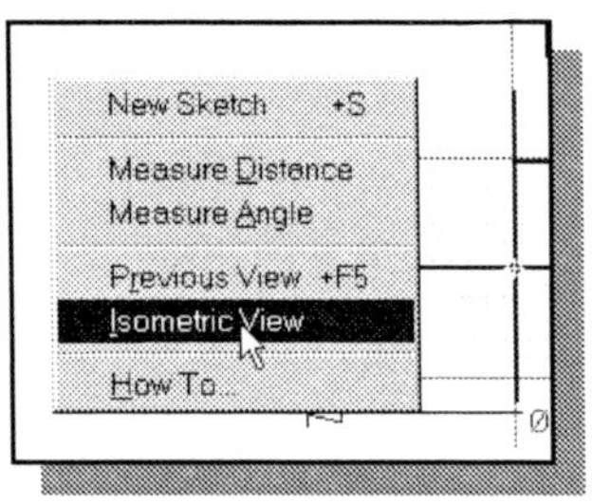

1. Inside the graphics window, right-mouse-click to bring up the option menu.

2. Select **Isometric View** in the option list to adjust the display of the 2D sketch on the screen.

3. Click on the ***Wireframe*** icon to set the display mode.

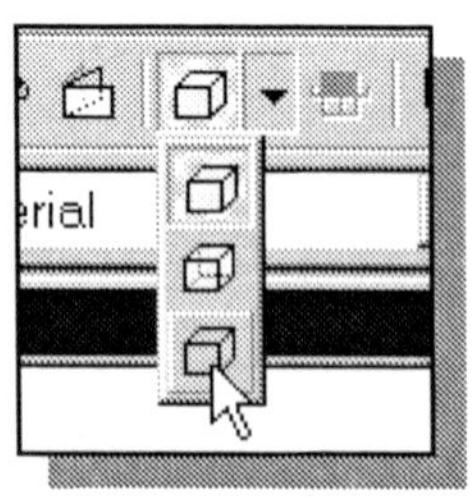

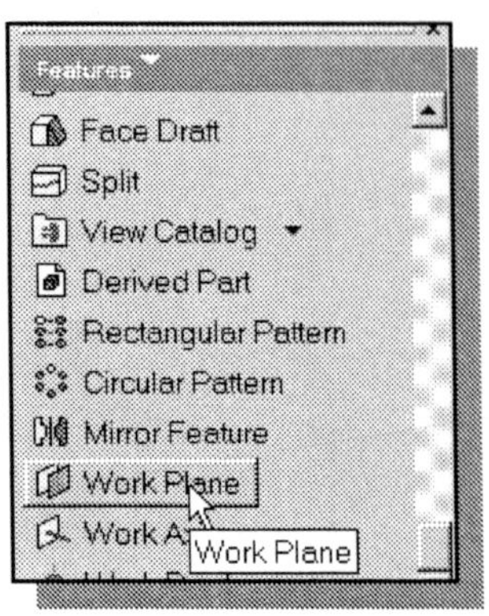

4. In the *Feature* toolbar, select the ***Work Plane*** command by left-mouse-clicking on the icon.

5. In the *Status Bar* area, the message: "*Define work plane by highlighting and selecting geometry*" is displayed. *Autodesk Inventor* expects us to select any existing geometry, which will be used as a reference to create the new work plane.

6. Inside the graphics window, move the graphics cursor next to the edges of the ***XY Plane***, until it is highlighted as shown below. Left-click once to select the *XY Plane* as the reference of the new work plane.

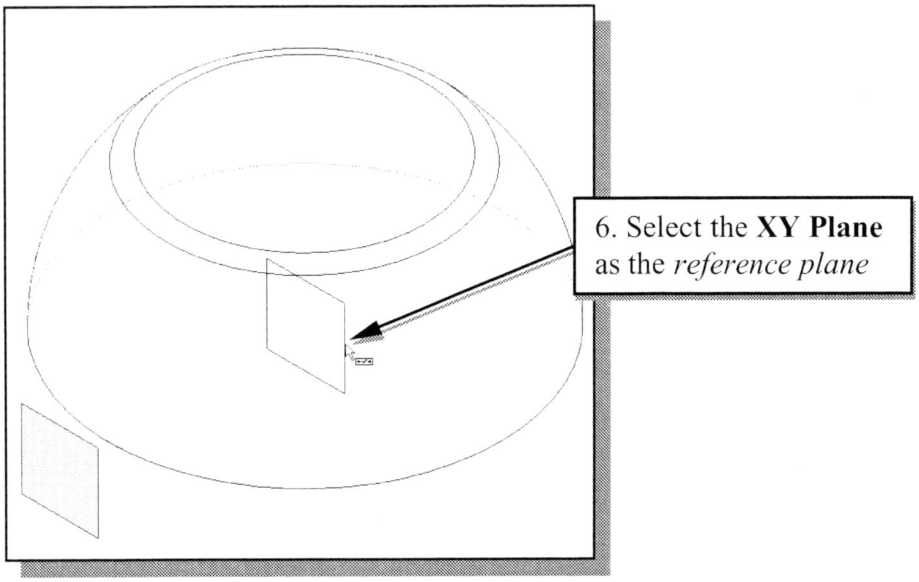

7. Use the left-mouse-button and drag toward the lower-left corner of the graphics window.

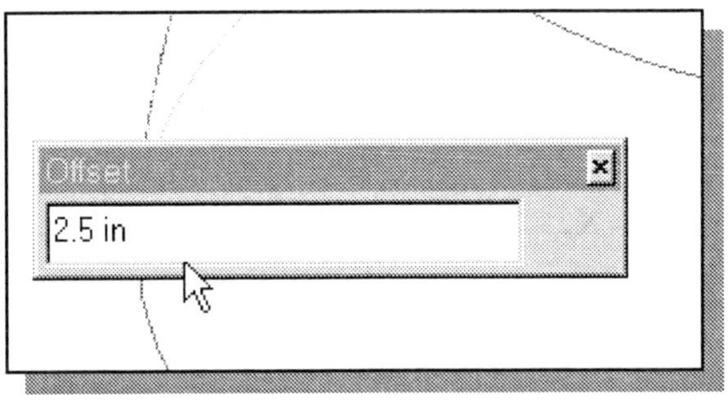

8. In the ***Offset*** popup window, enter **2.5** as the offset distance for the new work plane.

9. Click on the ***check mark*** button to accept the setting.

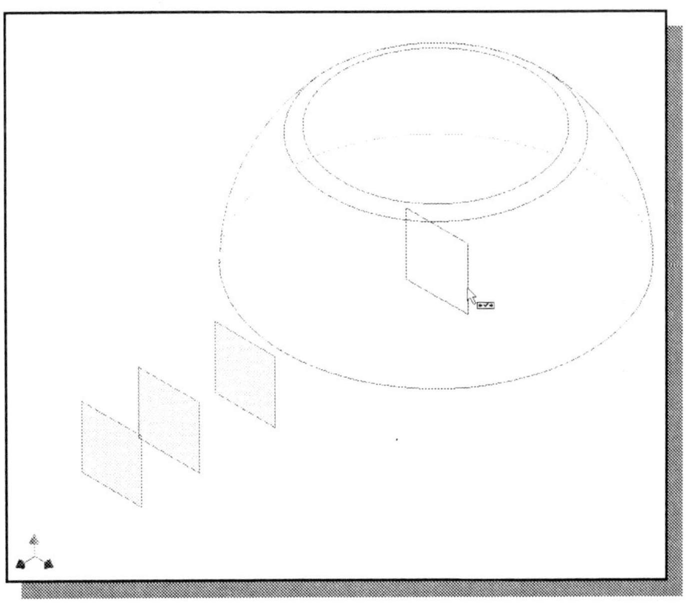

10. On your own, repeat the above steps and create two additional work planes that are **3.5** inches and **4.25** inches away from the XY Plane.

Creating 2D sketches on Work Planes

1. In the *Standard* toolbar select the ***Sketch*** command by left-clicking once on the icon.

2. In the *Status Bar* area, the message: "*Select face, workplane, sketch or sketch geometry.*" is displayed. Select the ***XY Plane*** by left-clicking once on any edges of the XY Plane in the graphics window.

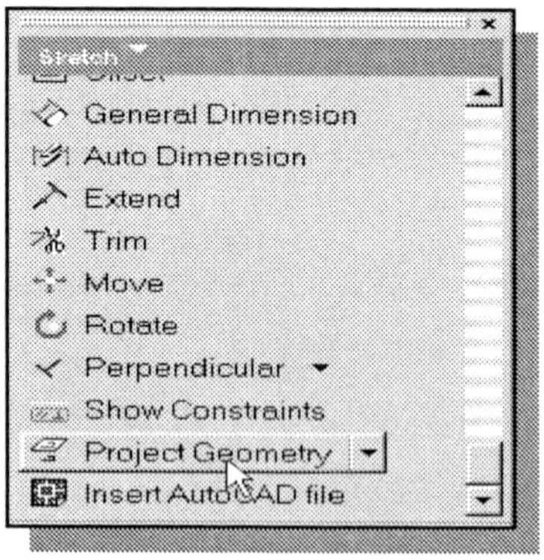

3. Select the ***Project Geometry*** command in the *Sketch* toolbar.

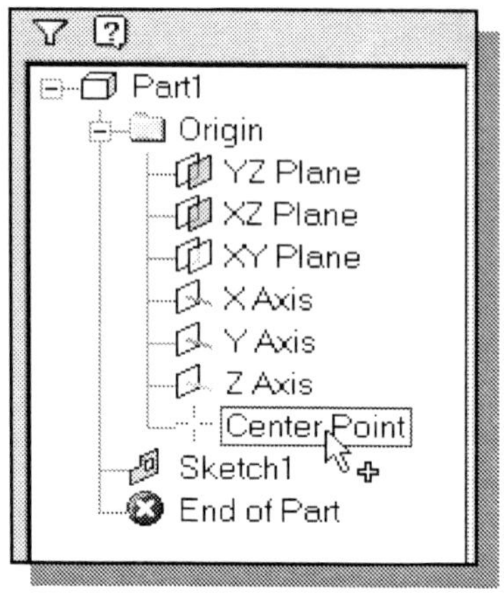

4. In the *Status Bar* area, the message: "*Select edge, vertex, work geometry or sketch geometry to project.*" is displayed. Inside the *Browser* window, select the ***Center Point*** to project the point onto the sketching plane.

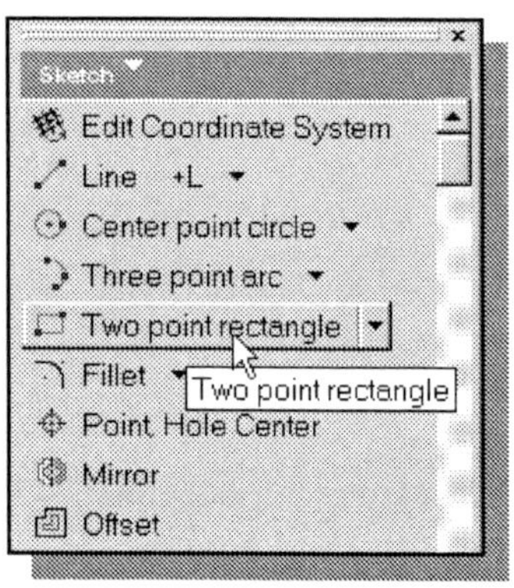

5. Select the ***Two point rectangle*** command by clicking once with the left-mouse-button on the icon in the *Sketch* toolbar.

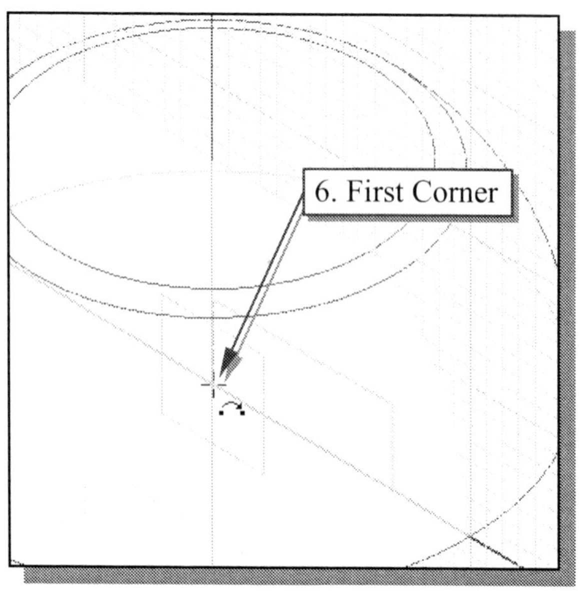

6. Click on the projected *Center Point* to align the first corner of the rectangle.

7. Create a rectangle of arbitrary size by selecting a location that is toward the right side of the graphics window as shown.

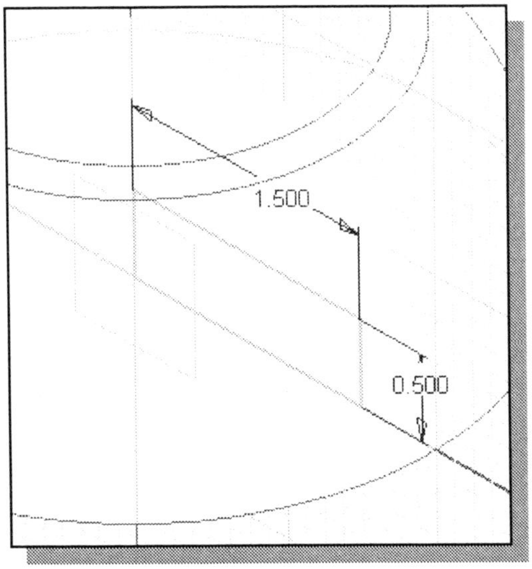

8. On your own, create and modify the two dimensions as shown in the figure.

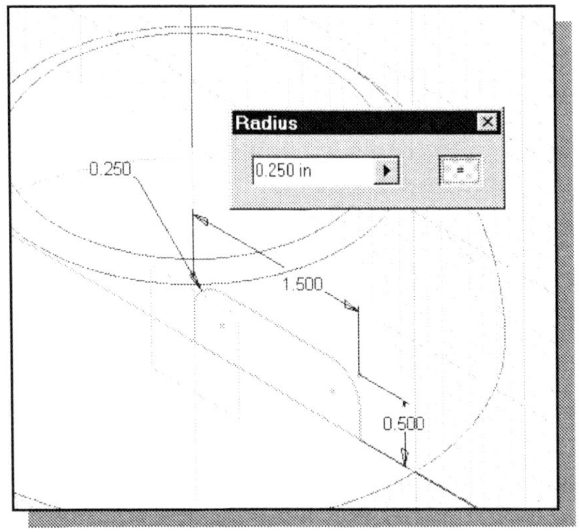

9. On your own, create two rounded corners (**radius 0.25**) as shown.

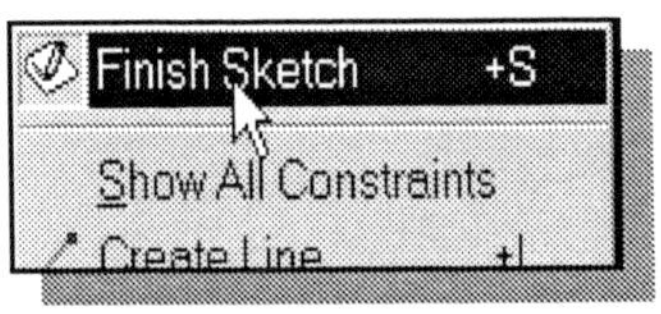

10. Inside the graphics window, click once with the right-mouse-button to display the option menu. Select **Finish Sketch** in the popup menu to end the *Sketch* option.

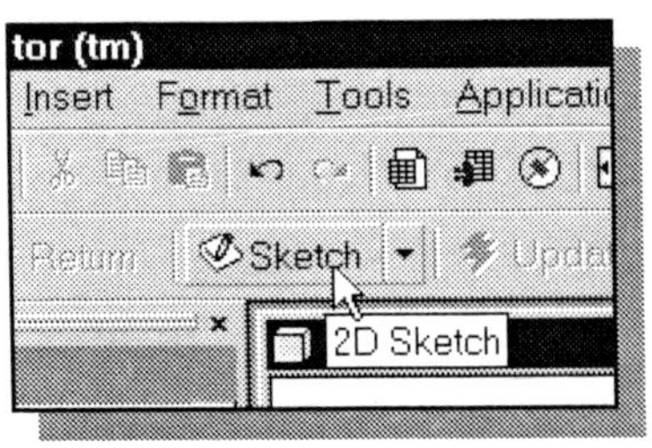

11. In the *Standard* toolbar select the ***Sketch*** command by left-clicking once on the icon.

12. In the *Status Bar* area, the message: "*Select face, workplane, sketch or sketch geometry.*" is displayed. Select the ***WorkPlane1***, by left-clicking once on any edges of the first offset work plane in the graphics window as shown.

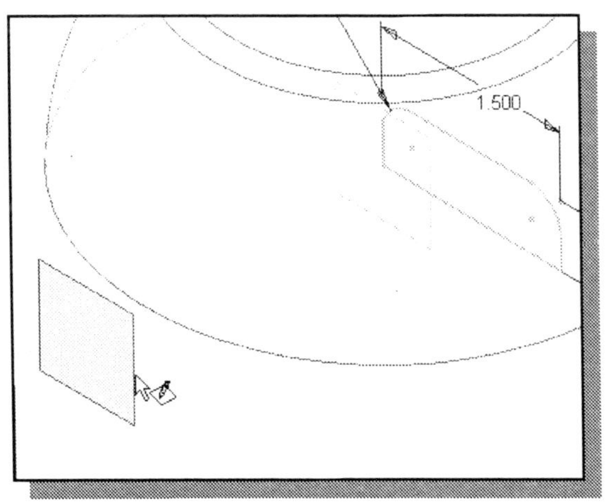

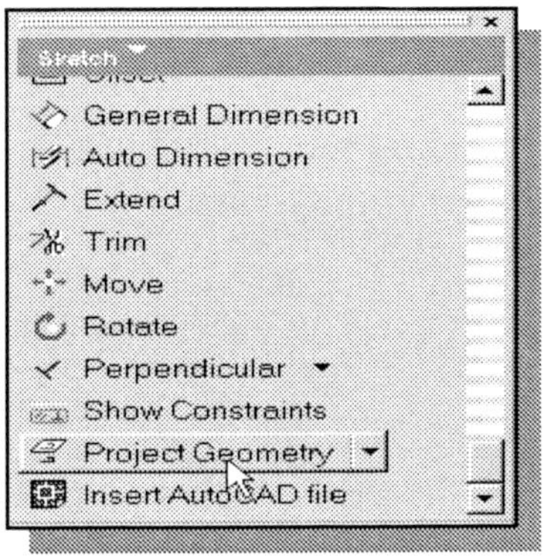

13. Select the ***Project Geometry*** command in the *Sketch* toolbar.

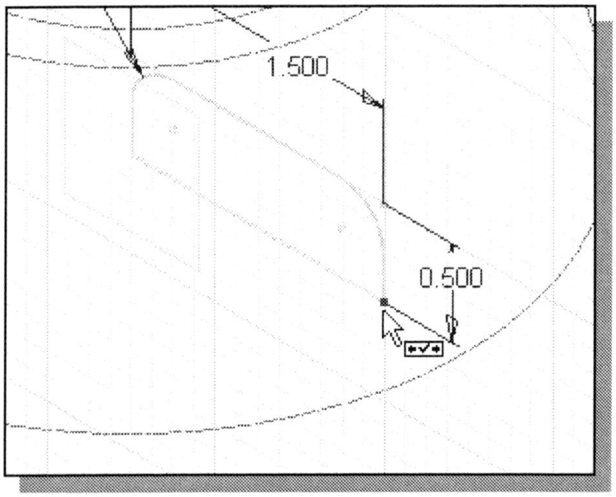

14. Select the lower right corner of the 2D sketch we just created, as shown in the figure.

15. On your own, create/modify the 2D sketch as shown in the figure. (The lower right corner of the sketch is aligned to the lower right corner of the previous sketch.)

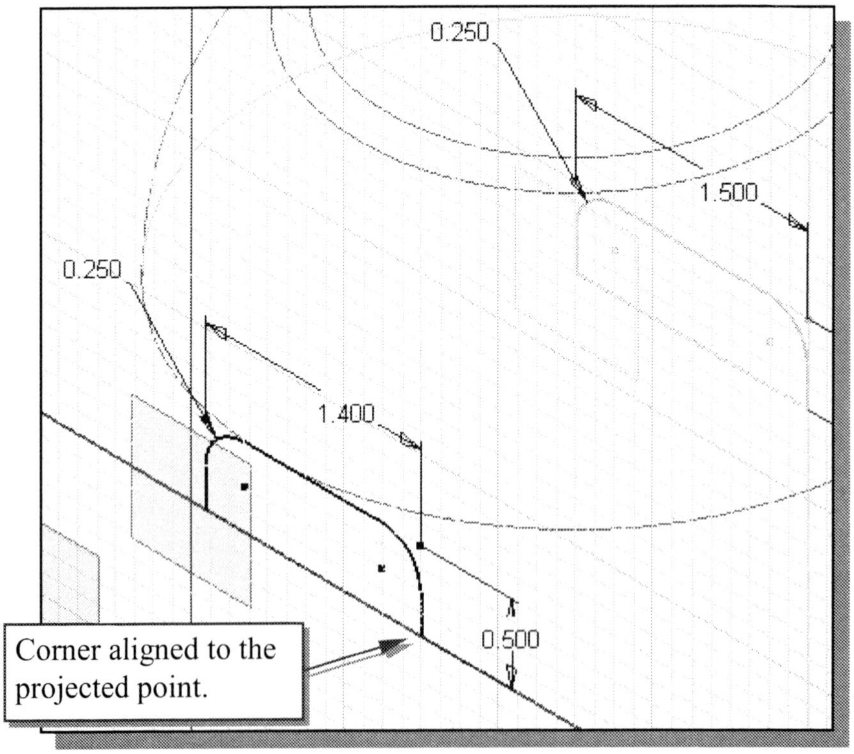

16. On your own, repeat the above steps and create two additional sketches on ***WorkPlane2*** and ***WorkPlane3*** as shown in the below figure. Note that the lower-right-corners of the four sketches are aligned in the Z-direction through the use of the projected center point.

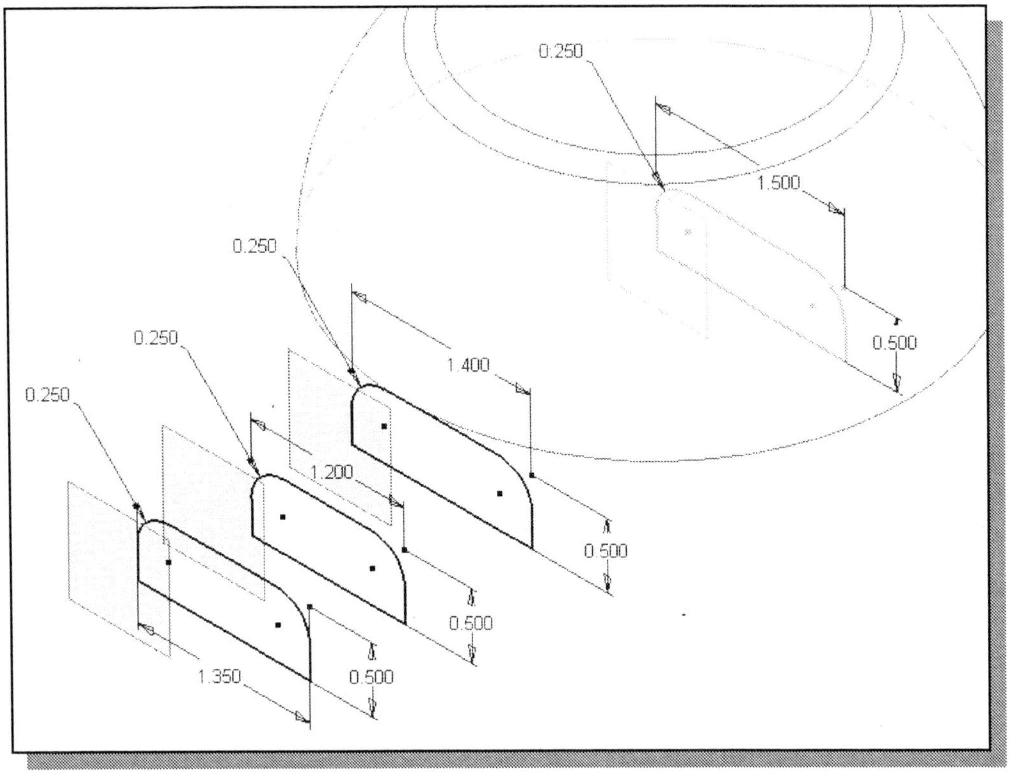

Creating a Lofted Feature

➢ The ***Loft*** option allows us to blend multiple profiles with varying shapes on separate planes to create complex shapes. Profiles are usually on parallel planes, but any non-perpendicular planes can also be used. We can use as many profiles as we wish, but to avoid twisting the loft shape, we should map points on each profile that align along a straight vector.

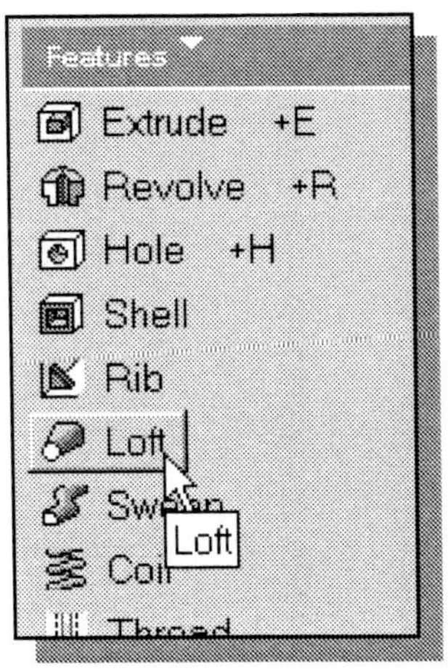

1. In the *Feature* toolbar, select the ***Loft*** command by left-mouse-click on the icon.

2. In the *Loft* dialog box, the ***Sections*** option is activated. *Autodesk Inventor* expects us to select any number of existing profiles, which will be used to create the lofted feature.

3. Select the four sketches, in the order that they were created, by clicking at the lower-right corners of the sketches. Three arrows are displayed showing the blending direction of the sketches. Note that to avoid twisting the loft shape, we are mapping the same corner points on the sketches to align along a straight vector.

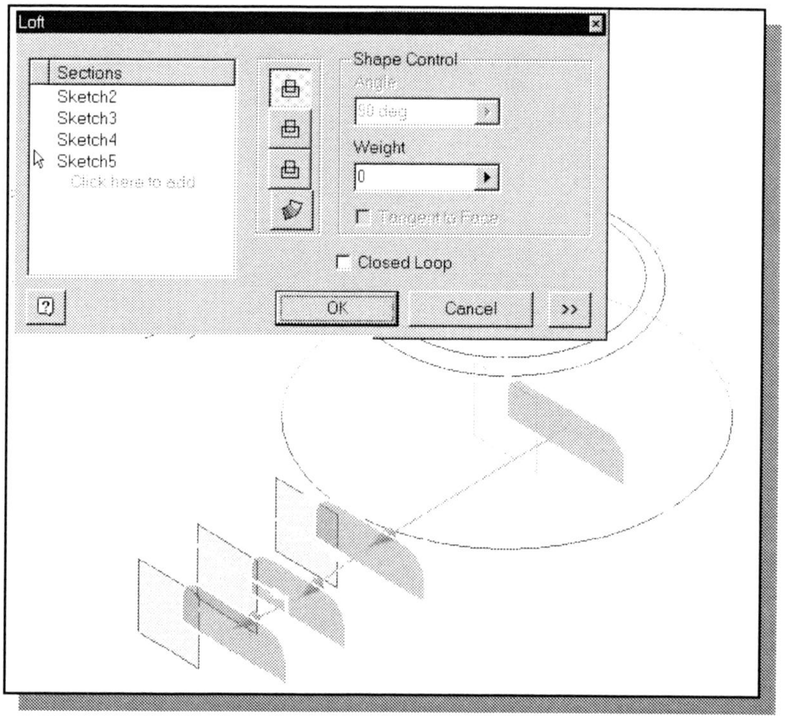

4. Click on the **OK** button to accept the settings and create the lofted feature.

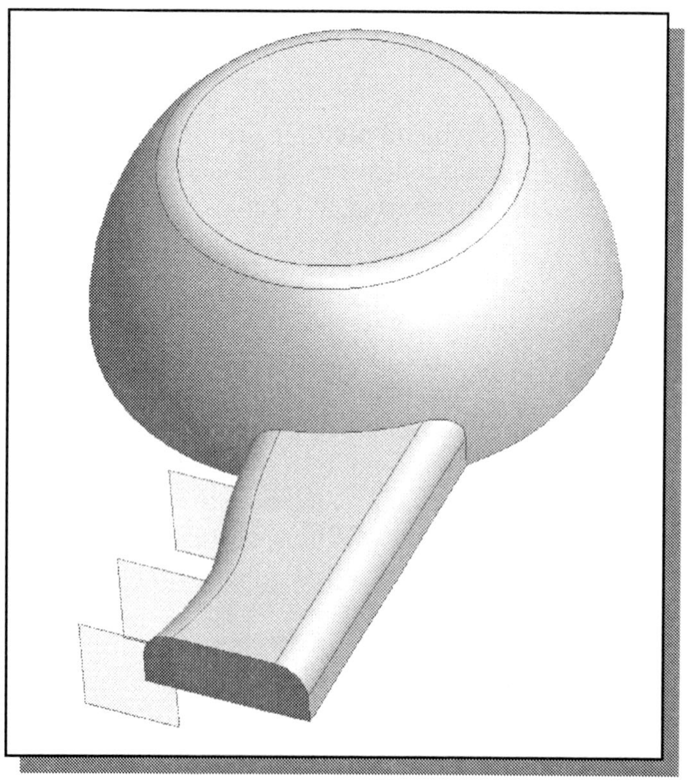

Creating a Swept Feature

The ***Sweep*** operation is defined as moving a planar section through a planar path in space to form a three-dimensional solid object. The path can be an open curve or a closed loop, but must be on an intersecting plane with the profile. The ***Extrusion*** operation, which we have used in the previous lessons, is a specific type of sweep. The ***Extrusion*** operation is also known as a ***linear sweep*** operation, in which the sweep control path is always a line perpendicular to the two-dimensional section. Linear sweeps of unchanging shape result in what are generally called ***prismatic solids***; which means solids with a constant cross-section from end to end. In *Autodesk Inventor*, we create a **swept feature** by defining a path and then a 2D sketch of a cross section. The sketched profile is then swept along the planar path. The *Sweep* operation is used for objects that have uniform shapes along a trajectory.

♦ Define a 2D Sweep path

1. In the *Standard* toolbar select the ***Sketch*** command by left-clicking once on the icon.

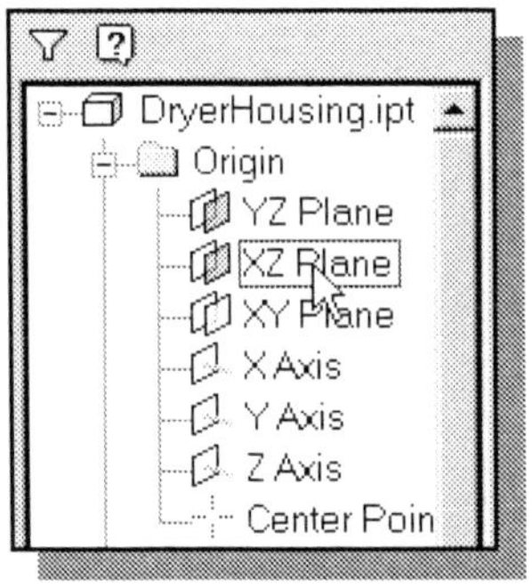

2. In the *Status Bar* area, the message: "*Select face, workplane, sketch or sketch geometry.*" is displayed. Select the **XZ Plane**, by left-clicking once on the *XZ Plane,* in the *Browser* window.

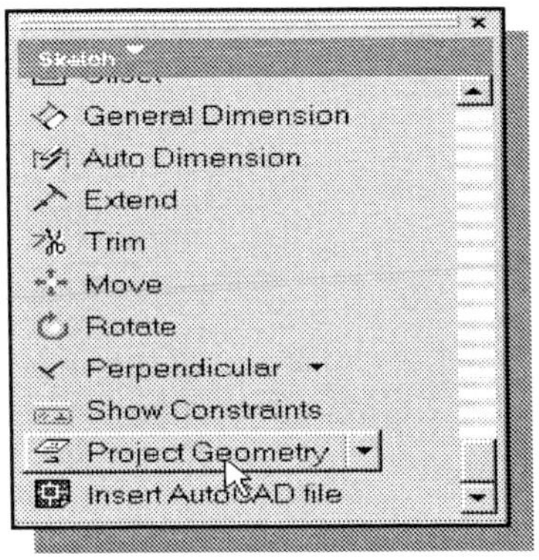

3. Select the ***Project Geometry*** command in the *Sketch* toolbar.

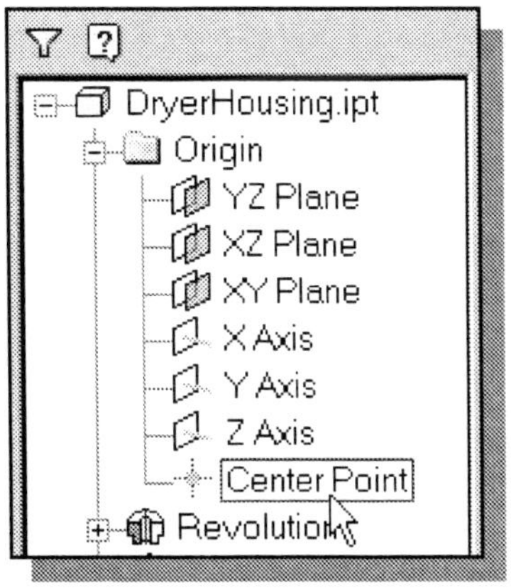

4. In the *Status Bar* area, the message: "*Select edge, vertex, work geometry or sketch geometry to project.*" is displayed. Inside the *Browser* window, select the ***Center Point*** to project the point onto the sketching plane.

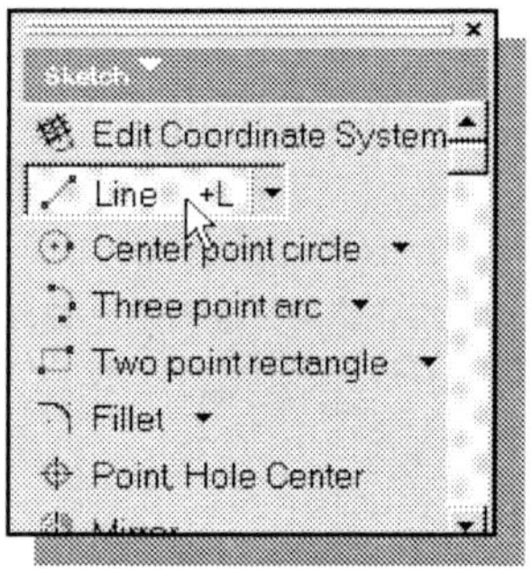

5. Click on the ***Line*** icon in the *Sketch* toolbar.

6. Create a line that is parallel to the XY Plane as shown.

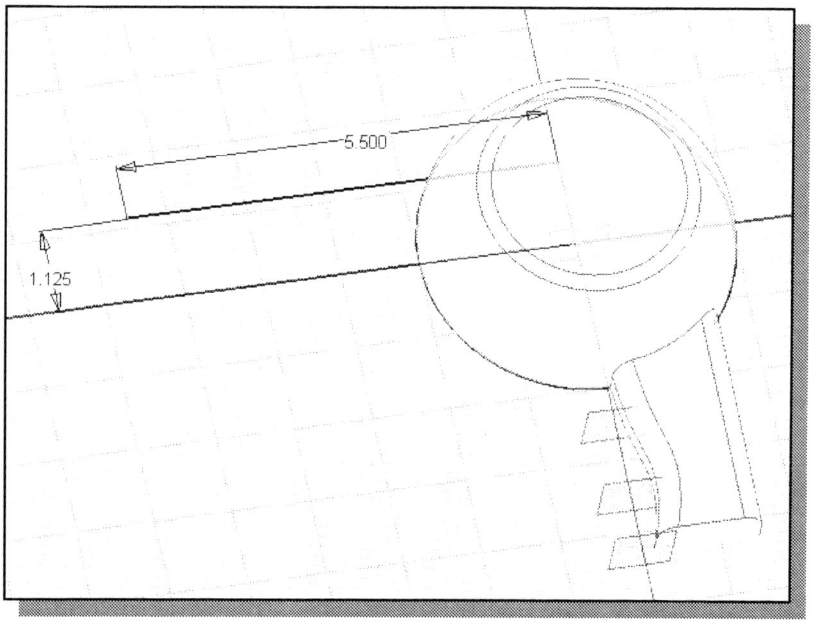

7. On your own, create and modify the two dimensions as shown in the above figure.

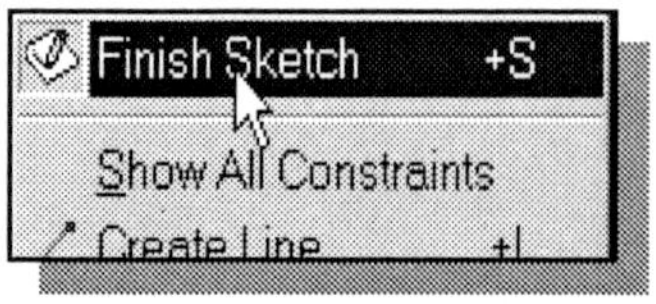

8. Inside the graphics window, click once with the right-mouse-button to display the option menu. Select **Finish Sketch** in the popup menu to end the *Sketch* option.

♦ Define the Sweep Section

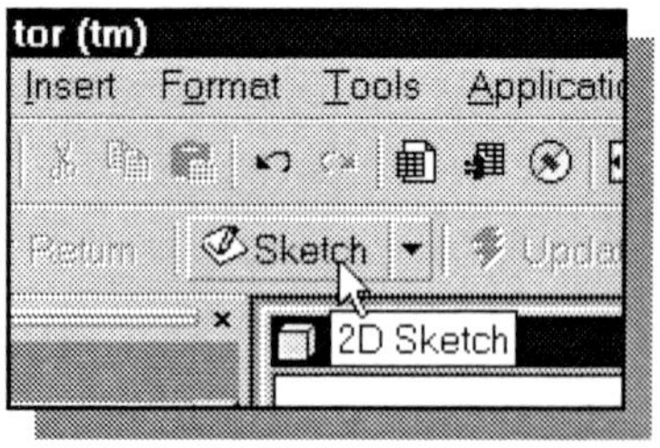

1. In the *Standard* toolbar select the ***Sketch*** command by left-clicking once on the icon.

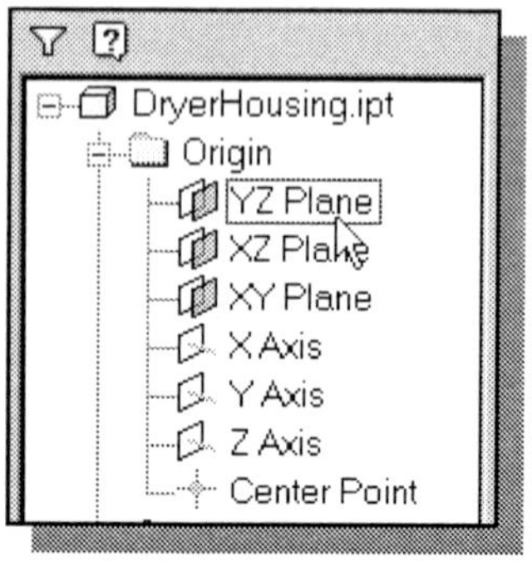

2. In the *Status Bar* area, the message: "*Select face, workplane, sketch or sketch geometry.*" is displayed. Select the **YZ Plane**, by left-clicking once on the *YZ Plane,* in the *Browser* window.

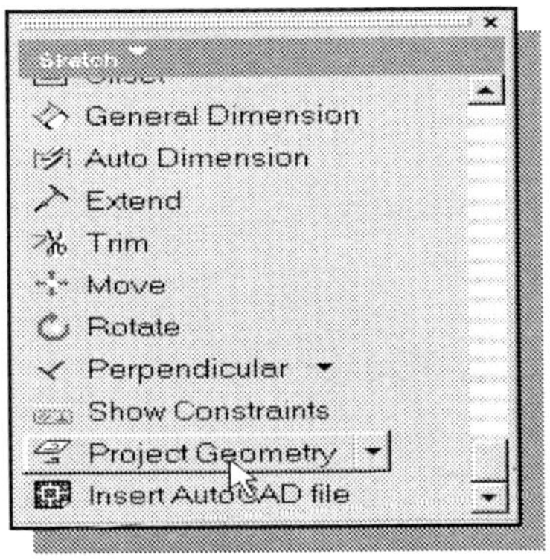

3. Select the ***Project Geometry*** command in the *Sketch* toolbar.

4. In the *Status Bar* area, the message: "*Select edge, vertex, work geometry or sketch geometry to project.*" is displayed. Inside the *Browser* window, select the line we created and project the line onto the sketching plane.

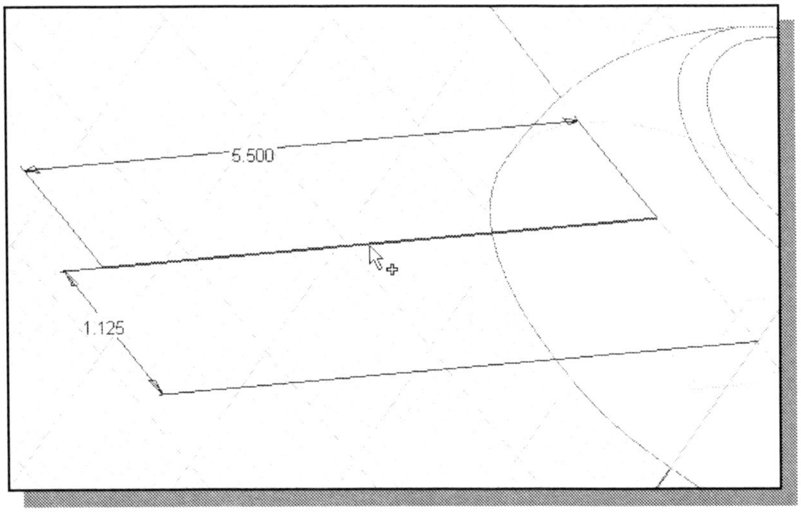

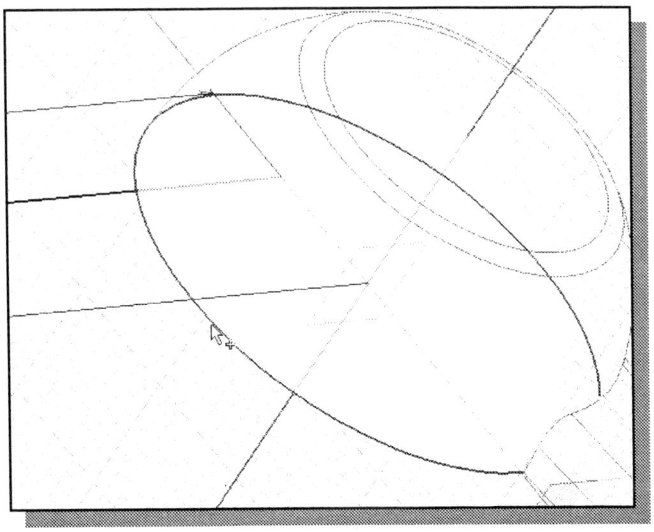

5. Click on the bottom face of the base feature to create a projected line, which will be used to align the 2D sketch of the sweep section.

6. Click on the **drop-down arrow** next to the **Arc** button in the *Sketch* toolbar area to display the available *Arc* options.

7. Select **Center point arc** from the drop-down list.

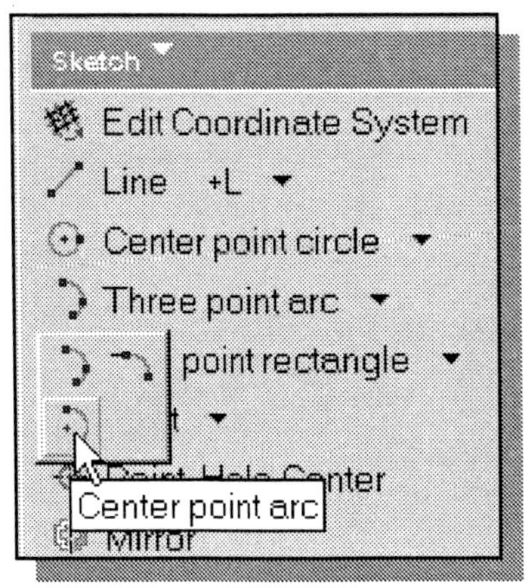

8. Click on the project point we created in step 4 to align the center of the arc to the sweep path. Watch for the alignment symbol to assure the proper constraining of the location. (Note that in *Autodesk Inventor*, it is not necessary to have the sweep path and the sweep section intersect with each other.)

9. Select two locations on the projected line to create an arc as shown.

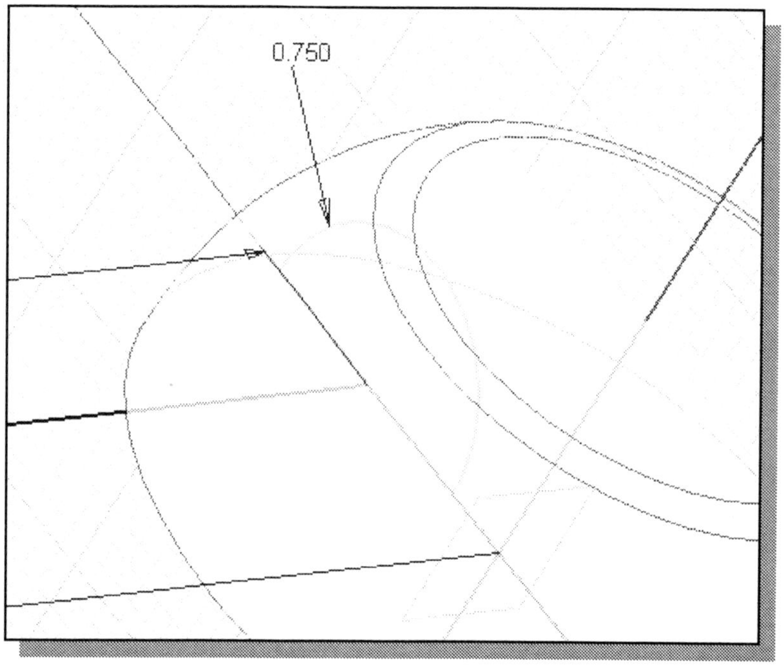

10. On your own, create and modify the dimension of the arc to **0.75**, as shown in the figure.

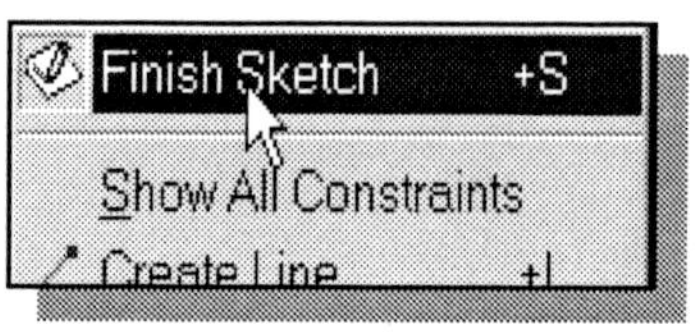

11. Inside the graphics window, click once with the right-mouse-button to display the option menu. Select **Finish Sketch** in the popup menu to end the *Sketch* option.

♦ Completing the Swept Feature

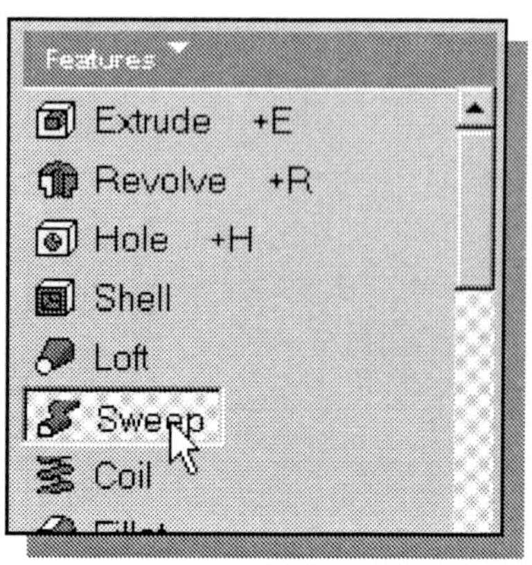

1. In the *Features* toolbar, select the ***Sweep*** command by left-clicking once on the icon.

2. In the *Sweep* dialog box, confirm the operation to ***Join***, and then click on the **OK** button to accept the settings and create the *Swept* feature. (Note that the *sweep section* and the *sweep path* are automatically selected.)

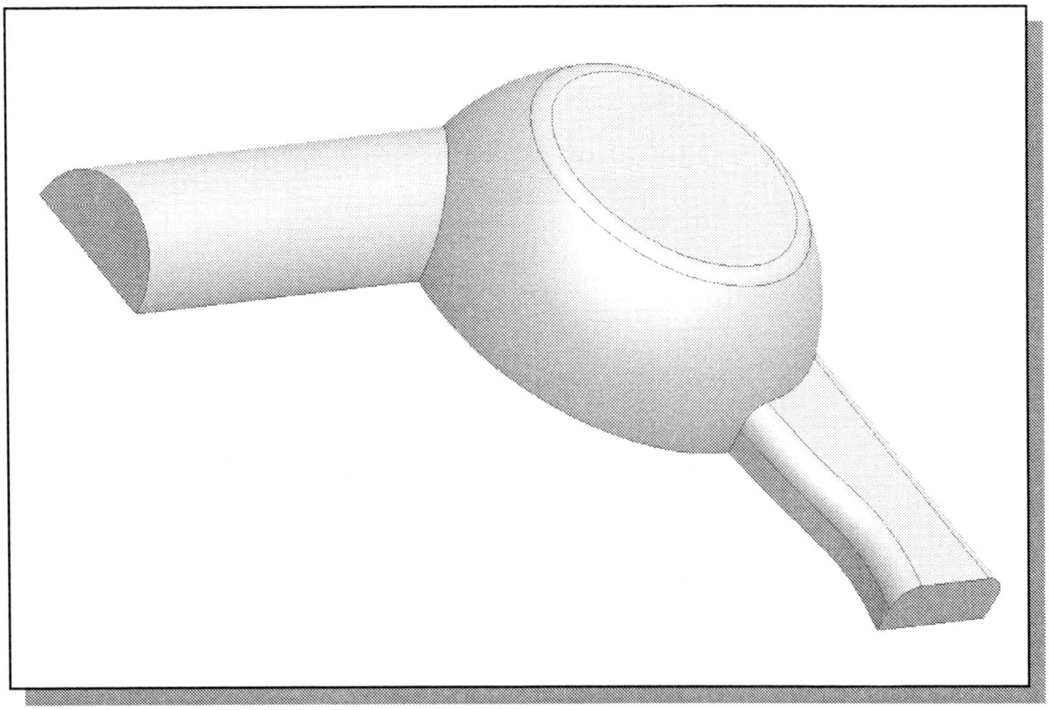

Effects of the Parent/Child Relationships

Note that the sweep section is linked to the sweep path and the bottom face of the base feature. Any changes to the base feature or the sweep path will change the sweep section. On your own, adjust and *update* the dimensions of the sweep path as shown below to examine the effects of the parent/child relationships. Reset the dimensions back to the **5.5** and **1.125** before proceeding to the next page.

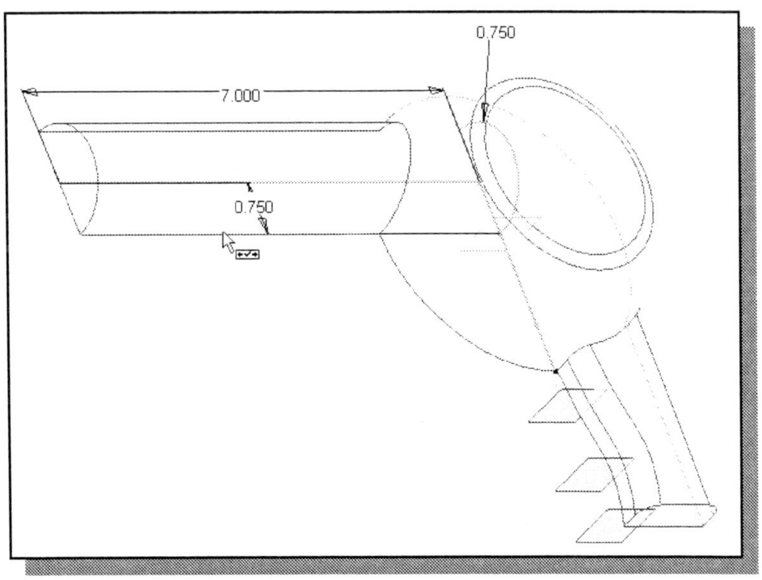

Create 3D Rounds and Fillets

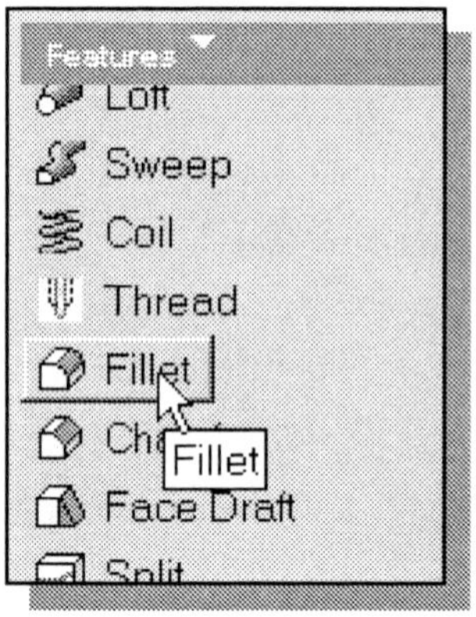

1. In the *Features* toolbar, select the ***Fillet*** command by left-clicking once on the icon.

2. In the *Fillet* dialog box, set the ***Radius*** option to a radius of **0.2** as shown below. (**DO NOT** click on the **OK** button.)

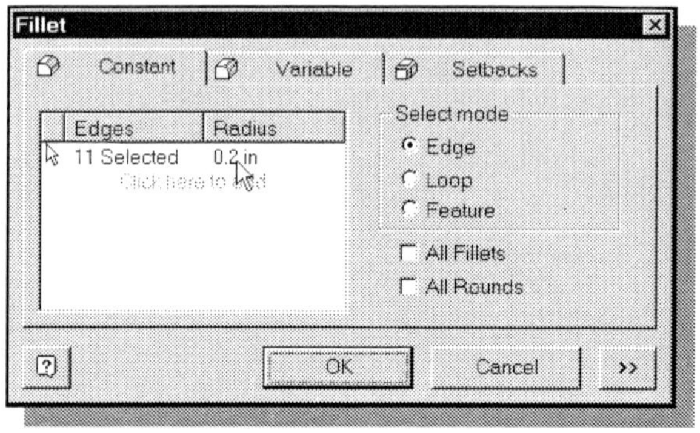

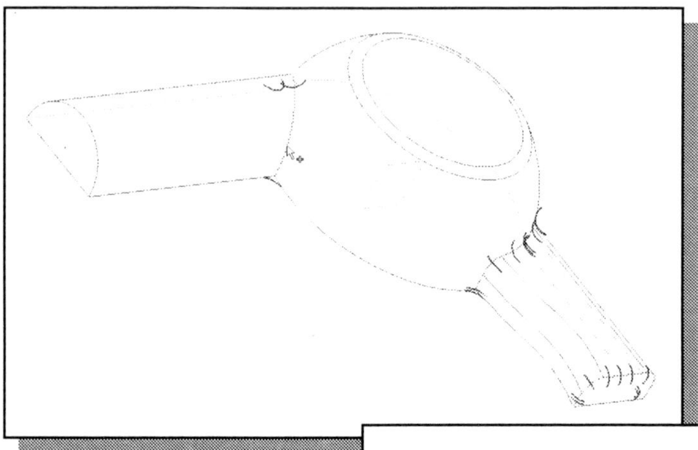

3. Click on the three edges as shown.

4. Click on the **OK** button to accept the settings and create the 3D rounds and fillets.

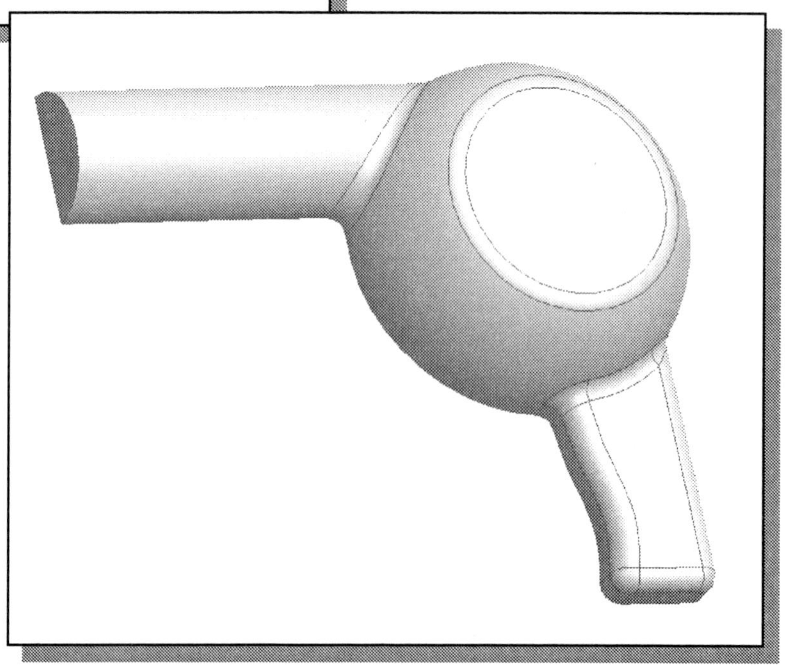

❖ On your own, examine the model history tree and determine the parent-features for the rounds/fillets in the design. If the sizes of the swept feature and lofted feature are changed, will the size of the rounds and fillets be maintained?

Using the Shell Operation

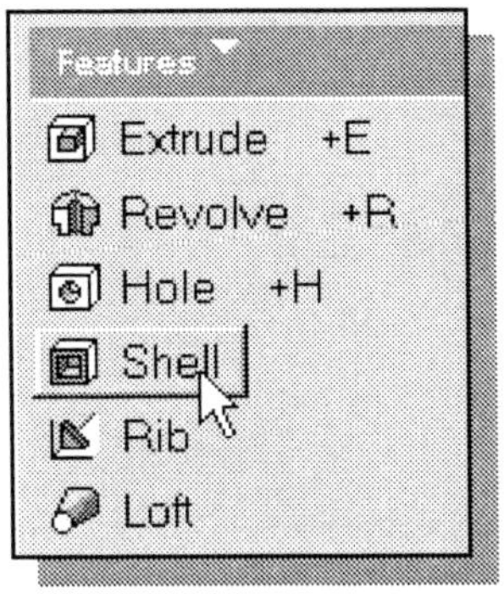

1. In the *Features* toolbar, select the ***Shell*** command by left-clicking once on the icon.

2. On your own, use the ***3D Rotation*** **quickkey** [**F4**] to display the back faces of the model as shown below.

3. In the *Shell Feature* dialog box, the ***Remove Faces*** option is activated. Select the two faces as shown below.

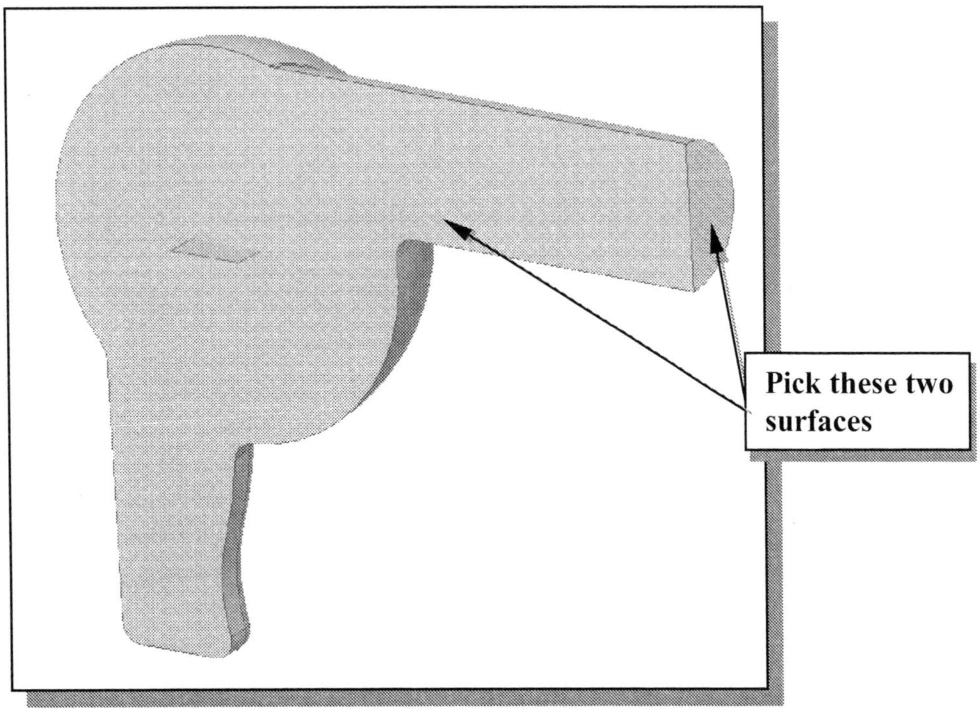

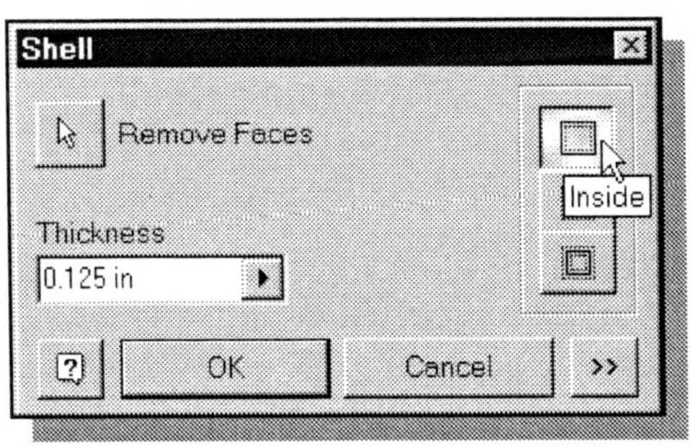

4. In the *Shell Feature* dialog box, set the option to **Inside** with a value of **0.125** as shown.

5. In the *Shell Feature* dialog box, click on the **OK** button to accept the settings and create the shell feature.

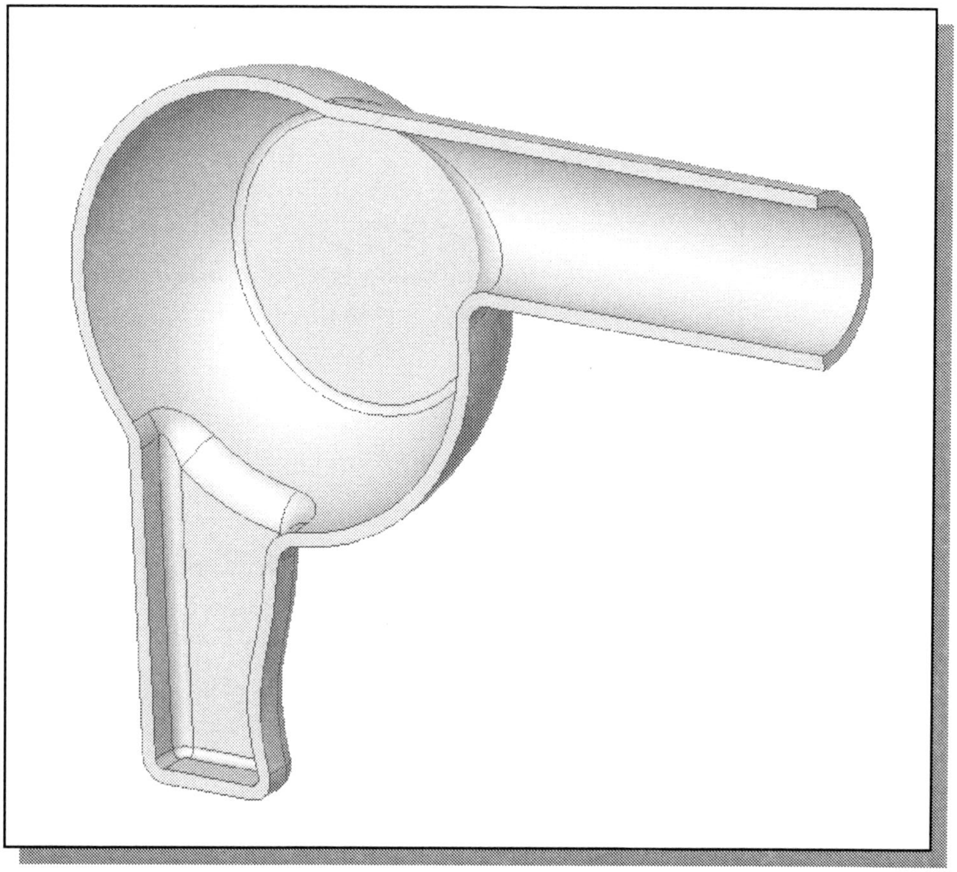

Create a Pattern Leader

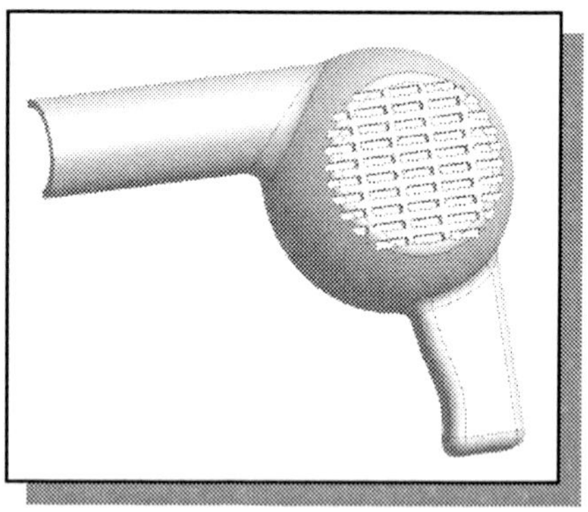

- The *Dryer Housing* design requires the placement of identical holes on the top face of the solid. Instead of creating the holes one at a time, we can simplify the creation of these holes by using the ***Pattern*** command to create duplicate features. Prior to using the *Pattern* command, we will first create a ***pattern leader***, which is a regular cut feature.

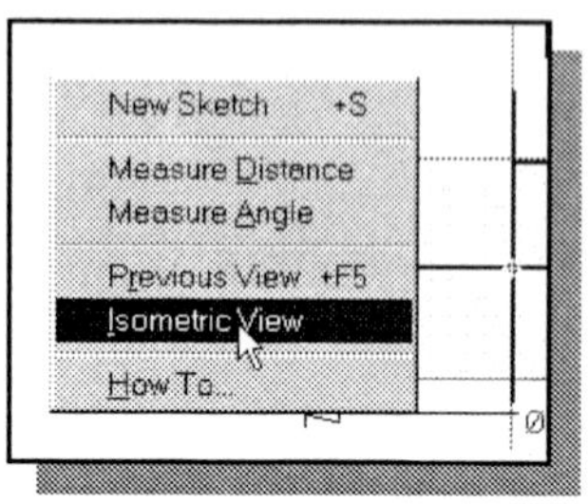

1. Inside the graphics window, right-mouse-click to bring up the option menu.

2. Select **Isometric View** in the option list to adjust the display of the 2D sketch on the screen.

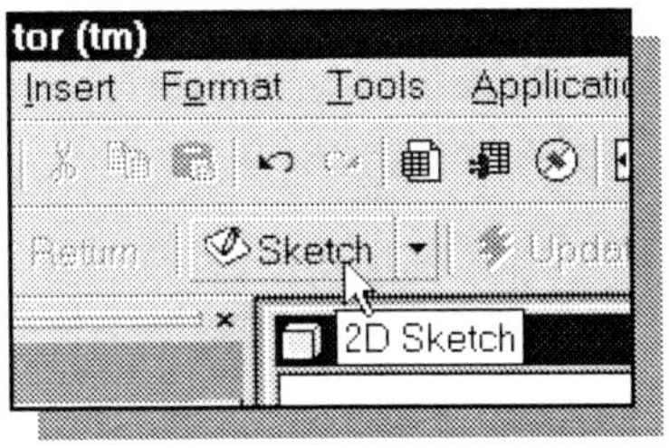

3. In the *Standard* toolbar select the ***Sketch*** command by left-clicking once on the icon.

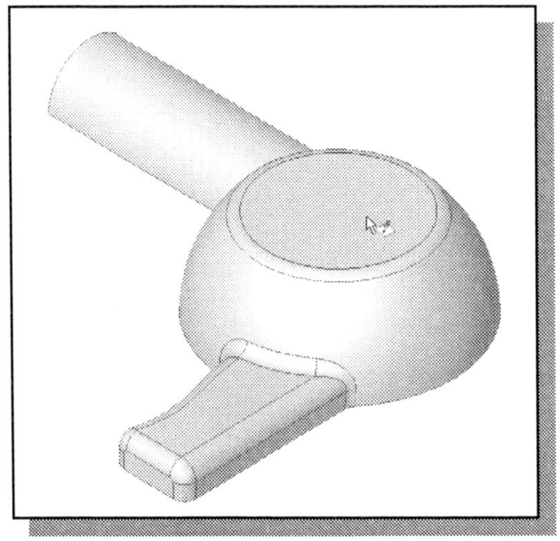

4. In the *Status Bar* area, the message: "*Select face, work plane, sketch or sketch geometry.*" is displayed. Pick the top face of the base feature as shown.

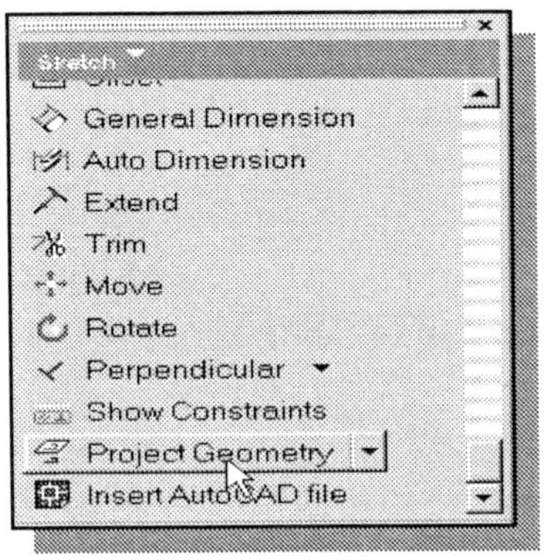

5. Select the ***Project Geometry*** command in the *Sketch* toolbar.

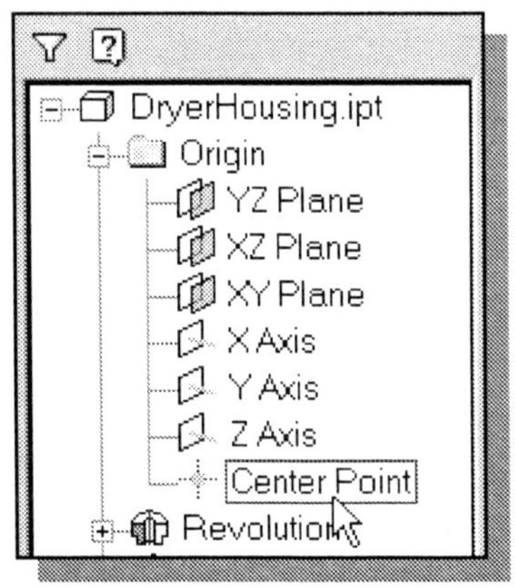

6. In the *Status Bar* area, the message: "*Select edge, vertex, work geometry or sketch geometry to project.*" is displayed. Inside the *Browser* window, select the ***Center Point*** to project the point onto the sketching plane.

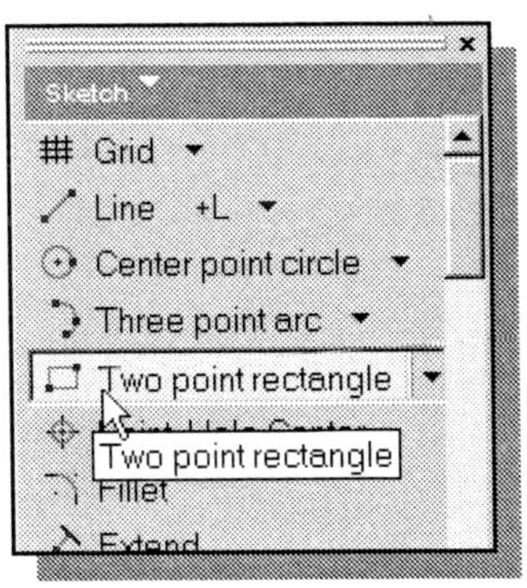

7. Select the ***Two point rectangle*** command by clicking once with the left-mouse-button on the icon in the *Sketch* toolbar.

8. Create a rectangle of arbitrary size that is toward the right side of the graphics window as shown.

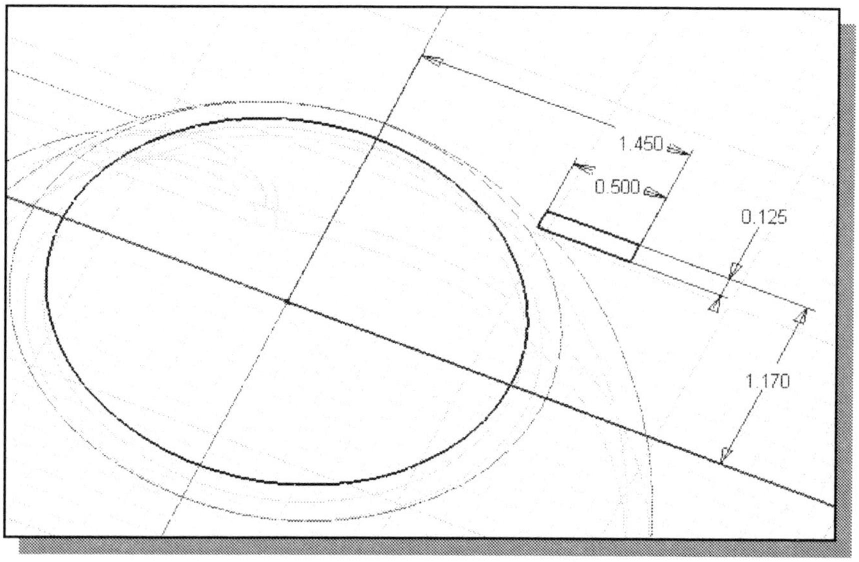

9. On your own, create and modify the dimensions as shown in the above figure.

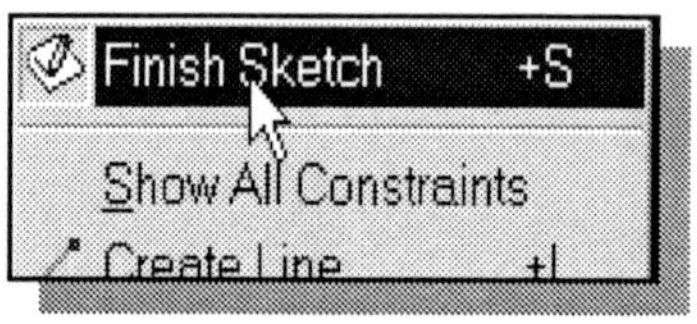

10. Inside the graphics window, click once with the right-mouse-button to display the option menu. Select **Finish Sketch** in the popup menu to end the *Sketch* option.

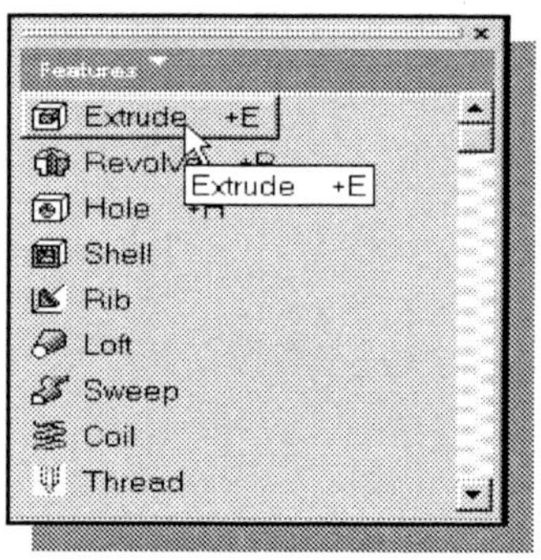

11. In the *Features* toolbar (the toolbar that is located to the left side of the graphics window), select the ***Extrude*** command by releasing the left-mouse-button on the icon.

12. Select the inside region of the rectangle as the profile of the extrusion.

13. Inside the *Extrude* dialog box, select the ***Cut*** operation and set the *Extents Distance* to **0.13 in** as shown.

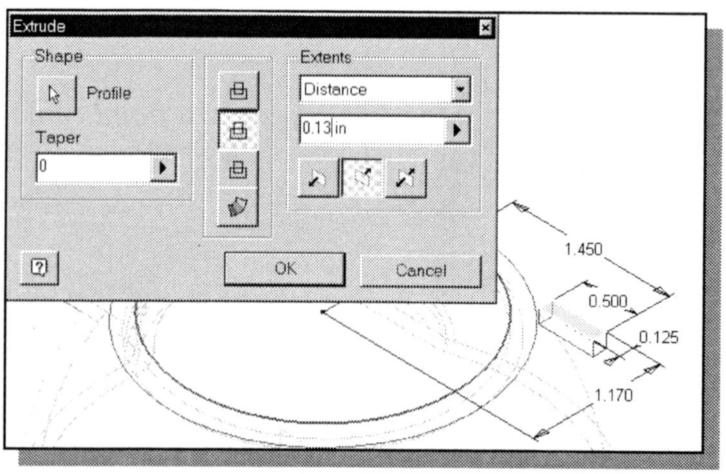

14. In the *Extrude* dialog box, click on the **OK** button to proceed with creating the cut feature.

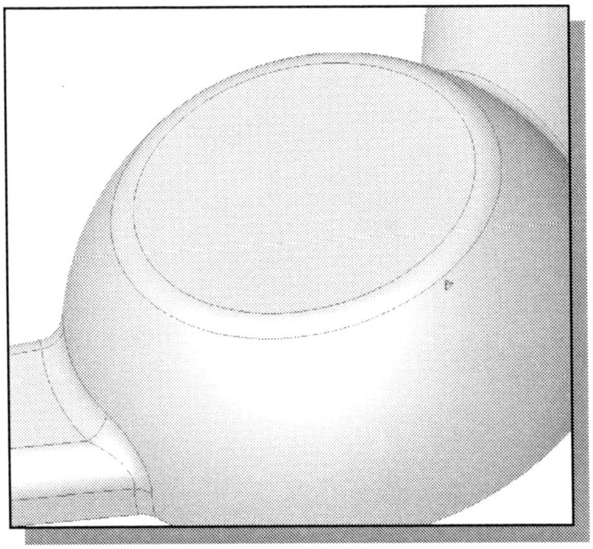

- Note that the pattern leader creates a fairly small cut on the solid model.

Creating a Rectangular Pattern

In *Autodesk Inventor*, existing features can be easily duplicated. The ***Pattern*** command allows us to create both rectangular and polar arrays of features. The patterned features are parametrically linked to the original feature; any modifications to the original feature are also reflected on the arrayed features.

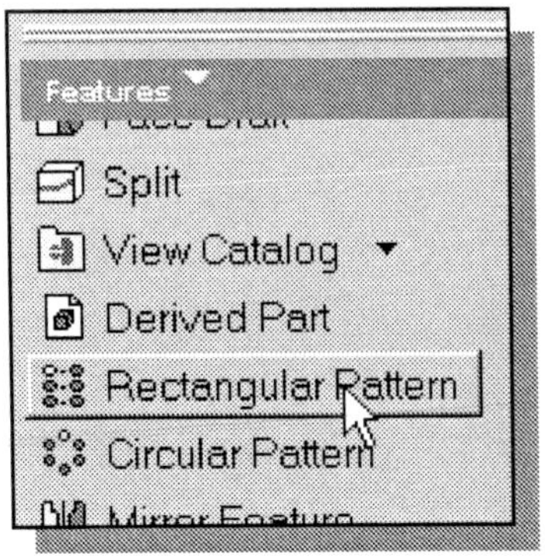

1. In the *Features* toolbar, select the ***Rectangular Pattern*** command by left-clicking once on the icon.

2. The message "*Select Feature to be arrayed*:" is displayed in the command prompt window. Select **Extrusion1**, the *cut feature created in the last section,* in the *Browser* window.

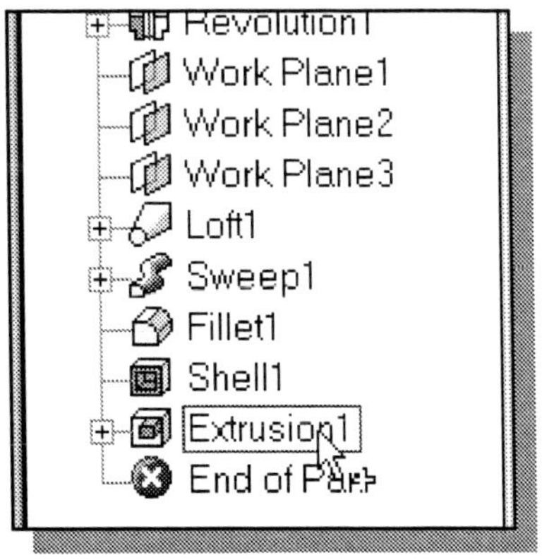

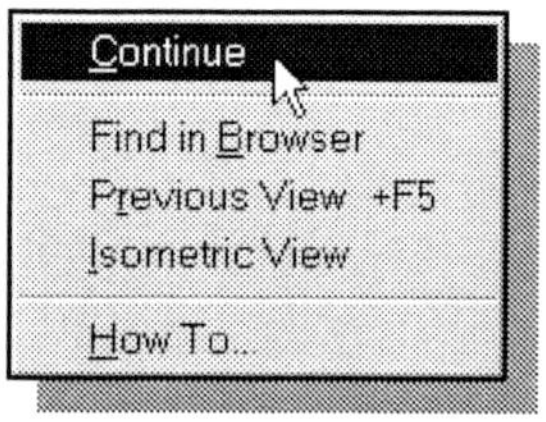

3. Inside the graphics window, right-mouse-click to bring up the option menu.

4. Select **Continue** in the option list to proceed with the *Rectangular Pattern* command.

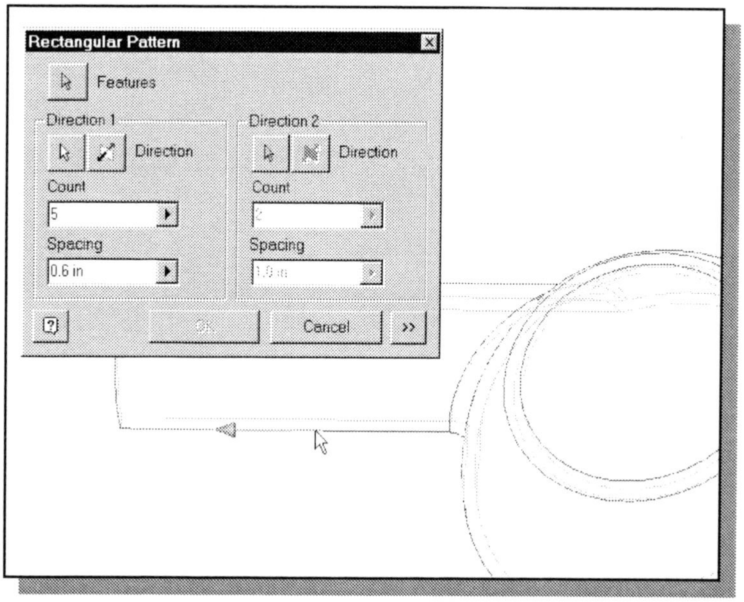

5. In the *Rectangular Pattern* dialog box, notice the **selection** option for *Direction 1* is activated. Click on an edge along the swept feature as shown in the figure.

6. In the *Rectangular Pattern* dialog box, enter **5** in the *Count* box and **0.6** in the *Spacing* box as shown.

7. In the *Rectangular Pattern* dialog box, click on the **direction selection** icon for *Direction 2*.

8. Click on an edge along the lofted feature as shown in the figure.

9. In the *Rectangular Pattern* dialog box, enter **10** in the *Count* box and **0.25** in the *Spacing* box as shown.

10. Click on the **OK** button to accept the settings and create the polar array.

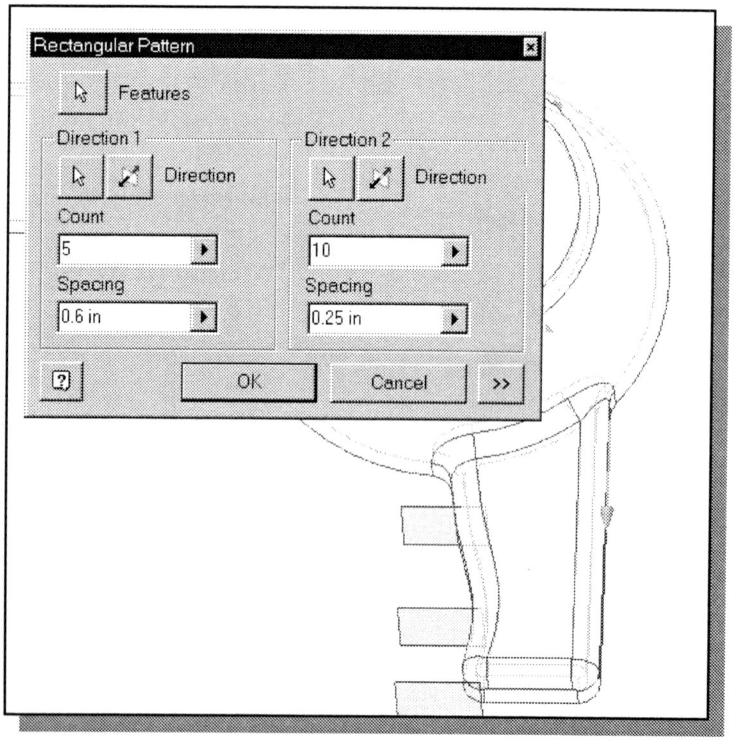

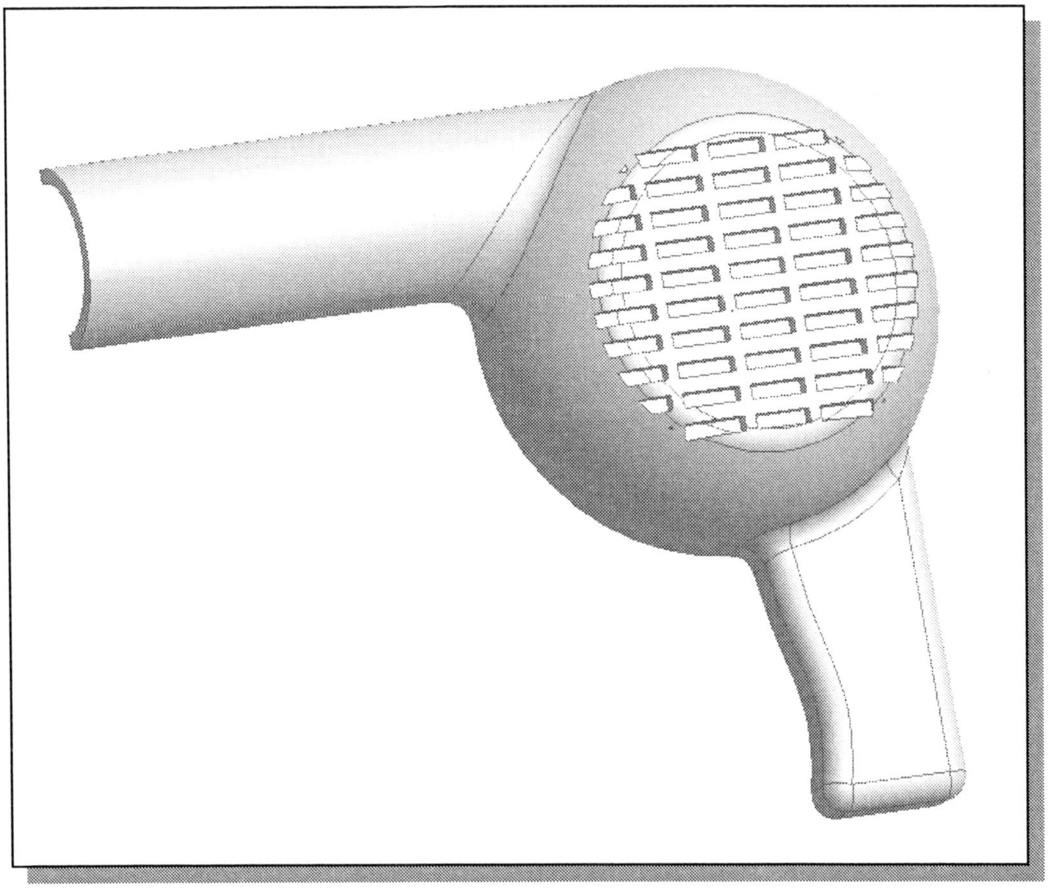

Examining the Parent/Child Relationships

The *Model Tree* now contains many items: work planes, work axes, work points, and four solid features. All of the parent/child relationships were established implicitly as we created the solid features. As more features are created, it becomes much more difficult to make a sketch showing all the parent/child relationships involved in the model. On the other hand, it is not really necessary to have a detailed picture showing all the relationships among the features. In using a feature-based modeler, the main emphasis is to consider the interactions that exist between the **immediate features**. Treat each feature as a unit by itself, and be clear on the parent/child relationships for each feature. Thinking in terms of features is what distinguishes *feature-based modeling* and the previous generation solid modeling techniques.

❖ On your own, *suppress* the ***Shell1*** feature and create another ***Shell*** as the last feature of the model. How would this addition change the result of the *Rectangular Pattern*?

Questions:

1. Keeping the *History Tree* in mind, what is the difference between *Cut with a Pattern* and *Cut Each One Individually*?

2. What is the difference between ***Sweep*** and ***Extrude***?

3. What are the advantages and disadvantages of creating fillets using the ***3D Fillets*** command and creating fillets in the 2D profiles?

4. Describe the steps used to create the *Shell* feature in the lesson.

5. How do we modify the *Pattern* parameters after the model is built?

6. Describe the elements required in creating a *Swept* feature.

7. Create sketches showing the steps you plan to use to create the model shown on the next page:

Exercise:

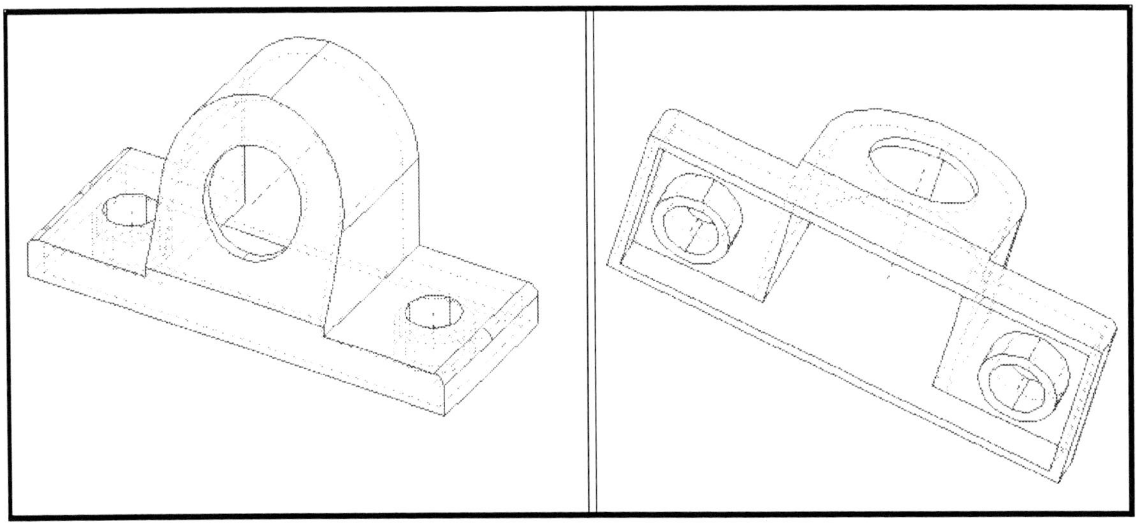

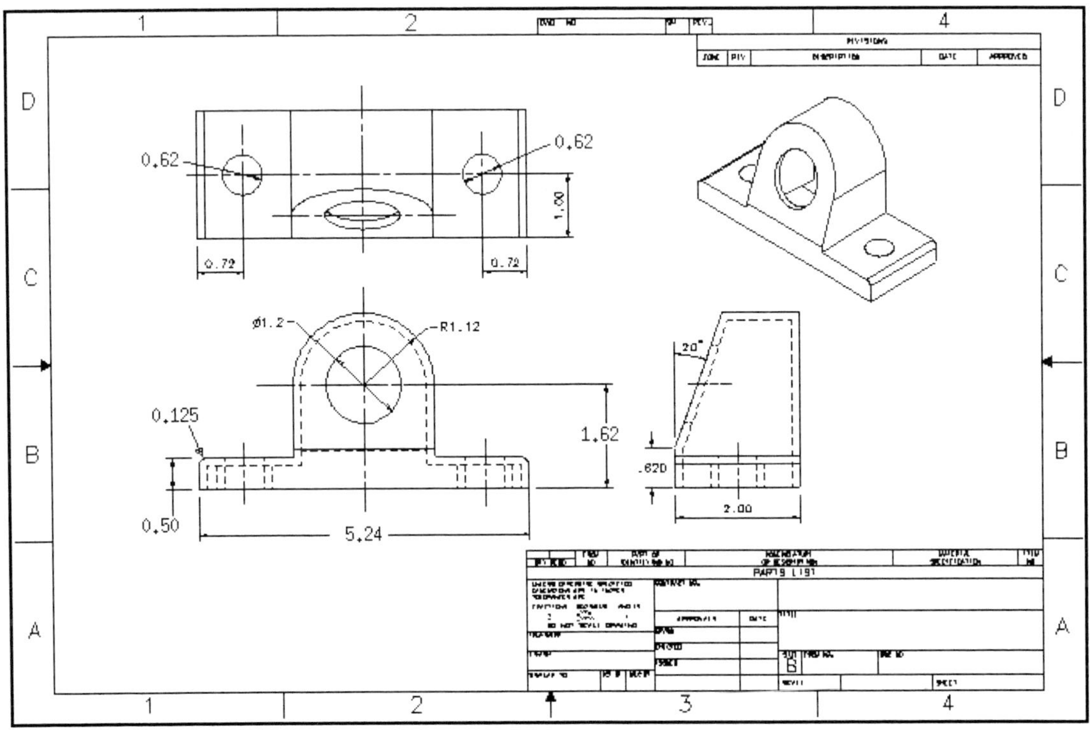
0.62
0.62
1.00
0.72
0.72
Ø1.2
R1.12
0.125
1.62
0.50
5.24
20°
.620
2.00
PARTS LIST

Notes:

Lesson 10
Assembly Modeling - Putting It All Together

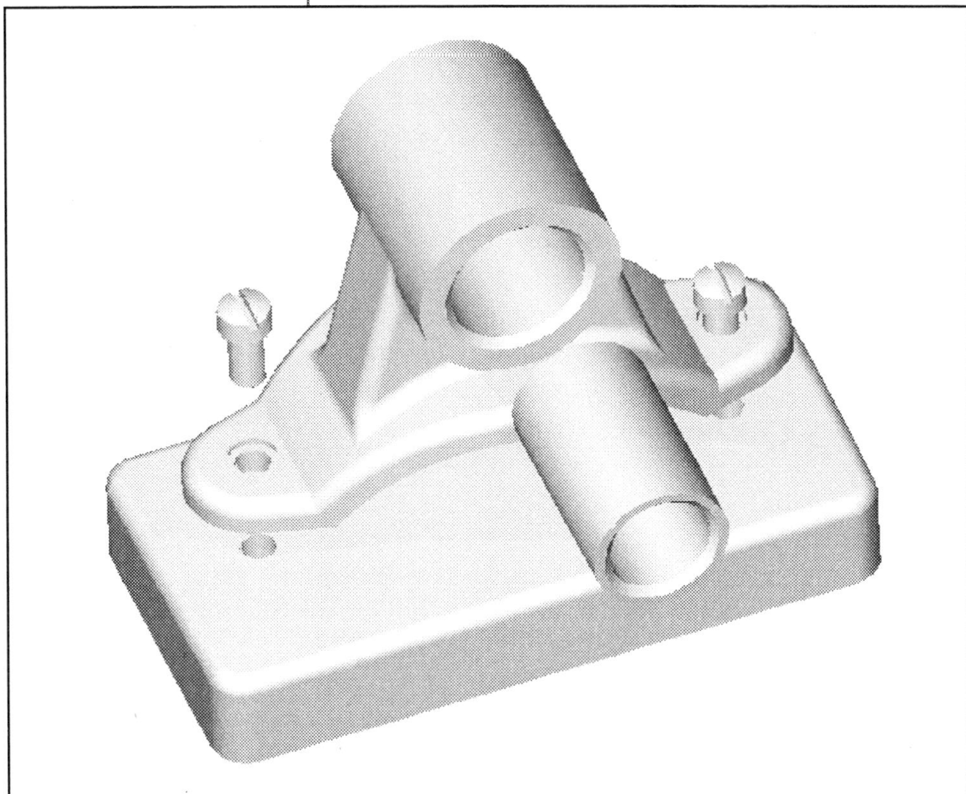

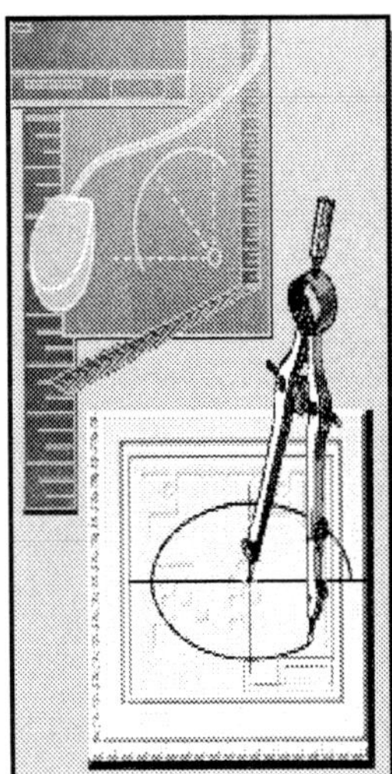

Learning Objectives

When you have completed this lesson, you will be able to:

- ♦ Understand the Assembly Modeling Methodology.
- ♦ Create Parts in the Assembly Modeler Mode.
- ♦ Understand and Utilize Assembly Constraints.
- ♦ Understand the Autodesk Inventor DOF Display.
- ♦ Utilize the Autodesk Inventor Adaptive Design approach.
- ♦ Create Exploded Assemblies.

Introduction

In the previous lessons, we have gone over the fundamentals of creating basic parts and drawings. In this lesson, we will examine the assembly modeling functionality of *Autodesk Inventor*. We will start with a demonstration on how to create and modify assembly models. The main task in creating an assembly is establishing the assembly relationships between parts. To assemble parts into an assembly, we will need to consider the assembly relationships between parts. It is a good practice to assemble parts based on the way they would be assembled in the actual manufacturing process. We should also consider breaking down the assembly into smaller subassemblies, which helps the management of parts. In *Autodesk Inventor*, a subassembly is treated the same way as a single part during assembling. Many parallels exist between assembly modeling and part modeling in parametric modeling software such as *Autodesk Inventor*.

Autodesk Inventor provides full associative functionality in all design modules, including assemblies. When we change a part model, *Autodesk Inventor* will automatically reflect the changes in all assemblies that use the part. We can also modify a part in an assembly. **Bi-directional full associative functionality** is the main feature of parametric solid modeling software that allows us to increase productivity by reducing design cycle time.

One of the key-features of *Autodesk Inventor* is the use of an assembly-centric paradigm, which enables users to concentrate on the design without depending on the associated parameters or constraints. Users can specify how parts fit together and the *Autodesk Inventor assembly-based fit function* automatically determines the parts' sizes and positions. This unique approach is known as the **Direct Adaptive Assembly approach**, which defines part relationships directly with no order dependency.

In this lesson, we will also illustrate the basic concept of *Autodesk Inventor*'s **Adaptive Design** approach. The key element in doing **Adaptive Design** is to ***underconstrain*** features or parts. The applied *assembly constraints* in the assembly modeler are used to control the sizes, shapes, and positions of ***underconstrained*** sketches, features, and parts. No equations are required and this approach is extremely flexible when performing modifications and changes to the design. We can modify adaptive assemblies at any point, in any order, regardless of how the parts were originally placed or constrained.

In *Autodesk Inventor*, features and parts can be made adaptive at any time during creation or during assembly. The features of a part can be defined as adaptive when they are created in the part file. When we place such a part in an assembly, the features will then resize and change shapes based on the applied assembly constraints. We can make features and parts adaptive from either the part modeling or assembly modeling environments.

The *Adaptive Design approach* is a unique design methodology that can only be found in *Autodesk Inventor*. The goal of this methodology is to improve the design process and allows you, the designer, to **Design the Way You Think**.

Assembly Modeling Methodology

The *Autodesk Inventor* assembly modeler provides tools and functions that allow us to create 3D parametric assembly models. An assembly model is a 3D model with any combination of multiple part models. *Parametric Assembly constraints* can be used to control relationships between parts in an assembly model.

Autodesk Inventor can work with any of the assembly modeling methodologies:

The Bottom Up approach

The first step in the *bottom up* assembly modeling approach is to create the individual parts. The parts are then pulled together into an assembly. This approach is typically used for smaller projects with very few team members.

The Top Down approach

The first step in the *top down* assembly modeling approach is to create the assembly model of the project. Initially, individual parts are represented by names or symbolically. The details of the individual parts are added as the project gets further along. This approach is typically used for larger projects or during the conceptual design stage. Members of the project team can then concentrate on the particular section of the project to which he/she is assigned.

The Middle Out approach

The *middle out* assembly modeling approach is a mixture of the bottom-up and top-down methods. This type of assembly model is usually constructed with most of the parts already created and additional parts are designed and created using the assembly for construction information. Some requirements are known and some standard components are used, but new designs must also be produced to meet specific objectives. This combined strategy is a very flexible approach to creating assembly models.

The different assembly modeling approaches described above can be used as guidelines to manage design projects. Keep in mind that we can start modeling our assembly using one approach and then switch to a different approach without any problems.

In this lesson, the *bottom up* assembly modeling approach is illustrated. All of the parts (components) required to form the assembly are created first. *Autodesk Inventor*'s assembly modeling tools allow us to create complex assemblies by using components that are created in part files or in place in assembly files. A component can be a subassembly or a single part, where features and parts can be modified at anytime. The sketches and profiles used to build part features can be fully or partially constrained. Partially constrained features may be adaptive, which means the size or shape of the associated parts are adjusted in an assembly when the parts are constrained to other parts. The basic concept and procedure of using the adaptive assembly approach is demonstrated in the tutorial.

The Shaft Support Assembly

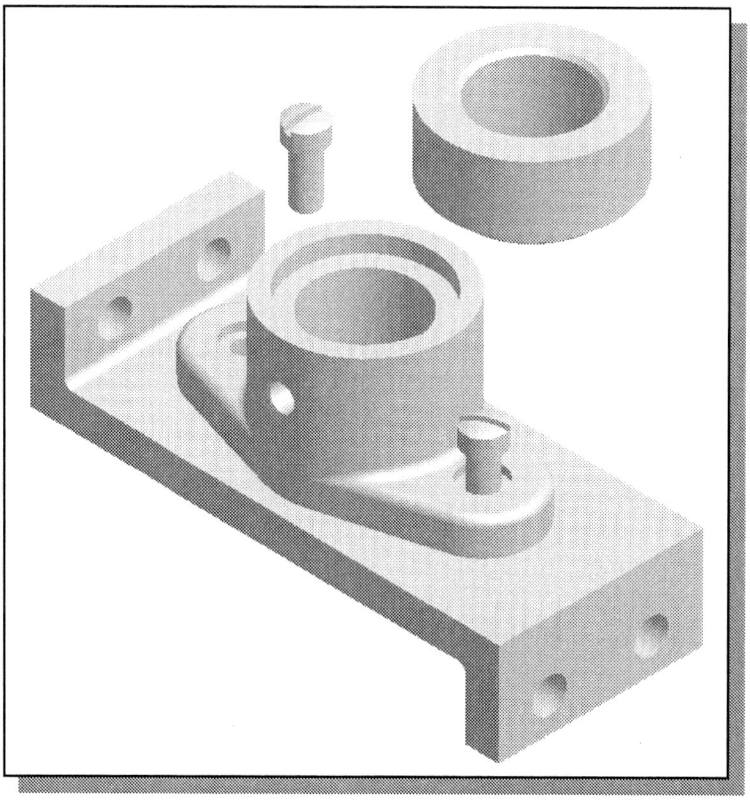

Additional *Parts*

- Four parts are required for the assembly: (1) ***Collar***, (2) ***Bearing***, (3) ***Base-Plate*** and (4) ***Cap-Screw***. Create the four parts as shown below, then save the models as separate part files: *Collar*, *Bearing*, *Base-Plate*, and *Cap-Screw*. (Close all part files or exit *Autodesk Inventor* after you have created the parts.)

(1) ***Collar***

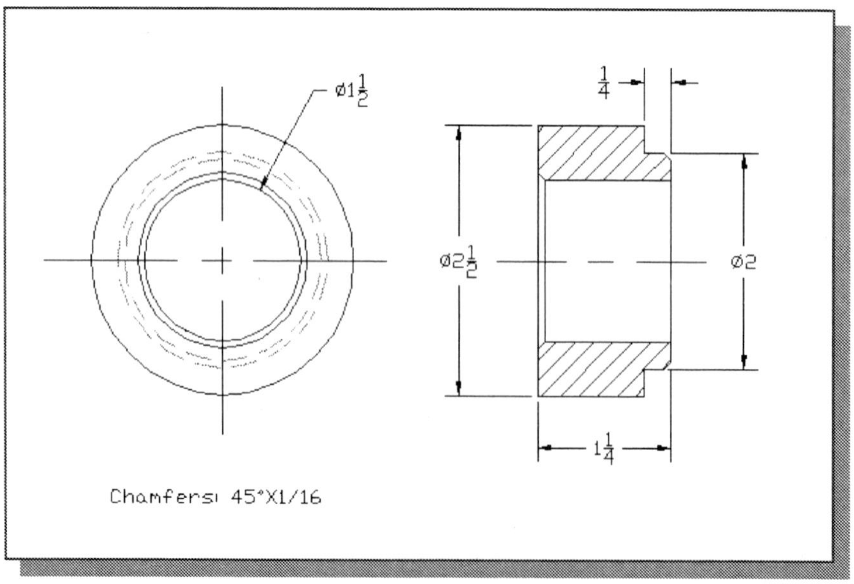

(2) *Bearing*

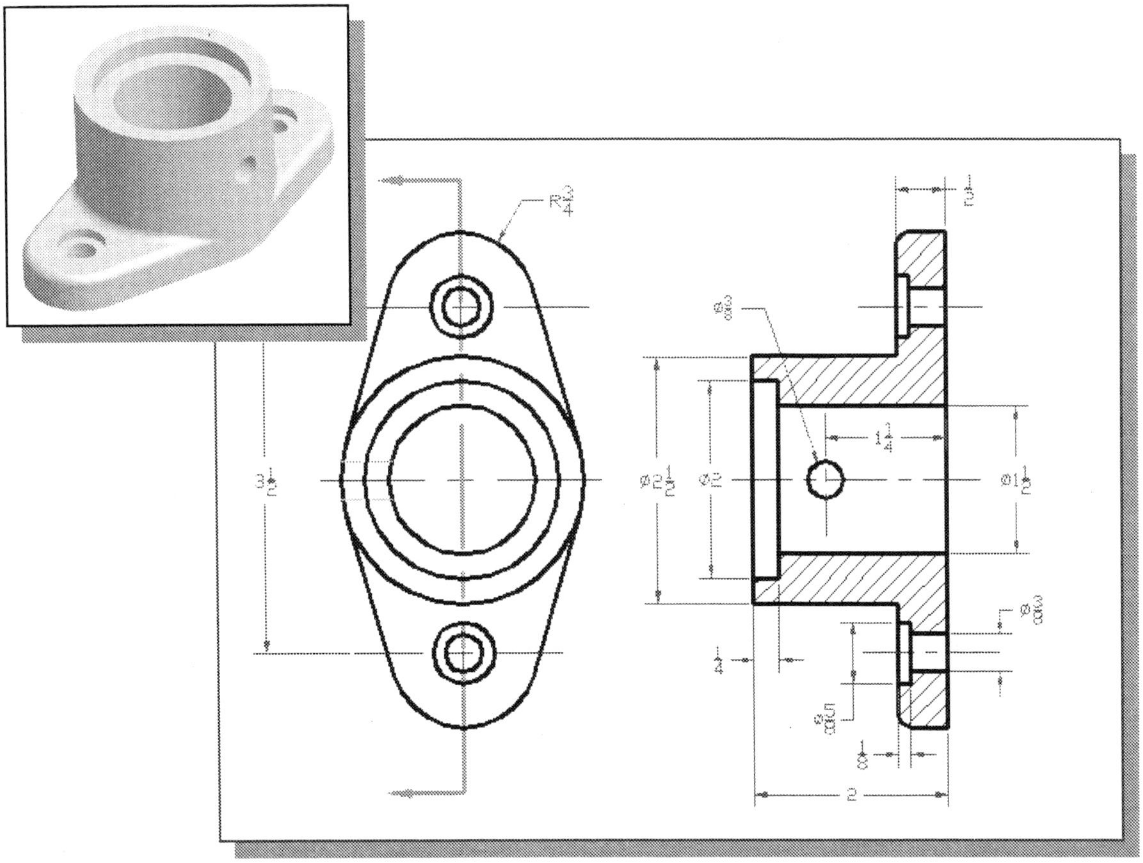

(3) Base-Plate

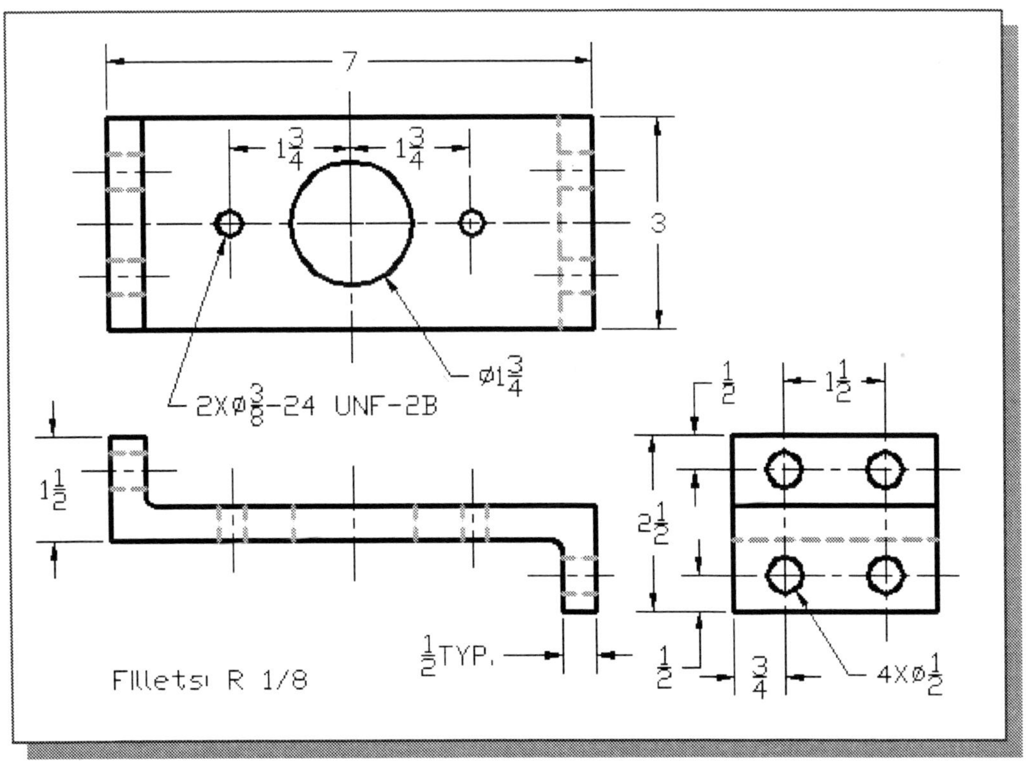

(4) ***Cap-Screw***

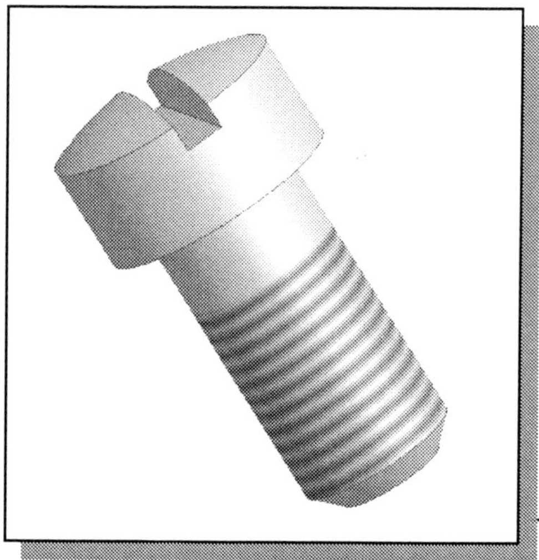

- Autodesk Inventor provides two options to creating threads: ***Thread*** and ***Coil***. The ***Thread*** command does not create true 3D threads; a pre-defined thread image is applied on the selected surface, as shown in the figure. The ***Coil*** command can be used to create true threads, which contain complex three-dimensional curves and surfaces. You are encouraged to experiment with the ***Coil*** command and the ***Thread*** command to creating threads.

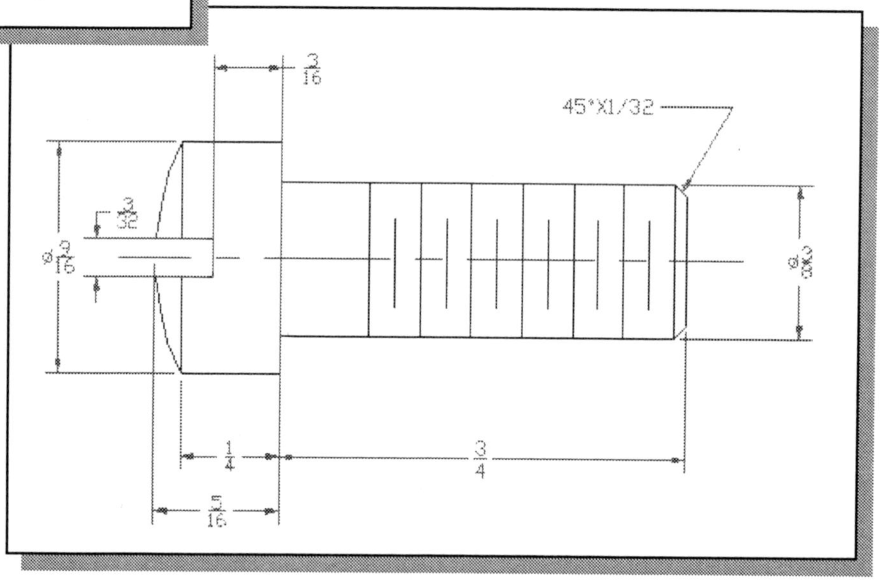

- Hint: First create a revolved feature using the profile shown below.

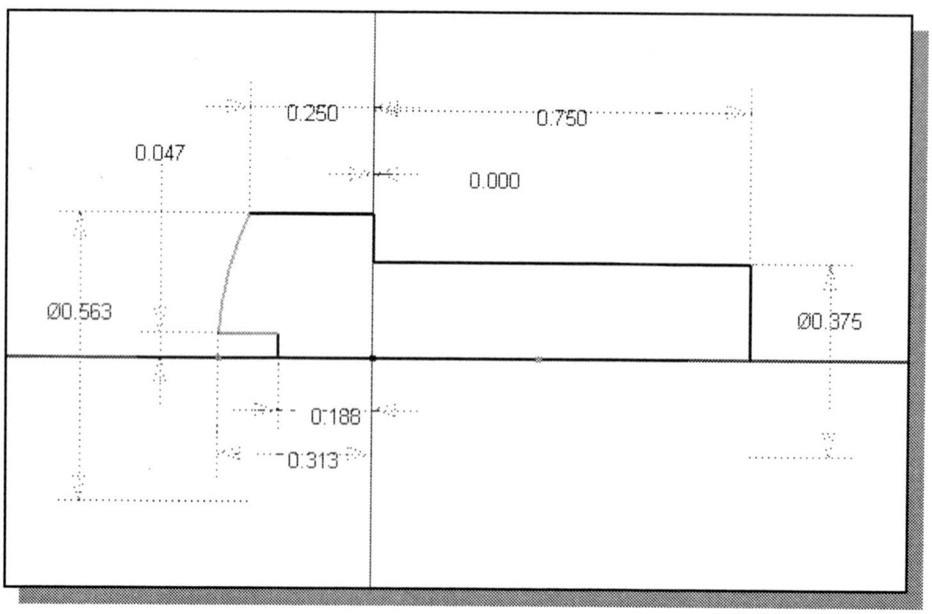

Starting Autodesk Inventor

1. Select the ***Autodesk Inventor*** option on the *Start* menu or select the ***Autodesk Inventor*** icon on the desktop to start *Autodesk Inventor*. The *Autodesk Inventor* main window will appear on the screen.

2. Once the program is loaded into the memory, the ***Startup*** dialog box appears at the center of the screen.

3. Select the ***New*** icon with a single click of the left-mouse-button in the *What to Do* dialog box.

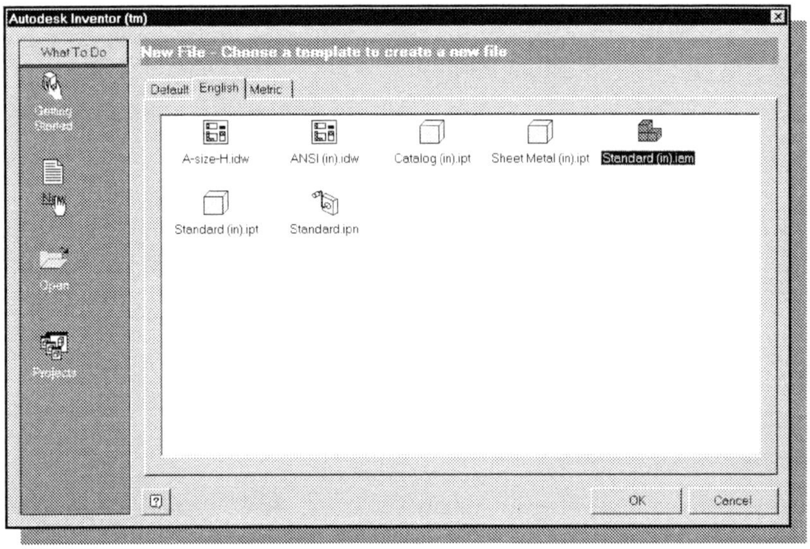

4. Select the **English** tab and in the *New - Choose Template* area, select **Standard(in).iam** (Standard *Inventor* Assembly Model template file).

5. Click on the **OK** button in the *Startup* dialog box to accept the selected settings.

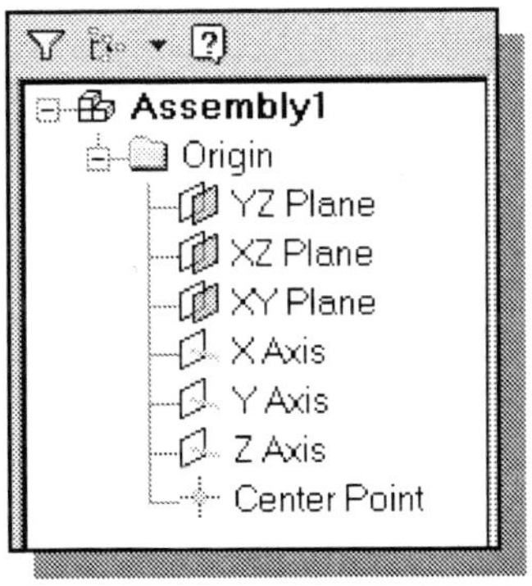

- In the *Browser* window, the *Assembly1* icon is displayed with a set of work planes, work axes and work point. In most aspects, the usage of work planes, work axes and work point is very similar to that of the *Inventor Part Modeler*.

- Notice that, in the *Assembly* toolbar, only two options are available: **Place Component** and **Create Component**. As the names imply, we can use parts that have been created or create new parts within the *Inventor Assembly Modeler*.

Placing the First Component

- The first component placed in an assembly should be a fundamental part or subassembly. The first component in an assembly file sets the orientation of all subsequent parts and subassemblies. The origin of the first component is aligned to the origin of the assembly coordinates and the part is grounded (all degrees of freedom are removed). The rest of the assembly is built on the first component, the ***base component***. In most cases, this *base component* should be one that is **not likely to be removed** and **preferably a non-moving part** in the design. Note that there is no distinction in an assembly between components; the first component we place is usually considered as the *base component* because it is usually a fundamental component to which others are constrained. We can change the base component to a different base component by placing a new base component, specify it as grounded, and then re-constrain any components placed earlier, including the first component. For our project, we will use the ***Base-Plate*** as the base component in the assembly.

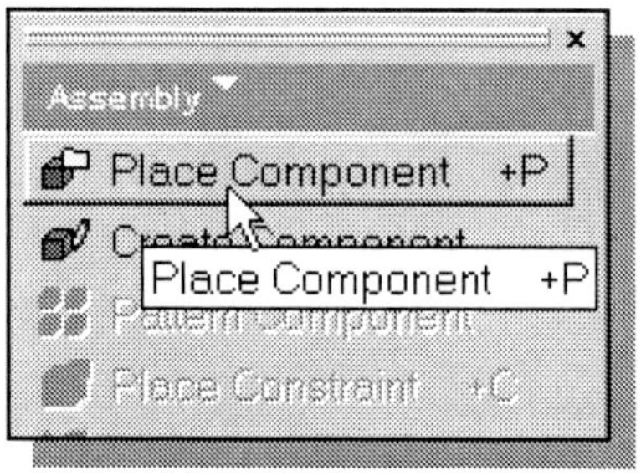

1. In the *Assembly* toolbar (the toolbar that is located to the left side of the graphics window), select the ***Place Component*** command by left-mouse-clicking the icon.

2. Select the ***Base-Plate*** (part file: ***Base-Plate.ipt***) in the list window.

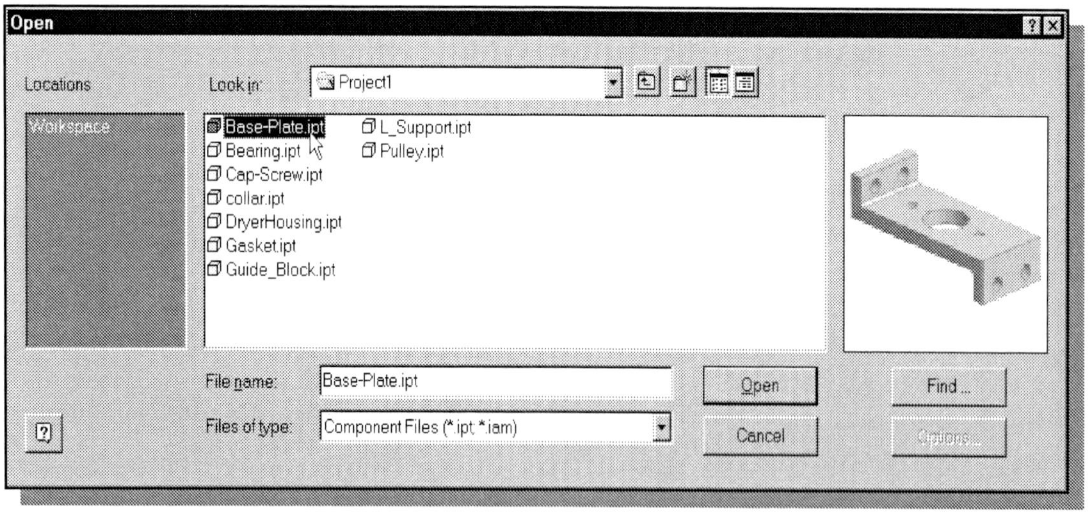

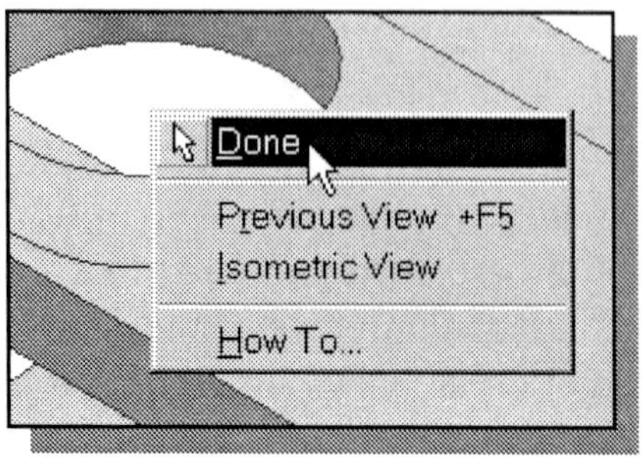

3. Click on the **Open** button to retrieve the model.

4. By default, the first component is automatically aligned to the origin of the assembly coordinates. We can also place multiple copies of the same component**. Right-mouse-click** once to bring up the option menu and select **Done** to end the placement of the *Base-Plate* part.

Placing the Second Component

➢ We will retrieve the *Bearing* part as the second component of the assembly model.

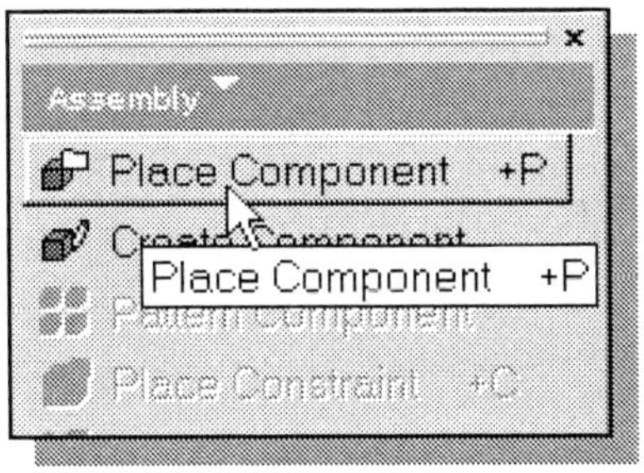

1. In the *Assembly* toolbar (the toolbar that is located to the left side of the graphics window), select the ***Place Component*** command by left-mouse-clicking the icon.

2. Select the **Bearing** design (part file: ***Bearing.ipt***) in the list window. And click on the **Open** button to retrieve the model.

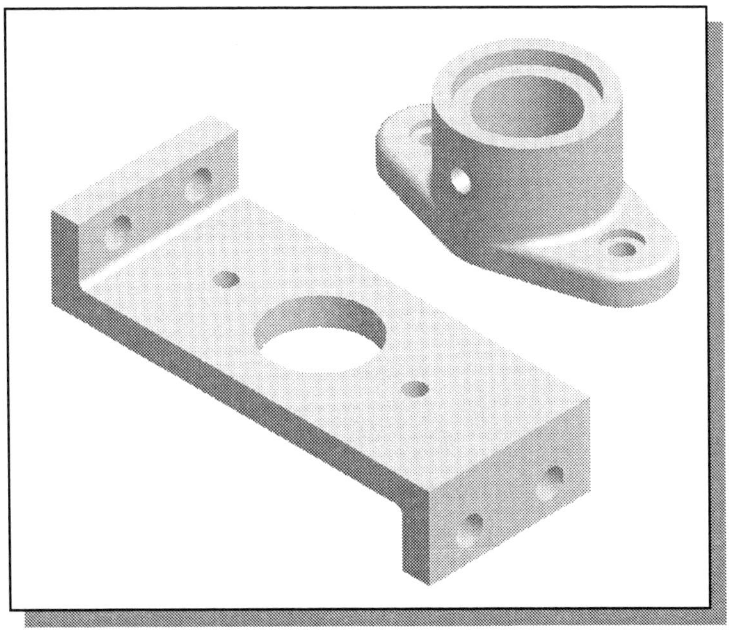

3. Place the *Bearing* toward the upper-right corner of the graphics window, as shown in the figure.

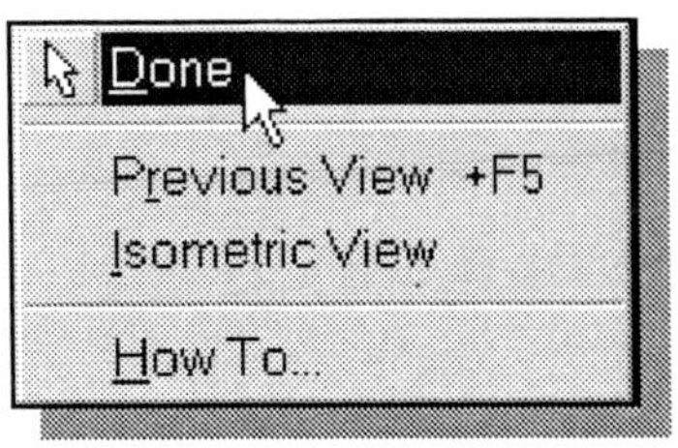

4. Inside the graphics window, right-mouse-click once to bring up the option menu and select **Done** to end the placement of the *Bearing* part.

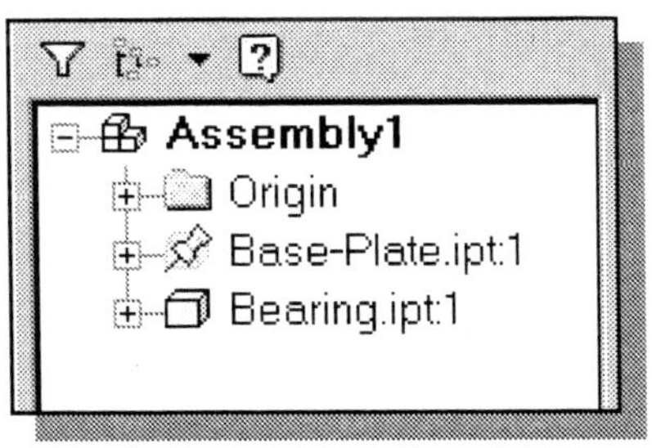

- Inside the *Browser* window, the retrieved parts are listed in their corresponding order. The ***Pin*** icon in front of the *Base-Plate* filename signifies the part is grounded and all ***six degrees of freedom*** are restricted. The number behind the filename is used to identify the number of copies of the same component in the assembly model.

Degrees of Freedom and Constraints

- Each component in an assembly has six **degrees of freedom (DOF)**, or ways in which 3D rigid bodies can move: movement along the X, Y, and Z axes (translational freedom), plus it can rotatation around the X, Y, and Z axes (rotational freedom). *Translational DOF*s allow the part to move in the direction of the specified vector. *Rotational DOF*s allow the part to turn about the specified axis.

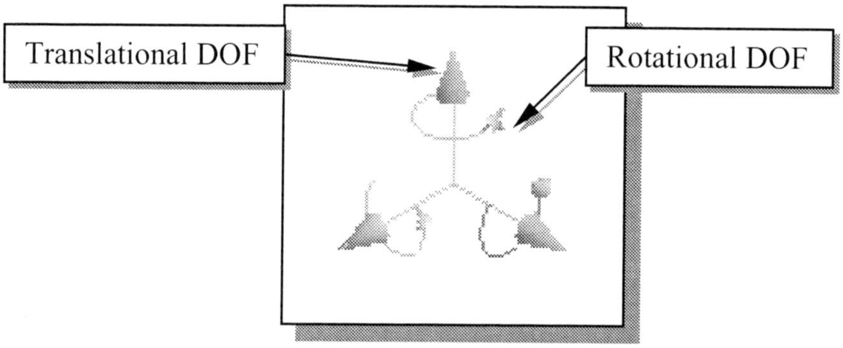

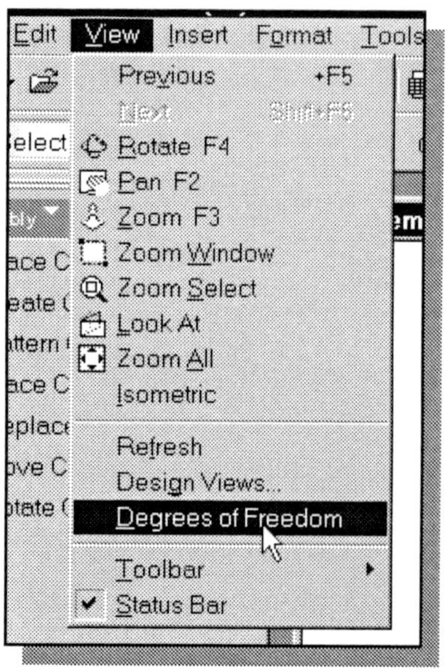

➢ Select the **Degrees Of Freedom** option in the **View** pull-down menu to display the DOF of the unconstrained component.

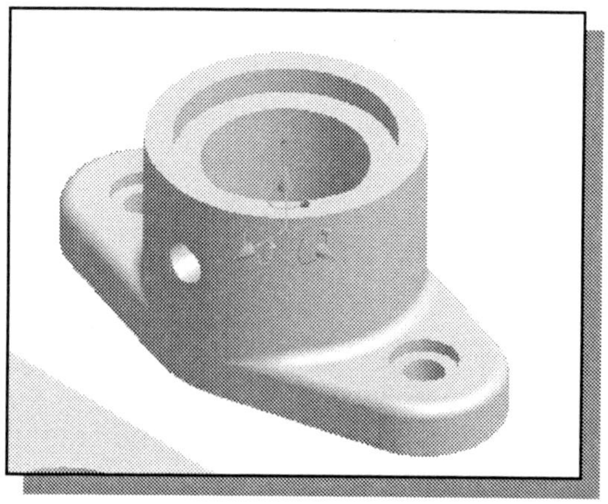

- In *Autodesk Inventor*, the degrees-of-freedom symbol shows the remaining degrees of freedom (both translational and rotational) for one or more components of the acti ve assembly. When a component is fully constrained in an assembly, the component cannot move in any direction. The position of the component is fixed relative to other assembly components. All of its degrees of freedom are removed. When we place an assembly constraint between two selected components, they are positioned relative to one another. Movement is still possible in the unconstrained directions.

- It is usually a good idea to fully constrain components so that their behavior is predictable as changes are made to the assembly. Leaving some degrees of freedom open can sometimes help retain design flexibility. As a general rule, we should use only enough constraints to ensure predictable assembly behavior and avoid unnecessary complexity.

Assembly Constraints

- We are now ready to assemble the components together. We will start by placing assembly constraints on the ***Bearing*** and the ***Base-Plate***.

  To assemble components into an assembly, we need to establish the assembly relationships between components. It is a good practice to assemble components the way they would be assembled in the actual manufacturing process. **Assembly constraints** create a parent/child relationship that allows us to capture the design intent of the assembly. Because the component that we are placing actually becomes a child to the already assembled components, we must use caution when choosing constraint types and references to make sure they reflect the intent.

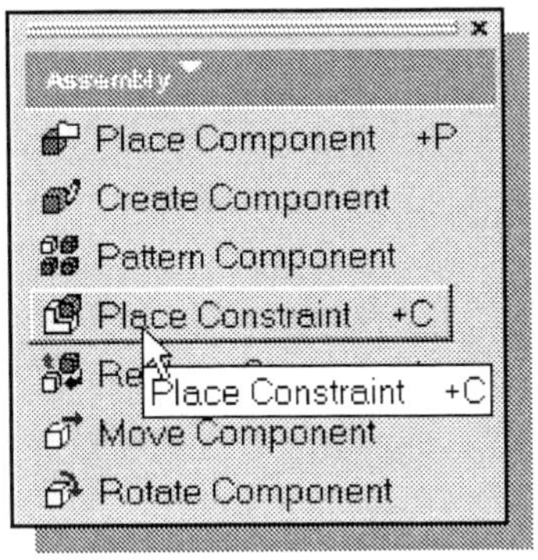

➢ In the *Assembly* toolbar, select the ***Place Constraint*** command by left-mouse-clicking once on the icon.

- The *Place Constraints* dialog box appears on the screen.

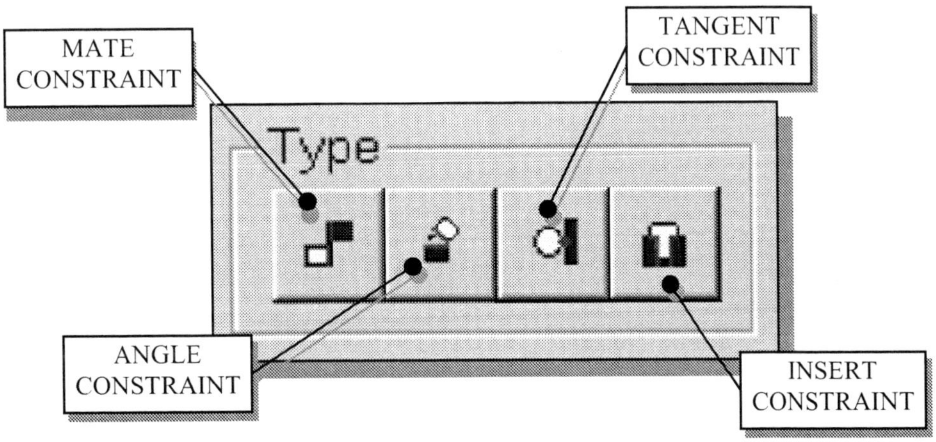

- Assembly models are created by applying proper *assembly constraints* to the individual component. The constraints are used to restrict the movement between parts. Constraints eliminate rigid body degrees of freedom (**DOF**). A 3D part has *six degrees of freedom* since the part can rotate and translate relative to the three coordinate axes. Each time we add a constraint between two parts, one or more DOF is eliminated. The movement of a fully constrained part is restricted in all directions. Four basic types of assembly constraints are available in *Autodesk Inventor*: Mate, Angle, Tangent and Insert. Each type of constraint removes different combinations of rigid body degrees of freedom. Note that it is possible to apply different constraints and achieve the same results.

➢ **Mate** - constraint positions components face-to-face, or adjacent to one another, with faces flush. Removes one degree of linear translation and two degrees of angular rotation between planar surfaces. Selected surfaces point in opposite directions and can be **offset** by a specified distance. Mate constraint positions selected faces normal to one another, with faces coincident.

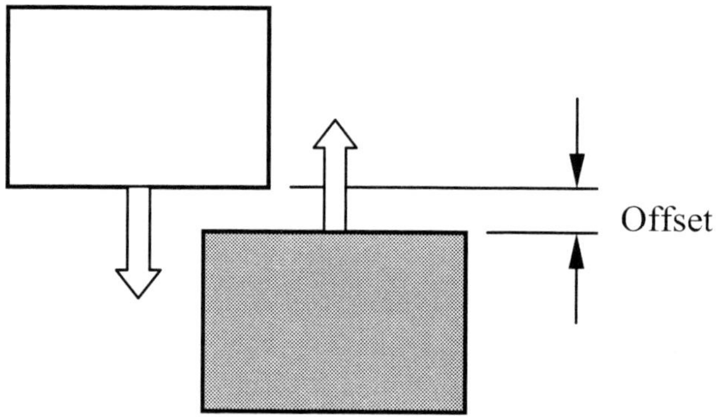

➢ **Flush** - Makes two planes coplanar with their faces aligned in the same direction. Selected surfaces point in the same direction and are offset by a specified distance. Flush constraint aligns components adjacent to one another with faces flush. Positions selected faces, curves, or points so that they are aligned with surface normals pointing in the same direction. (Note that the Flush constraint is listed as a selectable option in the Mate constraint.)

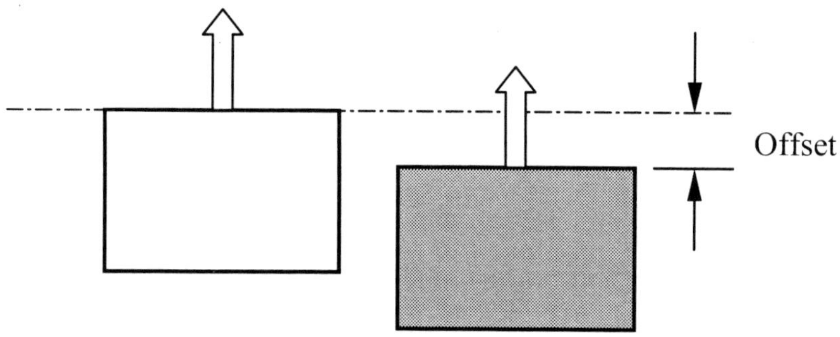

➢ **Angle** - Creates an angular assembly constraint between parts, subassemblies, or assemblies. Selected surfaces point in the direction specified by the angle.

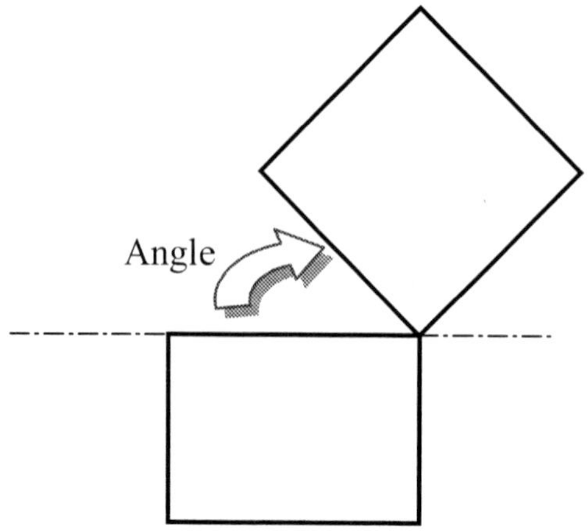

➢ **Tangent** - Aligns selected faces, planes, cylinders, spheres, and cones to contact at the point of tangency. Tangency may be on the inside or outside of a curve, depending on the selection of the direction of the surface normal. A Tangent constraint removes one degree of translational freedom.

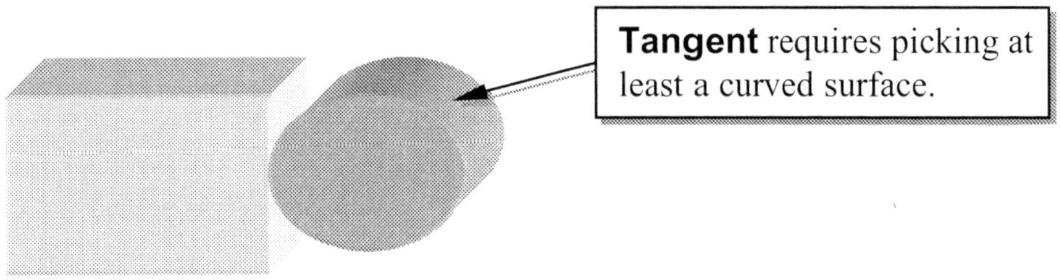

➢ **Insert** - Aligns two circles, including their center axes and planes. Selected circular surfaces become co-axial. Insert constraint is a combination of a face-to-face Mate constraint between planar faces and a Mate constraint between the axes of the two components. A rotational degree of freedom remains open. The surfaces do not need to be full 360-degree circles. Selected surfaces can point in opposite direction or in same direction and can be offset by a specified distance.

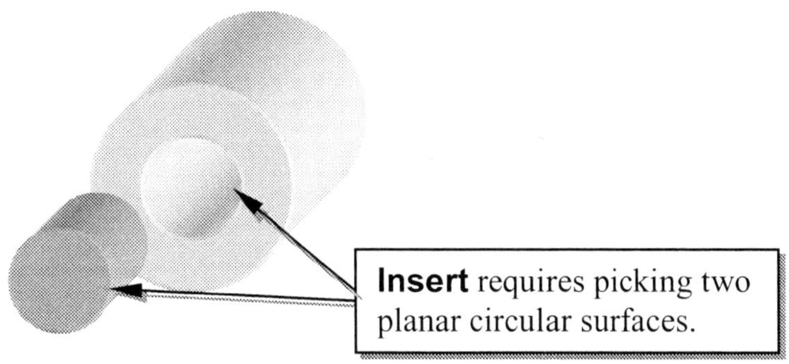

Apply the First Assembly Constraint

1. In the *Place Constraint* dialog box, confirm the constraint type is set to *Mate* constraint and select the top horizontal surface of the base part as the first part for the *MATE* alignment command.

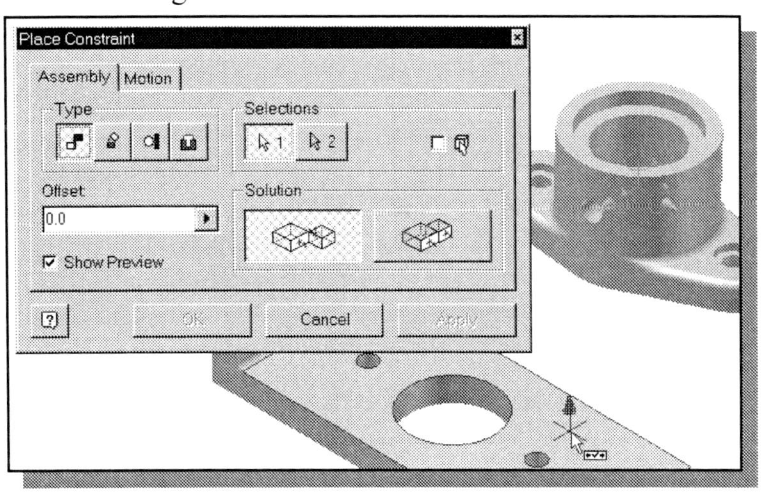

2. On your own, dynamically rotate the displayed model to view the bottom of the *Bearing* part, as shown in the below figure.

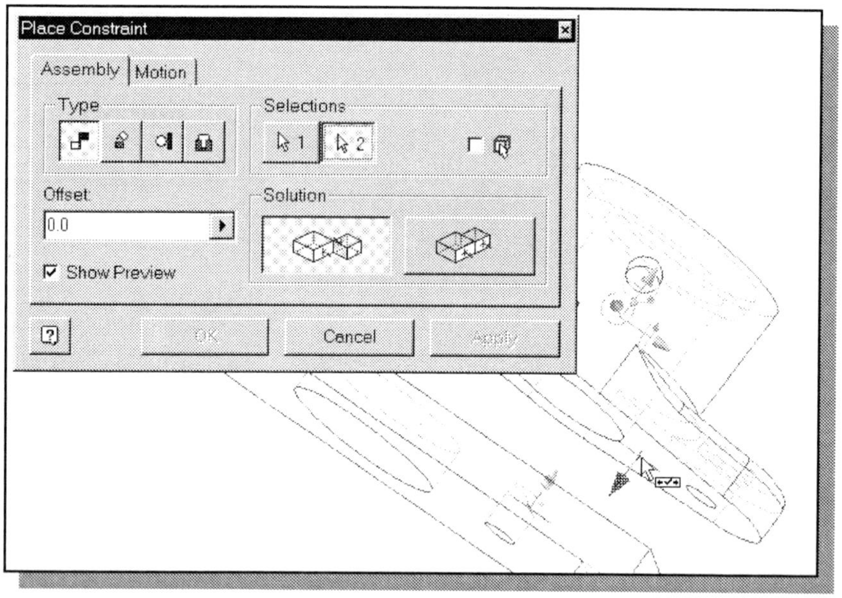

3. Click on the bottom face of the bearing part as the second part selection to apply the constraint. Note the direction normals shown in the figure, the **Mate** constraint requires the selection of opposite direction of surface normals.

4. Click on the **Apply** button to accept the selection and apply the **Mate** constraint.

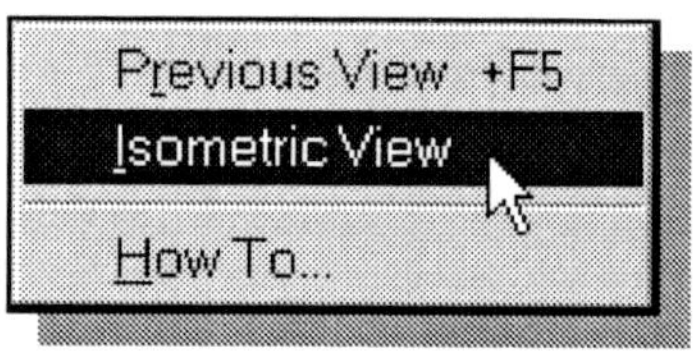

5. Move the cursor inside the graphics window, and then right-mouse-click to bring up the option menu.

6. Select the **Isometric View** to adjust the display of the assembly model.

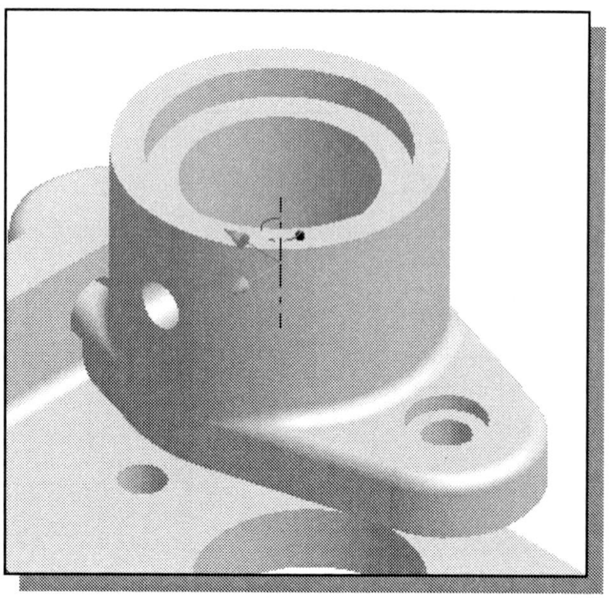

❖ Notice the DOF symbol is adjusted automatically in the graphics window. The Mate constraint removes one degree of linear translation and two degrees of angular rotation between the selected planar surfaces. The *Bearing* part can still move along two axes and rotate about the third axis.

Apply a Second MATE Constraint

❖ The Mate constraint can also be used to align axes of cylindrical features.

1. In the *Place Constraint* dialog box, confirm the constraint type is set to *Mate* constraint and the *Offset* option is set to **0.00**.

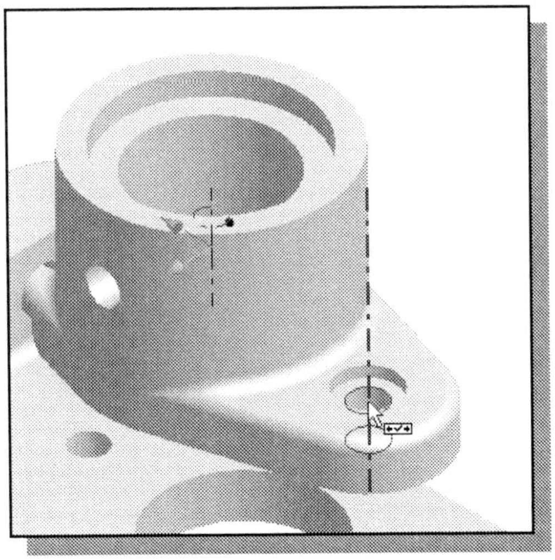

2. Move the cursor near the cylindrical surface of the right-counter-bore hole of the *Bearing* part. Select the axis when it is displayed as shown.

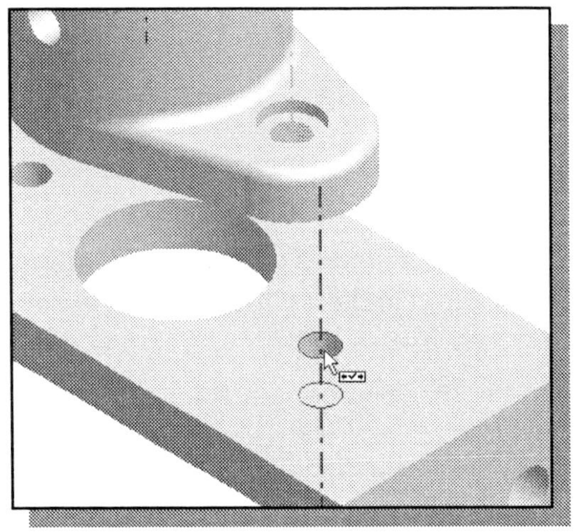

3. Move the cursor near the cylindrical surface of the small hole on the *Base-Plate* part. Select the axis when it is displayed as shown.

4. In the *Place Constraint* dialog box, click on the **Apply** button to accept the selection and apply the mate constraint.

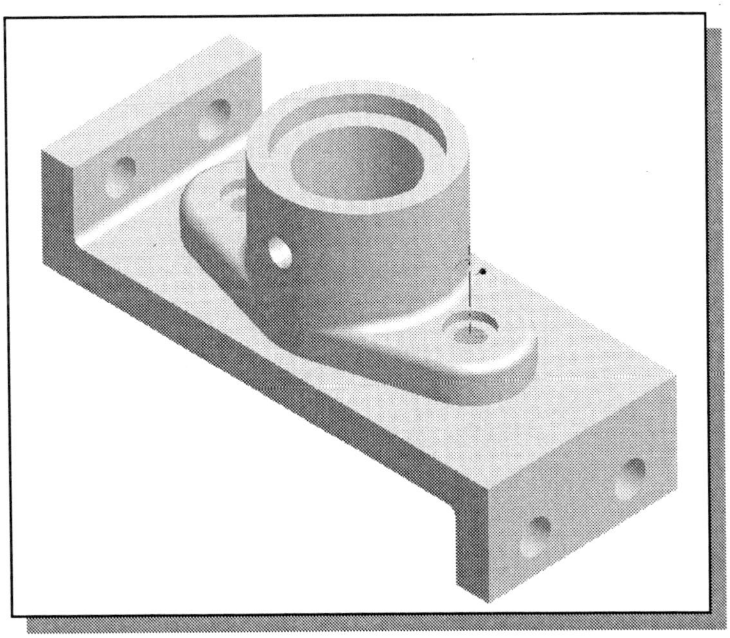

5. In the *Place Constraint* dialog box, click on the **Cancel** button to exit the *Place Constraint* command.

❖ The *Bearing* part appears to be placed in the correct position. But the DOF symbol indicates that this is not the case, the bearing part can still rotate about the displayed vertical axis.

Constrained Move

❖ To see how well a component is constrained, we can perform a constrained move. A constrained move is done by dragging the component in the graphics window with the left-mouse-button. A constrained move will honor previously applied assembly constraints. That is, the selected component and parts constrained to the component move together in their constrained positions. A grounded component remains grounded during the move.

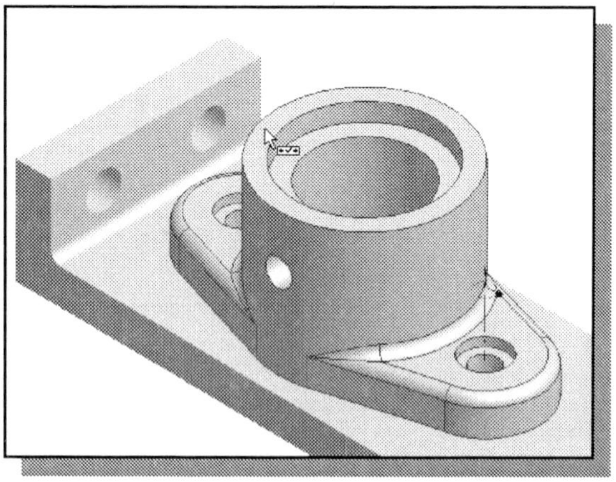

1. Inside the graphics window, move the cursor on top of the top surface of the *Bearing* part as shown in the figure.

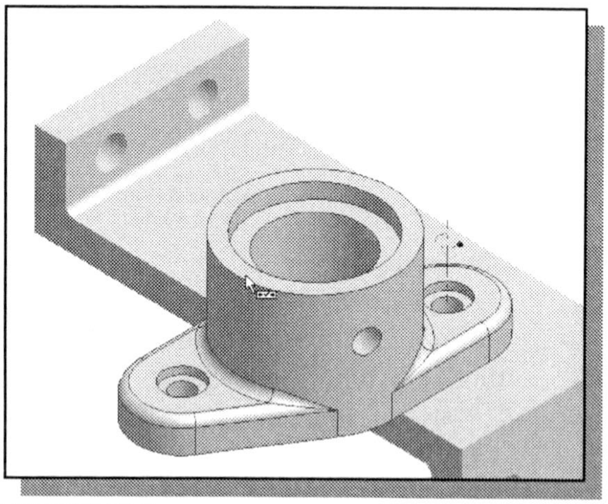

2. Press and hold down the left-mouse-button and drag the *Bearing* part downward.

❖ The *Bearing* part can freely rotate about the displayed axis.

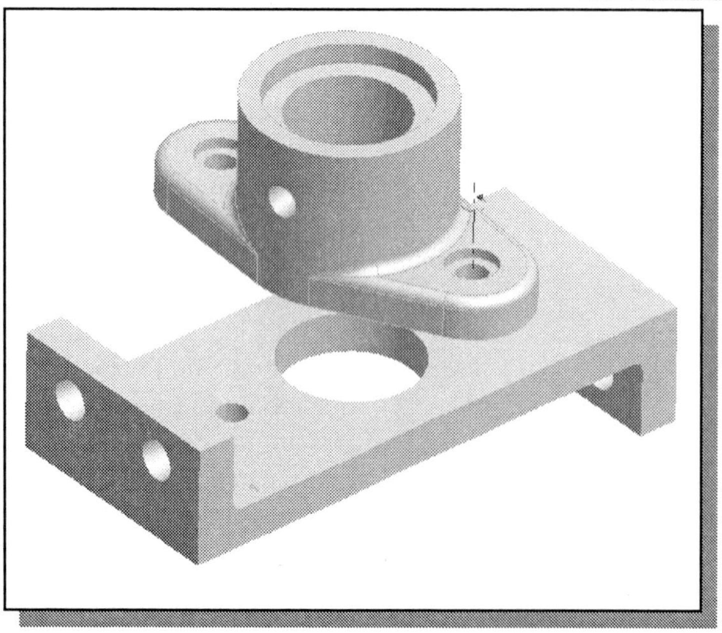

3. On your own, use the dynamic rotation command to view the alignment of the *Bearing* part.

4. Rotate the *Bearing* part and adjust the display as shown in the figure.

Apply a Flush Constraint

- Besides selecting the surfaces of solid models to apply constraints, we can also select the established work planes to apply the assembly constraints. This is an additional advantage of using the *BORN technique* in creating part models. For the *Bearing* part, we will apply a Mate constraint to two of the work planes and eliminate the last rotational DOF.

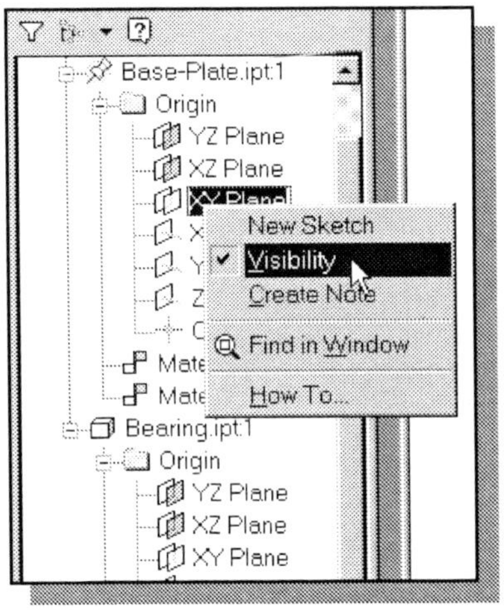

1. On your own, inside the *Browser* window toggle on the **Visibility** for the corresponding ***Work Planes*** of the *Base-Plate* and the *Bearing* parts.

2. In the *Assembly* toolbar, select the ***Place Constraint*** command by left-mouse-clicking once on the icon.

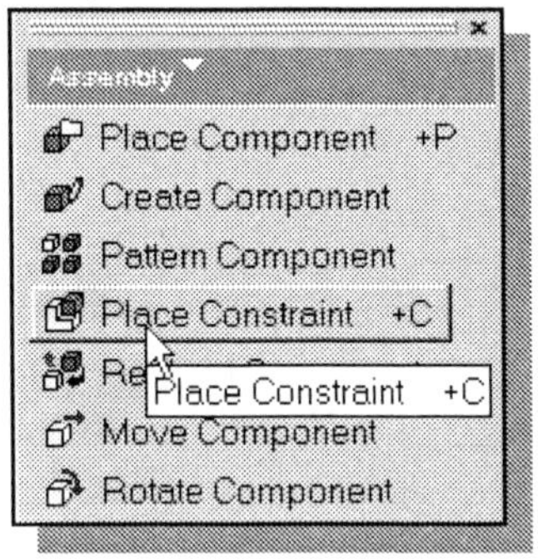

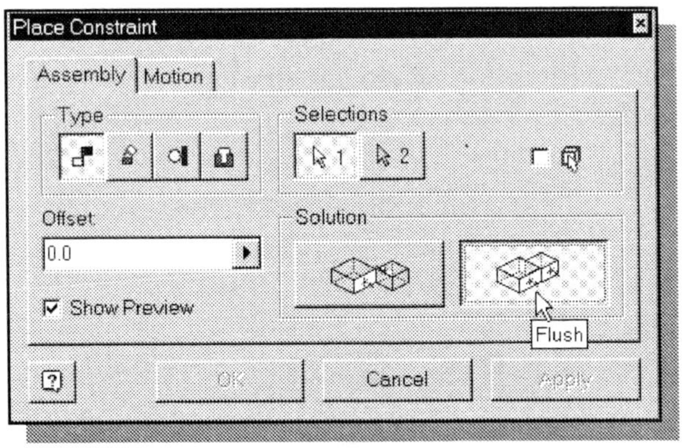

3. In the *Place Constraint* dialog box, confirm the constraint type is set to ***Mate*** constraint and the *Offset* option is set to **0.00**.

4. In the *Place Constraint* dialog box, switch the *Solution* option to ***Flush*** as shown.

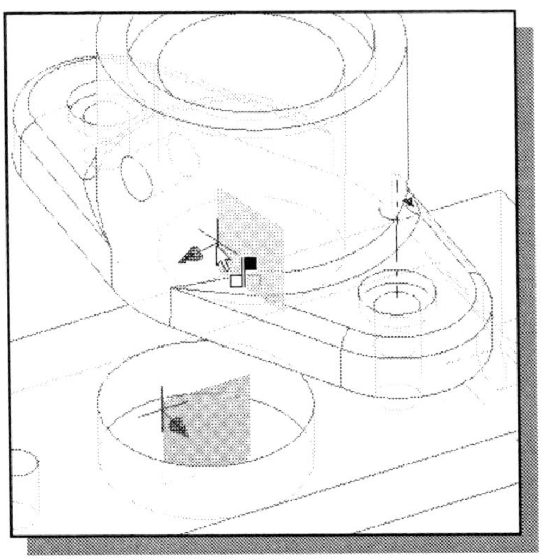

5. Select the *work plane* of the *Base-Plate* part as the first part for the *Flush* alignment command.

6. Select the corresponding *work plane* of the *Bearing* part as the second part for the *Flush* alignment command.

❖ Note that the **Flush** constraint makes two planes coplanar with their faces aligned in the same direction.

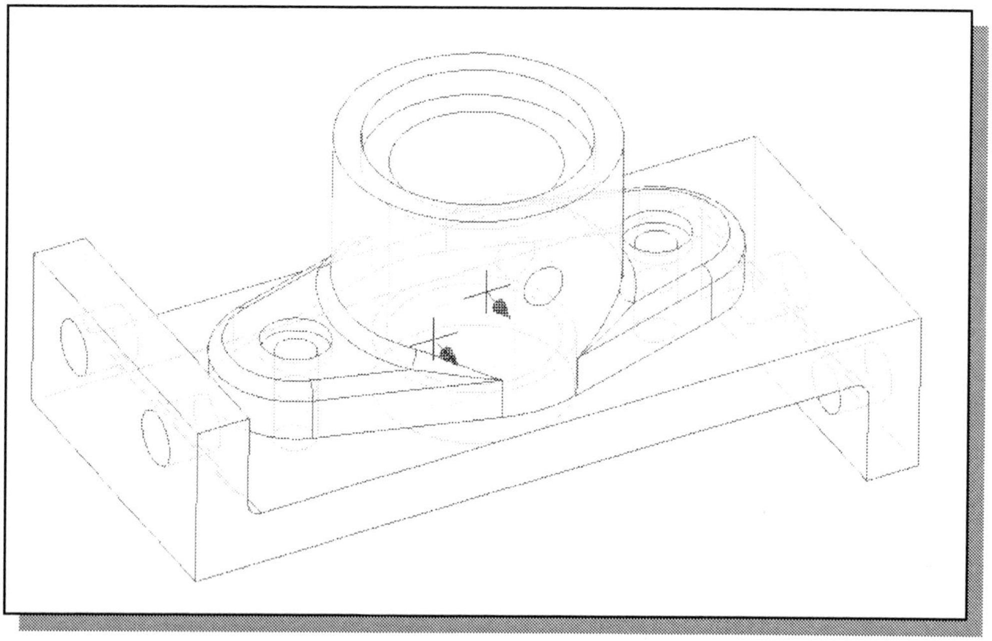

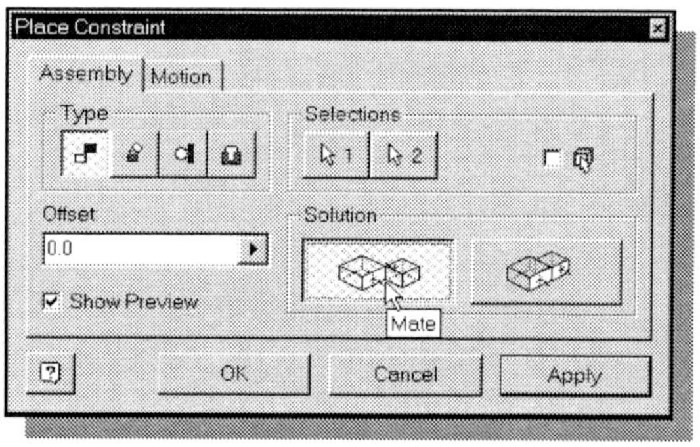

7. In the *Place Constraint* dialog box, switch the *Solution* option to ***Mate*** and notice the *Bearing* part is rotated 180 degrees to satisfy the Mate constraint.

❖ Note that the *Show Preview* option allows us to preview the result before accepting the selection.

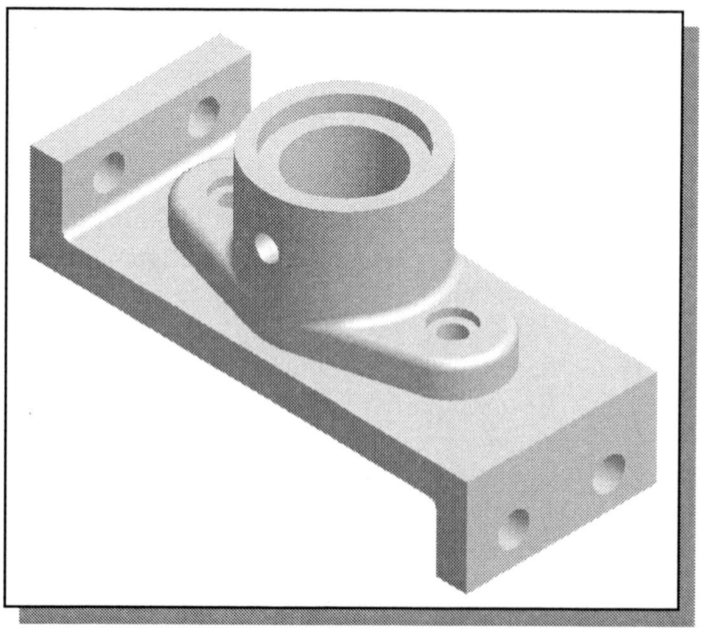

8. On your own, switch to the ***Flush*** option and click on the **Apply** button to accept the settings.

9. In the *Place Constraint* dialog box, click on the **Cancel** button to exit the *Place Constraint* command.

❖ Note the DOF symbol disappears, which indicates the assembly is fully constrained.

Placing the Third Component

➢ We will retrieve the *Collar* part as the third component of the assembly model.

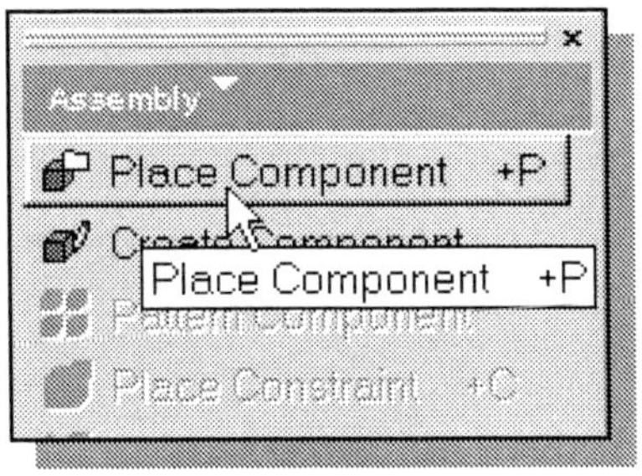

1. In the *Assembly* toolbar (the toolbar that is located to the left side of the graphics window), select the ***Place Component*** command by left-mouse-clicking the icon.

2. Select the ***Collar*** design (part file: *Collar.ipt*) in the list window. And click on the **Open** button to retrieve the model.

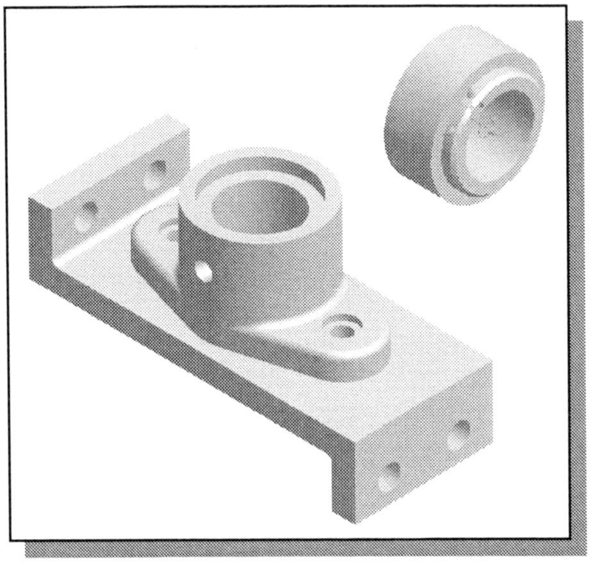

3. Place the *Collar* part toward the upper-right corner of the graphics window, as shown in the figure.

4. Inside the graphics window, right-mouse-click once to bring up the option menu and select **Done** to end the placement of the *Collar* part.

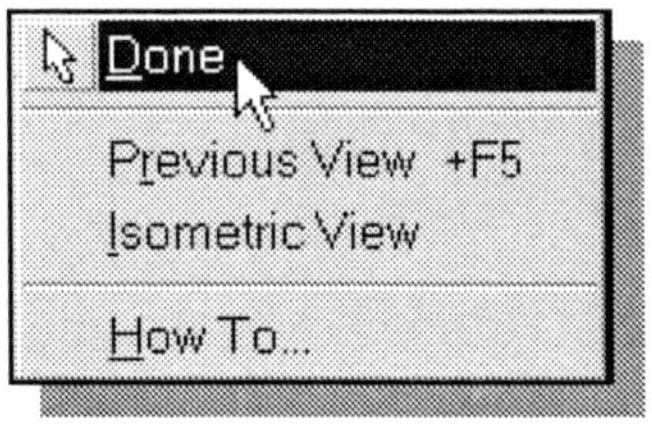

❖ Notice the DOF symbol displayed on the screen. The *Collar* part can move linearly and rotate about the three axes (six degrees of freedom.)

Applying a Insert Constraint

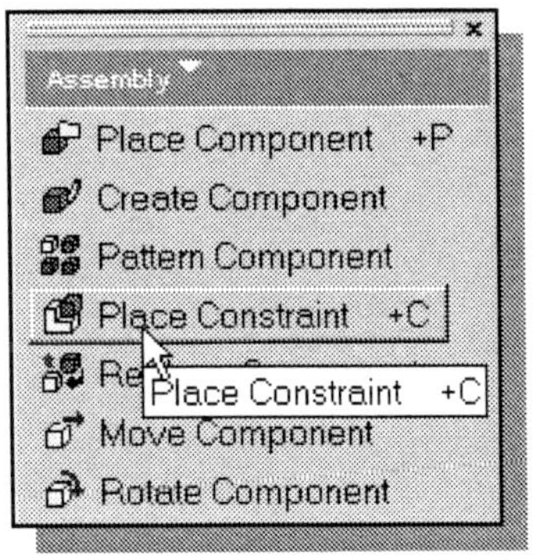

1. In the *Assembly* toolbar, select the ***Place Constraint*** command by left-mouse-clicking once on the icon.

2. In the *Place Constraint* dialog box, switch to the ***Insert*** constraint.

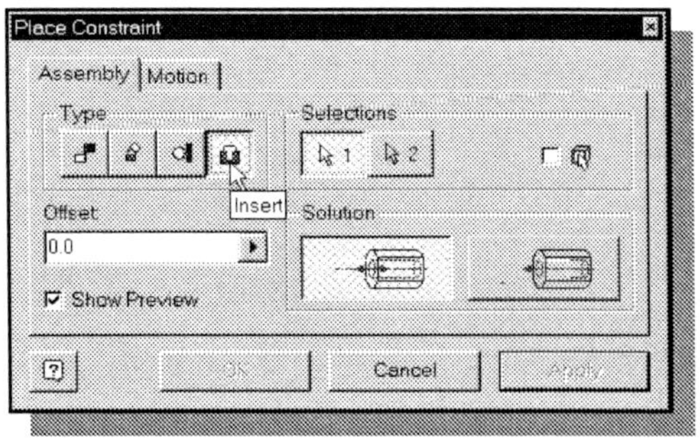

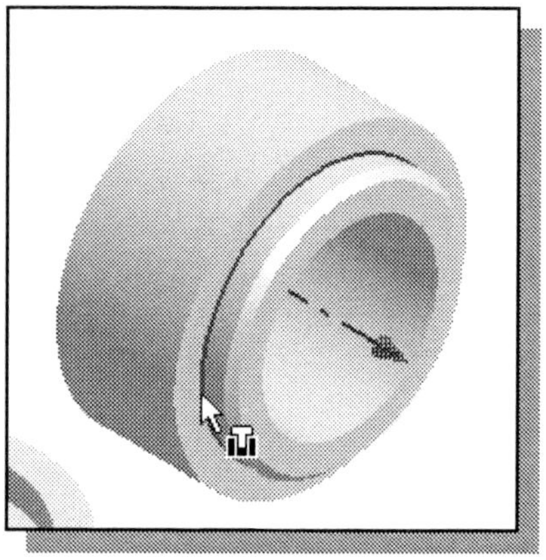

3. Select the inside corner of the *Collar* part as the first surface to apply the Insert constraint, as shown in the figure.

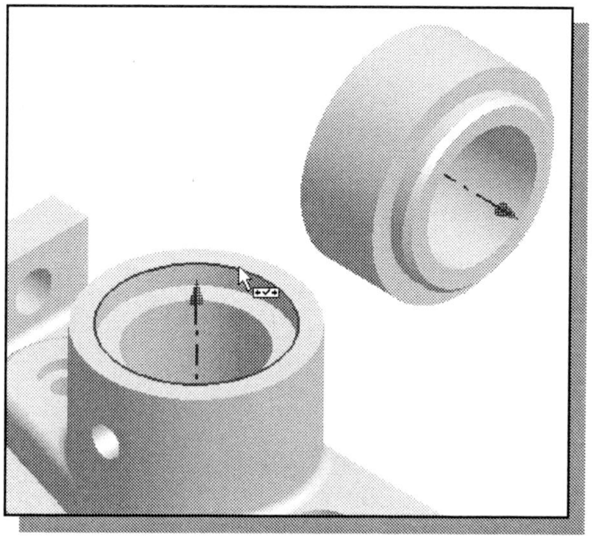

4. Select the inside circle on the top surface of the *Bearing* part as the second surface to apply the Insert constraint, as shown in the figure.

5. Click on the **Apply** button to accept the settings.

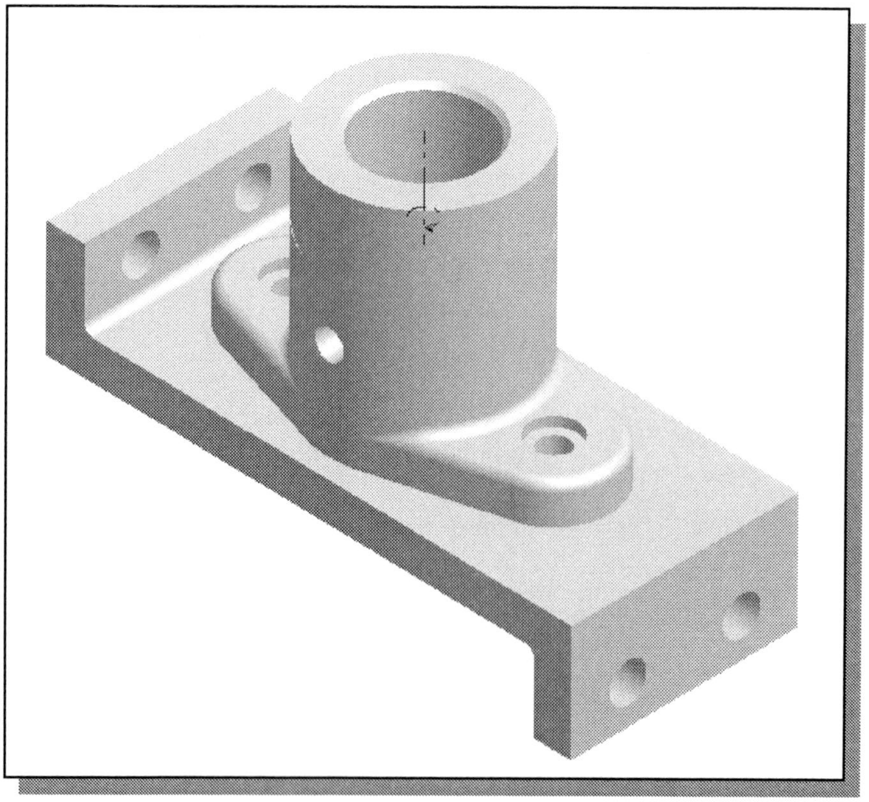

➢ Note that one rotational degree of freedom remains open; the *Collar* part can still freely rotate about the displayed DOF axis.

Assemble the Cap-Screws

❖ We will place two *Cap-Screw* parts to complete the assembly model.

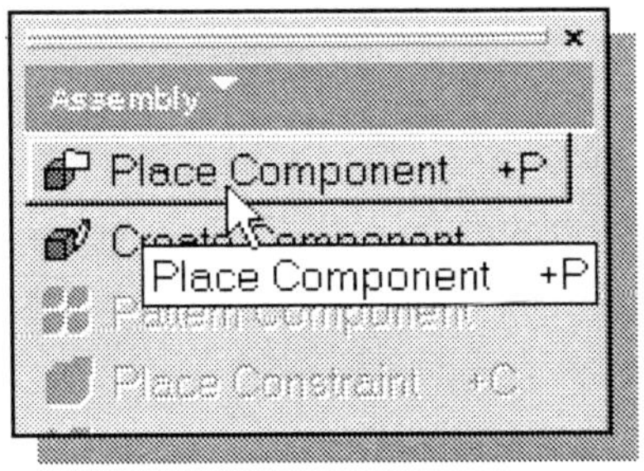

1. In the *Assembly* toolbar (the toolbar that is located to the left side of the graphics window), select the ***Place Component*** command by left-mouse-clicking once on the icon.

2. Select the ***Cap-Screw*** design (part file: ***Cap-Screw.ipt***) in the list window. And click on the **Open** button to retrieve the model.

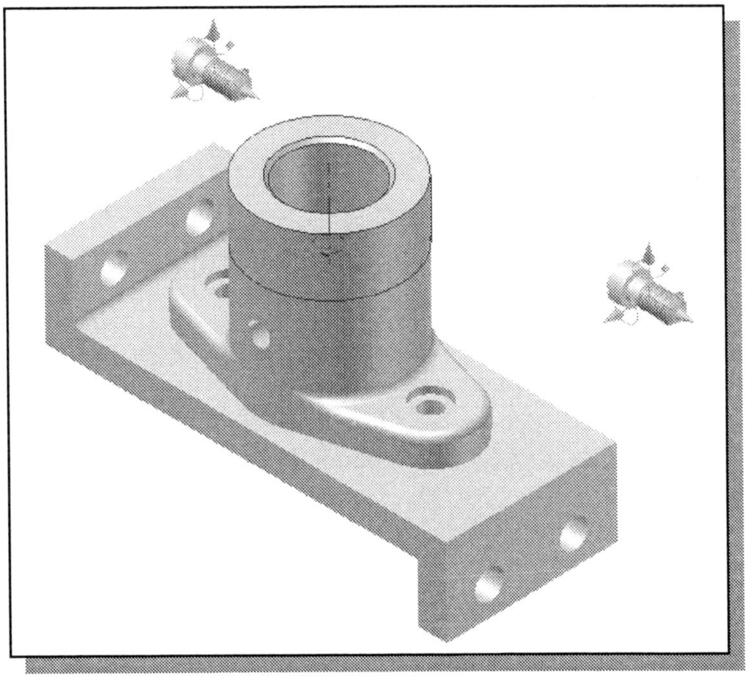

3. Place two copies of the *Cap-Screw* part on both sides of the *Collar* by clicking twice on the screen as shown in the figure.

4. Inside the graphics window, right-mouse-click once to bring up the option menu and select **Done** to end the *Place Component* command.

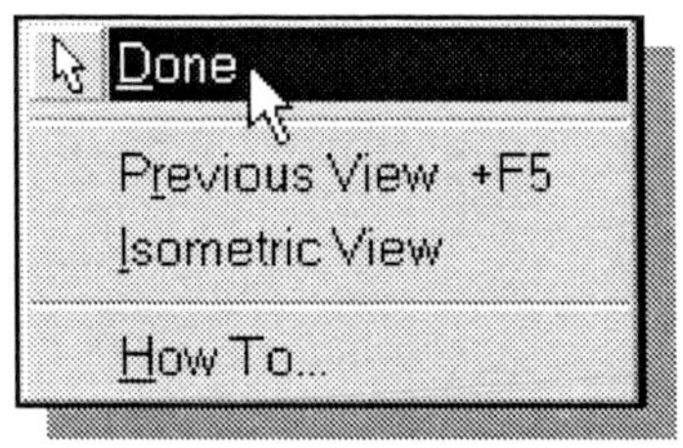

❖ Notice the DOF symbol displayed on the screen. Each *Cap-Screw* has six degrees of freedom. Both parts are referencing the same external part file, but each can be constrained independently.

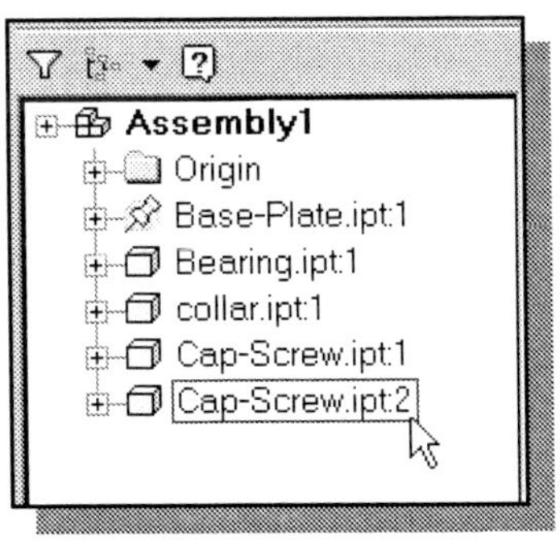

- Inside the *Browser* window, the retrieved parts are listed in the order they are placed. The number behind the part name is used to identify the number of copies of the same part in the assembly model. Move the cursor to the last part name and notice the corresponding part is highlighted in the graphics window.

➢ On your own, use the *Place Constraints* command and assemble the *Cap-Screws* in place as shown in the figure below.

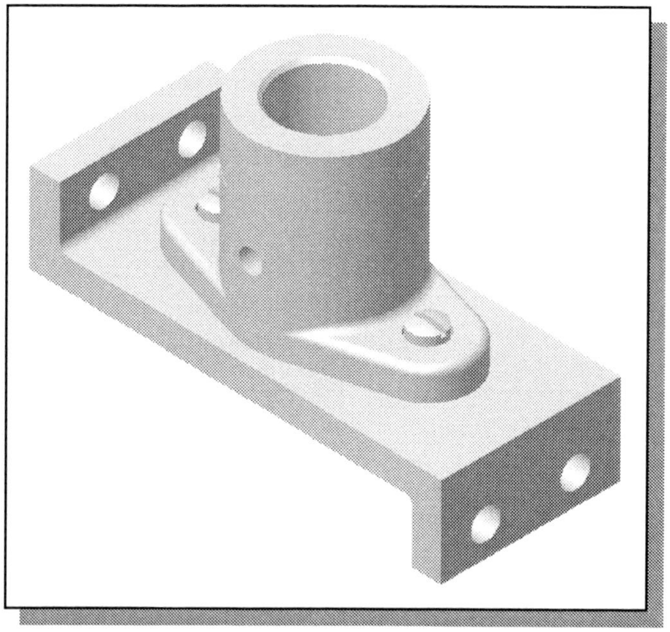

Exploded View of the Assembly

- Exploded assemblies are often used in design presentations, catalogs, sales literature, and in the shop to show all of the parts of an assembly and how they fit together. In *Autodesk Inventor*, an exploded assembly can be created by two methods: (1) Using the *Move Component* and *Rotate Component* commands in the *Assembly Modeler*, which contains only limited options for the operation but can be done very quickly; (2) Transfer the assembly model into the *Presentation Modeler*. For our example, we will create an exploded assembly by using the *Move Component* command that is available in the *Assembly Modeler*.

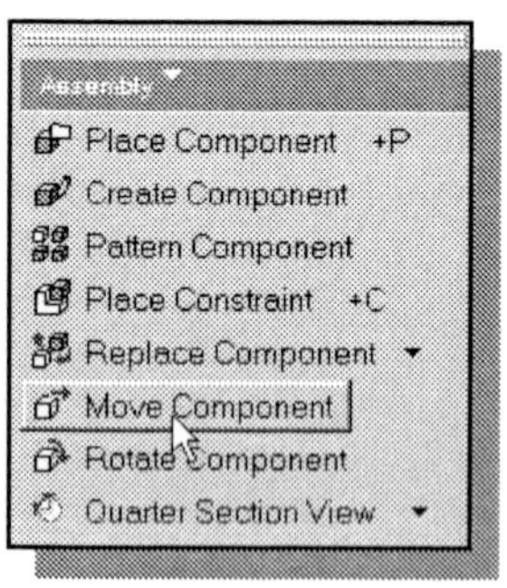

1. In the *Assembly* toolbar, select the ***Move Component*** command by left-mouse-clicking once on the icon.

2. Inside the graphics window, move the cursor on top of the top surface of the *Collar* part as shown in the figure.

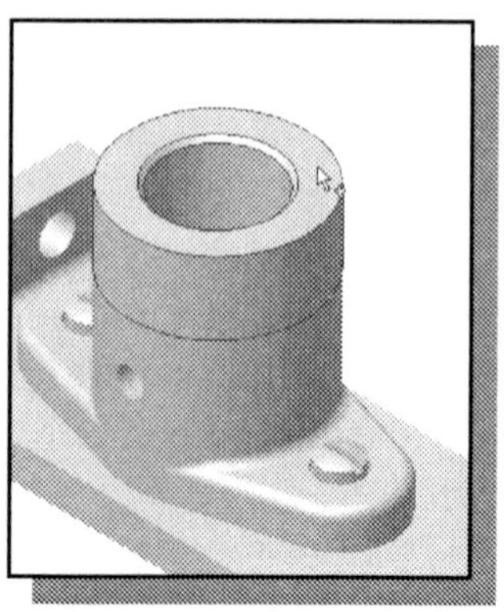

3. Press and hold down the left-mouse-button and drag the *Collar* part toward the right side of the assembly as shown.

4. On your own, repeat the above steps and create an exploded assembly by repositioning the components as shown in the below figure.

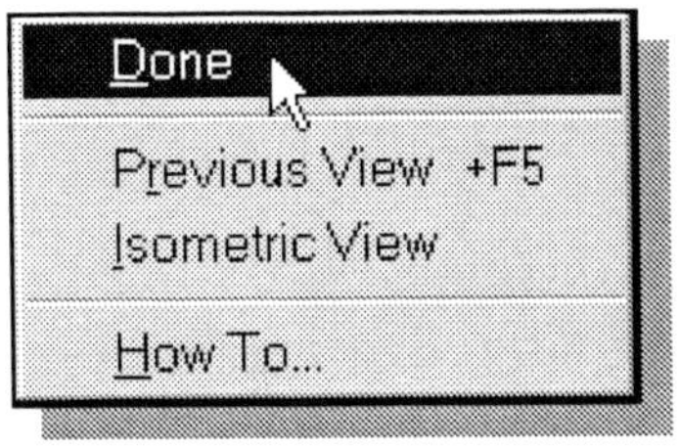

5. Inside the graphics window, right-mouse-click once to bring up the option menu and select **Done** to end the *Move Component* command.

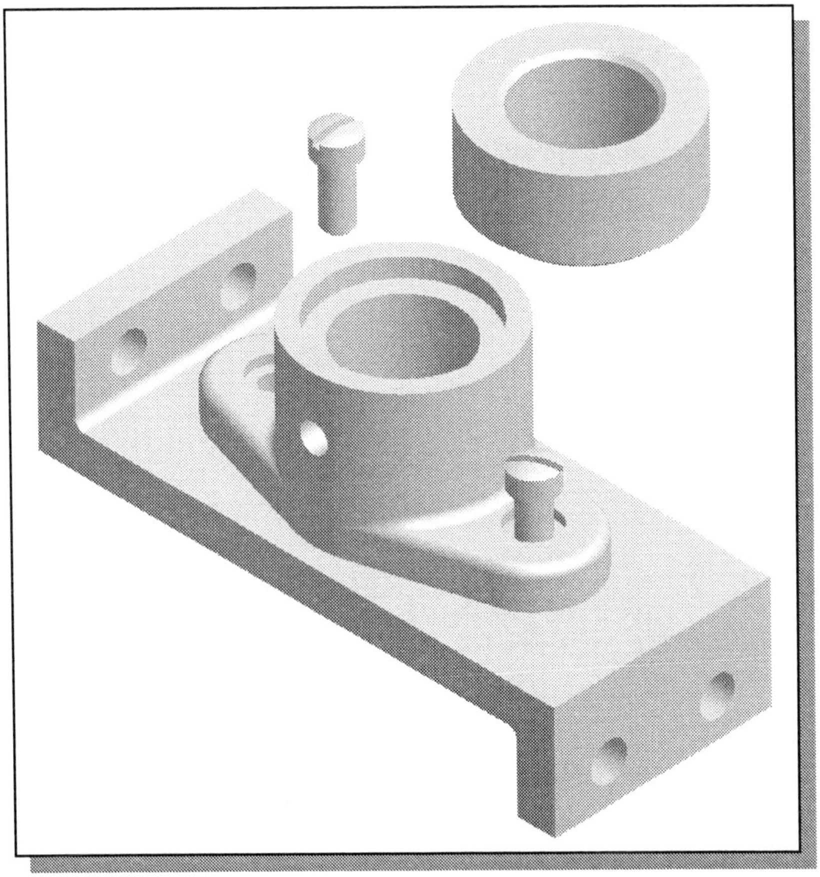

❖ The *Move Component* and *Rotate Component* commands are used to temporarily reposition the components in the graphics window. The displayed image is temporary, but it can be printed with the *Print* command through the pull-down menu.

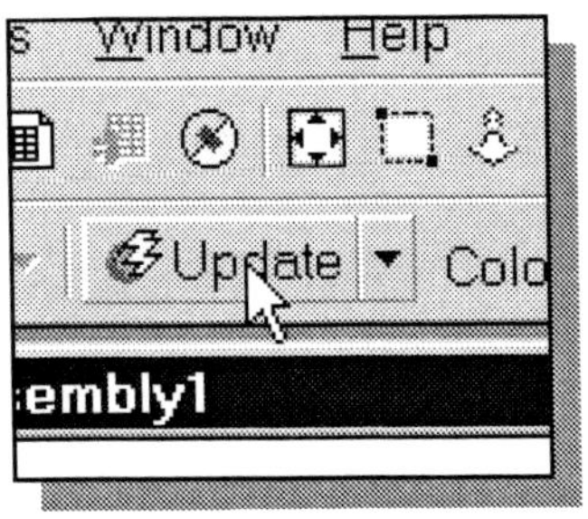

6. Click on the **Update** button in the *Standard* toolbar area.

❖ Note that the components are reset back to their assembled positions, based on the applied assembly constraints.

Editing the Components

- The *associative functionality* of *Autodesk Inventor* allows us to change the design at any level, and the system reflects the changes at all levels automatically.

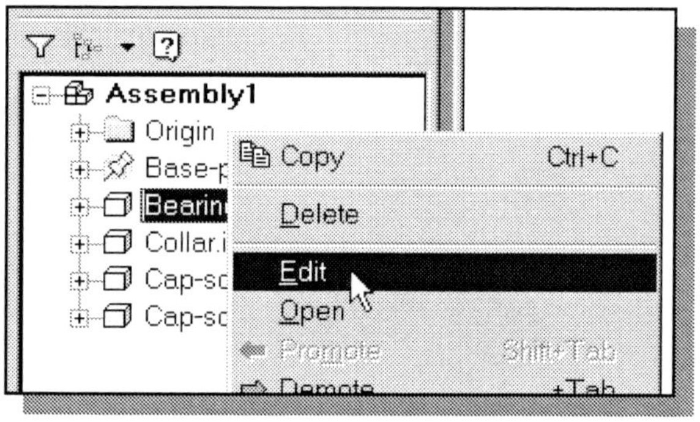

1. Inside the *Desktop Browser*, move the cursor on top of the ***Bearing*** part. Right-mouse-click once to bring up the option menu and select **Edit** in the option list.

❖ Note that we are automatically switched back to *Part Editing Mode*.

2. On your own, adjust the diameter of the small *Drill Hole* to **0.25** as shown.

3. Click on the **Update** button in the *Standard* toolbar area to proceed with updating the model.

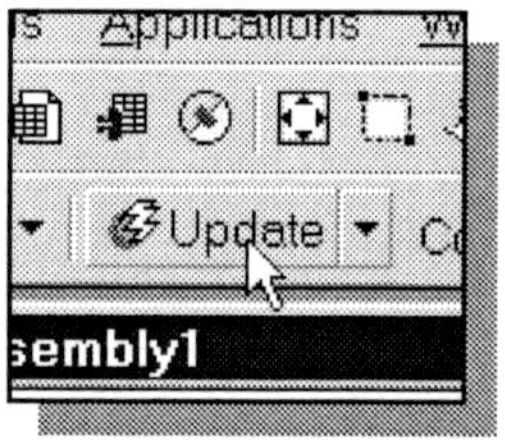

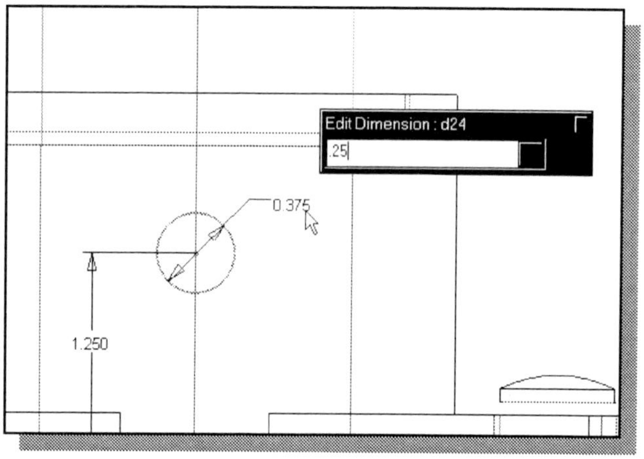

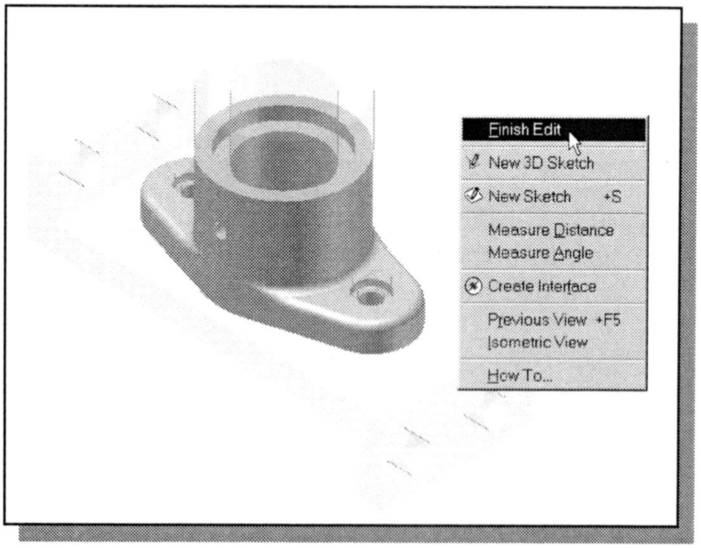

4. Inside the graphics window, click once with the right-mouse-button to display the option menu.

5. Select **Finish Edit** in the popup menu to exit *Part Editing Mode* and return to *Assembly Mode*.

➢ *Autodesk Inventor* has updated the part in all levels and the current assembly mode. On your own, open the *Bearing* part to confirm the modification is performed.

Adaptive Design Approach

- *Autodesk Inventor*'s ***Adaptive Design*** approach allows us to use the applied *assembly constraints* to control the sizes, shapes, and positions of ***underconstrained*** sketches, features, and parts.

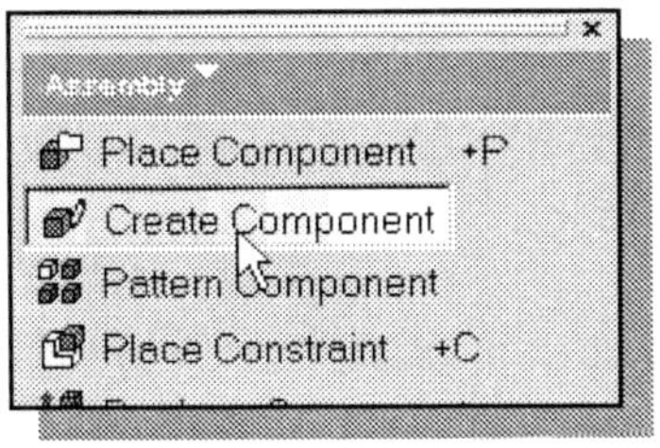

1. In the *Assembly* toolbar, select the ***Create Component*** command by left-mouse-clicking once on the icon.

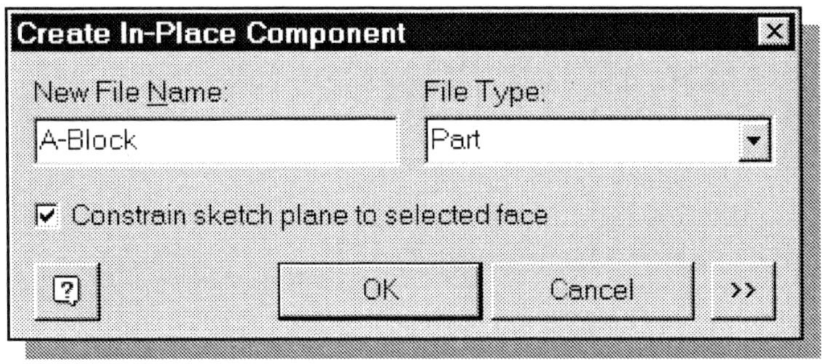

2. In the *Create In-Place Component* dialog box, enter **A-Block** as the new file name.

3. Click on the **OK** button to accept the settings.

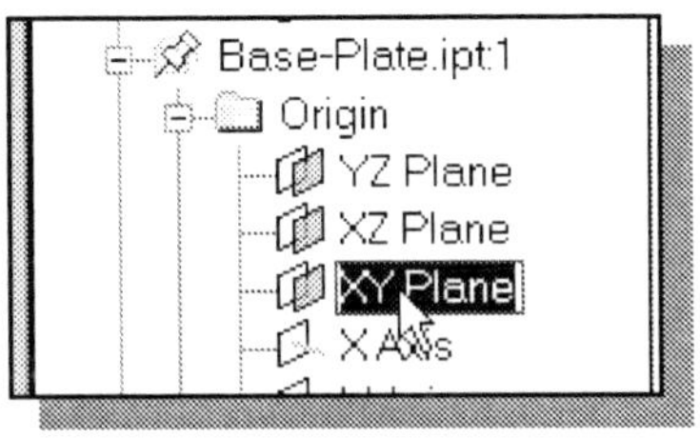

4. Click on the ***XY Plane*** of the *Base-Plate* part, inside the *Browser* window, as the sketching plane for our new part.

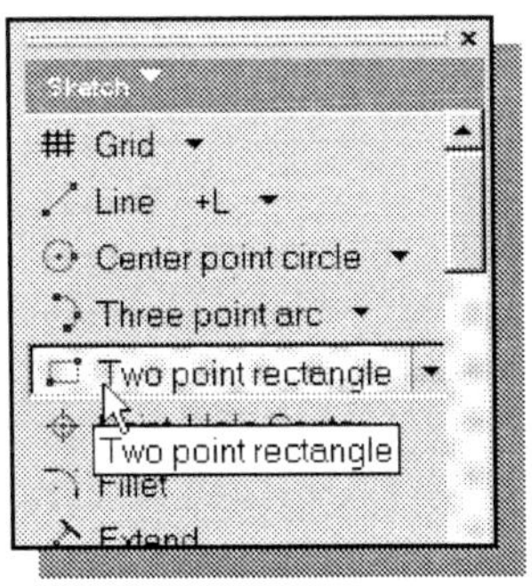

5. Select the ***Two point rectangle*** command by clicking once with the left-mouse-button on the icon in the *Sketch* toolbar.

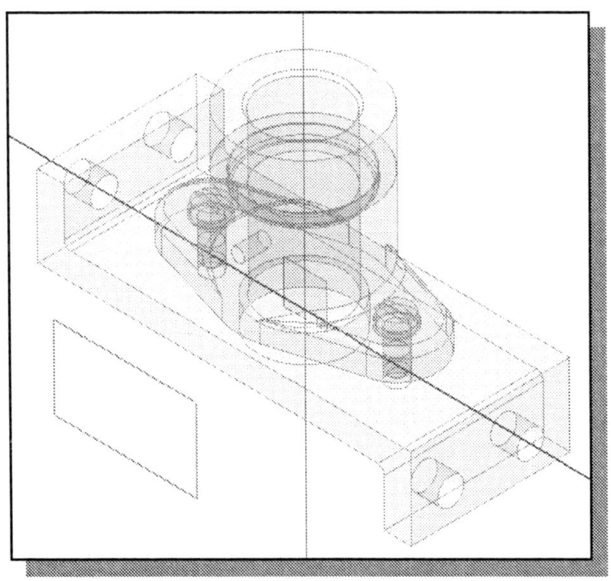

6. On your own, create a rectangle of arbitrary size below the assembly model as shown in the figure.

7. Inside the graphics window, click once with the right-mouse-button to display the option menu and select **Done** to end the *Rectangle* command.

8. Inside the graphics window, click once with the right-mouse-button to display the option menu. Select **Finish Sketch** in the popup menu to end the *Sketch* option.

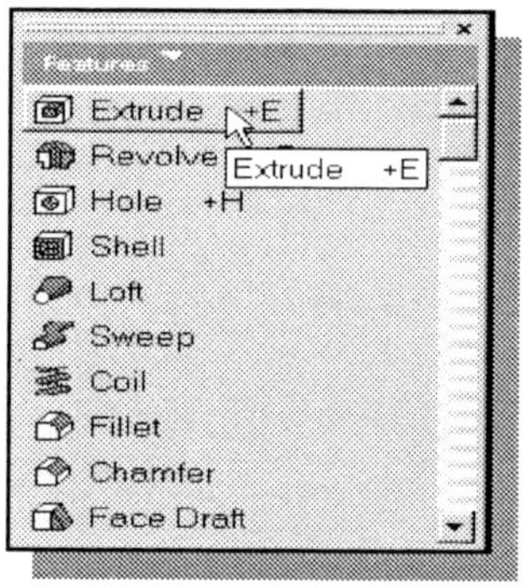

9. In the *Feature* toolbar, select the ***Extrude*** command by left-mouse-clicking once on the icon.

10. Inside the *Extrude* dialog box, select the ***Both Side*** option and set the *Extents Distance* to **3 in** as shown.

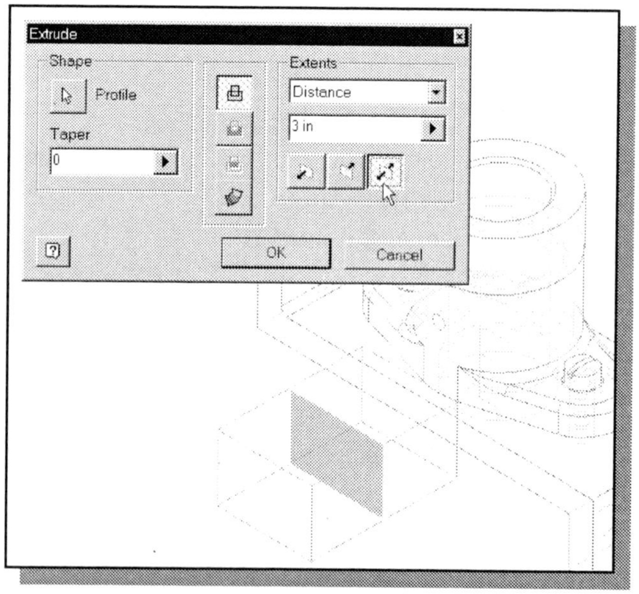

11. In the *Extrude* dialog box, click on the **OK** button to proceed with creating the feature.

12. Right-mouse-click on the ***Extrusion1*** feature of the *A-Block* part, inside the *Browser* window, and select **Adaptive** to allow the use of the adaptive design approach.

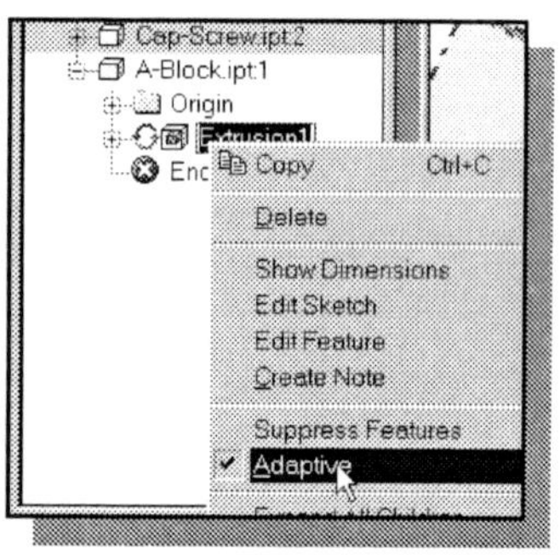

13. Inside the graphics window, click once with the right-mouse-button to display the option menu.

14. Select **Finish Edit** in the popup menu to exit *Part Editing Mode* and return to *Assembly Modeling Mode*.

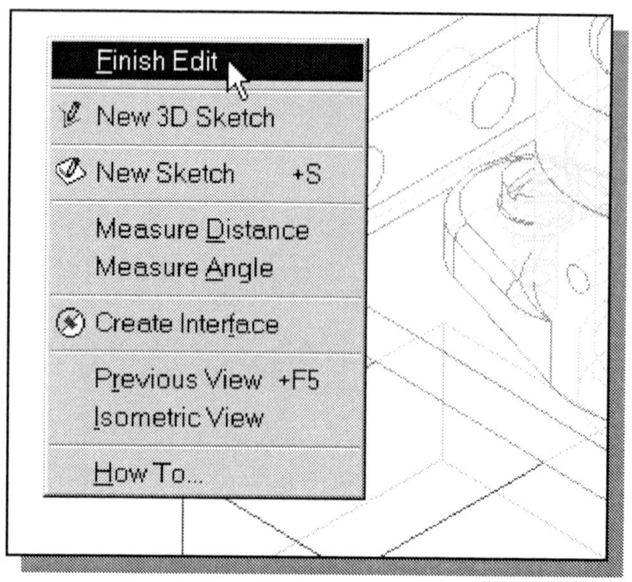

- Note that the rectangular block is created with only one dimension. The 2D sketch of the part is intentionally underconstrained.

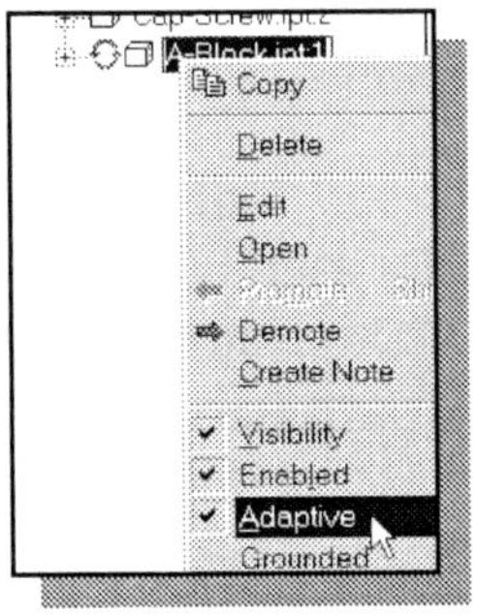

15. Right-mouse-click on the ***A-Block*** part, inside the *Browser* window, and confirm the **Adaptive** option is turned *ON*. This option allows the use of the adaptive design approach in the current assembly model.

- Note the ***Adaptive*** icon, the two-arrow symbol, appears in front of the part name in the *Browser* window.

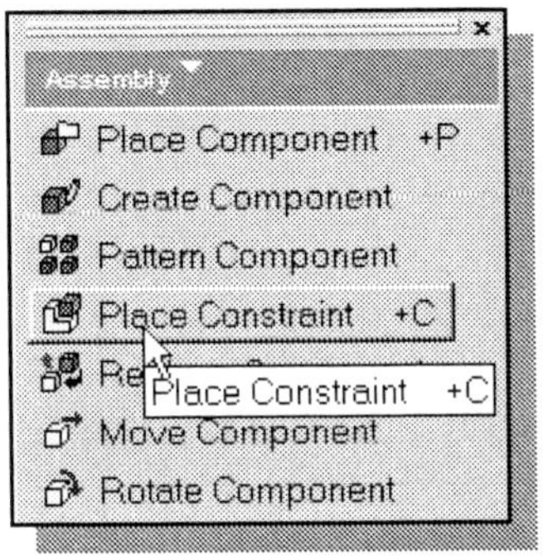

16. In the *Assembly* toolbar, select the ***Place Constraint*** command by left-mouse-clicking once on the icon.

17. On your own, use the **Flush** constraint to align the *A-block* to the left-edge and front-edge of the *Base-Plate* as shown below.

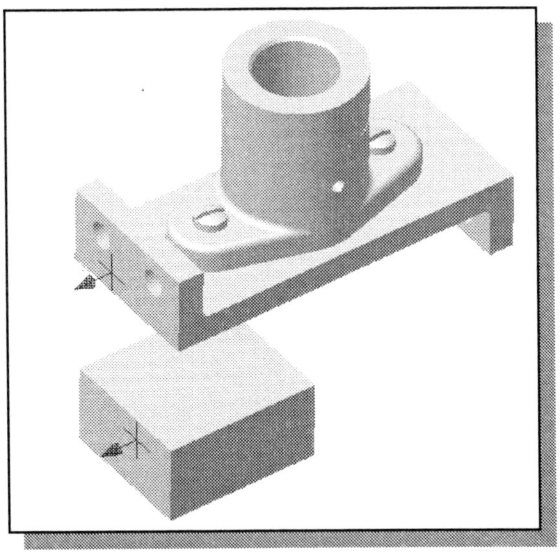

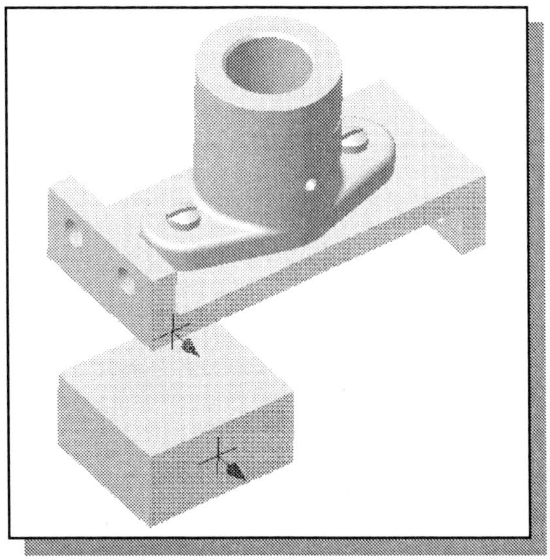

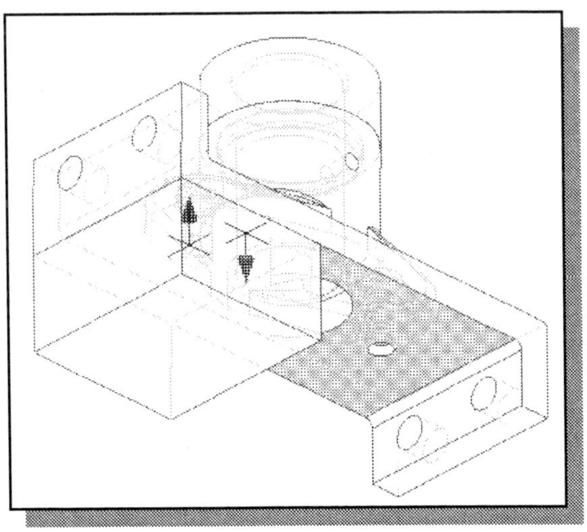

18. Use the **Mate** constraint and align the top of the *A-block* to the bottom of the *Base-Plate* part as shown.

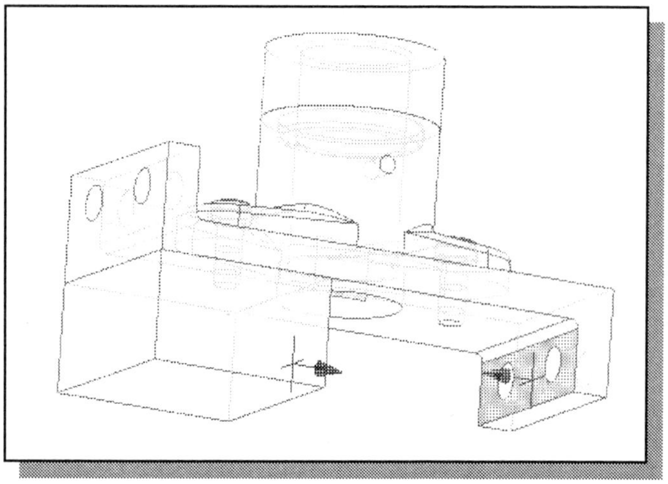

19. Use the **Mate** constraint and align the right surface of the *A-block* to the bottom-left surface of the *Base-Plate* part as shown.

- Note that the length of the *A-block* part is automatically adjusted to fit the defined constraint.

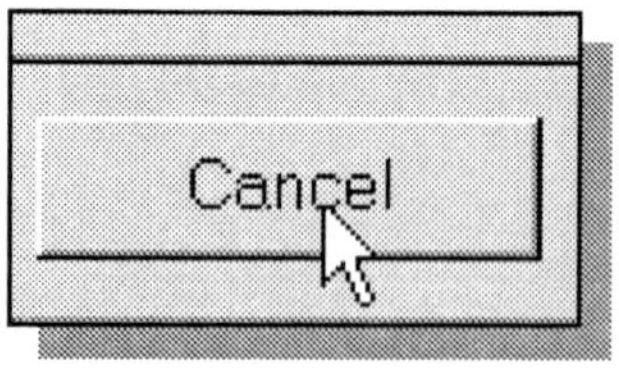

20. In the *Place Constraint* dialog box, click on the **Cancel** button to end the *Place Constraint* command.

Delete and Re-apply Assembly Constraints

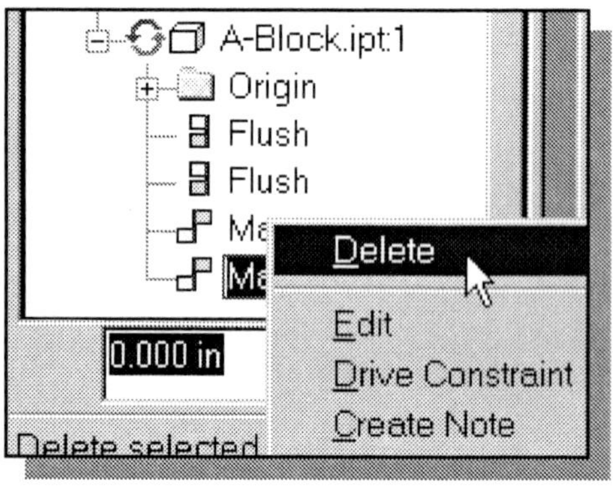

1. Inside the *Browser* window, right-mouse-click on the last **Mate** constraint of the *A-Block* part to bring up the option menu.

2. Select **Delete** to remove the applied constraint.

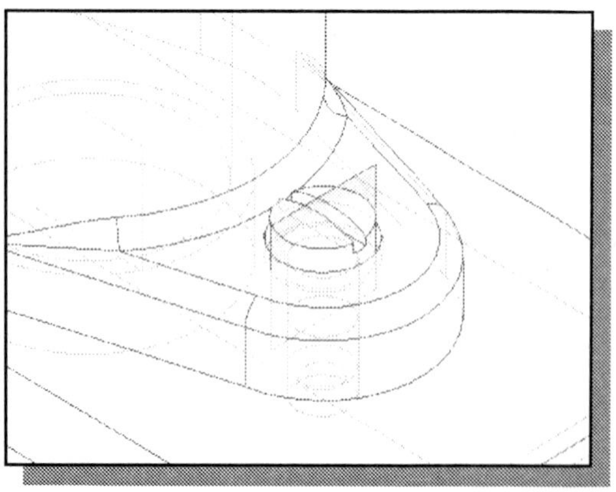

3. On your own, switch ***ON*** the **Visibility** of the vertical work plane of the *Cap-Screw* part as shown.

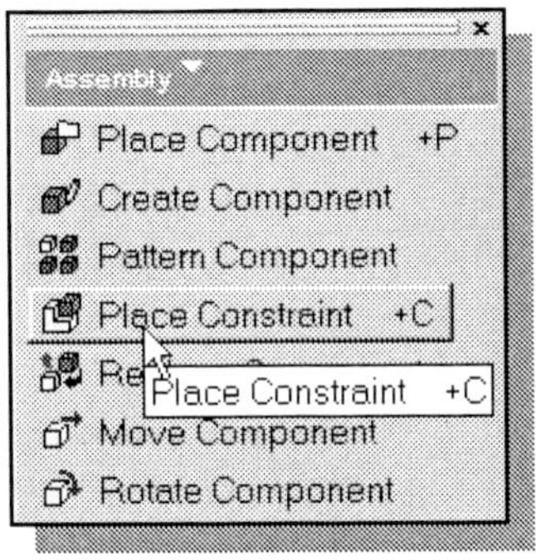

4. In the *Assembly* toolbar, select the ***Place Constraint*** command by left-mouse-clicking once on the icon.

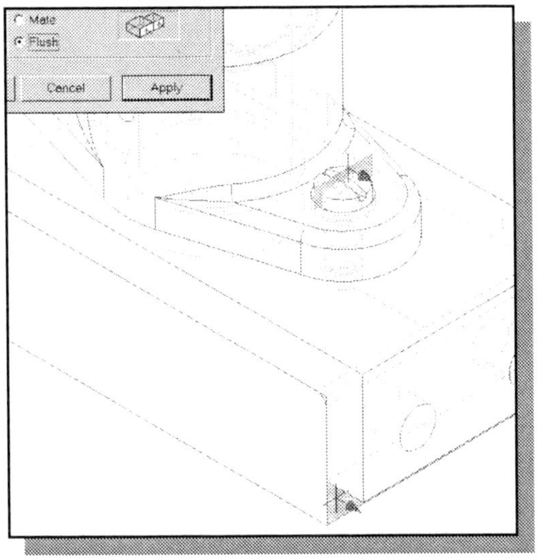

5. On your own, align the right-vertical surface of the *A-block* part to the vertical work plane as shown in the figure.

6. On your own, experiment with aligning the right-vertical surface of the *A-block* part to other vertical surfaces of the assembly model.

- As can be seen, the length of the *A-block* is adjusted to the newly applied constraint. The ***Adaptive Design*** approach allows us to have greater flexibility and simplifies the design process.

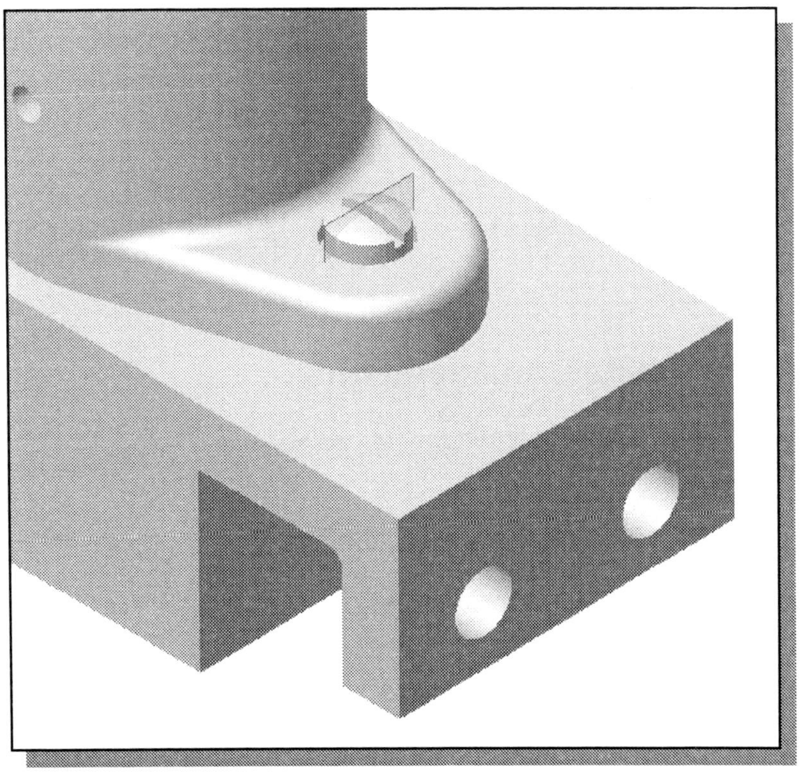

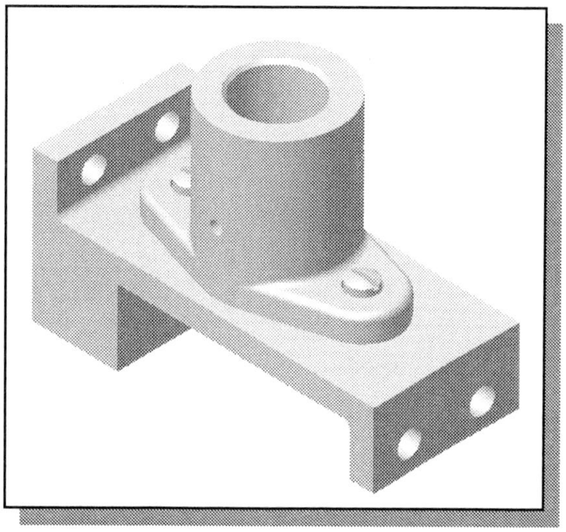

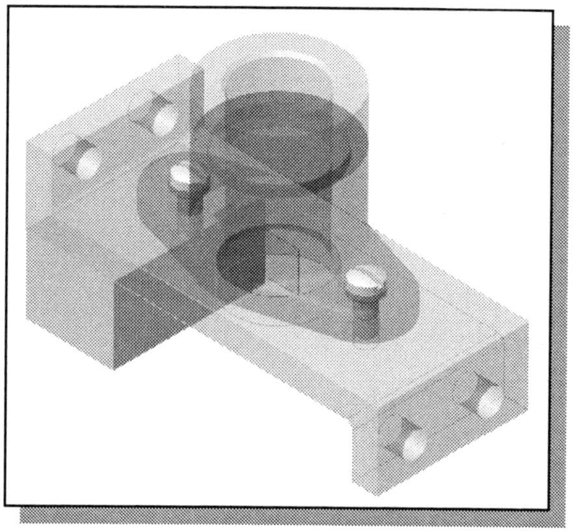

Conclusion

Design includes all activities involved from the original concept to the finished product. Design is the process by which products are created and modified. For many years designers sought ways to describe and analyze three-dimensional designs without building physical models. With advancements in computer technology, the creation of parametric models on computers offers a wide range of benefits. Parametric models are easier to interpret and can be easily altered. Parametric models can be analyzed using finite element analysis software, and simulation of real-life loads can be applied to the models and the results graphically displayed.

Throughout this text, various modeling techniques have been presented. Mastering these techniques will enable you to create intelligent and flexible solid models. The goal is to make use of the tools provided by *Autodesk Inventor* and to successfully capture the **DESIGN INTENT** of the product. In many instances, only a single approach to the modeling tasks was presented; you are encouraged to repeat all of the lessons and develop different ways of thinking in accomplishing the same tasks. We have only scratched the surface of *Autodesk Inventor*'s functionality. The more time you spend using the system, the easier it will be to perform parametric modeling with *Autodesk Inventor*.

Summary of Modeling Considerations

- **Design Intent** – determine the functionality of the design; select features that are central to the design.
- **Order of Features** – consider the parent/child relationships necessary for all features.
- **Dimensional and Geometric Constraints** – the way in which the constraints are applied determines how the components are updated.
- **Relations** – consider the orientation and parametric relationships required between features and in an assembly.

Questions:

1. What is the purpose of using **Assembly constraints**?

2. List three of the commonly used **Assembly constraints**.

3. Describe the difference between the **Mate** constraint and the **Flush** constraint.

4. In an assembly, can we place more than one copy of a part? How is it done?

5. How should we determine the assembly order of different parts in an assembly model?

6. How do we create an exploded assembly in *Autodesk Inventor*?

7. In *Autodesk Inventor*, how do we delete an applied assembly constraint?

8. Create sketches showing the steps you plan to use to create the four parts required for the assembly shown on the next page:

Ex.1)

Ex.2)

Ex.3)

Ex.4)

Exercise:

Leveling Device

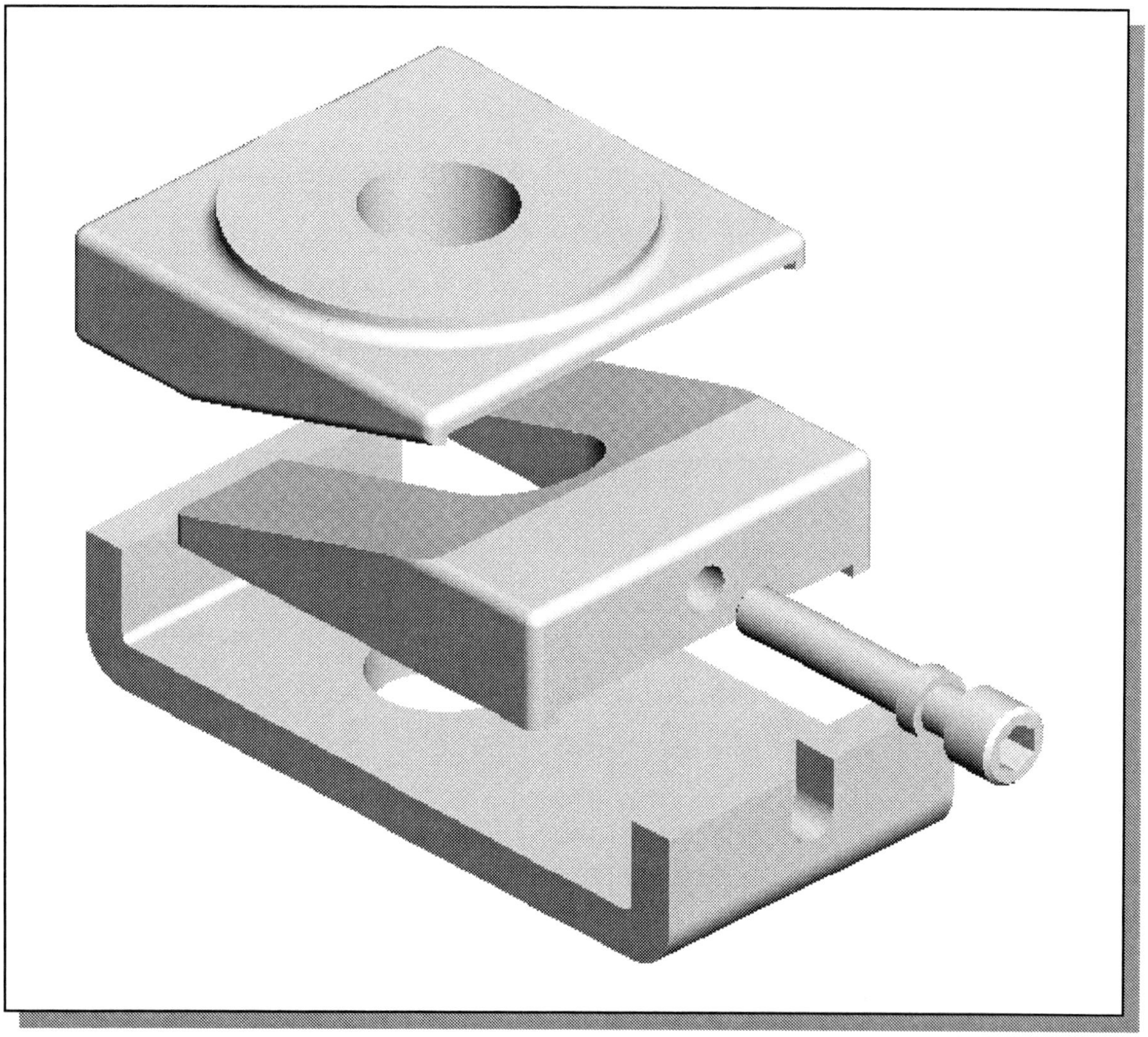

1. **Base Plate** *(All dimensions are in mm)*

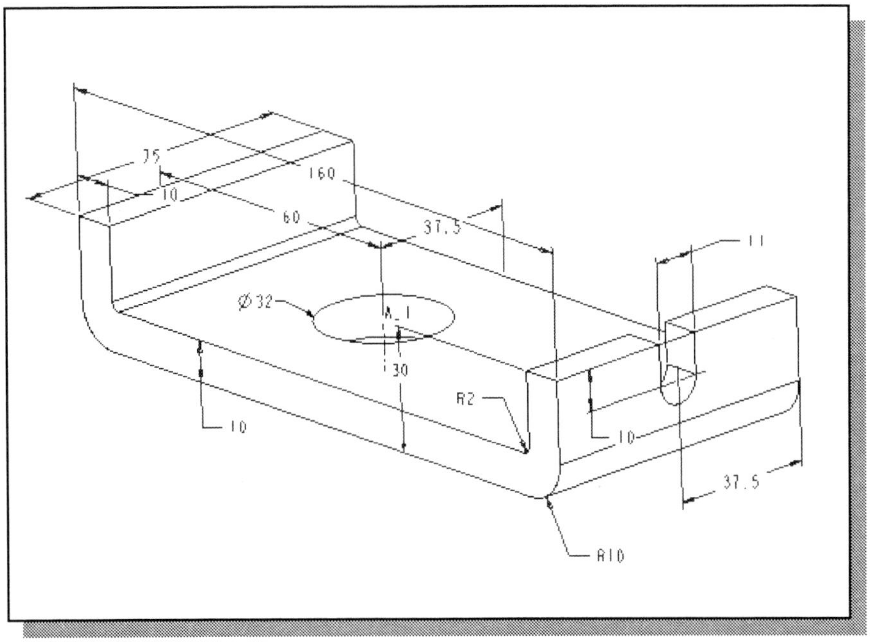

2. ***Sliding Block***

(Rounds & Fillets: R3)

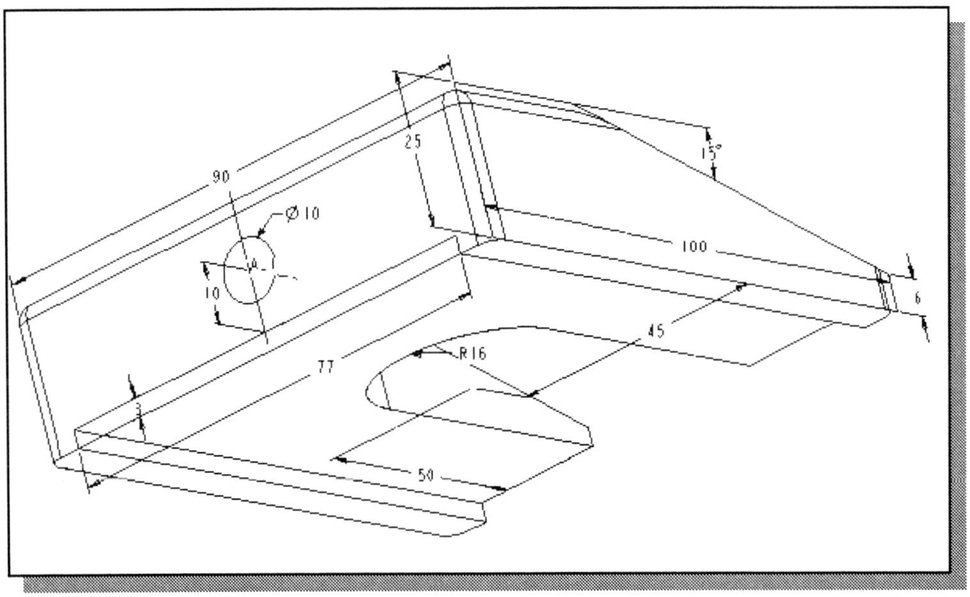

3. *Lifting Block*

(Rounds & Fillets: R3)

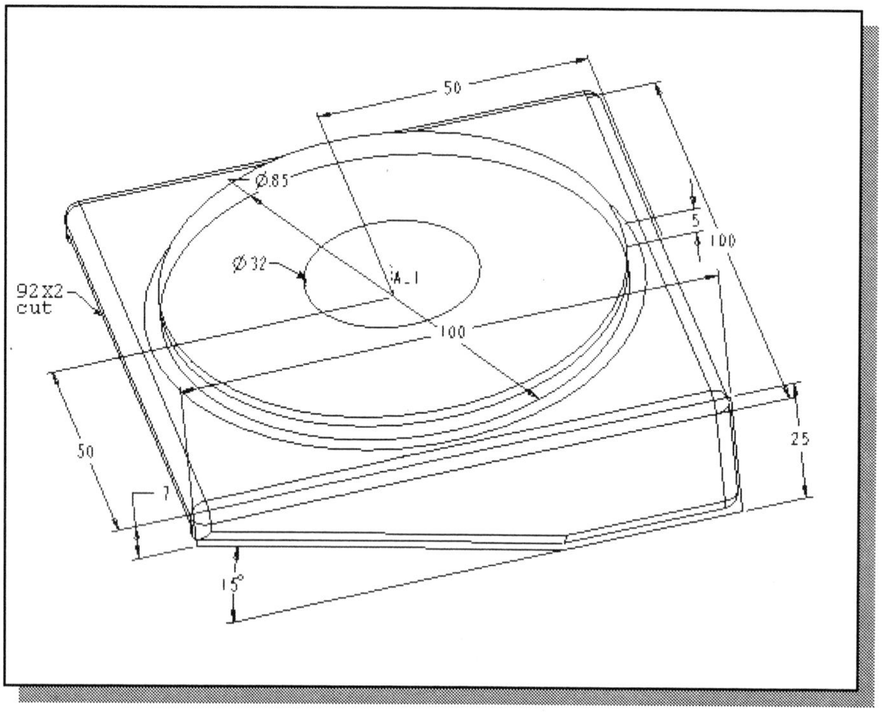

4. *Adjusting Screw*

(Threads Omitted)

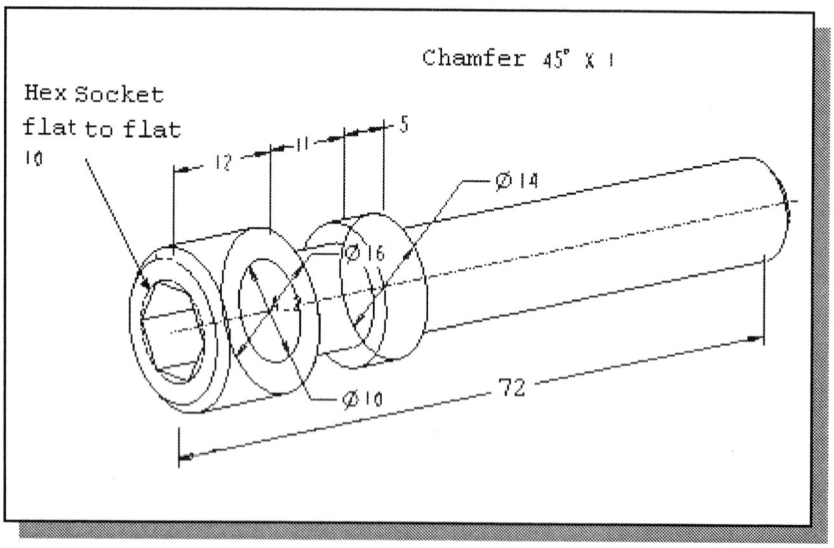

INDEX

W

X

Y

Z

Notes: